THE TWISTED MUSE

OTHER BOOKS BY MICHAEL H. KATER

Das "Ahnenerbe" der SS, 1935–1945: Ein Beitrag zur Kulturpolitik des Dritten Reiches (1974)

Studentenschaft und Rechtsradikalismus in Deutschland, 1918–1933: Eine sozialgeschichtliche Studie zur Bildungskrise in der Weimarer Republik (1975)

The Nazi Party: A Social Profile of Members and Leaders, 1919–1945 (1983)

Doctors Under Hitler (1989)

Different Drummers: Jazz in the Culture of Nazi Germany (1992)

THE TWISTED MUSE

Musicians and Their Music in the Third Reich

Michael H. Kater

New York   Oxford
OXFORD UNIVERSITY PRESS
1997

Oxford University Press

Oxford   New York
Athens   Auckland   Bangkok   Bogota   Bombay
Buenos Aires   Calcutta   Cape Town   Dar es Salaam
Delhi   Florence   Hong Kong   Istanbul   Karachi
Kuala Lumpur   Madras   Madrid   Melbourne
Mexico City   Nairobi   Paris   Singapore
Taipei   Tokyo   Toronto

and associated companies in
Berlin   Ibadan

Copyright © 1997 by Oxford University Press, Inc.

Published by Oxford University Press, Inc.,
198 Madison Avenue, New York, New York 10016

Oxford is a registered trademark of Oxford University Press

Library of Congress Cataloging-in-Publication Data
Kater, Michael H., 1937–
The twisted muse: musicians and their music in the Third Reich / Michael H. Kater.
   p.   cm.
Includes index.
ISBN 0–19–513242–4
1. Music—Germany—20th century—History and criticism.
2. National socialism and music.   3. Music and state—Germany—20th century.   I. Title.
ML275.5.K38   1996
780'.943'09043—dc20   96–6339

9 8 7 6 5 4 3

Printed in the United States of America
on acid-free paper

FOR BARBARA,
who has shared much of the reading and knows
most of the thoughts expressed in this book
from endless conversations over the years,
especially since she has contributed
several important ideas of her own

Preface

The themes of this study have only rarely been reflected in the existing literature. This book was written against the backdrop of four earlier ones that purported to tell the history of music in the Third Reich. The first of these, *Musik im Dritten Reich: Eine Dokumentation* (1963/1966), was an annotated collection of documents by Joseph Wulf which presented key materials from a few archives (then generally closed to many scholars) and music publications of the Nazi period. Valuable as these materials were, they were often published as mangled excerpts or otherwise distorted, and Wulf's running commentary was less than reliable. In 1982 the German musicologist Fred K. Prieberg published *Musik im NS-Staat*, which at the time looked like a monumental and all-encompassing history of music under the Nazi regime, and to this day has remained surprisingly current. But Prieberg had made even scarcer use of the archives than Wulf; he tended to draw his portraits in tones of black and white; his language was often shrill and accusatory; and he, too, made many mistakes, factual as well as interpretive. Compared to this work, *The Politics of Music in the Third Reich*, Michael Meyer's extended dissertation, published in 1991, took virtually no heed of almost twenty intervening years of research, paraphrased heavily from Prieberg's book without the benefit of any archival sources of substance, and contributed nothing that was new at the time. The latest of the four to arrive on the scene was *Music in the Third Reich*, a study by the British pianist Eric Levi. Though well intentioned, it too is but thinly documented with primary sources. Neither does the book properly weigh the importance of the various issues involved: for example, Levi pays equal attention to the place of opera and music publishing. It does not even resonate with music, nor does it seem to be populated by real people; the conductor Herbert von Karajan, for instance, is mentioned only once.

My own research was begun more than a decade ago, when I was still heavily engaged in my book on jazz. Unlike the four earlier authors, I attempted from the start to gain access to as many modern archives as possible, and surprisingly enough I sometimes succeeded where I thought I would never stand a chance. A case in point is the Richard Strauss family archive in Garmisch; another is the Pfitzner collection in the Austrian National Library at Vienna. Other depositories, such as the Rosbaud files in Pullman (Washington), the Schoenberg papers in Los Angeles, the Hindemith correspondence in Frankfurt, and the Kurt Weill collection in New York, were easier to gain access to, but not without the generous help of the archivists in charge. Altogether, I have visited and profited from twenty-five different archival collections from Los Angeles to Vienna.

My second source of information was contemporary music journals, of which *Die Musik, Zeitschrift für Musik,* and *Allgemeine Musikzeitung* were perhaps the most significant. Contemporary primary literature— many of these items odious propaganda pamphlets—was also important. In addition, I had the good fortune to interview and correspond with a number of witnesses from the Nazi era, whose insights often proved invaluable. If only I had been able to speak with a Karajan, a Schoenberg, or a Strauss! Significantly, one of the most accomplished artists of her time, the soprano Elisabeth Schwarzkopf, whose art I much admire, for reasons that only she herself can know refused to receive or even correspond with me despite repeated entreaties.

The secondary literature on overall aspects of my topic is both scarce and questionable in quality, as are some of the better-known memoirs; but specialized critical studies of the postwar era did prove useful. By contrast, compendium handbooks such as the multivolume *New Grove Dictionary of Music and Musicians* or *Musik in Geschichte und Gegenwart* turned out to be somewhat dated, rarely focusing on problems of interest to me. In addition, the latter work bore the stigma of having been edited by a former Nazi, who—typical of many of my leading characters—despite having compromised himself from 1933 to 1945, made a fabulous comeback after Zero Hour.

My thanks must go to all the witnesses who helped me solve my problems; they are identified individually in the notes. I also owe gratitude to all the archivists and their assistants in the United States, Germany, Austria, and Switzerland; I regret that they are too numerous to mention by name. A few, however, deserve special credit. Above all, I thank Richard and Gabriele Strauss for opening their family archive in Garmisch to me unreservedly; I had the entire run of the archive containing the correspondence of their grandfather. I fondly remember my many visits to their gracious home in Grünwald and to their house in Garmisch, where Frau Gabriele Strauss herself made copies of every single document I asked for. Hans Jörg Jans, the director of the Carl-Orff-Zentrum in Munich, went out of his way to provide both documentary material and sound advice of various kinds. Although I spent much less time at his institution, Giselher Schubert of the Paul Hindemith–Institut in Frankfurt was equally magnanimous. Last but not least is Daniel Simon, who, while director of the Berlin Document Center, opened the files of what is left of the Reich Music Chamber records there and consistently welcomed me back, as did his successor, David Marwell.

The help that I received from Joan Evans, a musicologist at Wilfrid Laurier University in Waterloo, was of a different but hardly less important kind. Being not a musicologist by training but a social historian with a strong and ever-growing interest in cross-cultural history, I needed firm guidance in the exposition of many of my subthemes, help in understanding music (short of technical analysis, which I hope to have successfully avoided), and direction in the use of musicological terminology. During many hours of her precious time, she not only gave me all this but also shared with me ideas on writing style, frequently probing the logic of some of my arguments. In addition, she steered me to the Rosbaud archives in Pullman. I owe her a great debt. If mistakes have remained (and no doubt they have), this is of course not at all on her account, nor on anyone else's but my own.

Many other friends and colleagues helped me along the way: Hellmuth Auerbach, Tamara Bernstein, Gerhard Botz, Albrecht Dümling, Saul Friedlander, Elke Fröhlich, Hans Otto and Ursula Jung, Lotte Klemperer, Gabriel and Joyce Kolko, Peter Loewenberg, Theresa Muir, Philip Olleson, Albrecht Riethmüller, Gerhard A. and Gisela Ritter, Adelheid von Saldern, Jürg Stenzl, Jill Stephenson, Joe Viera, Nike Wagner, William H. Wiley, and Warren Wilson.

It remains for me to thank important granting agencies. This book was researched and written while I was the recipient of a Walter A. Gordon Fellowship from York University, a Canada Council Senior Killam Research Fellowship from Ottawa, and, above all, the Konrad Adenauer Research Award of the Alexander von Humboldt Foundation in Bonn. These three fellowships freed me from my regular teaching duties and also facilitated necessary research stays in North America and Europe. In addition, I am particularly grateful to the Social Sciences and Humanities Research Council of Canada in Ottawa, which, as it has done consistently over the years, funded the bulk of my regular research costs, as well as to various colleagues at York University, who provided both funds and administrative aid.

Finally, a word about the midwives, without whom no book can see the light of day. Mary Lehane, Gladys Fung, and Joan McConnell as always provided hard-to-get books and articles through York University's interlibrary loan system. I never fail to be impressed by their ingenuity, in spite of, or perhaps because of, the computer gadgetry that I would be incompetent to handle. At Oxford University Press, Nancy Lane and Thomas LeBien granted much-needed advice and at one time came through with editorial and moral support for me when it was most needed.

Contents

Abbreviations

ADMV	Allgemeiner Deutscher Musikverein (General German Music Society)
AI	Arnold Schoenberg Institute, Los Angeles, Archive
AM	Amtsgericht München, Registratur S, Schwurgerichtsakten
AMR	*Amtliche Mitteilungen der Reichsmusikkammer*
AMZ	*Allgemeine Musikzeitung*
APA	Author's Private Archive
BA	Bundesarchiv, Koblenz
BBC	British Broadcasting Corporation
BDC	Berlin Document Center
BDM	Bund Deutscher Mädel (League of German Girls, within HJ)
BH	Bayerisches Hauptstaatsarchiv, Munich
BMW	Bayerische Motorenwerke
BS	Bayerische Staatsbibliothek, Munich, Handschriftenabteilung
CM	Carl-Orff-Zentrum, Munich
DAF	Deutsche Arbeitsfront (German Labor Front)
DAZ	*Deutsche Allgemeine Zeitung*
DDP	*Das Deutsche Podium*
DKW	*Deutsche Kultur-Wacht*
DM	*Die Musik*

EB	Elly-Ney-Nachlass, Staatsarchiv, Bonn
ETA	Ernst Toch Archive, Special Collections, Music Library, UCLA
GDT	Genossenschaft Deutscher Tonsetzer (League of German Composers)
GLM	*Das Grosse Lexikon der Musik: In acht Bänden*, 8 vols., ed. Marc Honegger/Günther Massenkeil (Freiburg, 1978–82)
HJ	Hitler-Jugend (Hitler Youth)
IBD	*International Biographical Dictionary of Central European Emigrés, 1933–1945*, ed. Herbert A. Strauss and Werner Röder (Munich, 1983)
IfZ	Institut für Zeitgeschichte, Munich
ISCM	International Society for Contemporary Music
JdM	*Jahrbuch der deutschen Musik, 1943/1944*, ed. Hellmuth von Hase (Leipzig and Berlin, [1943/1944])
KdF	Kraft durch Freude ("Strength-through-Joy," part of the DAF)
KfdK	Kampfbund für deutsche Kultur (Combat League for German Culture)
KSM	Klinckerfuss-Nachlass, Schiller-Nationalmuseum/ Deutsches Literaturarchiv, Marbach am Neckar, Handschriftenabteilung
LBI	Leo Baeck Institute, New York
LI	*Lexikon der Interpreten klassischer Musik im 20. Jahrhundert*, ed. Alain Paris (Munich and Kassel, 1992)
LP	Library of Washington State University, Pullman
MGG	*Die Musik in Geschichte und Gegenwart: Allgemeine Enzyklopädie der Musik unter Mitarbeit zahlreicher Musikforscher des In- und Auslandes*, 17 vols., ed. Friedrich Blume (Kassel, 1949–86)
MGM	Metro-Goldwyn-Mayer
MJV	*Musik in Jugend und Volk*
MK	*Musik im Kriege*
MMP	Münchener Stadtbibliothek, Monacensia-Abteilung, Pfitzner-Briefe
NG	*The New Grove Dictionary of Music and Musicians*, 20 vols., ed. Stanley Sadie (London, 1980)
NSBO	Nationalsozialistische Betriebszellenorganisation (National Socialist Shop Organization)
NSDAP	Nationalsozialistische Deutsche Arbeiterpartei (National Socialist German Workers' Party)
NSKG	NS-Kulturgemeinde (National Socialist Cultural Community)

NSV	Nationalsozialistische Volkswohlfahrt (National Socialist People's Charity)
NWH	Österreichische National-Bibliothek, Vienna (Wien), Handschriftenabteilung
NYA	New York Philharmonic Archives, Avery Fisher Hall, New York
OSW	Österreichisches Staatsarchiv, Vienna (Wien), Archiv der Republik
OW	Österreichische National-Bibliothek, Vienna (Wien), Musiksammlung, F68 Pfitzner
PA	Private Archive
PF	Paul-Hindemith-Institut, Frankfurt am Main
Promi	Reichsministerium für Volksaufklärung und Propaganda (Reich Propaganda Ministry)
REM	Reichsministerium für Wissenschaft, Erziehung und Volksbildung (Reich Education Ministry)
RG	Richard Strauss-Archiv, Garmisch
RKK	Reichskulturkammer (Reich Culture Chamber)
RMK	Reichsmusikkammer (Reich Music Chamber)
RRG	Reichs-Rundfunk-Gesellschaft (Reich Broadcasting Corporation)
RSK	Reichsschrifttumskammer (Reich Authors' Chamber)
RTK	Reichstheaterkammer (Reich Theater Chamber)
SA	Sturmabteilungen (Brownshirts; Storm Troopers)
SM	Stadtarchiv, Munich
SMK	Stadtarchiv, Munich, Kulturamt
SMM	Städtische Musikbibliothek, Munich, Pfitzner-Briefe
SS	Schutzstaffel (Security Squad)
Stagma	Staatlich genehmigte Gesellschaft zur Verwertung musikalischer Urheberrechte (State-approved Society for the Utilization of Musical Authorship Rights)
TG	*Die Tagebücher von Joseph Goebbels: Sämtliche Fragmente, 5* vols., ed. Elke Fröhlich (Munich, 1987)
TGII	*Die Tagebücher von Joseph Goebbels, Teil II: Diktate, 1941–1945,* 16 vols., ed. Elke Fröhlich (Munich, 1993–96)
UCLA	University of California at Los Angeles
UE	Universal Edition
Ufa	Universum Film–Aktiengesellschaft
VB	*Völkischer Beobachter*
WC	Weill-Lenya Research Center, New York
ZM	*Zeitschrift für Musik*
ZNF	Zentralbibliothek, Zurich, Musikabteilung, Nachlass Furtwängler

THE TWISTED MUSE

Introduction

It is some time after the Nazi invasion of Poland. SS troopers brandishing machine guns are storming the Jewish ghetto of a small Polish town. Shots ring out; men, women, and children fall to the ground. Two of the Nazi soldiers race up a flight of stairs. Against the din of shots and screams, they hear the sounds of a sonata being played somewhere on a piano. They arrive in a room, empty save for an upright piano, at which sits a young SS trooper, playing beautifully and with total concentration. Dumbstruck, his two comrades lean in through the open doorway. "Was ist das, Bach? Ist das Bach?" exclaims one. "Nein, Mozart! Mozart!" replies the other. But it is indeed Bach: the prelude from the A-Minor English Suite, composed around 1720.

This stunning scene from Steven Spielberg's celebrated film *Schindler's List* constitutes one of the most disturbing moments in the entire picture.[1] It juxtaposes the beauty of Baroque music with the mayhem of genocidal slaughter, both perpetrated by what had been hitherto one of the most civilized nations in the world. The brilliance of this scene is in its evocation of abject criminality, the serene sovereignty of music, and the obvious confusion of two SS men about matters cultural and by extension about the larger world in which they live and act. Classical music, of course. But Mozart or Bach? They are not sure. And does it matter anyway? Does it matter especially in the context of the machine-gunning of hundreds of Jews?

Writ large, does classical music matter in a Nazi cosmos of totalitari-

3

anism, fascism, dictatorship? If the pogrom scene from Spielberg's film encapsulates the greatest of extremes that characterized the Nazi regime, then aesthetically pleasing music had a logical place somewhere in this cosmos. But where was this place? Where and how did serious music fit into the pattern of culture in the Third Reich, and what kind of a culture was it? Most puzzling of all, who were the people that generated it? Were they SS troopers? Were they saints?

Maneuvering between these two polar opposites, this book attempts to answer some of those questions by examining serious, or "classical," music primarily through the men and women who created it during this period. If we return for a moment to the images from *Schindler's List*, it becomes obvious that aesthetics has no monopoly on morality, but yet the two are not mutually exclusive. Neither a negative nor a positive correlation exists between the two principles: egregiously fascist musicians may have made beautiful music, but they may also have played badly. Many shades of distinction existed in between.

There are additional perspectives from which this complicated subject can be approached. One involves the now decades-old dichotomy between "intentionalism" and "functionalism" in the interpretation of National Socialism.[2] If classical music existed in the Third Reich—and this is a given—by whose orders was it there, and whom did it benefit? This set of questions would posit the existence of an omnipotent source of power that utilized music for certain propagandistic ends. Indeed, much in the story that follows suggests that rational decision making was the wellspring for many of the policies that facilitated the playing and recording of and training in music during the period 1933–45. It is easy to imagine Joseph Goebbels as the president of the Reich Culture Chamber, which controlled the agenda of the Reich Music Chamber, dictating to conductors, composers, and musicians what music to compose and perform. One can envision Adolf Hitler as the ultimate Führer whose own tastes determined, in so many instances, what sort of music ought to be supported and what sort suppressed, perhaps even which musicians should be persecuted. Others also come to mind: Hermann Göring, who was head of the Preussische Staatsoper in Berlin; Alfred Rosenberg, who by 1933 had prescribed all manner of cultural tastes through his Kampfbund für deutsche Kultur; Robert Ley, who arranged festive music for his "Strength-through-Joy" celebrations.[3]

To the extent that much of the music that was heard in Germany after 1933 unfolded along these lines, the proponents of intentionalism are vindicated.[4] But far more musical events occurred almost in spite of state regulations, against the grain of Hitler's, Rosenberg's, Goebbels's, or Göring's personal taste, in contradistinction to newly established sets of aesthetic values yet continuous with certain lines of development from an earlier period that was now officially blacklisted. These countercurrents, then, would substantiate the theory of the structuralists, who maintain that governance of all matters in the Third Reich was sustained and propelled by virtue of dynamic radicalization, defaults, contradictions, forces colliding with those emanating from Nazi control towers, and, not least, pure happenstance.

Yet another vantage point from which to consider the topic is that of continuity versus discontinuity. Within a larger framework, historians have long been concerned with the question whether the Weimar Republic was merely a prelude to the Third Reich, or, conversely, whether the Third Reich simply manifested and cast into high relief tendencies first expressed during the republic. Whereas for some time after 1945 political historians tended to view 30 January 1933, the day of Hitler's assumption of power, as the end of the democratic, republican era and the beginning of the totalitarian, fascist one, in recent years much more structural overlap between the two eras has been detected. For example, if the presidential dictatorship of Chancellor Heinrich Brüning (1930–32) may be viewed as prefascist, then it becomes clear that Hitler's dictatorship was but a logical extension of this situation. And yet it may be argued that, despite appearances, Brüning's chronic extraparliamentarian sleight of hand, especially in economic matters, had as its objective the eventual salvation of the republic.[5] An authoritative study by Hans Mommsen manages to blend these seemingly irreconcilable views. Mommsen's characterization of the Weimar Republic as a "failed example of political modernization" implies the noble impulse toward progressive political change in the shape of a democratic republic (which became apparent especially during the early 1920s), but it also hints at the defeat of these modernizing forces by antidemocratic, authoritarian tendencies, some of them increasingly fascist, firmly lodged within the German body politic in the declining years of the Weimar experiment.[6]

In analogy to the earlier political-historical interpretation, cultural affairs were for a long time also viewed as having been progressive and democratic during the republic (as symbolized by the Bauhaus and Neue Sachlichkeit movements), in contrast to conservative, reactionary, and repressive developments after January 1933. At this level the classic interpretation of the Weimar Republic is Peter Gay's seminal *Weimar Culture: The Outsider as Insider*. By contrast, George L. Mosse, insofar as he dealt with culture, has painted a depressingly bleak picture of the Third Reich.[7] Younger historians, however, are now beginning to discover that matters were not so cut and dried but that there was a fair degree of confluence between the two cultural streams—between the republic on the one side and the Third Reich on the other. With respect to film, and notwithstanding wonderful surrealist experiments such as *The Cabinet of Doctor Caligari*, Gerald D. Feldman has spoken of the antidemocratic, potentially demagogic aspects of the largest film production company, Universum Film–Aktiengesellschaft (Ufa), which, as a ready tool of propaganda schemers, "owed its birth to initiatives taken by Germany's military leadership" during World War I, and toward the end of the republic was under the control of the antidemocratic Alfred Hugenberg.[8] What Propaganda Minister Goebbels did with the aid of film in manipulating public opinion can now be gleaned from his largely published diaries. With respect to music, Pamela Potter has written that many of the elements of backwardness and oppression said to be hallmarks of the Nazi period were also, or already, present in the republic, and that it is also difficult to identify a systematic Nazi "music police" whose job was to condone or condemn individual compositions, musicians, or composers.[9]

On close examination we can find in the Third Reich elements we would not expect in the dictionary definition of a totalitarian regime: a lack of controlling mechanisms, creative movements expressive of freedom such as jazz and swing, an extended influence of Jewish culture and its champions, even avant-garde attempts at modernism that may not have conformed with the modernist conceptions of the early republic but were nonetheless novel and were in fact officially welcomed and even subsidized as such.[10] And yet older traditions hailing from the Second Empire were by and large carried on as well, the best example being Richard Strauss. Thus, in the end, there was a mixture of aesthetic styles and forms, some of them mere copies of the tried and true, and bad ones at that, some syncretic and more interesting, and others bold new moves in the world of art and culture. These endeavors were motivated and frequently accompanied by various political convictions on the part of their creators; more often than not, and understandably in a time of party and governmental strictures, political opportunism and careerist considerations prevailed over moral ones. Hence, the men and women who leap from the pages of this book are rarely either saints or sinners, black or white. As ordinary Germans under stress who often wished to avoid oppressive political obligations, they tried to circumvent them as best they could; others played the new game more deftly and ended up on top. One and all—musicians and singers, composers and conductors, all of whom had to make a living as artists in the Third Reich—emerged in May 1945 severely tainted, with their professional ethos violated and their music often compromised: gray people against a landscape of gray.

1

—

National Socialism, the Third Reich, and the Music Scene

Music, Economics, and Political Opportunism

In March 1933 clarinetist Valentin Grimm found himself caught in a dilemma. Having learned of Hitler's victory in late January, he had returned to Germany after spending many years as a professional musician in New York City. Being a card-carrying Nazi Party member, he was now looking for a comfortable job in one of Germany's many well-known orchestras. No one offered to hire him, however, because there were no jobs. Grimm was facing a welfare existence unless things changed dramatically. They did not. In 1936 he finally landed a shaky part-time position with a Hamburg pops opera. The 185 marks he was paid every month was too little to live on and too much to starve. As late as 1938 Grimm was so poor that he could not even afford the dark suit he needed to play in the orchestra. Grimm seriously contemplated returning to New York.[1]

In Berlin the violinist Georg Kirchner did not fare much better. He had fallen victim to the tidal wave of unemployment sweeping across the waning Weimar Republic, and he also failed to make it back into the work force after Hitler's assumption of power. After several precarious years on the dole, he gave up all hope of a musical career and accepted work in a machine factory in 1938. The cellist Friedrich Walther was only slightly better off. Having served in the Bayreuth Festival orchestra from

7

1927 to 1933, he suddenly was discharged. Although Winifred Wagner, daughter-in-law of Richard Wagner and patron of the festival, offered to recommend him for a new job elsewhere, Walther was judged to be somewhat less than accomplished during auditions. Still, he managed to secure work as a backup cellist at the Deutsche Oper in Berlin, earning a mere 360 marks a month plus expenses and subject to dismissal with only two weeks' notice. In 1933 conductor Otto Klein was holed up in the capital awaiting a suitable job offer. With no such prospect in sight, he begged the government for support money. Five years later Klein had still not found employment. To pass the time and sharpen his skills, he composed the opera *Atlantis*, which was immediately doomed to oblivion. By this time both Klein and his wife had been struck by illness. They were supported solely by Klein's two brothers, who sent him 230 marks a month. Hanns Rohr, another conductor, had a doctorate in music. Having gotten by as an itinerant guest conductor from 1928 to 1934, he now accompanied his wife, a violinist, at the piano. If not for generous handouts from music-loving friends and the odd guest conductor's job, the couple would have gone under. By 1937 Rohr was suffering from a heart condition; a year later his distraught wife entered a sanatorium.[2]

During the first years of the Nazi regime, the fate of these musicians was hardly atypical; in fact, their personal difficulties were symptomatic of the widespread economic confusion that characterized the cultural scene in Germany following the last years of the Weimar Republic. The root cause could be traced back to January 1933. At that time the new Hitler regime had inherited from the republic a stagnant economy marked by high unemployment and low wages. This unemployment subsided only gradually; it was not until 1936 that it fell below that of 1928–29, and full employment was not achieved until 1938–39. In 1933 real earnings were a mere 87 percent of those in 1925–29, a relatively stable phase for the republic, and only in 1938 did they begin to surpass those of the peak years of republican prosperity.[3]

As difficult as these conditions were for the average German wage earner, they were much more onerous for the country's hundred thousand or so musicians, fewer than half of whom were devoted to the so-called classics, or "serious music." Not until about 1938 were they finally on an economic par with the national standard. One reason for this lag was that in tough economic times, matters of culture usually took second place. This made itself felt even in Germany, a country with a tradition of staunch public support for its cultural institutions, including opera houses and symphony orchestras. Such support, which had been gradually withdrawn as a result of the depression during the later years of the republic, was only haltingly restored in the first years of the Third Reich, as overall conditions improved.[4] In the summer of 1933, for instance, some members of the Berlin Philharmonic Orchestra, financially one of the best endowed of Germany's "culture orchestras" (those musical organizations dedicated exclusively to "serious music"), were still subjected to salary cuts of 40 percent. In 1935 unemployed Munich musicians were performing recitals in nursing homes on a volunteer basis just to maintain their skills.[5] Even as circumstances were improving, by late 1936 four out of five of Germany's gainfully employed musicians were bringing home less than 200 marks a month—which was less than what most blue-collar workers earned. The jobless rate still hovered above the 20 percent mark, more than twice the national average.[6]

Matters improved more quickly between 1936 and 1939 against the backdrop of general economic progress. More specifically, musicians of all kinds were needed after the establishment of Hitler's Wehrmacht in 1935 and the expansion of various government and Nazi Party organizations, notably the SS and the compulsory Reich Labor Service, all of which were eager to have their own bands. Moreover, geographic expansion caused by the annexation of Austria and, eventually, the Sudetenland and Memel created additional demands.[7] In March 1938 an impending shortage of qualified musicians[8] prompted the music lover Joseph Goebbels, head of all organized musicians under the Nazi regime, to promulgate a basic wage decree guaranteeing the profession's attractiveness. By this order, "culture orchestras" were favored over mere dance and light-entertainment bands. Orchestras were divided into five competency classes, and musicians' salaries and pension payments were standardized by law.[9]

These developments were reflected in an ascending salary curve for orchestra musicians, soloists, and conductors alike, with variations in each category based on qualifications, experience, and national prominence. Throughout the Third Reich, those musicians at the lowest end of the professional scale who were contractually employed consistently earned more in wages than any freelance work might net them. But at the upper end of the scale, an eminent artist might make as much from frequent guest appearances as from a guaranteed salary. If a musician was so fortunate as to be securely employed in 1933, his monthly earnings as an orchestra member could be as high as 450 marks. In 1936 the same salary could be as low as 350 marks per month, but it might well have risen, as it did for first violinist Hans Ortleb of the Deutsche Oper in Berlin, to over 600 marks by early 1939.[10] Concertmasters and soloists could expect to make at least double those amounts, depending on their opportunities for independent concertizing. This income placed them very close to the category of physicians, who, topping lawyers and dentists, were the highest paid of the self-employed professional groups in the Nazi era.[11]

Financially, conductors generally fared much better, with the world-famous Wilhelm Furtwängler the undisputed champion. In 1934 he received 1,000 marks per concert, contractually performing twenty-two of them in Berlin alone, in addition to touring, which fetched an equivalent amount per event. By 1937 Furtwängler was already getting 2,000 marks per appearance, and in 1938–39 this figure doubled again. For all of 1939 he earned well in excess of 200,000 marks, more than triple the 60,000 marks (including 20,000 marks in expenses) that his Austrian colleague Clemens Krauss was paid after assuming the directorship of the Bayerische Staatsoper in Munich in 1937.[12] Somewhat lesser-known conductors were still comfortably well off. For example, Hans Rosbaud in 1934–35 was earning about 13,000 marks per annum at Radio Frankfurt.[13] Other conductors employed for radio programs or as assistants throughout the Reich could be paid as much as a well-placed concertmaster, but less qualified ones were dependent on touring, and received as little as 200 marks per engagement.[14]

It is almost impossible to gauge the earnings of composers, many of whom doubled as conductors, soloists, or conservatory teachers. At one end of the spectrum was Carl Orff, who always tried to be fiercely independent. He subsisted for years on his publisher's advances, which he did not begin to make good on until the war, when Orff's operas finally began to bring him wealth.[15] No other composer of serious music earned as much as Richard Strauss, who in 1936—not one of his banner years—earned over 80,000 marks from all sources—high for a composer but noticeably trailing Furtwängler. Hans Pfitzner, who ranked just after Strauss in national importance, was making about half that much.[16]

Because in general terms the economic situation of musicians was so bleak until 1938, Nazi Party and government agencies tried to do what they could to help. Special symphony and chamber orchestras were financially supported and filled with jobless Nazi musicians.[17] When the British jazz band leader Jack Hylton applied to tour Germany in 1934–35, he was allowed to do so only on condition that he contribute one quarter of his earnings to unemployed German colleagues.[18] The Reich made grants of thousands of marks to aid the unemployed and facilitate the dignified retirement of older musicians. At Carnival time in Febrary 1935, a musicians' ball was organized in Munish's posh Four Seasons Hotel for the benefit of impoverished musicians,[19] and in 1936 Goebbels instituted Künstlerdank, a social-assistance program backed with millions of marks, from which the chronically indigent, such as involuntarily retired musicians and other artists, were to profit. From the fall of 1937 to the fall of 1938, Künstlerdank benefited more than three thousand musicians with up to 300 marks each.[20]

The program's work did not cease after economic conditions for musicians had improved. Even during World War II, when many musicians were in a position to exploit their unique talents, Goebbels called on musicians to entertain the troops and participate in various cultural schemes, to the extraordinary financial advantage of the musicians.[21] But the very fact that Künstlerdank was a creature of the regime raises the question of a possible interrelationship between economic performance and pro-Nazi political deportment, and specifically the question of opportunism. That is, did their financial straits motivate musicians to join the Nazi Party between 1933 and 1945? Given the insufficient evidence to date, the answer can only be equivocal. From a largely north German sample of musicians of all stripes and qualifications between 1933 and 1938, most of whom joined the party in 1934, it may be concluded that about one fifth of the profession was in the Nationalsozialistische Deutsche Arbeiterpartei (National Socialist German Workers' Party [NSDAP], or Nazi Party) before the war. Moreover, those who were employed showed a stronger tendency to join the NSDAP than those who were idle.[22] Still, this does not rule out destitution as a possible motive for Nazi Party membership. In 1934, for instance, though about one third of all musicians were jobless, more than half of the employed ones had a monthly income of 100 marks or less.[23] It may have been only these who show up as NSDAP members in the statistics. But why, then, was the proportion of Vienna Philharmonic musicians (among the best paid in the Reich) who were Nazi Party members also equal to one third after the Anschluss of Austria in 1938, and why did this membership rise over the years, even with the economy on the upswing?[24] It is clear that in this case factors other than purely economic ones were causing many artists to jump on the Nazi bandwagon.

To be sure, interference in music professionals' lives by the Nazi regime was considerable, and not only in economic terms. Official dictates called for the nazification of music to the extent that art generally had to be "put to the service of an idea," which in this case meant the ideology of racist National Socialism.[25] At the height of the war Wolfgang Stumme, chief of music in the Hitler-Jugend (Hitler Youth), still described German music as an antidote to "dangerous poison threatening the blood," that is, stimuli from the "Jewish, materialistic, Bolshevist environment."[26] In theory, then, only narrowly defined "German music" was to be produced and listened to. In 1938 Hans Pfitzner, under the impression that creative freedom was being stifled, remarked sarcastically to Hermann Göring, the boss of the Preussische Staatsoper, that in present-day Germany "any criticism is forbidden, indeed abolished, so that you cannot write it if a soubrette sings badly, even when it is really so."[27] Of course, Pfitzner knew well that such policies represented merely the ideal condition called for by Nazi fanatics, and that they could not be enforced with any degree of consistency. Goebbels knew this also when he pronounced in February 1934 that however tightly a government might rule, it had to keep loose reins on artistic and intuitive activities.[28] Richard Strauss, as president of Goebbels's Reichsmusikkammer (Reich Music Chamber, or RMK), took his cue from Goebbels when in 1935 he listed the desirable qualities of a music director: he had to have good ears, he had to be able to play the piano well, he had to understand the art of singing, and he had to comprehend the dynamics of modern opera (especially Strauss's own). Significantly, in this catalog of virtues Strauss failed to mention anything about Nazism or the Hitler regime.[29]

These two conflicting tenets, censure and toleration, turned out to be the guidelines for music creation and administration in the Third Reich.

While they expressed opposite intentions, neither one in its pure and unadulterated form dominated the musical life of the nation. Typically representing compromise in combination, they tempered each other, ensuring that some degree of artistic freedom would always obtain. Such a fluctuating system of balances, as we know today, was characteristic of the overall policy structure of Hitler's Third Reich and served to keep it going.[30]

Germane to the question of artistic opportunism, or the premeditated blending of art and politics in the first years of the regime, the principle of compromise found its practical embodiment in a three-stage process of policy making: first, if a musician proved to possess artistic talent and loyalty to the regime in more or less equal measure, then professional success could be virtually guaranteed; second, if a lack of musical competence was painfully obvious, then no amount of political dedication could warrant artistic survival; third, even if a musician's ties to the regime were minimal or nonexistent, he could still forge an impressive career for himself if the quality and quantity of his musical output were high by any standards, unless he went out of his way to insult the regime. The third stage explains the relative success of conductors such as Rosbaud and Furtwängler, of composers such as Strauss, and of performers such as the bass-baritone Hans Hotter.

Officially, then, as with many occupations in the Third Reich, Nazi affiliation of one kind or another was held to be a prerequisite for career advancement in the serious-music business, and prospective employers often applied pressure to individual musicians to join the Nazi Party.[31] This prompted many artists of solid but not outstanding ability to find jobs or improve their situation on the basis of existing or newly earned Nazi credentials. The conductor Gerhart Stiebler was out of work and judged to be merely competent as a musician, but because he had joined the NSDAP in 1932 and been very active as a party speaker, he was hired as musical director of the Görlitz theater in June 1933. Regime officials as highly placed as Prussian Minister of Education Bernhard Rust had seen fit to intervene on his behalf.[32] Although in 1936 the consensus was that Wilhelmine Holzinger, a freelance pianist always in search of a job, was but a mediocre musician, she had befriended Gauleiter Julius Streicher of Nuremberg and other party leaders and finally was deemed worthy of further support in the form of a job at Radio Nuremberg.[33] And in Berlin in 1936 there was Walter Lutze, a repertory conductor at the city's Deutsche Oper, which was within not Göring's but Goebbels's own jurisdiction. Lutze, too, was able but not brilliant and, like Stiebler, had joined the party in 1932. In addition, he was an old friend of Heinrich Hoffmann, Hitler's personal photographer, and father-in-law of Hitler Youth leader Baldur von Schirach. When Lutze was served notice on artistic grounds, Goebbels personally intervened and prevented his dismissal; although the conductor was slated for removal during the war, when musicians were scarce, the propaganda minister protected him up to the end of the regime.[34]

The entire Schirach family exemplifies Nazi patronage in the arts. Baldur's father, Karl von Schirach, long retired as Generalintendant of the Weimar stage but an old follower of Hitler since the 1920s, was made intendant of the Wiesbaden theater in 1933.[35] Rosalind, Karl's daughter, was a run-of-the-mill soprano at the Berlin Deutsche Oper. Together with her lover Gerhard Hüsch, the well-known baritone, she organized a powerful Nazi cell there that wielded much influence. One trade journal hailed her as the "ideal image of a Nordic-Aryan singer."[36]

Baldur himself wrote melodramatic poems, many of which venerated the Führer and were set to music, giving cantatas such as those by the unexceptional Hans Ferdinand Schaub timely and very convenient content.[37] In fact, gearing the thematic content of a musical composition to the spirit of the times could bring rich rewards to its creator; Schaub found himself elevated to the position of "state composer" by the Gauleiter of Hamburg and was granted an unconditional sinecure.[38] Friedrich Leiboldt of Naumburg composed his *Horst Wessel Cycle* in part on verses by von Schirach; it was scheduled to be premiered by a mixed choir in 1934. Rudolf Bockelmann, another famous baritone, acted as soloist in the song "For the Führer," written by the little-known Hans Gansser and marketed by Electrola Records in 1935. Paul Winter, who perhaps deservedly was to rise to the rank of general during World War II, crafted a hymn-fanfare and had it performed at Vienna Radio in April 1938, after Hitler had marched his troops into Austria; it was inspired by his profound joy over the "magnificent consummation of the union of Greater Germany."[39] Frequently, such politically inspired compositions were generated because venal regime leaders—Göring, Goebbels, or Alfred Rosenberg—had commissioned them.[40]

But even though in the twelve years of Hitler's rule some twenty thousand compositions with political applications were produced, the large majority, written by crass dilettantes of undoubtedly sterling party reputation, were never recognized.[41] Hitler himself, while admitting to only moderately sophisticated musical tastes, at least was shrewd enough to see through the most blatant cases of opportunism. Hence, he "disliked the newly composed party rally music," and by 1935 he had forbidden the inflationary practice of personal dedications to the Führer.[42]

Not only career-conscious composers but also instrumentalists and conductors who, for lack of talent, had been failures in the pre-Nazi period now attempted to use the party badge or other regime paraphernalia to pursue their goal. They still failed because of incompetence. Doris Kaehler, at thirty-eight not the youngest contralto in the business, traveled from Berlin to Berchtesgaden, where she beleaguered Hitler at his Berghof, hoping that a chance to sing for him might lead to a spot at state radio. Kaehler was a Nazi "Old Fighter"—one of those who had joined the party before January 1933—and the daughter of a minor party functionary, but her artistic credentials were wanting.[43] Paul de Nève, who in the "Marxist-Jewish Reich" had directed musical events for the party for free, was hoping for restitution; yet he remained merely a candidate for Künstlerdank, for in 1938 he was already fifty-seven and had no particular artistic merits.[44] Party comrade Otto Wartisch, a conductor, failed dismally to land a contractual post at the Munich Philharmonic in 1936, as did party comrade Fritz Müller-Rehrmann, hoping for a post as conductor, composer, or music professor anywhere in Germany, in 1937.[45] Typically, artists such as Wartisch and Müller-Rehrmann overestimated their chances and, on the basis of their Nazi pedigrees, aspired to positions they could never do justice to, even at the pleasure of benevolently minded dictators, as Goebbels himself correctly observed in late 1936. The composer Paul Hindemith at the start of the Nazis' regime declared that "bad works can't be pushed indefinitely, and the people they are now digging out are all complete mediocrities."[46]

Nazi Agencies of Music Administration

One reason why the compromise between suppression and toleration was workable was the relative impotence of, and the lack of cooperation between, the agencies set up to administer music in the regime. The first of these agencies was the Kampfbund für deutsche Kultur (Combat League for German Culture). The Kfdk, founded by the Nazi Party ideologue Alfred Rosenberg in February 1929, was a political lobby aimed at rescuing German culture from what the National Socialists considered pornography, Bolshevism, international Jewry, and the "gutter press"—all symbolized by Bauhaus art, critical writings in the left-wing *Weltbühne*, and modernist (or "atonal") music.[47] It was aimed at Germany's educated elite during Hitler's rise to power, at a time when he was eager to court the upper strata of society. Until January 1933 conservative, nationalistic, and race-conscious Germans, most of them from academic circles but also performing artists, had joined its various regional cells. In the realm of music, the local Kampfbund leaders would stage recitals and concerts, frequently with the help of unemployed musicians (such as a Kampfbund choir), and Nazi sympathizers with an interest in high culture would attend, as well as contribute money.[48]

For administrative purposes the Kampfbund leadership created elaborate subdivisions, including sections for serious and for light music, for opera, for instrumental and vocal music, for composition, and, not least, for music education.[49] After January 1933 the Kampfbund's ambition to be the sole regulator of music in the Third Reich became stronger, fueled by Rosenberg's own sense of mission as the party's official philosopher and warden of all things cultural. As job-creation schemes became ever more important, local music events featuring unemployed or underemployed instrumentalists, vocalists, even entire orchestras or choirs took precedence in all the German provinces, such as in Halle, where an evening of Brahms sonatas and Wagner's *Wesendonk Lieder* was organized in March 1933. The inclusion of Wagner signaled the Kampfbund's uppermost purpose, that of sweeping "the last bits of Jewish rot out of our German house, quickly and thoroughly."[50] This belligerent agency acquired some official currency when it managed to put on a celebration in honor of Hitler's birthday on 20 April 1933 in Berlin, on which occasion Rosalind von Schirach's paramour Gerhard Hüsch presented songs by Bach and Schubert. Similarly unadulterated German fare was offered a month later in Leipzig, when Kampfbund organizers penetrated the famous Gewandhaus Orchestra hall to stage works by Brahms—supposedly in honor of the centenary of Brahms's birth. And in early summer a special arts festival in Berlin afforded Gustav Havemann's national Kampfbund Orchestra the chance to present selections from Wagner's *Tristan und Isolde* and *Der Fliegende Holländer*.[51] To emphasize the Nazi Party backing, at a Kampfbund festival in Stettin in the fall the pianist Annemarie Heyne, a niece of Deputy Führer Rudolf Hess, participated, and in Plauen so did Heinrich Bienert, a reciter of poetry as well as a Standartenführer in the SA.[52]

The Kampfbund was weak, however, and its domination over German music was tenuous and short-lived for two reasons. First, it was an unofficial, unauthorized party organization, founded on impulse by one Nazi leader ambitious for overall cultural control, and without Hitler's committed backing. Throughout its existence the Kfdk had its organizational and financial base only in the Nazi Party and was never grounded in government. Soon after the regime had been installed, Rosenberg's reign was challenged by Goebbels, Göring, and Prussian (later Reich) Culture and Education Minister Bernhard Rust, because of his jurisdiction over music education. Second, despite Rosenberg's historic role as founder and spiritual figurehead, the Kampfbund never enjoyed strong central leadership, either from Berlin or from Munich, the seat of party headquarters. Instead, it was directed locally and regionally by mid-level party bosses, not all of whom were musicians, and who were likely to be engaged in internecine feuding. Every provincial hamlet seems to have had a Kampfbund dictator "who issued directives capriciously," as Hindemith's frustrated music publisher wrote him in April 1933.[53] And so, as a consequence of the Kampfbund's shaky beginnings and lack of authority, centralization, and coordination, Rosenberg eventually was surpassed by stronger contenders for cultural control, the most persistent of whom turned out to be Goebbels.

During 1933 and early 1934 the Kampfbund sought to fortify its influence with the aid of local delegates who held key positions in municipal music circles. In Rhenish Krefeld it was conductor Walther Meyer-Giesow who lorded it over the municipal orchestra, a collegium musicum, and a madrigal choir, and who throughout 1933 planned virtually all the musical activities in town.[54] In Munich, Kampfbund dictator Paul Ehlers so usurped the traditional Bach-Verein and its choir and orchestra that Carl Orff, who before the Third Reich had played a key role in it, withdrew in early 1934.[55] And in Marburg the Kfdk chief used his power to organize as many musical events as possible, for the greatest number of party faithful, at preferential ticket prices.[56]

The undoing of Rosenberg's combative organization began as early as spring 1933, for it was taking liberties in music policy and administration for which it had no mandate, thus embarrassing not only civil but party authorities as well. In April a Rhenish Kampfbund cell, allegedly with Rosenberg's authorization, offered Munich composer and conductor Hans Pfitzner the directorship of the Düsseldorf Opera. But when Pfitzner checked with the lord mayor of Düsseldorf, who was ultimately responsible, he received no commitment. The Kampfbund then explained that it had merely tried to act on a suggestion from Rosenberg, but that, naturally, Pfitzner would have to deal with the mayor himself. The Kampfbund had lost face, and Pfitzner was chagrined.[57]

In north German Schwerin, meanwhile, concertmaster Karl Krämer was summarily dismissed from the Mecklenburg state theater for displeasing one of his superiors. Krämer had the Kampfbund intercede with the Gauleiter, but since it was without authority, nothing came of the action.[58] In Hamburg, Kapellmeister and Kampfbund member Willi Hammer set down a definition of art meant to serve as a general directive for the Reich, but no sooner had it been promulgated than it sank into oblivion.[59] By spreading lies, a Berlin Kampfbund functionary in February 1934 tried to discredit the noted music critic Hans Heinz Stuckenschmidt, but was forced to apologize after Stuckenschmidt's vigorous protest.[60]

By this time Goebbels, who not only was in charge of propaganda for the party but also since March 1933 held a ministerial position authorizing him to oversee matters of culture almost everywhere, had put his Reichsmusikkammer (Reich Music Chamber), or RMK, firmly into place, and it was now applying heavy pressure on Rosenberg's disparaged Kampfbund cells. Although Rosenberg was given an "Office for the Supervision of the Total Spiritual and Philosophical Education and Development of the NSDAP," his remained a marginal party agency, in contrast to Goebbels's dual functions in the party and the state. Within this new office Rosenberg created yet another music control post, hoping to redouble the efforts of his lackluster Kampfbund on the strength of party legitimacy while coupling the impotent Kfdk with the Kraft durch Freude (Strength-through-Joy) organization, or KdF, of Robert Ley. The new control post, known as the Main Office for Music, was handed over to Herbert Gerigk, an ambitious musicologist and music critic with impressive Nazi credentials.[61] Meanwhile, the Kampfbund für deutsche Kultur in its new guise became known as the NSKG, or NS-Kulturgemeinde (National Socialist Cultural Community); henceforth, it would perform merely as a music (and theater) lobby, purchasing cheap blocks of tickets for its many, now entirely passive, members throughout the Reich. It also organized concerts of its own.[62] The NS-Kulturgemeinde was totally absorbed by Strength-through-Joy in 1937 and thereupon ceased to exist as one of Rosenberg's cultural platforms.[63] During the war especially, the KdF organized mass events for the sake of armaments production and troop entertainment; in its service German musicians performed for BMW workers as well as for Waffen-SS soldiers and civilians on the home front. Here music's new calling as an instrument of politics and war had been fully realized.[64]

Significant defections from the Kampfbund had occurred in the spring of 1933, when four leading functionaries left to organize a Nazi cartel of musicians in Berlin under violinist Gustav Havemann.[65] Their Reichskartell der Deutschen Musikerschaft was organized along neocorporatist lines, using notions borrowed in part from Italian Fascism, ideally thought to serve the collective interests of a professional group and popular long before Hitler with spokesmen for other occupations, such as lawyers and physicians.[66] In the fall this Reichskartell became the nucleus for the Reich Music Chamber.[67]

In March 1933 Goebbels was still indicating his support for Rosenberg's Kampfbund, but by then it was already clear that he intended to take over the reins of culture in the Reich himself.[68] Goebbels fully realized this claim when, in late June, he was officially authorized to set up the machinery for such control, utilizing his new Reichsministerium für Volksaufklärung und Propaganda (Promi, or Reich propaganda ministry), and hence endangering any and all of Rosenberg's preexisting party institutions.[69] Former Rosenberg sycophants such as Havemann were beginning to drift into Goebbels's camp, and Hans Hinkel, once a Kampfbund secretary, was already in his employ.[70]

The founding of the RMK was formally announced on 1 November 1933 as part of an umbrella organization, the Reichskulturkammer (Reich Culture Chamber, or RKK) presided over by Goebbels. There were similar subchambers for visual arts, theater, literature, journalism, radio, and later also for film. Membership in the RMK, as in the other chambers, was compulsory for all professionals in their respective categories.[71] Havemann and other cronies from the Kampfbund—such as Heinz Ihlert, a Berlin businessman, occasional piano player, and Nazi Old Fighter since 1927—commenced to staff the various sections, Havemann himself taking charge of musicians after merging his Reichskartell, and Ihlert becoming the executive secretary. Hans Hinkel became responsible for the RMK in 1935, when he was appointed secretary-general of the Reich Culture Chamber. This much larger culture chamber was ceremoniously inaugurated on 15 November 1933, with Richard Strauss conducting his own *Festliches Präludium*. This was no accident, for at Goebbels's behest Strauss had agreed to serve as president of the subordinate RMK.[72]

Since 1945, and even before, there has been much speculation as to why the world-famous composer consented to take on this—to say the least—questionable job. Strauss certainly did not have to do so for financial reasons, for he was a wealthy man; he was in no need of additional publicity; and in 1933 he was not yet under any sort of political pressure. The answer is not, as one German musicologist has contended,[73] that he was a power-hungry, dyed-in-the-wool National Socialist, but that he saw in the dictatorship of Hitler a convenient if somewhat distasteful tool to realize goals he himself had been anticipating for decades. Admittedly no friend of the democracy of Weimar,[74] Strauss believed that a dictatorial regime could finally implement the changes toward neocorporatism that would benefit the German musical profession, and in particular composers, on behalf of which he had been toiling since the beginning of the century. As newly available documents from the Strauss family archive in Garmisch reveal, three goals were foremost in his mind. First, he wanted to upgrade musical culture in the country by instituting throughout the highest level of training and performance. Second, he wished to increase the profit share of serious composers vis-à-vis light-music composers, among whom he most detested the creators of operettas such as Franz Lehár, a constant object of his vilification. Third, he aimed to extend the period of copyright for serious-music compositions, for the sake of composers and their heirs.[75]

His was a specialized agenda, sharply skewed toward the immediate concerns of people like himself. Significantly, Strauss chose to head the RMK section for composers personally. It is doubtful whether Goebbels recognized the potential for conflict when he appointed the maestro—a conflict that inexorably developed over time. But for now, in the fall of 1933, he merely wished to exploit Strauss's immense prestige nationally and especially internationally, for Hitler's regime craved recognition abroad, just as Strauss intended to exploit the powers of a dictatorship.[76] In any event, because of Strauss's professional self-interest in the RMK and his reluctance to exchange the comfortable life of a composer in Garmisch for a functionary's presence in Berlin, he delegated most RMK affairs to underlings, in particular to his business manager Ihlert, becoming personally involved only in matters dear to his heart. Strauss's letters to the few men in Berlin whom he trusted and regularly corresponded with, notably Ihlert, Hugo Rasch, and Julius Kopsch, demonstrate contempt for their daily routines, which he deemed far beneath him.[77]

One immediate result of this absentee presidency was a lack of direction in the upper ranks of the Berlin RMK, leading to confusion, corruption, and infighting. At Berlin headquarters Ihlert and Havemann especially were soon feuding with their colleagues; Ihlert himself was accused of protectionism and inefficiency, others of tardiness and sexual misconduct.[78] A second result was a conspicuous absence of firm RMK controls throughout the Reich, normally manifested in the fascist strictures and repression that even then typified Nazi policy in other areas.

It is true that under Strauss's arm's-length presidency the RMK initiated what became its traditional policy of conscripting professional musicians and demanding monthly membership fees. The RMK also instituted musical competency tests in order to weed out amateurs and frauds and thereby help define a professional code—all in the spirit of neocorporatism that was a hallmark of the era. Moreover, the RMK granted—and withheld—permission for musicians to travel abroad and spend a predetermined amount of hard currency. And to continue the job-creation programs already begun, on a much smaller scale, by the Kampfbund, it limited the number of foreign instrumentalists allowed into Germany, who might snatch jobs away from natives.[79]

Meanwhile Goebbels, in order to assuage musicians' concerns, and in keeping with his stated principle of relative artistic freedom, maintained a fairly low profile as cultural enforcer in the early days of the regime. Hence, Strauss himself was able to hold controls and censorship to an absolute minimum. This, in fact, was one of the few areas of RMK policy that still interested him and over which he tried to reserve decisions for himself, certainly whenever he could make it his business to be informed. This was evident not only in the matter of the proscription of Jewish colleagues, which he soft-pedaled, but also with regard to the nature of the music to be performed. For instance, when in March 1934 the fanatical Nazi critic and RMK presidium member Fritz Stege wished to censure a concert pianist with a penchant for modern works, the presidium opposed him on the grounds that "in principle, the Reich Music Chamber cannot forbid works of an atonal character, for it is up to the audience to judge such compositions."[80]

The immediate circumstances of Strauss's dismissal from his post by Goebbels in July 1935 are well known: in 1932 he had employed the Austrian Jewish novelist Stefan Zweig as librettist for his opera *Die schweigsame Frau,* and that was looked upon as an affront to the National Socialist regime. Moreover, when Zweig, finding his situation increasingly distasteful if not downright dangerous, attempted to extricate himself from the ongoing working relationship, Strauss wrote him on 17 June 1935 stating that he was only playacting as RMK president to prevent the worst from happening. Long suspicious of Strauss, the Gestapo intercepted the letter, and a disgusted Goebbels compelled him to resign. Public announcements indicated that Strauss had done so because of "old age" and "severely strained health."[81]

Although in the postwar literature this has become the standard explanation of Strauss's break with the RMK,[82] the deeper and more important reasons were structural. During Strauss's denazification hearings in 1947, it was said that the dismissal symbolized a "change in the system," of the chain of command between Goebbels as cultural overseer and his chamber leaders, and of the overall policy to be observed within a chamber.[83] The fact was that Strauss, although prestigious, was simply too single-minded and egotistically independent to serve the Nazis well over the long run. His absence from Berlin and his general lack of interest in the day-to-day administration of the RMK had already caused disruptions; and his skeptical attitude toward the "Jewish Question" made it clear that although he was authoritarian, he was by no means ruthless enough to implement the censorship and other controls Goebbels wanted to see applied throughout the RMK. This had surfaced as a problem during the Hindemith affair of 1934–35, when Strauss advised his council that the composer should not be ostracized from the RMK.[84] Hindemith's as yet unperformed opera *Mathis der Maler* hitherto had been the only contemporary serious-music composition to be declared unwanted, not by any new aesthetic-ideological criteria but for political reasons, not the least of which had to do with Hitler's long-standing dislike of that composer, with his modernist reputation. It had not been Strauss who indicted him but the highest-level regime leaders themselves.[85]

Strauss was replaced by Peter Raabe, the retired Generalmusikdirektor of Aachen and a professor emeritus at the technical university there. He was sufficiently nondescript to serve as Goebbels's ideal puppet. Born in 1872, he had enjoyed a respectable if not spectacular career as conductor, and had earned a doctorate with a dissertation on Franz Liszt. He had just begun his retirement when the minister's call reached him. Raabe had a personal motive for accepting this post, for his conducting career was in the process of being eclipsed by the meteoric rise of Herbert von Karajan, who, though active only a few months in Aachen, had outshone him there chiefly as conductor of the municipal opera.[86] Although Raabe did not apply for Nazi Party membership until 1937, he was a fanatical follower of Adolf Hitler and, by all accounts, was deeply committed to Nazi cultural policy.[87] Unlike Strauss, however, and probably influenced by his idol Liszt, whose harmonic innovations anticipated the atonality of Arnold Schoenberg, Raabe was partial to the more modern composers, a weakness Goebbels liked to ridicule, and which made Raabe even softer putty in the minister's hands.[88]

Raabe's far more subordinate position as president of the RMK became obvious in a number of ways. Unlike Strauss, Raabe was made to wait in the antechambers of Goebbels's ministry when ordered to report to his lieutenants, and Raabe's protest went unheeded.[89] Deciding to tighten his policy of public controls somewhat while still favoring persuasion and conversion over outright restriction, Goebbels met with no objections from Raabe when he instituted closer monitoring of concert programming. In September 1935 a limited blacklist of works by Jews and foreigners was issued, something Strauss most certainly would never have consented to.[90] In 1936 Raabe, despite his protest, finally had to acquiesce in Goebbels's decision to absorb into the RMK the Allgemeiner Deutscher Musikverein (General German Music Society), Liszt's creation of 1859, in which Raabe played a leading role and whose independence he wished to preserve. (It was at the ADMV's annual functions that Raabe had been observed to favor "modernism.") The ADMV was duly liquidated in 1937.[91] In the matter of Hindemith's proscription, it was Raabe who at Goebbels's insistence in October 1936 signed an order placing all of Hindemith's works on a public-performance index, something that could never have been entrusted to Strauss.[92]

By this time, however, Raabe was no longer the minister's sole plenipotentiary in matters of musical culture in the Reich, for in late 1936 Goebbels had appointed Heinz Drewes, the Generalmusikdirektor of Altenburg, to head a department of music in the Propaganda Ministry.[93] The reasons for this move are not entirely clear, but it can be surmised that Goebbels wished to have some sort of guarantee that Raabe would be held in check to avoid a repetition of the extreme embarrassment that Strauss had caused him. This would have been wholly in keeping with the National Socialists' practice of establishing a "fragmented administration," with double and triple levels of jurisdiction, duplication of responsibility, and crossed chains of command. Ultimately, the higher leaders benefited from such institutionalized chaos, since only they could act as arbiters in seemingly endless disputes or in cases where government efficacy was seriously at stake. Invariably this strengthened their position. This, incidentally, was the major reason why Hitler himself did not intervene in the initial rivalry between Rosenberg and Goebbels, for in the final analysis it was he who emerged supreme.[94]

Goebbels made sure that he would always have the last word by artfully entangling the responsibilities of Raabe and Drewes. His scheme was clever enough: Raabe as president of the RMK came under Goebbels as president of the Reich Culture Chamber, of which the RMK was a part. The RKK was of course rooted in Goebbels's Promi. Drewes, while an official of the Promi, was not given responsibility for Raabe, whose formal superior was Goebbels. On the contrary, just to keep Drewes in his place, he was cross-appointed to the RMK's presidium, thus making him nominally subordinate to Raabe.[95] Predictably, Drewes and Raabe were constantly at each other's throats regarding "the leadership in music," which made Goebbels happy, for he could always threaten either man with ammunition derived from the intrigues of the other.[96]

In theory, Drewes's department was to have powers of policy creation and Raabe's agency powers of policy enactment.[97] But in practice, in those areas that really mattered to him Goebbels towered over both men, conveying his wishes in person or using as his conduit a state secretary of his ministry. As long as it lasted, this delineation meant that Raabe continued to exercise responsibility in practical matters such as coopting and regulating RMK membership and devising technical rulings.[98] In terms of ideological and content controls, however, Raabe seems to have been comparatively disadvantaged, or to have taken his cue from Drewes's department, if not—as in the case of Hindemith's banning in 1936— directly from Goebbels. This is evident from the details of the long battle Raabe waged against jazz, a battle he could not win till the end, not least because Goebbels himself divined that jazz served certain propaganda functions, especially in wartime.[99] In the serious-music realm Raabe's subservience became transparent in the summer of 1937, when Carl Orff, whom Rosenberg's Kampfbund had been battling since 1932, premiered his scenic oratorio *Carmina Burana*. Drewes took an immediate dislike to Orff and, while never censuring outright any of the composer's current or future works, successfully intimidated him, keeping him in abeyance until well into the war. Raabe's office merely echoed Drewes's authority.[100] Almost certainly it was Drewes, too, not exactly a champion of modern music, who had prevailed on Goebbels to dissolve the ADMV against Raabe's wishes; this in fact cemented the eternal enmity between the two functionaries.[101]

Under the presidency of Peter Raabe, the Reich Music Chamber was to experience several personnel changes. The most important of these were the appointment of the composer Paul Graener as head of the composers' section, which Strauss himself had led until the summer of 1935, and then Graener's own replacement six years later by Werner Egk, a former student and friend of Carl Orff and disposed, like Orff, toward the composition of more modern music.[102] As we shall see, this change occurred over differences concerning the place of popular music, and because Goebbels, in the hope of establishing a uniquely Nazi musical style, had found it imperative to grant some leeway to the more progressive of Germany's composers. The traditionalist Graener, whom the minister had derogatorily described as a "Santa Claus" back in 1936, could give no such assurances.[103] In any event, Egk's appointment at a nominally inferior but in fact extremely influential level after July 1941 reduced the power of both Drewes (who intermittently found himself at the war front) and Raabe, who performed his duties rather perfunctorily, delivering speeches and conducting concerts throughout the Reich.[104] Off and on Goebbels considered replacing both Drewes and Raabe, for he could not say who was the duller of the two. Furtwängler was reportedly interested in the RMK post.[105] In the end both men proved indispensable for carrying out the practical chores that had become their everyday routines in a period of scarce new talent. At the close of 1943 it was Drewes whom Goebbels credited with having resuscitated Berlin's musical scene after a year of severe British air attacks. But Raabe, too, had to postpone his plans to retire to private life "in order to write a couple more books." Ironically, one of his final tasks was to decree, during late summer 1944, the dissolution of all major culture orchestras in the Reich, save for a fortunate few, such as the Berlin Philharmonic, that were still needed to uphold civilian and troop morale.[106]

Nazi Musical Careers

The example of the two successive RMK presidents, Richard Strauss and Peter Raabe, might suggest that overall, in the Third Reich superior musicians tended to spurn National Socialism, while confirmed Nazis were lacking in musicianship. But such was not necessarily the case: there was no consistent correlation between political conviction and musical talent. In the Third Reich excellent musicians could also be fanatical Nazis, and, conversely, mediocre musicians could be ardent defenders of democracy and the inalienable rights of man. There were, of course, various permutations in between these two extremes, with the ratio of musicianship to politics not easily determined.

Whether the violinist Gustav Havemann actually was a true Nazi after 1932 may be doubted by some, for he had been known as a left-winger until his sudden conversion to Hitler's movement in the spring of that year, which took many of his colleagues by surprise.[107] Havemann could already look back on a prominent career. A former student of the legendary Jewish violinist Joseph Joachim, he had been apointed professor at the Hochschule für Musik in Berlin at the age of thirty-nine in 1921, and in 1932 he received an honorary doctorate from the University of Greifswald.[108] During the republic he led one of the foremost string quartets, specializing in modern music including works by Schoenberg and Hindemith.[109] It is, however, not unlikely that in early 1932 Havemann experienced a genuine conversion to National Socialism (if so, he would not have been alone among German artists), even if later it became easy to charge him with opportunism.[110] To all intents and purposes Havemann tried to serve his new masters well, chiefly as conductor of the Kampfbund's symphony orchestra of unemployed musicians, and by January 1933 the Berlin Kampfbund concerts were scheduled every Sunday.[111]

As a confirmed Nazi, Havemann soon found that his once formidable reputation as a violinist was suffering because of his preoccupation with conducting, which in his grandstanding manner he did badly, but also because of his incessant meddling in politics. About his conducting it was said that "he is performing in absolutely empty halls; it is a laughable event artificially propped up by yawning Brownshirts."[112] He alienated Rosenberg by extricating himself and other musicians from the Kampfbund, as well as other Nazi figures such as Robert Ley, whose Deutsche Arbeitsfront (German Labor Front), or DAF, supported its own orchestra of indigent Nazi musicians. Havemann even went so far as to ingratiate himself with Deputy Führer Rudolf Hess, claiming a place in his hierarchy. In addition, Havemann was constantly being accused of being not only a former Marxist and crony of the Jews but also a squanderer of money, a friend of the bottle, and an obsessive womanizer. Even after he had found what looked like a permanent home as head of musicians in the RMK, malicious tongues charged that he was protecting the violinist Maria Neuss, the illegitimate child of his earlier liaison with a Jew. All the while Goebbels was backing Havemann, no doubt because he still needed capable allies in his own struggle against Rosenberg and other regime leaders.[113]

Eventually, still uncertain over his place in the pecking order but craving recognition as a bona fide Nazi, Havemann stumbled into the Hindemith affair, which became a test for so many musicians and administrators early in the Third Reich. For Hindemith, his colleague at the Hochschule in Berlin, Havemann harbored genuine loyalties; he once had championed his innovative music.[114] Thus, he wrote to Hess in December 1933 that Hindemith, already suspect, was not of the same ilk as "the Jewish Schoenberg and Weill."[115] Havemann was about to join forces with Furtwängler, then the chief defender of Hindemith, notwithstanding the fact that he had denounced the conductor, along with Strauss, for omitting the Hitler salute during a performance of the Brownshirts' beloved "Horst Wessel Lied."[116] On 16 November 1934 Havemann, in his capacity as RMK section leader, delivered a much-publicized address at the annual meeting of the Prussian RMK, in which he placed Hindemith on a par with the national icons Strauss and Pfitzner. He insisted on "the protection of true genius" and expressed "opposition to petty strife and infighting." But a few days later Goebbels, probably under pressure from Hitler, ineluctably came around to Rosenberg's long-standing view that Hindemith could no longer be tolerated, and this meant trouble for his supporters.[117] When Hindemith fell from grace early in 1935, Furtwängler and Havemann fell along with him, albeit not so far or so hard. Havemann tried his utmost to support the composer after Hindemith took temporary leave from the Hochschule für Musik and became active on behalf of the German Reich as a music educator in Turkey. But then in July, during the Strauss debacle, Havemann too lost his RMK portfolio, though not his Berlin professorship.[118]

It could be said that the corrosive powers of the Third Reich succeeded in corrupting a talented but nevertheless weak character such as Havemann and turned him into its lackey, whereas in a true democracy the violinist would have been forced to stand on his merits and might well have excelled. Having barely escaped expulsion from the party in 1937, throughout the remainder of the regime Havemann had to fall back on what was left of his musicianship without the aid of politics.[119] He abandoned his Nazi orchestra, which soon found itself in hopeless competition with similar groups, and once more tried his luck as a concert violinist, albeit one who was especially fond of performing his own trivial compositions. No wonder that from even the official press he garnered no more than polite applause.[120] By wartime, when a revived Havemann Quartet of undistinguished string players was performing for the troops, Havemann had in any case been overshadowed nationally by the much younger Max Strub and Wolfgang Schneiderhan, to say nothing, internationally, of his now exiled Jewish colleague Carl Flesch and rising newcomers such as Jascha Heifetz, Yehudi Menuhin, and Isaac Stern.[121]

The composer Paul Graener was if anything, an even more tragic figure than Gustav Havemann, who was his junior by ten years. This epigone of Brahms—who, as a budding yet largely self-taught artist, had once been told by the aging master, "You still have a lot to learn"—led a checkered career as conductor and composer in the decades before the Third Reich.[122] During the republic, unlike Havemann, he was anything but the darling of an educated music audience, and Graener blamed his eclipse—for he was always in the shadow of Strauss and Pfitzner, not to mention the modernists—on Jews and Marxists. He had the extraordinary misfortune of having his (thus far) most important composition, *Hanneles Himmelfahrt*, premiered in 1927, the year of triumph for Ernst Křenek's sensational jazz opera *Jonny spielt auf*. Graener's was a maudlin, religiomystical opera based on Gerhart Hauptmann's much harder-hitting social realist play of the same title, and it paled in comparison with Křenek's iconoclastic musical score and plot.[123] Indeed, Graener's was a deadly serious syncretic style of composing, sometimes reminiscent of Bruckner or Reger, at other times of Strauss or Graener's idol Brahms. An inveterate foe of modernism, he modeled his operas on conventional and well-worn literary and historical themes (*Don Juans letztes Abenteuer; Friedemann Bach*).[124] A former director of the Mozarteum Conservatory in Salzburg, Graener headed the Stern'sche Konservatorium in Berlin from 1930 to 1934; and as an early Kampfbund official he joined the NSDAP in March 1933 and made it to the presidium of the RMK in November of that year. Strauss reacted with sarcasm after learning that it was Graener who would take over his office as head of the composers' section in 1935.[125]

Why did Goebbels choose Paul Graener, who was virtually unknown outside Germany, to succeed the celebrated Richard Strauss? The most plausible answer is that with Hindemith out of the line of succession, by the traditional standards of the period Graener ranked third in the hierarchy of German composers, after Strauss and Pfitzner, and the minister still wanted a credible figurehead. Since Pfitzner was notoriously difficult and not likely to cooperate with the Nazis in cultural politics, Graener seemed the logical choice, for, like Raabe, he was too insignificant to cause serious trouble, and what national prestige as a composer he did have could easily be utilized in the service of the regime.

Graener used his office mostly to announce policy decisions made over his head by Goebbels, Hinkel, Raabe, and Drewes, and the surviving correspondence reveals that he soon came to loathe the job. Even the fact that he was simultaneously a vice-president of the RMK did not help. Yet these positions had one advantage: he could now get his chronically neglected works performed, both in the concert hall and on the radio. As the most dedicated Nazi follower of the three leading German composers, Graener had already seen an impressive revival of his works after Hitler's rise to power, and his own standing in the Kampfbund für deutsche Kultur had been a boon.[126] But although in 1934 Graener managed to receive the coveted Beethoven Prize,[127] the critics were not altogether happy with him. Frankfurt's Karl Holl, for instance, sounded less then enthusiastic when, in February of that year, he noted that in his

Friedemann Bach, although making a sincere effort, Graener had not achieved any depth. Regarding his newer opera, Der Prinz von Homburg, Richard Strauss was predictably more scathing. And Goebbels, too, assigned Graener merely a passing grade.[128]

Faithful to his assertion that the German people "once again want Romanticism," the pro-Hitler Graener got even more of his works performed after his elevation to high office in summer 1935; in fact, government agencies were now requesting his music.[129] But he had two weaknesses. One was an inability to manage money. By 1936 financial irregularities had driven him deep into debt. Using his office, Graener evidently applied pressure to several German radio stations to get his works scheduled more frequently in an attempt to collect more royalties.[130] The other weakness was his failure as head of the RMK composers' section to stand up to Goebbels in internal discussions regarding the place of serious versus light-entertainment music. As president of the RKK, Goebbels himself advocated a change in emphasis from serious music (Ernste, or E-Musik) to light music (Unterhaltungs-, or U-Musik). The minister, who had some elitist tastes and certainly scorned the masses, nonetheless was a consummate politician and realized that if he was to coopt the largest number of people to satisfy the aims of the regime, they would have to be wooed, and this could be achieved only with the help of popular culture, not Bach or Beethoven. Hence, in setting rates for royalties and the like, Goebbels decided to favor composers of popular music over those of classical works. This conflict had originated not under Raabe and Graener but under Richard Strauss, and had in fact contributed to the tensions that resulted in Strauss's eventual dismissal.[131]

Graener's indecision in this matter, as well as his financial improprieties, proved to be an embarrassment to Goebbels and his stalwarts. Although Graener's prestige, such as it was, still was needed to maintain a unified front among the Reich's composers—a front for which he was a useful figurehead during annual composers' conferences and similar congresses—regime insiders belittled him as "Papa Graener" and devised schemes to lower his profile. Within the Promi this was accomplished in April 1937, when his leadership of the composers' section was reduced to a nominal role, which meant that only for appearances' sake was he still being touted as the "leader of German professional composers."[132]

At the same time, measures were initiated to salvage his finances. Eventually Goebbels himself guaranteed a loan to Graener in the amount of 30,000 marks, an extraordinary sum at the time.[133] Reich Culture Chamber Secretary Hans Hinkel also applied pressure on German opera companies (except for the Preussische Staatsoper in Berlin, controlled by Göring) to perform more operas by Graener. This policy seems to have worked, for an increasing number of Graener's works were now being staged, to polite critical acclaim.[134] All of a sudden there were "Graener Morning Celebrations" for the Hitler Youth and "Paul Graener Festivals" dedicated to contemporary German composers.[135] Before long, radio stations were regularly broadcasting cycles of Graener's works.[136] In January 1942 Graener's seventieth birthday was commemorated nationally with great fanfare, and later he received a onetime composer's bonus from the RMK in the amount of 6,000 marks, as did Strauss and Pfitzner.[137]

This was an official reminder that for ceremonial purposes Graener still held high rank as a politically accredited artist of the Third Reich. But as an administrator of the official culture, Graener continued to be a failure. With his great love for nineteenth-century music, Graener had not, after all, created conditions conducive to the invention of a true National Socialist musical style. And he continued to withhold his support from popular music, in the absence of a decisive policy regarding E-Musik. Hence, during a policy meeting in Goebbels's Berlin office early in 1941, the minister forced a showdown on the issue of serious versus light music. This was at a time when millions of ordinary soldiers with average tastes were in the trenches, and hundreds of thousands of workers were toiling on the home front for a Nazi victory. This time Graener, with some help from the RMK staff, took a more determined stand for the classics, supporting demands for higher royalties for serious composers. After Goebbels refused, Graener formally gave up the post of RMK section head, which he had already relinquished de facto in 1937, and the much more flexible and much younger composer Werner Egk replaced him.[138]

Graener's end was ignominious. Plagued by illness and bombed out of his house in Berlin, he and his wife (they had already lost their three children) moved to a temporary home first in Metz and then in Salzburg, financially supported by Goebbels's cronies. Feeling cheated of fame and fortune, he was still hoping for a house of his own in the suburbs of the capital. His final composition was Deutsche Hymne, which he had had performed while in Metz but was unable to sell to his powerful friends in the Promi for national radio distribution. Embittered, he died in Salzburg in November 1944, neither mourned by colleagues nor ritually remembered by a regime that had already bankrupted itself culturally and politically.[139]

Other musicians succeeded in the Third Reich through a combination of respectable talent and demonstrable National Socialist conviction. Not unlike Graener, Berlin composer Max Trapp, already middle-aged in 1933, had been thoroughly steeped in the late Romantic tradition, his works reflecting the influence of Brahms and especially Strauss. His professional beginnings after World War I had been quite auspicious. He was a professor at the Akademie der Künste in Berlin by 1920, and the premiere of his Second Symphony a few years later gave rise to very high hopes.[140] But, like Graener and others laboring in the shadow of the modernists, he could not make much headway with a critically discerning public, even though well-established traditionalists such as Furtwängler and the popular pianist Elly Ney were on his side [141]

Typically, Trapp's lack of public acclaim had much to do with his conversion to the Nazi movement, which occurred in the last years of the republic, when the Hitlerites were gaining ground. He became a Nazi Party member and, while it lasted, joined Rosenberg's Kampfbund für deutsche Kultur, where he was put in charge of serious-music composers. After that it was noted that his music made "a real impact."[142] Indeed, the Third Reich brought him a spate of official successes, some extraordinary honors, and invariably the polite, noncommittal critiques of Nazi commentators. As a composer Trapp was reckoned among the privileged members of the late Romantic Old Guard, who ranked below Pfitzner and Graener.[143] Among other works, he wrote a piano and a cello concerto, a Divertimento, and symphonic suites, and renowned figures such as Furtwängler, Herbert von Karajan, and Karl Böhm conducted them. He was singled out by radio and concert halls as a paragon of contemporary musicianship and duly received the national composition prize of 1940.[144] But although the large majority of reviews were most favorable, every once in a while a more daring critic reminded music lovers of the obvious: that for all their craftsmanship, Trapp's works were hardly original and far from the level of genius.[145]

There were several similarities between Max Trapp and Georg Vollerthun, a composer of lieder and operas who had also been influenced by Strauss, had been snubbed by Weimar audiences, and had joined the Kampfbund in 1932, there to be put in charge of opera. With Trapp and Graener he shared the dubious distinction of being singled out, weeks before Hitler's takeover, as part of "a selection of mediocrity" by the critic Stuckenschmidt.[146] Suffering, like Graener, from the revolutionary impact of modernists such as Křenek and Weill on German opera, Vollerthun conceived of himself as a restorer of traditional musical language in opera and song. In a program note he once wrote: "I view it as a mandate to write the kind of music which, if not understood, will be loved and especially sung by every fellow German. This should be my contribution to the musical culture of our time."[147]

Early in the Third Reich he earned some accolades with a "national" opera entitled Der Freikorporal; it was set in the seventeenth century at the court of August the Strong, king of Saxony, and for its performance at Goebbels's Deutsche Oper, Vollerthun was given leave to use as stage extras exceptionally tall members of Hitler's SS bodyguard.[148] The opera made the rounds in Germany to courteous reviews, but in circles that really mattered reaction was mixed at best. Goebbels himself thought it well intentioned but bereft of melody and altogether "too thin," while Strauss asked in mock amazement whether that sort of work represented "the new Germany."[149]

Nonetheless, throughout the Third Reich Vollerthun plodded on, mostly with new vocal compositions, often accompanying at the piano while singers rendered his own new songs. Predictably, he too collected his fair share of prizes and official distinctions, until in 1936 his career was almost cut short by a sex scandal after the sixty-year-old artist, married since 1912 to a general's daughter and the father of four children, had been discovered in bed with a coachman.[150] But because Vollerthun took care to deliver a distinctly "Nordic," National Socialist message in his songs and stage works—and did so with an acceptable combination of ideological conviction and musical competence—he proved difficult to get rid of. Early in the regime he had been lauded as a politically valuable artist. "In his creations we witness National Socialist music," wrote one Nazi reviewer approvingly. And so, like Trapp and some others, he remained a fixture of the Nazi cultural scene, only to fall into the abyss of extinction at its end.[151]

Deservedly, the same fate befell two others who, though not without artistic merit initially, exploited the National Socialist regime ruthlessly for the sake of their careers, with varying success. Wilhelm Rode, who had been one of Germany's better-known Wagnerian baritones during the 1920s joined the Nazi Party in the spring of 1933 at the age of forty-six. Possibly because Hitler had liked his singing, and SA chief Ernst Röhm also was very fond of him, in 1934 Rode was appointed intendant of the (formerly municipal) Deutsche Oper in Berlin, a position he maintained despite much controversy until 1945, with Goebbels's acquiescence.[152]

Rode's unpopularity with the Deutsche Oper company stood in odd contrast to his former celebrity as a singer. Over the years he did much to alienate his colleagues there. Once, seeking to curry favor with the homosexual Röhm, he proposed to dress his orchestra musicians in drag during a special concert for leaders of the Brownshirts. He was unreliable as an employer and constantly embarrassed his fellow artists with tall tales about his friendship with the Führer, whom he slavishly admired. Compared to Göring's Preussische Staatsoper repertoire under chief dramaturge Heinz Tietjen, Rode's was strictly second-rate, a fact that could not escape Goebbels. Until well into the war, the Gestapo kept a file on Rode, and eventually a conductor nominally inferior to him saw to the day-to-day business, yet for outward appearances, Hitler maintained his support.[153]

To what extent a hatred of Jews had been a factor in Rode's attraction to National Socialism is not known. This factor, however, was very instrumental in motivating the conductor Leopold Reichwein to become a follower of the Nazis. Born in Silesian Breslau in 1878, a conductor of the prestigious Vienna Hofoper before World War I, he had been cashiered by the Austrians in the early 1920s, most likely for lack of brilliance, though in his own recollection the Jews had been at fault. Moving over to the symphony of the Gesellschaft der Musikfreunde in Wien, a respectable if not the premier orchestra in Vienna, he harbored this resentment against Jews until, in September 1930, he published a vicious article in Rosenberg's *Völkischer Beobachter* in which he claimed that Jews, including Felix Mendelssohn-Bartholdy and many others, had become involved in music strictly to make money. Reichwein had joined the NSDAP in Germany six months earlier and had become the Viennese chieftain of Rosenberg's culture league.[154] So, notwithstanding his mixed German-Austrian background, as Michael Tanner puts it, Reichwein can be considered the prototypical "Nazi conductor."[155]

He was certainly not the most fortunate, however. Eager to leave behind the aggressively nationalistic climate of clerico-fascist Austria, which, till March 1938, was becoming increasingly anti-Nazi, Reichwein sought permanent posts in several German cities. The fact that he was rejected each time may have had much to do with his insider's reputation: Strauss deemed him average, a mere "cobbler" as a musician; the Viennese music critic Victor Junk, himself an ardent National Socialist, thought him insufficiently flexible as an orchestra leader.[156] After the 1938 Anschluss of Austria, it was not difficult for Reichwein to return to Germany, albeit merely for guest appearances; he remained based in Vienna, honing his reputation as an interpreter of Bruckner, Wagner, and Pfitzner.[157] Reichwein's life ended in 1945, coterminously with that of the Reich he had been so eager to serve.

This cross-section of Nazi musicians would be incomplete without a discussion of two women, Li Stadelmann and Elly Ney. Both were keyboard artists (as were most German female instrumentalists), and befitting the regime's character as a male-supremacist society, they were without any party, state, or other institutional office. Yet they were confirmed National Socialists nonetheless, and they had an impact on the musical life of the nation.

In both cases these women's National Socialist beliefs were driven by genuine anti-Semitism, stemming from what they regarded as bitter experiences in preregime days. Li Stadelmann was a Munich-based harpsichordist specializing in Baroque music, especially that of Bach. Even in the 1920s she was sufficiently accomplished to be invited to concert engagements abroad. In 1929, while on a tour of West Prussia (which then belonged to Poland), she had played with the violinist Andreas Weisgerber, a Jew. Stadelmann reacted angrily when Weisgerber's sensitive interpretation of the classical German composers was enthusiastically accepted by their audiences. In 1933 she hailed the coming of Hitler, rejoicing that "our German masters will find German interpreters."[158] She immediately joined the Nazi Party and, subsequently, at least three additional Nazi organizations. After the Munich Bach-Verein was usurped by the Kampfbund to cleanse it of "Jewish influence," church-music recitals relied heavily on Stadelmann. The harpsichordist continued to make her name as one of the most sought after chamber musicians of the Nazi period.[159]

Elly Ney's case is much more significant because she was both a greater artist and a more fanatical National Socialist. Born in 1882 in Düsseldorf, the daughter of an active imperial army sergeant and a music teacher, she was a child prodigy, giving public concerts as a teenager and touring the

United States extensively from 1921. By 1930 she had performed as a piano soloist in all the larger cities of the union and in many other countries as well.[160] Most probably her intense nationalism derived from the narrow-mindedness of her petit bourgeois military home, which appears to have rendered her entirely xenophobic. When, as a ten-year-old, she trained under the Jewish Cologne Conservatory piano teacher Isidor Seiss, she immediately took a dislike to him because of his "racially alien" qualities. As she later recalled, she made up for this unpleasant experience by spending more time in the choir of conservatory director Franz Wüllner, a Gentile. During her concert tours she was keen to propagate German values abroad, as in the United States, where she fancied herself fighting for "spiritual ideals and for *German* music," and in Switzerland, where she had German poems recited before her concerts. Characteristically, she was skeptical of the newer composers such as Schoenberg and Ernst Toch, but deeply appreciated the German-rooted Pfitzner, with whom she shared a general suspicion of Jews.[161]

Even before 1933 Elly Ney had developed a personal idealism that was not without its eccentricities. Like Hitler, she was a fervent vegetarian; she valued special herbs and juices and explored the spiritual powers of hydrotherapy.[162] She subscribed to a sort of humanitarian ethics, which her admirers today interpret as having been universal, but upon closer examination turns out to have applied only to racially pure and patriotic Germans—in a word, to fellow Nazis.[163] Indeed, within the Third Reich she was altruistic to the point of self-sacrifice, performing virtually free of charge for young German audiences; but they tended to be members of the Hitler Youth. On those occasions when she played for blue-collar audiences, it was for workers in the German Labor Front of Robert Ley; and when she entertained soldiers, they frequently included the Waffen-SS.[164] Her chosen medium was Beethoven, whose compositions she interpreted impressively, and after whom she styled herself physically, displaying that same heroic facial expression and that well-known untamed mane. Beethoven, of course, was in vogue in the Third Reich; he stood for the heroic spirit with which Hitler himself identified. Ney came to enjoy the appellation of high priestess that music critics bestowed upon her, for the aura of the quasi-divine was very much to her taste. Nor does she seem to have minded the translation of that concept from an originally Christian setting to a neo-pagan Germanic one.[165]

With her exuberant talent and thoroughly professional background, Ney would have flourished no matter what political regime she found herself in; indeed, the distinguished trio that she headed, along with cellist Ludwig Hoelscher and violinist Wilhelm Stross (later Max Strub), had been founded in the final phase of the Weimar Republic. But, given her personal and political predilections, she was fated to do particularly well in the Third Reich, to the point where many regarded her as the proto-typical National Socialist musician. For her own commercial benefit she exploited the national Beethoven mania for all it was worth, performing the master's works repeatedly in concerts and making many record-ings.[166] And though at least one knowledgeable foreign observer found her approach insensitive, she became something of a Mozart specialist as well, with the help of an adjunct faculty position at Salzburg's famous Mozarteum Conservatory.[167]

But Ney's ambition reached beyond the music that was her life. She aimed to become the personal friend of as many Nazi regime leaders as possible, for she regarded them as Germany's true saviors from all the perceived ills besetting it, particularly Judaism. Ney's abiding anti-Semitism is probably unique among the outstanding German musicians of the time. She was obsessed with Jews as firmly as she believed in the curative powers of medicinal herbs. Early on in the regime she claimed to have realized how insidiously the Jews had oppressed the Gentiles, with-out using any force at all, and later, once she had read Richard Wagner's treatises on the so-called Jewish Question, she became even more con-vinced. Over time she came to accept all the vicious prejudices proliferat-ing in Nazi Germany: that a disagreeable interpretation of a Bruckner symphony could have been the result of Jewish manipulation; that the writings of Stefan Zweig, Richard Strauss's librettist, were "ugly, Jewish-demonic"; and so on. She also regarded the art of jazz as racially degener-ate and "dangerous, precisely because technically it is of such great virtu-osity." Not surprisingly, these sentiments influenced her career decisions. As early as spring 1933, when she was asked to perform in Hamburg in place of the young Jewish pianist Rudolf Serkin (who, then living in Switzerland, had already been banned), she regarded this as an insult. In a letter she claimed that the thought of sitting in for a Jew was distasteful to her and that she could bear it only by concentrating "on the work alone."[168]

For Ney, Adolf Hitler was the cure to rid Germany of this alleged disease. She welcomed his early attempts to remove Jews from influential positions. "He is proceeding slowly yet radically," she remarked. Of course, she was aware that she herself was one of the beneficiaries of such measures. Upon recording Schubert's *Forellenquintett* for Electrola, she commented on the absence of "Jewish recordings" with great satisfac-tion. She was equally delighted that foreign Jewish soloists of the stature of Carl Flesch, Jascha Heifetz, and Vladimir Horowitz had all "played themselves out."[169]

Ney's tireless public service for the benefit of any conceivable party organization, especially the Hitler Youth, found a natural complement in her persistent lobbying for the favor of the leaders. With Goebbels, the chief of the Reich Culture Chamber, she does not seem to have had any notable rapport, while at the same time he appears to have been indif-ferent to her artistry.[170] In any event, she was interested first and foremost in the Führer. Enthralled by several of Hitler's early broadcast speeches, she was determined to play for him in private, and she was beside herself with envy after learning that her colleague Wilhelm Backhaus had already managed to do so by May 1933.[171] In the summer of 1936 the pianist, who in her public addresses never neglected an opportunity to praise Hitler, finally enjoyed his vicarious presence when she was seated close to the Führer's box at the Bayreuth Festival.[172] Barely a year later Hitler bestowed upon Ney, who had dutifully held a number of party organization memberships, the honorary title of professor. Finally, in the summer of 1938, she met him during an official dinner, where he shook her hand warmly. Thus encouraged, she asked outright to be allowed to play for him, but again this came to naught. By the fall of 1939, when war had broken out, Ney had to resign herself to the fact that "the Führer is occupied."[173] All those other party eminences she communed with—Hinkel, Frick, Hess, Rust, von Schirach—could never quite make up for this disappointment.[174]

Whatever its extent, nothing could better demonstrate the nazification of the music profession in the Third Reich than two unique institutions, each comprising artists who by themselves reflected the potential as well as the limits of Nazi cultural coordination. Although a considerable qualitative difference existed between them, they both ultimately became tools of Nazi indoctrination through music adapted for and aimed at specific target groups. The first was the National Socialist Reich Symphony Orchestra, and the second the Wagnerian festival at Bayreuth.

The Nazi symphony was formed around 1931 in Munich by Franz Adam, who apparently was authorized by Hitler himself, presumably because Adam, like Havemann in Berlin, intended to employ only out-of-work Nazi musicians. Much earlier he had played a pioneering role at Radio Munich, where in 1928 he nonetheless seems to have lost his job owing to incompetence. At that time a noted Munich music pedagogue accused Adam of an "uneven musical education," "uncertainty of taste," and "mediocrity." Still, in the last few months of the Weimar Republic, approximately seventy musicians gathered around Adam, who used them for various concert tours in the Bavarian hinterland.[175] According to one early follower whom Adam later fired, these concerts were a fiasco, from an organizational as much as from an artistic perspective. Whenever a concert had been played in some provincial backwater, the orchestra's treasurer would count the meager earnings for the evening, a process that reportedly took hours, and during which orchestra members had to while away their time in some pub until each of them finally received a few marks. Musically, the repertoire was restricted to a few stock selections, such as Bruckner's Fourth Symphony and Beethoven's "Leonore" Overture; and they were so badly played that the overall standard was said to be considerably below that of Havemann's Berlin Kampfbund orchestra.[176]

Adam also served Rosenberg's Kampfbund at first but left himself open to other possibilities, until in 1935 his itinerant unit became the official symphony orchestra of Ley's German Labor Front, concertizing mostly within the framework of its Strength-through-Joy program. Sponsored by the regime, it specialized in regional concert series, for which party cadres of all descriptions, from Hitler Youth to Reich Labor Service personnel, were coopted. The Reich Symphony Orchestra turned into a sort of National Socialist Boston Pops. Since Adam's purpose was to reach as many uneducated people as possible (and thereby claim a growing degree of popularity with the masses), the repertoire remained fairly traditional, including much early and hence relatively uncomplicated Wagner; the Romantic German masters Bruckner, Brahms, and Reger; the mainstay Beethoven; and later also Adam's own unassuming creations. It is indicative of the quality of this orchestra that none of Germany's reputable soloists ever joined it, nor did Adam (or later his deputy Erich Kloss) ever host a guest conductor of note. But it kept showing up at high-profile regime functions such as the annual Nuremberg party rally, and when German troops began their invasion of Poland in the autumn of 1939, it was in their rear guard.[177] In 1940 the orchestra performed for a motor squadron of the SA near the Esterwege concentration camp, and in the years to come it regularly entertained both factory workers supporting the war effort and SS and Wehrmacht soldiers, the latter increasingly in occupied territory. Hopelessly mired in convention to the point where even Nazi critics mocked it for its lack of daring, it chalked up a ten-year performance record of some 1,500 concerts by December 1941. Its activities ceased only after Goebbels's proclamation of Total War in the early fall of 1944.[178]

If Adam's programs were designed as conventional classical fare for the palate of the common man, the spectacles celebrated on the Green Hill of Bayreuth constituted high culture harnessed, initially at least, for the edification and continued ideological indoctrination of the social elite. In the decades since the German catastrophe of 1945, apologists for Wagner and the Bayreuth Festival have attempted to whitewash the reputation of the composer and his oeuvre by emphasizing the aesthetic integrity that Bayreuth has always stood for and stressing the differences between the original phenomenon and anything that smacked of National Socialism. Hence, it has been claimed that Wagner's Judeophobia, if subjected to careful qualification, proves less than virulent.[179] The hypernationalism with which Bayreuth came to be identified in the chauvinistic era before World War I, it is implied, originated after Wagner's death and was the product of unconscionable manipulators of the master's heritage. According to this carefully crafted legend, it was the Nazis, especially Hitler himself, who grafted the evils of fascism, extreme nationalism, and anti-Semitism onto the Wagner–Bayreuth legacy. Hence, these issues did not originate with Wagner himself but with National Socialists guilty of improper historical judgment and manipulative abuse. Moreover, Wagner's heirs—namely his son Siegfried and Siegfried's English-born wife, Winifred (née Williams)—have been portrayed as innately innocent and gentle souls. Siegfried, although in many ways a weak character, is viewed as a cosmopolitan man not interested in German fascism and its causes;

and Winifred as an altruistic impresario who developed a purely personal friendship with Hitler. The Führer appears, if at all, as a man personally obsessed with Wagner and Bayreuth, whereas his cronies—chiefly Rosenberg and Goebbels—are reported by some apologists to have been impervious to the lure of the Green Hill, even loathing it and everything it represented.[180]

The reduction of the relationship between Bayreuth and the Third Reich to a level of personal friendship between its two principals is intended to deny any official institutional links and thus any formative effect of the Wagner cult on Hitler and the Nazi regime. In addition, it is meant to obscure the political prostitution of Bayreuth, which to an extent had already begun in Wagner's own time but accelerated in the presence of the Nazi Party leader, reaching its zenith in 1944. Both factors are germane to this analysis, since in fact nothing has ever quite managed to illustrate the potential consequences of a marriage between culture and fascist politics as graphically as the symbiotic relationship between Bayreuth and the Nazi hierarchy.

According to his grandson Wolfgang Wagner, "Richard Wagner believed to have wrought for the Germans a self-reliant national art, by having created Bayreuth."[181] But the "national art" inherent in his *Gesamtkunstwerk*, as the elder Wagner must have been aware, was open to political manipulation even in his lifetime, as the unified German Reich moved gradually yet steadily toward nationalist megalomania.[182] Wagner himself, of course, especially in his last years, was less a German nationalist than an anti-Semite. His hatred of Jews straddled the dividing line between the traditional and the modern, as Wagner exhibited everything from a social and aesthetic to a racist and religious anti-Semitism, and was in fact a pioneer of that late nineteenth-century movement. Although it is possible that early jealousy of and rivalry with his contemporary composers Mendelssohn and especially Meyerbeer steered him in this direction, their Jewishness as such is not what inspired Wagner to publish his first anti-Semitic tract, *Judaism in Music,* in 1850. But it was republished in a much more vicious form in 1869, at a time when German Jews had benefited from greater emancipation after Bismarck's early wars of unification. This fact, as well as Wagner's almost daily anti-Jewish diatribes communicated to his companion Cosima, suggests the increasing force of his anti-Semitism as a personal credo, one that was even reflected in the composer's artistic works. In fact, at least one current critic of Wagner's operas interprets the notion of redemption in *Parsifal* as symbolized by a non-Jewish Christ, to such a degree that "in *Parsifal* the new Wagner religion is manifested most explicitly; its fundament is the Bayreuth brand of anti-Semitism."[183]

In any event, the young Hitler, growing up in fin de siècle Linz and Vienna, was impressed as much by Wagner's music and staging as by the implied philosophy. Hitler steeped himself in Wagner's mythical world of a sacred Germanic past. Wagner soon set the standard for Hitler as artist and human being. "For him nothing counted but German ways, German feeling and German thought," as a friend of Hitler's Linz and Vienna days, Austrian music student August Kubizek, later recounted.[184]

As a Bavarian soldier during World War I, Hitler would keep the piano score of *Tristan* in his knapsack as others kept their Nietzsche. After the war, as Hitler began his political career in Munich, it was his mentor, the habitually drunk and odiously anti-Semitic Dietrich Eckart, once a critic in Bayreuth, who further fanned the flames of his enthusiasm for Wagner. Ernst ("Putzi") Hanfstaengl recalls how, in those heady days of early Nazi Party growth, Hitler would pattern his public speeches on the dynamics of the *Meistersinger* prelude to achieve the greatest possible effect. In addition to Wagner's Germanocentrism, Hitler also came to adopt the composer's idea of struggle—a struggle, as some of Wagner's followers and later also Hitler interpreted it, essentially against the Jews. Hitler spoke of his early total devotion to Wagner in his prescient autobiography, which he started writing while imprisoned at Landsberg in 1924–25, naming it *Mein Kampf,* not accidentally after Richard Wagner's own *Mein Leben.*[185]

There is no question that Hitler, continuing his rise to power in the mid- to late 1920s, considered himself Wagner's direct successor, a man of genius and a hero who would save the German people, who in turn were defined and united by a purity of blood.[186] During this period Hitler's ties with the Wagner family of Bayreuth were cemented. Hitler had visited Wahnfried, the Wagner shrine, in October 1923 and was deeply moved by both Wagner's grave and what he considered the personal grace and charm of Siegfried and Winifred Wagner. That couple happened to be in Munich a few weeks before Hitler and Erich Ludendorff staged their Beer Hall Putsch in early November 1923, but they were not in the center of the, by then, fully developed Wagner cult centered in Bayreuth. Other self-anointed intellectuals and seers were, such as Hans von Wolzogen and Wagner's son-in-law Houston Stewart Chamberlain, whom Hitler had also visited in 1923 and who wrote to him in Landsberg.[187]

Until 1933 Hitler's relationship with Bayreuth grew mostly through a personal friendship with Winifred Wagner, who shared his pan-Germanic views and joined the NSDAP in 1926, and her husband, Siegfried, who, while decidedly an enemy of Weimar and hence on the right of the political spectrum, was personally less interested and not at all involved in day-to-day politics. Much later Hitler thought him to have been at the mercy of the Jews. The Nazi Führer, who for tactical reasons during the republic had attended only the festival performance of 1925, often liked to stop over in Bayreuth on his journeys from Munich to Berlin. He developed a special fondness for the couple's four children, although it seems unlikely that he, though a bachelor with a professed erotic love for his half-niece Geli Raubal, would have sexually abused Wieland, the firstborn, as has recently been claimed. Nor is it likely that he ever had a clandestine sexual relationship with Winifred, even though her husband, who died in 1930, suffered from his early reputation as a promiscuous homosexual. For Uncle Wolf, as Hitler was called by the Wagner children, Bayreuth in 1932 was a kind of secondary home and the Wagner family his surrogate family. To Hitler, Richard Wagner was prophet, archetypal German polymath, and artist as well as political leader.[188]

Members of the extended Wagner family in particular have insisted that apart from Hitler himself, leaders of the Nazi movement were not merely uninterested in Wagner and Bayreuth but strenuously opposed to both.[189] This is patent nonsense. In *The Myth of the Twentieth Century* (1930), chief party ideologue Rosenberg repeatedly refers approvingly to Wagner, his ideas, and his musical creations. "The cultural accomplishment of Bayreuth is perennially beyond discussion," he writes.[190] By 1929 Rosenberg's Kampfbund für deutsche Kultur had already made such an impression on Winifred Wagner that she became one of its earliest open supporters, and she was "greatly pleased" to be offered honorary membership in the league three years later.[191] As long as it lasted, the Kampfbund organized regional Wagner celebrations and touted the composer's works in its journals. Rosenberg himself alluded to Wagner's genius at the annual meeting of the NS-Kulturgemeinde in Düsseldorf in 1935.[192]

Rosenberg's powerful rival Joseph Goebbels was no exception. The future propaganda minister had met and been very moved by Chamberlain in Bayreuth in 1926 and, according to his rambling diary, enjoyed Wagner's music a great deal, both at the festival and during other performances. After Hitler had instituted official support for Bayreuth in 1933, Goebbels's Promi became an integral part of that effort. In July 1936 Goebbels stated categorically that "Richard Wagner's music conquered the world because it was consciously German and did not wish to be anything else."[193] Two years later Goebbels justified his anti-Semitic RMK measures in terms of Wagner's hatred of Jews.[194] Wagner's music also was ostentatiously admired by Franconian Gauleiter Hans Schemm (in whose precinct Bayreuth lay and who got his Nazi Teachers' League involved), Gauleiter Adolf Wagner of Munich, and Munich's party-appointed lord mayer Karl Fiehler. Schemm, Wagner, and Fiehler co-signed a letter of protest published in April 1933 against Thomas Mann, in defense of Richard Wagner.[195] Westphalia's Gauleiter Alfred Meyer and Winifred Wagner jointly patronized a Richard Wagner festival in Detmold annually from 1935. Other notorious vessels of Wagner culture were von Schirach's Hitler Youth and Röhm's Brownshirts.[196]

Wolfgang Wagner continues to maintain that even during the Third Reich his mother's relationship with Hitler was primarily that of a "private person" who got along well with the Führer and to whom she felt some kind of fealty. He also repeats his mother's earlier assertion that Bayreuth, instead of losing its former independence, actually was able to strengthen it.[197] It must be granted that underneath the official network linking Berlin and Bayreuth there was that old, warm feeling of friendship between the Reich chancellor and the Wagner family, which had first flowered in the mid-1920s. Winifred Wagner enjoyed a direct line to Hitler; she was invited to official functions in Munich and Berlin, especially when international guests, notably English ones, were present. Hitler considered Winifred, who is said to have had a sexual liaison with Berlin and Bayreuth dramaturge Heinz Tietjen in those years, one of the ladies to show off with in public, along with filmmaker Leni Riefenstahl and one or two others.[198] He maintained a personal interest in the Wagner children, particularly Wieland, the eldest, who was allowed to waive military service.[199] The Führer's protection even extended to sheltering the deceased Siegfried Wagner from ridicule: when one of his outlandish operas was performed in Berlin, the press was warned "not to treat this as a matter of minor importance."[200]

But given the extent to which Hitler used not only the ideas of Richard Wagner but also the Bayreuth Festival for the purposes of party and state, Winifred Wagner was reduced to a mere handmaiden in all but the narrowest of artistic regards. "You know," she reminded Strauss in June 1935, "that nothing happens in Bayreuth that does not originate with the Führer or has not been confirmed by him."[201] On Hitler's initiative the Bayreuth Festival was scheduled as an annual rather than a biennial event from 1936 on. From 1933 it was financially supported by the regime; scores of young people, either Hitler Youth or university students, were invited to attend for free.[202] Hitler needed the festival as a permanent celebration of National Socialism and its Third Reich. His own appearances at the festival, starting in 1933, became national spectacles of the highest order and were treated as such by the controlled media. Like the Führer's birthday on 20 April or the Beer Hall Putsch commemoration of 9 November, this was another opportunity for Hitler to put his regime on public display. Hence Wagneriana and National Socialist symbolism became inseparably intertwined at Bayreuth annually for several days during the summer. In August 1933 the reporter for the *Manchester Guardian* noted: "Bayreuth this year resembles a Hitler festival. The china shops are full of Hitler plaques, and 'Mein Kampf' has replaced 'Mein Leben.' From every flagstaff and nearly every window a Swastika flag is flying. Brown shirts are almost de rigueur." Three years later a Bayreuth native echoed this sentiment: "Swastika flags, wherever the eye may roam. . . . Flowers, garlands, welcome signs. And many brown uniforms. . . ."[203] The festival was converted to special wartime use after the fall of 1939, when, with the help of Ley's Labor Front, tens of thousands of soldiers and SS men, as well as armaments workers, were brought to Bayreuth in special trains to have their resolve for further battle or tank construction firmed by heroic Wagnerian tenors.[204]

There were what might be called ancillary events that gave the illusion of a perfect marriage between art and politics, Wagnerism and Hitlerism. As early as spring 1933, around the time of Hitler's forty-fourth birthday and the fiftieth anniversary of Wagner's death, German opera houses obliged the Führer with performances of Wagner's works; all national radio stations played Siegfried's "Forging Song," from the opera of that name. A separate Wagner celebration in Hohenschwangau, south of Munich, provided an additional opportunity for the new chancellor to become a producer himself. A year later Hitler, in full public view, laid the cornerstone for a Richard Wagner national monument in Leipzig. That year also featured a special broadcast series on Wagner and H. S. Chamberlain, with commentary by the likes of Hans Schemm, Leopold Reichwein, and Baldur von Schirach. In 1938 Hitler declared that a new Richard Wagner memorial site would be erected, and that henceforth on the Führer's birthday some German opera house would offer a special Wagner program.[205]

Since this was a reciprocal relationship, the advantages were mutual. The phenomenon known as the Green Hill took on a fascist ambience, but it also gained publicity, important not least for commercial reasons, and a virtual guarantee against insolvency. The evidence shows that although public stagings of Wagner operas nationally had been decreasing long before the onset of the Third Reich, and even more so after 1933, in absolute figures these performances still topped the list until 1942–43, with works by composers such as Verdi, Puccini, and Strauss well behind.[206]

For the Nazi regime the benefits were more complex and more far-reaching. If Wagner's personality had made an indelible impact on the young Hitler, the Bayreuth cult was able to embellish and buttress the mature politician's weltanschauung. In December 1933 Hitler's followers were reminded once again of the Führer's long-standing conviction that "National Socialism was anchored in the works of Wagner."[207] Indeed, Wagner's conception of opera as *Gesamtkunstwerk* could be intentionally misinterpreted as containing a strong totalitarian notion that conformed with Hitler's view of totalitarian politics. It is true that much of Wagner's irrationality was mirrored in Hitler, and his anti-Semitism matched and enhanced Hitler's own, to the same extent that the composer's neo-pagan mythology bolstered Hitler's ideas about a new German secular state. Most important, through his own example Wagner had shown the world how art could be mixed with politics, could in fact be highly politicized. In this regard Hitler had shown himself to be a faithful student of the master, for if necessary Bayreuth could serve as an example of how music and musicians were to be politicized in an era of fascism. Nonetheless, the observation by one German music critic certainly amounted to an over-statement when, early in the Third Reich, he said of *Meistersinger:* "The relationship between politics and art, which is reflected therein, is significant and highly indicative of the situation of art in the new state."[208] For Bayreuth, even with its high degree of indoctrination, remained an exception. That the politicization of music ultimately remained incomplete may have been due less to any policies set by Hitler or Goebbels than to the fact that by its very nature true art remains inviolable.

2

Musical Professionalism and Political Compromise

Hitler's Bias: Knappertsbusch and His Nemesis Krauss

Conductor Hans Knappertsbusch was a blond, blue-eyed giant, the very picture of a Nazi male. He was so chauvinistic that following World War I he refused to perform in Paris since France was one of the Allied victors. Later he claimed to have been constantly under attack by Marxists and to have moved "exclusively in nationalist circles of society."[1] Suspicious of Jews and other, allegedly corrosive elements in the cultural life of the republic, he was coopted by the National Socialists as one of their own years before Hitler assumed power. In 1933, when several of his colleagues emigrated for political or racist reasons, he is reported to have said that he would rather toil in a quarry than leave Germany.[2] But instead of achieving great success in the Third Reich as one of Germany's most prominent conductors, he lost importance steadily throughout the Nazi regime. The principal reason for this was that Adolf Hitler never liked him.

Possibly Knappertsbusch's hypernationalism stemmed from the early 1910s, when the conductor, then in his early twenties, was an assistant at the Bayreuth Festival and came into contact with the Wolzogen and Chamberlain circle. In 1922 he became the successor to Bruno Walter as Generalmusikdirektor of the Munish-based Bayerische Staatsoper. There he proved extremely popular with the culture-loving public; he was familiarly known as "Kna." This German from Elberfeld was outspoken, with a less than subtle wit. As a conductor he was less interested in details than in the overall structure of a work. One of his trademarks was his contempt for rehearsals; this sat well with lazy musicians in the orchestra but caused suspicion among purists and perfectionists.[3]

Most Munich-based Nazis of the 1920s immediately claimed Kappertsbusch as one of their own, especially since he had replaced Bruno Walter, a Jew whose original name was Schlesinger. They well remembered, as did Knappertsbusch himself, that during his Munich tenure from 1913 to 1922, Walter had suffered severely from local anti-Semitism and that the novelist Thomas Mann had been one of the few notables to defend him; it was said that as a Jew Walter simply was not qualified to conduct Wagner. Knappertsbusch was thought able to redress that deficit, as he himself believed more than anyone else.[4] In early 1929 Alfred Rosenberg and his lieutenants moved Knappertsbusch, for their own devious purposes, into the center of an argument involving another Jew, an editor of Munich's influential daily *Münchener Neueste Nachrichten*. This man of letters was Paul Cossmann, a converted Catholic, former pan-German and strident nationalist, and a very close friend of Hans Pfitzner. The scandal broke out after the paper had criticized a performance by Knappertsbusch of Beethoven's Ninth Symphony, whereupon the conductor had charged its editors with narrow partisanship. In taking up the cause of Knappertsbusch, the Rosenberg clique brought into play a charge of Jewish conspiracy, which was easy enough, since Cossmann had earlier befriended Bruno Walter. Knappertsbusch did not encourage, but neither did he stop or protest, various tendentious articles in Rosenberg's *Völkischer Beobachter* purporting to champion the blond maestro. Another vicious attack against Jews was launched in June 1929 by Nazi delegate Rudolf Buttmann in the Bavarian Landtag, and by that time Rosenberg's Kampfbund für deutsche Kultur had also taken up the cudgels. Whether he had planned it or not, Knappertsbusch now had irrevocably maneuvered himself into the position of a candidate of the extreme right.[5] The conductor himself became part of this campaign once the National Socialists took power in January 1933. He commenced a chain of events in Munich's highest cultural circles, the full details of which are only now becoming clear, and the ultimate consequence of which was the permanent exile of Nobel laureate Thomas Mann from Germany.

This affair grew out of three related sets of circumstances: the historic enmity between Walter and Knappertsbusch; the tenuous friendship between Knappertsbusch and Pfitzner, which was fraught with difficulties; and Pfitzner's long-standing and complicated relationship with Thomas Mann. In his nationalist phase until the early years of the Weimar Republic, Mann had been an unstinting admirer of Pfitzner and his music. But the two men became estranged when Mann came to the defense of the republic, while Pfitzner became entrenched in his opposition to it. Both had been, and still were, close friends of Bruno Walter; as early as 1917

Mann had defended Walter, and as late as September 1932 Pfitzner had wished to entrust Walter with the premiere of a new symphony.[6]

Knappertsbusch was chagrined at Mann's and Pfitzner's patronage of Walter, who in early 1933 was director of the Leipzig Gewandhaus Orchestra. In addition, Knappertsbusch's musical relationship with Pfitzner was clouded by the Cossmann affair and Pfitzner's idiosyncrasies as a regular but careless guest conductor of the Munich opera.[7] Perhaps to legitimize his ambition to become an intellectual leader of the newly constituted cultural right wing in the Bavarian capital (whose interests could not entirely be left in the hands of the troglodyte Rosenberg), Knappertsbusch decided to launch an attack against Mann. At the time the famous author was on a lecture tour outside Germany, the subject of which was Knappertsbusch's hero Richard Wagner. By the conductor's reckoning, with such an attack he could reconcile himself with Pfitzner and at the same time compromise Walter by smearing the character of Walter's friend Mann.

The novelist had always maintained an informed interest in music and had been a devoted admirer and often a critical scholar of Wagner for decades.[8] As an undaunted defender of the republic, however, he also had publicly attacked the Nazis, who in turn had placed him on their blacklist. In 1929 Mann had been targeted by Rosenberg's newly founded Kampfbund, and a year later he had rated a derogatory mention in Rosenberg's pamphleteering Myth of the Twentieth Century. In October 1930, when Mann had openly lectured against the Nazis in Berlin, it was Walter who whisked him away from hostile Brownshirts in his car. The next day the Nazi press had officially labeled Mann a German traitor.[9]

Mann's lecture on Wagner had been commissioned by the Goethe Society of Munich for 13 February 1933, the fiftieth anniversary of the composer's death. It was first delivered on 10 February at Munich University and eventually published, under the title "The Sorrows and Grandeur of Richard Wagner," in a prominent Berlin newspaper. The purpose of the lecture was to warn of "the Nazis' appropriation of Wagner for an unholy alliance of Macht and Kultur."[10] In late February this address was repeated on Mann's lecture tour in Amsterdam, Brussels, and Paris.[11]

Mann said mostly positive things about Wagner, but to a fanatical Wagnerian some of his observations would have seemed outrageous, and even his carefully worded criticism was found objectionable. He described Wagner as a precursor of Sigmund Freud for having adopted, in tracing all forms of love to a sexual origin, something akin to a psychoanalytic method. He chided the elderly Wagner for having dismissed, in the pages of the reactionary Bayreuther Blätter, "much of beauty," including Mendelssohn's music. Mann's speech admitted the possibility that Wagner's genius was "just an amalgam of dilettante accomplishments." He attacked the Bayreuth circle's proclivity for kitsch, likening Wagner's art to the "dried-flower arrangements" of bourgeois vulgarity. And he really stung the nationalists by condemning the abuse of Wagner's music "in order to achieve an added patriotic effect," as Wagner's own nationalism had been "totally intellectual and apolitical." Indeed, as a political animal Wagner had been "more of a socialist and cultural utopian" than "a patriot in the aggressive, nationalistic sense." Mann ended on a universal rather than chauvinistic note when he said: "Let us be content to honour Wagner's work as a powerful and complex phenomenon of German and Western European life, which will ever continue to serve as a profound stimulus to art and knowledge."[12]

At the time and for many decades thereafter, it was merely suspected by critics and scholars, including Mann himself, that Knappertsbusch was the force behind the massive protest that was launched in the *Münchener Neueste Nachrichten* on 16 April 1933.[13] Pfitzner's private correspondence, preserved in the Austrian National Library, has made that conjecture a certainty. Knappertsbusch had successfully solicited pillars of Munich's conservative society, among them Richard Strauss (who had supported him in the Cossmann affair),[14] Akademie der Tonkunst president Siegmund von Hausegger, chief art curator Friedrich Dörnhöffer, chief dramaturge Baron Clemens von Franckenstein, and the noted artist Olaf Gulbransson. But established Nazis with an interest in Richard Wagner had also been approached, including Bavarian Minister of Culture Hans Schemm, Munich Gauleiter Adolf Wagner, and Munich's lord mayor Karl Fiehler. Wilhelm Matthes, a fervent Nazi music critic who had scathingly attacked jazz and the modernists in the Weimar Republic and was lionized by all musical reactionaries, jumped on the bandwagon. Mann had maligned a "German genius," wrote Knappertsbusch. Since he was in charge of the Wagner heritage as far as Munich was concerned, Knappertsbusch felt honor-bound to defend the composer. "Whoever dares publicly to belittle the man who like few others has represented the power of German *Geist* to the world," he threatened, "will have something coming to him."[15]

The conductor's initial appeal had been to Pfitzner, who wholeheartedly supported the planned statement but thought that Knappertsbusch was being overly abrasive. He therefore urged the conductor to delete several phrases and the final sentence, which, characteristically of Knappertsbusch, brandished a broadsword rather than a rapier. It read: "Who is Richard Wagner, and who is 'Herr' Thomas Mann?"[16] The published protest began with references to Germany's "national revolution," praised Wagner as the expression of "the deepest German feeling," and finally berated Mann on account of his "cosmopolitan-democratic views." Someone like Mann, who for years had revealed himself as unreliable and inexpert in his writings, had no right to criticize "perennial German spiritual giants."[17]

It is still commonly believed that soon after these events Hans Knappertsbusch fell victim to intrigue, with the result that the reigning National Socialists in late 1935 prematurely annulled his Munich contract. After 1945 Knappertsbusch himself claimed that he had been sacrificed on the altar of fascist politics and racism.[18] All this is far from the truth. Knappertsbusch lost his position in early 1936 on account of a combination of factors, only one of which could possibly be traced to anything resembling opposition to the Third Reich (during a stay in The Hague he had apparently made an unflattering reference to the Nazis, though this was probably motivated less by the conductor's political convictions, which were unshakably right-wing, than by his well-known penchant for impulsive tongue-lashings).[19] In fact, after Hitler's rise to power Knappertsbusch continued to serve the Nazis well, doing the Kampfbund's bidding and directing politically charged Wagner festivities in and around Munich.[20]

The two main reasons why Knappertsbusch was dismissed were his rather dilatory handling of the Staatsoper's business over a period of years and Hitler's personal dislike for his art, which the Führer did not judge capable of advancing his long-standing plans for a grandiose beautification of his beloved Munich, the so-called capital of the Nazi Movement.

It was alleged that Generalmusikdirektor Knappertsbusch had been responsible for irregularities in the directorship of the opera since 1927, and his problems with guest conductor Pfitzner—which predictably resumed after the Mann affair—constituted one of several telling symptoms.[21] Charges surfaced that Knappertsbusch had neglected orchestra recruitment, had handled artists' contracts in a negligent manner, and had authorized opera productions that were much too opulent in times of financial restraint. He had committed many of the errors jointly with opera Generalintendant Baron von Franckenstein, who was due to retire in the fall of 1934.[22] Knappertsbusch had also been too cavalier in accepting numerous guest engagements outside Munich.[23] There had in fact been objective complaints about the last years of the Knappertsbusch era; in the opinion of music publisher Willy Strecker of the Schott firm in Mainz, for example, the conductor had done nothing to educate the Munich audience toward an appreciation of more progressive works.[24]

Franckenstein's replacement as Generalintendant was Oskar Walleck, a member of the SS from Brunswick. In all likelihood he stoked the fires of intrigue against Knappertsbusch, though hard evidence for this is still lacking. But after the fall of 1934 he suddenly reversed opera production arrangements he had made with Knappertsbusch earlier; the conductor himself complained about a constant "policy of needle pricks."[25]

In November 1935, however, Knappertsbusch still felt a special allegiance toward Hitler, who, as he well knew, "wanted Munich to be the city of German art."[26] Nonetheless, effective 1 January 1936 Knappertsbusch became a Bavarian state pensioner—not by dint of political unreliability, as spelled out in the fourth paragraph of the Nazi law of 7 April 1933 for the reconstituion of the bureaucracy (as was suggested by his apologists thereafter), but for purposes of administrative simplification (sixth paragraph).[27] This pill which the fifty-four-year-old conductor had to swallow was all the more bitter as legions of Munich fans were very reluctant to see him go; his pension was kept deliberately low, and any further professional activity in Bavaria was forbidden.[28]

Knappertsbusch retired to Vienna, ironically now also the sometime refuge of his erstwhile rival Bruno Walter, and there assumed the function of a permanent visiting conductor at the Wiener Staatsoper. Although he had recently received good press after guest-conducting there, he supposedly complained, just before leaving Bavaria, that in Kurt Schuschnigg's Austria he would once again become the prey "of the Jewish mob," a fate he claimed to have suffered earlier in Munich.[29]

If Generalintendant Walleck was actively behind any of these machinations, he was under pressure from Goebbels, who received him in Berlin at the end of December 1935.[30] Goebbels, in turn, most certainly was instructed by Hitler, who simply loathed Knappertsbusch as an opera conductor. It is possible that Hitler had had to tolerate the conductor during his "bohemian" years in postwar Munich and that, not sufficiently knowledgeable himself, he had been influenced in his judgment by friends with educated musical tastes, such as Putzi Hanfstaengl. In any case, at the time of Walleck's new appointment in autumn 1934, Hitler was heard to say that Knappertsbusch was "not a suitable conductor for the Munich opera. He was more fit for concerts." At the end of 1935, when Knappertsbusch's discharge was imminent, Hildegard Ranczak, a sympathetic Munich singer, took a plane to Berlin to speak directly with the Führer, but to no avail. "That military bandleader must go!," she was told. As late as 1942 Hitler was heard to say that it was sheer punishment to be forced to listen to one of Knappertsbusch's opera performances. But again it is possible that even then Hitler did not know what he was talking about.[31]

Though not strictly speaking a Nazi, but no democrat either, despite this professional and personal slight Knappertsbusch continued to serve the Third Reich above and beyond the call of duty. Although Munich remained closed to him almost to the end, he was indisputably in charge of the Vienna opera until Karl Böhm's regular tenure began in January 1943.[32] The Anschluss of Austria in the spring of 1938 seems not to have affected him one way or the other, and the summer of that year found him at the Salzburg Festival conducting his hero Wagner's *Tannhäuser*.[33] All over the German Reich, and later in the occupied countries as well, Knappertsbusch was a frequent guest performer, and he led the very best orchestras, including the Berlin Philharmonic.[34]

This musician, who no doubt wished to be a good National Socialist if only the rat pack would let him, continued to oblige the regime faithfully as Hitler's war dragged on. In February 1940 he conducted the Vienna Philharmonic (identical with the orchestra of the Staatsoper) in a concert sponsored by the NSDAP. A few months later he conducted his Viennese musicians as they played Wagner to commemorate the Nazi stalwarts who had fallen during Hitler's putsch of November 1923. In September

1941 he accepted an invitation by Hans Frank, the music-loving but nonetheless ruthless governor of occupied Poland, to conduct the Berlin Philharmonic in Cracow, only a few miles from Auschwitz.[35] And however much Hitler may have sneered about Knappertsbusch at the dinner table among his entourage, he did allow the conductor to perform with that same orchestra on the occasion of his birthday in April 1943. The Führer was never able to dismiss Knappertsbusch completely because Eva Braun, his mistress, kept admiring the conductor's "masculine appearance." In due course Knappertsbusch received the Martial Order of Merit (along with arch-Nazi Elly Ney) and so was ready to play again for the Führer's birthday jubilee in Berlin the following year, though Hitler still kept insisting that Knappertsbusch was no good as an opera conductor. One of the last routine services the subservient Knappertsbusch rendered was for the edification of Waffen-SS units (of the kind that Dr. Josef Mengele belonged to while at Auschwitz), which were stationed in Vienna, in March 1943.[36] A few months before the regime's collapse, the security service of the SS judged Knappertsbusch to be "a decent man, in personal as well as political respects. Though not exactly an active National Socialist, he has always shown true German conviction."[37]

For all intents and purposes Knappertsbusch seems to have been vindicated when the new Munich Gauleiter Paul Giesler invited him to direct the Munich Philharmonic in a special concert during the summer of 1944. Still, the blond and blue-eyed giant had his pride. After nine long years Giesler's generous offer would break the ice, he retorted, but wouldn't his old orchestra from the Munich opera be offended if he were not allowed to conduct it? Not even the accommodating Giesler could help him here, for the Bayerische Staatsoper orchestra under Clemens Krauss was off-limits by that time, and qualitatively it was in an altogether different category.[38]

Approximately six months after Hitler had voiced his opinion of Knappertsbusch in the fall of 1934, he told Oskar Walleck that Krauss was the right conductor for the Bayerische Staatsoper.[39] In retrospect, if Knappertsbusch appears to have been an artist of narrow nationalist and racist inclinations, who in 1933 was predestined to become the National Socialist musician par excellence but was derailed en route, Clemens Krauss emerges as something of a pawn. By upbringing and attitude he was cosmopolitan, originally a conductor with wide musical interests who embraced the moderns, a man with the most cultivated universal tastes—in short, anything but a narrow chauvinist. And yet it was Krauss who seems to have been lured to National Socialism and the Third Reich almost against his will. Early on he was a favorite of the Führer, but by 1944 he had become Hitler's captive. The question is, to what extent did Krauss succumb to Nazism, and in what way did this surrender compromise his art?

Krauss was the tropical palm to Knappertsbusch's German oak. Rumored to be the illegitimate child of a beautiful Viennese actress and, as his physiognomy betrayed, Archduke Eugen von Habsburg,[40] he had the manner of a Spanish conquistador and the charm of a Venetian gondolier. Both at the podium and in private he could be haughty and yet disarmingly engaging at the same time. His sense of theatrics, on stage and off, was proverbial. As Hans Heinz Stuckenschmidt once noted in the late Weimar years: "Even his exit is a well-studied pose. The hero thinks of himself. Himself last and as the ultimate one." He was highly educated and well read to the point where he was able to write a libretto for Richard Strauss, surely the most demanding of modern opera composers.[41]

This sophisticated musician, after the usual journeyman routine, became director of the Frankfurt Opera in 1924 at the age of thirty-two, and in 1929 he was appointed director of the Wiener Staatsoper as well as, a year later, the city's philharmonic concerts. In January 1935 he replaced Furtwängler as permanent director of the Preussische Staatsoper in Berlin, then under Göring, until in January 1937 he became the new opera director in Munich. After taking over Oskar Walleck's title of intendant in 1938, he became one of the most powerful musicians of the Third Reich.[42]

It is possible to interpret Krauss's professional biography from 1929 to 1944 as that of a man who practiced art for art's sake and who, despite official accolades, was never touched by the poison of fascism. In fact, in Vienna Krauss obviously attempted to swim against the current of convention and reaction that was increasingly becoming a hallmark of Austro-Fascism after the ascendancy of Chancellor Engelbert Dollfuss in the fall of 1932. He was autocratic, using his own infallible judgment in musical and theatrical direction. Thus, he performed Hindemith, Stravinsky, and Alban Berg, and showed interest in new scores by Křenek and Weill. His long and intense friendship with Strauss, whose newest work he was ever eager to premiere, was not a facet of his modernism but rather bespoke his sense of tradition—a tradition he mastered as a matter of course. It was Strauss, whose own modernism had peaked with the composition of *Elektra* in 1909, who had been behind his move from Frankfurt to Vienna in 1929, at a time when Krauss was proud of the reformist course he had steered at the Frankfurt Opera.[43]

At the end of 1934, and in the immediate aftermath of the Hindemith affair, Krauss accepted a much better paid position offered to him by Göring at the Preussische Staatsoper, not least because his one-man rule in Vienna had begun to irk influential members of the opera company, some of whom were bedfellows of the increasingly authoritarian Austro-Fascists. In addition, Krauss had been waiting to hear from the Viennese Culture Ministry regarding an extension of his present contract, but this was not forthcoming.[44] When Krauss left, he was cunning enough to take certain prominent members of the Austrian opera whom he had come to like along with him. Chief among them was his own wife, Viorica Ursuleac, originally a Romanian, whom Krauss had met and worked with as early as the Frankfurt years. (Baroness Gerta Louise von Einem, a child-hood friend of Göring and his sisters, who was visiting the Prussian minister-president in his sumptuous office around the end of 1934, was triumphantly told by Göring that Frau Ursuleac was waiting in the lobby, "and she is about to bring me the Wiener Staatsoper.")[45] Other famous singers who left with Krauss included Josef von Manowarda, Franz Völ-ker, and Erich Zimmermann.

Göring may have been indifferent to Krauss, although his absolute trust in Generalintendant Heinz Tietjen could temper any such feelings. When the Austrian conductor moved to Berlin, he was assured of the friendship of an old protector, though he also gained two new enemies who immediately complicated his life in the capital. The trusted friend was Strauss, then still president of the RMK, who was glad to be able to use a former protégé to strengthen his musical influence vis-à-vis his old rival Furtwängler. Strauss knew how much Krauss liked to perform his music. Tietjen told the composer in February 1935 that he could now rest assured "that the Strauss renaissance, under Clemens Krauss, will be in the very best hands."[46]

But the maestro was far away in Garmisch, and this gave free rein to Krauss's two new enemies, Tietjen and Furtwängler. Each had a different axe to grind. Tietjen soon recognized Krauss's indubitable organizational and dramaturgical genius and thus saw his own position endangered. He also feared constant interference by the suspicious Strauss.[47] Furt-wängler, of course, had been the immediate victim of the Hindemith scandal in December 1934, as a direct consequence of which he had been replaced by Krauss as principal conductor and director of the Preussische Staatsoper, a post he had held since September 1933. Furtwängler, who had preceded the Austrian in several important positions before, pro-fessed to have an insultingly low opinion of Krauss's musicianship. His letter to Strauss in the spring of 1936, at a time when Krauss was already on his way out of Berlin, is a model of personal defamation. Furtwängler wrote that even in Vienna the level of Krauss's performances had been "modest" at best, and in Berlin he had not been able to do justice to the sophisticated tastes of the operagoing public. In London and Paris, too, he had failed as guest conductor: "He possesses a certain cold elegance and a technique that is not without interest to experts, but beyond that he has nothing, not even the slightest, to offer, and he lacks even a trace of force and warmth." In the terminology of the Nazis, Furtwängler thought that Krauss could "in no way relate to great German music" and hence could not conduct Beethoven, Wagner, or the classics. "It is simply im-possible to describe Krauss as an essentially German artist": this was Furtwängler's verdict on a man whom he, rightly or wrongly, saw as a potential successor to himself in all of Germany.[48]

It has correctly been suggested that with such odds against him, Krauss, a man of Mediterranean temperament, with his coterie of Austrians and his Promethean artistic ambitions, simply could not have made a success of his tenure in Berlin, try as he might. He was bound to feel uncomfortable as Furtwängler was being readmitted as guest conductor of both the Berlin Philharmonic and the Staatsoper on a relatively permanent basis in the months ahead.[49] Consequently Krauss did not try very hard; indeed, forces beyond his control—and even that of Furtwängler, Strauss, and Tietjen—had begun to conspire early in 1935 to remove him from Berlin to a more propitious place in the Reich. These forces were none other than Goebbels and Hitler.

It will be remembered that Hitler was convinced that Krauss, whose Austrian style he had obviously come to like, would be the right successor to the faltering Knappertsbusch in Munich as early as the spring of 1935, at a time when Krauss was already conducting in Berlin.[50] There is nothing to suggest that Hitler or anyone else in Germany—least of all Göring—called Krauss to Berlin so that he might be groomed there to replace Knappertsbusch in Munich.[51] When the occasion arose, Hitler, and with him Goebbels, simply tried to solve two parallel but independent problems using one and the same agent. That Krauss should actively have lobbied for a change from Berlin to Munich is also unlikely, given his rather limited access to the Berlin power brokers, yet at least one historian has plausibly suggested that once he knew of the impending change, he himself did not place any obstacles in its path.[52]

Hitler clearly delegated Goebbels to exploit the existing tensions in the Berlin music scene with the aim of installing Krauss as Knappertsbusch's successor in Munich. In so doing the propaganda minister had to deal with Munich's new Generalintendant Walleck, who in turn communicated with Krauss; Knappertsbusch and Krauss, however, seem never to have discussed the matter. In the fall of 1935 Hitler and Goebbels apparently decided in favor of Krauss, although at least one document also mentions Furtwängler as a possible candidate, further reason for the perennial friction between the two musicians.[53] During the negotiations between Walleck and Krauss over several months beginning in December 1935, plainly at Goebbels's urging, the conductor finally settled for the same salary he had been paid in Berlin, though he demanded significantly larger stipends for his artists.[54]

Krauss's debut in the Bavarian capital occurred early in January 1937, and in keeping with the lofty goals Hitler himself had set for Munich, his performance of works by Wagner, Mozart, Verdi, and Strauss was attended by the highest regime and party officials, including Deputy Führer Rudolf Hess and Munich's Gauleiter Adolf Wagner.[55] Krauss's start in such an official setting was auspicious. He was mindful of Hitler's mandate to beautify Munich, and he took that as license to augment his own prerogatives as opera director. One that he wished for himself was the position of intendant, which Walleck understandably was loath to give up. Yet Krauss knew that he was supported in this by his patron Strauss.[56] The actual contract between the Bavarian Ministry of the Interior and Krauss, which was finalized and signed by both parties in early

September 1936, specifically mentioned Krauss as the "future artistic director of the new great opera in Munich, whose construction has been decided upon." It thus predestined Krauss for higher duties and, even at this date, effectively neutralized Walleck.[57] The stunning arrangement constituted a novelty in modern German opera history.

Without a doubt Hitler was serious about embellishing Munich and supporting Clemens Krauss's role in this. Krauss was to receive no less than 400,000 marks annually in operating funds for this momentous task, over and above the generous salaries for all the artists involved, including himself.[58] Fully conscious of his designated position, Krauss immediately started a progressive theater regime, supported by his loyal troupe; at his insistence the Munich opera orchestra was placed in a higher salary category, closer to Berlin's and Vienna's, and he always fought on behalf of his singers. But he also had the unequivocal support of Strauss, whose works he naturally favored, and in which his wife invariably played a lead role, to the unstinting admiration of the composer.[59] One of Krauss's coups was to hire away from Hamburg Germany's most promising bass-baritone, the magnificent Hans Hotter, who immediately became Strauss's favorite.[60] As a result, the comparative dullness of the Munich opera scene gave way to a glamour rivaled only by Berlin. The singer Hildegard Ranczak, once the defender of Knappertsbusch, recalls that under Krauss it was not long before "the glitter of the productions could hardly be surpassed."[61]

Just before signing a new contract with Munich in the spring of 1938, Krauss reiterated his commitment to the Führer's mission of establishing a new Reich opera in the Bavarian capital. This meant continued reform of the existing theater to the point where it would be able to assume "first rank."[62] In a symbolic move Walleck, with whom friction had been inevitable, was now removed and sent to Prague, and Krauss himself took over the intendant's functions; there was no more powerful man in German opera at this time.[63] By March 1939 a resident of Switzerland, Gertrud Hindemith was being only partly sarcastic when she wrote to her husband Paul in America that Krauss, with his frequent guest appearances throughout the Reich, seemed to be the only "attraction" on the German music scene.[64]

And yet Krauss was not truly satisfied. Despite all his difficulties there, Vienna had been his first love, and he wanted to return. Berlin had given him trouble, and even in south German Munich—better suited to his Austrian temperament—public dislike for him after the demise of "Kna" was so strong that vicious gossips kept identifying him as a "half-Jew."[65] Others, such as Elly Ney, were constantly holding his friendship with Richard Strauss against him.[66] Such opposition made Krauss even more determined to shift his center of operations away from Munich, back in the direction of Vienna. He knew he could not leave Munich completely—Hitler's trust in him commanded continued dedication to the cause of Munich's cultural aggrandizement—but by April 1938 the

Anschluss of Austria appeared to open new possibilities for Krauss, perhaps in a dual capacity in Munich and Vienna. Thus, on 25 April in a personal letter to Hitler he proposed himself as the needed reformer for the Viennese opera, since "in the interest of a quiet development of the Munich and the Vienna institutes a forced mutual competition would be very detrimental, so that, quite on the contrary, a common artistic direction should be sensible, both from an artistic and economic point of view." Krauss showed no false modesty in asserting that he would be the natural choice for such a joint responsibility.[67] But Hitler was not to be persuaded. He still infinitely valued Krauss as his champion for Munich, and he loathed Vienna; Krauss was not to be wasted on a metropolis that, during his own miserable existence there, had harbored "almost two hundred thousand Jews."[68] In 1940, after the sympathetic and culture-conscious Baldur von Schirach had become Gauleiter of Vienna, Krauss tried a second time, and was once again rebuffed.[69] He was barely mollified by the fact that, first, Strauss now required his presence more often in Garmisch, south of Munich, where both could work on the libretto for *Capriccio;* and second, in April 1940, Salzburg, one third of the way between Munich and Vienna, offered him the presidency of its famous Mozarteum Conservatory.[70]

There was every indication that Hitler was actively pursuing his plans for Munich. Characteristically, he was obsessed with a gigantic reconstruction of the Bayerische Staatsoper, and he commissioned more and more technical experts to design the buildings and committed ever larger amounts of money to the project.[71] Under no circumstances was Krauss to leave Munich. He was duly appointed to Walleck's former position of Generalintendant; his contract was slated for renewal with a sizable salary increase; and the staff of the Munich opera was finally put in the same salary category as those of Berlin and Vienna.[72]

In contrast stood the continual deterioration of the existing local opera culture as a result of the physical destruction wrought by war. Krauss, who had been destined to become the omnipotent opera tsar of Nazi Germany, found himself fighting daily battles to preserve costumes and props, then, as the bombs kept falling, stage sets and, eventually, the singers, musicians, and technical staff he needed for his performances, now that war production service and duty at the front were beginning to claim them.[73] Motivated by the combination of two factors—his long-standing desire to leave Munich for Vienna and his realization that opera in Munich as he had imagined it was becoming an impossibility—Krauss tried to avoid exposing his company in places acutely endangered by bombs while still trying to accommodate the megalomaniacal Hitler, all the while attempting to move himself in a somewhat easterly direction. Hitler, however, insisted that Krauss remain at the Bayerische Staatsoper rather than transfer, say, to Salzburg, and he ordained the use of lesser Munich stages should the opera be bombed out of its own theater.[74] Three days after that order was issued, the opera building did indeed go up in flames; but instead of moving his operation into an acceptable alternate location, Krauss, ever ready to leave Munich, bided his time with improvised concerts in whatever local hall was free.[75] In July 1944, after Strauss's new opera *Die Liebe der Danae* had been rehearsed by Krauss's ensemble for a performance at that year's Salzburg Festival, Goebbels canceled the event. At this point a disgruntled Krauss began to stall over signing an extension of his Munich contract, even though he was now to earn 80,000 marks annually, double the salary he had started with in early 1937. Hitler, bent on rebuilding the state opera house, hoped to tie him into his cultural reconstruction scheme till the summer of 1949.[76]

Krauss knew that his career was at an end in September 1944, when he found himself forced to write to Hitler, after trying to save most of his staff from compulsory war service, that "as far as I myself am concerned, I have to face the fact that any artistic work in Munich will be quite impossible. To inform you of this is merely my duty."[77] At this point, with Allied troops poised to cross the Rhine, Hitler had more serious problems to deal with than following up on his chimerical cultural plans and disciplining his wavering servant. On the brink of ultimate destruction, Richard Strauss lamented that because of the bombing of Munich's theaters, "the joy of my old age, the exemplary performances of my works under Clemens Krauss, at least for me have been submerged by ashes and rubble" (Strauss spoke of the ruin of no fewer than twenty-eight new productions), even as Martin Bormann issued his terse order, echoing the erratic Hitler, that the Bayerische Staatsoper orchestra "be kept at its present artistic strength." As an afterthought, Bormann wished to reemphasize "in what high esteem the Führer was holding Clemens Krauss."[78]

In retrospect, was Krauss really a Nazi? On strictly formal grounds it can be safely affirmed that he was not. To be sure, there were early reports that in Vienna he and his wife had held Nazi views and that he had aligned himself with regional National Socialist leaders such as Alfred Eduard Frauenfeld.[79] In April 1933 a Viennese Nazi insider reported that Krauss had applied for Nazi Party membership but had been turned down as an obvious opportunist, though this report may be apocryphal.[80] Krauss may, however, have concluded a tactical alliance with certain Austrian Nazis as a form of opposition against representatives of the authoritarian Austrian regime, who were hampering his progress; at the time before the Anschluss such an alliance was deemed to be one of the most effective methods of resisting the Dollfuss–Schuschnigg regime.[81]

Nevertheless, there is not a shred of hard evidence that Krauss was ever a nominal let alone a confirmed Nazi, before or after 1935. On the contrary, three witnesses who knew Krauss well as fairly young men have maintained that he was indifferent to Nazi ideology and shunned party membership. One is a fellow Austrian, the composer Gottfried von Einem, who saw him intermittently toward the end of the war and insists that "Clemens Krauss was no Nazi." A second is bass-baritone Hans Hotter, himself beyond reproach, who knew him well professionally in the Munich era and has voiced the same opinion. The third is Krauss's Munich administrative assistant Erik Maschat, who claims that his boss was entirely above Nazi Party issues, declined membership for himself, and paid absolutely no heed to the party in his dealings with other artists.[82] Nazi Party judgments about Krauss at the height of the war, for what they are worth, were invariably negative, or at best neutral; they also mention nothing about possible pro-Nazi involvements back in Vienna. Alfred Rosenberg's office for the supervision of spiritual development in the party, for instance, criticized the conductor's "ideological unreliability as manifested through ever new examples."[83] Not surprisingly, the cosmopolitan Krauss felt uncomfortable in the company of Nazi bigwigs and evaded their invitations; his social elitism and eclectic tastes were anathema to the simplistic worldviews of Gauleiter and other Nazi officials, who at their raucous parties were wont to drown themselves in alcohol.[84]

But for an artist in the Third Reich, even the best, one's political reputation did not rest merely on Nazi Party membership and mental or physical proximity to regime leaders. Like Knappertsbusch, Krauss compromised his professionalism in the Third Reich, at least partially, and he did it in more subtle ways than his cruder predecessor. With the goal of boundless artistic influence in the Reich ahead of him, certainly as far as opera was concerned, he committed both moral and aesthetic sacrifices for the benefit of fascist politics. The aesthetic compromises were not heavy ones, yet they were significant. The conductor who had planned to premiere Ernst Křenek's new atonal opera *Karl V.*, and had left Vienna in protest when Austrian cultural authorities opposed that, in the Third Reich very quickly became known as a proponent of the older, more traditional style of opera. Of course, Krauss's decisions may have been entirely tactical, a means of ensconcing himself more firmly. Several months after arriving in Munich he declared that his first priority was to present classical works and "at best performances of extremely notable newer compositions." Once the champion of Alban Berg, Krauss now denounced the "fallacies of atonality" and decried the "fruitless musical experiments of the moderns."[85] Such words benefited him, but they were also grist for the mill of Nazi reactionism.

In October 1941 Werner Egk, a cautious modernist himself, who had just been appointed to the post of composers' section leader in the RMK, complained to his chief Joseph Goebbels (who himself favored a strictly German model of modernity) that since beginning his tenure in Munich, Krauss had performed the works of three older contemporary composers, as opposed to only one of the younger generation. The three older men were Strauss, Pfitzner, and Ermanno Wolf-Ferrari; it is not certain whom Egk thought of as the younger man, for in fact Krauss had presented the works of at least three young composers, including Egk's own

Zaubergeige in March 1937, in addition to Norbert Schultze's *Schwarzer Peter* and Carl Orff's *Der Mond*. Nonetheless, Egk was clearly implying that Krauss lacked a commitment to younger, more modern composers.[86]

By using the example of Orff's opera, it can be shown that Egk's complaint was not far off the mark. Although a Nazi handbook informed its readers in 1944, not without a touch of flattery, that Krauss's premiere of this fairy-tale opera on 5 February 1939 constituted the one "essentially progressive" element in Krauss's musical repertoire, Orff himself, who also regarded his work as modern, considered Krauss's production a failure, clearly attributable to Krauss's reluctant identification with the aesthetics of modernism rather than to any lack of understanding of its nature. It followed, then, that at the end of 1942, by which time Orff's pioneering progressive work *Carmina Burana* had had many successful performances in Germany, Krauss was dead set against staging it at the Salzburg Festival.[87]

Krauss's main political sin was that he knowingly exploited the Führer's predilection for his art, to the point of alienating the rest of the Nazi hierarchy; this, however, in no way weighed in his favor as a form of moral resistance. For the sake of Hitler's largesse Krauss was prepared to take on all other enemies, even the leading National Socialists. Although his two years in Berlin had been unpleasant but still bearable, in 1937 a storm broke around Krauss. The conductor tempted the devil when in his letter to Hitler of April 1938 he suggested that he would be ready "for the combined leadership of two important institutions" situated "in the leading cities of the, by now, united southern realm of culture in the Reich."[88] Colleagues of renown, such as Hans Pfitzner, were beginning to see what he was up to and lost no opportunity to castigate the Austrian, thus generating further adverse publicity for him at a time when he least needed it.[89]

Krauss's ruthless use of his direct access to Hitler annoyed first Munich's Gauleiter Wagner and then Goebbels, who was, after all, his superior as president of the Reich Culture Chamber. In 1943 Krauss sought nothing less than a plenipotentiary leadership status similar to Göring's vis-à-vis his Prussian state theaters, which, as far as Munich was concerned, would have outstripped the power of Goebbels, Drewes, and Raabe.[90] But if the growing animosity between the conductor and Hitler's immediate underlings did not amount to an act of political defiance on the part of Krauss, it did tend to bolster his self-image as the omnipotent culture dealer in the land, and this, with its potential for abuse of all kinds, not excluding personal enrichment, was a dangerous token of irresponsibility in a dictatorial environment. (The enrichment, incidentally, was apparent less in the case of Krauss himself, who was always extremely well off, than that of his wife, for whom he demanded every possible contractual benefit whenever the occasion presented itself.)[91]

Certainly by the last few years of the Third Reich, Krauss, while in a formal sense preserving his high standards of musical professionalism, ended up giving as much to National Socialism as he got from it, perhaps in a somewhat quieter way than his less competent predecessor Knappertsbusch but nonetheless equally discreditably on moral and political grounds. He performed concerts for Robert Ley's Strength-through-Joy organization and for the Gauleiter of Salzburg.[92] In the spring of 1940 Krauss was coopted into Drewes's Promi agency for the control and revision of objectionable music, which, among other tasks, "Aryanized" older texts by changing geographic and political settings. Goebbels himself was making full use of his skills by June.[93] Also in 1940 Krauss conducted a concert for the Waffen-SS, and he went repeatedly to Cracow to entertain Hans Frank, that butcher of Poles and Jews and lover of German *Kultur*.[94] For several weeks in 1942 Krauss took the Berlin Philharmonic Orchestra on a tour of fascist Spain, Portugal, and Vichy France, but in Marseilles and Lyons he met with opposition from what appeared to be members of the Resistance. Did that stir his conscience?[95] Krauss conducted radio programs in honor of his patron Hitler's birthday, and even paid his musical respects to the otherwise despised Munich Gauleiter Adolf Wagner upon his death in April 1944.[96] Thus, not unlike Knappertsbusch, he ended his Third Reich career in May 1945 with his professional skills undiminished but, after so long in Hitler's political orbit, with an indelible stain on his artistic ethics.

Political Allegiance and Career Enhancement

By the time National Socialism took hold in Germany, both Knappertsbusch and Krauss were enjoying international reputations established years before. Although they entered into working alliances with the regime of Adolf Hitler for different reasons and with varying degrees of success, they were not dependent on any formal ties with the Nazi regime to ensure their professional future. Significantly, neither one of them was a member of the Nazi Party or any of its affiliated organizations.

But there were two other groups of musicians in the Third Reich who could not afford such relative independence, and they had to seek some, often formalized, association with the regime for the sake of furthering or maintaining their careers. The first group consisted of younger musicians, perhaps with talent comparable to that of the two conductors, but who were on the bottom rung of the career ladder and therefore had to take out some kind of political insurance, as it were, in order to make it to the top. To this group belonged musicians such as the young conductor Herbert von Karajan and the very promising coloratura soprano Elisabeth Schwarzkopf. A second group included more mature musicians, some also of international reputation, who nonetheless did not match the range of accomplishments of a Furtwängler, Knappertsbusch, or Krauss, and could be tripped up by political issues, perhaps at the instigation of an envious colleague, if they were not careful. One who comes to mind is the pianist Wilhelm Backhaus, who was the object of intense jealousy on the part of the Nazi virtuoso Elly Ney.

We begin with Herbert von Karajan. One finds three themes in his Third Reich career that run more or less parallel to one another and are to some extent interdependent: first, the unfolding of an extraordinary musical talent; second, a series of formal political commitments; and third, what might be called personal and, by Nazi standards, political irregularities that held the potential to endanger his professional progress.

Karajan was born in 1908 in Austrian Salzburg, the son of a well-to-do physician of partially Greek-Macedonian ancestry whose forebears had been ennobled while in the service of the Saxon kings. A child prodigy at the piano, young Herbert studied conducting. In 1928 he became choir director and, until 1934, orchestra conductor at the state theater in Ulm. After he conducted works by Tchaikovsky and Richard Strauss at the Salzburg Mozarteum in 1929, the local press praised his "suggestive power" and musical "intuition," later to become the constituent elements of his legendary magic. Karajan's opera repertoire in Ulm was conventional, not modern, appropriate for a young musician who was hoping to make his mark in the trendsetting musical establishment. He was extremely hardworking, presenting no fewer than 125 productions in just over thirty-three months.

Nonetheless, his contract ran out in 1934. While seeking opportunities in Berlin, he met the new intendant from Aachen, who was looking for an opera conductor in that small Rhenish-Prussian frontier town, which, though in many ways provincial, was renowned for its well-established musical tradition. After a complicated audition and a year's probation, Karajan was hired as tenured conductor of the Aachen Opera in April 1935. At twenty-seven he now was the youngest Generalmusikdirektor in Germany. A few months later he also took over the Aachen Symphony, an event that hinged on Peter Raabe's retirement there and subsequent appointment as Strauss's successor in Berlin at the RMK.

Over the next few years Karajan acquitted himself so well in Aachen that he came to the attention of Generalintendant Heinz Tietjen in Berlin. After some involved deliberations and several extremely successful appearances as guest conductor, the Austrian was installed in April 1939 as a Kapellmeister at the Preussische Staatsoper, which Clemens Krauss had left more than two years earlier. He kept his Aachen position for a while, commuting back and forth, until he finally gave it up in 1941 to dedicate himself solely to his demanding responsibilities in the capital.[97]

The indisputable fact was that, from 1939 to 1945, Karajan became the most interesting and attractive of an entire generation of young conductors in the Reich, including Eugen Jochum, Hans Rosbaud, and Karl Böhm. His success had to do not only with his personal magnetism but also with his unique style of conducting and, gradually, with his interest in more contemporary works. He was famous for learning orchestra scores by heart very quickly, so that he always conducted from memory. This astonished the public and, deservedly or not, underlined his reputation as a genius.[98] As for his interest in contemporary music, he was known for his fresh interpretations of Strauss's works, and the verve with which he took on conceptually more daring modern compositions such as those of Carl Orff. Tietjen was reminded of the young Hans von Bülow upon seeing Karajan conduct Strauss's *Elektra* in the spring of 1940. After a performance of Strauss's *Zarathustra* in October of that year, Tietjen reported to the master that "the audience had gone berserk with enthusiasm" for the young conductor. Delighted by this good news, Strauss was pleased to acknowledge the "magnificent Karajan."[99]

Early in 1941 Karajan conducted a spectacular concert performance of Orff's *Carmina Burana,* which had gained national fame through Böhm's Dresden premiere in October 1940 (it was first performed in Frankfurt in 1937). Later in 1941 Karajan staged the full opera version at the Staatsoper in Berlin. Werner Oehlmann, one of the more credible critics still active, wrote in *Das Reich* that for a composition with such "primitive energies," Karajan had managed "controlled dynamics" and emphasized the "tenderness of the score." The composer himself was even more impressed. "The orchestra under Karajan sounds fantastic," Orff rhapsodized from Munich after having observed his work's resounding success.[100]

But there was still that darker, politically determined theme in Karajan's *vita.* To take the most distasteful aspect first, long after the war, when confronted with incontrovertible proof that he had joined the Nazi Party twice—on 8 April 1933 in Salzburg, while already holding a job in the Third Reich, and then three weeks later in the Swabian town of Ulm— Karajan brushed it off as lies and falsifications. He admitted only to joining the NSDAP in Aachen because the local authorities had made this a condition for permanent employment there.[101] Here he was repeating a bill of goods that he had first successfully sold to Austrian authorities in March 1946.[102] The only element of truth to it is that Karajan's Ulm party membership was acknowledged as valid for Aachen NSDAP purposes, and his Reich membership was transferred there (as it was later to Berlin) under the same registration number.[103]

One key to Karajan's political opportunism certainly lay in his personality. He was an obsessively ambitious man who felt he had to be first in almost everything he did. He is in this respect reminiscent of another notorious Nazi careerist, SS General Reinhard Heydrich, a superb violinist, master fencer, aircraft pilot, and consummate womanizer. In Karajan's case the list of accomplishments began with his conducting, but later it included his achievements as a businessman (he marketed his own records and pioneered compact discs), a skier, an airplane pilot, and a race-car driver, not to mention his notorious sexual exploits.[104] In contemporary musical terms the visible manifestation of this ambition was a perfect match for the Nazi ideal—vitalism wrapped in the cloak of the demonic—precisely the Mephistophelian trait that characterized Karajan's image as a conductor.[105]

Karajan's ample capacity for opportunism even gave rise after the war to the suspicion that he had gone so far as to join Heydrich's SS security service to advance his own purposes.[106] But though the conductor did use as his agent Rudolf Vedder, an unsavory SS member who represented many high-ranking artists in the Reich, he had no other contacts with the SS, and his alleged collaboration not only was never proved by the postwar Allied denazification authorities, but in fact, in light of Karajan's musical activities, is now thought to have been highly unlikely.[107]

Given the available evidence, it makes sense to take a closer look at the circumstances surrounding Karajan's duplicate party membership in April and May 1933 and the eventual transfer to Aachen. It has been observed that Karajan joined the NSDAP in Salzburg on 8 April 1933, the very day when Jews in public positions, including municipal orchestras, were notified of their impending dismissal by the German Reich just across the border. Karajan must have known, as did so many of his "Aryan" colleagues, that his chances of future professional success might well double if he, as a bona fide party member, were able to profit directly from the consequences of this ordinance. In fact, at the beginning of 1933 he himself had been given his notice in Ulm, a measure that was temporarily suspended to take effect a year later. At the same time, however, his concerts in Ulm had been well received in the Nazi press. In any event, after first joining the party in his hometown of Salzburg, and as the Austrian Nazi Party was facing proscription under the authoritarian Dollfuss regime (the ban finally was issued in mid-June), Karajan joined again a few weeks later at his place of employment in Ulm. There he had a Jewish colleague, Otto Schulmann, who was also a potential rival. Schulmann was soon dismissed, whereupon he emigrated to America. But both Karajan and Schulmann subsequently claimed that they had been the best of friends, and that Schulmann's Jewish background and Karajan's party membership never entered into their relationship. Still, there is a lingering suspicion that the multimillionaire Karajan bought Schulmann off.[108]

Karajan's party membership may have stood him in good stead when he moved from Ulm to Prussian Aachen via Berlin. Edgar Gross, the town's new intendant, who had scouted Karajan in Berlin, was a party member, as was Aachen's alderman and the culture warden Albert Hoff. These men eventually tipped the balance, and the final decision was made in favor of the ambitious Austrian.[109]

Karajan's subsequent move from Aachen to Berlin must also be evaluated within a political framework, albeit not a narrow one contingent on party membership (it is true, for example, that Karajan never flaunted his membership and never wore the party badge).[110] In those years Karajan, almost by default, benefited from political rivalries between Goebbels and Göring, exemplifed in this case in the continuing friction between Goebbels's (and Hitler's) favorite Wilhelm Furtwängler and Göring's confidant

Heinz Tietjen. After Furtwängler had given up his prominent position at the Preussische Staatsoper in late 1934 (though he was soon guest-conducting there and overseeing Philharmonic concerts) and Generalintendant Tietjen had lost Clemens Krauss about two years later, Tietjen was on the lookout for a replacement at the Prussian opera. With Göring's support that eventually led to Karajan's making more frequent guest-conducting appearances in the capital, to the enthusiasm of the national press. (It has also been said that Rudolf Bockelmann, the singer and one of Göring's stalwarts, had had a hand in bringing Karajan to Berlin.)[111] What settled Karajan's hiring as conductor of the Preussische Staatsoper was a sensational critique entitled "Karajan the Miracle," written by Edwin von der Null, one of Berlin's more perceptive critics, which appeared in 1938 in the *Berliner Zeitung*. It described Karajan, who had just conducted *Tristan und Isolde*, as someone whom even fifty-year-old conductors could learn from—a massive affront to Furtwängler. There is compelling evidence that this article was written at the insistence of Göring, and published by his minions at that widely read Berlin daily, for the express purpose of compromising the politically neutral Furtwängler, with the attendant side effect of exalting the much younger party member Karajan.[112]

It seems ironic that even in the Third Reich, rife with default, compromise, and contradiction, two such geniuses as Furtwängler and Karajan could not coexist. But the fact remains that in metropolitan centers such as Berlin (or, as we have seen, Munich), art was so politicized for the benefit of the fascist regime that natural competition which would otherwise have been conducive to overall creativity suffered. Personal rivalries and petty politics had already poisoned the relationship between Tietjen and Krauss (to say nothing of Furtwängler and Krauss, whom Karajan admired),[113] and now this tension was to be repeated all over again, not necessarily to the benefit of the often bewildered music connoisseur. As Furtwängler and Karajan kept exchanging barbs and musically assaulting each other's bastions, invariably with the sanction and certainly to the amusement of their respective regime patrons,[114] the public did not know whose side to take, or whether to take sides at all. "Later I went on to the opera to hear Karajan," noted the exiled Russian Princess Marie Vassiltchikov in her diary in December 1940. "He is very fashionable and some people tend to consider him better than Furtwängler, which is nonsense. He certainly has genius and much fire, but is not without conceit."[115] By 1942 Karajan had fallen on hard times as Furtwängler managed to strengthen his position in Berlin, not only by gaining strong sympathy from his traditional patron Goebbels but also because Tietjen, the master of intrigue (in that respect besting even the Mephistophelian Karajan) envious of the Austrian's success, cunningly ingratiated himself with the propaganda minister. "Furtwängler virtually regarded Karajan as Satan and seized every opportunity to vilify him," a contemporary Berlin stage producer recalled.[116] At any rate, it was clear that Furtwängler was once again increasing the number of his irregularly scheduled guest appearances at the Preussische Staatsoper, while Karajan was moving out of the national limelight.[117]

Given his calculating disposition, Karajan served the Nazi system in ways no different from those of Knappertsbusch or Krauss, whether it meant conducting orchestras for party functions, playing in occupied Paris, or performing for Hitler's birthday.[118] But, in addition to the wiles of colleagues such as Furtwängler and Tietjen, his career faced other risks as well, though it would stretch the argument to say that these were genuinely political. Karajan once encountered a musical problem that further complicated his relationship with Hitler and Goebbels, who already favored his rival Furtwängler. Notwithstanding his own difficulties with the regime, Furtwängler invariably had the upper hand because of his direct access to the propaganda minister and the Führer, who both loved hearing him in concert.[119] In 1940 in Berlin Karajan conducted *Die Meistersinger*, with Bockelmann singing the part of Hans Sachs. As was his custom, Karajan directed without a score. Unfortunately, Bockelmann missed his entry, apparently because he was drunk. Skillfull as he was, Karajan saved the evening through forceful intervention, but the mistake had been noticeable. Although this was a misfortune that might befall any conductor without serious consequences, this time Hitler happened to be seated in his "Führer's box." He was furious. In Karajan's own words: "Someone told Hitler this came to pass because that man Karajan has to conduct his music by heart. I think it was Minister Goebbels who then had somebody tell me that from now on I was to conduct from the score. Sure enough, next time there was a score on the conductor's stand. I just turned it over and continued as usual." Among his entourage Hitler did not hold back his criticism, and this seems to have contributed to Karajan's eventual failure to succeed Karl Böhm in Dresden in late 1942. Here Karajan was outmaneuvered by Karl Elmendorff, a Generalmusikdirektor from Bayreuth and Wiesbaden seventeen years his senior, who had schemed to get the position with the help of an acquaintance, Gerdy Troost, the widow of the Führer's architect Paul Ludwig Troost and herself a close friend of Hitler.[120]

Karajan's star fell even further when in October 1942, after having divorced his first wife, an operetta singer from Aachen, he married Anita Gütermann, heiress to a textile fortune, but who had a Jewish grandparent and therefore was classified as of "mixed blood to the second degree" under the Nuremberg Race Laws of 1935. Karajan's postwar claim that because of this questionable marriage he was dragged before a Nazi Party court whereupon he resigned his party membership is certainly false. His party papers in the archives are intact, and there is no record of any resignation, a move that would have placed anyone who attempted it in the greatest danger and was therefore, throughout the Third Reich and especially during the war, extremely rare. The denazification authorities believed him, however, and once again this opportunistic ploy helped to revive Karajan's spectacular career after World War II.[121]

One who would often join him on his musical progress in the future was the coloratura soprano Elisabeth Schwarzkopf. Seven years younger than the conductor, she was born in Jarotschin near Poznan in what once was and today is again Poland. She was the daughter of a German Social Democratic Gymnasium teacher, known to oppose the Nazis. In 1953 she married the English impresario Walter Legge and became a British citizen, eventually settling in the outskirts of Zurich. According to her official letterhead, she is now known as "Kammersängerin Prof. Dr. Elisabeth Legge-Schwarzkopf, Dame of the British Empire."[122]

On the occasion of her eightieth birthday in December 1995, it was observed that she was still haunted by "dark tales that should be clarified and finally laid to rest if untrue." Like Karajan after the war, she wanted to obscure whatever Nazi ties she had maintained during the Third Reich, so in an immediate postwar declaration for the Austrian authorities she downplayed any suspected Nazi connections and virtually presented herself as an innocent captive of the regime.[123] When in 1992 I asked her for help in clearing up that part of her biography, she first kept me waiting for two years and then suddenly declared that she had no time to think over my proposal, what with her life flowing quickly away and so many other matters concerning singing and helping young performers fully occupying her attention. Her lawyer later indicated that she might be ready to cooperate; but after I had mailed a list of questions, as requested, I heard nothing further from either of them.[124]

Schwarzkopf's credo has been and still is that "I don't have to set things straight. I'm not responsible—in no way." And so early in 1983 Schwarzkopf repeatedly denied to journalists from the *New York Times* that she had ever joined the Nazi Party; only when the reporters persisted on the basis of evidence they possessed did she admit it. Yet her explanation that "everyone at the opera joined" was patently false.[125] Joining the party was not a routine affair; like Karajan, Schwarzkopf made sure to join early in her life in order to guarantee continuing success at a time when she had already made her mark as one of the best promising young singers in the German music world. As early as 1935 she, along with two others, had been singled out by one of her teachers at the Hochschule für Musik in Berlin as an exceptional student, and three years later a state examination administered by the Reichstheaterkammer (Reich Theater Chamber), or RTK, as part of Goebbels's Reich Culture Chamber qualified her as an opera singer "summa cum laude."[126] Despite her obvious talent, Schwarzkopf wanted to buy some political insurance; in 1935, while at the Berlin Hochschule, she joined the Nazi Student League for a time and became a section leader in the women's wing, a position of exceptional influence in the national student population.[127]

After having assured the authorities of her faultlessly "Aryan" pedigree (this was routine), Schwarzkopf secured her first contract as a novice

soprano, "singer (beginner)," under Intendant Wilhelm Rode at Goebbels's Deutsche Oper in Berlin in May 1938 at the modest annual salary
of 2,400 marks.[128] Rode took an immediate professional interest in the
artistic progress of the young soprano, who in 1939 was training privately with Maria Ivogün, a retired coloratura of great fame.[129] It was in
April 1939 that Schwarzkopf, barely twenty-four years old, began to
engage in a pattern of capricious behavior. This soon compromised her
superior Wilhelm Rode, who considered himself personally responsible
for her performance at the opera and hoped to reap the benefit of her
outstanding work. Her first infraction was to arrive late for a performance of Eugen d'Albert's popular opera Tiefland, for which she was
fined 20 marks. A few weeks later she took a longer work break than
authorized, injured her foot, and this time was late for a rehearsal. Perhaps the already exceptionally proficient singer was bored by rehearsals;
she began asking her supervisors every time if she was really "needed" at
them. At the beginning of June she was notified that a con-
tinuation of such behavior could lead to immediate dismissal, seriously
hampering her career. Schwarzkopf, however, did not change her attitude, appearing without shoes in a performance of Tannhäuser at the end
of October.[130]

The singer's postwar rationalization of these escapades as her way of
defying National Socialism, especially Goebbels,[131] is without foundation, for three reasons. First, it would have been foolish for even the most
talented of Germany's young and promising artists to endanger his or her
future just for lack of personal control, particularly in a dictatorial regime. Second, Schwarzkopf herself wrote obsequious letters to Rode,
feigning full contrition. Third, and most important, rather than acts of
symbolic defiance by a potential victim of the Nazi regime, these were
the actions of a prominent Nazi student leader during her university
days, and of a woman who eagerly offered further signs of political
compliance, such as joining both the Nazi Party (1 March 1940) and
the NSV, or Nationalsozialistische Volkswohlfahrt (National Socialist
People's Charity).[132]

The real reason for Schwarzkopf's behavior was that she was trying to
use a number of schemes to advance herself. Her rebellious high jinks
occurred at the Deutsche Oper, a company controlled by Goebbels, who
himself considered their productions "somewhat clichéd."[133] So with
some reason she might have considered herself a notch or two above her
colleagues there, and her capers were apparently a ruse calculated to
improve her working conditions or get her transferred to a more promising environment, such as Göring's Preussische Staatsoper. Her demonstration of unshakable political allegiance was another such opportunistic
ploy, for it would have been difficult for anyone to stand in the path of a
singer, already a trailblazer in the field of opera and later lieder, who had
at the same time a proven record as a Nazi. Finally, Schwarzkopf knew
that she had friends in high places who would help her to escape from the

influence of uncouth men such as Rode, whose patronage she had endured only to get started. Among them was Hans Erich Schrade, secretary of the RTK in Berlin. Another was pianist Michael Raucheisen, husband of Maria Ivogün, a solid Nazi and personal friend of Goebbels, who often worked with Schwarzkopf. A third was Hans Hinkel, the powerful secretary of the overarching Reich Culture Chamber, whom she, with many other artists, obliged by entertaining the troops at a safe distance from the front lines.[134]

During the war Schwarzkopf consistently improved her working conditions and contractual compensation until by 1942 she was taking on so many guest engagements that Rode was genuinely afraid of losing her.[135] Late in 1942 Schwarzkopf decided to break away completely from Berlin and sign a contract with Karl Böhm, who was set to take over the Wiener Staatsoper. Artistically this would have placed her at the zenith of her career. But this was too much for Goebbels, who sympathetically received the protests of Deutsche Oper officials and for the time being ordered both Böhm and Schwarzkopf back into line.[136]

The singer, already widely acclaimed by the critics, contracted tuberculosis and was inactive in 1943–44 but still did not fail to cultivate her regime connections.[137] During a "music week" organized by the conquerors of Poland for political reasons in connection with the SS-led "Reichsuniversität" of Posen (Poznan) in September 1942, Schwarzkopf sang under the direction of Hans Pfitzner at the university, not far from her place of birth. Gauleiter Arthur Greiser, whose wife was a concert pianist, and who himself would be executed by the Poles in 1946 for war crimes, spoke of grandiose plans for National Socialist music education as a correction of twenty years of "alien" (Polish) rule on originally German soil after World War I. Schwarzkopf later thanked Pfitzner personally for having invited her there to interpret his compositions.[138] In December 1942 the soprano again took part in one of Hinkel's troop entertainment schemes, giving a solo recital for the Waffen-SS on two separate occasions.[139] And by 1944, when she finally was able to make her debut under Böhm in Vienna singing arias by Rossini, Verdi, and Wagner, she was not wanting for support. According to Ernst Lothar, the American theater and music officer for U.S.-occupied Austria in 1946, theater-loving SS General Hugo Jury, the Gauleiter of Lower Austria, residing in Vienna, had established a personal relationship with the singer.[140]

In the case of Knappertsbusch, Krauss, Karajan, and Schwarzkopf, it is possible to draw up a sort of balance sheet indicating both pluses and minuses. If these areas are viewed in combination, one discerns many shades of gray rather than just black and white, a pattern that seems to have been typical of the majority of musical artists in the Third Reich. In the biographies of two other Austrian-born artists we also find conflicting elements of resistance, accommodation, and service to the regime, so that in the end they cannot be definitively painted as either Nazis or non-

Nazis. These men are the conductors Karl Böhm and Hans Rosbaud, born in 1894 and 1895, respectively, and classmates from Graz. They both enjoyed normal careers in the period before the Nazi takeover, as well as after 1945. In this sense they resemble Knappertsbusch and Krauss, who had no need to rely on Nazi support, but they also suggest parallels with Karajan and Schwarzkopf because, given their relative youth, they were not yet well enough established to carry on as if in a total political vacuum.

To be sure, there were shades of gray for both. To Karl Böhm's credit was his aesthetically faultless and sometimes politically daring choice of repertoire. Böhm had built his reputation prior to the Third Reich as a Kapellmeister under Bruno Walter in Munich and as Generalmusikdirektor in Darmstadt; he then came to Hamburg, and in 1934 to Dresden as successor to Fritz Busch. His art was that of an expert in all the classics, but increasingly specializing in Mozart and Richard Strauss.[141] Böhm's closeness to Strauss, which later included a personal friendship second only to Strauss's relationship with Krauss, was such that even Strauss's musical enemies—Hans Pfitzner for one—became his own.[142] Böhm was more daring than Krauss in that he always liked conducting works as modern as was tolerable in those times, such as Rudolf Wagner-Régeny's *Günstling* (premiered in 1935), Stravinsky's ballet *Jeu de cartes* (European premiere, 1937); or the controversial *Carmina Burana,* which was a huge success in 1940.[143] Böhm actually risked the opprobrium of the regime in premiering Richard Mohaupt's *Die Wirtin von Pinsk* in February 1938, for Mohaupt was married to a Russian-Jewish violinist and had close ties to the hated jazz culture.[144] Furthermore, Böhm collaborated with the progressive (and anti-Nazi) Oskar Fritz Schuh, an artistic director, and Caspar Neher, a stage designer, and he supported composer Boris Blacher, who was not fully "Aryan," when Blacher began teaching a composition class at the Dresden Conservatory in 1938.[145] When Böhm antagonized Goebbels by signing Schwarzkopf to sing for his Wiener Staatsoper in 1942–43, the minister's right-hand man Hans Hinkel threatened "appropriate measures against the Vienna opera and its Generalmusikdirektor." One of those measures appears to have been, for a few months at least, the proscription of Böhm as a performing artist on Goebbels's national radio network. At the time Böhm's stance could have been interpreted by enemies of the Nazi regime as a brave attempt to preserve the principle of artistic freedom.[146] Böhm himself later claimed to have sent his son Karlheinz to Switzerland in anticipation of his own flight from the Third Reich, and to have tried to save his Vienna artists—much in the manner of Clemens Krauss in Munich—from conscription for any form of war service.[147]

But Böhm had his Achilles' heel. His two main career moves—from Hamburg to Dresden in early 1934, and from there to Vienna in early 1943—occurred under political auspices that tended to taint his post-1945 reputation. In accepting the music directorship of the Dresden

Opera after Fritz Busch's politically motivated dismissal, which Böhm himself later termed an "unsavory departure," he showed not only a lack of tact and compassion but also extreme careerist opportunism at the expense of personal morality. Hitler, in fact, had smoothed his path from Hamburg to Dresden by facilitating an earlier contractual release than was possible under the law. Significantly, Böhm later wrote in his memoirs that it was "the decision of the Führer" which prevented him from leaving Dresden prematurely, in this case for Berlin.[148]

Once in Dresden, Böhm poured forth rhetoric glorifying the Nazi regime and its cultural aims. When, in the summer of 1935, owing to the rise of pro-Habsburg sentiment backed by Vice-Chancellor Rüdiger Starhemberg and possibly Mussolini, Nazi fortunes were sinking in his native Austria, Böhm declared to regime authorities that he had many followers in Vienna, especially in the National Socialist camp, and that he could be of propagandistic service to Nazi interests by giving concerts there.[149] A few months later he praised the "deep comprehension by the Führer of artistic problems," and later still he announced that the path of present-day music, as far as symphonic work was concerned, was "prefigured by the weltanschauung of National Socialism."[150]

Repeatedly Böhm conducted Wagner's *Die Meistersinger* in opening ceremonies for the Nuremberg Nazi Party rally.[151] He also conferred with Goebbels, who, until the end, seems to have been rather fond of him. Contrary to what Böhm himself maintained, Hitler did not consistently oppose his move from Dresden to Vienna from the time when the question was first broached in 1941 (according to Goebbels's diaries, Böhm had been fairly unhappy in Dresden since at least 1937, though his difficulties there were to some extent of his own making).[152] The propaganda minister approved of the change in any case, though in March 1942 Goebbels and Hitler agreed that Böhm should not violate any contractual agreements binding him to Dresden. By July 1942 Hitler wanted Böhm in Vienna, and so the maestro took up the post of Generalmusikdirektor of the Wiener Staatsoper on 1 January 1943, with the Führer granting him the Martial Order of Merit on 30 January, commemorating ten years of Nazi rule in Germany.[153] Like Knappertsbusch, Böhm reciprocated by officiating at local festivities in honor of Hitler's birthday in April 1944.[154]

Hans Rosbaud was an even greater champion of modern music than Karl Böhm, both in the Weimar Republic and, insofar as this was feasible, during the Third Reich. The same age as Paul Hindemith, Rosbaud was his fellow student at the Hoch'sche Konservatorium in Frankfurt between 1912 and 1918, where both studied composition with the Jewish composer Bernhard Sekles. The two were friends, a tie that resulted in Rosbaud's visit to Zurich in 1938, the only conductor to come from Germany for the world premiere of Hindemith's opera *Mathis der Maler*.[155] Rosbaud revered Arnold Schoenberg and was the acknowledged conductor of Schoenberg's works in Germany till his death in

1962.[156] After he had assumed his first significant position as music director of the Frankfurt radio station in 1929, Rosbaud strengthened his commitment to the cause of modern music, using his position at the radio station to support, albeit unsuccessfully, Stravinsky's bid to be played in the Third Reich.[157] Other favorites of his were Orff (he directed *Carmina Burana* enthusiastically as Generalmusikdirektor in Westphalian Münster during the 1939–40 season), as well as Prokofiev, Debussy, and Ravel.[158]

Rosbaud's stand on music was certainly not an easy one. As early as 1935 he had commented from neutral Switzerland to Béla Bartók, whose music was somewhat suspect in Germany, on the Hungarian composer's difficulties in being regularly performed there. Recalling that he, Rosbaud, had presented some of Bartók's works in the past, he explained to the composer that most German conductors and producers were afraid to touch them. As for himself, he knew that his presentation of non-German music could always be held against him, and he would have to be prepared to ward off "the most vehement attacks."[159] In 1937 he wrote to Schoenberg, again from outside Germany: "I would like to write you more often, but it is not always very easy; you do understand."[160] Unlike Böhm, who claimed that he had no opportunities to leave Germany, there is evidence that from 1934 to 1937 Rosbaud would gladly have emigrated to the United States, if only he had received more consistent support from the New York concert agent Arthur Judson and conductor Arturo Toscanini, who initially showed themselves to be sympathetic.[161]

Nonetheless, his love for and support of a type of music defamed by the Nazis and his growing uneasiness in the Third Reich do not automatically qualify Rosbaud as having been an anti-Nazi or even a non-Nazi artist. Like colleagues before and after him, he accommodated himself to a totalitarian regime that guaranteed him some artistic latitude and a regular source of income by making certain concessions in return. The records show that Rosbaud, for the sake of an uninterrupted career in Germany, maneuvered from one step to the next, rendering unto Caesar as much as he thought he could justify, undoubtedly hoping to emerge from those troubled times unscathed. He seems to have been a man of circumspect and guarded nature, with a calculating sense of generosity. Shortly before the Nazis came to power, Matyas Seiber, the Hungarian Jew who had taught a jazz class for Sekles at the Hoch'sche Konservatorium, remarked, seemingly paradoxically, that Rosbaud had impressed him as "cold and unapproachable . . . although very friendly."[162]

Rosbaud justly spoke of "vehement attacks" in his letter to Bartók, for he was much beleaguered in Frankfurt. After 1933 at the radio station, as a result of Nazi rule, serious music was incrementally neglected, specifically that of modernist composers.[163] And yet Rosbaud contributed his own share to creating the climate of cultural repression from which he so carefully distanced himself in his letter to Bartók and later. When in the fall of 1935 jazz was placed on the index of the national radio network, the Nazi broadcast administrators prepared a polemic that was aired on the Frankfurt station on 9 December 1935; it mentioned "the perverse erotic side of jazz," among other vices. Rosbaud assisted in this effort by selecting appropriate musical examples that "proved the contradiction between nigger jazz and German individuality."[164]

Although Rosbaud was at that time generally perceived by some as enjoying quite an "unfettered" reign at the Frankfurt radio station,[165] he did have one enemy who hated his modernist proclivities and tried to unseat him on a charge of being Jewish. This man was a conductor subordinate to Rosbaud, an Old Fighter of moderate talent and scant influence who, not least out of professional envy, launched an intrigue against Rosbaud in 1936 and at one point appeared to enjoy the support of the local Gestapo. But Rosbaud protested vehemently against what he took to be a vilification of his reputation and in the end was vindicated.[166] As early as 1933 rumors that Rosbaud was Jewish had abounded, a reaction to his modernist leanings, a slightly Jewish sounding name, and his Austrian origins. At that time Rosbaud had been defended by his friend and erstwhile patron Prince Alexander Friedrich von Hessen, a minor composer who, in his correspondence with the conductor, comes across as an egregious anti-Semite. On behalf of Rosbaud the prince affirmed in April 1933 that "under no circumstances can he be accused of being Jewish or possessing anything less than a German sense of patriotism."[167]

After Rosbaud had moved to Münster in the fall of 1937, he gave no indication that the prince might have been mistaken. Not without some justification Rosbaud later claimed to have made this move because he could expect greater artistic freedom there than in Frankfurt.[168] In all likelihood money was also a factor, for in Münster he was to receive 18,000 marks a year, more than any radio music director could earn.[169] But in Münster Rosbaud also accommodated the Nazi hierarchy by conducting concerts for the local party organization, including a "Führer Celebration" in April 1939.[170]

"German art, too, has its war objectives," said Münster's Gauleiter Alfred Meyer during "Gau Culture Week" in May 1940, which was launched with a performance of the *Meistersinger* Overture conducted by Hans Rosbaud.[171] This was a political program, setting a standard that was applied even more stringently at Strasbourg, where Rosbaud became Generalmusikdirektor of the opera in 1941. In 1940 Alsace, with its capital of Strasbourg, had been taken by the Nazis from the French, and along with its sister province of Lorraine had been annexed to the Reich in contravention even of the humiliating Nazi armistice with Paris in June.[172] The aim now was to eradicate from Alsace anything that smacked of French influence and replace it with all things German; by summer 1943 this could be accomplished only with an inordinate number of death sentences. In the realm of culture, the newly constituted "Reichsuniversität Strassburg," a Nazi-politicized version of the old French-led institution, was to play a major role in a manner similar to

that of the new SS University of Posen in former Poland.[173] The same
Germanization policies applied to music. In this area, the hypernationalist Hans Pfitzner had worked in Strasbourg before World War I, so newly
established German practices could be connected to this "tradition."[174]
Against this highly politicized background, a Generalmusikdirektor
placed in Strasbourg by the German authorities had to be eminently
reliable politically, in addition to possessing artistic excellence. On both
counts Rosbaud qualified. The Nazi authorities, who sanctioned his appointment, thought him capable of furthering the "continued blooming
of German culture" by doing the kind of work that would "radiate into
the whole of Alsace and the newly added western parts of the Reich."[175]
The imperialist function of his new position was not lost on the conductor, who remarked in the summer of 1943: "The significance and standing of the Strassburg Opera is mainly contingent on the fact that it serves
as an extremely important agent of culture, strongly projecting the German character and German art into the western realm."[176]

Hence, it comes as no surprise that Rosbaud found it difficult to ratio-
nalize this "politically charged" office after 1945.[177] This was especially
so since he must have known that several musicians of the Third Reich,
Furtwängler included, were now priding themselves, accurately or not, on
having refused to perform as representatives of the German government
in any of the newly occupied territories.[178] Rosbaud's self-defense in this
regard was threefold: that he had brought joy to the poor, occupied
Alsatians; that he had risked his own safety in helping some of them out
of various political difficulties; and that he had insisted on keeping fran-
cophone Alsatians, with whom he preferred to speak French, in his orchestra rather than let them be conscripted into the Wehrmacht and
replaced by Germans.[179]

On the first count, it would be somewhat presumptuous to claim that
occupied Alsatians, after their own conductors had been banished, received nothing but delight from a Nazi-supervised music scene, even if
French composers (whom Rosbaud had favored before the war) were
being played—by an orchestra which, even before 1940, was increasingly
pro-Nazi and anti-Semitic. But this was not even the case; on the contrary, Rosbaud introduced the works of Nazi composers such as the
Hitler Youth music instructor Cesar Bresgen, and of contemporaries
who, like Rosbaud himself, had made their peace with the Nazi regime,
such as Johann Nepomuk David, Kurt Hessenberg, Hermann Reutter,
and Winfried Zillig. Those "Alsatian" composers whose works Rosbaud
featured bore German names, not French ones, and so far there is no
evidence that they were not sympathetic to the Nazi cause. The rest of the
program was traditionally German, with Pfitzner well represented, a list
safely tailored not to antagonize the authorities. In fact, in the spring of
1944 Rosbaud went out of his way to oblige the German rulers by speaking at the university, whose highly political nature could not have escaped
him, about the music of Frederick the Great of Prussia. The Prussian king,

who had enlarged his realm by waging aggressive warfare against the Austrian empire of Maria Theresa in the middle of the eighteenth century, was a Nazi icon, and so his lecture sat well with the official propaganda.[180]

On the second point of having helped individual Alsatians, we have Rosbaud's own post-1945 assertion to go by, as well as statements by others who corroborate the conductor's claim. But so far there is no hard evidence dating from the time of the Third Reich.[181] Finally, on the claim of having saved musicians from war service, as the war dragged on orchestras throughout the Reich were being depleted of (German) musicians, who were needed at the front. By March 1942 the RMK was remarking woefully on the scarcity of good German musicians.[182] Therefore, in many musical organizations, particularly in the entertainment industry, foreigners were being hired. It is thus highly unlikely that pressure would have been applied on Rosbaud to keep only German citizens in his Strassburg Opera orchestra, since by that time it was permissible to use (politically unreliable) natives. And if he did try to save musicians from Nazi war service, this was nothing that his colleagues Böhm and Krauss were not also doing. It was commendable but not out of the ordinary for a German conductor of rank to do so.[183]

The examples of these four prominent German musicians illustrate how, during the Third Reich, one could compromise oneself politically to varying degrees for careerist reasons. Many other artists in similar situations can be shown to have entered into comparable compromises, on comparable grounds, although individual circumstances and the exact nature of their compliance may have differed. Many did in fact join the Nazi Party, including the gifted young violinist Wolfgang Schneiderhan, who started paying his party dues as a twenty-five-year-old professor in 1940, or singer Rudolf Bockelmann, who had joined three years earlier. Bockelmann also acted as a functionary of the Nazi actors' union at his opera company in Berlin. When asked early during the Nazi regime why he had decided to cast his lot with the Nazis, he is said to have replied, if you can't fight them, join them![184] Bockelmann had good personal rapport not only with Göring but also with Goebbels, who enjoyed surrounding himself with congenial artists, including the pianist Michael Raucheisen, who was every singer's choice as an accompanist. Like Bockelmann, Raucheisen was invited to official dinners over which Hitler presided. He entered the Nazi hierarchy when in early 1942 he became chief of the soloists' section at the national radio network, where he was also involved in program planning. As such he had real influence, as on the day in September 1942 when a decision was expected on whether bass-baritone Paul Bender could be played on the radio, as he was married to a non-"Aryan." Unlike the great majority of his colleagues, not only was Raucheisen allowed to do as he wished professionally, but beyond that he was richly rewarded for his display of fealty to the Nazi cause. In 1941 he received 3,500 marks for just three days of work entertaining the troops, secure behind the trenches in German Halberstadt. At the end of 1943, because his Berlin residence had been bombed out, Raucheisen was allowed to resettle himself and his family, complete with maid, on beautiful Lake Ammer, a safe distance south of Munich. Hitler conveyed personal congratulations to the pianist on his fifty-fifth birthday in February 1944.[185]

Collaboration with Nazi institutions was practiced by the best of these artists, even if it was only of a token character. But, like Raucheisen, others also tried for special favors. The cellist Paul Grümmer had been eager to play for Rosenberg's NS-Kulturgemeinde, was the Führer's dinner guest at least once, and was sent on an official cultural mission to Portugal by the Propaganda Ministry. In 1941 he took advantage of his status by trying to benefit from the expropriation of the estate of Roszi Marton, an Austrian Jew who had been forced to emigrate. Grümmer wished to purchase, on highly favorable terms, her evacuated Alpine villa.[186] Walter Gieseking, touted as "one of the greatest pianists in the world," recognized interpreter of Debussy, champion of Paul Hindemith, and a musician with an ear for jazz, joined Rosbaud in a German Labor Front concert at Radio Cologne in October 1939. He appears to have countenanced Rosenberg's Kampfbund für deutsche Kultur as early as 1933, and as late as 1940 performed for the NS-Kulturgemeinde, its successor organization. In 1933, like his pianist colleagues Wilhelm Backhaus, Edwin Fischer, and Wilhelm Kempff, he expressed a desire to play for the Führer and very much wanted to have an audience with him. Gieseking's career flourished, and he received a bonus when in March 1944 he was awarded the Martial Order of Merit.[187]

A few musical artists appear to have done nothing at all to ensure professional survival. One wonders if they were really so outstanding or only naive. One of them was the bass-baritone Hans Hotter. This awesomely gifted singer, who won national fame early in his career, was twenty-four when, during Hitler's first year of power, he was employed at the Deutsches Theater in Prague, then still the capital of the sovereign Czechoslovak Republic. At a New Year's Eve party (1933–34) open to the public, Hotter participated in a sketch in which he parodied Don Quixote. In a doggerel verse he imitated Hitler's voice, repeating over and over that he wished to bring peace to the world. Prague was at that time filled with anti-Nazi German refugees, and the audience howled with laughter, but the German embassy was not amused. As a German citizen Hotter was threatened with the confiscation of his passport and was told he would be stopped at the border if he tried to return to the fatherland. A friend, Wilhelm Nonnenbruch, professor of medicine at Charles University, helped him out of the mess, and the embassy let him travel. He was then hired in Hamburg and later in Munich under Krauss, and his meteoric career was launched. Hitler, who frequently attended his performances, was especially fond of him, at one time telling him the exact date, place, and opera role in which he had last seen him. As late as May 1942 the Führer regarded Hotter as "the great baritone of the future." After 1933 Hotter is not on record for having paid particular respects to the regime or for having sought preferential treatment from it. Nonetheless, a secret police report of 1943, perhaps taking its cue from Hitler, gave him a clean political bill of health, stating: "Hotter is one of the most important heroic baritones in Germany. As far as politics is concerned, H. is one of the most assertive figures of the Munich art scene. Even though he does not belong to the NSDAP, he consistently displays a very positive attitude to the Nazi state, and this includes the war events. His attitude is not at all opportunistic, but is the natural expression of a character that is thoroughly straightforward."[188]

This leaves one last category of behavior to consider, and it is the hardest to document: a combination of professional opportunism and political belief. Here the questions are many. For instance, even if the combination is plausible, which of the two ingredients would have been the stronger one, opportunism or conviction? Only a few examples come to mind, the most convincing ones for purposes of this study being those of Bruno Stürmer and Anton Webern.

Stürmer was born in 1892, studied music in Heidelberg, and after holding various intermediate posts around Germany settled in Kassel in 1930, where he directed a chamber orchestra and madrigal choir and freelanced as a pianist and composer. Something of a specialist in choir music, toward the end of the Weimar Republic he showed the influence of Peter Erwin Lendvai, who as a teacher in Hamburg until his forced emigration to England in 1933 concentrated on compositions designed for choirs. Although Stürmer had experimented with Futurism in music, with his unorthodox *Messe des Maschinenmenschen* (1930), he entered the Third Reich as a strong proponent of conventional tonality.[189]

Throughout the Nazi period Stürmer always maintained a solid but not brilliant reputation as a musician and composer, particularly through the Stürmer Trio (in which he played piano), the composition of chamber music, and his active, often didactically motivated involvement with choirs, especially male choirs.[190] But Stürmer also wrote and performed tendentious music, and here the vital question poses itself whether his pro-Nazi tendency was more calculated or more genuinely heartfelt and sincere. Whereas the former can always be assumed for the sake of argument, the latter could have been true in the case of a man who had injured an arm as a soldier in the trenches of World War I and hence was somewhat predisposed toward nationalism, a political conviction that, in the case of an artist who also upheld the ideal of the male choir, could easily merge with the extremist Nazi creed. A second factor here was Stürmer's authentic pedagogic intent, which cast him in the same mold as most of the other Hitler Youth composers and musicians (discussed in chapter 4): subjectively well-meaning, they were seduced by Hitler's heroic schemes and then played along.[191]

In the musical workshop of Bruno Stürmer this possible combination of opportunism and faithful adherence to dogma generated, as early as the summer of 1933, an a cappella work for male choir, *A People's Call,* in anticipation of the 1935 Saar plebiscite. A few months later a Düsseldorf male teachers' choir performed Hermann Unger's *Nights in the Trenches,* under Stürmer's direction. In May 1935 Stürmer's cantata for male choir *Our Soul* was presented at the regional Aachen Nazi Party rally, in which Herbert von Karajan also participated.[192]

Hence, the tendentiousness resulted from both the content or theme of Stürmer's works and the organizational framework within which they were published and performed. In Hitler's Germany, compositions largely for male choir, with titles such as *German Confession, From the War, Pilot's Cantata Free Flight, German Concert, Germany's High Bloom, The Hour Has Struck,* and *Song for Heroes,* all spoke volumes as nationalism intensified, dictatorial strictures strengthened, and, after September 1939, a martial aura suffused all aesthetics.[193] As for the institutional aspect, Stürmer had his titles included in required songbooks for the Hitler Youth and in a special compendium volume to help Nazi functionaries celebrate specifically Nazi holidays. He served on Hitler Youth panels judging young Nazis' songs, voices, and compositions, and he participated actively in cultural events staged by neighboring Marburg's Nazi Student League. His "Pilot" cantata had been commissioned by Göring's Air Ministry upon the commencement of the war.[194] And so it was only fitting that in 1943 Stürmer should win a politically inspired prize of 2,100 marks offered by the town of Solingen for a cantata for male choir suitable for Nazi ceremonies, his "Germany" cantata, based on lyrics by Hermann Claudius, who was experienced in furnishing texts for Nazi celebrations.[195]

The case of Anton Webern is both more bizarre and more tragic than Stürmer's because of his established place in the music world. As late as 1990 one historian of music could still write that this outstanding pupil of Arnold Schoenberg and proponent of serial music had been indifferent toward National Socialism. Given Webern's background one would like to think so, yet it is far from the truth.[196] The Austrian Webern, who originally had left-wing ties, was shocked at first by the Nazis, who had forced the departure of his beloved teacher Schoenberg from the Preussische Akademie der Künste and from Berlin. But then he slowly came to sympathize with what he saw as an interesting experiment engendered by National Socialism. According to his chief biographers, the composer "maintained for years that Hitler, after satisfying his followers with an initial display of raw power, would moderate his policies."[197] Webern associated Hitler with everything that was positive in Germany, for, as the American violinist Louis Krasner has observed, "he was passionate about his belief in the superiority of German culture and its destined, historic role."[198]

Schoenberg, in exile, remained in touch with Webern by mail, telling him from Paris in August 1933 about his resolve to reconvert to Judaism.

Then, on New Year's Day 1934, Schoenberg wrote him from America that he was worried about him and his friend Alban Berg, neither of whom had written lately. "Since, after all, we Jews have experienced it a hundred times in these days that the unbelievable has happened, that people had suddenly become Nazis who yesterday were still friends, I could not at all explain to myself your silence . . . other than that you, too, had fallen in line," wrote Schoenberg. Webern quickly allayed his teacher's worries, and for a while Schoenberg felt at ease.[199]

Thereafter Webern fell on hard economic times, as musically he found less and less acceptance. And, as Schoenberg had feared, his empathy with National Socialism intensified, so much so that one day he exclaimed that someone should attempt "to convince the Hitler regime of the rightness of the twelve-tone system." Whether there was a connection between the two factors at the time—penury on the one hand and pro-Nazi sentiment on the other—must be doubted, for Webern was living in the Vienna suburb of Mödling and had no chance of finding employment or any kind of reward in the German Reich. So his feelings must have been genuine rather than opportunistic. This is borne out by a story his Jewish acquaintance Louis Krasner told. In April 1936 Webern, accompanied by Krasner on his way to the ISCM (International Society for Contemporary Music) festival in Barcelona, instead of traveling directly from Vienna through Switzerland, intentionally made a detour through Munich. There he took Krasner to the railway station pub for a beer. Back in the train compartment he asked him: "Did anyone do anything to you? Did any harm come to you?" He continued: "This proves that what we've been hearing about all these excesses in Germany is not true. It's all propaganda!" Later, in June 1937, Schoenberg again demanded to know whether there was substance to new rumors that Webern had become "a follower of or adherent to the Nazi Party," to which Webern quickly protested "No, no, no!!"[200]

March 1938 brought the Anschluss of Austria, and Webern became a citizen of the Reich. Within a few weeks Webern's daughter was in the Hitler Youth and quickly married to an Austrian Storm Trooper. Webern was a legal witness to the ceremony, at which the groom wore his party uniform. The composer's own son Peter and another son-in-law also were actively drawn to the Nazi movement. Soon the Nazi fight against "degenerate" music was extended to the newly annexed Austria, and Webern's music was so branded. When the Nazis organized their exhibition of degenerate music later that year in Düsseldorf, they included a picture of Webern, identifying him as a twelve-tone composer even more extreme than Schoenberg. Webern himself maintained personal relationships with Jewish friends, a dangerous thing to do, yet they nevertheless suspected him of sympathy for the Nazis' cause.[201]

Even though the Nazis had caused Webern to sink deeper into poverty by making performances of his work impossible and taking Jewish students away from him, he developed an almost psychotic sense of German patriotism that grew odder still after the outbreak of World War II. In 1940 he found reading Hitler's *Mein Kampf* exhilarating and observed every German victory on the western front with great enthusiasm. "Are things not going forward with giant steps?" he wrote to a friend in May. "This is Germany today! But the *National Socialist* one, to be sure! This is exactly the *new* state, for which the seed was already laid twenty years ago. Yes, a *new state it is,* one that has never existed before!! *It is something new!* Created by this unique man!!!" This in the same year that a Nazi music critic equated Webern's music with "the violation of all natural feeling."[202]

Webern's financial situation deteriorated further, leading to bouts of depression, and he may finally have made the tactical decision to cash in on his documented affection for the Nazi regime.[203] On 9 November 1940, a day of commemoration for Hitler's Beer Hall Putsch and a Nazi holiday in the Reich, he wrote to a functionary of the Reich Music Chamber, of which he was a member in good standing, complaining that he found himself "in complete isolation." He pointed to his success as a composer and teacher of music and noted how he had suffered under the Austro-Fascist regime of Dollfuss and Schuschnigg, hoping for an improvement after the Anschluss. This, however, did not happen "despite all the willingness to cooperate." Although he did not say so outright, he was obviously asking the Nazi rulers for a handout.[204] He was immediately sent an application form for Künstlerdank, Goebbels's Nazi charity for needy artists. In addition to indicating that he was "Aryan" and not a member of the Nazi Party, Webern also wrote that he was currently earning no more than 225 marks a month, and that on only an irregular basis. The Nazi music administrators registered without emotion that his mode of composition was generically related to Schoenberg's and was therefore the cause of his present problems. Since he himself was politically beyond suspicion, however, and his son was a (formerly illegal) Austrian Nazi Party member, a gift of money would be possible. Hence, it was proposed to allot Webern the sum of 250 marks as a onetime contribution. As it turned out, this would help Webern allay starvation for a little more than four weeks.[205] Nonetheless, Schoenberg's worst fears appear to have been realized.

3

Persecuted and Exiled Jewish and Anti-Nazi Musicians

Nazi Anti-Semitic Policy in the Music Sector

On 7 April 1933 the anti-Semitic Nazi government promulgated the so-called Law for the Reconstitution of the Civil Service. It called for the dismissal of Jewish employees in the public realm, excepting at first only a very few, such as veterans of World War I. By the fall of 1935 those exceptions were, by and large, canceled.[1] Many private and semipublic institutions in the Third Reich, such as medical health insurance boards, took advantage of these regulations to rid themselves of unwanted Jewish members, in this case nurses, hospital orderlies, and physicians, whom Gentiles envied not least for their competitive earning power.[2] In the arts, too, Jews were beginning to be fired by the spring of 1933, for to the same degree that Jewish physicians had been dominant in the health-care delivery system of the Weimar Republic, Jews had been influential in the cultural life of the nation, especially in music.[3] By 1935 the Bayerische Staatsoper in Munich had let go all of its Jewish artists save three, and after the Anschluss of Austria in March 1938, the Wiener Staatsoper lost its twelve non-"Aryan" members almost overnight.[4]

In terms of ideology, oppressive action by agencies of the Nazi state against Jewish musicians was predicated on a supposed antithesis between what was officially regarded as discrete categories of German music on the one side and Jewish music on the other. "Jewry and German music are opposites," proclaimed Joseph Goebbels in 1938; "by their very nature they exist in gross contradistinction to each other."[5] But try as they might, the Nazis could not define either German or Jewish music on the basis of empirically discernible evidence.[6] Deep down they knew, as a prominent Jewish music educator had stated at the beginning of the Third Reich: "Invariably we find that Jewish composers, wherever they might have worked, have exhibited those characteristics typical of their period and of their environment."[7] The Nazis tried to escape from this quandary by imputing certain arbitrary properties to one or the other category and then positing the axiom that the music of the "Nordic race" was vastly superior to its "Jewish" counterpart, and that the two were irreconcilable.[8] This dictum was ceaselessly honed by the Reich's musicologists and expert publicists until it became an unshakable Nazi truism and an ideological premise for persecution of the hated cultural minority.

The musical differences, wrote Friedrich Blume in 1939, were anchored in immutable racial differences that were yet to be fully identified by German science.[9] In the absence of the anticipated "scientific" revelations, it fell to German music scholars of all stripes to determine the true nature of "German" music so as to denounce convincingly its detested inverse. But, as the Berlin musicologist Albrecht Riethmüller has recently observed, from the beginning this task was destined to fail.[10]

Stereotypically, German music was equated with traditional values of the perceived national culture: heroism and love of battle (as in the Reformation) in sixteenth-century chorales, Handel, or Beethoven; profundity in Brahms, as also found in Kant, Hegel, or Schopenhauer; after great tension a resolution and the Faustian drive to creation, apparent in composers such as Bach, Mozart, and Schumann; introspection of the kind found in Reger (or the late Biedermeier period); and rootedness in "blood and soil," as evidenced by Schubert's lieder, the works of Bruckner, and the humble but honest Volkslied, judged to be endemically German.[11] Quintessential elements of Occidental music were the triad, the tonal system, and the specifically "Aryan" rhythm as marked by the succession of weak and strong beat accentuations and the syncopations of Bach and Brahms. Motif repetitions in German music were said to be always sequential, moving from one level of intensity to a higher, more dramatic one. All of Occidental music was ipso facto German, having originated in northern European, Germanic lands, once played there on the mighty lur, that "highly distinctive lip-vibrated instrument dating from the late Nordic Bronce Age."[12]

After generous references to Richard Wagner and Alfred Rosenberg, and for lack of authentic criteria, Jewish music was conveniently defined as everything that German music was not.[13] The worst that could be said about Jewish musicians was that they worked chiefly for money—as Wagner's sometime patron Jakob Meyerbeer was alleged to have done and the opera singer Richard Tauber was now accused of doing—or created cheap effects, such as using sex in opera and passing it off as love, a criticism leveled at Kurt Weill's Weimar period work.[14] Underlying the

Nazis' constructs was the thesis that Jewish musicians, especially composers, could not bring forth anything original because they lacked an indigenous culture. According to Willy Strecker, of the Schott publishing firm in Mainz, Jews as a race had no creative potency; Bach, Beethoven, Handel, and Mozart could never have been Jews. In imitation, however, Jews were said to be masters, often showing off a superior technique to cover up a lack of substance. But this exterior brilliance, while attractive, could lead to a mannered style and overall superficiality, betraying the triviality of the music as it was being performed. Hence, Mendelssohn wa *s* often charged with infusing his compositions with a saccharine flavor, notorious in his melodic lines. Works such as his *Ein Sommernachtstraum* were suspect because of their shallow, "eel-like smoothness."[15]

Plagiarism was also said to be common, for example, that Mendelssohn and Mahler copied Schubert, Schoenberg copied Brahms, and Wolfgang Erich Korngold copied Puccini and Strauss. In a Jewish composer's music, genuine feeling of the German kind was said to degenerate into banal sentimentality (again Mendelssohn was the chief culprit here). Thematic repetitions would be mechanical and tediously monotonous, not redolent of deep emotion and executed in meaningful curves of ascent and descent as in "Aryan" German music. Even worse, sentimentality could engender a whining femininity, quite the opposite of the heroic quality of Beethoven's "Eroica" Symphony for example. All told, the Oriental origin of such music, with something of the "Negroid" thrown in as well, was allegedly recognizable, stemming from venues diametrically opposed to the historic homes of Germanic lurer.[16]

Three Jewish composers gave the Nazi musicologists particular trouble, for their works were already internationally acknowledged as being embedded in the admired German musical tradition of the nineteenth and twentieth centuries. These composers were Mendelssohn, Mahler, and Schoenberg. The kindest judgment about them by well-intentioned "Aryans" was that qualitatively their music could not be distinguished from that of contemporary national worthies, so that their works were the equal of acceptable Gentile ones in every respect. Such judgments irked the Nazis, and hence they rationalized the inferiority of these three composers in particular ways. The works of all three were said to have acquired a German veneer for two reasons: first, because at the early stage of their careers these composers really wanted to be German instead of Jewish; and second, because as very clever Jews they had mastered almost to perfection the technique of insinuating themselves into an alien culture. Almost, but not quite: a very well trained ear could discern the difference between them and the work of true-blooded Germans. Yet such a refined ear was not possessed by ordinary citizens of the Reich. Therefore, it behooved the Nazi musicologists to engage in *völkisch* enlightenment.

Mendelssohn was portrayed as having begun the process of artificial "Germanization" of Jewish musicians through total acculturation, including adherence to the Christian faith. In his particular case, Mendelssohn allegedly used Protestant church music as his medium until he developed his own, essentially mawkish brand of secular music, thereby thoroughly exposing his Jewishness. Mendelssohn's love of vocal music was shared by Mahler, who cherished the German *Volkslied*, which in his hands, claimed the Nazis, was perverted to a kitsch form similar to Mendelssohn's. Through constantly trying and failing to become German, Mahler developed "deep inner turmoil" in both his private and his musical persona, and in due course this was manifested as a trademark of all of his music. Mahler's deracination led him on a desperate search for "exceptional effects," which eventually ended in a "negative expressionism and narcotic Nirvana," as exemplified by his *Lied von der Erde*. Finally there was Schoenberg. The characteristic that Schoenberg shared with Mahler was decay. Schoenberg allegedly completed the process of musical ruin begun by Mahler. As a young man Schoenberg had not expended much effort in assimilating his style to a German mold, although he did try. The modernity he came to espouse later was based on abstract intellectuality, a dismantling of the Germanic tonal structures into something international and thus antinational. For the Nazis, Schoenberg's twelve-tone system stood for destruction and chaos. Indeed, with particular reference to Schoenberg's pupil Hanns Eisler, it has been said that one reason why the Nazis were so afraid of twelve tone dissonance was that it countermanded the notion of a harmonious *Volksgemeinschaft*—the pure, racially defined people's community.[17]

But how to demonstrate all this to the average German music lover? Some of these arguments were voiced, in a scholarly setting, by Germany's leading musicologists, such as Karl Hasse, Ludwig Schiedermair, Friedrich Blume, and Gotthold Frotscher, on the occasion of an exhibition called "Degenerate Music," held in May 1938 in Düsseldorf.[18] Organized by Hans Severus Ziegler, Karl von Schirach's successor as Generalintendant of the Weimar theater, it was based on the notorious exhibition of defamed art presented in the Munich Haus der Kunst by Goebbels a year before. Paul Sixt, the Weimar musical director, was Ziegler's collaborator.[19] In his official address Ziegler agreed with leading musicologists and administrators of German culture that "atonality is the result of the destruction of tonality and hence represents degeneracy and artistic Bolshevism. Moreover, since atonality forms the basis for the harmonic system of the Jew Arnold Schoenberg, it has to be specified as a product of Jewish thought."[20] Individual audio-booths enabled visitors to listen to samples of the "degenerate music." Indeed, some of these booths were mobbed by eager German listeners, especially the one featuring music from Weill's *Dreigroschenoper*, a stark comment on the effectiveness of the musicologists' propaganda.[21]

The conference organizers picked up where Richard Wagner, the archetypal anti-Semite in the field, had left off, as they proceeded systematically to indict Jewish musicians of rank.[22] In addition to Weill and Schoenberg, the German-Jewish musicians represented there were men such as Ernst Toch, Franz Schreker, and the conductor Otto Klemperer, like Schoenberg now a resident of Los Angeles. Special sections were reserved for Jewish composers of operetta such as Leo Fall and Oscar Straus, and "Aryan" but nonetheless defamed composers of classical music such as Křenek, Stravinsky, and Hindemith. There also was a section on jazz, which the Nazis traditionally linked to a Negroid-Jewish subculture.[23]

After January 1933, as in the case of physicians, there were "Aryan" musicians who tried to speed up the pace of anti-Semitic efforts by denouncing Jewish colleagues, usually those whose jobs they coveted for themselves.[24] But at least in the beginning, the regime wanted controlled anti-Jewish legislation, not hasty and emotionally charged pogroms. Its leaders, most notably conservative bureaucrats held over from various Weimar administrations, wanted their policies to appear legitimate because they knew the world was watching. So despite an anti-Jewish boycott in early March and the anti-Semitic civil service law of 7 April 1933, Nazi experts on the "Jewish Question" at first proceeded at a measured pace.[25] It was difficult enough for them to handle the negative publicity surrounding the brutal dismissal from their jobs in Berlin, Leipzig, and Dresden of the Jewish conductors Bruno Walter and Otto Klemperer, as well as Fritz Busch, who was not himself a Jew but was friendly with many Jews and was known to be opposed to dictatorship. "A general panic" had set in, warned a Nazi writer, and if the regime proceeded too radically, "our artistic life would soon resemble a giant mortuary." Hans Hinkel, the Berlin leader of the Kampfbund für deutsche Kultur (KfdK), who had been appointed special commissar for Jewish affairs in Göring's Prussia, conceded in the spring of 1933 that several Nazi agencies had overreacted in regard to the danger posed by Jews, and assured those who were gravely concerned that the baby would not be thrown out with the bath water. Despite an unemployment rate of fifty thousand among German musicians, the rights of Jewish artists would be respected, assured Hinkel, so long as they paid their respects to the new German state. Wilhelm Furtwängler, who feared that foreign Jewish musicians would be barred from German concert halls and that German artists would be boycotted in retaliation abroad, seconded Hinkel when he wrote to Minister of Education Bernhard Rust that "in Germany in the future every artist, no matter of which nation or race, must have a chance to be heard."[26]

Such caution was supported by protests from prominent musicians from abroad. Led by Arturo Toscanini, a group of conductors in the United States, several of them Jewish, sent a cable to Hitler on 1 April 1933 protesting the well-publicized dismissal of Walter, Klemperer, and others. The cable read in part: "The undersigned artists who live and execute their art in the United States of America feel the moral obligation to appeal to your Excellency to put a stop to the persecution of their colleagues in Germany for political or religious reasons." In a symbolic gesture Hitler commanded the head of the national radio network to proscribe performances by the artists concerned, in effect banning their records. Though comparatively mild, this countermeasure was sufficient to cause Toscanini to cancel his upcoming visit as conductor of the 1933 Bayreuth Festival; not even a letter from the Führer himself, who was besought by Winifred Wagner, could change his mind.[27]

A second protest came from the Jewish violinist Bronislaw Huberman, who, although not a German but a Polish citizen, had experienced many triumphs on German concert stages. According to the music connoisseurs Erika and Klaus Mann, the children of the exiled Thomas Mann, he regarded Germany as "his beloved second home." While in Vienna, Huberman responded to an entreaty by Furtwängler, who had wished him to accept the assurances of Hinkel and others at face value and return to Germany to perform. Reflecting on Toscanini's recent action, Huberman refused, writing on 31 August 1933: "The question is not just of giving violin recitals; it is not a question concerning the Jews as such. No, the issue touches on the elementary preconditions of our European culture, of freedom of personal expression regardless of class or race." Huberman then lent emphasis to his words by undertaking European concert tours for the benefit of German exiles from Nazism. Another open letter from him to German intellectuals in March 1936, published in the *Manchester Guardian*, was considerably stronger, but by then Nazi anti-Jewish measures had visibly escalated.[28]

The very process of implementing anti-Jewish measures against musicians was cumbersome and slow; one informed historian has rightly spoken of "the creeping institutionalization of this cultural purge."[29] The causes lay as much in an inefficient apparatus as in a certain degree of wariness on the part of key administrators and musical personalities. Winifred Wagner, for one, was not at all prepared to cooperate with Goebbels, Göring, and Hitler in this matter. In the early months of the regime she impressed the Führer with her determination to retain her Jewish opera stars for the upcoming festival season, and for the time being she prevailed.[30]

The bedrock of anti-Semitic legislation in the musical sector was Article 10 of the first implementation decree of 1 November 1933, subsequent to the law that had established the Reich Culture Chamber (RKK) in September 1933. This article stipulated that members of the chamber's subsections, such as the Reich Music Chamber (RMK), could be expelled or refused entrance if they did not possess the required "reliability and suitability." This clause, rather than constituting a strict law to be immediately applied, resulted in a surprisingly large degree of latitude in an attempt to solve the "Jewish Question," for it provided no rationale or mechanism for focusing on Jews, who remained undefined, nor did it automatically exclude them from the RMK. Quite to the contrary, in order to get anywhere with this provision, Jews and "Aryans" alike were implicitly treated as members of that chamber until a screening process had identified the undesirables, who were then individually declared inadmissible by the RMK president. The screening necessitated sending out questionnaires that asked members many personal questions, including two relating to racial identity and religion. These forms went out from late 1933 until the entire process was halted in 1938 for reasons of impracticality; in the meantime, years could elapse before decisions on a particular member's expulsion were finalized.[31]

Some of this delay was due to Richard Strauss, the first president of the Reich Music Chamber, who was unenthusiastic about the regime's anti-Jewish stance. He consistently refused to have anything to do with drafting an anti-Semitic clause in the RMK's statutes, claiming that the tenth paragraph violated "all established rules of decency." It is probable that because of his obstinacy, Jews were not expressly mentioned in the paragraph when it was finally put into law in Berlin in November 1933. Henceforth, he distanced himself from its anti-Jewish implications, never once signing personal expulsion letters throughout his tenure as president (through July 1935). This he left to the RMK's executive secretary Heinz Ihlert, who complained bitterly to Hinkel about Strauss's recalcitrance in May 1935.[32]

After the complicated process of identifying Jews had got off to a slow start, it continued to be impeded along the way. One part of the actual execution of the task was left to local representatives of the RMK, and because they were slack they had to be reminded of their duties by the RMK central office in Berlin. President Raabe, who otherwise signed the exclusion orders quite willingly, acknowledged in May 1937 that the total number of RMK members in the Reich was so large that a thorough examination of each musician's racial pedigree was virtually impossible. So many Jews and other undesirable musicians, such as those playing the loathed jazz, still managed to keep working that in the largest cities special RMK police had to be employed, usually former musicians of one sort or another, who made regular checks on nightclubs, orchestra pits, and other venues of musical performance, seeking out offenders. It was only after the Nuremberg Race Laws were passed in September 1935 that a legally binding definition of "Jew" could be referred to, and subsequently Goebbels, as president of the RKK, found that so-called half-Jews, who might or might not enjoy the rights of "Aryans," depending on the circumstances, posed an additional problem for the RMK.[33] Meanwhile, parallel to the RMK, functionaries in the national radio network were also slow to work out binding regulations with a view to a consistent anti-Jewish policy insofar as future broadcasts were concerned.[34]

To be sure, the radicalization of anti-Semitic policy making that set in around 1937, leading up to the terrifying climax of the multiple pogroms of 9–10 November 1938, took its toll on the remaining Jewish musicians—those who had not yet emigrated or been incarcerated or killed. By way of a diabolical prelude to what today is known as Kristallnacht, the Jewish musicians of Austria were driven out after the annexation in March 1938, and they were given no quarter. In fact, none of the delays which had afforded a certain degree of protection to Jewish artists in the Old Reich were evident in the newly created Ostmark during the months following the Anschluss, and when the November pogroms hit Berlin, Frankfurt, and Hamburg, they also struck Vienna with a vengeance.[35] Still, there were seemingly inexplicable delays and contradictions. In December 1939, a year after RMK leaders had proudly spoken of the "extirpation" of the Jews from "the cultural life of our people," Goebbels complained that "Jews are attempting once more to enter the cultural life," with particular reference to artists of mixed parentage.[36] That was after yet another reminder had gone out to regional RMK functionaries in February, and then again in July, to get on with the business of scrutinizing musicians' family backgrounds. By October 1939 the RMK's regional office responsible for Berlin had checked ancestry documents for a mere 789 of its 13,085 musicians. And even in 1943, at the height of the war, when the crematoria at Auschwitz were going full blast, Goebbels had occasion to lament that "the Reich Culture Chamber is still not as purged of Jews as I had originally intended."[37]

Again, Goebbels thought that the large number of "half-Jews" who had remained in the music chamber were to blame, in addition to "quarter-Jews" and Gentile musicians married to Jews.[38] Indeed, in the decade from 1933 to 1943 near-perplexity reigned in the Nazi racial mapping stations as far as Germans with fewer than three Jewish grandparents and those with non-"Aryan" spouses were concerned. All save fully Jewish persons remained relatively unmolested until the Nuremberg Race Laws of September 1935 established some official guidelines, although Jewish spouses in so-called privileged marriages (those dating from before January 1933) and their "Aryan" partners were often already at risk both professionally and socially. This state of affairs was persistently reflected in the Reich Music Chamber. In the fall of 1933, for instance, the Jewish wife of Wiesbaden Generalmusikdirektor Carl Schuricht was quite willing to divorce her husband lest he suffer professionally at the hands of the regime. But at that time, because they had married before January 1933, Schuricht was assured by the authorities that no divorce was necessary. In a September 1933 letter he was also told that the Preussische Staatsoper was still employing "non-Aryan artists, just as it did before."[39]

At this point exempted non-"Aryan" artists were either so-called Hindenburg exceptions (those who had fought in World War I) or what the Nazis liked to call persons of mixed blood (*Mischlinge*). As a matter of fact, there were many musicians in the Third Reich with one Jewish grandparent who nonetheless fared relatively well; still, only a very few of them (such as the Munich composer Carl Orff) would have been able to deceive the party officials about their identity indefinitely.[40] The composer Heinrich Kaminski—who, like his one-time pupil Orff, had a Jewish grandmother—was not able to escape racial registration, yet he still emerged unscathed. Although the party had condemned him because of his opposition to the regime in 1933–35, it noted to its satisfaction that by 1940 Kaminski had four children in the Hitler Youth, and he himself was now said to be "politically beyond reproach."[41] Indeed, after the promulgation of the Nuremberg Race Laws in 1935, it seemed to be written in stone, at least for a while, that in many respects "quarter-Jews" were to be treated like "Aryans" (with the exception of holding certain offices, in the party or in government), whereas "half-Jews" *might* enjoy such protection, but could also be counted as full Jews.[42] Goebbels decided very quickly that as far as his Reich Culture Chamber was concerned, a "compromise" was called for "quarter-Jews over to our side, half-Jews only in exceptional cases."[43] But still there were no guarantees for anyone. An RMK list of 1936 had marked 2,202 members for expulsion: 1,738 as full Jews, 413 as half-Jews, and 48 as quarter-Jews.[44]

With regard to mixed marriages, the Nazis vacillated for a while before they made it clear that artists with Jewish spouses were jeopardizing their position. Significantly, the 1936 expulsion list had contained the names of only three *jüdisch Versippte*, as the official argot had it. In the same year, on the occasion of the traditional press ball in Berlin which he hosted, Göring made a point of chatting amiably with state opera members who were attending the function with their non-"Aryan" spouses. Göring, of course, had said earlier, "I shall decide who is a Jew," and forthwith had elected to keep in his employ Generalmusikdirektor Leo Blech, who had four Jewish grandparents.[45] By early 1938 at least, the Reich Radio Chamber, part of the RKK, was following a policy of not broadcasting the works of composers married to Jewish women, with some exceptions such as Franz Lehár and Eduard Künneke, whose operettas Hitler loved, the cocaine-addicted Künneke being the husband of a half-Jew.[46] Early in 1939, after Kristallnacht, Goebbels decreed that any musician with a Jewish spouse must be treated "like a half-Jew" and expelled from the RMK immediately.[47]

The outbreak of the war, on the one hand, complicated the studious attempts of the Nazi bureaucrats to determine to what extent a person was "Aryan" or Jewish, since there were now many more pressing matters to be attended to. But, on the other hand, this problem pushed itself to the fore again because the "Final Solution of the Jewish Question," as a program to be implemented, made more precise definitions obligatory. At the infamous Wannsee Conference, chaired by Himmler's lieutenant Reinhard Heydrich on 20 January 1942, and at the behest of Göring, the problem was tackled head on, but conference participants still came away with the realization that if a "half-Jew" were to be extinguished, a "half-Aryan" would also perish. That Gordian knot was never cut, and racial *Mischlinge* received yet another reprieve.[48]

After this event Goebbels was nowhere near resolving the conundrum for the purposes of his own chambers. "What will happen to the half-Jews?" he asked. "What to those related to Jews, in-laws of Jews? Or to those married to Jews? We obviously still have a lot to do, and in trying to solve these problems, a multitude of personal tragedies will undoubtedly ensue."[49] His indecisive diary musings of early March 1942 translated into even more loopholes for potential victims of racist dragnets. In 1942–43 Alfons Ganss, a half-Jewish violinist and light-music combo leader, had obtained special permission to work in the Wehrmacht's troop entertainment program under the protection of the SS–undoubtedly because draftable musicians were becoming scarce.[50] Jews married to "Aryans" avoided deportation to the eastern liquidation camps by a hair's breadth in 1943, at a time when Goebbels himself was eager to review their situation once again for his own purposes. By August of that year Goebbels and Armaments Minister Albert Speer were planning the conscription of Mischlinge in work battalions to clean up after air raids, an assignment not without particular danger to sensitive musicians.[51]

This erratic policy was partially caused by, and manifested in, a common inability on the part of regime officials to identify correctly individual Jewish artists. Symptomatic of this inability were the cases of Frida Leider, Alfred Cortot, and Theo Mackeben. The Prussian Kammersängerin Leider was an opera star at Covent Garden, La Scala, and Bayreuth who was married to a Jewish conductor but was herself not Jewish. In August 1935—one month before the Nuremberg Race Laws—the SS tabloid Schwarze Korps reported that "the Jewess Frida Leider" had given a recital in Kissingen; a week later the paper had to affirm in great embarrassment that Leider was an "Aryan." The French pianist Alfred Cortot, thought by Hinkel to be a non-"Aryan," was prohibited from concertizing in Hamburg at the same time. Only after French ambassador André François-Poncet had vouched for his non-Jewishness was he allowed to honor his commitment. The composer Theo Mackeben had collaborated with Brecht and Weill in their late Weimar productions. During the Third Reich he slowly rose to become one of the most important writers of German film music. His wife was Loni Heuser, a cabaret comedienne with a sardonic political wit. As late as February 1938 the national broadcast network suspected both of them of being Jewish, since neither had as yet reported on their ancestry.[52]

To remedy this confusion, Munich's own Hans Brückner, a fanatical Nazi simpleton and personal friend of the Nuremberg Jew-baiter Julius Streicher, who once plied his trade as an operetta tenor, together with an equally befuddled Düsseldorf dentist's wife by the name of Christa Maria Rock, in 1935 published and marketed an index of Jewish musicians, which claimed absolute infallibility. It listed mostly interpreters of light music, but focused on widely known serious musicians as well. Yet a few months after its appearance, Rosenberg's party organ Die Musik noted that this handbook was anything but reliable. For example, it had described German composer Max Bruch (1838–1920) as a Jew and claimed that the famous conductor Erich Kleiber, said to be Erich "Klaiber," was also Jewish. After reading that he was a Jew, Ralph Benatzky, the composer of popular operettas, protested so vigorously that Goebbels himself became upset.[53] The mistakes, including many omissions, were so embarrassing that Brückner and his associate were forced to publish a revised edition in 1936, though it too was faulty. The details regarding Bruch, Kleiber, and Benatzky had been corrected, but omissions had remained (for example, composer Alexander von Zemlinsky and cellist Matyas Seiber).[54] Meanwhile, officials of Goebbels's national radio network were also in the dark owing to their failure to organize a file of Jewish artists. As late as 1938 and 1939, respectively, total ignorance reigned with respect to the ethnic origins of American conductor Leopold Stokowski and French composer Camille Saint-Saëns, who were not Jewish.[55]

Finally, in 1940 and subsequently Theo Stengel and Herbert Gerigk, two stooges of Alfred Rosenberg, who still thought himself responsible for such matters, published a party-sanctioned handbook of Jews in music that had many reprintings and was distributed in the thousands. It corrected most of the earlier blunders and omissions. For instance, composer Anton Rubinstein (1829–1894), who, as one of the two authors had complained elsewhere, was often referred to as not Jewish (although Brückner had described him correctly), was now definitively listed as a Russian Jew.[56] But there was at least one further misunderstanding. Although this time around Zemlinsky was cited as the half-Jewish brother-in-law of Arnold Schoenberg, he was really fully Jewish, and a review of the book in the Rosenberg-beholden journal *Die Musik* maintained that Zemlinsky was Schoenberg's father-in-law.[57]

Because of these conceptual and procedural uncertainties, the "Jewish content" in German music did not vanish overnight, and neither did the Jewish artists. Music publisher Willy Strecker's observation early on in the Third Reich that the aim of the Nazis was "to suppress everything Jewish and Bolshevik" certainly was correct, but his somewhat later observation that "the danger has now passed and that the guidelines set down by the new music commission will prove to be quite rational" was overly optimistic. In retrospect, Hans Heinz Stuckenschmidt rendered a much more accurate assessment when he stated after World War II that the Nazi directives were "totally woolly, really incomprehensible," so much so in fact that in the first few years of the Hitler regime the works of Jewish composers could still be performed, and Jewish musicians themselves were still at work.[58]

Again, levels of tolerance varied under the regimes of two consecutive RMK presidents, Strauss and Raabe. While Strauss was by no means free of a certain brand of anti-Semitism characteristic of many members of the haute bourgeoisie, he was selective as far as the musical arts were concerned, choosing as his special targets the composers of operetta, all of whom he hated without qualification and whom he regarded as overwhelmingly Jewish. But "Jewish content" as such was not an article of faith with Strauss. His own opera *Salome* (1905), which in 1939 was attacked as a "Jewish ballad," he thought entirely appropriate for German audiences, for he had it on good authority that the Führer himself as a youth had once hiked to Graz just to hear this work.[59] Raabe, by contrast, was much more dogmatic. Within a year of having been appointed RMK president, he professed to be fighting for "a purge and continuous reorganization of German musical life."[60]

In any event, during the first two years or so of the Third Reich, all manner of musical performances of entirely non-"Aryan" character continued to be staged. In 1933, of course, several events had already been planned before Hitler came to power and could not be canceled. Hence on 12 February Arnold Schoenberg, at the behest of Hans Rosbaud, gave a radio lecture on the Brahms centenary over the Frankfurt broadcast network. Schoenberg's *Pelleas und Melisande* was conducted by Heinz Unger, a Jew, in Berlin on 2 March; the composer himself was still in the capital. Seven days later in Munich, on the very day of Bavaria's formal coordination with Nazi rule in Berlin, the Jewish conductor Max Reiter presented an Italian program at the Odeon Theater. Two weeks after that, Hans Rosbaud scheduled a waltz by Josef Lanner on Radio Frankfurt, in an adaptation by the young Jewish pianist Erich Itor Kahn, whose arrangements were featured again in early 1934. In October 1933 the Mendelssohn-Bartholdy Prize was awarded in Berlin to the evidently "Aryan" Dresden pianist Karl Weiss. The Jewish Kolisch Quartet and pianist Artur Schnabel also performed in Nazi Germany before they left the country, and again in 1934 Zemlinsky's opera *Der Kreidekreis* was staged in Berlin. "Its 'non-Aryan' authorship was still not conspicuous, the work being repeated several times, as was the norm then," recalled Rudolf Hartmann, who had had a hand in the staging. Mendelssohn's *Ein Sommernachtstraum* was given routinely in Krefeld during 1934–35, but, with Raabe about to take office, that seems to have been the last Jewish work to survive in German repertory theaters.[61] This did not put a stop to the Jewish influence, as Wolfgang Stumme, the music supervisor for the Hitler Youth, lamented as late as 1944.[62] In that year a music critic from Solingen was astonished to find that Berlin violinist Robert Schultz was still indulging in cadenzas originated by the Jewish virtuoso Joseph Joachim when playing Beethoven's Violin Concerto. Nazi censors, while agreeing with the critic, thought that disciplining this behavior would be impossible, if only on practical grounds.[63]

Indeed, in trying to control the Jewish influence in music, the Nazis had problems in three specific areas: first, with the content of texts that could be historically traced to Jews; second, with Jewish musical scholarship, which was of very high caliber; and third, with phonograph recordings of "Jewish" music or artists.

As to musical texts, the problem arose chiefly with opera and oratorios. As an outstanding example, Mozart's libretto for *Il Nozze di Figaro* was found objectionable because the original had been authored by a Jew, Lorenzo da Ponte, and translated into German by conductor Hermann

Levi. Strenuous efforts were undertaken by corrupt music scholars to preserve the Mozartean character of the text while "Aryanizing" it sufficiently to satisfy stern Nazi censors.[64] Still, this was in stark contrast with a 1936 directive from the Promi that allowed for the text of lieder to stand if the composer was as important as, for instance, Robert Schumann, even if the text's author was Jewish.[65] The rationale for this was that many German verses, especially those by Heinrich Heine, were so well known, and their authors' identities generally so submerged, that very little was at risk. It appears to have escaped the Nazis that this directive in itself challenged the very validity of their anti-Jewish arguments. Handel was also problematic, and not only because of his predilection for England. During the Olympics in 1936 his oratorio *Hercules* was performed; it was later found that the storyline was based on "material from Jewish history." This was thought to count against Handel, no matter how great his music. In general, music with Jewish plots had to go, and therefore Handel's oratorios should not have been performed.[66] There were exceptions, however, as when Handel's *Judas Maccabeus* was reissued under the new title *Commander* in 1939 with the text carefully rewritten, because the work fit so well into the war effort.[67]

As to scholarship, whereas the Nazis were able to relieve Jewish musicologists of their duties under the law of April 1933, it was much more difficult to negate hitherto accepted accomplishments on the part of Jewish scholars and musicians of earlier decades. Let it suffice here to mention Felix Mendelssohn as the musical giant that he was. The Nazis had to wrestle with his reputation not only as a composer but also as a music historian and editor, instrumental in the Bach revival.[68]

Finally, recordings of Jewish musicians and composers were generally not banned until 1 April 1938, a respite owing solely to the multinational character of the record industry, on which the German cultural establishment still depended for some years.[69] Until this key date many foreign Jewish artists, who might not have been easily identified as such in Germany, as well as Austro-German Jews whose background was well known, were marketed by recording companies such as Electrola and Telefunken. This was true for both composers such as Mendelssohn and instrumentalists and conductors such as Bruno Walter, Fritz Kreisler, Artur Schnabel, Simon Goldberg, and the Russian-born cellist Gregor Piatigorsky, who before his emigration had resided in Berlin. But the bell was tolling for those artists. Significantly, the year of the race laws, 1935, seems to have initiated the gradual reversal. Schnabel's records were still being offered "with huge hype in all the German cities," as Werner Kulz charged in *Zeitschrift für Musik;* he felt that such sales ought to be prohibited. But even after the sales boycott had been ordered in the spring of 1938, some popular recordings of Mendelssohn could still be had, surreptitiously, under the counter at Berlin's better record stores.[70]

Jewish Musicians under Nazi Rule

Kreisler, Schnabel, and Goldberg were among those Jewish musicians who managed to get out of Germany fairly easily, and early, as soon as they sensed which way the wind was blowing. This prescience was not shared by the majority of Jewish musicians who were born in Germany, held German citizenship, and regarded themselves as ordinary Germans. Often attached to property they had accumulated in better times but also because they loved their country, they rationalized that things would soon turn around. Indeed, most German Jews who stayed in the Reich for years when they could have escaped comparatively quickly suffered from this delusion, seeing Nazism as just a nightmare that would soon pass, so long as one was patient.[71]

What helped artists such as Kreisler and Schnabel was that they had never taken out German citizenship, although they may have lived in the Reich for years and were generally regarded as German. More often than not, they were self-employed, freelance professionals who, if they were famous enough, could command their honorariums in any country that valued the pursuit of culture, rather than having to depend on salaries and pensions from a corporate German employer such as a municipal orchestra. Kreisler, for instance (who had only one Jewish parent), had been born in Vienna in 1875 and had never surrendered his Austrian citizenship, although he had resided in Germany for years and, when the Nazis took over in January 1933, was the owner of a villa in Berlin's fashionable Grunewald district. Kreisler was on an Amerian tour at the time, not returning to Berlin until summer; then, after declining yet another written invitation by Furtwängler to perform with him, he left to take his vacation in Italy and France, never to see Hitler's Reich again.[72] The bass Emanuel List, also an Austrian, had lived in Berlin since 1923, singing often in the capital's opera houses as well as at Bayreuth; he was among those singers protected by Winifred Wagner for the 1933 festival, after which he emigrated to the United States. That particular move may have been easier for him than others, for he had been living in America since before World War I and had even applied for citizenship there.[73] The Beethoven expert Schnabel, a Pole, was another who held Austrian papers; he had lived in Berlin since 1900, and although he taught at the Hochschule für Musik there, his main income derived from international concertizing. After his final Berlin recital on 28 April 1933, he immediately left for Italy and then migrated first to England, then to the United States.[74] Simon Goldberg, also a Pole and, since 1929, the concertmaster of the Berlin Philharmonic under Furtwängler, resigned from the orchestra voluntarily rather than submit to being fired during a vacation break in 1934. Although technically an employee, he enjoyed the status of an independent artist and stayed on in Europe, performing as a soloist in various countries, until 1938, when he made his New York debut.[75]

Kurt Weill, a German Jew of independent albeit modest financial means originally from Dessau, had seen the political handwriting on the wall since the last years of the Weimar Republic, when the performance of his operas *Aufstieg und Fall der Stadt Mahagonny* and *Die Bürgschaft* had been physically impeded by Storm Troopers. His latest work, *Der Silbersee,* had been staged to positive reviews on 18 February 1933 in Leipzig, with Detlef Sierck as director (he would soon make his name in Hollywood as Douglas Sirk). But as important a city as Hamburg had declined to present *Silbersee,* and frightful Nazi threats were in the air when the work was performed in Erfurt and Magdeburg, the latter on 27 February, the day of the portentous Berlin Reichstag fire. Weill, having filed for divorce from his "Aryan" wife, Lotte Lenya, abandoned a newly acquired house in Berlin and left Germany for Paris in the expectation of better prospects on 21 March.[76]

For some Jewish musicians the catastrophe of being dismissed from what had seemed to be secure employment, often followed by forced exile, was attenuated owing to the built-in delay mechanism of the anti-Jewish bureaucracy described earlier, to some instances of mistaken identity (or, rather, pedigree), or to sheer luck. Several of the more fortunate artists were *Günstlingsjuden,* or Jews in legally privileged situations through birth or marriage. In many cases such delays afforded no more than a few years' grace, which could, however, often be used to prepare for a more secure future abroad than if one had to flee on only a couple of months' notice.

There were two fully Jewish musicians who, because of the protection of key Nazis, were able to stay on in the Third Reich unharmed, at least for a number of years. Conductor Leo Blech was the celebrated exception among all the able Jewish musicians who did not have a hope in the world of remaining in Germany as they might have wished. Nothing in particular distinguished the famous Blech from, say, Bruno Walter, Otto Klemperer, or Jascha Horenstein, all of whom were doomed, except for the sheer coincidence that Heinz Tietjen, head dramaturge of the Preussische Staatsoper (who was an opportunist rather than a full-fledged Nazi), had decided that he simply could not do without him. At sixty-two Blech was close to retirement age when Hitler came to power. He had vast experience abroad, including in the United States and in Sweden, where he had risen to the post of royal court conductor, and at the Staatsoper the idiosyncratic maestro had made himself popular with German and international visiting artists alike. It appears to have been the, at that time still valid, international reputation of the opera which convinced Tietjen that for its sake alone he had to keep Blech on. Blech was also dearly loved by his Berlin audience: after conducting Wagner's *Die Götterdämmerung* one night in June 1933, to the dismay of a fanatical Nazi observer, Blech received a standing ovation. How easily Göring, who craved international attention in those early years, was persuaded is not known, but Tietjen always did have an uncanny hold on him. In any event, it was not until the summer of 1938, as the Nazis' hatred of the Jews was about to discharge itself in the pogroms a few months later, that the pensioner Blech was prevailed upon to leave the country. German guards escorted him and his family to Riga, the capital of independent (and quasi-fascist) Latvia, where he conducted the national opera until that country's invasion by the Red Army, whereupon Blech returned to Stockholm.[77] Early on Blech proved a singular embarrassment to diehard Nazi officials abiding by the laws, such as they were, as they found it difficult to justify his continued employment to other designated victims of Nazi racial policy.[78]

The other privileged Jewish musician was Otto Manasse, a Munich composer and pupil of Max Reger. He was seventy-nine in July 1939, when Paul Graener, then still nominal chief of the composers' section in the RMK, asked his friend Hinkel to safeguard Manasse's small apartment, the lease of which was just expiring. Hinkel asked Munich's lord mayor Karl Fiehler to attend to the matter. What finally happened to Manasse is unknown: an economically independent artist, the composer, a convert to Christianity whose Protestant church music was frequently performed in Munich, could neither be dismissed from a post he did not hold nor forcibly evicted from the country of his birth. It is likely that he fell victim to the Munich deportation raids after 1941, unless he had the good fortune to die before they occurred.[79]

A few German musicians married to Jews either escaped the various anti-Semitic dragnets in Germany or else left the country. To the first category belonged the opera star Frida Leider, who was married to the Jewish violinist and Kapellmeister Rudolf Deman. Leider was too prominent to be touched, although in similar cases the 1933 cut-off date for marriages, from which Schuricht had benefited, was increasingly being ignored, especially after the Nuremberg Race Laws were instituted. After the Anschluss the prima donna continued to live in Germany, while her Austrian-born husband attempted to ride out the storm in Switzerland, though he had no work permit. Harassed and under political pressure, Leider found maintaining her career in Germany an almost impossible task, but she did not think it necessary to leave the country.[80] Another German artist with a Jewish spouse was the violinist Karl Klingler, leader of the noted Klingler Quartet. The quartet itself was dissolved because its cellist, Ernst Silberstein, was Jewish. Klingler himself received special permission to continue working after it was learned that his wife was not entirely Jewish, as had first been thought. Good musicians being scarce at the height of the war, Klingler, already over sixty years of age, was used for much-needed troop entertainment.[81]

The case of Franz von Hoesslin was more complex. A well-known Bayreuth conductor, Hoesslin was married to his second wife, a Jewish singer, in 1935, when his contract as Generalmusikdirektor of Breslau was allowed to lapse for that reason. In a personal conversation the Wagner acolyte Hitler granted Hoesslin protection on condition that his wife leave Germany. Once she had moved to Italy, Hoesslin applied for new positions but was getting nowhere (apparently Goebbels was one of his main opponents). Winifred Wagner, whose late husband, Siegfried, had been a friend of Hoesslin's, continued to back him, and since Hitler himself no longer objected, Hoesslin was able to assist Generalintendant Tietjen in Bayreuth until 1940. Hoesslin thanked the Führer in a hand-written letter of August 1939: "How can I find words of gratitude for all this generosity rendered unto me?" The conductor expressed a wish to reciprocate by toiling for national and international recognition of German culture, thereby serving his fatherland and its Führer. Alas, things were to take a different turn. After having moved first to Switzerland and then to Italy at the height of the war to be close to his wife, Hoesslin decided to defy the fatherland after all. In 1944 he applied to cancel his German citizenship. Taking its cue from the SS, which characterized Hoesslin as palpably "hostile to Germany," the Reich Music Chamber ensured that Hoesslin's name was struck from its registry forever.[82]

Soprano Hilde Güden was expelled from the Reich Culture Chamber, but luckily for her it happened so late as not to matter anymore. Her case was a bizarre one. In 1941 the attractive twenty-four-year-old was a member of Clemens Krauss's famous Bayerische Staatsoper company when the race investigators decided that instead of one Jewish grand-parent, as she had stated, she really had three. Under the Nuremberg Race Laws, one Jewish grandparent had placed the singer comfortably within the "Aryan" camp; but three put her at acute risk of being judged fully Jewish. There was a wrinkle in this case in that since 1938 Güden, though Austrian-born, had become a Turkish citizen by a former marriage to a Turkish diplomat. In August 1943 an anthropological institute in Vienna determined that "in terms of her racial appearance she exhibits none of the characteristics typical of Jews"; yet at the same time, the SS security service came to the absurd conclusion that Güden was a spy. By then the soprano, long divorced, had moved to Rome. That far the arm of Goebbels's henchmen could not reach. Güden was expelled not from the RMK but from the theater chamber in September 1943. Had these questions regarding her ancestry arisen a few years earlier, and had she remained in Germany, she probably would have been killed.[83]

Güden's colleague Sabine Kalter, a contralto at the Hamburg Opera since 1915, knew that she had four Jewish grandparents; that point had been spitefully driven home by anti-Semitic cartoons in the local press as early as 1930. By the civil service law of 7 April 1933, Kalter should have been dismissed immediately; but she was so popular with her Hamburg audience, having received a standing ovation in early April, that the authorities hesitated to act. Opera Intendant Albert Ruch took personal responsibility for shielding her so that she could stay on while looking for permanent work abroad. In January 1935, under the shadow of further threats, she moved to England, where she soon triumphed at Covent Garden.[84]

Despite all the loopholes and administrative inconsistencies, however,

most musicians governed by the provisions of the April 1933 law and the
September 1935 Nuremberg race legislation were dealt with mercilessly
and in short order. Reflecting on this state of affairs, and anticipating the
worst as early as May 1933, the Mannheim composer Max Sinzheimer
wrote to his Munich colleague Carl Orff, who himself was powerless to
help: "I have become depressed to the point where I find it difficult to
write." Sinzheimer was nevertheless still wondering how it could be that
"every bungler of a better race may hamper my own work."[85]

This was the sentiment of Jewish musicians high and low, even in the
early stages of the Nazi regime, as many were sensing, despite Hinkel's
apologetic rhetoric of spring 1933, what its leaders were truly intending.
The highly placed ones generally had much more latitude to act, even if
they had to move quickly, as they were anticipating or actually experienc-
ing the termination of employment contracts. The cases in point here are
those of Schoenberg, Klemperer, and Walter.

Arnold Schoenberg had keenly felt the reverberations of anti-Semitism
in the dying days of the Weimar Republic, and he was under no illusion as
to the significance of Hitler's advent as chancellor on 30 January 1933.
For a few weeks after that event the composer still entertained hopes of
visiting Spain, as he had done before, this time in order to collaborate
with the cellist Pablo Casals on a new work, a concerto for cello and
orchestra. But the plan came to nothing, and on 1 March, even before the
law of 7 April, composer Max von Schillings, in his capacity as president
of the Preussische Akademie der Künste, made a humiliating announcement at a session attended by Schoenberg that the Jewish influence would
have to be broken. Schoenberg acted on this cue and resigned his professorship at the academy, where he had taught since 1925, in a letter
dated 20 March. Throughout April and May he made plans to move,
along with his second wife, Gertrud, and baby Nuria, to Paris, ostensibly
for his regularly scheduled holiday and for reasons of health. As an alternative Nice also crossed his mind. On 17 May the Schoenbergs traveled to
Paris. A week later Schillings sent him an official confirmation of his
resignation. To all intents and purposes Arnold Schoenberg, born in the
Austro-Hungarian Empire, had been expelled from the German Reich.[86]

Conductor Otto Klemperer had a somewhat different experience, for at
first he refused to leave the country of his birth. Klemperer had lost his
position at the innovative Berlin Kroll Oper in 1931 and was working
under Tietjen at the Preussische Staatsoper when Hitler came to power. A
man of many moods, Klemperer was unhappy in this post. Still, he proved
his originality on 12 February 1933 with his daring new version of
Tannhäuser, presented in collaboration with his old friend the avant-
garde producer Jürgen Fehling. This unorthodox interpretation, which,
incidentally, was marred by bad singing, provoked outcries of disgust
among the Nazis in the audience. Goebbels thought it a travesty, for
"Jews just don't understand Wagner." Nonetheless, Klemperer believed
that his conversion to Catholicism and his staunch anti-Bolshevism

would save him, as Blech was being saved. In fact, he contracted a few more engagements within Germany, then in early March departed for a concert tour of Hungary and Italy, expressing to foreigners a "euphoric view of Germany under the Nazis." On his return to Berlin at the end of the month, hoping to keep his job, Klemperer made patriotic overtures to Tietjen, insisting that "he was in complete agreement with the course of events in Germany." When Tietjen signaled the end of their working relationship, Klemperer asked for an audience with Göring, which never was to materialize. Klemperer still remained optimistic, writing to his "Aryan" wife, Johanna, that it was not his Jewishness that was the problem but rather the mistaken perception of his leftist leanings. Manic as he was at that point, for he was already suffering from a severe mental imbalance, he insisted in the company of friends that the "Jewish Question" was not a racial but a religious issue and that Hitler had to be granted a Jewish Palatine guard. Then on 4 April, after learning of the sudden arrest of a Berlin Jewish physician, Klemperer hurried to get out of the country, trying to take with him a pretty Russian-Jewish girl he had become infatuated with. He finally entrained for Zurich that afternoon, alone, and with a weeping wife bidding him farewell. To add insult to injury, the German press printed a malicious notice months later charging that the conductor had fled from a tax debt in the thousands of marks.[87]

And then there was Bruno Walter, who was maneuvered into the center of a national scandal involving Richard Strauss. Several conflicting versions exist, but the gist appears to be this. Born in Berlin, an Austrian citizen since 1911, Walter was permanent conductor of the Leipzig Gewandhaus Orchestra as well as a regularly scheduled guest conductor with the Berlin Philharmonic, in addition to his regular responsibilities in London and New York. Walter was returning from New York to his Berlin apartment in March 1933, after Hitler had taken over, when he learned that there was trouble in Leipzig, where he was to conduct in a few days. Although the Gewandhaus officials were attempting to salvage his performance, it was clear that massive political pressure would force him out. This was in fact accomplished by the already nazified Saxon Ministry of the Interior. Walter then returned to Berlin to await his next concert with the Philharmonic on 20 March. This series was being watched by the just-created Reich Propaganda Ministry. Walter's booking agency learned that Propaganda Minister Goebbels had suggested canceling the performance to avoid unpleasant repercussions. Taking this as the threat to his personal safety that it indeed was, Walter, who must have known he was intensely hated by Hitler, had his agents telephone Goebbels's state secretary Walter Funk, who assured them that order could not be guaranteed if Walter went ahead with conducting. At that point Strauss was requested to stand in for Walter. (Who had asked him to do so is still at issue.) Strauss at first refused without giving any reasons, but when prevailed upon by Walter's prominent Berlin agency (whose proprietors were Jewish), the maestro agreed on economic grounds: in order to save the cash-strapped orchestra, he pledged his conductor's honorarium as salary to be distributed to the needy Philharmonic musicians. Strauss then conducted the event, while Walter canceled yet another impending German concert, this time in Frankfurt, and immediately moved back to Austria, his former home for many years (and then via Italy to America), henceforth avoiding Europe until after the war.[88]

Low on the scale of professional fortunes were Jewish or half-Jewish musicians who had found a niche in the entertainment marketplace in happier times, but with the advent of the Nazi regime were suddenly caught off guard. As they were struck by sundry anti-Semitic decrees, most of which they hardly understood, they were excluded from the music world but, because of their professional training, had nothing else to fall back on as a livelihood. This produced a vicious circle in which they became fatefully entangled. After receiving an initial RMK warning to cease engaging in musical activities for the purpose of earning money, which in two of our documented cases occurred in 1935, they nonetheless continued to play in public, typically in corner pubs, where RMK control personnel easily caught them, or teaching pupils, in order to survive on minimal wages. Inevitably they would be sentenced to a fine, which, while not yet exorbitant, was high enough to drive them back to the illegal trade to make enough money to pay it. Caught time and again, the musicians faced fines that increased exponentially, placing the culprits in an ever greater quandary. One hapless man was confronted with penalties increasing from 25 to 300 marks in a span of two and a half years. After their passports were confiscated by the authorities to prevent them from emigrating and defaulting on their payments, these wretched people would eventually be sent to a concentration camp as asocial non-"Aryans," a doubly fatal designation.[89]

Between the marginal players and the famous were many accomplished musicians, practitioners of serious or classical music, who lost their gainful employment not quite as anonymously as the parlor artistes but with much less fanfare than a Schoenberg, a Klemperer, or a Walter. They had to start casting about for something else to do, preferably, if possible, after emigrating. Some, like the conductor and composer Berthold Goldschmidt, had been harassed by the Nazis long before the official sea change and were already marked as pariahs. Born in 1903 in Hamburg, Goldschmidt had won the Mendelssohn-Bartholdy Prize and in 1931 had come to the municipal opera in Berlin (after January 1934 the Deutsche Oper under Goebbels). There he was taunted by "Aryan" colleagues for collaborating in the production of works by Jacques Offenbach, the nineteenth-century French composer of light opera. The so-called Röhm Purge of June 1934, which eliminated radical elements, instilled in him, and so many others, the hope that things would change for the better. The directors Jürgen Fehling and Gustav Gründgens, both experimentally minded Gentiles determined to remain in Germany, persuaded him to stay on. But change was not in the offing, and eventually Goldschmidt was interrogated by the Gestapo. He escaped to England in 1935.[90]

The conductor Joseph Rosenstock was thirty-eight when he was suddenly driven from his post as Generalmusikdirektor in Mannheim, a few days after passage of the 7 April 1933 law. Rosenstock wrote to Strauss in the hope of getting help, but Strauss was not yet RMK president, and it is doubtful that he could have done anything. For a few years Rosenstock worked as musical director for opera production in the Jewish Kulturbund, a questionable haven for Germany's remaining Jews (discussed later in this chapter), until he emigrated to Japan in 1936.[91] Local Nazis suddenly removed the singer Rose Pauly (who had been born in Hungary in 1895 and whose Jewish parentage could not even be decisively ascertained by lexicon authors Stengel and Gerigk as late as 1940) from the Dresden production of Strauss's opera *Die Frau ohne Schatten* early in May 1933, thus coming close to ruining the show.[92] At about the same time, Frankfurt's opera intendant Josef Turnau was relieved of his duties on the basis of the April law. The city's lord mayor rubbed salt into Turnau's wounds when in July he wrote him that his opera stagings had been "alien to the German spirit and had violated the people's national sentiment." Within weeks Turnau had moved to Vienna. His Frankfurt colleague Hans Wilhelm Steinberg, who was the musical director, was fired in a similar manner and with virtually identical justification, betraying the often stereotypical routine of the purges at that time. In Steinberg's case (as in Rosenstock's), his World War I record was discounted, despite the exemptions President Paul von Hindenburg had originally insisted upon. Steinberg, a former assistant to Otto Klemperer, first worked for the Kulturbund and then went to Palestine before achieving great success as William Steinberg in San Francisco, Pittsburgh, and Boston.[93] Generalmusikdirektor Jascha Horenstein was also removed almost immediately from his post in Düsseldorf. Once again the stock argument was that Jews were incapable of conducting Wagner, but Horenstein's interpretation of Beethoven's music was also turned against him. Horenstein actually went to court for breach of contract, and, amazingly enough, won a tidy sum before embarking for Australia. So unstable was the anti-Jewish legislation that in one case its very own exemption clauses could not carry any weight, while in another it could still be overriden by conservative-minded courts used to established administrative rulings.[94]

Time and again there were oddities occasioned by these imprecise laws, whereby individuals could benefit or suffer doubly for their status. Some examples are hair-raising, for they betray pro-Nazi sympathies on the part of the musicians concerned. Two instrumentalists whose records have survived were half-Jewish yet, undetected, had been members of the Nazi Party before January 1933. One of them evidently did not learn of his true "racial" identity until he had to present papers; his subsequent disbarment from the professional ranks in 1935 shattered this thirty-year-old clarinetist. The other man, a former local Nazi leader, was conscripted for heavy labor a few weeks before the war broke out; he was hoping to receive a special dispensation.[95] Yet another half-"Aryan" musician, on the verge of exclusion from his livelihood as he had known it, complained to his old friend Hinkel in summer 1935, reminding him that "many years ago I offered my services to the National Socialist movement free of charge."[96] Another musician, a Gentile, after closer scrutiny in 1938, found that the woman he had married three years earlier had a Jewish mother. This now compromised his post with the Radio Stuttgart Orchestra. Although the violinist insisted that his wife was "free of the miserable Jewish traits and, like myself, hates and abhors the Jewish race," the authorities at first did not accept his explanation that he had been duped by his in-laws. Only by 1939, as the shortage of qualified professionals was becoming painfully obvious everywhere, did he receive special permission to keep working.[97]

Indeed, the problems with so-called mixed marriages were coming back to haunt the Nazi administrators more than they had originally predicted. A particularly grotesque case was that of the noted conductor Ernst Praetorius, a man who could not, like his better-known colleague Franz von Hoesslin, command the special admiration of the Führer and then simply turn his back on the Third Reich. Praetorius had been Generalmusikdirektor in Weimar since 1924, when he was informed early on in the Third Reich that his contract would not be renewed, as confidants of Hitler's such as Hans Severus Ziegler were to assume key posts in that culturally important town. Praetorius was not without the requisite connections; a former member of Rosenberg's KfdK, he knew well the Berlin Nazi musicians Gustav Havemann, Paul Graener, and Georg Vollerthun and considered himself a friend of Weimar's own Elisabeth Förster-Nietzsche, Friedrich Nietzsche's younger sister and a resolute National Socialist and fierce anti-Semite. But in addition to his problems with the Hitler clique that claimed his job, Praetorius was married to a Jew. By early 1935 he was reduced to working as a chauffeur in Berlin, and in May, in order to improve his chances for an appropriate position, he divorced his wife, thereby bowing to the well-publicized stipulations of the Nazi government. He then became a member of the team of exiles Paul Hindemith had helped to organize, under the full authority of the Nazi bosses, who were sent to Ankara to assist the Turkish government in the construction of a music education system patterned after Germany's. By 1936 Praetorius was in Ankara, extremely successful professionally, conducting and putting into place a whole array of reforms designed to spawn an indigenous, albeit German-inspired, Turkish high-music culture. But he also was without his former wife, who remained back in Berlin, neither able to practice her medical profession nor allowed to join him, for in his official position he still fell under the jurisdiction of the German diplomatic representatives in Turkey and, by extension, of the Reich. Praetorius did not earn enough to pay for the education of his children, as well as the economic support of a first wife and their daughter and subsistence for his second wife, Käte. His belongings had been sent from Berlin but were being held in storage pending the appearance in Ankara of his divorced wife, since the shipment was in her name. Praetorius seems to have realized the absurdity of his situation, for which he himself had to assume a large part of the blame. Pangs of guilt must have dictated to him a policy of deceit, for he told his exiled friends that he had had to leave Germany because he had *refused* to divorce his Jewish wife.[98]

Before their emigration—or extermination—Jewish musicians, like other Jewish artists, were temporarily allowed to exercise their art within the framework of the Jüdischer Kulturbund, or Jewish Culture League. After negotiations between leaders of the Berlin Jewish community and the Prussian commissar for Jewish affairs, Hinkel, the regime granted permission in June 1933 to found this specifically Jewish organization, to be staffed by Jewish artists and financed by Jews themselves for the exclusive benefit of Jewish audiences. Eventually Hinkel was to represent the Prussian minister-president (Göring), the Prussian minister of education (Rust), and the Reich propaganda minister (Goebbels). The moving spirit on the Jewish side was Dr. Kurt Singer, a Berlin neurologist, very knowledgeable about music and himself a conductor, who had founded the Berlin Physicians' Choir in the final days of the Hohenzollern empire. The honorary presidium of the league was to include Jewish notables such as Leo Baeck and Martin Buber. The league was to be managed on a month-to-month basis for specially coopted members, who would pay 2.50 marks (later 2.85 marks) monthly. The Kulturbund administrators considered applications from some two thousand artists and auxiliary personnel (including non-German and Christianized Jews), of whom they hired no more than two hundred. They opened the season with a staging of Gotthold Ephraim Lessing's play *Nathan der Weise* in the Berliner Theater on 1 October, and two weeks later the new Kulturbund orchestra under Michael Taube gave a concert.[99]

Berlin's example was quickly followed by regional Kulturbünde for the Rhine-Ruhr area, with their seat in Cologne, and Rhine-Main with a seat in Frankfurt. Smaller institutions were then formed in Hamburg, Munich, Breslau, Kassel, and other locations, so that in March 1935 the Nazi regime saw fit to put altogether forty-six local associations under a Berlin-led umbrella union, the so-called Reichsverband der jüdischen Kulturbünde, or Reich Association of Jewish Culture Leagues, soon shortened to Jüdischer Kulturbund (Jewish Culture League). The adherence of the individual local leagues to this association was made obligatory. Of those, the one in Berlin remained the largest, with twenty thousand active and passive members by early 1934; the one in Prussian Küstrin was the smallest, with only twenty-four members.[100]

Contemporary pronouncements by Jewish functionaries may lead one to believe that the responsibility for founding these organizations lay

equally with the Nazis and the Jews. It was said that the Jüdischer Kulturbund afforded Jews an opportunity to ponder their national and cultural
origins, to reflect on the question of their assimilation with non-Jewish
Germans or their difference from, or likeness to, eastern European Jewry.
They talked about a great new beginning, which would require "strength,
energy, endurance, and time."[101] But these were glib phrases, designed to
please or at least placate the Nazi rulers, for there was no doubt in
anybody's mind that the regime leaders were the true originators of this
scheme, notwithstanding the degree of cooperation by individual well-
intentioned Jews.

The Nazis had acted from a variety of self-serving motives. First, potential social unrest among Jews as a result of severe and sudden economic
displacement could be channeled and contained by providing a new
source of income, at least for some of them, who could act as models for
others. This held true even if, ultimately, it was not "Aryans" but other
Jews, the passive league members, who were forced to provide for those
artists. Significantly, one prerequisite for being hired as a Kulturbund
artist in Berlin in 1933 had been acute financial need; the honoraria paid
to solo artists, though comparatively low, were sufficient for subsistence.
In Frankfurt, for instance, performers received 20 marks for an appearance. It was in line with this policy that in April 1938 the Promi decreed
that only those Jewish musicians could be taken on who were league
members and who had no other regular income. Even with SS troops
standing by, Hitler did not wish economic discontent among disadvantaged Jews to erupt into revolt.[102]

Second, the propaganda value of the Kulturbund outside Germany was
high. If Jews could be shown to have some sort of cultural autonomy, the
Nazis could claim that generosity, not oppression, was the guiding philosophy of their *Judenpolitik,* no matter how severe were foreign charges
of anti-Semitism. This was the official tenor of speeches by Goebbels,
Hinkel, and their minions.[103]

Third, the cultural ghettoization of Jews anticipated their physical
ghettoization, and later facilitated tighter policing.[104] This complemented
the purging of the culture chambers which had been spearheaded by
Goebbels and Hinkel since their foundation, coterminously with the creation of the Jewish culture organizations. It was not by accident that
Hinkel played a key role in both Nazi-spawned ventures. Nor was it an
accident that many Jewish musicians, upon being ejected from or formally barred entry into the Reich Music Chamber, were routinely told to
go to the Jüdischer Kulturbund for possible employment.[105]

Predictably, the authorities meted out capricious and cruel treatment to
those German Jews who tried to remain in the mainstream of a national
culture they had been accustomed to for decades. In an area of cultural
endeavor painfully circumscribed by the new rules regarding "Jewish"
content, the Jewish Kulturbund planners had to exercise self-censorship
to abide by the official guidelines, had to seek Hinkel's or his underlings'

approval for any schedules, and always risked SS or Gestapo penalties for infractions.[106] The regime used Jews as hostages whenever something went wrong, as when Wilhelm Gustloff, the Nazis' representative in Switzerland, was murdered by a Jew in early 1936 and by way of reprisal, the entire Kulturbund was totally immobilized on Goebbels's orders for several weeks. In November of that year a revue by Leo Raphaeli planned for Hamburg was abruptly prohibited for no apparent reason. After Kristallnacht on 9–10 November 1938, all activities of the Kulturbund were again suspended until Goebbels saw fit to order the Jews back to work in the theaters for fear of inciting an international backlash.[107]

At the time not many Jewish artists were able to comply with this ruling, as many were detained in the camps. Of course, their audiences had also dwindled. And Kulturbund events never having been a money-making proposition, their producers found it increasingly difficult to break even as the passive membership diminished year after year, owing to emigration, pauperization, incarceration, natural death, and sometimes murder of Germany's Jews. Periodic reminders to musicians to pay up and stay active as supporting members bore little fruit. If there were fifty thousand Jews organized in culture leagues throughout the Reich in 1936–37, this would have constituted just over 10 percent of all Jews then still living in Germany.[108]

The end was nearing once the Jews of Germany had become pawns of the Nazis during the official pogroms of November 1938. To be ordered back to producing culture now was much harder than had been engaging, even under pressure, in such activity in 1933 of one's own free will. The Nazis' aim of keeping the Jews locally centralized for purposes of control was still paramount; hence, lacking actors and musicians, the reopened leagues were reduced to showing films. In the larger centers sometimes there was an occasional solo recital or a string quartet debut, but nothing more than this. The Gestapo dissolved the Kulturbund nationally on 11 September 1941. By July SS security chief Reinhard Heydrich had received orders from Göring for a master plan toward the "Final Solution of the Jewish Question." Russian Jews were already being shot by special SS squads in the rear guard of the advancing Wehrmacht. As of 19 September all Jews in the Reich were required to wear the Star of David, and on 1 October any further emigration was interdicted. When deportations of Jews to the East began on 14 October of that year, the idea of the Jüdischer Kulturbund had become obsolete.[109]

Against heavy odds, music stood out in the Kulturbund's overall program as the major activitiy; in combination, operetta, opera, and concert music commanded the largest number of performances and, especially in the case of opera, used up the bulk of the budget.[110] Some of the musicians who worked for the Kulturbund were outstanding: in Berlin the conductors Joseph Rosenstock and, after his departure, Hans Wilhelm Steinberg, aided by Kurt Singer's own choir and Michael Taube's chamber players, as well as soloists such as the pianist Leonid

Kreutzer and the singer Paula Lindberg.[111] Hamburg, too, had fine musicians, as did Frankfurt, including the pianists and composers Rosy Geiger-Kullmann and Bernhard Sekles (until his death in 1934), Hindemith's and Rosbaud's former teacher.[112] Stuttgart was home to the eminent pedagogue and choirmaster Karl Adler, and even in Mannheim for a few months Max Sinzheimer found a new raison d'être as coordinator of music activities in the region. "The 'business' here at least keeps me going," he informed Orff early in 1934. "I do planning and directing and fancy myself as some sort of Jewish Generalmusikdirektor."[113] There was also a record firm, Berlin-based Lukraphon, which produced Jewish folk music, sacred music, some unpretentious swing for dancing, and music by Beethoven, Mozart, and Mendelssohn.[114]

Two interrelated difficulties chronically plagued all these music endeavors. One was that the better the performing artists, the more likely they were to emigrate, as music is not bound by language. Thus, the Kulturbund began to lose ranking musicians as early as 1933, and many more later, never to be replaced: in Berlin, Kreutzer went to the United States, and the Hungarian-born violinist Ödön Partos returned to Hungary; in 1934 Taube left for Palestine. The singer Beatrice Freudenthal emigrated to America in 1936 from Hamburg, and a year later Hamburg's general director Robert Müller-Hartmann sought refuge in Great Britain. By 1938 few professionals were left, one exception being the opera singer Wilhelm Guttmann, who was to die during a performance in Berlin early in 1941. Ludwig Misch, a teacher, conductor, and music critic there, in 1936 looked favorably upon the attempt to found a music school in order to educate recruits, but because of the high rate of emigration by musicians, the venture was destined from the start to fail. Misch himself taught groups of pupils in what functioned as ghetto "Jewish schools" in the capital, obviously with some encouraging results, for the last survivor of one class (all the others had perished) thanked him in 1965, recalling that "during that dark period, when we were excluded from concerts and every enjoyment of art was denied us, you introduced us young people to music and awakened in me personally a great love for music, which did not desert me in the war years to come and ever again thereafter."[115]

To alleviate the dual problems of attrition and recruitment shortages, Kulturbund leaders were keen to hire Jewish stars from abroad, which would have had the added effect of acting as a magnet for some of the more jaded concertgoers. A favorite was the bass Alexander Kipnis of Berlin opera and Bayreuth fame, who had emigrated to the United States in a timely move in 1933 but, cutting short a European tour, was back in Berlin in 1934, appearing annually in various German cities until, three weeks before Kristallnacht, he gave a presumably final recital in Karl Adler's Stuttgart Kulturbund quarters.[116] Contralto Sabine Kalter, now living in London, performed in Berlin in the spring of 1937 and then in Hamburg that winter, singing songs by Mendelssohn, Mahler, and

Dvořák, and arias by Handel.[117] Violinist Carl Flesch also came from London to Berlin, where he had once lived. By the summer of 1936, however, these visits had became too difficult. As much as he loved to entertain his "race companions," the Gestapo had to authorize each visit, and Flesch's basic honorarium of 1,200 marks could no longer be met by an ever-decreasing German-Jewish audience. "Since time is money," as he put it, the star resolved to decline all further invitations.[118]

With the possible exception of Berlin in the early years of Nazi rule, this would have been an impossible amount to raise for any of the satellite culture leagues. In addition to paying meager stipends to their own artists, they also tried to subsidize other causes, such as charity for needy Jews, including out-of-work physicians and artists. In Berlin a separate orchestra was organized for the newly unemployed (such as businessmen who had once learned to play an instrument as a hobby), and a studio was dedicated to younger Jewish composers. Several times the culture leagues suffered the unexpected loss of money, as when performances were indiscriminately canceled by the Gestapo.[119]

To complicate matters further, the culture leagues were hampered by progressively severe rulings regarding the thematic content of their programs. The German censors' ideal was totally Jewish music for totally Jewish audiences. But that was difficult to achieve for, like the Nazis, the Jews were discovering that "Jewish music" was not an artistic genre in and of itself. Hence, derivative definitions were used: libretti written by Jewish authors, a story line from the Old Testament, or the works of any Jewish or baptized-Jewish composers, among whom Mendelssohn remained preeminent. Significantly, the very first concert of the Berlin Kulturbund in October 1933 included works by Handel, Mozart, and Tchaikovsky, and from then on generous mixes of Jewish and non-Jewish content were common. Of the thirty-nine orchestra pieces and oratorios staged by the Berlin league up to February 1938, nineteen were composed by Jews; similar ratios obtained for Frankfurt and Breslau, and undoubtedly for other venues.[120]

Jewish musicians practiced self-censorship when they, of their own volition, forsook the works of Wagner, Richard Strauss, and Weber, thought to be proprietorily German. In 1936, after the inception of the race laws, the playing of Beethoven by Jews was proscribed. In May 1937 Hinkel berated Jews for performing Beethoven and Mozart, so the latter was ruled off limits in 1938. Foreigners, including non-Jews, remained on the authorized list till the end, but in the last few months of the League, performance of German composers was absolutely forbidden.[121]

Ironically, Arnold Schoenberg, the composer thought to be the epitome of Jewish culture by Hitler's regime, was just as unpopular among German-Jewish music audiences as among "Aryans." Only rarely were works of the great pioneer of modern music performed anywhere—by Erich Itor Kahn early on in Frankfurt, in Hamburg in 1935, in Berlin in 1934 to celebrate Schoenberg's sixtieth birthday, and in 1937. These remained isolated events, however, dedicated mostly to his early works, especially *Verklärte Nacht* (1899). Ludwig Misch, the most influential Berlin diaspora critic, set the tone; he disliked Schoenberg, whose music had shown "only slight resilience in our living times." Lesser modern composers, such as Karol Rathaus, fared even worse.[122]

Instead, the works of contemporary but, by international standards, hardly memorable Jewish composers, often local celebrities, were featured, including the likes of Max Kowalski, Rosy Geiger-Kullmann, and Ludwig Rottenberg, Hindemith's father-in-law, in Frankfurt, and another Schönberg (this one named Jacob), as well as Gerhard Goldschlag, Edvard Moritz, and Heinrich Schalit in Berlin. Apart from the inevitable Handel with his Old Testament motifs, Yiddish and Hebrew synagogue compositions, some artfully contrived, were presented, to mixed receptions.[123] Mozart's *Il Nozze di Figaro*, not a Jewish work by any stretch of the imagination despite its libretto by da Ponte, was the Kulturbund's first opera production, in late 1933. It was followed, in April 1934, by an opera with a genuinely Jewish plot, namely, Verdi's *Nabucco*, which was succeeded a couple of weeks before the November 1938 pogrom by *Die Pioniere*, hailed as the first truly Jewish opera, a Zionist-inspired eastern Jewish-Palestinian stage work by one Jakob Weinberg.[124]

As if things were not already complicated enough, even the Jewish and other non-German productions sometimes did not go smoothly. Once Gustav Mahler's song cycle *Lieder eines fahrenden Gesellen* was arbitrarily proscribed for Jewish audiences by a new censor in Hinkel's central office. It turned out that this ill-informed man liked Mahler so much that he thought the composer could not possibly be Jewish, so he put him on the list. No sooner had this mistake been discovered than it was corrected. There was a particularly sordid incident involving Willy Strecker, the powerful music publisher from Mainz. The Berlin Kulturbund had requested permission to mount Stravinsky's *Histoire du soldat*, but Strecker did not wish to go along with this, lest Stravinsky, whose "Aryan" reputation in the Third Reich was shaky in some circles, suffer at the hands of avid Nazis. Strecker told Stravinsky, "If you permit the Jewish Kulturbund to perform it, your enemies will gleefully term you, as well as your art, 'Jewish,' spoiling everything we have managed to nurture." To avoid the performance—and to avoid telling why—Strecker planned to charge the Jews a higher fee than they were able to afford for the work. Fortunately for the Kulturbund, the publisher later reversed himself. This was a stark example of how Gestapo, Promi, and private "Aryan" interests could conspire to make the Jews suffer, all to benefit their enemies' greed and ideological fanaticism.[125]

As part of the general downfall of the Jüdischer Kulturbund, the retrenchment of its musical divisions was most visible because these had been proportionally the largest and most significant. To be sure, despite the occasional musical highlight, there had always been deficiencies, such as the chronic shortage of wind players and an overrepresentation of string players.[126] Hence, the orchestras of Hamburg and Munich consisted mainly of string sections, a problem Hamburg tried to solve by joining forces with its Frankfurt counterpart, which regularly took to the road.[127]

The creeping failure of the culture league's musical productions was disheartening to sympathetic observers, but not to the cynical manipulators in Goebbels's and Hinkel's train. Frankfurt had to give up its accomplished orchestra at the end of the 1935–36 season, mostly for lack of funds. Throughout the Reich music performances decreased by 26 percent, compared to a total decline in artistic activities of 20 percent, in the period from September 1936 to September 1937.[128] By June 1939 the Berlin Jewish opera had been disbanded, even though a scaled-down opera choir, now renamed a "chamber choir," continued to present Mendelssohn, Monteverdi, and eastern Jewish and Hebrew chants and hymns. What was left of the Berlin orchestras and singers congregated, for the last time, for a Verdi celebration in July 1941. When the end came, Nazi functionaries redistributed Kulturbund instruments to SA and SS units; pianos went to Nazi welfare organizations and Wehrmacht sanatoriums. Confiscated phonographs and records were recycled, the latter in the form of bakelite from the German recording industry, which increasingly marketed marches as well as a good deal of Beethoven to steel the German people's will toward achieving final victory.[129]

Although most Jewish musicians were able to leave the Reich before the deportations began, a significant number of them could not do so and ultimately perished. For many, concentration camp became a terrible way station as anti-Semitism institutionalized itself, whether they eventually made it out of the country or not. In trying to reconstruct the Via Dolorosa of these musicians, the historian is frustrated by a dearth of documentation. The educator and composer Erich Katz of Freiburg is one of the few about whom something is known prior to his arrival in the United States. Vilified by Nazi musicologists early on, Katz was dismissed from a Freiburg municipal music conservatory in 1933. His subsequent letters bespeak his desperation. With his future uncertain in July 1933, Katz wrote to Orff: "As far as I am concerned, I don't know what will become of me. I guess I won't be able to stay in Germany, not only for reasons of subsistence, but because I have no more business being in this country as a non-member of the people's community (who is said to be lying whenever he writes in German). After all, at thirty-three I cannot allow myself to be buried alive, as it were, culturally and musically. But on the other hand, you will know how willing other countries are to accept people without money like myself, Switzerland, for instance, which would be a place of first choice. It really just comes down to one thing: the rope." As it turned out, Katz was offered a temporary job in Switzerland, but he stayed in Germany until the 1938 November pogrom, after which he was shipped off to a concentration camp for several months. From England in 1939 he was able to emigrate to New York in 1943, but not until 1959 was he comfortably established, in Santa Barbara.[130]

Not far from Freiburg, in Stuttgart, lived Karl Adler, the choirmaster. If, as I have said, the Nazi system was so capricious that some Jews could take advantage of its inconsistency, this system could also turn against them. Adler was taken into "protective custody" in March 1933, when anti-Jewish activities were generally still low-key. Like Katz, he was arrested again in November 1938, but was released after one week. He too emigrated, to New York, where he started a new career.[131] Other musicians who were temporarily incarcerated were the Frankfurt tenor Hermann Schramm, the Viennese violinist Josef Geringer, and the young Berlin pianist Edith Kraus. She was sent to Theresienstadt with her husband, where she entertained her fellow inmates on an old piano that she found in an attic. Although her husband was sent to Auschwitz to be gassed, she was able to return to her native Prague.[132]

Musicians who took their own lives out of sheer desperation must be counted among the victims of the Holocaust. These included Gustav Brecher, who was born in Austrian-ruled Bohemia in 1879. His symphonic poem *Rosmersholm*, an early work, was conducted by Richard Strauss when Brecher was still a boy. He came to national prominence when he premiered Křenek's *Jonny spielt auf* in 1927 and the Brecht–Weill *Aufstieg und Fall der Stadt Mahagonny* in 1930, both in Leipzig. He was director of the opera there in 1933 when he was discharged. He and his wife killed themselves in Belgium in May 1940, as soon as they knew that the Wehrmacht was drawing near.[133] Josef Lengsfeld, a leading member of the Munich Kulturbund orchestra, committed suicide with his wife in Munich after the events of Kristallnacht.[134]

Many German-Jewish musicians died in Theresienstadt and other Nazi concentration camps, as did Kurt Singer, the Berlin founder of the Jüdischer Kulturbund, as late as 1944, as well as Therese Rothauer, a singer, and Richard Breitenfeld, a member of the Frankfurt Opera ensemble. Composers Hans Walter David and Erwin Schulhoff died, one in Maidanek, the other in the Bavarian concentration camp of Wülzburg. Of some musicians we have no record other than that they perished in a camp somewhere—the Viennese violinists Viktor Robitsek and Max Starkmann, for instance. Of others we know only that they vanished without a trace, as did Hamburg Kulturbund pianist Richard Goldschmidt.[135]

No one has served as a finer symbol of the pride and suffering of these Jewish musicians than the composer Viktor Ullmann, who, the son of an Austrian officer, was a resident of Prague. Born and educated in Vienna, where he studied with Schoenberg, he was part of the Austro-German music tradition. Ullmann, just over forty years old, was in Theresienstadt in 1944 when he composed his opera *Der Kaiser von Atlantis*, performed for the first time in New York in 1977 and then again in Mainz in 1994, the year it was released as a recording. The opera is a thinly veiled indictment of a deranged despot who eventually surrenders his life so that Death can return and re-create natural order in society. Ullmann also composed a piano concerto, a symphony, piano sonatas, and a string quartet. Before he was sent to Auschwitz to be murdered one day in the fall of 1944, he had been urged by his friends to leave his Theresienstadt works behind for posterity.[136]

Auschwitz also claimed the life of baritone Erhard E. Wechselmann, who, after fleeing Germany, served as cantor of the Jewish congregation in Amsterdam. Alfred Kropf, a Kapellmeister from Stettin, managed to conceal his identity with the help of forged ancestry papers but was found out and sent off to be gassed. Frankfurt contralto Magda Spiegel was taken first to Theresienstadt but, like Ullmann, met her death in Auschwitz. Composer James Simon, a student of Max Bruch, had taught in Berlin and thereafter was freelancing. He fled to Holland, was caught and sent to Theresienstadt, then transferred to Auschwitz, where he died. Most moving is the fate of Alma Maria Rosé, niece of Gustav Mahler and daughter of the well-known Viennese violinist Arnold Rosé, whose pupil she was. A first-rate soloist, she fled to France in 1938, only to be interned in the Drancy concentration camp a few years later. She was deported to Auschwitz, where she directed an orchestra of young female players, including her deputy conductor, the singer Fania Fénelon. Rosé was thirty-eight when, in 1944, she contracted meningitis and typhus, which evidently caused her untimely death.[137]

Jewish Flight and Exile

Most Jewish musicians managed to escape from the Nazi Reich if they had the financial means to do so and were able to find willing sponsors and continued support in countries where they wanted to live. As in the case of other Jewish professions and occupations, there were three primary places of sanctuary, with the United States heading the list; virtually one out of every two emigrants went there. England accepted one out of ten Jews seeking protection, and Palestine slightly less than that.[138]

There were several categories of musical professionals likely to emigrate, and their eventual success depended largely on what field they were engaged in. Because music communicates its message through an international language, conductors and instrumentalists had the best chance. Singers did well, too, because most of them were multilingual on account of performing opera repertories in several languages. Composers had a harder time of it because they often needed to feel the support of their roots in order to be creative. For instance, Carl Orff, with one Jewish grandmother, is said to have considered emigrating in 1938 but quickly decided against it because he knew that away from his native Bavarian soil, his musicianship would prove barren. The hardest group to transplant were music professionals dependent on language—scholars, musicologists, critics, teachers. Most could prevail only if they had an instrumental sideline or knew how to compose.[139]

England was the closest country for the musicians to flee to, but, because of its economic depression and resultant unemployment, they had to contend with an ever-increasing degree of indigenous anti-Semitism, to the great delight of Goebbels, who ruminated about this in his war diaries.[140] Even though it is doubtful that anti-Semitism was the reason why the Hamburg contralto Sabine Kalter participated in only twenty or so concerts by the London Royal Opera, she was in competition with singers such as the Swedes Kerstin Thorborg and Karin Branzell.[141] England also received the conductor Erwin Stein, a Schoenberg pupil, who joined the music firm of Boosey and Hawkes; the violinist Nikolai Graudan, once concertmaster of the Berlin Philharmonic; and Arnold Rosé, Graudan's counterpart at the Wiener Staatsoper.[142] Of some significance to Britain's musical life was the arrival of Egon Wellesz and Berthold Goldschmidt. Like Stein, Wellesz had studied composition under Schoenberg, and at the time of the Anschluss he was vice-president of the Austrian Composers' League and a professor in Vienna. This composer of nine symphonies, sundry string quartets, and ballet music was able to teach Byzantine music history at Oxford. Goldschmidt, by contrast, after some experience as director of an orchestra of unemployed musicians in the Berlin Kulturbund, fell on hard times in London because—typical of England's immigration policy—he did not receive the required musician's work permit. Hence, he secretly gave lessons until in 1944 he was hired by the BBC for its anti-German propaganda. After a hiatus of decades Goldschmidt, who lost twenty-two relatives in the Holocaust, once more became a significant composer in old age, and in the early 1990s was a darling of the international media.[143]

The British-ruled mandate of Palestine was fraught with economic difficulties in that, at the high point of Jewish immigration after 1933, it already had a relative surplus of white-collar professionals; what it really needed was a large influx of manual laborers. The German and Austrian musicians, along with doctors, lawyers, and academics, found few positions to suit their training. Politically, there was mounting friction with Arab residents, some of whom were professionals themselves, if not Western-trained musicians. Because of this and other variables, the British enacted restrictive immigration controls. So unless they were willing to retrain, Jewish musicians had only a slight chance of finding a place in Palestinian society. After 1938 British regulations were so severe that one out of every three newcomers to the land was a clandestine alien, always at risk.[144]

Much of this did not affect the early migrants, for example, Karl Salomon from Heidelberg, who found work as a music educator officially sponsored by the University of Jerusalem as early as summer 1933. Amused, he wrote home to Germany about the clash of cultures, of

English teachers in the territory's schools trying to coach unwilling Arab students in three- or four-voice harmony. Grand opera, he wrote later, was impossible for lack of resources. By 1936, undaunted, Salomon was active in radio programming as well.[145]

Munich-born Paul Frankenburger, who had studied piano, violin, and composition, was to become at least as influential in the Israeli music world as Salomon; he is regarded as the father of modern Israeli composition. Thirty-five in 1933, he too emigrated after careful planning and a very conscious preoccupation with Hebrew and Zionist forms of culture. Renaming himself Paul Ben-Haim, he commenced to teach composition at Tel Aviv Conservatory, but he also served as an important role model through performance. In 1936 it warmed his heart to be reunited with his eighty-year-old father, soon to die, on a visit to Palestine, but years later he had to mourn the death of his sister Rosa in Auschwitz.[146]

Newly arriving musicians such as Salomon and Ben-Haim, as well as others such as Hanoch (Heinrich) Jacoby and Joseph Tal (Gruenthal), both of whom emigrated in 1934, received a tremendous boost from the founding of the Palestine Symphony Orchestra, which in 1935 was accomplished by the visiting violinist Bronislaw Huberman, and with which Toscanini performed in 1936 and 1938. The orchestra instantly attained a very high standard because it was composed largely of recently expelled German-Jewish instrumentalists with superb credentials.[147]

Somewhat atypical of this group was the composer Stefan Wolpe, not only because of his penchant for twelve-tone music (after his initial flight from Berlin he had studied briefly with Anton Webern in Vienna), but also because of his communist convictions and antibourgeois attitude. This may also have led him to adopt an anti-Zionist stance, which rendered his integration into Palestine problematic after his arrival there in 1934. But though his serial compositions had little resonance among his newfound peers, he was positively influenced by the Sephardic folklore he encountered in the mandate's kibbutzim, and he incorporated some of this material into his Palestinian works. It was the communal experiment of the kibbutzim that soothed his Marxist conscience. Still, he felt stifled, especially by the formality of the Jerusalem Conservatory. Logically, Wolpe should have moved on to the Soviet Union, but he sought refuge in the United States instead. Arriving there in 1938, he eventually worked at some of New York's music schools, sometimes coaching aspiring jazz musicians such as clarinetist Tony Scott.[148]

Before reaching Austria in 1933, Wolpe had in fact gone to his spiritual haven, Moscow, and had been tempted to stay there, but, as one of his biographers suggests, at that time the need for formalized instruction such as Webern could provide was stronger.[149] Indeed, very few German or Austrian Jewish musicians went to Russia, and even fewer stayed there and lived to tell about it. Probably the most prolific of those who did was the Austrian-born Fritz Stiedry, known, among other things, for his collaboration with Kurt Weill in the late years of the Weimar Republic.

From 1933 to 1938 Stiedry conducted orchestras in Leningrad and Moscow but then moved on to New York, citing Soviet xenophobia as a reason. Lotte Schlesinger, a composer from Berlin, taught at conservatories in Charkov, Kiev, and Moscow between 1937 and 1938 before settling in Massachusetts. The Polish-born conductor Paul Klecki also worked in Charkov in 1937–38, then went to Lausanne and finally to Liverpool. It may be assumed that leftist political leanings played a role in motivating these musicians, as they motivated the (non-Jewish) actress and singer Carola Neher, who had been close to Weill and was the mistress of the socialist conductor Hermann Scherchen. But beyond that, they were well aware that there was a market in the East that could be commercially exploited. Some of the musicians who took advantage of these opportunities had to pay for them with their freedom, and even their life, as they became caught up in Stalin's purges. This happened to Neher and to the unbendingly communist Bruno Schmitzdorf and Salomon Katzenellenbogen.[150]

By one reckoning 465 musicians emigrated from Germany or Austria to the United States during the Hitler period, most of them Jews.[151] Although a traditional haven for the persecuted around the world, America was not the most accommodating country to arrive in during the 1930s and 1940s. Under the constraints of isolationism in the wake of World War I, among the immigrants it still favored were those from northwestern, not eastern or southern, Europe, and certainly not Jews. In the words of the crude Kansas congressman J. M. Tincher, there existed considerable prejudice against "Wops, Dagoes, Kikes and Hunkies." And although incoming Jews after 1933 fell under the rather favorable immigration quota for German nationals, the effects of the Great Depression militated against a friendly reception for Jewish professionals, difficulties that were often exacerbated by capricious anti-immigration legislation in individual states. Only by 1937 did immigration laws begin to relax somewhat, which tended to favor the Jews. But by that time the American consuls' waiting lists were quickly being filled up with German and Austrian Jewish names, so that for many, onerous years of waiting lay ahead. After Kristallnacht more Jews were allowed into the country, as the 1939 and 1940 statistics were to show. But once the United States entered the war, internal anti-Semitism created hardship for the Jews already there.[152]

America's budding musical culture welcomed the Jewish musicians in principle, but its proponents often were so ill-informed or naive as to cause pain to the more sophisticated German artists. The sardonic Arnold Schoenberg was particularly scathing in his criticism. On the occasion of his sixtieth birthday at the end of 1934, when he was already living in California, whose moderate climate he cherished, Schoenberg complained about the ignorance of U.S. musicians and their agents. Of conductor Serge Koussevitzky he said that he was so uneducated as to be incapable of reading scores. And he called symphony-orchestra musicians on the West Coast conservative, "for they have to conserve their own incompetence, ignorance and cowardice: these they conserve so well that nobody can recognize them." Sometimes the Jewish musicians had cause to doubt the sincerity of their American hosts, who claimed to support their fight against universal fascism. The wealthy Elizabeth Sprague Coolidge, for instance, a founder of the Berkshire chamber music festival in 1918, acted as a most generous patron to exiled musicians such as Schoenberg and Ernst Toch. But she also offered a prize for an original chamber work by a German composer in Nazi Germany (as she would during the war to Italian Fascist composers); the announcement was posted by Goebbels's own Reich Music Chamber.[153]

In the United States only a few Jewish musicians achieved a noteworthy measure of success. Fritz Kreisler did reasonably well as a soloist (he died in New York in 1962). Hanns Eisler, a former student of Schoenberg, might have had a more prolific career if he had stayed in Hollywood, where he was intermittently successful composing film scores. But he was a dedicated communist who had chanced a few sojourns in the Soviet Union and the Spanish Civil War theater before coming to the East Coast in 1938. After being denied a U.S. immigration visa, Eisler temporarily moved to Mexico. From 1940 to 1942 Eisler again lived in New York, teaching at the New School for Social Research. Thereafter his spate of Hollywood accomplishments began, until in 1948 he became a victim of Senator Joseph McCarthy. By way of Vienna, Eisler left for the newly created German Democratic Republic.[154]

Artur Schnabel, who moved to Michigan in 1939 via Italy, England, and France, never regained his former European reputation as one of the foremost pianists of his time. He was to die in 1951 in Switzerland. A much younger pianist, Erich Itor Kahn, was typical of the many promising young musicians uprooted at the beginning of their careers. He and his wife finally reached American territory after a life of deprivation and exile in Paris and internment in Vichy French camps. In New York from 1941, he became a founding member of the Albeneri Trio, which enjoyed some national acclaim and even made recordings. Itor Kahn's compositions were significant but today are hardly remembered; regrettably there is no entry for him in the authoritative *New Grove Dictionary of Music and Musicians* (1980). After his immigration, Stuttgart's Karl Adler was fortunate enough to be offered a chair in music pedagogy at Yeshiva University in New York. Synagogues supported Manfred Lewandowsky and Oskar Guttmann, both of whom had been cantors and choir directors at temples in Berlin.[155]

The most important Jewish musician in exile was of course Schoenberg, a position in keeping with his official place at the top of the Nazi index. Fundamentally, Schoenberg was unhappy in his new home, but there was justification for this unhappiness, and the circumstances in which it was fostered must be understood with compassion. He had contracted with the private Malkin Conservatory in Boston in late summer 1933, which facilitated his transfer with his new young family from France. By 1935 he had started teaching composition at the University of Southern California, and by 1936 was a professor of music at the University of California, Los Angeles (UCLA). On more than one occasion, especially at the beginning of his stay, Schoenberg could not help admitting that his new country had been good to him and that he was lucky to live in such a beautiful house, in suburban Brentwood, in California's temperate climate.[156] Nevertheless, his teaching job was demanding, leaving him little time to compose. And when his works were performed, they were his early, nonserial compositions, as happened on 16 March 1934, when he himself was able to conduct his *Pelleas und Melisande* (1903) with the Boston Symphony. But his epochal twelve-tone oeuvre was neglected.[157]

Schoenberg's discontent thus stemmed from two interrelated problems, as he correctly perceived them: his local and national lack of recognition as one of the foremost composers of the twentieth century, and his lack of financial security. There is no denying that it took Schoenberg much longer than it ought, both to be offered an acceptable academic position and to be accorded homage as an eminent composer. He became embittered by the failure of the U.S. music establishment to recognize his decades-long importance as the father of modern European music. And he was also increasingly disappointed by the lack of interest shown in his pioneering twelve-tone compositions on the part of fellow émigrés who could have introduced them to American concert audiences, notably Bruno Walter and Otto Klemperer. These conductors, who had never really warmed to his serial works, were at best content to present his earlier, tonal compositions, such as *Verklärte Nacht*. As Schoenberg lamented from Los Angeles in November 1935, he did not "find appreciated what I am doing in favor of the future state of musical culture in this city." In June 1938 he waxed enthusiastic about the prospect of a Schoenberg festival to be held in New York, hoping it would increase the popularity of his works, but was all the more disappointed when this plan fell through. To an executive at RCA Victor he insisted a few months later that his music ought to be widely distributed on records, since "I am the only living composer of a reputation like mine." Perennially unimpressed with the "second- and third-rate" orchestras of America and conductors who were "third-class, at the most," he, with good reason, reproached the influential American Society of Composers, Authors, and Publishers in New York: "Certainly, it was not vanity and it was not hunger for publicity, when I now tell you: I wonder why my name is never mentioned in your publications."[158]

Even though to the end of his life Schoenberg did not suffer from poverty, he never amassed riches or even received the rewards that should have been his due. Before assuming his post at UCLA he determined that he would have to teach at both Los Angeles area universities to approximate the salary he had been receiving from the Berlin Akademie der

Künste alone. But this was impossible, and so by July of 1936 his UCLA salary was fixed at $4,800 per annum, no less than that of many full professors, yet not enough to allow him to recoup his European losses or save money for a not-so-distant retirement. With the help of private students, who would pay him anywhere from $15 to $25 per lesson, he still had enough funds to send occasional checks to his son Georg in Europe; he drove a decent car, and at social gatherings at his house he even went out of his way to serve opulent meals. In 1935, when asked by Metro-Goldwyn-Mayer to consider writing a score for the film *The Good Earth*, Schoenberg asked for $50,000, at which the film moguls recoiled, with Schoenberg admitting to Alma Mahler-Werfel later that he had requested such a large amount because it would have enabled him to stop teaching and devote time to his composing—a legitimate desire, for there were major works to finish. Since, upon his retirement in 1944, he had been teaching for only eight years, Schoenberg's pension from UCLA came to less than $30 a month, a humiliatingly meager sum, and until his death in 1951 he found it hard to make ends meet, all the more so when a much-coveted Guggenheim Fellowship, which he would clearly have deserved, failed to materialize. Altogether, Schoenberg's economic situation was a very sad one, for it stalled his productivity as a composer, and in comparison with that of Igor Stravinsky, who was immeasurably richer, truly made him appear neglected and disadvantaged.[159] To make matters worse, toward the end of his tenure at UCLA he had a falling out with the university administration, which resulted in his withdrawal of an earlier promise to deposit his private papers there. He was so disenchanted at the time that he considered moving to New Zealand, where he thought his dollars might go farther.[160]

In a critical but sympathetic account Dika Newlin, a former wunderkind and an American musicologist and composer, has amply documented Schoenberg's bitterness, which frequently manifested itself in the classroom at UCLA. Schoenberg's acerbity in interpersonal relations was indeed so trying as to become legendary. Even a musicologist of Richard Taruskin's stature sees fit to describe his personality as nothing short of "absolutist and despotic."[161] Nevertheless, Newlin has also spoken of the other facets of Schoenberg's character, such as his sense of humor, his childlike or avuncular charm, and his genuine desire to teach the young conventional, if not atonal, music.[162]

Schoenberg showed these more endearing qualities to close friends such as Franz and Alma Werfel and fellow composer George Gershwin.[163] He was also on cordial, if at times reserved, terms with Thomas Mann, who lived in nearby Pacific Palisades and saw the Schoenbergs on several social occasions, even though Frau Mann disliked this "tyrannical man." "For dinner at the Schoenbergs in Brentwood," reads Thomas Mann's diary of 27 August 1943, "hospitable reception. Naughty children," a tart reference to Schoenberg's two young sons from his second marriage.[164] Schoenberg and Mann conferred about the problems of present-day

Jewry, to which Mann could well relate, since his own wife, the former Katia Pringsheim, hailed from a prominent Munich Jewish family, and in his present exile he was surrounded by many Jewish acquaintances. Mann took care in advising Schoenberg about the prospects of publishing an article on the Jews, in which the composer, not so incidentally, exhibited his long-held right-wing political convictions. They were such that the liberal-democratic novelist ascribed to Schoenberg's overall ideology "a somewhat fascistic bent," born of "a certain will to terrorism." Politely, Mann counseled revision of the essay.[165]

Here Mann referred to Schoenberg's preoccupation, ever since he had left Germany for Paris in May 1933, with Judaism and the situation of contemporary Jews during the onslaught of Nazism. With authoritarian conviction embedded in central European hierarchical thinking, Schoenberg determined that a new political party should be formed to further the cause of the Jews—if need be in a militant manner. As Asians, not Westerners, said Schoenberg, Jews should concentrate on their own ethnicity and, in particular, their religious roots. Taking his inspiration from his reconversion to Judaism, Schoenberg, like many deeply religious Jews, held that the Jews were being punished by God for having forsaken him. As a first consequence of such musings, Schoenberg believed that the emigration of Jews from Germany, the land of their present predicament, should be facilitated. Though without job prospects at the time, Schoenberg wanted to invest all of his personal and professional energies in bringing about such a movement.[166]

Such a conviction, which culminated in Schoenberg's dictum that "Jews have to relearn how to hate and pursue the enemy to the last drop of blood," was roughly coterminous with the composer's opera *Moses und Aron*, written in 1930–32 but not finished at that time, and in fact never to be finished, to which in this context he made specific reference.[167] In the United States Schoenberg continued to think about such a scheme, though it remained barely theoretical, occasionally surfacing, as in letters to friends or the correspondence, containing the draft article, with Thomas Mann in 1938–39.[168] Instead, Schoenberg converted his intellectual momentum to music, as when he sketched out a "Jewish Symphony" in four movements at the beginning of 1937. Schoenberg's "Four-Point Program for Jewry," written in October 1938 and evidently serving as the basis for his communication to Mann, harked back to his Paris proposition. Its musical complement was *Kol Nidre* (1938), a work for reciter, chorus, and orchestra, which carried out his belief that Jewish liturgical music should be modernized.[169] One may view as a more politically articulated derivative of this composition Schoenberg's later *Ode to Napoleon* (1942), based on Lord Byron's hymn and symbolizing political dictatorship of any era. "I knew it was the moral duty of intelligentsia to take a stand against tyranny," said Schoenberg later.[170]

None of the Jewish exiles in America could have suffered more from Schoenberg's difficult personality than the conductor Otto Klemperer, who had first come to Los Angeles in 1933 eventually to assume the directorship of the Los Angeles Philharmonic Orchestra, still in its fledgling years. Klemperer was an admirer of Schoenberg when the composer arrived there several months later. But by the end of 1934 Schoenberg was allowing his prejudices to get in the way of his relationship with this colleague. He refused to attend a banquet in Klemperer's honor because that would have meant acknowledging those Americans of influence who had ignored Schoenberg's own works for decades. Nonetheless, despite occasional squabbles usually caused by Schoenberg, Klemperer continued to conduct the composer's works for a number of years, albeit merely the earlier, tonal ones, and he also had a hand in gaining Schoenberg more satisfactory employment on the UCLA music faculty.[171]

In 1939 the manic-depressive Klemperer was operated on for a nonmalignant brain tumor, and thereafter his precarious state of health contributed to a further deterioration in the relationship between the two émigré musicians. By now Schoenberg was convinced that Klemperer did not like him or his music because he was still conducting only Schoenberg's earlier compositions. Schoenberg called Klemperer's musical choices "reactionary" and avoided seeing the conductor on many occasions, even though he could not snub him altogether. Aware of Klemperer's illness, however, Schoenberg did not want to compound his problems unnecessarily. "Although I am full of spite against Klemperer on account of his attitude to my music," he wrote, "and although I am convinced that he cannot understand my music, I presently do not wish to insult him. . . . For who knows whether he will ever fully recover." In September 1940 Klemperer substantiated Schoenberg's suspicion that much of the composer's music was foreign to him, and both men were now wondering "how the demolished artistic bridge could ever be repaired." As if their conceptual differences were not serious enough, the two great musicians were also quarreling about personal favors exchanged in the past, such as money Klemperer had lent to Schoenberg which had never been paid back. Schoenberg, in his Old Testament stubbornness, continued to believe that Klemperer was behind the currents of reaction in the Los Angeles area, which, as he saw it, denied him a performance of his works at every opportunity. The sordidness in which this relationship became mired, and remained almost till the end of World War II, is a sad comment on the egocentricity of both artists, as well as on the hardships inflicted on two creative souls by enforced exile.[172]

Quite apart from the problems with Schoenberg, Klemperer's unbalanced mental state meant that sustaining a musical career at the highest level in the United States seemed uncertain. Even though he was fortunate enough to be offered the conductor's chair at the Los Angeles Philharmonic, until the 1934–35 season this was only a probationary situation. Although he appreciated the orchestra, like Schoenberg, Klemperer deplored the "spiritual niveau" of his new environment. On his first trip to Los Angeles in 1933, he had had to leave his wife and two children in

Vienna, where he himself would rather be. Yet he was acutely aware of Austria's home-grown anti-Semitism, and he was hampered by the Nazis' confiscation of sizable life insurance funds due him. Homesickness plagued him, on top of a sense of futility. "I am thinking much of the future," he wrote to his wife in November 1933, "since I do want to return to Europe." And, about Vienna in February of the following year, "I don't think that we will be able to stay in this beautiful city, in which I gladly would have felt at home." After his own futile attempts to resettle in Europe, his family joined him in Los Angeles in June 1935.[173]

Once established there, Klemperer had his share of concert engagements, mostly on the West Coast but not infrequently also in New York. He reorganized the Pittsburgh Symphony Orchestra and even toured Europe. From New York he took the side of Paul Hindemith in that composer's brewing conflict with the Nazi regime over *Mathis der Maler,* offering to inaugurate the work in New York. In Los Angeles he not only conducted Schoenberg but also premiered works of their fellow exile Ernst Toch. Klemperer, too, was readily received into the sophisticated circle of German émigrés unofficially presided over by Thomas Mann, whom, like Schoenberg, he saw socially on several occasions. When his old colleague Hindemith arrived in Los Angeles in March 1939, Klemperer featured him as viola soloist in a pair of subscription concerts he conducted. But the onslaught of disease later that year ended his regular employment with the Los Angeles Philharmonic, although he stayed on as guest conductor. As a consequence of his partial paralysis and a severe personality disorder, which proved particularly trying for his family, he fought with many of his former friends. February 1941 found him in a New York mental home; when he left it after two days, its director had the police issue warnings describing Klemperer as "dangerous and crazy." Klemperer did not make a full professional comeback until his post-war career chiefly as conductor of the Budapest Opera and the Philharmonia Orchestra in London. In the words of his daughter Lotte Klemperer, a return to Germany for him simply was "out of the question," and he finally settled in Zurich.[174]

Another émigré musician, Bruno Walter, enjoyed a success in the United States that was much more conspicuous than that of either Schoenberg or Klemperer, for professional and personal reasons. Walter had long been familiar with American customs and culture, and he spoke English well. Like his friend Toscanini, he respected what the Americans were capable of doing, and he was grateful for their unflinching appreciation of his art. He was financially somewhat better off when he left Europe to settle in Los Angeles in 1939, and he did not suffer from Klemperer's illness or the misanthropy of the resentful Schoenberg, who, although he claimed to relish Walter's musicianship, in late 1934 hyperbolically referred to him as "a repulsive pig."[175]

Walter had first visited the United States as a mature conductor in 1923. In 1932, at the height of his career in Europe, he was invited to become associate conductor, with Toscanini, of the New York Philharmonic, a position he held for three consecutive seasons. These engagements paid him approximately $1,000 per concert for an average of forty performances a season. After his ouster from Leipzig and Berlin in March 1933, the Philharmonic cabled him sympathetically in Amsterdam: "After all you have given to the world of art we send our sympathy for the unjust treatment accorded you." Thanking the American musicians, the Berlin-born Walter movingly replied: "All countries in Europe except one are open to me and pour down the invitations on me. But you will understand that my experiences just with this one country are very sad, because it has been my home country where and for which I worked all my life."[176]

In 1933 Walter moved to Salzburg, making it his home base for numerous appearances as guest conductor all over Europe, including Vienna, while he maintained his American ties as best he could. A schedule for his European season from January to May 1934 includes no fewer than fifteen major centers, starting and ending with London, and not counting the Salzburg Festival in August. For his New York engagement he was able to sign three other prominent refugees from Nazi injustice: the violinist Bronislaw Huberman, the cellist Emanuel Feuermann, and the pianist Artur Schnabel.[177]

Yet in his case, too, one aspect of his continued career in Europe was troublesome, and that was his naive trust in the authoritarian Austrian regime of Chancellor Kurt Schuschnigg, with whom he was friendly, and his willingness to concertize in Italy, disregarding its own Fascist framework and Mussolini's growing friendship with Hitler. While he sincerely believed that Schuschnigg, possibly with the backing of Mussolini, would save Austria from Hitlerism, Walter evidently overlooked the seeds of fascism in his adopted country. As for Italy, his long-standing admiration of that country was oddly reminiscent of Schoenberg's openly stated sympathy with dictatorship as a means of controlling people.[178] Yet, unlike Nazi Germany, Fascist Italy, despite Mussolini's tyranny, remained attractive to musicians, including Walter and even Hermann Scherchen, for the Italians loved traditional as well as modern music, sponsored modern-music festivals, and showed no official signs of anti-Semitism until 1938.[179]

It has been plausibly suggested that Walter's proximity to Schuschnigg was the cause of the arrest of one of his two daughters by the invading Nazis while he and his wife were away in Amsterdam during the Anschluss.[180] Eventually she was freed, and after several more sojourns in unoccupied Europe, and after their other daughter had been murdered by her husband, the Walters embarked for New York from Genoa in October 1939. In America he was to become a regular guest conductor of the Los Angeles and New York Philharmonic orchestras, also performing frequently at the Hollywood Bowl, at the New York Metropolitan Opera, and in an NBC Symphony series. His old friend

Thomas Mann, with his unerring sense of integrity, punctiliously re-corded in his diaries the many times he went to hear the conductor in Los Angeles or New York; and Walter's surviving daughter, Lotte, was a frequent guest of the Manns in Pacific Palisades. In 1942, at the age of sixty-six, Walter was offered the musical directorship of the New York Philharmonic, but the conductor, busy as usual, declined the honor owing to fatigue. This recurring weakness led to illnesses, and in November 1943 Walter was forced to ask a young beginner from Lawrence, Massa-chusetts, a student of Koussevitzky, to stand in for him. Leonard Bern-stein, a mere twenty-five years of age, gave a thrilling rendition of Strauss's tone poem *Don Quixote* with the New York Philharmonic, greatly impressing the visiting Mann. So far, Walter's stay in the United States had been a full one, so much so that in 1944 his New York col-leagues regarded him as "a leading custodian of a precious heritage and as a guide and patron of later trends." Walter acknowledged that he was grateful to have found "a new home and such opportunity to contribute to American musical life."[181]

In contrast to Schoenberg, Klemperer, and even Walter, there was Kurt Weill. He adapted to the United States better than any of the other refu-gees, and he knew how to take the downturns in stride. Weill, long a fan of American jazz, and particularly Louis Armstrong, as early as 1931 had hoped that Leopold Stokowski might be interested in staging his opera *Die Bürgschaft* in Philadelphia, a somewhat farfetched plan which did not materialize. While in Paris in April 1933, he again hoped that he might soon set foot on American soil.[182]

After finally arriving in New York in September 1935, Weill became successful as a composer of sophisticated Broadway musicals and the occasional film score. A couple of his hits—"September Song" from *Knickerbocker Holiday* and "Speak Low" from *One Touch of Venus*—were popularized on radio by Bing Crosby and Frank Sinatra.[183] In 1943 Weill almost succeeded in featuring an old acquaintance, Marlene Die-trich, in the role of Venus on Broadway, but the eccentric actress got cold feet about having to appear on stage; besides, she hoped to star in the film version expected later from Hollywood. The greater the triumph was for Weill when Mary Martin accepted the role, to enthusiastic reviews.[184] Another highlight of Weill's revived artistic career in America was his collaboration with the lyricist Ira Gershwin, who saw in Weill an accept-able replacement for his brother, George, who was felled by cancer in 1937.[185] Weill was paid $10,000 by Paramount for a film score in 1939; the enormous success of his Broadway musical *Lady in the Dark* in 1941 assured him a weekly income of $900 from that source alone, while the movie rights sold to Paramount for over $42,000. With the even greater success of *One Touch of Venus*, Weill was clearing $100,000 in 1943. A year earlier he had complained wistfully that he was liable for a "very high income tax," quickly adding that that was an easy chore, "as long as one has the good fortune to live in this wonderful country." This statement was symptomatic of the composer's attitude toward his newly chosen home: he was head over heels in love with it. In 1936 he had written, "The longer I am here and the better I get to know this country, the more I like it," and he never looked back. He kept his good humor even in adversity. When his musical *The Firebrand of Florence,* with Lotte Lenya in the lead, did poorly in 1945, he consoled himself that he was used to the "ups and downs of success," and that setbacks were unavoidable.[186]

Weill's commercial achievements in New York and Hollywood have raised the legitimate question of a lapse of artistic integrity in the composer's career, which in Europe, some critics say, was originally dedicated to serious music rather than light entertainment. Insisting on the qualitative dichotomy between "classical" and light music, including jazz, these critics continue to charge Weill with leaving behind his fine European achievements in order to sell his soul to American commercialism.[187] More sympathetic scholars have lessened the charge by implying that the "American Weill" took advantage of greater freedom in creating his works in the United States than he had been afforded in Europe, saying that his music "was flowing more freely," and that the choice of thematic content—psychiatrists, cowboys, fashion magazines, American vaudeville—signaled his enthusiasm as a recently arrived U.S. resident.[188]

As Stephen Hinton has remarked, such analyses are at best patronizing and at worst faulty, for they are predicated on the customary dichotomy of "the European versus the American, the critical versus the commercial, the highbrow versus the middlebrow."[189] Weill himself, eminently conscious of his talent for writing music for the theater, saw no lapse at all in terms of either genre or quality. In America he wished to "continue what I had begun in Europe," as he professed in 1937. At that time he was pleased to discover that some Americans were interested in his earlier concert and stage works.[190] In 1941 he even viewed his occasional Hollywood scores as "a new type of intelligent musical picture, just as *Lady in the Dark* was a new type of musical play."[191] He obviously equated the quality of his work for Broadway (and for film) with that of his Weimar social-critical operas, which were certainly not at the qualitative level of cheap operetta.

His longtime collaborator in epic theater, Bertolt Brecht, clearly saw this similarly when he attempted to rekindle his professional relationship with Weill upon moving to America in the summer of 1941. Weill was tempted to renew the partnership, at one time contemplating an Afro-American version of *Die Dreigroschenoper* in which Paul Robeson was to have performed. But, in addition to problems with Robeson, the scheme foundered on the shoals of past bad memories and continued mistrust, for the crafty Brecht, as Weill suspected, was up to "his old tricks again."[192]

Weill was remarkably consistent in his long-term musical development, which was not interrupted but rather continued in America, on the basis of past European experience. Accordingly, Weill kept as his social and professional company artists of the sort he had worked with back in Germany and France, first and foremost Lotte Lenya, his once and future wife and mistress, who understood the rhythm of his life; after divorcing in Berlin, they maintained an on-and-off relationship, remarrying in 1937.[193]

Weill's European perspective did not prevent him from standing behind America's war effort, which he wanted to fortify culturally.[194] Moreover, he invested much energy in his sense of Jewishness, therein paralleling Schoenberg. Yet, unlike the Viennese composer, he spurned the pen, delivering his message solely through music. In his youth Weill had been blasé about his Jewish roots, but he had never left Judaism as Schoenberg had done.[195] Hence, his earnest concern with his religion during the spring of 1934 in France lacked both the militancy and the commitment that had characterized Schoenberg's reconversion a year earlier. The Eternal Road, which was being shaped at that time, was to be a scenic oratorio based on the Old Testament; "Ruth" and "David" were constituent sections, "Isaac's Sacrifice" and "The Dance Around the Golden Calf" leading themes. Franz Werfel had written the text, and Max Reinhardt was in charge of stage direction. Weill had written a song or two for Helene Thimig, Reinhardt's companion. The Reinhardts and Werfel were still living in Austria, safe for the moment, and a production in Europe seemed just as viable as one in America. In the end, the text of this epic musical proved as long and as cumbersome as the production was costly; the work was a failure when it was finally produced in New York in 1937, with resounding financial losses.[196] But this did not dampen Weill's commitment to the Jewish cause. At the height of the Holocaust, in 1943, he was again at work on music for a commemorative demonstration in honor of Hitler's Jewish victims, in which many liturgical themes were employed. The event, mourning the violent death of 2 million Jews, took place in New York City, well attended by a crowd of forty thousand. Weill deemed it "a giant success." The war against Hitler had been over for a year when Weill's specially written "Kiddush" was performed at the Park Avenue Synagogue. At that time the composer had but four years to live.[197]

By all accounts Kurt Weill was a far happier man than Ernst Toch. This composer's American phase encapsulates the many tragedies of a musician's exile more strikingly than any other in the records, exhibiting few of the personal joys and professional highlights of more successful men such as Weill. If anyone could serve as a paradigm for the ultimate futility inherent in endless suffering, Toch might. One of the most profound and also one of the saddest confessions made by any émigré musician about this trying period surely is his: "You lose your old home and do not gain a new one, once you emigrate."[198]

Toch was born in Vienna in 1887, and after World War I came to teach at the conservatory in Mannheim. Having earned a doctorate from nearby Heidelberg in 1921, he lived in Berlin from 1929 to 1933, teaching piano and composition. Toch was considered a brilliantly promising composer of the new school, one who essentially retained the conventional tonal modes, and his compositions—string quartets and other chamber music, an opera, and a piano concerto—were performed at new-music festivals in Prague and Frankfurt to great acclaim. He had already been to the United States several times when he arrived in New York as a refugee in 1935, having been invited there, via Paris and London, to teach at the New School for Social Research.

In England Toch had written the music for the film *Catherine the Great,* and in 1937 he took up George Gershwin's advice to move to Hollywood, where he began composing for grade-B American films. It is said that he did this expertly, but he came to suffer more and more from the intellectual emptiness such labor entailed, growing increasingly despondent as he regarded himself an artistic prostitute. His circle of friends was small, for he preferred the life of a recluse, often hiding with his dog in a cabin made from two huge containers his possessions had arrived in from Germany, which he had deposited on the sands of Malibu. Although Mann met him and appreciated what he had to say, his relationship with Schoenberg was tenuous. One reason for this was that Schoenberg had gotten nowhere with the independently minded Toch when he had tried to enlist his help in Paris, during his 1933 attempt to found a "Jewish Party." Another and more significant reason was that Schoenberg was jealous of Toch's success as a film composer, the bane of Toch's existence, and at least on one occasion Schoenberg surprised his friends when he stayed away from a concert featuring the work of both men, presumably because Toch's works were "getting a little more attention than they ought." Eventually Toch gave up his Hollywood career and became a teacher of composition at the University of Southern California. While he continued to make a living for himself, his wife, and his daughter, he was unhappy for the rest of his stay in America, recognized by few of his peers, neglected by most. Some years before his death in 1964 Toch told the musicologist Nicolas Slonimsky: "I am the most forgotten composer of the twentieth century."[199]

Exiled Non-Jewish Musicians

Jewish musicians felt compelled to emigrate because they feared first for their jobs and then for their lives. Non-Jewish musicians, however, were not nearly as strongly motivated to leave Nazi Germany. Hence, the number of "Aryan" refugees from Hitler's Reich is significantly smaller, in music as in other professions.[200] When in 1938 Erika and Klaus Mann described the case of a non-Jewish physician who left his wife and child behind to go to Shanghai because he saw no alternative, they were citing an atypical incident. Even though they claim that the doctor was driven by political motives, they may have ignored some other factors that could have played an additional, decisive role: perhaps the man was estranged from his wife, or was psychotic.[201] It is not normal for a man of even the noblest convictions to leave his family behind in a situation of uncertainty or danger. What is normal is to stand by one's loved ones and face adversity together.

If the motives of this physician were questionable, neither were those of even the few "Aryan" musicians who became émigrés entirely beyond reproach. The Prussian-born opera singer Lotte Lehmann had a much-publicized altercation with Hermann Göring in 1933 before she ended up at New York's Metropolitan Opera and then on the shores of Southern California, where she became a member of the vaunted circle surrounding Thomas Mann. She may have been genuinely anti-Nazi, refusing ever again to perform in the Reich, but she also was married to a Jewish banker, and when she fled from Berlin to Vienna, were she lived, she allegedly was accompanied by her lover.[202] In 1944 Carl Schuricht finally left the Third Reich for Switzerland, apparently because he could not countenance Hitlerism any longer. But he had served the Nazis for over a decade and had placed his marriage to a Jewish woman in jeopardy. By 1944 one did not need many "political" reasons to move out of Germany, what with the bombs falling on every city and an Allied invasion at hand.[203] With Toscanini's help, Hugo Burghauser, a bassoonist in the Wiener Staatsoper, made it to the United States after the Anschluss, but Burghauser himself was suspect, having been a collaborator with the Austrian authoritarian regime of Dollfuss and Schuschnigg.[204] Even Hans Heinz Stuckenschmidt, the leading modernist music critic, could not retain his intellectual independence till the end. Short-circuited in his career for altruistic reasons in the early years of the regime, he became subject to a journalistic gag order in 1934. He was vehemently attacked by Fritz Stege, an arch-Nazi and rival for the power of the pen, and was shunned by the Reich Culture Chamber. In 1937 he had found work as a music critic in Prague, but by 1940 the occupying Germans had caught up with him again and enlisted his services as a critic in German-controlled Romania. In this capacity Stuckenschmidt permitted himself to bend the truth and, though not loudly, blew the horn of Nazi propaganda. Finally drafted into the Wehrmacht, Stuckenschmidt spent the end of the Third Reich as a prisoner of war in American hands.[205]

One of the best-known non-Jewish musicians to leave Germany early in the regime was Fritz Busch, conductor of the Sächsische Staatsoper in Dresden, an enthusiastic participant in World War I and politically right of center. Both Busch and his wife, Grete, recorded for posterity the dramatic tale of his fundamental opposition to the Nazis as early as the Weimar Republic, describing SA and regional Saxon government machinations to have him dismissed on the evening of 7 March 1933, just as he was about to conduct Verdi's *Rigoletto*. They tell, too, of his subsequent self-imposed exile and continued work in Buenos Aires, Copenhagen, and Glyndebourne.[206]

Without a doubt, from the Nazis' perspective there were several counts against Busch even before January 1933. He was the older brother of Adolf Busch, who in 1925 was hailed as "the greatest German violinist" and who, married to a Jew, had taken up residence near Basel in 1926, making no secret of his dislike for the Nazis and receiving into his household, and later as his son-in-law, a talented young Jewish pianist by the name of Rudolf Serkin.[207] In the Saxon Landtag since the final months of the republic, a large faction of National Socialists, against Fritz Busch's opposition, had wanted to cut the cultural budget affecting the state opera much more severely than he himself thought necessary. Busch was then accused by the Nazis of favoring Jewish friends and artists, of spending too much time as a guest conductor, mainly in Berlin, and of collecting an inordinately high salary along with overly generous vacation time—the latter privileges documented as charged, but contractually granted to him during the republic. A number of personal intrigues against Busch and his family in Dresden were the prelude to his eventual dismissal in early March.[208] This not entirely unexpected turn of events angered not only the Busches but also Richard Strauss, who had planned to have his new opera *Arabella* premiered under Busch in Dresden later that summer, an opera that was dedicated to the conductor but eventually had to be staged under Clemens Krauss.[209]

That Busch was framed for the sake of parochial party politics was clear both to his loyal opera following and to many highly placed Nazis. Members of the opera company were pressured into signing a declaration certifying that "in terms of artistic merits, Busch was wanting." Although most musicians and singers agreed to this or, like coloratura soprano Erna Berger, gave their oral consent because they were out of town, they all knew, as one of them wrote to Strauss, that Busch had always been "very popular with the orchestra."[210] The letter writer also conceded, however, that there may have been some irregularities, minor enough to be easily settled with a minimum of good will on either side.[211] Nazi music publisher Gustav Bosse averred that Busch may have stepped out of line in constantly striving, as was alleged, to get away from mere opera work and seek more concert performances, especially in Berlin. Nevertheless, Bosse deplored the fact that an artist of Busch's caliber had been "smeared in this fashion."[212]

Bosse certainly did not see through the cabal that had spawned this affair. Behind the scenes a link was being forged between Busch and Göring, who, under the influence of his mistress Emmy Sonnemann and Tietjen, was interested in attracting the conductor to Berlin. As a very personable young actress, Sonnemann had been a friend of the Busches during their years in Stuttgart, and when Busch had moved to Dresden in 1922 and Sonnemann to nearby Weimar, the friendship had not lapsed,

Sonnemann taking her "chap," the stunt flyer and businessman Hermann Göring, to Dresden with her to meet the Busches socially on at least one occasion prior to Hitler's takeover. Before the disaster of 7 March she had telephoned Busch from Berlin that Göring, then acting Prussian minister of the interior and designated minister-president, was very interested in securing for the conductor a major position in the capital, and Hitler, who admitted as late as 1942 that, after Krauss and Furtwängler, Busch "would have become the best German conductor," seems to have been in favor, so long as his patronage of Furtwängler was not disturbed.[213]

In the weeks following the Dresden debacle Busch saw Göring in Berlin at least three times, with Göring evidently holding out hope that the conductor might be able to assume the directorship of the Preussische Staatsoper, which the future Prussian premier was hoping to control. The available sources suggest there is every reason to assume that Busch would have been delighted to accept this post and would not have left Germany at all. But Furtwängler stood in the way (he would rather have seen Busch in Hamburg or as Bruno Walter's successor in Leipzig), and he had the backing of Hitler, against whom Göring, in the final analysis, could not act. The Führer himself tried his best, through personal intervention, to change his Saxon deputies' minds about Busch, but he got nowhere: additional proof of the imperfect chain-of-command structures in the Nazi gubernatorial fabric at that time, certainly insofar as culture was concerned. An alternative solution, for the 1924 Bayreuth veteran Busch to assume the musical directorship of the festival instead of the pesky Toscanini, did not suit Busch's current plans, and besides, he had already been approached by the Nazis to do some publicity work for them in South America.[214]

In their separate memoirs the Busches allege that the cable inviting Busch to stage a German opera season at the Teatro Colón in Buenos Aires came as a godsend just as he was being forced to surrender his Dresden post.[215] This is an outright fabrication, for although he had been asked to come to Argentina in the 1920s, this particular invitation had been rigged with the help of Reich authorities after Busch had repeatedly consulted with Hans Hinkel. Hinkel was then also still employed by Göring, and there is every reason to believe that the future minister-president used this opportunity to save face in the matter. The plan was for Busch, in the company of other German artists, including ostracized Jews, to give several performances in Buenos Aires to promote the Nazi regime there, for such a controversial company of artists, including known regime opponents, officially sponsored by the German government, would suggest to the Argentinians a much larger degree of Nazi tolerance than actually existed. Whether he knew it or not, on his tour to South America, which lasted until late 1933, Busch was constantly watched by a specially assigned Nazi stooge.[216]

Archival documents suggest that after his return from the Argentinian capital, Busch hoped to be rewarded with the coveted post in Berlin.[217]

But since that did not happen, he had to content himself with European offers, repeated tours of South America, and private visits to his brother Adolf's residence near Basel. By 1934 his assumption of the musical directorship of the Glyndebourne opera company in England turned out to be a prestigious if not a lucrative venture; Busch earned his principal income at the Metropolitan Opera in New York, in Buenos Aires, and at the Royal Opera in Copenhagen. Having failed to obtain Swiss citizenship, even with the help of Thomas Mann, who was a close friend of his brother, he took out Argentinian papers in 1936. Until the outbreak of the war Busch received numerous offers from the Germans to conduct in the Reich, but as a political exile, supported by his U.S.-resident brother Adolf and his family, he spurned them. Busch worked first in Denmark, then in Sweden; in 1941, in the most definitive move of his career since 1932, he left for Argentina via Russia and the United States.[218]

When Fritz and Grete Busch returned to Buenos Aires in 1941, he took over as opera director at Teatro Colón from Erich Kleiber, with whom he had already alternated a few times.[219] Busch and Kleiber, both born in 1890, had both reached the highest rung of the conducting ladder around 1923—Busch in Dresden and Kleiber as Generalmusikdirektor at the Preussische Staatsoper in Berlin. Moreover, both had been partial to newer composers such as Hindemith, with Busch the more conservative of the two. Both had a sense of democratic values and unerringly opposed the Nazis, not least because of their anti-Semitic policies. The Danish tenor Helge Rosvaenge later said that Kleiber condemned "the silencing of famous Jewish composers, such as Meyerbeer, Mendelssohn, Mahler, and Offenbach."[220]

Yet beyond those striking similarities there were significant differences. Whereas Busch was a hardy blond Westphalian somewhat resembling Knappertsbusch, though more stockily built, Kleiber was a bald, diminutive Viennese, more flexible in interpersonal relations and perhaps more intuitive in his musical interpretations. Kleiber was more seriously committed to modernism, to the extent that conservative composers such as Hans Pfitzner declared that they were no friends of his. But Kleiber could hardly have cared less, for his distinct favorite was a fellow Viennese, Schoenberg's master pupil Alban Berg. This had led him again to conduct Berg's *Wozzeck* at the Berlin Staatsoper in 1932 (he had also conducted its premiere there in 1925), and this, along with the earlier introduction of the French Jew Darius Milhaud's *Christophe Colombe* in 1930, had brought down the wrath of the Nazis upon him. Early in 1933 Kleiber, whose name was persistently if mistakenly assumed to be Jewish, was denounced by Theo König, a Berlin opera musician, for dismissing him and certain of his colleagues, all of them Nazi Party members. The dismissal had merely been one of the routine measures of necessity being taken everywhere in Germany on account of the economic depression.[221]

Obviously Kleiber, like Fritz Busch, did not go out of his way to please the new rulers, but unlike Busch, he resigned his position on his own accord after presenting works that were anathema to the Nazis, and he could not be kept in Germany for love or money. The occasion was, predictably, the premiere of a composition by Berg. The Viennese composer, though not Jewish, had been placed on the Nazi index along with the other members of the so-called Second Vienna School, Arnold Schoenberg and Anton Webern. This was a terrible blow to Berg, for he was suffering financially and needed profitable performances of his music in the Reich, what with the authoritarian Austrian cultural bureaucracy (supported by Bruno Walter) spurning his avant-garde works. And so, constantly protesting his racial "Aryanism," Berg kept imploring his friend Kleiber to promote him. In particular, he wanted Kleiber to stage his new opera Lulu, with his own libretto based on two controversial plays by the pre-expressionist writer Frank Wedekind, a risqué plot involving a femme fatale, a sex-crazed physician, a lesbian countess, and Jack the Ripper—the sort of thing the Nazi censors would instantaneously brand as degenerate art. The immediate judgment of Furtwängler, Kleiber's senior colleague, was one of discouragement, yet Kleiber chose to push ahead with the venture. He knew that although many Nazis disliked him, the leading politicians were increasingly dependent on him as a non-Jew, internationally capable of upholding the musical culture of the Reich at least as well as the ostracized Walters and Klemperers would have done. In fact, Kleiber had been mentioned as a possible successor to Busch in Dresden; Strauss, Tietjen, and Göring thought the world of him.[222]

For the sake of his own success, Berg was somewhat apprehensive about the fact that Kleiber was not a Nazi Party member, yet the conductor knew about the obstacles in the way of an opera such as Berg's, which, in any event, was still unfinished (and was to remain so). Therefore, with the acquiescence of Göring, Kleiber settled for orchestral excerpts from the opera score, the so-called Fünf symphonische Stücke aus Lulu für den Konzertgebrauch, which was premiered at the Berlin Staatsoper on 30 November 1934. It turned out to be written in the twelve-tone style. The critics were divided, with even some Nazis among them having to cede partial credit to Berg. Although Alfred Burgartz thought that the work was lacking in substance, characterizing Berg's melodic lines as "nothing but a nervous commotion," he had to applaud the composer's "subtle ear for harmony, his masterful handling of artistic style, his instrumentation akin to the highest art." Nevertheless, the old prejudices still obtained, with the American ambassador William Dodd again mistaking Kleiber for "a Hebrew" and Alban Berg, too, for a Jew.[223]

After the concert, amid jeers and bravos, someone shouted "Heil Mozart!" Kleiber called back: "You are mistaken: the piece was by Alban Berg!" The conductor took the entire incident as a sign of worse things to come. He resigned his post with the Preussische Staatsoper four days later, although for contractual reasons his last concerts in Berlin were required to take place in early January 1935. He told his Berlin superiors that he felt constrained under the Nazi regime, unable to carry on with his work. His resolve to take leave of Berlin was coterminous with the Hindemith–Furtwängler affair, resulting in Furtwängler's own retreat from his regular employment as director of the Staatsoper and Hindemith's continual fall from grace as a composer and professor at the Berlin Hochschule für Musik.[224]

Göring and Tietjen both made overtures to Kleiber in an effort to change his mind, but the conductor remained firm and began what turned out to be a lengthy vagabond journey through Europe and South America. Still an Austrian, the citizen of a country that did not want him before or after March 1938, Kleiber settled permanently in Buenos Aires in 1939 and became an Argentinian citizen like his German colleague Fritz Busch. In contrast to Busch, however, he made a very strong impression as an antifascist from 1933 on, a conviction he articulated for the last time on European soil when he refused to direct *Fidelio* at Milan's La Scala during the 1938–39 season after learning that, owing to the Fascist-directed onslaught of anti-Semitism, Italian Jews were not to be admitted to the theater.[225]

The case of the Austrian Ernst Křenek, composer of the sensational opera *Jonny spielt auf* of 1927, was somewhat special. He never actually had contact with the Nazis, since after working in Kassel and Wiesbaden he had returned to his native Vienna in 1928, and after January 1933 avoided the Reich. But for National Socialists everywhere *Jonny* remained the epitome of the Weimar gutter culture they so despised, and they kept referring to him as "that Jew" or "Jew bastard" Křenek, although he was of undeniably "Aryan" lineage, even though his first wife, Anna, whom he divorced in 1929, was the daughter of Gustav Mahler. Like Schoenberg, Hindemith, and Weill, Křenek figured in the Nazis' exhibition of "degenerate" music in the spring of 1938 at Düsseldorf, and had the composer not steered clear of Germany between 1933 and 1938, his safety might have been at risk. Of course, had he remained in Austria after the Anschluss, he would certainly have been persecuted.[226]

Hence, he is a proper subject for inclusion in this study. Křenek, like his Austrian modernist compatriots Webern and Berg, fell into dire economic straits primarily because all of his works were under attack in Nazi Germany (and were not being played much anywhere else in Europe). In addition, he was being harassed by Austrian Nazis in Vienna. His idea for a twelve-tone opera, *Karl V.*, which he planned to mount in collaboration with Clemens Krauss, had been scuttled because of intrigues by Austrian Nazis, who thought the work degenerate. Yet, unlike Krauss, Křenek did not oppose the authoritarian Viennese regimes of Dollfuss and Schuschnigg but rather accommodated himself, certainly to Dollfuss, in the hope of a Catholic restoration and a neocorporatist system of state and society based upon it. Hindered in his musical activities, he turned more and more to text writing, and by 1934 had placed his publicity value in the service of the Fatherland Front of Engelbert Dollfuss.[227]

Although Křenek, like Walter and others, developed a certain predilection for Fascist Italy, where he was attracted "to the way in which modern art was treated by the Italian state"—a clear reference to the success of modernist music there—he soon realized that his own artistic progressivism and the reactionary political goals of the Austrian regime were irreconcilable. As one of his biographers has observed, he saw that in Austria "the same artists remained pushed back to the wall who were also defamed in the Third Reich." By 1936 it was clear to him that Chancellor Schuschnigg would not be able to ward off the aggressive advances of Hitler much longer, and this and the realization that he was getting nowhere economically prompted his decision to emigrate.[228]

Křenek traveled to the United States in 1937 on a cross-country tour with an obscure company called the Salzburg Opera Guild, ostensibly to perform and lecture, but in reality to check out conditions with a view to a permanent move. America was actually an unlikely home for him, since *Jonny*, the only work of his that was known there by name, had failed in 1929. Furthermore, as the example of Schoenberg already showed, twelve-tone music was either unheard of or terribly suspect. Křenek also had an aversion to English and initially refused to learn it. He hated American food, subsisting mainly on orange juice, cigarettes, and whiskey. On top of all that, the organization of the tour was not to his satisfaction. On this trip, which took him from New York to San Francisco, he lectured on atonality and played his own new Piano Suite and Schoenberg's *Sechs Kleine Klavier-Stücke* (1911). There were some enthusiasts, recorded Erika and Klaus Mann, "but the rest of the audience remained politely cool." Křenek, however, had friends in America: Hans Heinsheimer, formerly of Vienna Universal Edition music publishers, now ensconced in New York; Roger Sessions, who was teaching at Princeton; and Schoenberg in Los Angeles. They arranged future recitals for him, introduced him to radio, and kept an eye out for a teaching position. Somehow Křenek came to like the country, especially California.[229]

Křenek returned to Europe in February 1938, a crucial time for his native Austria. Having just renewed his Austrian passport at the consulate in New York, he did not dare enter Vienna again, but instead worked on emigrating to America from Holland and England. September saw him back in the States. Once again his friends toiled on his behalf, and later in the year, with the help of Heinsheimer and Koussevitzky, Křenek played his aggressively atonal piano concerto in Boston. Heinsheimer was sitting next to an elderly lady who "joined in the polite applause and then looked at the program. After a while she turned to her husband and said: 'Conditions in Europe must be dreadful!'" In 1939 Křenek taught summer school at the University of Michigan and wrote a surprisingly positive report about his unspoiled students to Schoenberg. He believed that not they but the "so-called experts" would make trouble.[230] Indeed, after he had started teaching at Vassar College in September 1939, he chanced upon an article by a colleague who maintained that central European twelve-tone composers now in America only pretended to be refugees from fascism; in reality Hitler had sent them over in order to corrupt American youth through their teaching.[231]

Conditions improved for Křenek after his suspicious Vassar colleagues had him fired in 1942 and he was able to assume the directorship of the music program at Hamline University in St. Paul—not an illustrious institution, but Křenek had the moral support of the admiring conductor Dimitri Mitropoulos, who was based across the river in Minneapolis. In 1947, aged forty-seven, and after excruciatingly hard work as a college teacher, Křenek finally was able to join his old friends in Los Angeles, where he kept himself busy as a guest lecturer and writer. As in the case of Schoenberg, his move to America had taken a heavy toll on his creativity as a composer.[232]

In the early 1920s Křenek's modernism was supported by the conductor Hermann Scherchen, who was nine years his senior. Scherchen premiered Křenek's first symphony at Frankfurt in December 1922, and a year later he presented the composer's Piano Concerto no. 1 in Winterthur, a small town in Switzerland where Scherchen had taken the position of music director of its centuries-old Musikkollegium.[233] Scherchen subsequently made a name for himself as the foremost champion of modernism in Germany, one of his main feats being the cofounding of the avant-garde music journal Melos, which he served as its first, trendsetting editor in 1920. Among modernists in German music, both aspiring and established, Scherchen soon was a power to be reckoned with. In 1919 the nineteen-year-old Kurt Weill had considered Scherchen's advice to look up Arnold Schoenberg in Vienna, and Weill was enchanted to learn in 1930 that Scherchen had been asked by a Munich theater to mount his Aufstieg und Fall der Stadt Mahagonny, although this production never materialized.[234] Scherchen, who was known for his objective approach to conducting as well as his pedagogic intensity, enjoyed vast prestige not only among comrades on the modernist front such as Schoenberg, Hindemith, and Orff, but also with established icons such as Hans Pfitzner, who seriously asked him as early as 1920—touching in such a dyed-in-the-wool conservative—to explain the compositions of Schoenberg to him.[235]

What set the conductor apart from most other modernists was that he stood unabashedly on the political left and was universally regarded as a great friend of the Soviet Union, although he never joined the German Communist Party. Scherchen did not think it contradictory to introduce one of the signature songs of the Russian Revolution to a Berlin audience in 1920 and to give the first German performance in Frankfurt of Stravinsky's Histoire du soldat, the celebrated work of an exile from Bolshevism. This early admirer of Dimitri Shostakovich made it his business to visit the Soviet Union on several concert tours throughout the Weimar Republic, although later, hard-core Stalinists shunned him.[236]

By virtue of his modernism and his socialist proclivities, Scherchen was an early natural foe of anything vaguely associated with National Socialism, and was recognized as such by the Nazis. His Swiss platform in Winterthur served him in good stead when the time came for him to avoid Germany permanently for fear of being arrested. One of his last German posts (his Swiss appointment had always been untenured) had been as Generalmusikdirektor with the Königsberg Radio Orchestra under its Jewish intendant Hans Flesch, who was related by marriage to Hindemith. All this early personal history the Nazis used in 1933 to brand Scherchen a "darling of Marxists and Jews," characterizing his influence as "poisonous."[237] From his precarious base in Winterthur, Scherchen embarked on a peripatetic journey throughout non-German Europe, always in the vanguard of modern musical developments, which took him to avant-garde festivals in Strasbourg (August 1933), Florence (April 1934), Prague (September 1935), and Barcelona (April 1936). Most of these were organized by the antifascist International Society for Contemporary Music, which prized new compositions, and which Scherchen sometimes served as a juror. One of his more remarkable accomplishments during the early years of Hitler's rule was to assemble an orchestra of unemployed musicians in Vienna, many of them Jews who were themselves discriminated against by anti-Semitic forces within Schuschnigg's circle, until March 1938. Scherchen honed this ensemble to perfection, so that it was admired even by the conservative Bruno Walter. Until the war the conductor's various guest appearances took him as far afield as Moscow, Jerusalem, and London.[238] During the war, however, Scherchen remained more or less permanently moored in Switzerland.[239]

Whether or not Scherchen was typical of non-Jewish émigré artists fleeing Hitler may well be debatable, yet even in light of the available evidence, two particular observations are of interest. First, for all his prodigious activity, he was in constant financial straits, although he was patronized by Werner Reinhart, a wealthy burgher of Winterthur. The reason seems to have been twofold, in that he had to pay alimony to a number of women and their numerous children (the unstable Scherchen had no fewer than five wives, outdoing Carl Orff by one), and that he lost money on Ars Nova, a music-publishing firm he had founded in Brussels. Second, as the poet Elias Canetti has scathingly noted, Scherchen was difficult to the point of being capriciously offensive to his friends, although at the same time he could be extremely engaging.[240]

Even before Hitler came to power, tension between Scherchen on the one side and Hindemith and Orff on the other is well documented, but it was the young composer Karl Amadeus Hartmann, whose works Scherchen admired and championed, whom he especially made to suffer for it.[241] Hartmann, who was fourteen years younger than Scherchen, acknowledged before his premature death in 1963 that the conductor had pointed the way for him musically, yet in the same breath Hartmann also spoke of the "vacillations" in Scherchen's character and intellect. Hartmann's widow, Elisabeth, went further when, in 1994, she remarked to me that "it was terrible to see how mean Scherchen could often be."[242]

Some of this is borne out in the preserved correspondence. In 1935–36 Scherchen had fulsome praise for Hartmann, who in his native Munich saw himself pushed into total isolation because he himself could not abide by any of the new Nazi rules of professional comportment. Scherchen seems to have supported Hartmann on ISCM prize committees outside the Reich and expressed interest in premiering the composer's newest work, the chamber opera *Des Simplicius Simplicissimus Jugend*, in the conception of which he had had a strong hand. Hartmann communed with Scherchen at the ISCM festivals in Strasbourg and Prague and visited the conductor in Winterthur.[243] But by mid-1937 things had changed: Scherchen was accusing Hartmann of being dishonest with him, while still holding out the promise of the *Simplicius* premiere. When in 1938 Karl and Elisabeth Hartmann traveled to London to see Scherchen at the ISCM gathering there, the conductor treated both of them in a demeaning manner. London almost led to a parting of the ways for the two men when Scherchen declared a lack of interest in *Simplicius*. But with the outbreak of World War II, Scherchen turned around again, sending friendlier communications to his acolyte. In 1944 the Hungarian composer Sándor Jemnitz, a mutual friend, wrote to Hartmann that Scherchen's fundamentally spiteful attitude seemed to have reversed itself.[244]

Throughout the Third Reich Jemnitz tended to attribute Scherchen's forbidding air to a growing sense of egotism, whereas the Swiss composer Heinrich Sutermeister, as early as 1934, hinted at political motives, since Scherchen seemed to be spurning all of his former German friends.[245] In its very complexity the conductor's case is intriguing, for it may very well be that for all his ostentatious socialism and antifascism, Scherchen was internally torn and plagued by self-doubts. After all, a once world-renowned music pioneer, he was now tucked away in a small provincial Swiss town; there were serious complications in his relationships with women; and economically he was ailing. As Germany was making good strides in the war and Switzerland became an obvious future target, might it not be wise to go back? Indeed, as has recently been revealed, by about 1941 or so there were contacts between Scherchen and Furtwängler, who acted in the role of a messenger from Goebbels, offering to let bygones be bygones if Scherchen returned to an appropriate position in the Reich; the Gewandhaus in Leipzig was mentioned. There is evidence that the conductor considered the offer seriously, but, for reasons known only to Winterthur archivists who will not divulge the information, nothing came of it.[246]

This episode illustrates the tragedy of exile, but it also points to the need for a renewed inquiry into the motivation of several known refugees from Nazi Germany. Whereas by definiton all Jews were enemies of the Third Reich, the same cannot be said in the case of Gentiles who, because of a history of right-wing leanings or an authoritarian personality, might otherwise have arranged a détente with the Third Reich, had a fortuitous combination of circumstances favored their return.

4

Music in the Institutions

Family, School, and Hitler Youth

From the moment it came to power in 1933, the Nazi regime was bent on reviving and coordinating musical practice in conventional institutions such as schools and even the churches as well as the family, which continued to be regarded as the smallest cell in the racially determined body politic. Music was viewed as a convenient form of cement between the rulers and their people. As Joseph Goebbels had long since found out, music possessed vast propagandistic potential through which the collective mood of the subjects could be controlled; it also could be used to dress up important nationalistic incentives for presentation to the public, and it could serve as a vehicle for various regime messages and slogans. Martial songs to be sung in Nazi formations, by the SS, or by the Wehrmacht in war were one striking example; another was the secular cantata of the kind that Bruno Stürmer might try his hand at, specifically composed to honor the Führer on his birthday, during specially tailored National Socialist ceremonies.

Starting at the lowest echelon of communal living, the primary social unit of the family, the medium to effect this musical bonding was *Hausmusik*, that is, music performed in one's own house or home. The term *Hausmusik* was not an invention of the Nazis, nor of course was the

130

actual article, but it had never before been politicized to the extent that they would attempt. Chamber-style music had been played in the home by moderately well trained lay musicians throughout the eighteenth and most of the nineteenth century. This was a time when the creations of composers such as Johann Nepomuk Hummel and Beethoven were popularized, musical instruments were becoming cheaper and more accessible, and sheet music could be supplied by music publishers, purchased by the public, and studied at home. To own a piano and be able to show off at least one accomplished family member, usually an adolescent daughter performing standard pieces, became one of the hallmarks of the German bourgeoisie which thrived on *Bildung*, as indeed many Germans came to believe more and more that it was really they who had invented and now owned the Western musical tradition. Such hubris was nourished by composers of the stature of Richard Wagner, who once said: "The German has the exclusive right to be called 'musician.'"[1]

Hausmusik fell into decline toward the end of the nineteenth century because of a growing public obsession with concert hall virtuosity. This decline was exacerbated by the rise of the German youth movement at the turn of the century. Young people now wished to be at one with nature, and they scorned bourgeois accoutrements of culture such as pianos, cellos, and flutes. World War I and the Weimar Republic encouraged these developments: wartime was not an appropriate time for *Hausmusik;* and the strong anti–nineteenth-century bias of the 1920s, largely influenced by youth groups, militated against the once-fashionable idea of music in the home, with its traditional connotations of an elite class.[2]

Expediency dictated by postwar economic strictures favored the purchase of cheaply manufactured portable instruments such as recorders and guitars instead of pianos. Early republican youth movement leaders, utilizing the simpler instruments, adapted elements of *Hausmusik* to an outdoor environment and hence continued to strip it of its bourgeois symbolism. Farther down the road, these youth leaders organized the first "Tag der deutschen Hausmusik" in 1932; the emphasis continued to be on group and choral singing as well as on affordable portable instruments suitable for accompanying communal singing, ideally in the outdoors.[3] After January 1933 Nazi music functionaries cleverly enlarged on this idea by holding *Hausmusik* events annually, but not without moving this music, in part at least, back into buildings. Beginning in 1940 these events were held under a special theme inspired by one of the great German composers: in 1940 it was Schubert, in 1941 Mozart, and in 1942 Bach; Max Reger and Brahms dominated national events in 1943 and 1944.[4]

In addition to the general linkage between certain forms of music and political propaganda, there were several specific reasons for the Nazis to favor *Hausmusik* in changing contexts over the years. The most immediate one was economic, tied to an early Nazi Party election platform accommodating small and medium-sized businesses.[5] Because of the mainstream youth movement and other forces during the Weimar Republic, as well as the deteriorating economic conditions toward the republic's end, instrument manufacturers and to some degree music publishing firms had suffered and, by the time of Hitler's takeover, needed regeneration. This applied particularly to the piano industry (here one is reminded of Hitler's early friendship with the Bechstein family). Pianos had lost popularity, a process that was exacerbated by the advent of the sound film which obviated the need for pit orchestras in cinemas, where pianos had been ubiquitous. At one point hundreds of discarded pianos were offered as firewood. Only used instruments were being purchased by consumers, if at all, and piano manufacturers and dealers were near bankruptcy.[6] Significantly, early on in the regime instrument and music-publishing lobbies assisted in staging Hausmusik competitions, and Hans Edler, a violin maker from Munich, donated one of his better instruments as an official prize.[7]

Another related factor was that many private music educators had been idle for years, since families could no longer afford to have their offspring trained, and instruments to teach them on were unaffordable. Whatever music instruction there had been during the republic the youth movement had taken care of free of charge, and in Prussia, Leo Kestenberg's cultural reforms had assigned a large part of music education to the public school system. Hence, not surprisingly, private music instructors also rallied behind the new Hausmusik initiative. Contingent on that were expectations that musicians as a profession—most of them solidly middle class, who had long suffered both economically and in terms of lost social prestige—were to be elevated to new occupational heights.[8]

The third reason for the Nazis' espousal of Hausmusik had to do with archaic impulses that resisted certain aspects of modernity such as advanced technology, which many equated with American culture, in this case in the area of radio and the recording industry. Hausmusik was said to be threatened by mechanically reproduced music, on records and over the airwaves, because the relative perfection of the latter would discourage more modest personal efforts.[9] As much as Goebbels, for his propaganda purposes, was aware of the uses of the modern electronic media (here paralleling the Führer's own interest in fast cars and airplanes), there was a substantial faction of "Blood-and-Soil" purists rooted in the Nazi Party who condemned what they saw as symptoms of false, merely mechanical progress.[10] Not surprisingly, Goebbels's old adversary Alfred Rosenberg was in the forefront here. Through original Kampfbund connections, antitechnical notions took hold in the realm of culture, at least until the advent of World War II.[11]

This theme of the human versus the mechanical—which at the time was paralleled by similar trends in other areas of human endeavor, such as medicine—precipitated a character factor that was easily exploitable for totalitarian purposes: that is, proponents of Hausmusik idealized the lay element inherent in it, insisting that Hausmusiker should develop only limited instrumental skills, noticeably short of professional perfection.

The deeper reason here was to keep the lay players at a level of semiac-complishment that would leave them susceptible to manipulation from above, not only of the musical-technical kind but also ideologically, as *Hausmusik* became a quasi-political duty. In accepting his amateur sta-tus, the home musician, by implication, acceded to the need to be molded; and since *Hausmusik* now had a strong political slant, such molding could legitimately take place through political channels. In *Hausmusik* no single performer excelled; it was the collective group that counted, and this was but a mirror of the larger concept of gemeinschaft. In the final analysis, *Hausmusik* constituted a depersonalizing apparatus that served well the overall aims of the *Volksgemeinschaft,* especially since the most malleable citizens were expected to take part in it: boys and girls, as well as mothers of young children. Not every member of the people's commu-nity was credited with having the minimum requisite talent, but almost everyone was urged to participate.[12]

There was an additional, aesthetic motive, in that undesirable music could be more easily contained and desirable music introduced. To the first category belonged all manner of "Jewish" compositions, whether simple pieces composed by Mendelssohn or the detested jazz. Among the second were compositions by newer German composers who had gained the regime's favor, such as Bruno Stürmer and Ernst Pepping, who com-posed for the sometimes lucrative *Hausmusik* functions. This was a chance for the regime leaders to demonstrate to the public what sort of music they preferred them to engage in, once a minimal consensus on that question had been reached.[13]

The family was widely acclaimed at the archetypal vessel for *Haus-musik,* for in the organicist view of National Socialism it was a kind of preschool for Nazi life, before and while Nazi organizations such as the Hitler Youth and later the party, SA, SS, and Wehrmacht took over. The family was supposed to provide the individual the first chance to learn how to subject himself to the larger goal of the community. Nobody subscribed to this idea with greater conviction than RMK president Peter Raabe. In 1936 he spoke of the sacrifices individuals would have to incur as members of their families. In 1941 he even said that "the systematic eradication of the family would logically lead to the loss of individual *völkisch* life and consequently to a general cultural decay."[14]

But in reality, the family never served in that prescribed National So-cialist role; it continued its time-honored functions, which often enough placed it in opposition to overarching rival Nazi organizations such as the Hitler Youth.[15] Hence, the call of leading Nazis at the beginning of the regime for *Hausmusik* to be performed within the family circle remained largely unheeded, as Nazi celebrations in private homes were the excep-tion rather than the rule.[16] In 1938 one Nazi spokesman openly dis-counted the family as a carrier of *Hausmusik,* instead praising what the Hitler Youth had done for the genre thus far.[17]

Indeed, it was true that whereas the *Hausmusik* movement was, in organizational terms, taken under the wing of the Reich Music Chamber as one of its sections, important events were almost always staged in a Hitler Youth context and, to a lesser degree, the schools.[18] *Hausmusik* being a peculiarly Nazi phenomenon after 1933 and by its nature ideally suited to serve the character-building aims of the Hitler Youth, it was the Nazi Youth leaders who soon longed to monopolize it, to the detriment of the schools, with which they were engaged in a permanent rivalry.[19]

With the outbreak of war in 1939, public and official interest in *Hausmusik* subsided temporarily, for two primary reasons. First, some of the original aims of the *Hausmusik* movement had been fulfilled, such as alleviating the plight of the music industry and propagandizing the value of the family, for whatever that had been worth. Second, the main proponents of the movement—mostly young men from the schools, the Hitler Youth, and the conservatories—were now in the trenches.[20] But *Hausmusik* had proved valuable as a propaganda tool in the recent past. Hence, it took the regime leaders only a few months to revive it, albeit in a somewhat different form. Although the RMK and Hitler Youth remained its leading champions, other Nazi organizations now also joined in the organizing and staffing of the events, and in coopting audiences for numerous contests, notably Strength-through-Joy and Nazi women's groups, representatives of the SS, and party Gau (the largest regional) administrations acting as sponsors.[21] If anything, the mandate of *Hausmusik* to exert a totalitarian influence on its contestants was solidified, with the war providing a higher purpose and Wehrmacht soldiers serving as allegedly eager listeners.[22] More and more, *Hausmusik* lost its outwardly amateur character as professional musicians exploited the events to peddle their own artistic wares.[23] Thus, in some respects it became merely another commercial platform, albeit one highly sanctioned by the state.

The low profile of *Hausmusik* in the nation's classrooms was symptomatic of the inferior position of the teaching and practice of music in both the lower and upper schools of the Third Reich. Although music was looked upon as a basic instrument for molding National Socialist youth, it simply did not find the proper platform to achieve this purpose within the conventional school system. Compared to purely party institutions such as the Hitler Youth and the Reich Labor Service, the schools tended to lag behind as shapers of Nazi men and women in almost every respect. Their administration was still largely conventional, not revolutionary; typically Nazi reforms did not set in until comparatively late, and often they were timid.

The reform measures in music education were a case in point; the first came only in 1938, five years after the "revolution" and just one year before the war, which would reintroduce inertia. Music instruction was traditionally a secondary subject, ranking with "technical" courses such as drawing, art appreciation, and sewing, and not many hours were set aside for it. Qualified music teachers were rare even in the secondary schools; in the first years of the regime mostly lower-school teachers were used to instruct in these Gymnasia until a new breed of Nazi-trained upper-school music teachers could be hired. That new training was slow to produce results, however, and the lower-school teachers were not specialists, for in the primary schools they had had to teach everything from the three R's to sports. Although there were ambitious programs on the drawing boards for music education at both levels, the actual instruction remained limited, consisting chiefly of communal singing on the model of the *Volkslied,* very basic theory lessons, and rudimentary music appreciation. Only minimal instrumental skills were taught, such as guitar accompaniment to choral singing; rarely, in some upper schools, violin; and playing on out-of-tune pianos. Schools, under the Reich Education Ministry rather than the Reich Music Chamber, were strictly for educating passive listeners, not for turning out accomplished instrumentalists, as RMK president Raabe noted in 1936. As a countermodel he may well have had in mind the Hitler Youth which was rivaling the schools in so many of the fresh, bold National Socialist initiatives, and early on in the regime had taken the lead in helping to mold a new type of German, well versed in the Nazi-defined arts, the new style of communal, physical, and political deportment, and some martial arts.[24]

In the early years of the regime Hitler Youth training was already the chosen alternative to public school education. In addition to the classical disciplines of conventional instruction such as mathematics and languages, this training included dynamic character-molding subjects such as physical education and the arts, in particular music. Given the devastating spectacle of uniformed Hitler Youth supervising the humiliation of Vienna after the Anschluss in March 1938, when elderly Jews were forced to clean the city's sidewalks with toothbrushes, one wonders what music had to do with that. But, of course, music was said to be a racial matter, reflecting the positive properties of a superior race and the negative properties of an inferior one, as the Jews were held to be. Also, many Nazi elders believed that artistic endeavors and political awareness were not incongruous but were eminently reconcilable within the National Socialist persona. Indeed, even the martial ideal fit in here, for "the soldier and the artist are not opposites, but are blended in a harmonious union to produce the leader. Spiritual depth and physical power: these two qualities render Germany invincible."[25] Hence, the Hitler Youth leadership embarked early on the artistic education of its charges, which for its purposes was also always ideological. In particular, it commenced "systematic music instruction."[26]

The aim of the Hitler Youth was twofold: to utilize music, with its ideological and character-building potential, within its ranks in order to raise better leaders, and to infiltrate the existing music establishment with a view to planting its representatives there and bending existing standards to suit its own revolutionary needs. As the head of the Reich Youth Leadership, Baldur von Schirach, said in June 1939, he wanted to assume total responsibility for orchestra recruitment by testing the talents of his young followers and sifting out the most gifted.[27] In terms of sheer numbers, this aim stood a good chance of succeeding; by December 1935, even though enlisting in the Hitler Youth was not yet compulsory, it had coopted almost half of all teenagers in the Reich. In March 1939 membership was made obligatory for young people between the ages of ten and eighteen, twenty being the cutoff age for girls.[28]

As a first step the Reich Youth Leadership founded music schools and conservatories specifically for the Hitler Youth after music lessons had been declared an integral part of Hitler Youth service in 1937.[29] They were augmented with music training camps and rallies periodically organized throughout the Reich.[30] These institutions were dynamic and unconventional, attracting not only potential leaders but also young men and women already engaged in youth education and Nazi social work, such as kindergarten and public school teachers, private music teachers, and even future professional musicians. The classroom emphasis was on pedagogy and craftsmanship in music, instrumental as well as vocal, and much attention was paid to "rhythmic education." The schools were regionally dispersed and administered within a specially created music section in the Hitler Youth Leadership, which, after 1934, was under the care of former music student Wolfgang Stumme. There were thirty-five of these schools in 1939, and many more at the height of the war. In 1943, for example, the Musikschule of the Hitler Youth command in southeast Austrian Carinthia was instituted; after four years of training and a final examination, its graduates received a special Hitler Youth diploma as professional musicians.[31]

In 1940 Schirach moved to Vienna to act as regional Gauleiter. His replacement as head of the Hitler Youth was Artur Axmann. To all intents and purposes, the organization's ideology and policy were continued. Schirach's ideal of a monopoly over orchestral training in the Reich was advanced when in 1941 special Hitler Youth orchestra schools were created for boys between fourteen and eighteen, which concentrated solely on orchestral music education. These schools took the place of state colleges originally planned by the Reich Education Ministry, but which, for lack of initiative on the part of the often alcoholic Minister Bernhard Rust, had never progressed beyond the planning stage. The pupils at these schools all had to be incorporated into the Hitler Youth and were supervised by full-time Hitler Youth leaders. They wore uniforms, had to engage in sports and paramilitary exercises, and, in addition to learning their craft, had to serve in regional Hitler Youth functions, as did their teachers. The Reich Education Ministry assisted in recruiting candidates for these institutions at all levels of public schooling. Potentially this meant that in ten to fifteen years all the major culture orchestras of the Reich would be staffed with former Hitler Youth, who would, after continued political conditioning, then all presumably be members of the party, the SA, or the SS.[32]

Apart from instituting its own non–university-level academies, the Hitler Youth got to be very good at infiltrating existing conservatories and universities, and even created rival institutions. In 1944 there existed in the greater German Reich, including the Sudetenland, fourteen degree-granting conservatories, all of which were under at least partial Hitler Youth influence, and three of which—in Berlin, Weimar, and Graz—possessed facilities especially dedicated to qualifying "music educators of the Hitler Youth."[33] The Akademie für Kirchen- und Schulmusik in Berlin (later termed Hochschule für Musikerziehung)[34] had started its regular Hitler Youth course of studies in 1936, Weimar's Hochschule für Musik followed in 1937, and the Graz Hochschule für Musikerziehung in 1939–40. By 1942 the full range of programs at these institutions took three years to complete; they could also be taken in combination with other, conventional curricula offered there. These conservatories picked up where the nonacademic Hitler Youth orchestra schools left off; one had to be eighteen (seventeen in the case of women) to become a conservatory student.[35]

In Berlin, Stumme himself served as an adjunct lecturer from 1934, specializing in courses such as "Music in the Hitler Youth" and later "Festivals of the Year."[36] Weimar retained the services of the young and enthusiastic Wilhelm Twittenhoff, who in the early 1930s had trained with Carl Orff and worked on his Munich *Schulwerk* project.[37] In terms of serving Hitler Youth needs, the Mozarteum in Salzburg was not quite as prominent as the institutions in Berlin, Weimar, and Graz, but eventually it had as its director the noted Berlin musicologist Eberhard Preussner and as its president Clemens Krauss, and by 1940 its Hitler Youth music instructors included the promising Nazi composer Cesar Bresgen and the former youth movement music pioneer Fritz Jöde. Helmut Bräutigam, one of the most dedicated of Hitler Youth composers, was invited for recitals there, until he fell at the eastern front.[38] In the Hitler Youth sphere of these conservatories all the conventional music subjects were taught, with a strong emphasis on the didactic, but the largely ideological courses are noteworthy: "German Musicology" was to impart all the newly contrived pseudo-science regarding German versus Jewish music; Stumme's "Festivals of the Year" course covered mostly Nazi political holidays; "Border-Territorial Incursions" alluded to colonialist ventures into areas to be forcefully Germanized, such as western Poland and Alsace. Female students were offered "Culture Work in the BDM" (the Bund Deutscher Mädel, or League of German Girls, was the female wing of the Hitler Youth); and there were courses in "Schooling in Weltanschauung" and "Commando Action in Leadership Schools and Formations."[39]

The model for all the higher schools of music education in the Hitler Youth was the institution at Graz in southeast Austria. Founded as an associate school of the long-existing Graz Conservatory in 1939, this Hitler Youth music training center in scenic Eggenberg Castle was fully functional by 1940. This elite conservatory prided itself on the constant readiness of its faculty to serve other National Socialist organizations, such as the Nazi Student League, Reich propaganda offices, and the Reich Music Chamber.[40]

Graz had on its staff Ludwig Kelbetz, once, in the regimes of Dollfuss and Schuschnigg, an illegal Austrian Nazi youth leader and Hitler Youth songwriter, who, like Bräutigam, in 1943 was to pay for his fascist beliefs with his life at the front. Music theory was taught by Kelbetz's close friend Karl Marx, born in Munich in 1897 and a former student of Orff, who remained in touch with him throughout the war. At the time of the Nazi takeover in 1933, Marx and Orff had co-directed the Munich Bach-Verein, until it had been usurped by the Kampfbund für deutsche Kultur. After 1939 Marx excelled, like so many of his regime-pleasing colleagues, in the composition of music for the new Nazi ceremonies, such as a cantata to be sung by Hitler's uniformed boys and girls on the occasion of Thanksgiving festivities, which, in the Third Reich, were ideologically tied to the German Blood-and-Soil cult. This composer, who otherwise excelled at compositions for the organ, contributed routinely to songbooks for the Hitler Youth.[41]

Who, then, were the students at these music schools and conservatories, and what were their motives and objectives? In ordinary times they might well have been regular music students aiming for a career in primary or secondary school education or church-music work. Now they could still target these more traditional goals, but careers in the party's manifold organizations were open to them as well, first and foremost the Hitler Youth itself. Others were studying toward a nonmusical profession, such as law, and were using the Hitler Youth music connection as a convenient means of upgrading their political credentials. Yet, no matter what the purpose, to be admitted to any of Hitler Youth courses, whether for a few semesters or an entire degree program, students had to have a certain amount of party or Hitler Youth experience. With such service on record, and in combination with proven musical aptitude, even a modicum of formal schooling could open the gate to one of the party's music-training centers. A modest family background was no obstacle. Not least through the medium of music, then, the Hitler Youth frequently proved to be a vehicle of upward social mobility in the Third Reich.[42]

Spurred on by specially trained music educators, Hitler's khaki-clad teenagers toiled to at least age eighteen, singing and making music throughout the Reich as part of their prescribed curriculum. By 1944 they had grown to include nine hundred separate groups. They played at every conceivable Hitler Youth function, for instance, during rallies, but also undertook special missions abroad, such as to fascist Madrid and to collaborationist youth organizations in occupied Paris in 1944. One of their more pleasurable duties was to regale the Führer at his Berghof retreat. More often than not, they performed the specially composed works of their instructors, such as Karl Marx and Cesar Bresgen, and of dedicated Hitler Youth songwriters such as Erich Lauer and Hans Baumann. It is likely that without the Third Reich and the many Hitler Youth music organizations formed after 1933, hardly anyone would have taken notice of the compositions of most of these older Hitler Youth acolytes. In this way, otherwise nonpolitical musical events were penetrated by the ideologized music of the Hitler Youth, as was the "Niederbergische Music Festival" in Rhenish Langenberg during May 1936, which featured "songs of our time" sung by a mixed Hitler Youth choir. In addition, the BDM prepared a "morning sing-song," and *Pimpfe*, youth just over ten years old, presented the songs they had memorized for an evening celebration. Some of these music events were highly competitive, with performances and compositions by the various regional groups being rated. Here the aim was to spot the most gifted for further grooming either in the Hitler Youth educational institutions or for *Menschenführung*, the political leadership of men, in Stumme's words the most exalted purpose of the Nazi movement.[43]

The composers Baumann and Lauer, typical figures on the Third Reich cultural scene, already came close to Stumme's ideal. Hans Baumann was the more gifted of the two, capable of both writing lyrics and setting them to music. His work was characterized, in the words of his chief biographer, by a natural feeling for "harmony, grace of style, and a marriage of adolescent enthusiasm with epic political goals." He was "the quintessential songwriter of the Hitler Youth." Of ninety-eight songs in a single Hitler Youth songbook, Baumann had written no fewer than twenty. Nineteen years of age in 1933, this Catholic from a provincial Bavarian town had offered his most famous song, "Today Germany Belongs to Us, and Tomorrow the Whole World," even before the Nazis' rise to power. His Catholicism became submerged as this primary-school teacher embarked on a full-time career in the Hitler Youth in 1934. Ideologically, his mellifluous songs well conditioned Germany's young for the destruction that was to follow, in which he himself took part as a lieutenant of the Wehrmacht.[44]

Three years older and from Baden, Erich Lauer studied music at Heidelberg and joined Hitler's movement in 1930. After 1936 his main posting was as a music consultant in the brownshirted SA. His specialty was less the composition of songs than the creation of entire cantatas and celebratory suites for Nazi ceremonies, in which the Hitler Youth was featured. He too joined the Wehrmacht at the start of the war, participating in the campaigns against Poland and the Western Allies and in the Balkans. He became an expert at compiling songbooks for the Nazi Party and the SA, and his own songs were among the most politicized ever written in the Third Reich.[45]

Significantly, the entire phenomenon of Hitler Youth music organizations originated with radio, where choral or instrumental groups were needed for the enhancement of largely political broadcasts, as well as cultural programs of the Blood-and-Soil type. Radio, of course, was the preeminent fascist tool of propaganda and ideological insemination. Before the war it featured bimonthly "Hours of the Young Nation" during the evening prime time. Here youth leaders received advice on the current goals and methods of youth education; but there were also special programs for young children, strategically broadcast in the afternoon. By 1939 the Hitler Youth was responsible for nearly all the *Volkslied* programming in radio, which under the Nazis was highly politically charged; the secondary aim was to steer the taste of Germany's young away from popular hits, shallow operetta, and jazz. And radio was yet another vehicle for Hitler Youth composers such as Marx, Bresgen, and Armin Knab, who profited handsomely from royalties and directing. It could also serve as a platform to prominence for ambitious musicians such as the eighteen-year-old Wolfgang Sawallisch, who was in charge of a choir of *Pimpfe* at Munich Radio in 1941. Yet within truly artistic circles, the radio-music groups of the Hitler Youth were suspect. When "Radio Group 5" of the Hitler Youth at the Munich station planned a public recital in early 1939, the organizers were aware "that it would be quite a struggle to interest the authoritative music circles of the capital of the movement in attending such a concert."[46]

Certainly the most important task of all the music groups in the Hitler Youth was to help celebrate the new Germanic Nazi festivals, arranged throughout the year by the party. There were two basic cycles. The first of these involved the replacement of traditional Christian ceremonies such as Christmas and Easter with pagan feasts celebrating the seasons, such as summer and winter solstices. Long-popular Christmas carols were to be supplanted by new Nazi hymns such as Baumann's clever "High Night of Clear Stars Above." Protestant and Catholic confirmation ceremonies were to be replaced by special Nazi youth consecrations, marking political rites of passage, in which youths swore a personal oath of allegiance to the Führer. Christian Thanksgiving gave way to pagan peasant feasts. As late as April 1944, Goebbels even entertained hopes of replacing conventional funerals, such as the one for Munich's Gauleiter Adolf Wagner, with new Nazi rituals featuring "temples of honor" instead of the Christian cross.[47] The Nazi regime was clearly intent on eradicating the Christian churches and the traditional values they stood for, even if this was a long and arduous task; and the Hitler Youth, exposing the young to a Nazi rather than a Christian value system, was the ideal conversion agency. It is significant that several composers, such as Marx, Twittenhoff, Armin Knab, and Fritz Büchtger from Munich, all skilled Baroque chamber musicians, for whatever reason were now willing to devote their talent to composing and performing secular instead of sacred cantatas. Moreover, these ceremonies called for an increasing use of the organ.[48] Another boost to this effort was the Hitler Youth's usurpation, for these and other purposes, of the traditional elite boys' choirs, all of which were world-famous for rendering traditional sacred music. With one fell swoop the Thomaner-Chor of Leipzig, the Dresdner Kreuzchor, the Wiener Sängerknaben, and the Regensburger Domspatzen were collectively taken over by the Hitler Youth command, without so much as being asked. Along comparable lines, the Hitler Youth created a Mozart choir in Berlin from its best talents.[49]

The second cycle of Hitler Youth music embraced new political rituals and the Führer cult. Five new Nazi holidays had been created, which were to be celebrated in a fashion attractive to all segments of the population, and here enthusiastic uniformed youths and their music were fundamental. The first of these holidays was the anniversary of the Nazi assumption of power on 30 January. The second was Hitler's birthday on 20 April. The third was 1 May, which as a former socialist memorial day had been refashioned to appeal to all "productive Germans of the mind and the fist." The fourth was the day of the Reich party rally in Nuremberg, usually held in September. And the fifth was 9 November, not only the anniversary of Hitler's 1923 Beer Hall Putsch (during which Nazis were shot dead) but also—even more far-fetched—Remembrance Day in honor of the fallen of World War I. The ninth of November had already become the day on which Hitler Youth graduates were accepted into the Nazi Party, and on both this day and Hitler's birthday members of the SS were regularly promoted. Frequently, the Hitler Youth celebrations on those five occasions were institutionally supported by other party administrations, such as the KdF or the SA. Again, trusted composers were given career-enhancing opportunities to create special instrumental and vocal music for these festivities. This was serious business. To give but two examples, during the 1934 party rally on 8 September Hitler spoke to sixty thousand Hitler Youth, telling them that "everything we demand from the Germany of the future we demand from you, boys and girls!" The boys and girls then broke into the song "Our Flag Ahead Shows Us the Way." Four years later eighty-five thousand youths attended, among them a thousand trumpet players and drummers, and seven hundred additional musicians. Hitler Youth virtuosos performed between the speeches, its choirs led communal singing, and there were fanfares for special emphasis.[50]

The ultimate purpose of Nazi education, in the schools and notably the Hitler Youth, was the production of heroes to fight Nazi Germany's offensive wars, and of their future mates—healthy broad-hipped women ever ready to give birth to more heroes while demurely occupying their places in home and hearth.[51] Music in the Hitler Youth was geared to these goals. The educational approach was cumulative, as Hitler Youth leaders began by teaching boys to play martial fanfares on the trumpet and ended by sending them into the Wehrmacht or the Waffen-SS to fight the enemy. Music educators made not a single move without these aims, and the methods to achieve them, firmly in mind: this is precisely what they had learned to do at the academies in Berlin, Weimar, and Graz.

At the first stage of this process, well before World War II, Hitler Youth music cadres came to adopt military forms of organization borrowed from the Wehrmacht. The favored instruments were those of the army: fifes, trumpets, and drums. During the war the Hitler Youth leadership expended a lot of energy on selecting suitable boys with "strong lungs and healthy, proper teeth" to train on the trumpet; the drummer "had to be physically capable of carrying the parade corps drum, even on longer marches."[52] At the second stage it was the music itself that mattered. Songs were often soldiers' songs, some of them centuries old and revived by the youth movement of the 1920s, others newly composed by the likes of Hans Baumann, Heinrich Spitta, and Gotthold Frotscher, and designed to inspire marching. Quite apart from its military purposes in war, the march was a conditioner of totalitarian rule. "The more uniformly and rhythmically all are marching in step, the greater will be the inner unity of the troops," preached Ludwig Kelbetz; "for the musician this physical-rhythmic basic training is of particular significance."[53]

From there one graduated, once the war was on, to the cultural entertainment of the troops behind the lines. Hitler Youth chamber orchestras played works by Vivaldi, Haydn, and Mozart; the choirs presented songs and cantatas by Baumann and Spitta and their colleagues; and there was communal singing with the soldiers. Such activity familiarized the future warriors with the front, and indeed, once inducted into the armed forces, Hitler Youth musicians influenced much of the martial music performed in air, navy, and army units. Not surprisingly, former Hitler Youth cadres were said to have been the most fanatical Nazis in the Wehrmacht, with the musicians among them not only taking care that the proper songs were chosen but also fighting valiantly and dying exemplary heroes' deaths, as the much-publicized examples of Bräutigam and Kelbetz demonstrate.[54]

The ultimate combat experience for Hitler Youth was in the SS, whose units also had marching and concert bands. As early as January 1934 the SS musicians gave a public concert in the Berlin Sportpalast, with a program of music devoted entirely to Hitler's exemplar Frederick the Great of Prussia. After its founding in 1941, the music school of the Waffen-SS became a natural receptacle for Hitler Youth veterans, who later joined the vanguard of Hitler's elite troops in the fighting at the fronts.[55]

Meanwhile, the BDM girls contributed to the war effort in their own gender-specific way: specializing on recorders and in singing, they were eternally popular with soldiers at the front, primarily with the wounded, who reportedly did not care how badly the girls performed so long as they made an appearance. As the war dragged on, all soldiers were suffering from a lack of regular sexual activity, evidenced by their sometimes scandalously promiscuous behavior when at home on furlough, no less than by the obliging licentiousness of local teenage girls, queuing up at train stations to greet them and pick a mate for the night. Hence, ironically, there was a double edge to the biological purpose that had been drummed into the young women of the Hitler Youth early on, with music acting as the food of love, though a love increasingly illicit and contributing to juvenile delinquency.[56]

The three most important men on the Hitler Youth music scene were Wolfgang Stumme, Cesar Bresgen, and Fritz Jöde. Stumme, born in Prussia in 1910, studied to be a music teacher at the primary-school level, and from 1932 to 1933 he taught school. Having joined the Hitler Youth in April 1933, he was put in charge of its music operations by Schirach the following year. He was married in April 1936 and a male heir, always sure to please Nazi superiors, arrived in November. His Nazi Party membership dates from May 1937. Holding the rank of Oberbannführer, one of the highest in the Hitler Youth, he organized musical education and activities, assisted by Karl Cerff, who also was liaison to the SS and to Goebbels's Propaganda Ministry. Stumme himself, who never even had the equivalent of a full university education let alone an academic degree, began teaching courses at Berlin's Akademie für Kirchen- und Schulmusik, an accredited conservatory and later one of the three Hitler Youth music showcases, in an adjunct capacity in the fall of 1934. His specialty then was in the area of "Music in the Hitler Youth," but it was later broadened. He took frequent leaves in order to look after his Hitler Youth responsibilities, some of which called for propaganda trips inside and outside the Reich, even before the war. In addition, Stumme published profusely on issues relating to his general field; most of his writing is of a decidedly propagandistic nature. In December 1939 he joined the Wehrmacht for active service in France and later Russia, where he was wounded. Having received several decorations, he returned to Berlin in September 1942 as a second lieutenant (ret.). Because Stumme was credited with having extended the period of academy instruction for Hitler Youth music educators from one to three years by 1942, he was recommended for a regular professorship in 1944.[57]

Cesar Bresgen served the cause of Hitler Youth music in three capacities: as a composer, an organizer, and an educator. He was born the son of a Munich painter in 1913 in Florence. Bresgen experienced cosmopolitan influences during his childhood in Salzburg, Prague, and Munich, where he was acquainted with artistic friends of his parents. From 1930 to 1936 he studied at the conservative Munich-based Akademie der Tonkunst under Joseph Haas and Siegmund von Hausegger, and until 1935 he also played the church organ at St. Rupert's. He met progressive composers early on in his formative years—Stravinsky, Orff (whom he called his friend throughout the Third Reich), and Hindemith. In 1934 he experienced "the new youth of Adolf Hitler." Three years later he met the Führer himself at the Berghof, being impressed by "an almost magical image" as Hitler blessed children against the backdrop of the Salzburg mountains. By his own admission, Bresgen became a fervent National Socialist.[58]

A talented young composer, Bresgen over the years produced a fair share of legitimate works, but as he was drawn into the vortex of fascist politics and ideology after 1934, his oeuvre became contaminated with tendentiousness to the same degree that he profited materially from the new regime. Safely avoiding the bolder idiom of Stravinsky's or Hindemith's works, which had so impressed him earlier, he specialized in neo-Baroque genres: songs, chamber works, concerti, and later cantatas. One of his first creations was *Songs of May* in the unornamented vein approved by the Nazis, which he had performed, accompanying himself at the piano, as a member of Haas's master class in the Munich Conservatory in June 1934.[59]

Two choruses for brass, composed by the Munich-based Bresgen, were performed in honor of the Olympic Games in August 1936. The same festival that had featured his friend Orff's *Carmina Burana* in June 1937 saw the introduction of his *Symphonic Suite* in Darmstadt, heard previously only in Mannheim. Later that year a "Munich Music Week" premiered his Sonata for Viola and Piano; Rosenberg's *Völkischer Beobachter* lauded its "contemporary life direction." Another Nazi, Richard Eichenauer, also praised Bresgen's undisturbed conventional tonality, as expressed in his "polyphonic attitude." Along with Werner Egk and others, Bresgen was a star at the Düsseldorf Reich Music Festival of 1939, following on the heels of the previous year's festival, to which the exhibition of degenerate music had been attached. The simplicity and songlike character of his compositions consistently met with positive responses. A highlight of his career as a serious composer was the premiere of his fairytale opera *Dornröschen* (Sleeping Beauty), in Strasbourg under Hans Rosbaud in 1942; Bresgen completed two additional operas before 1945.[60] Earlier, in 1937, the music publisher Strecker had doubted whether the young composer "already has the maturity necessary for larger works." But five years later Strecker willingly accepted *Dornröschen* for his list.[61]

In 1943 the prominent Nazi critic Herbert Gerigk observed approvingly that some of Bresgen's music was reminiscent of the cantatas presently being cultivated by the Hitler Youth.[62] This reference to Bresgen's mainstream work pointed to his other function, that of a major Hitler Youth composer. Although after World War II Bresgen maintained that he had not written music for political purposes nor had any of his compositions been performed within a political context, upon graduating from the conservatory he had commenced to produce music for the Hitler Youth like clockwork.[63] This political output started around 1938 with his *Bläsermusik*, written for trumpets, trombones, tuba, and kettledrums, thus mirroring the new Nazi interest in martial instruments. The work was presented in Munich on the occasion of a "German Day of Song: One People, One Reich, One Führer." A year later a Hitler Youth songbook edited by Erich Lauer contained verses set to music by Bresgen that were written for Blood-and-Soil harvest ceremonies, glorifying the German peasant. *Kindelfest*, a cantata celebrating the birth of a baby on a farm, a distinctly biopolitical event, was premiered in Munich in 1940;

over the years it had several revivals. In 1941 Bresgen's admirers witnessed the publication of a cantata for soldiers, an orchestral work commemorating Germany's fallen, and a festive instrumental piece, like *Kindelfest*, with a modest degree of technical difficulty especially designed for Hitler Youth bands. He collaborated with Baumann in the creation of a festive oratorio, *Der Strom*, and accepted a mandate from the Salzburg Hitler Youth command to present special arrangements of *Volkslieder* suitable for communal singing, both in 1943. The following year, the twilight of Nazi Germany, got off to an auspicious start for Bresgen with a new trombone concerto played under the anti-Semitic Generalmusikdirektor Paul Sixt by the Berlin Philharmonic in a concert dedicated to the Hitler Youth. There was also a new harvest cantata for instruments and choir, as well as a *Fanfare* for six brass instruments commissioned by and for the SS. This piece recalled the structure of the *Bläsermusik* of 1938, with an almost identical instrumentation, "entirely in the polyphonic style of early German times."[64]

Again, Bresgen's postwar assurances that he had been pressured by the regime to put his talents at its service and that he nonetheless "never had much to do with politics" are lies.[65] The evidence shows that Bresgen's first political office after graduation was that of a musical adviser for Hitler Youth programming at the Munich radio station. He had much opportunity to schedule and direct many of his own works and those of other regime-championed composers, usually with the help of Hitler Youth musicians of all stripes. This activity continued well into the war years. In the spring of 1938 Bresgen also was in charge of Anschluss celebrations organized by the Hitler Youth in Salzburg. Bresgen's second, rather more important post was as a music educator in the Hitler Youth wing of the Salzburg Mozarteum Conservatory, newly opened under Nazi patronage in 1939. As such he assumed the respectable rank of Obergefolgschaftsführer. Bresgen, who wanted to interest his friend Orff in joining the Salzburg venture, beckoned him enthusiastically: "Looking at it from the outside, we are very successful, since all our instrumental and vocal classes are filling up, enabling us to establish local branches in the countryside. In part, the students are very gifted, so that we can really build up splendid choral and instrumental groups." In his capacity as lecturer (he was made a professor in 1944), Bresgen spoke on "Music Education in the Hitler Youth" at sister institutions such as the one at Graz (1939), provided music for Nazi book exhibits such as "The Book and the Sword" (1941), and led his uniformed boys and girls at Nazi music festivals, including the Tonkünstlerfest held in Munich under the aegis of Nazi Lord Mayor Fiehler and the KdF (1941). His opera *Dornröschen*, just premiered under Rosbaud in Strasbourg, opened in Salzburg in May 1942 during a special culture festival of the Hitler Youth, presided over by Schirach and other Austrian Gauleiter. In the same year the Hitler Youth leadership sent him to Fascist Italy as a special emissary, and he was appointed to serve on specifically Nazi cultural panels.[66]

Such manifold commitments brought their rewards. A thorough study of the music journals of the period conveys the impression that Bresgen was the most industrious and most popular Hitler Youth composer ever to be performed. He could do no wrong, either with critics or with serious fellow musicians such as Rosbaud, Orff, and Egk. His financial compensation must have been considerable, from both royalties and the educational and leadership functions he performed. And then there was the prize money that quite naturally accrued to him as one of the brightest hopes of the new German music establishment. In 1936 Bresgen received the Felix Mottl Prize from the Bavarian regional government for various of his early compositions. Two years later he won a prize in the amount of 1,000 marks put up by the city of Munich. Then, in 1941, came another prize from Munich; this time his teacher Joseph Haas and Richard Strauss were jurors. Along with Orff, Bresgen was among the recipients of a one-time RMK award given to him by Egk and Heinz Drewes in 1942. Finally, in 1942 Bresgen collected the newly funded "culture prize" of Salzburg, worth a handsome 7,000 marks, as a "cultural-political pioneer who goes to the source of a racially conscious German music tradition."[67]

Of the three principals on the Hitler Youth music scene, Fritz Jöde was by far the most complex. As historians are discovering ever more strands of continuity between the Weimar Republic and the Third Reich, it is becoming clear that to a certain extent the German youth culture constituted one of them. There were similarities between the Weimar youth movement and the Hitler Youth before and after January 1933 that were founded either on logical developments of given situations after World War I or on their absolute immutability and durability over time. The elements of nationalism of the Weimar youth leagues known as Bündische Jugend and that of the Hitler Youth were congruent, as were both youth movements' expressions of love for the outdoors and a healthy disrespect for their elders.[68] An additional common factor, until the Nazis further racialized and militarized it, was music, expecially between 1925 and 1939. More than anyone else, Fritz Jöde was responsible for the musical commonalities, until by World War II his influence in the Third Reich had become somewhat attenuated.

Jöde was born in Hamburg in 1887. He studied to become a primary-school teacher and was instructing schoolchildren before World War I. In 1920–21 he did postgraduate work in musicology at Leipzig; then in 1923 the influential administrator Leo Kestenberg, who intended to reform music pedagogy in Prussia, called him to Berlin, where Jöde became a professor at the Akademie für Kirchen- und Schulmusik. As director of the German Youth Music School, which was affiliated with the academy, Jöde set out to extend certain changes in the music of the German youth movement already initiated by Walter Hensel and Hans Breuer. Some aspects of this reform were very much in keeping with the new trends of the Weimar Republic, which the Jewish Kestenberg himself supported. One was the observance of sobriety and objectivity (also inspiring the

Weimar and later Dessau Bauhaus), as well as the application of minimalism to cultural expression, as in the later canvases of Paul Klee; another was Jöde's attempt to move away from the excessive ornateness of nineteenth-century musical compositions, especially the late Romantic works. Jöde wanted to return to the simple roots of creativity, which he saw in every one of his pupils; he eschewed virtuosity and certain instruments associated with it, such as the piano. His antidote was the human voice: natural, uncontrived communal singing, away from the stuffy bourgeois home, was his recipe for healthy, wholesome living. Hence, it was he who in a very personal sense opposed the private music teachers and piano manufacturers and who contributed decisively to the temporary demise of *Hausmusik*. Jöde's specific measure of accomplishment was command of the round, as sung by groups of children and older youths alike. By its very nature the canon called for a community of members, not the showcasing of an individual, highly skilled soloist. His musical communities were intended to defeat the rationality and liberalism of the nineteenth century which had begun with the Enlightenment; instead, Jöde wished to rely on irrational elements, on natural impulses, on the organic, and on uncomplicated lay music-making after the most basic formal and, ideally, free public instruction.[69]

Although Jöde had been called to Berlin by Kestenberg, the representative of the staunchly Social Democratic government in Prussia, he himself was not a Marxist, nor did he belong to either of the two established left-wing parties. In fact, there were several elements of his pedagogical philosophy that predisposed him to the political right, although he was always very careful to demonstrate friendship and good will toward as many ideologically and culturally diverse groups as possible in the fractured society of Weimar. (Hence, he is on record as professing sympathy for communists, friendship with the Jewish pedagogue Karl Adler in Stuttgart, and admiration for the Austrian-Jewish poet Franz Werfel, whose verse he hoped to see set to music.) Jöde's antirationalism meshed with the anti-intellectualism of German right-wingers during the republic, and several of his like-minded music pedagogue friends, such as Georg Götsch and Fritz Reusch, both of whom Kestenberg had equally favored in the public education system, later became active Nazis. The rejection of the brand of liberalism reflected by the Weimar system and the complementary idea of a strong state that would take public music instruction in hand, which Jöde espoused, were potentially right-wing, even though Jöde's benign critics argue today that by this he always meant democracy—an assumption wholly unproved. In any event, this strong-state decisionist philosophy was also shared by Eberhard Preussner, the influential Berlin musicologist, later director of the Salzburg Mozarteum, who found adjusting to the Nazi system not too difficult for his own purposes.

Jöde's belief in gemeinschaft—organic community as opposed to rational society—was one of the mainstays of right-wing, prefascist thought in

Weimar Germany (also upheld by intellectuals such as Othmar Spann, Carl Schmitt, and Ernst Jünger), and here Jöde was strongly supported by, and in turn very much relied on, Ernst Krieck. This philosopher was also a former public-school teacher turned professor who at the end of the Weimar Republic had authored an influential book, *Musische Erziehung* (1933), that contained many parallels to Jöde's ideas. During the early stages of the Third Reich, Krieck became the quintessential Nazi professor, serving, sequentially, as rector of Frankfurt and Heidelberg Universities. Jöde and Krieck both were applauded by Georg Kallmeyer, an important publisher of youth movement music and literature, who in the republic was rightist enough to become, after 1933, the house publisher for music in the Hitler Youth. When Jöde, in many ways a product and exponent of the republican educational system, was coming under increased attack by dyed-in-the-wool Nazis, mostly from Rosenberg's Kampfbund faction during the last years of Weimar, Kallmeyer and Krieck defended him against the charges of Marxism and patronage of Jews, while Jöde himself, ever so carefully, seems to have made overtures to sympathetic representatives of the Nazi Party. There were indeed other Nazis, particularly among public-school teachers, who would have welcomed Jöde's total and open conversion to their creed. "What a pitiful spectacle is this campaign against Jöde," lamented one teacher, "for should not every National Socialist teacher be able to find out for himself that Jöde has instilled the youth music movement with *völkisch* power, an archetypal power, and that National Socialism and the youth music movement share the same ground?" No wonder that in one corner of Germany, in the summer of 1932, a rumor had started that "Jöde had become a card-carrying member of the NSDAP," a rumor that, at that particular juncture, was still unfounded.[70]

Sensing which way the wind was blowing after January 1933, and afraid of losing his chair at the Berlin academy, Jöde was at pains to make overtures to representatives of the new regime; but he also knew he could rely for support on effective friends such as Krieck and Kallmeyer. Kallmeyer especially was active on Jöde's behalf, writing to Prussian Education Minister Rust, among others, lest Jöde lose his Berlin tenure, and identifying among Jöde's firm Nazi backers Richard Eichenauer, the anti-Semitic musicologist; Hans Freyer, a Leipzig Nazi sociologist; Herman Wirth, soon to establish Himmler's SS "Ahnenerbe" research foundation; Johannes von Leers, another egregious anti-Semite (who would later advise the post–World War II Egyptian government how to conjure up another anti-Jewish holocaust); and of course Krieck and Reusch. Jöde himself suddenly discovered hypernationalist leanings: not only did he engage in a great deal of networking, trying to rally as many Nazi advocates to his cause as possible, but also he issued statements that could have come from a long-term, bona fide Nazi. Publicly he declared that he welcomed "the new *völkisch* movement"; to prove it he contributed money to a Führer portrait for the Berlin academy on Hitler's birthday in 1934. Indeed, one of Jöde's new official lines was that German youth music had, from the very beginning, been a "*völkisch* movement," that it had veritably soared toward "a new Germany," and that now there was "a reawakening of our people." Jöde's newfound conviction was that the music of the youth movement as one had come to know it had had to be submerged in the revolution led by Adolf Hitler and then was reborn, with its spirit essentially intact, in a new form.[71]

If put to the test, Jöde could have proved this, for several of his former students, Stumme among them, had joined the Berlin Hitler Youth in 1933 at his urging and, as the music pedagogical experts that they were, soon rose to positions of significance under Schirach. One consequence was Stumme's own appointment at the Berlin academy in 1934; another was the Hitler Youth's issuing of songbooks for the entire organization, all on the Jöde Weimar model, first stressing the vocal, and only later the instrumental, aspects of music-making. Other supporters soon included Kelbetz, Bräutigam, Twittenhoff, Marx, and Herbert Napiersky, another hard-hitting Nazi youth composer. Kallmeyer, meanwhile, profited as the favored publisher.[72]

Many Old Fighters of the Nazi movement were suspicious of Jöde's change of heart and sensed what was indeed the case: that he had merely bent some of the more pliable planks of his own assorted ideological platforms to adapt to the new rulers. Hence, he continued to be assaulted by adherents of the idea of *Hausmusik*—private music teachers and conventional music publishers, as well as exponents of musical virtuosity—especially those who were members of Rosenberg's Kampfbund für deutsche Kultur for as long as it was powerful in the first few months of the regime. He found it difficult to shake off the "Marxist" label, especially since he took seriously the "socialist" component of National Socialism. Jöde's prized image of the recorder, that quintessential lay instrument of the Weimar youth movement, was derided by some; at the same time, through the action of others, it was becoming the instrument of choice for the BDM. "The chameleonlike qualities of Fritz Jöde," complained Rosenberg's *Völkischer Beobachter,* "whose artistic, political, and confessional convictions are subject to such noticeable changes, should, after all, counsel caution."[73]

In February 1935 Jöde suddenly was put on paid leave from the Berlin academy, and in October 1936 he was dismissed. This sequence of events has been interpreted by his many post–World War II followers as revenge on the part of his long-standing political enemies, but that is only partly true. Although the Reich Music Chamber later admitted that "political grounds" contributed to the dismissal, it also exposed the real cause: Jöde, unhappily married since 1913, had been found to have sexually approached at least sixteen girls in his circle, some of them under eighteen, over the past several years, although in all cases these had been consensual encounters, and he had had sexual intercourse with only one, a more mature young woman. On the basis of the surviving evidence, which mentions names, dates, and circumstances, there can be no doubt that the charges were entirely justified. Yet it may also safely be surmised that Jöde was not the only popular youth movement leader who succumbed to such carnal temptations. If so, why was he exposed while most of the others made their way through the Hitler Youth without complications? A strong faction within the Nazi movement did believe that Jöde was not credible as a proselyte from the Weimar era, and they never forgave him. Although Jöde was removed from the Berlin academy at 75 percent of his rightful pension for the next five years, criminal proceedings were mercifully stayed.[74]

In the years following his dismissal, Jöde, whose pension amounted to merely 3,500 marks annually, found making a living difficult, even though he had stated to the authorities that he must be given credit for training an entire generation of "music leaders," who were now serving "in the new Reich." As far as he was concerned, he was continuing to further the "cultural-political goals of the Third Reich." Meanwhile, he was living from hand to mouth, he said, for his earlier publications were not selling as well as they used to. While this may have been true, his name continued to crop up in the National Socialist literature, and some of his work was expressly recommended for Nazi ceremonies. Jöde found cultural odd jobs, some of which were in broadcasting in Munich, and he applied for membership in the Nazi Party in 1938 to improve his chances of economic and political survival. The Nazi authorities left him alone, provided "he would not be receiving a chance to come into contact with defenseless adolescents."[75]

But Jöde's old friends in the Hitler Youth had not forgotten him. In 1940 the director of the Mozarteum in Salzburg, Eberhard Preussner, who had thought highly of Jöde back in Berlin and shared many of his goals, called him to the Salzburg Conservatory. Preussner's associate Cesar Bresgen, a new admirer, fully supported this action. Just in time, Jöde's party application was approved in January of that year. Jöde immediately joined Bresgen in the Hitler Youth music wing of the Mozarteum at a respectable rank: his full Nazi title was "Music Delegate of Gau Salzburg of the Hitler Youth." On a day-to-day basis he was involved not only in Hitler Youth education work, but also in Nazi university student performances. Citations of his published output increased even more in the official literature. In 1943, for reasons not specified but possibly having to do with his exalted ego, Jöde retreated to Brunswick to a lesser Nazi educational institution; dismissed from there as a total-war measure in 1944, he rode out the Third Reich in Bad Reichenhall, a stone's throw from Salzburg. Like many Nazis and collaborators, he was anticipating opportunities for re-employment in the postwar era.[76]

The Academies and the Protestant Church

Whereas the Hitler Youth was an integral part of the revolutionary Nazi movement, institutions of higher learning, like the primary and secondary schools part of a time-honored governmental bureaucracy, lacked that movement's dynamic momentum, and so they were always lagging behind in the development of a specifically Nazi curriculum. As late as 1944 Felix Oberborbeck, the rector of the Graz-based Hochschule für Musikerziehung, stated that the traditional university system, its faculty, and course offerings were "still below the National Socialist standard of education," even though some form of amalgamation was being striven for. The multiple aim was, of course, to create a new type of music educator, indeed, a new type of musician, as well as entirely new areas of study, such as music for the armed forces or music-making within the National Socialist community.[77]

To bring about the realization of those goals, not only did Jewish instructors have to be removed, but also the authority of the small albeit dependable core of Nazi music educators had to be established and fortified. On the one hand, these educators were encouraged to cooperate closely with the Nazi movement's representatives such as Wolfgang Stumme, and on the other, they were to wield influence over their less than Nazi-minded colleagues with the objective of turning them around. Last but not least, they had to help in the shaping of a new Nazi student body.

This called for the suspension of Jewish faculty members. Jewish professors of all specialties were among the first professionals removed from their places of work by the civil service law issued on 7 April 1933, and professors of music were no exception. The boom was lowered on every conservatory and the faculty of music of every German university; because the instructors, unlike some practicing musicians, were employees of the state or senior civil servants, the law could automatically be applied, and no exceptions were made. Hence, Hans Gál was forced to leave his post as director of the conservatory in Mainz; he returned to his native Vienna, and from there was able to emigrate to England in 1938. At the Bayerische Akademie der Tonkunst, violin teacher Jani Szanto, renowned for his master classes, and director Hermann Wolfgang von Waltershausen were driven out, over the objections of Richard Strauss. And the Frankfurt Hoch'sche Konservatorium fired both the cellist and jazz instructor Matyas Seiber and the longtime director, Hindemith's and Rosbaud's teacher Bernhard Sekles.[78]

The anti-Jewish purge, largely fueled by Rosenberg's Kampfbund für deutsche Kultur, was most noticeable in Berlin, first, because of the capital's concentration of higher-level music schools, and second, because most of the Jewish teachers there were internationally renowned artists. Such was the case with the previously mentioned professor of piano Leonid Kreutzer, who had taught at the Hochschule für Musik since 1921. In June 1933 he insisted that although he was originally from the Baltics, his mother tongue was German and he was a German citizen. His accomplishments, so he reminded Göring's commissar for Jewish affairs Hans Hinkel, were to have trained a younger generation of German pianists and to have exemplarily interpreted German composers such as Max Reger in Germany as well as abroad. But this did not help him. He was dismissed, along with his colleagues the cellist Emanuel Feuermann; Hugo Leichtentritt, a professor of composition; Erwin Bodky, who taught piano, harpsichord, and musicology; and others. Confirmed Nazis took their place, as did the song composer Georg Vollerthun in the case of Schoenberg's former teacher Alexander von Zemlinsky.[79]

Subsequently, until he was sacked from the Prussian State Hochschule für Musik because of a homosexual indiscretion in 1936, Vollerthun excelled as an instructor in the art of lieder writing and performance, using as his teaching aids his own and Paul Graener's songs as well as those of more famous nineteenth-century Romantic composers.[80] Vollerthun's comrade-in-arms was the composition teacher Max Trapp, since 1934 Schoenberg's successor at the Preussische Akademie der Künste. An Old Fighter of the Nazi movement from the dying days of the Weimar Republic, he taught the sort of traditional composition that the Nazis—unjustly—thought Schoenberg incapable of doing. That factor, in combination with his unshakable political conviction, made him an ideal conservatory teacher for the hardliners in the Third Reich. But, like Vollerthun, Trapp came close to stumbling over a sexual affair in 1935, this time with a student, the wife of a local party clerk who was intent on having him excluded from the party as well as on ruining his professorial career. Furtwängler, Goebbels, and Hitler all intervened with the Education Ministry, and Trapp's dismissal was reversed. Until 1945 he remained a most faithful servant of the regime.[81]

Teaching on the music faculty of the University of Berlin after 1935 was Gotthold Frotscher, part of whose work involved Protestant church music. As for secular music, Frotscher was obsessed with the notion that Germany's entire culture had been contaminated by Jews. He wanted to revive the folk songs of the Romantic period, the vehicle of their reincarnation in the Third Reich being the "racially determined life community of the people." During the war he was one of the most fanatical spokesmen for musical education in the Hitler Youth, believing that a musical soldier was a better soldier. German culture, said Frotscher, was a weapon in the fight for the survival of European culture, broadly defined. After an anticipated "Final Victory," much more research would have to be done into the correlation between race and music.[82]

Well before the war the Nazi regime had succeeded in installing a few powerful professors of music in strategic positions across the Reich. At the University of Tübingen in Württemberg, Karl Hasse taught music; he was one of only two music professors who openly tried to implant the ideas of Rosenberg's Kampfbund in institutions of higher learning months before the Nazi takeover. As in the case of Frotscher, this associate professor's fight was with anything that he identified as Jewish in German music, in particular jazz and the works of the Weimar moderns. Taking advantage of the political change after January 1933, Hasse moved to the Cologne Conservatory as its new director and full professor in early 1935.[83]

Munich had two exponents of Nazism: Karl Blessinger and Richard Trunk, both of whom taught at the Akademie der Tonkunst. Blessinger had been there since 1920. He joined the Nazi Party in 1932, in the 1930s authored an odious treatise on Mendelssohn, Meyerbeer, and Mahler, and as late as 1944 published a vicious diatribe on Jews in music.[84] Trunk, another epigone of the Romantics, came to the academy from the Cologne Conservatory in 1934. How he got there is characteristic of Nazi promotions, for in the manner of Intendant Wilhelm Rode of the Deutsche Oper in Berlin, Old Party Fighter Trunk used his good connections to SA Captain Ernst Röhm. After Trunk, just to be on the safe side, had memorialized in song both Hitler and Horst Wessel, the Brownshirts' early martyr, those same Brownshirts prevailed on Bavarian Culture Minister Hans Schemm, who then summoned Trunk to the academy as its new president. In 1942 Trunk, who had already set some of Schirach's Hitler Youth verses to music, succeeded Bresgen as recipient of Munich's Music Prize.[85]

And so it went. At the University of Königsberg, the associate professor Josef Müller-Blattau, who during the Weimar Republic had actually sympathized with the modernists, also chose as his subject of interest the Nazi hero Horst Wessel, about whom he wrote a pseudoscientific article in 1934. In it he stylized the "Horst Wessel Lied," that irrepressible SA marching hymn of Wessel's own making, as the "never to be lost property of the people, a true *Volkslied.*" This calculated act won him advancement to Frankfurt (1935) and then Freiburg (1937). After publishing a book on "Germanic music" in collaboration with the SS, he was given a chair at the new Reichsuniversität Strassburg in 1942.[86] Meanwhile, Müller-Blattau's former professor at Freiburg, Wilibald Gurlitt, in 1933 had already hailed the newly acceptable racist approaches to the study of Bach, even though Gurlitt himself had a non-"Aryan" wife and had to leave his post two years later. Still, he and Kiel University's Friedrich Blume played key roles in the authoritative Deutsche Musikgesellschaft; Blume, moreover, functioned at the musicological convention that scientifically adumbrated the anti-Semitic Düsseldorf exhibition of degenerate music in 1938.[87]

The proportion of Nazi professors in all the music faculties of the Third Reich is difficult to determine until more extensive studies have been made. Because by far the largest number of universities and conservatories were exclusively state institutions, some of which had been founded centuries earlier, they tended to cling to old, proven patterns and had to be forcefully drawn into the Nazi realm before they could be deemed "revolutionary"; this took considerable time.[88] In that sense they were quite different from original Nazi organizations such as the Hitler Youth, SA, or SS, with their respective training centers; almost anyone who was working within these groups has to be considered a Nazi. In the universities, however, there still were islands of genuine scholarship and academic freedom, and academic appointments were still being made that were justifiable by objective standards. Furtwängler, for instance, accepted a position at the Prussian Hochschule für Musik in early 1941, where he was asked to supervise master classes.[89] The great conductor may have collaborated with Hitler's regime on various issues, but he was not a Nazi.

Whereas the contrasting types installed at the state institutions are easily defined at the extremes—here a Furtwängler, there a Hasse—there also were hybrid types, in whom Nazi and non-Nazi ingredients mingled in various ratios. Georg Schünemann was the example of a type in which many of the old values of a traditional German university professor had been preserved, but who, like Jöde, exhibited the symptoms of compromise and even conversion. His mirror image Fritz Stein, by contrast, exemplifies the type who had embraced Nazi revolutionary tenets even before January 1933, behaved like a confirmed National Socialist with an impressive degree of consistency throughout the Third Reich, and yet still showed sympathy with conventions that had been in place since before the political sea change.

By all accounts Schünemann was an engaging, personable, witty man, who was well liked by his contemporaries in the 1920s. Born in Berlin in 1884, he received a comprehensive musical education, studying the flute and the piano as well as music theory and composition, the last for a while with Pfitzner. He received a doctorate in 1907, took his university lecturer certificate in 1919, and became a professor at the Berlin Hochschule für Musik in 1920. By 1923 he was its acting director as well as a chairholder at Berlin University. As such he found himself in the Kestenberg camp, and, like Jöde, he sympathized with the political left. Among other works, he published an important book on the history of conducting, and, being the excellent, progressive teacher that he was, he patronized promising young composers of the modern school, such as Ernst Křenek when he was studying in Berlin in the early 1920s. By the end of the Weimar Republic Schünemann had made a name for himself as a musician, a theorist, and especially an editor and historian of pre-Romantic music.[90]

In 1932, with the removal of the Jewish Franz Schreker, Schünemann assumed the full directorship of the Berlin Hochschule. The situation was bound to be an uncomfortable one for him because he knew that the same hypernationalist forces that had toppled Schreker (and, incidentally, Kestenberg as well) might soon become much stronger and threaten even him.[91] Schünemann therefore tried to get on the good side of Nazi colleagues such as violin professor Gustav Havemann, who was himself a recent turncoat, and whom he had brought into the faculty. The circumstantial evidence suggests that after the political changeover in January 1933, Schünemann attempted to join the Nazi Party but was rejected because he was too easily identified with the Kestenberg era and his show of nationalism was mistrusted. He did manage to join a petty Nazi outfit, the National Socialist Workshop of State Officials. He also tried to offer the chair of a dismissed Jew, Oskar Daniel, to Hugo Rasch, a rock-solid Nazi and minor composer who later became Richard Strauss's RMK factotum in Berlin. Rasch, no less conscious of his academic deficiencies than of the political leverage this act accorded him, with Hinkel's complicity rejected Schünemann's overture in a show of mock indignation, citing Schünemann's friendship with Kestenberg. Schünemann then tried to placate Hinkel by helping him install at the Hochschule student representatives of the KfdK, which step, because of internecine tangles, turned other Nazis against him. Several of the National Socialist students still vouched for him, however, citing "the purity of his convictions, so social and so national, his glowing love for the fatherland," as one young woman enthusiastically put it. But by April it had become clear that this scholar had boxed himself into a corner, so much so that his close friend Hindemith feared that "because of his vacillations, he has spoiled everything." In early May 1933 Schünemann lost his job at the Hochschule, though he kept his professorship at the university; as a music historian he was now put in charge of the music division of the Prussian State Library, evidently much to his own displeasure.[92]

Over the following years Schünemann tried to get by as best he could, undoubtedly resenting the Nazi state and what it had done to him, and also avoiding the kinds of political loyalty statements that Jöde was using to ingratiate himself with the men in power. In 1937 he seems to have considered emigration, perhaps to the United States, but ironically his scholarship proved so indispensable to the Nazis that they did their best to appease him. After Schünemann had unearthed a forgotten violin concerto by Robert Schumann and the cultural establishment had performed it, the professor received full credit. Schünemann agreed to cooperate in purging "Jewish" librettos and replacing them with acceptable texts; the most notable was Hermann Levi's translation of Mozart's *Il Nozze di Figaro*, which by 1940 had outlived its usefulness as an appropriate opera to be performed by the now deteriorating Jüdischer Kulturbund. In 1940 Schünemann also acted as an expert appraiser of musical artifacts looted from occupied France. All the while he continued in his valuable role as an editor and publisher of works such as Beethoven's conversation notebooks. Moreover, various specialist functions that Schünemann fulfilled benefited the offices of Education Minister Bernhard Rust and Promi music overseer Heinz Drewes, among others. In 1943 the professor lent academic credence to Hans Frank's mistaken assumption that Chopin was of partly German ancestry and publicly proclaimed in Cracow that the constructive elements of that composer's music were due "to a core of German music, which, in the final analysis, is traceable to Chopin's German music education." When this scholar turned sixty in March 1944, he rated special mention in the Nazi press, but he never got back his old position at the conservatory, nor is it likely that he ever asked for it. He had resigned himself to a comparatively mild form of accommodation with the Nazi regime, which in turn was content to tolerate him. Nobody's hero and nobody's villain, Schünemann died, unsung, in January 1945, amidst the ruins of what had once been the capital and his beloved home.[93]

Fritz Stein survived the national collapse of early May 1945, so that people who had known him during the Third Reich could tell the Western Allies in Berlin that Stein had been an "enemy of jazz music," an idiom he had defined as "a mixture of Negro raunchiness and Jewish impertinence." Stein was also reported to have told Wehrmacht soldiers that "a people which possesses a Bach and a Beethoven will never lose the war."[94]

These two statements sum up much about the scholar who was Georg Schünemann's successor as director of the Berlin Hochschule für Musik after April 1933. Like the equally gifted Schünemann, Stein had had a choice as to where to go early in his professional life. Born in 1879 near Heidelberg, he had studied Lutheran theology and passed the qualifying examination as a pastor by 1902, but then he returned to the university and took full academic training as a musician, specializing in church music and organ. By 1913 the young Ph.D. was an associate professor of musicology at Jena. He became a Generalmusikdirektor in 1925 and a full professor at the University of Kiel in 1928, where his expertise was in Bach, Reger, and choral music. In the mold of many of his male cohorts, Stein derived his strong sense of German nationalism from the twin sources of Lutheran theology and voluntary service in World War I. It may have been this hyperpatriotism that prompted him to support the Nazis clandestinely from 1925 (the republic's civil servants risked dismissal if they joined an extremist party openly) and tied himself to the Kampfbund in 1932. Unlike Schünemann, Stein did not countenance the works of any of the moderns beyond Reger, and his later friendship with Hindemith was probably not based entirely on that composer's music.[95]

Stein revealed the rudiments of a musical-political program during a Berlin meeting of the Kampfbund weeks after Hitler's new appointment, a meeting that was chaired by the local Kampfbund general, Hans Hinkel. The German people had to be led back to real, mellifluous music, said Stein. Singing, particularly choir exercises, was fundamentally important. Music in the schools, of the kind that the Kestenberg era had championed, had to be reformed. After Stein had replaced Schünemann at the Hochschule für Musik, he continued his cooperation with the Kampfbund, supporting Hinkel's ongoing efforts to launch student representatives of that league at the Hochschule. Later, however, like Havemann and others, Stein was shrewd enough to move into an executive position at Goebbels's new Reich Music Chamber in the fall of 1933.[96]

Like Schünemann and Jöde, Stein had to tread carefully on Nazi soil because he, too, had a skeleton in his closet. This was his Jewish son-in-law, who was living in England.[97] It is therefore quite possible that many of the concessions Stein had already made and was yet to make to gratify the regime were purposely designed to protect himself; had Stein been completely invulnerable, he might have been less accommodating. Nevertheless, there is no denying that Stein was extremely ambitious and, at the age of fifty-four, thought that many of the cultural leadership functions in the new Reich were cut out for him. Interestingly enough, it was Stein who, before accepting the Berlin directorship, insisted that the Jewish faculty members Kreutzer and Feuermann be replaced with "Aryans." Beyond that, he emphasized the National Socialist "leadership principle," the mission of "German artists," and the "holy, folkish, spiritually and ideologically anchored cultural tasks ahead."[98]

Stein proceeded to buttress his position at the Hochschule by engaging in extramural activities, mostly in conjunction with the expanding RMK, and always by seeking the blessing of Goebbels's immediate representative, Hinkel, or that of the two RMK presidents, Strauss and Raabe. If in the case of the former he still found it necessary to make personal visits to Garmisch, he could afford to be somewhat more casual in his dealings with the latter, since, though seven years his senior, Raabe had been his doctoral student at Jena in 1916.[99] One of the first major efforts Stein expended was to coordinate all the choirs in the Reich in true Nazi fashion, officially an assignment from the RMK, but one that he had had a hand in creating. This project possessed ideological significance because it spelled the organizational dissolution of workers' choirs, many of them formerly communist, of the kind that Hermann Scherchen had conducted. To all intents and purposes Stein had accquitted himself of that responsibility, in the interest of creating "a new choir culture in the Third Reich," by the summer of 1935.[100] Furthermore, Stein sought and eventually gained membership in the Nazi Party, and, just to show that he was on the right track, hurled invectives against the renowned republican music critic Hans Heinz Stuckenschmidt, who currently was very much on the defensive.[101]

In contrast to his colleagues Jöde and even Schünemann, Stein prospered throughout the Third Reich. He was placed in charge of important musical events during the 1936 Olympics, and recordings of choral and chamber works he conducted were marketed by Electrola.[102] His post as a presidial counselor in the Reich Music Chamber remained unassailable. For his sixtieth birthday in December 1939 he received accolades nationwide, including the Goethe Medal from Hitler's own hands. During the war the professor made himself useful by supporting all manner of party associations, including the SS, whose elite Leibstandarte Adolf Hitler corps he schooled in choral singing.[103]

As a National Socialist academic Fritz Stein went further than most of his ilk, providing more than sufficient proof of his loyalty to the dictatorial regime. But perhaps his Jewish son-in-law also caused him to have a bad conscience, for occasionally he suppressed the Nazi side of his personality, for the benefit of his politically less sheltered colleagues. The most prominent of these was Hindemith, on Stein's very own faculty at the Hochschule, whom he admired and whose plight from 1934 to 1937 he sought to lessen, hoping all the while that he might be able to guarantee Hindemith's professional survival in Germany. Another redeeming impulse was his offer to employ Carl Orff at his conservatory, around 1938, when that composer's star had not yet risen to exalted heights. Orff had his own peculiar problems of adjustment to the Nazi system that Stein most certainly knew nothing about. Nonetheless, what intrigued him about Orff was the individualism of an artist who, while not a Stravinsky or a Schoenberg, appeared to be bold and modern, and could not easily be tarred with the brush of craven Nazi collaboration.[104]

In late 1933 Stein joined forces with leading members of the Confessional Church, who had been striving for a renaissance of Lutheran sacred music. This revival movement within the German Protestant Church, to which more than 60 percent of the population belonged, was directed against trends and tendencies in the officially supported establishment of the so-called German Christians, who had permitted themselves to be turned into complete pawns of the Nazi regime. From their beginnings, which predated 1933 by several years, the platform of the German Christians was not entirely distinguishable from Alfred Rosenberg's ideology, although after January 1933 the party philosopher's position was not to permit any form of institutionalized Christianity, as in the two main churches, but to fight it. Nevertheless, many of Rosenberg's early views on Christ and Christianity, if not the churches themselves, were congruent with the views of the German Christians.

At the core of Rosenberg's critique of Christian beliefs was his primitive neo-Nietzschean disdain for the religious persona of Jesus Christ. Rosenberg rejected the New Testament version, inspired by Saint Paul, of Christ as the meek sacrificial lamb whose mission it was to atone for the sins of hereditarily sinful humankind. He replaced this with the image of a strong, heroic Christ, not God's son but a resourceful human warrior of Nordic countenance and disposition: blond, blue-eyed, tall, and invincible. The religious myths of Calvary, the Cross, and the Resurrection were Paulist fabrications; instead, Christ was said to have been a proto-Germanic hero, and of course he had never been Jewish. In this way Rosenberg not only secularized but actually racialized Jesus Christ; such a de-Christianized Christ would aid him in the instrumentalization of his future battles against the established churches.[105]

The German Christians embodied a form of Lutheran Christianity which, after the *Diktat* of Versailles in 1919, was highly nationalistic and xenophobic, and in particular anti-Semitic. Not unlike Rosenberg, they believed in a blond, "Aryan" Christ, a Faustian man of action, and, especially from 1927, they were bent on purging the Bible of its Semitic traits, totally obliterating the Old Testament and manipulating the New Testament so as to laicize it. Purist adherence to the acknowledged veracity of the Reformation Bible gave way to neopagan exegesis that was politically and even racially informed. As a projection of de facto political currents, this approach was programmatically termed "Positive Christianity." After January 1933 the new Nazi regime, with no professed love for either of the two main churches, the Lutheran Protestant and the Roman Catholic, but not yet preaching their extinction, attempted to utilize recent developments by forcing, through tightly controlled synodal elections in September, the formation of a government-controlled Protestant Reich Church, the ruthlessly autocratic element in this being the German Christians. A majority of Protestant bishops and pastors opposed this program and separately constituted themselves first as the Pastors' Emergency League and then, at the Barmen Convention in May 1934, as the Confessional Church. Institutionally still tied to the officially favored German Christians and their Reich Bishop Ludwig Müller, a dour ex-army chaplain, the Confessionalists differed from their heretical Nazi brethren in that, as a matter of principle, they rejected the efforts of the Nazi government to control them (something the political authorities eventually failed to do even with the initially pliable German Christians). Contending with Martin Luther, who had believed that the church ought to respect the state, whatever it might stand for, but that in turn the state should refrain from interfering in strictly church affairs, Confessional Church leaders such as Martin Niemöller and Friedrich von Bodelschwingh insisted on institutional and theological inviolability.[106]

The separation of the two spheres—church on the one side and state on the other—from the vantage point of the Confessional Christians implied the freedom to determine the nature of the sacraments and to define the liturgy, as well as resistance to any attempt on the part of outsiders to impinge on this freedom. Essentially, the Confessionalists continued the pietistic approach to Evangelical Lutheranism, which had been upheld, prior to January 1933, in order to check the aberrations of what had always been, and continued to be, the Positive Christian minority. This entailed a purist interpretation of the Scriptures, including the Old Testament; a desire to restore the authentically religious, scripturally felicitous persona of Christ as the Son of God; and a resolution to observe the original, unadulterated liturgy, with a view to undoing the deplored corruptions. In addition to sovereignty in matters affecting their creed, the Confessionalists insisted on their right to render unto Caesar individually in any manner they chose, and for many—who were just as nationalistically minded as the German Christians—this meant voting for and becoming members of the Nazi Party. Neither did Confessionalist Christianity preclude anti-Semitism, since many of its followers had long hated Jews, if merely on religious grounds. What they objected to, however, was being told by government or party authorities how to deal with the issue of the Jews, whether individually in interpersonal relations, institutionally, or in dogma. As the church struggle in the Reich unfolded after 1934—a struggle in which Rosenberg was to play a most sinister role—the mainstream Confessionalist movement drifted ever farther away from the officially sanctioned yet decreasingly significant faction of German Christians. Meanwhile, within the Confessional Church itself divisions proliferated, with various shades of Nazism and anti-Nazism coexisting side by side. Hence, at the height of World War II the situation had polarized to produce doctrinaire Confessionalists who came to see in Hitler and his Nazis evil incarnate, and pro-Nazi Confessionalists who, although also under threat of incarceration, still claimed the independence of religious dogma as a matter concerning only individual believers and their God, while at the same time they thought nothing of serving the government in whatever fashion it desired. In 1944 at one end of this spectrum one could find men such as Dietrich Bonhoeffer, who fought Hitler literally to the death (they were murdered by the Nazis), and at the other men such as Otmar Freiherr von Verschuer, a genetics specialist in Berlin who ordered his assistant Dr. Josef Mengele to provide him with heterochromatic eyeballs of Jewish prisoners from Auschwitz.[107]

What all of this amounted to in terms of music was that church-music experts in the camp of the Confessionalists objected to the way in which the German Christians had treated sacred music, which they deemed to have been tampered with and falsified. Thus, the Confessionalists wished to restore the original liturgical quality of sacred music to a state of purity—analogously to theology—as had existed in the post-Reformation times of Schütz, Telemann, and Bach. In order to accomplish this, they enlisted the help of musicians and composers who themselves had a professional—that is, musical or musicological—interest in this "revival," who nominally could be counted to a greater or lesser extent among the Confessionalists, who occupied positions of influence at church or secular conservatories, and who maintained their political cover through various degrees of collaboration with Nazi authorities. Fritz Stein, an ordained pastor, expert church musician, and enthusiastic National Socialist, was a perfect example. Beyond such professional help, the Confessionalists also sought the organizational support of the Reich Music Chamber under Stein's former student Peter Raabe, and, to prove that they were entirely beyond suspicion of being enemies of the state, they did their best to comply with certain provisions of anti-Semitic legislation when it affected baptized Jewish church musicians. Accurately if cynically, one critical church-music historian has characterized the sum total of these machinations as a campaign in which the Confessionalists allied themselves "with Hitler against the German Christians."[108] A major demonstration, to signify decisive progress in those efforts and expose the relative weakness of the despised German Christians, occurred in 1937 in Berlin, when the Festival of Protestant Church Music was organized. Whatever those festivities may have accomplished in the cause of purifying liturgical music and the rebirth of traditional polyphony, the keen observer could have no doubt that above all it represented a shabby compromise with the regime leaders on the part of calculating composers such as Wolfgang Fortner, Ernst Pepping, Hugo Distler, Johann Nepomuk David, and Armin Knab.

Hence, it appears that in their reformist zeal the Confessionalists proceeded to exorcise the devil with the help of Beelzebub. Their leader in this was Oskar Söhngen, a theologian and church musicologist, born in 1900, who taught at the Berlin Akademie für Kirchen- und Schulmusik and took a keen interest in liturgy. In May 1933 he and his confreres, among them the professors Frotscher and Gurlitt and the composer Distler, set the tone when they publicized a declaration in which they laid out the tenets for a revival of Protestant church music. They stated that such music had to be removed from the concert hall and that its aesthetics, allegedly as in Luther's time, had once more to be subordinated to the primacy of the liturgy; this meant that the music itself was to become more a part of the liturgical process in the church. Musical virtuosity, whether on the part of organists or choirmasters, was to be eschewed. Such church music was to relate once more to its Reformation archetypes, either through recourse to music by masters such as Schütz, Buxtehude, Pachelbel, Hassler, and of course Bach, or through the creation, by young German composers such as Distler, of neo-post-Reformation works. This music would be tied to the congregation, which was now viewed in analogy to the *völkisch* community of the Nazis. The entire movement was positioned against the nineteenth century and its music, and against "the corrosive forces of liberalism and individualism," a value system associated with that century. "Cosmopolitan art" that was not rooted in German soil could never function as Protestant church music. Church music, and with it the church organ, had to be regarded organically, that is to say, in organic union with the congregation, with the people.[109]

Göring's commissar Hinkel got busy, charging the highly vaunted Stein and Stein's colleague in Tübingen, Karl Hasse, with the task of creating order, for a situation in which Nazi Confessionalist church musicians were at war with Nazi German Christian church musicians was embarrassing at best. The problem was a delicate one, for Hinkel was the original leader of the Berlin chapter of the Kampfbund für deutsche Kultur, to whose northern and southern wings Stein and Hasse also belonged. The German Christians, against whom the Confessionalists ranted, were also strongly anchored in the Kampfbund. By June 1933 Hasse had rendered a cautious assessment of the situation. He did not deny his personal predilection for the Kampfbund's mission, the German Christian Movement, and its church-music and political goals. But he was expert enough to concede that aberrations of the kind the German Christians were prone to, such as "Schubert songs with organ accompaniment, cello solos and things of this nature," could in no way be justified as contributions to Christian ritual if performed as part of a Lutheran church service. By September the wily Hinkel had enticed Stein to agree to an appointment as president of a new Reich League for Protestant Church Music, along the lines of Söhngen's Church-Music Rejuvenation Movement, formed earlier. Not least because of his own ties to the German Christians and Kampfbund membership, Stein accepted this office only reluctantly. Moreover, by October Hinkel had used his personal influence with Bishop Müller to have this Reich League legitimized and therefore made binding on both of the antagonistic camps. Realistically speaking, Hinkel, Hasse, and Stein all had made very politic moves, for this clearly marked the beginning of twilight for the Kampfbund as well as for the German Christians. After the founding of the Reich Music Chamber, the Reich League for Protestant Church Music was integrated into it, and from then on membership in it as well as in the RMK was made compulsory for every German Protestant church musician.[110]

The thematic bone of contention between German Christian and Confessional church musicians has already been alluded to. It remains, however, to clarify these differences further and, more important, to show why the music program of the Confessionalists was essentially fascistic. As I have noted, Söhngen and his friends objected to the employment by the German Christians and their post–World War I forerunners of what was to a large extent Romantic music from the post-Napoleonic period of the nineteenth century, which was bereft of original church ties, conceived for secular concert audiences, and executed with virtuoso panache, often by star performers. Much of this struck the reformers as bathos and, if the quality was poor, as downright kitsch as, in their eyes, piety gave way to sentimentality and sober artistry to noise and bombastic posturing. Conventional church choir practices reminded Söhngen's compatriot the music critic Fred Hamel of the gauche hymn culture of beery burgher glee clubs; as far as he was concerned, in most churches the pipe organ tended to function as "the tractor of a perennially dragging congregation." Confessionalist believers saw in these entrenched customs a perilous departure from simple piety as originally dictated by orthodox Lutheranism, where nothing intercedes between the believer and his God, least of all overblown art. The worst example of this kind of church music was offered in September 1933 to Goebbels by an aristocratic lady from the German Christian fold, who had composed a cantata in honor of Adolf Hitler to verses she herself had written. In this "Almighty God" figured no more prominently than the beloved Führer, whom God had "awakened" for the sake of the German people, whom Hitler in turn wished to "liberate from every hardship." Another, more harmless example was the popular Christian hymn "Silent Night," which, because it harked back to the nineteenth century and was regarded as campy, was to be banned. To Söhngen, Hamel, and now Stein these sorts of offerings amounted to objectionable paganism.

Instead, the reformers wanted to find the way back to the preaching of the Gospel, as contained in the Scriptures, and church music was to aid this transmission as an integral part of church liturgy. This new liturgical consciousness, in opposition to the false liberalism of the Romantic nineteenth century, was seen to ally itself with the revolutionary impulses emanating from the new nationalist awakening commanded by Hitler. It promised organic, *völkisch* unity rather than the disingenuous spirituality of a bygone century. The sobriety of sixteenth- or seventeenth-century chorales was anti-Romantic, anti-emotional, and close to the sort of spiritual militancy that had motivated Luther; the singing of the congregation, the community, indeed the corporative and the military combat unit (as later in the war), was to be a potent symbol of the new awakening and, springing from it, the new organic unity.[111]

This kind of thinking exhibited obvious parallels with the sociopolitical aesthetics of Ernst Krieck and Fritz Jöde (who were persona non grata with both the German Christians and the Kampfbund); indeed, these aesthetic commonalities throw into stark relief the susceptibility of the church-music reformist ideology to Nazi weltanschauung. This weltanschauung, as paradoxical as it might seem, given the initial mandate of the Confessionalists, was regarded not as in opposition but rather as complementary to the Confessionalist church-music aesthetics. The authoritarian Nazi government was hailed as assisting the Confessionalists in their cultist purification. As Hamel explained: "In light of the unqualified national and progressive intention of the National Socialist program all guarantees have been put in place for future developments. The path is cleared—our work can begin!"[112]

Both the new euphoria and the Nazi contacts became obvious during the previously referred to Festival of New Church Music, organized by the Confessionalists in Berlin during October 1937. Works by the new school of restorative church musicians—Distler, Pepping, Fortner, David, Müller, Chemin-Petit, and Micheelsen—were performed; significantly, they all had, or were to have, some compromising Nazi connection. Some musicians, such as the organist Fritz Heitmann, were staunch preregime National Socialists. The event was co-financed by the Nazi government; one of the orchestra conductors was Peter Raabe of the Reich Music Chamber, another the ubiquitous Fritz Stein. Old hymns included some purged of their "Jewish" content. In press releases and surrounding publications Söhngen stressed the affinity between the reinvented church music and the Hitler Youth, remarking that several of the featured composers were active in that organization. He made much of the fact that all of the works performed at the festival were created *after* 30 January 1933, thus reemphasizing the similarity between the political and church-music awakenings. As he opened the three-day event on 7 October in the Potsdam Garnisonkirche, Söhngen proclaimed: "The Protestant church music, in the coming days, is awaiting the judgment of the public. Moreover, it is doing so in the happy contention not only that it owes an important service to Adolf Hitler's new Germany, but also that it is ideally qualified to render it." Söhngen then sent a devout telegram to the Führer, who immediately responded with thanks.[113]

The theologian kept his part of the bargain. In the years following these festivities, under Söhngen and his staff Protestant church musicians who were baptized Jews were unprotected and thus fell afoul of the Nazi race laws, and Söhngen's new brand of church music was put to good inspirational use in the aggressive Nazi Wehrmacht. With respect to the "racially" Jewish church musicians, Söhngen prided himself on the fact that there were only a few problem cases, since fortunately it could be proved "how *judenrein* the church music had kept itself to begin with."[114]

For Söhngen, the most important avant-garde church composers represented at the 1937 festival were Johann Nepomuk David (1895–1977), Ernst Pepping (1901–1981), and Hugo Distler (1908–1942).[115] They may have been church musicians, and as such they should have been in opposition to the Nazi regime—as should have been the Confessional Church in *everything* it did. But they were sufficiently close to the regime to hold teaching positions at institutions of higher learning that enjoyed official protection. Their music, sacred or profane, was also performed publicly throughout the Third Reich and, for the most part, applauded. The regime accorded them its respect by nominating them for generous prizes, at the level of the Reich Music Chamber, in 1942. Moreover, toward the end of the war David and Pepping were placed on a most-favored-artist list, which meant preferential treatment such as being shielded from military conscription. When Distler committed suicide in 1942, the regime-beholden *Zeitschrift für Musik* called him "a strong talent" and deplored his loss, and the Hitler Youth Thomaner-Chor of Leipzig sang his hymns in his memory.[116]

Distler, who wrote for sacred as well as secular occasions, composed in a neo-Baroque style patterned on his great exemplar Heinrich Schütz, and he preferred a cappella choirs. His was a polyphony establishing autonomy for all voices and often entering into bold harmonic terrain. His music was definitely an antipode to the luxuriant sounds of nineteenth-century Romanticism, but he also was careful to draw the line between his oeuvre and the legacy of the modernists. Indeed, Weimar-style modernity was firmly rejected by these church-music restorers. Distler regarded atonality in particular as "going against nature."[117]

Post–World War II claims that Distler's music was defamed by the Nazis are easily disproved by the evidence; still, it is entirely possible that he killed himself because the political pressures were weighing on his conscience.[118] He may have been crushed between the demands of the Nazi state and loyalty to his Protestant faith, for he could not serve both. Distler's ties to the National Socialist regime were subtle ones, though firm at first. From 1931 to 1937 he was Kantor and organist at the Jacobi Church in Lübeck, thereafter at the conservatory in Stuttgart, and from 1940 to 1942 at the Akademie für Kirchen- und Schulmusik in Berlin, where he would have had regular contact with Hitler Youth music students of the kind Wolfgang Stumme was cultivating. Back in Lübeck, a party member since 1933, Distler was coaching young girls and boys, at least one of whom opted for entry into the Hitler Youth at a time when this was by no means obligatory. Distler himself spoke with conviction of the "bold" new political awakening, "the greatness of the patriotic events" after 1933, and he saw in Hitler's state a proper framework for the creation of contemporary Gothic music against the backdrop of politico-pedagogical responsibilities. Although he wrote most of his work for the church, he also dedicated some of it to "potentially all ceremonials and communal celebrations"—an open invitation to the planners of the new political festival cycle. Not surprisingly, one of Distler's compositions was later earmarked for the 9 November rituals commemorating Nazi victims of the Munich Beer Hall Putsch; his song "Awake, Oh German Land" conjured up loyalty to the Third Reich; and yet another, the "Song for Men" for a capella male choir, was deemed suitable for 30 January, the anniversary of the commencement of Hitler's regime.[119]

Ernst Pepping ranked with Distler as a neopolyphonic pioneer of the first order. He too walked the fine line between post-Romantic tonality and modernism. In 1926 he participated at the Donaueschingen modern-music festival, where his serenade for military band and a suite for trumpet, saxophone, and trombone were played. But in the 1930s he disclaimed anything "atonal," although he conceded the inadequacy of traditional functional harmony dictated by tonic and dominant, with its dependence on the leading note; for him salvation once again lay in the seemingly primitive, Gothically austere structures of Baroque-style music. Pepping took seriously the parallelism between the new political and musical awakenings; to him the community imputed to the social fabric and the community allegedly found in a church congregation were congenial and deserving of more than just lip service. He passionately subscribed to the new organicist view. "Art as much as the politics of the day is inspired by the same will," he wrote in 1934, "the will to collect the dispersed parts, to form a new community. The rudder of the spirit has been turned around. There has hardly ever been a time when the objectives of the past have been opposed as ruthlessly as today." "The new art" that he and his colleagues now stood for meant a fresh departure, no less so than did "the new political persuasion." With such utterances as background, Pepping articulated strong objections to the artistic customs of the past century, with its overblown concert business, its scattered and useless "individualisms."[120]

Besides his sacred-music compositions so cherished by his mentor Söhngen, Pepping composed weighty secular works; both genres were popular well into 1944. He had written a choral mass, *Deutsche Choralmesse*, in 1928. The use of the adjective "German" at that time was not suspect, for it was in the tradition of composers such as Brahms, who wrote his *Deutsches Requiem* between 1857 and 1868.[121] But when, in 1938, Pepping titled a newly composed mass of his *Deutsche Messe*, he must have known, as did all German intellectuals and artists, that under Hitler "Deutsch" had moved beyond its original, neutral function of regional or national denomination and had become freighted with heavy ideological—that is to say, National Socialist—baggage. Hence, as in the case of Bruno Stürmer and others of a similarly calculating disposition, any composition that after 1933 was explicitly designated "Deutsch" could now be interpreted as an obeisance to the Nazi regime.[122]

And so it was not by accident that in 1938, four years after his appointment to a Berlin Protestant church-music conservatory, works by Pepping were deemed suitable to celebrate Hitler's assumption of power—evidently with such success that in 1942 the lord mayor of Essen commissioned him to compose new pieces for political ceremonies. At the same time, two new symphonies of his were premiered under Böhm in Dresden (1939) and under Furtwängler in Berlin (1943). Pepping wrote a secular opus, Das Jahr, which in its thematic naturalism corresponded tendentiously with the artificial festival cycle of the regime (rather than with Haydn's famous brainchild), glorifying the organic sequence of the seasons, hailing the Blood-and-Soil qualities of the German archetype rooted in the land—a work staged, moreover, by brown-shirted Hitler Youth of Dresden's elite Kreuzchor in 1941. Although the Nazi Party was aware of Pepping's close ties with the Confessional Church, the composer was never suspect. With a sense of satisfaction its exponents noted that his music had progressed from a once "cacophonic" style to a "moderately modern" level. And "as a teacher, he is generally judged quite favorably."[123]

Johann Nepomuk David was originally a Catholic primary-school teacher from Austria, but he became an instructor at the Leipzig Conservatory in 1934, and by the time of the Berlin Protestant church-music festival he ranked with Distler and Pepping as one of the new polyphonic giants. His specialty was music for the organ and symphonic orchestra, although he composed for choirs as well. In retrospect it is difficult not to be overwhelmed by the official reception of his works in the supervised press. Review after review, one more positive than the next, identified him as one of the most respected composers of the Nazi cultural establishment, no matter how much these works may have revolved around religious subjects. Therefore, David's complaint to Carl Orff in 1943 that he felt neglected shows either a man of great naiveté or an artist with an enormous ego.[124]

Actually, the fact that David kept all his irons in the fire suggests anything but naiveté. The Völkischer Beobachter devoted a positive critique to him on the occasion of the Berlin church-music festival as early as 1937. As in the case of Distler and Pepping, he allowed one of his motets to be recommended for Nazi celebrations—for the ninth of November—a few years after the political takeover. When in the summer of 1941 Minister Rust converted the Leipzig Conservatory to an academy of university rank, this amounted to an upgrading from which David could only benefit. Appropriately, he took part in the ceremonies, celebrating the Nazi minister's presence with the help of his neoclassical art. It was reaffirmed that music education in the future would be totally geared to National Socialist standards. Soon after, David became the director of the upgraded institution and a full professor. Subsequently he composed a motet, based on an aphorism of the Führer invoking "fealty" to the "Volk," for choir and three trombones, and had it premiered on campus under his own direction. He also organized a commemorative choir service in honor of the fallen Nazi hero and fellow musician Helmut Bräutigam. This was around the time when he, along with the Nazi Max Trapp and his Berlin colleague Pepping, received a state subvention from the RMK in the not so paltry amount of 4,000 marks. The composer reciprocated by aiding the war effort in the only way he knew, sketching *Symphonische Variationen über ein Thema von Heinrich Schütz* in four movements, which was bluntly conceived as "martial music." There were warriorlike sections entitled "Battle Procession," "Fear and Worship," "Portent for the Enemy," and "Battle, Victory, and Thanksgiving." Like a few others, this work symbolized the mixed marriage between aggressive fascism and chauvinistic, bigoted religion.[125]

The silent alliance between National Socialism and Protestant Christianity through the medium of church music had significant repercussions for education, at the university student level, and filtering down from there to the schools and, more important, the highly impressionable Hitler Youth. At their own institutions of higher learning David, Pepping, and Distler trained future educators and Protestant Kantoren who were to become active in Nazi-adapted churches, nazified schools, and Hitler Youth organizations. As far as is known today, the three men did not contribute directly to the body of hymn music that was especially designed to be internalized on a day-to-day basis by every Hitler boy and girl in the land. This rather more amplified National Socialist function was the preserve of yet another group of church musicians, whose most prominent and insidiously dangerous representatives were Heinrich Spitta, Armin Knab, and Wolfgang Fortner. If, as has been observed, the contrived minor-mode songs practiced in the Hitler Youth were sounding more and more like old church hymns, it was these men and their students who were chiefly responsible.[126]

As late as 1953 Heinrich Spitta (1902–1972) was remembered by Oskar Söhngen as someone who worked "from the bosom of the church, from the fulcrum of the faith." Söhngen described Spitta's compositions as "real church music, because here faith itself has become an integral constituent of creativity."[127]

Faith in what? Heinrich Spitta, nephew of the famous church musicologist and Bach biographer Julius August Philipp Spitta, and whose grandfather and father had also been church musicians and theologians, had begun as an interpreter of Schütz and received a Ph.D. from Göttingen at the age of twenty-two. His early and extreme nationalism—surely a factor that drew him to Hitler—stemmed from his just having missed serving in the imperial army (he had that in common with Heinrich Himmler) and witnessing the French repossession of his home town, Strasbourg. Influenced by Jöde and his movement, he was apparently captivated by the mysteries of the German *Volkslied* as early as 1926. The imperative of simplicity, which compelled him to choose the vocation of a primary-school teacher, also informed his taste for basic structures in instrumental music and song. His preoccupation with post-Reformation music forms was thus a foregone conclusion, but so was his predilection for fascism, promising law and order and an anti-Allied national restoration. In 1934 Karl Cerff hired the young composer for the Hitler Youth; in February 1935 Spitta had succeeded his role model Jöde at the Berlin Akademie für Kirchen- und Schulmusik, where from now on he cooperated closely with a kindred spirit, Hitler Youth music chief Wolfgang Stumme. Spitta soon proved equal to the task of being both a church musician and an educator for the Hitler Youth: at a music-training camp at Erfurt in November 1935 his *Thanksgiving Cantata* was performed, and the profound piety of this work was said to give the lie to those who "blabbered about the incompatibility of God and Hitler's youths."[128]

In a very short time Spitta advanced to become one of the most fashionable Hitler Youth composers of the Nazi era. Youth camps, music schools, and conservatories sang his compositions, all of which resonated with the chauvinism of Hans Baumann, Helmut Bräutigam, and Erich Lauer. But they also distinguished themselves through a pseudosacred quality grafted from the chorales of Spitta's childhood as well as the churches and sacred-music schools where he had studied earlier and now taught. The mixture was as alluring as it was hypocritical, catering to the needs of the impressionable young, those who constantly had to be reassured of a bond with their proclaimed political rulers, particularly Hitler himself, but at the same time were not yet ready to throw overboard the trusted bourgeois Christian value system of a shaken and perhaps bygone era. One of the earliest Hitler Youth songs Spitta created was "The Führer Has Called Us," whose lyrics conjured the drums, the standard, the drone of marching army boots and horses' hooves. But there was also reference to children and women to be protected by the Lord God, since the menfolk, busy at the military front, were now incapable of doing it. Demonization of imaginary adversaries, the "saucy scum," was aimed squarely at the Jews, whose "randy hides" would have to be properly treated. The primitive metaphors from the realm of family, religion, and war, specifically the polarization of good versus evil, an effective scare-mongering device employed by the churches from time immemorial to keep their flocks in submission, was thus optimally utilized in this and many similar hymns by Spitta, who remained just as active as an author of "serious" works. His most famous one came to signify both the sacred and the profanely political in that it was entitled *Holy Fatherland*.[129]

Yet another Hitler Youth music educator whom Söhngen admired was Armin Knab, a doctor of jurisprudence born in 1881, who had spent an entire career in the public legal system in Bavaria until he was called to Berlin's Akademie für Kirchen- und Schulmusik in 1934. Knab, too, was devoted to the resurrection of archaic modal music, "the simple, essential polyphony," and his main interest centered on the creation of oratorios and other choral music. Today he is remembered, if at all, as a composer of songs, of both a Christian and a secular nature. But he also wrote chamber music, examples of both genres being widely performed in public concerts all over the Reich well into 1944. In 1942 samples of Knab's works were featured in a national broadcast series, said to be representative of Germany's southern regions, along with those of Bresgen, Egk, and Knab's friend Orff. When in 1944 Knab was released from his duties at the academy, he was commended for his pedagogical work on behalf of his many students, for he was among very few composers "whose labors have been widely recognized and who have founded the style, which today we may regard as the pace-setting expression of our artistic ambitions."[130]

Those words supply the clue for Knab's multifaceted commitments to the cause of National Socialism and the Hitler Youth, whatever else he may have accomplished for Söhngen's Protestant church-music reform. Knab's own and the post–World War II assertions of his friends that he stayed aloof from the Nazi movement and that, in particular, he "withstood" the "pressures" of the regime to join the Nazi Party are typical of the strategic falsehoods meant to exonerate the culprit that we have seen before. The fact is that Knab was able to ignore the Nazi Party because he had already become a member of the Nazi Jurists' League, on 21 December 1933, while still in the public prosecutor's office in Würzburg. That was tantamount to Nazi Party membership.[131]

Like Spitta and Distler, Knab participated in the official support activities for integrating *Hausmusik* into the new Nazi culture. He, whose lieder were soon favored for classroom instruction by his Nazi colleague Vollerthun at Berlin's sister conservatory, was himself instrumental in educating future Hitler Youth leaders such as Ludwig Kelbetz. He collaborated with the Nazi poets Will Vesper, Erwin Kolbenheyer, and Hermann Claudius in composing Nazi-conformist songs; his works figured prominently in all manner of neopagan Nazi celebrations and in songbooks specifically designed for the Hitler Youth. The verses to which he set his music were redolent of Nazi weltanschauung, of struggle, angst, and death, and as a church composer he came as close as anybody to replacing the received Christian usage with Nazi symbology. "Oh Germany, Germany, Fatherland," "The Germans' Liberation Song," "A German Morning," "Young Germany," "Thou Must Believe in Germany's Future," "Dead Soldiers," "Who Can Kill Our Soul?," "German Spring," "Speak Not of Your Own Sorrows": in their obvious suggestiveness these works and many others catered to the Nazis' ideology of Blood-and-Soil, of submission by the individual to the totalitarian community, of the martial mien and invincibility of superior Germans via-à-vis racially degenerate foes, of ultrachauvinism and Adolf Hitler's greatness. They were recommended for and performed at Nazi functions staged by the Hitler Youth, the Nazi Student League, the SA, Wehrmacht, and SS.[132]

Commensurate with his efforts on behalf of the dictatorship, Knab, like most of his gifted associates who sold out to the fascist regime, was handsomely rewarded. Gauleiter Otto Hellmuth of Main-Franconia, with the express sanction of Goebbels, awarded him the Max Reger Prize in 1940. Along with Trunk and Orff from Munich, Knab received the 2,000 mark RMK prize in 1942. And the town of Erfurt commissioned him and Claudius to write a *Cantata for the German Year* a few months later. If Knab did not appear on Goebbels's vaunted war service exemption list, it was simply because he was already too old for conscription.[133]

The last composer in this group of church and Hitler Youth musicians, much treasured by Söhngen, was the Heidelberg conductor, composer, and professor Wolfgang Fortner. Indeed, Fortner's compositions were crucial for the success of the Berlin 1937 church-music festival. But Fortner was also involved with various Nazi institutions. Thus, the assertion of the post–World War II musicologist Ulrich Dibelius that Fortner sought "refuge" from Nazism in the church is as embarrassing today as another expert's statement that the Nazi period had confined the composer's sacred music to a place "behind the church walls." Instead, in Fortner's case as in others, his efforts on behalf of the National Socialist regime developed in lockstep with whatever he may have felt called upon to render unto the church. This was an exemplarily Lutheran and, for the Confessional church, a Nazi-sanctioned credo.[134]

Fortner, born in 1907 in Leipzig and raised in that city's formidable church-music tradition, took the Gymnasium teachers' examination in 1931, and in the very same year was appointed to the faculty of Heidelberg's Protestant conservatory as an instructor of music theory and composition. His activities were prodigious, including directing the noted Collegium Musicum and later on founding the Heidelberg Chamber Orchestra. His predilection for church modes and pentatonic and whole-note scales soon became apparent; and he cherished linear counterpoint, the canons and fugues of the Baroque period—those halcyon years of Lutheran-inspired church music—even treading on pre-Bach terrain. Fortner came to prefer sparse instrumentation and linear voice-leading, professing these to be dry, sober, objective antidotes to Romanticism (and, as Jöde and Söhngen would add, to liberalism, pomposity, and virtuosity). As in the case of many of his contemporaries, such music was in the new mold of neoclassicism, which had evolved after World War I all over Europe in reaction to "the increasingly exaggerated gestures and formlessness of late Romanticism." Its most prominent exponent certainly was Stravinsky, but in Germany its practitioners included Hindemith and others. Here, neoclassicism articulated itself specifically, and characteristically, through the "Back-to-Bach" movement, to which, both before and after January 1933, Fortner, Spitta, Pepping, Distler, and their friends solidly adhered.[135] The purist simplicity in religion (and its liturgical music) striven for by Söhngen and his cohorts was to merge with the simplicity of neoclassicist revival structures.

In the Third Reich the austerity of Fortner's music—like that of his friends—naturally matched the authoritarianism of the political rulers and the Protestant church elders alike. The fascist thought processes were in gear by then; already in 1931 Fortner had created a musical school play entitled *Cress Is Drowning,* which evoked the sacrificial altruism of the individual for the sake of the greater community. In 1932 he collaborated with the anti-Semitic harpsichordist Li Stadelmann, another Baroque purist; Rosenberg's Kampfbund für deutsche Kultur sponsored the German premiere of his new concerto for string orchestra in nearby Mannheim a few months after Hitler's takeover. Then followed guest-conducting for the Nazi labor union Nationalsozialistische Betriebszellenorganisation (NSBO), and the staging of specially composed works for a spectacular Nazi celebration at the University of Göttingen in 1937 (the year of Fortner's Berlin Festival publicity), not to mention his *Eine deutsche Liedmesse* (1934), meant to keep the Confessionalist congregations in line. In 1939 one Nazi musicologist called Fortner a master of "uncompromising archaic-polyphonic styling."[136]

Around this time Fortner, who was just as adept at composing "celebratory cantatas" for the anniversary of Hitler's 1933 coup as at writing religiously inspired music, was one of the most promising musicians of the Third Reich. Most probably he did not even perceive his balancing act between church and dictatorship as the shabby compromise it was. Courted by the church authorities of Baden, who did not wish him to move to Berlin, and praised as politically "reliable and spotless" by the regional Nazi authorities for an abiding commitment to the conductorship of the local Hitler Youth orchestra, Fortner could say that he had achieved the best of both worlds. But his one, carefully hidden blemish was his homosexuality, which was a biopolitical crime in the Third Reich. Does this factor explain his obsequiousness to both kinds of potentially threatening authorities?[137]

Ostensibly content, Fortner joined the party early in 1940. He served in the Wehrmacht long enough to be moved by the death of comrades in the trenches, which he then was able to solemnize in song. Objectively speaking, this was the ultimate cynicism: the church musician's work which had prompted young men to fight for Hitler in the first place, as Stumme, Marx, and Kelbetz would have it, was quickly turned around to celebrate the victims, perhaps the very same young men. Till the end of the national struggle Fortner remained politically correct, maligning Schoenberg's twelve-tone system as "evidence of uprootedness" (this from a man who after the war would himself write serial music), contributing to numerous Hitler Youth songbooks, collecting convenient prizes alongside his colleagues, composing and concertizing in sacred and secular environments: in short, the model career of a Confessionalist church musician outwardly at peace with the fascist state.[138]

The combination of polyphonic reformism, Hitler adoration, dogmatic and liturgical restoration, and anti-Romantic crusading reached its apex in conjunction with the "Organ Movement," which originally was also associated with the Back-to-Bach drive. It was sustained by most of the previously mentioned zealots and led by true masters of that king of instruments such as Karl Straube, Gotthold Frotscher, and Günther Ramin. It became tightly aligned with the Confessionalist church-music crusade, which it predated by some years, for, as a subsidiary development of neoclassicism, it had its origins in the early 1920s. At that time Straube, Wilibald Gurlitt, and the doyen of German musicologists Arnold Schering had wanted to restore the organ to its Baroque foundations, demanding for it a drier, cleaner sound than that with which the practitioners of the Romantic period had allegedly corrupted it. Essentially, this called for a renaissance of the original simple pipe organ as an instrument reduced to its basic technology. It was claimed that whereas an original organ could and should be played with a maximum of transparency, the modern, technically overequipped instrument was wrongly being used to simulate the sound of huge symphony orchestras, to muddle linearity, to drown out precision, and to effect mawkish melodrama and tearful sentimentality. At a 1927 Freiburg conference focusing on reform, these issues were signally raised. But it was also made clear that a clean Baroque tone rather than an opulent nineteenth-century sound was the equivalent of true "German" music (as German as Bach himself had been) and furthermore, that American commercial influences, as in the ubiquitous Wurlitzer cinema organ, would have to be fought. This lent the movement a nationalistic, even xenophobic quality which later served it well in its merger with the Confessionalist music reform and its overall integration with the Nazi system.[139]

For purposes of the May 1933 declaration, co-signed by Gurlitt and Distler and their colleagues and calling for a revival of Protestant church music, the concerns of the Organ Movement were part of the agenda. Henceforth the struggle of the organ reformers came to be ever more closely identified with that of the Confessionalist church musicians under Söhngen's leadership, with comparable invective hurled against the German Christians, who were accused of nurturing the "Romantic" organ. Distler and David, both superb organists themselves, provided the strongest personal linkage between those two sets of objectives, and that close relationship became manifest during the 1937 Berlin church-music festival, a second Freiburg organ conference in 1938, and the "Berlin Organ Days" held in 1942. The aims were, consistently, a return to Schützian or Bachian organ style as archetypally both Protestant and German, a reconciliation of the organ's role with orthodox Lutheran liturgy in the churches, and a fruitful interaction between astringent neo-Gothic organ music and congregational singing, to exemplify unity and community.[140]

On the occasion of the Berlin organ festival, however, it was also declared that the organ must not be pushed into a corner, for the use of a mere handful of specialists, but that it should be "directly in touch with today's general musical cosmos." This was a clear reference to the political role the organ had begun to play, since about 1935, with the approval, even connivance of churchmen such as Knab, David, Fortner, and the Leipzig Thomaskirche organist Ramin.[141]

At the time of the infamous party rally of September 1935, which ushered in the anti-Semitic Nuremburg Race Laws, Hitler decided to construct Europe's largest organ in the Nuremberg rally grounds for the next year's celebrations. This turned out to be a Walcker organ with 16,000 pipes, 220 registers, and 5 manuals, amplified by giant loudspeakers—quite the antithesis of a simple Back-to-Bach organ. Franz Adam of the Nazi Symphony Orchestra had a hand in the overall planning. The entire concept of the organ as the king of instruments, truly a monumental organ, was now linked to Albert Speer's vision of the party rally site and its events as a colossal edifice for the Nazi regime. The majestic sound of that organ was literally to overwhelm the attending Nazi faithfuls and put them in awe of Hitler. Ramin, Germany's best organist and once a pioneer of the Organ Movement, was then chosen to demonstrate the instrument in a private sitting for the Führer, and he also worked the manuals, pedals, and stops during the 1936 party rally.[142]

The symbolic value of this action cannot be overestimated, for now, beyond narrow neoclassicist and church-liturgical objectives, it had inexorably established the organ as a preeminent tool of Nazi ceremonials. Moreover, the pairing of the organ with Hitler's Führer persona is telling: the most powerful musical instrument known to humankind was linked to the most powerful politician ever. As Müller-Blattau said, the organ was "the total instrument of a total state"; the allusion to Hitler as the "omnipotent organist" was hypnotic.[143] This was not lost on Himmler, when in early July 1937 he ordered the organist of Potsdam's Garnisonkirche to play the organ in a special ceremony at Quedlinburg in the Harz Mountains. Here, before a congregation of high SS leaders, the rediscovered (alleged) skeleton of the medieval King Heinrich I of Germany, whose reincarnation Himmler fancied himself to be, was finally laid to rest.[144]

At the second Freiburg organ festival of 1938, the paradigm of the organ as the "total instrument" was reiterated and engraved in stone when it was decided that a permanent Hitler Youth organ workshop should be created. This would benefit many of the music students who had been training at the conservatories and academies with a view to becoming church organists or Hitler Youth music instructors. From then on, and into the war, the organ became an integral part of the Hitler Youth music scene, especially as far as the young musicians' involvement in specifically Nazi celebrations was concerned. A tall, blond Youth leader in a smartly tailored brown uniform, flawlessly able to rattle off a Bach toccata on the organ, would possess all the desired social and political attributes; he would be universally admired, popular with the girls (to aid master-race procreation), a contemporary idol, the prototype of a new Führer.[145] He was the model for the machine gun–toting SS soldier displaying his fine piano skills in Spielberg's movie *Schindler's List.*

After the Freiburg conference church and party men agreed that the organ was a quintessentially "political" instrument, suited for all manner of Nazi celebrations. And the connection with the Back-to-Bach impulse was not forgotten. In the words of Confessionalist church official Herbert Haag, "most of Bach's organ works lend themselves to festival planning without any reservations," perhaps as interludes between speakers and choir, as on 30 January of each year.[146] Furthermore, he noted with reference to the church congregation: "Which instrument could better serve a total weltanschauung and the will expressed in its festivities than the organ, which is, at the same time, the symbolic instrument of the community?"[147] And Müller-Blattau asserted that the Organ Movement's original goal—to remove the organ from exclusively church property and place it within the German community—was finally being realized.[148]

During the war, when Spitta's hymn "The Führer Has Called Us" was performed by choir, it was done to the accompaniment of brass and organ. By the spring of 1942 Hamburg's Music Hall possessed a very large pipe organ which, as Generalmusikdirektor Eugen Jochum noted, was particularly suited for "momentous party celebrations." Months later Richard Strauss, the composer of *Also Sprach Zarathustra*, with its majestic organ introduction, was asked by the Gauleiter of Silesia to compose a special festive piece for another giant organ in Breslau, fit for "the largest and most significant political and cultural-political stagings of the Reich."[149] Strauss never even replied. Church counselor Haag's recommendation of 1939 was put into practice on 30 January 1943, when Berlin's Akademie für Kirchen- und Schulmusik had its organist perform Bach's *Präludium und Fuge in G-Moll*, after which followed Nazi addresses and then Spitta's third movement from the partita *Heilig Vaterland*, again played on the organ; a "Führer Service" concluded the event. By this time "Open Organ Celebrations of the Berlin Hitler Youth" at Charlottenburg Castle had been strategically designed to replace regular church observances on Sunday mornings. Also during 1943 more regional organ workshops and festivals were organized, under the aegis of the party. At one of these, in Heidelberg, the current work of church musician Wolfgang Fortner was mentioned as a shining example. Cesar Bresgen and Gotthold Frotscher issued new "organ primers." Moreover, both Frotscher and Ramin participated in an organ workshop in Vienna, which in spirit was beholden to National Socialist revelry; appropriately, it concluded with a hymn and greeting to the Führer.[150]

This was only one of several occasions on which Frotscher and Ramin collaborated for the sake of rejuvenating both organ and church-music practices. They had been co-signatories for the cause in May 1933 and jointly conducted an organ workshop for the Reich Music Chamber in Vienna in 1940.[151] And yet, though representatives of the combined Protestant church and new organ movements, the two musicians were cut from different cloth. Although they were both the sons of clerics and were raised in the Lutheran tradition, Frotscher's first loyalty was to National Socialism, to which he always subordinated his church-music interests. Ramin, by contrast, was first and foremost a church organist, who found that he could take advantage of the Nazi movement over time.

Frotscher joined the party in 1933 at the age of thirty-six, while still teaching musicology at the Danzig Conservatory. Like Fritz Heitmann, that other organ expert and Söhngen friend, he had been close to the Kampfbund für deutsche Kultur. But after his promotion to professor at the University of Berlin in 1936, he placed himself at the disposal of the Reich Music Chamber and, in an advisory capacity, of Goebbels himself. Subsequently, he became highly instrumental in both the development of an organ movement for the Hitler Youth, wherein he assisted Stumme, and the related drive toward utilizing the organ in various Nazi regime functions, "without its confessional connotations." Toward the end of the war Frotscher was well known for his specialty, research into the interrelationship of "music and race."[152]

Ramin positioned himself rather differently. Uncommonly gifted, this favorite student of the venerable Leipzig Thomaskantor Karl Straube was teaching at the university by 1919, at age twenty-one, a year after he had become the Thomaskirche organist. He became a professor two years later.[153] It is true that from 1933 to 1945 Ramin presented many examples of masterly musicianship. He did this at the organ, on the harpsichord, and after his appointment as Thomaskantor in late 1939, the most important church-musician post in all of Germany, as director of the Thomaner-Chor and Baroque orchestras. One of his extraordinary feats was to learn Bach's *Goldberg-Variationen* in only four days.[154] Moreover, we can probably believe his widow's assertion that he "strongly abhorred" National Socialism.[155] All the more strange, therefore, at least at a superficial level, is Ramin's calculated resolve to accommodate himself politically to the rulers in order to advance his own career. Yet after appreciating the function, for church and state, of the organ and Protestant music movements, in both of which Ramin was firmly anchored, the private distaste for Nazism might have appeared to him as something to be subordinated both to the arcane aesthetics of those movements, which were sacrosanct, and to his own, very personal goals.

Ramin began to compromise himself in circumstances surrounding a concert tour to the United States. He had already toured there, very successfully, just before Hitler came to power, and the Americans wanted him back. In December 1933 Ramin ingratiated himself with the new regime by advertising his repertoire as one of "purely German" (as opposed to French) organ music, asking in false modesty whether a concert tour would be "desirable, in the interest of German cultural propaganda." He was clearly playing on the fact that Jewish émigrés were creating a bad name for Nazi Germany abroad and that he, with his art, could correct this. Thus, he solicited special official support. The Propaganda Ministry replied that Ramin's planned mission would be "warmly welcomed" and promised logistical assistance. Goebbels personally intervened with the city of Leipzig to effect the organist's temporary release. Predictably, Ramin's American concerts were a rousing success. One German Nazi living in California, with ties to the Foreign Office, who followed the tour reported that the virtuoso had indeed performed "German organ music. This is the kind of propaganda for Germany that cannot be contested."[156]

In California, Ramin's artistic offering at the cultural level had been complemented at the technical one by the presence of Elly Beinhorn, a charming young airplane pilot and wife of famed race car driver Bernd Rosemeyer. Beinhorn, who had flown up from Mexico, was well acquainted with Minister of Aviation Göring, and this probably led to an invitation for Ramin to play at Göring's wedding to the actress Emmy Sonnemann on 12 April 1935, at which Hitler was a legal witness.[157] Next came Ramin's role as organist for the 1936 Reich party rally; a year later he played at Söhngen's church-music festival. Apparently he understood how to serve both God and Caesar.[158]

Especially Caesar. Around this time he also collaborated closely with Rosenberg's NS-Kulturgemeinde in local cultural matters at Leipzig. In 1940 Straube is alleged to have resigned his office as Thomaskantor in protest against the regime. When Ramin only too willingly took over the post, tension is said to have resulted between the two men because of Ramin's accommodating ways. The Nazis thought—correctly, as facts were later to show—that Ramin would be better suited to lead a Thomaner-Chor that now consisted entirely of Hitler Youth.[159]

Until the end of the war Ramin went along with the rest of his accomplished colleagues in the realms of the church and concert halls. He conducted "Heroes' Requiems" and "German Masses," and joined Johann Nepomuk David and Reich Minister Rust at the commencement of the Leipzig Conservatory in 1941. He took the Thomaner-Chor to the Nazi Protectorate of former Czechoslovakia and Fascist Italy to demonstrate the "victory of European art, German style." The Third Reich honored him, as it did others, with ostentatious prize ceremonies. One of Ramin's most significant regime functions at the climax of the war was to direct his Thomaners in a concert of music by Bach for the benefit of a company of SS soldiers about to follow the call of duty. This was in 1942 at Thomaskirche in Leipzig; the SS men were the very same troops, or at least comrades of those troops, putting in service at the eastern liquidation camps. Anyone who witnessed this spectacle could not have escaped the realization that Bach, Hitler, concert musicians, and the churches had all entered into a strange and unholy alliance.[160]

5

Dissonance and Deviance

The Nazi Struggle for Modernity in Music

When I visited the Austrian composer Gottfried von Einem in his Viennese apartment in November 1994, I asked him what sort of music the Nazis, in principle, wanted German composers to create. Without a moment's hesitation von Einem answered: "The opposite of Schoenberg—music in C major."[1] At a superficial level this is of course true. But an exhaustive answer to this question would be more complicated than that. For since the Nazis conceived of themselves as political, social, and cultural revolutionaries, they expected changes, not to say revolutions, to take place in the arts in conformity with all other changes they might cause.[2] As Joseph Goebbels specified in a Munich speech in 1936: "The National Socialist weltanschauung is the most modern thing in the world today, and the National Socialist state is the most modern state. There are thousands of motifs for a modern art in the spirit of this weltanschauung."[3]

Yet how long these changes would take, how thoroughly they would break with the recent German past, who would generate and supervise them, was never programmatically planned but was left to the initiative of individual artists and officials, and finally became a matter of contention between regime leaders as, for instance, between Goebbels (Promi) and

177

Rosenberg (KfdK–NS-Kulturgemeinde). The role of Hitler as the ultimate Führer in these processes was also not clearly circumscribed. Consequently, gray areas developed in which most artists and many politicians moved with less than absolute certainty, leaving themselves open to attacks from various quarters. Yet the lack of precise definitions and official guidelines allowed some artists to tread on what was by orthodox Nazi standards shaky ground, and permitted individual politicians and administrators to offer patronage and protection to musicians who were, strictly speaking, fettered by an intolerant dictatorship. Because the competing ideological canons that were being upheld—whether Rosenberg, Goebbels, Göring, Himmler, or Hitler himself was behind them—could always be modified or neutralized by day-to-day pragmatism, niches of artistic freedom were able to evolve and survive, often surreptitiously, yet just as often in the name of one governmental priority or another. This pattern of cultural-political Darwinism[4] accounts for much of the friction between Rosenberg and Goebbels early on in the Third Reich, which has already been described in some detail, but it also explains why modernist composers such as Carl Orff, Werner Egk, Rudolf Wagner-Régeny, and, to a certain extent, Paul Hindemith were able to carry on throughout the regime.

Against this backdrop, three precepts of Nazi cultural administration must be understood, which were, in unequal measure, shared by Goebbels and Hitler, and which, after only a few months of the regime, turned out to be more durable and efficacious than any policy directives emanating from other regime sources. These were, first, that German culture, including music, was a direct reflection of the German soul and had to be protected and encouraged sui generis. Second, beyond its intrinsic properties, German culture possessed the potential for practical application, for instance, as Goebbels repeated many times, as a palliative to soothe the general population or as a tonic to condition the fighting morale of the troops. Third, culture had to remain largely autonomous, meaning that artists, not ideologues or politicians, had to be in charge of its development—a certain degree of government censorship notwithstanding. Within this general framework, culture—and, in our particular case, music—was expected to develop from older forms to something more contemporary (the Nazis always hesitated to use the term *modern,* which smacked of the ideologically saturated modernism that the hated Weimar Republic had spawned and become associated with). Contemporary graphic art under Nazism, whatever the medium, was not permitted to be anything but clearly descriptive, as was exemplified in the exhibition of degenerate art opened in 1937. By the same token, contemporary music was not permitted to be atonal, especially of the twelve-tone variety personified by Schoenberg, as the Nazi music exhibition in Düsseldorf demonstrated a year later. Both modern, abstract (as in much Expressionist) art, and modern, atonal music were ultimately condemned as Jewish. As the preeminent overseer of German culture in the Third Reich,

Goebbels wanted quality within the legitimate representational modes that were rather loosely defined, and he favored innovation. Realizing that geniuses did not fall from the sky even at the command of the Führer, Goebbels and his men had to content themselves with waiting for great artists to work their way to the front of the pack by virtue of superior creations, although this could of course take years of the envisioned Nazi millennium. Failing that desirable but highly unrealistic goal, the state could attempt to encourage budding young artists, through public competitions and the like, until a few gifted ones shone through, to be subsequently honed to a state of perfection according to prescribed Nazi criteria. As it turned out, from 1933 to 1945, after the Nazis had expunged all the Jews, they fell rather short of both these objectives.[5]

At the start of the regime, the most likely candidate to serve as a role model for innovation in German music was Paul Hindemith; for several months influential National Socialists saw in him the cultural standard bearer toward revolutionary change without iconoclasm. In one sense Hindemith was preordained for this position. Among the leading modernists during the artistic experiments of the Weimar Republic, even before 1933 Hindemith had modified his earlier style, at least sufficiently to placate many Nazis. Although at times he thought that National Socialism was but a transient phenomenon one could easily endure and outlive through circumspect behavior, at other times he was tempted to collaborate with representatives of the Hitler Youth, the German Labor Front, and especially the Kampfbund für deutsche Kultur, in its early capacity as both art broker and art police. There was talk about the composer's being put in charge of the entire German music scene for the sake of reorganizing it, news that even reached Alban Berg in Vienna. "I have been asked to cooperate and have not declined," Hindemith wrote to his fellow composer Ernst Toch in September 1933, already in exile in London. Various new compositions by Hindemith were performed all over the country, and benign critics touted him as the "leader of the younger, contemporary modern movement." After the founding of the Reich Music Chamber, his offical status was enhanced when he was appointed to the RMK's "leadership council" in February 1934. A preview of what looked like a propitious career was the premiere of his symphonic version of *Mathis der Maler*, for when it was presented under Wilhelm Furtwängler in Berlin on 12 March 1934, it was greeted with accolades nationwide, even by Nazi critics.[6]

The symphony consisted of excerpts from a full-scale opera on which Hindemith was still working, and which he was hoping to have staged later. Altogether this music was somehow emblematic of the altered style of the composer. The rededication to conventional tonality, rich triadic harmony, polyphonic vocal passages, diatonic and old church modes of the kind Distler, Pepping, and David espoused: all these in the recent judgment of Claudia Maurer Zenck, "conformed very precisely to the official expectations for modern German music in the Third Reich." At the time, critic Heinrich Strobel spoke of a "totally new simplicity and plasticity of the musical language."[7] The libretto for the opera, written by Hindemith himself, and harking back to the time of the Reformation, the historic ideal for the Nazis, was anything but anathema to the zeitgeist, especially since the hero was Matthis Nithart, popularly known as Matthias Grünewald. Nithart was considered to be an arch-Gothic painter much beloved by Nazi art historians such as Wilhelm Pinder and Expressionist artists such as Emil Nolde, who early on empathized with the Nazis (even though, as in the case of Gottfried Benn, a fellow Expressionist and writer friend of Paul Hindemith, a lasting positive relationship with the regime never developed—a delicious irony that could not have escaped the soon-to-be émigré composer).[8] If Nithart—or Mathis, as Hindemith called him—ever served as an autobiographical paradigm for the composer (and advocates for this interpretation exist), he was not a symbol of "inner emigration," recoiling from tyranny, as some Hindemith admirers have insisted, for at the end of the plot he arranged himself with his alter ego, Cardinal Albrecht. Elements of the story, such as the Peasants' War, accorded with the Nazi ideal of "struggle for the Reich." And Hindemith's Mathis exhibits typically German attitudes, not the least of which is his eventual acquiescence to the powers that be, as, repeatedly, the cardinal extends to him favors and understanding, ultimately causing the introspective Mathis to resign himself to temporal authority.[9]

Hindemith's success under Furtwängler, however, was only one facet of his professional life. Another was that he had made deadly enemies in the Nazi camp before 1933, significantly not for musical but for ideological reasons. The initial source of this opposition was Hitler himself, who allegedly had seen the soprano Laura in Hindemith's opera Neues vom Tage, in a flesh-colored bodysuit, sitting in a bathtub on a Berlin stage in 1929, and was disgusted. (It may be assumed that the music had not helped.) Hindemith's collaboration with Bertolt Brecht in the late 1920s was also spitefully remembered. Not surprisingly, the composer had Rosenberg and his league against him on principle because he was married to a partly Jewish woman (her father, Ludwig Rottenberg, had played a leading role on the Weimar cultural scene as conductor of the Frankfurt Opera), and he was said to be the protégé of Jews. Gertrud Hindemith's Jewish brother-in-law Hans Flesch was a broadcast executive until he was shipped off to a concentration camp in 1933. Hindemith himself, at home and abroad, continued to perform with the Jewish virtuosos Goldberg, Feuermann, and Huberman in various string groups. Throughout 1933, therefore, there were voices that, appealing to the Nazi weltanschauung, maintained that Hindemith was out of the question "as leader of the new German music in the spirit of Hitler, which we so ardently desire."[10] Rosenberg's culture-hustling followers, in the summer of 1934 reorganizing themselves into the NS-Kulturgemeinde, were fanatically motivated to step up their campaign against Hindemith after his Berlin success in March; and Hindemith himself made derogatory remarks about Hitler while in Switzerland, which caused a proscription of his works on German radio. More seriously, Hitler forbade a planned premiere of the opera *Mathis der Maler*, again not for musical but personal reasons. Largely to countermand the destructive activities of the NS-Kulturgemeinde, whose leaders appeared to be obsessed with Hindemith, the composer's supporter Furtwängler, aided by Hindemith's professorial colleagues Gustav Havemann and Fritz Stein, at first planned to speak to Hitler personally but then on 25 November 1934, rushed into print an article in a prominent Berlin newspaper that precipitated the "Hindemith affair," the first cultural scandal of the Third Reich.[11] In this ill-considered piece the conductor tried to excuse Hindemith's earlier, more stringent essays into modern music as youthful follies, but defended the musician as "purely Germanic" and as essentially apolitical, and as a man who was, first and foremost, an extremely productive artist.[12]

Apart from Rosenberg and his NS-Kulturgemeinde, Hindemith's weightiest opponent after Hitler himself was now RKK president Joseph Goebbels, assuredly not because he hated his music (Goebbels's diaries are silent on this issue), but probably because the vengeful Führer had put him up to it and Goebbels could not abide cultural-political criticism coming from such a man as Furtwängler—his subordinate as vice-president of the RMK and chief conductor of the Berlin Philharmonic. Rosenberg himself followed up a speech by Goebbels with polemics of his own in the *Völkischer Beobachter* (a rare show of unanimity between these chronic adversaries), and Göring, Furtwängler's boss at the Preussische Staatsoper, personally telephoned Hitler. Finding the deck stacked against him, Hindemith took a temporary leave of absence from the Hochschule für Musik, where his duties were assumed by Max Trapp. This was the beginning of his leave-taking.[13]

It has been averred that Hindemith bravely resisted the temptation to make concessions to the Nazis of any kind from the moment they came to power.[14] This is not quite true, for he had accepted the RMK council position. Creatively, however, there had been no concession, since his changes in musical style were incidental rather than calculated. But he did find himself in a difficult spot. If some regime representatives welcomed him for artistic reasons, others would rebuke him on political-ideological grounds. It is possible, as some scholars have suggested, that Hindemith might have made his peace with the regime had it exerted itself on his behalf and made generous amends.[15] But Hindemith's list of sins in Nazi eyes was much too long for this to happen, and he himself was never sufficiently opportunistic to meet the Nazis even halfway. The years from 1935 to 1940 saw the gradual eclipse of his music, examples of which were duly, if for the wrong reasons, included in the 1938 exhibition of degenerate music. These years witnessed Hindemith's intermittent absence from the Reich in Turkey and in Switzerland, his resignation from the Berlin conservatory, and finally in 1940 after several tours there, his assumption of permanent residence in the United States.[16] But the fact that well into the war Germans of diverse positions and influence time and again expressed interest in his oeuvre was testimony not only to his pre-1935 prominence, which had been universal, but also to the continuing need the Nazis had for good contemporary music, since no one else in their midst seemed to be able to provide it quite so inventively and authoritatively.[17]

The Nazis' pathological association of "modernist" with "Jewish," rather than with any objectively measurable musical qualities, was borne out once more, for a time at least, in the case of Igor Stravinsky. His was an ironic one, for whereas he was a foreigner, he was not Jewish, his music was never atonal, and as an exile from Russian Bolshevism, he could have been acceptable in Germany, as were many other Russian musicians of all stripes, such as Serge Matull, a hard-drinking Berlin jazz guitarist. Most important, Stravinsky was not known to be a friend of the Jews, and he was a declared admirer of Mussolini and was positively disposed toward the Third Reich.[18]

Because of the fanaticism of Rosenberg's Kampfbund, however, Stravinsky had been persona non grata in right-wing German circles since the late 1920s. The antagonism was based on his perceived Jewishness and his identification with modernist Weimar art—what was mistaken for atonality, an alien rhythm, and an affinity with jazz. Rosenberg's temperament pervaded the musical climate in a period when Goebbels's Reich Music Chamber was either nonexistent or in the throes of uncertain gestation, and when the search was on for an outstanding modern German composer, yet the attitude toward Hindemith's creativity was increasingly ambivalent. Hence, the musicologist Joan Evans has spoken of an unofficial boycott of Stravinsky in the first three years of the regime, broken only occasionally by intrepid figures such as Hans Rosbaud at Radio Frankfurt and Erich Kleiber and Hans Heinz Stuckenschmidt in Berlin.[19]

This situation was changing by 1936, as Stravinsky was gaining more acceptance throughout Germany, on concert stages and in recordings, for a number of reasons. For one, xenophobia had died down as more and more laid-off musicians were finding work. By that time, too, Stravinsky's "Aryanism" and his generally profascist leanings may have become more common knowledge. Also, before the Olympic Games in Berlin, ideological belligerence was giving way to an outwardly friendly tolerance; hence, the former Russian now living in Paris was not unwelcome. Finally, while the orthodoxy of Rosenberg's circle was on the wane and Goebbels's hand became ever stronger, the Hindemith situation still rested in the balance insofar as that composer could hope that his opera *Mathis der Maler* might yet be performed. For several months he was free from a general ban on his music and technically was only on leave from the Berlin Hochschule für Musik, officially advancing the Reich's cultural objectives in Turkey as a visiting professor at the behest of the German authorities. In terms of Goebbels's and Hitler's search for that unique musical innovator, this meant that the competition was still open. Stravinsky, now recognized as not so atonal, although Rosenberg acolytes such as Herbert Gerigk were still wary of him, while obviously not a candidate for the Reich's resident genius, might provide some welcome inspiration. Thus, some Nazi and many non-Nazi cognoscenti were looking to Stravinsky, as he and his son Soulima performed his concerto for two pianos at the music festival in Baden-Baden in early April 1936. One National Socialist lover of modern music recalled hearing an "interesting" Stravinsky, in contrast to the "boring" Egk, Fortner, and Pepping, and a sadly "resigned" Hindemith. From then on, until the outbreak of World War II, Stravinsky's music was played frequently in the Reich, despite occasional and largely inconsequential bickering by reactionary Nazi crusaders, including his prominent place at Ziegler's exhibition of degenerate music.[20] Would Stravinsky's example produce homegrown progeny?

Beginning with Rosenberg and his Kampfbund, the Nazi regime in 1933 started a series of loosely connected efforts to foster the development of local music talent. By early 1934 Goebbels and his newly founded RMK had maneuvered themselves into position behind this drive, as the minister exhorted broadcast executives in particular to be on the lookout for unknown but promising contemporary German composers. The key word was "contemporary," the underlying assumption being that a recruitment of neophyte artists would generate a "new" style acceptable to Nazism: bolder than the Romantic genre of the past but stopping short of "Jewish" atonal or twelve-tone construction. In addition, wealthy municipalities such as Munich were encouraged and obediently complied with the directive; renowned orchestras such as the Berlin and Munich Philharmonic joined in; special composers' conferences were organized. The ideal was a Hindemith or even a Stravinsky, but without the ideological and foreign stigmas attached to their names. A Nazi-style Reich music festival, the successor to the traditional meeting of the Allgemeiner Deutscher Musikverein, was organized in Düsseldorf for late May 1938. Programmatically, it was connected to Ziegler's rather more peripheral exhibition in that it was meant to illustrate results of the past few years and point the way ahead. But as Goebbels delivered the main speech, which consisted of mere rhetoric imploring the new music talent to make an appearance, it became clear that prior efforts had by and large failed.[21]

Early on in the regime, the composer Werner Egk pinpointed the problem: since "contemporary" did not necessarily connote "modern" or "revolutionary," older living composers whose music, in the traditional style, had been around for years and was well known, could try to answer the call and pass themselves off as champions of the new era.[22] With chronic predictability, proven warriors such as Paul Graener, Georg Vollerthun, Max Trapp, and Richard Trunk—all of them established mediocrities—as well as regnant artists such as Strauss and Pfitzner, would be drawn into concert programs or music competitions simply because they were still active, only to crowd out the younger men. Of those, too, the majority tended toward the unremarkable: composers such as Kurt Stiebitz, Otto Besch, Albert Jung, Hermann Simon, Ulf Scharlau, Gottfried Rüdinger, Bruno Stürmer, and Cesar Bresgen.[23]

But for unreconstructed connoisseurs of modern music this strange dialectic also produced an interesting, if entirely unexpected, result. For riding safely on the coattails of the "revolution," and for reasons of their larger search not altogether rejected by Goebbels's henchmen, were impresarios of smaller new-music events, such as those of the Baden-Baden Festival in 1936, which drew Stravinsky, Hindemith, Egk, and the innovative though largely unknown Gerhard Frommel. In Frankfurt, Generalintendant Hans Meissner attracted for the opera and concert scene the forward-looking conductor Bertil Wetzelsberger, the Swiss stage director Oscar Waelterlin, and set designer Caspar Neher, that old friend of Brecht and Weill. At the last performance of the ADMV in 1937, Meissner's team produced one of the most modern stage works to be heard in Germany for years, Orff's *Carmina Burana*, which, influenced by Stravinsky, initially met with enough negative responses, especially from the Rosenberg camp, to scare the composer. Rosbaud, an admirer of Stravinsky and Schoenberg, was at the time trying to use his Frankfurt radio station to accommodate as many truly modern works as possible. In Dresden in 1938 Karl Böhm staged the opera *Die Wirtin von Pinsk* by jazz aficionado Richard Mohaupt (who, with his Russian-Jewish violinist wife, left for America at the end of the year), and conducted music by Bartók, who as a citizen of Nazi-friendly Hungary was still deemed acceptable.[24]

From this small, comparatively modernizing trend, which was embedded within yet ran counter to a much broader reactionary Nazi tendency in the arts, three or four musicians benefited, one by design and the others more or less by accident. Perhaps naively, Paul von Klenau and Winfried Zillig composed music that was atonal, and hence nominally violated the Nazis' instructions to break neither the triad nor the IV–V–I progression.[25] But analysts found that their serialism was based on a model different from Schoenberg's twelve-tone rows. Still grating but less offensive to conventionally trained ears, Zillig's series were "capable of generating a sense of tonal center." Klenau, a Danish-born Schoenberg student who had divorced his Jewish wife some time earlier, made a case in 1933 for officially ascribing the invention of twelve-tone theory to Josef Matthias Hauer, a somewhat younger Viennese contemporary of Schoenberg who was "Aryan," worked mainly as a theorist, and composed very little (which helped to relegate him to obscurity).[26]

Dresden composer Gottfried Müller, born in 1914, studied in Edinburgh and with Karl Straube in Leipzig, and was discovered by Fritz Busch. The son of a clergyman, he was in close touch with Oskar Söhngen's Confessionalist church composers; works of his also figured prominently at the 1937 Berlin church-music festival. Müller composed church as well as tendentious political music in a polyphonic style akin to that of Pepping and Distler, so to the extent that those polyphonists and neoclassicists were considered modern, so was Müller. In 1933 Stuckenschmidt had wryly observed: "The developments in European music during the last twenty years have passed over him without a trace. In his variation technic he is related to Reger, his harmony is influenced by Brahms, his phrasing is academic in the barren sense of the word." Because of all this, and perhaps also because he was so obviously young, he had the good fortune to find favor with Goebbels and Hitler as early as 1936. "Maybe a really great talent for the future, the Führer is quite taken," noted Goebbels in his diary. Müller, now slated for a professorship by Hinkel, was commissioned to write a piece for the 1938 party rally, based on a Führer aphorism. The musician enthusiastically embraced this opportunity "to transfigure artistically the great National Socialist community."27

If the relatively immature Müller could not be the musical deus ex machina the Nazis were praying for, perhaps Egk could. How much of his prolific career during the Third Reich must be attributed to happenstance and how much to his own design is not yet clear, but there can be no doubt that early positive reaction to his works primed him to aspire to official standing. The Swabian Egk, born in 1901 and an erstwhile pupil of Orff, was closely associated in the waning Weimar Republic with modernists such as Hermann Scherchen; he also knew Hindemith, Kurt Weill, and Heinrich Kaminski and was strongly impressed by Stravinsky. Working in the Munich area, he caught his first lucky break in late 1933 when his radio opera *Columbus* was broadcast, to be restaged in the concert hall in 1934. Like Stravinsky, whose influence he always acknowledged, Egk had a propensity for tone color and for pronounced rhythm. His music sounded vaguely dissonant and acerbic, harsh to some, but was staunchly diatonic. "Will Werner Egk succeed in the creation of a new style," asked a Bavarian daily in 1934, "or will he merely exhaust himself in endless experimentation?" His major opera *Die Zaubergeige*, premiered by that corps of progressives in Frankfurt in May 1935, again showed the influence of Stravinsky (critics also detected allusions to Mozart and Strauss), but it had the incalculable advantage of being a light, popular work based on a fairy-tale motif. That suggested a closeness to the people; it also contained the essence of melody that Goebbels so loved, and it rejected the "overblown" modernism the minister hated. An unbeatable combination was shaping up. Notwithstanding some barbs from the Rosenberg camp, which naturally objected to the Stravinsky touch, Egk was fingered by Goebbels as a potential winner at an international music competition on the occasion of the Berlin Olympic Games in July 1936, which, unsurprisingly, he proceeded to win. Again, the critics lauded his "providential, genuine folksiness." In 1938 Fritz Stege, arguably the most hawkish of Nazi critics, credibly paraphrased Egk's assertion that any German brand of music to be written these days would have to be suitable for a Nazi Strength-through-Joy event.[28]

In 1936, three years before discovering Herbert von Karajan, Prussian Generalintendant Heinz Tietjen had installed Egk as a Kapellmeister at the Preussische Staatsoper. Egk's new opera *Peer Gynt,* based on Henrik Ibsen's drama, was premiered there on 24 November 1938, conducted by the composer himself. It had a craggy but still conventionally tonal flavor, which was tolerated by most critics. They generally disliked Egk's plot, however, because it featured not a heroic protagonist (as in the earlier play by Dietrich Eckart, Hitler's besotted Munich friend) but rather a down-and-out loser. Egk's Peer Gynt cavorted with whores in Latin American bars (there were hints of tango reminiscent of the dangerous jazz) and had to contend with unsavory underworld trolls: he was anything but a Nazi superman. Still, with the help of his new patron Tietjen, Egk weathered the doctrinaire Nazi critics' storm. A performance in January 1939 was attended by Goebbels and Hitler and, surprisingly, admired by the Führer, although later he too questioned the libretto. The work was then ostentatiously chosen by the minister as one of two official opera presentations for the Düsseldorf Reich Music Festival later in May. Programmatically it was said to be "indicative of a pure and Nordic conception of art." After the festival Goebbels singled out Egk by awarding him a composition contract worth a whopping 10,000 marks. By 1940 Egk appears to have been a recognized leader among the new German composers, and in the artistic media he was beginning to spout cultural-political maxims that sounded flattering to Nazi ears. His next opera, *Columbus,* converted from the earlier radio piece, much less original and spectacular than *Peer Gynt* and also less controversial, opened in Frankfurt in January 1942.[29]

Had the Nazis found their golden boy of contemporary German music? At the height of World War II, after Hindemith's chances had been wrecked, Egk was only second-best. Moreover, he was pursued by three or four others, any of whom could overtake him. In 1939 Gertrud Hindemith sarcastically observed that one of them, Gottfried Müller, was omnipresent: everywhere you go you hear "Müller the great symphonist." Indeed, Müller became a fixture on Germany's concert scene and usually earned accolades; still, none of his works had the singular effect of Egk's very best efforts, such as his *Peer Gynt,* and he did not write operas, the Nazis' favorite genre. By April 1944 Goebbels informed the Führer that his protégé's latest composition for choir and orchestra, again inspired by Hitler, had fallen short of expectations: it was "too polyphonic"—whatever the minister meant by that.[30] Müller's fame, unlike Egk's, did not survive the final catastrophe.

Then there were Carl Orff, Paul Höffer, and Karl Höller. They all shared the distinction of being hounded by Rosenberg's stooges at the beginning of the regime, which could have qualified them as progressives without much further scrutiny.[31] Orff's impressive *Carmina Burana* success of 1937 was duplicated in Dresden under Karl Böhm in 1940, but not repeated with subsequent works of his, although he did manage to build a solid career. Even though he composed operas and also had a folksy side, however, his decided disadvantage was that, unlike Egk, he was not personally recognized by Goebbels or Hitler reasonably early in the regime and, since he was not fully "Aryan," could not expose himself in public office, as Egk was soon to do.[32]

Paul Höffer, born in 1895, a former student of Franz Schreker and subsequently influenced by Hindemith, had written a piano concerto, a couple of symphonies, and several chamber works, when he, like Egk, received an official commission at the 1939 Düsseldorf Festival, but it was only half the amount of Egk's advance. Although he made political concessions by writing pieces for the Wehrmacht and the Luftwaffe and musically sang the praises of Hitler's *Volksgemeinschaft* like any Stürmer, Bresgen, or Spitta, his style may have so obviously resembled that of the mellifluous nineteenth-century giants as to have rendered him not merely "contemporary" but "modern" by Nazi standards.[33]

Karl Höller was twelve years younger than Höffer; in Munich's reactionary atmosphere he had undergone a much more conservative training than either Höffer or Orff. Influenced by Bruckner and Reger, he too opened himself up to influences by Hindemith and Stravinsky, but he also liked the French Impressionists. Commensurate with his youth, Höller did not become prominent until World War II: his works, clearly harmonic rather than angular or dissonant, often found themselves in the company of those by other Nazi "avant-gardists," such as Müller and David, as well as Respighi, Fascist Italy's favorite composer. What may have blocked Höller's path to Nazi prominence was the fact that in April 1944, most certainly unjustly, Hitler considered his compositions sufficiently discordant to brand them "atonal," even though Goebbels tried to change the Führer's mind.[34] Like Werner Egk, Müller, Orff, Höffer, and Höller all were candidates for generous state prizes dispensed by the RMK in 1942, and their names were included in a favored-composers' list for broadcast purposes as late as April 1944.[35]

The 1939 state commissions for Egk and Höffer were, of course, in the Nazi tradition of encouraging homegrown talent through various public incentives. Although the works of these five composers had not all come about as a consequence of such overt government stimulus, the subsidies were continued almost to the end of the war, and with the same, generally dismal results as in the past. Moreover, multiple quota systems were introduced, designed to force recently written works into the concert halls and, especially, onto opera stages. Whatever else these routines may have meant, they do suggest that in the final analysis the Nazi cultural wardens were not unreservedly happy with the likes of Orff and Egk, even less so with Müller, Höffer, and Höller, and any of the polyphonic neoclassicists of the Söhngen school. At the same time, they realized the limitations, for their purposes, of older contemporaries such as Strauss, Pfitzner, and

Graener, to say nothing of the producers of comparative trivia such as Vollerthun, Trapp, and the thoroughly self-deluded composer Wilhelm Furtwängler.[36] That pattern did not change when, in the summer of 1941, Graener was replaced as head of the RMK composers' section by the ambitious Egk. Appointed personally by Goebbels, Egk continued to repeat his mantra that more contemporary composers must be performed, the better to express the spirit of these revolutionary times, which now were "comfortably removed from the period of Expressionism and atonality."[37] Whether Egk was turning into a genuine Nazi, opportunistically attempting to advance his own career, or merely doing the Nazis' bidding in order to shield his avant-garde composer friends (Orff, von Einem, Blacher, and Wagner-Régeny) remains to be determined.[38] To be sure, Goebbels was not in a state of unmitigated bliss when, in July 1944, virtually at the final hour, he demanded from his broadcast network that "music by modern composers" be played, and the broadcasters had to confess that such music was not available, as none had been commercially recorded in the recent past. Even to the cynical Goebbels this must have signaled the overall cultural bankruptcy of the Reich.[39]

The Ambiguities of Dissidence: Orff, Wagner-Régeny, and Furtwängler

Contrary to conventional interpretations of the nature and function of totalitarian dictatorship,[40] German musicians in the Nazi era had a surprising degree of latitude in the creation and performance of their works. This, as we have seen, was due to a number of circumstances. One was the difficulty leading Nazis had devising a binding definition of "German" music, or music that was, without reservation, acceptable in the concert halls, on the opera stages, and in the recording studios. As in the case of "Jewish" music, "German" music, especially that composed by the contemporary generation, was ultimately not definable. Another factor was that even though subjective notions about politically acceptable music ruled the minds of Nazis such as Rosenberg, Goebbels, Göring, and Hitler himself, their reactions to what was considered passable were never clearly and consistently articulated, much less coordinated. Hence, their standards were never manifested in coherent control programs to be executed by efficient censorship agencies, and even when such agencies existed, at least early in the regime, they were riven by intraparty rivalries, such as the running feud between Goebbels and Rosenberg, instead of being logically interrelated and mutually complementary.

As I have mentioned, Rosenberg was the first to assert official claims to the licensing of art, but his Kampfbund für deutsche Kultur lacked authority and by 1934 had been emasculated. Its successor, the NS-Kulturgemeinde, issued "directives for music production," which, in the shadow of Goebbels's already extant Reichskulturkammer, sounded like exercises for a fascist utopia.[41] But the only notable success the NS-Kulturgemeinde ever scored was against Hindemith in 1934–36, and only because the Promi's RMK happened to be fighting alongside it. Until the summer of 1935 the RMK itself was hampered by Strauss's reluctance to provide dynamic National Socialist leadership, and thereafter, Raabe frequently proved less than able to act in a decisive, authoritative manner. From 1936 on, he was encumbered by the installation of Heinz Drewes at another level of the Promi hierarchy, so that, undoubtedly with Goebbels's acquiescence, a comprehensive policing of the musical scene became impractical. Director of a special Reich music censor's office by December 1937, Drewes turned out to be interested mainly in screening foreign works as well as popular dance and jazz music, while "Jewish" compositions, since 1933, continued quite routinely to be discarded by parallel mechanisms. Drewes's activities assumed real significance only after the outbreak of World War II. In everyday practice this censor's office did not automatically demand that a score or a libretto be submitted for examination before a premiere, yet, given justifiable suspicion, it could request it. Then again, composers were encouraged to make such submissions on their own, especially when in doubt. Upon composers and conductors Drewes's agency seems to have had a self-regulatory effect, for in 1944 it was noted that, remarkably, only a few works had had to be expressly banned by the office, including "not even one example of so-called serious music."[42] Was the element of fear a sufficient instrument of cultural control for Drewes's boss, Joseph Goebbels?

As Alan Steinweis has keenly observed, apart from the problem of definitions, there was simply too much musical activity in the Reich, and it was too decentralized, to be effectively controlled over an extended period of time.[43] Generally, Goebbels allowed subordinate offices, those of Raabe and Drewes, to supervise day-to-day musical activities, with little personal interference. He was, of course, fully aware that Drewes was less favorably disposed than Raabe, the onetime champion of the ADMV, toward the kind of modern music that he himself was seeking. As it turned out, it was to Goebbels's advantage to play off these underlings against each other. The crucial point, however, is that in those artistic matters that Goebbels genuinely cherished, he always reserved final judgment for himself, regardless of any previously institutionalized decisions. In fact, since he was convinced that by temperament and disposition all artists are apolitical—a condition he, along with his Führer, deplored but accepted with a sense of resignation—he believed it necessary to intervene only occasionally in the artistic processes of the nation, in order to keep the political ship on course. Because music, comparatively speaking, had its limitations as far as political applicability was concerned, however, and because the minister himself lacked the necessary musical training, he reserved his own censorial discretion for art forms that he was more qualified to judge, and which he thought were even better suited for propaganda than music. These were in the areas of film, broadcasting, and journalism, and, to a lesser extent, literature and the graphic arts.[44] Hence, commensurate with its comparatively abstract and nondescriptive character, music in the Third Reich proved to be the least licenced and the most autonomous of all the arts.

This is not to suggest, of course, that every composer and conductor was fully cognizant of these conditions and could comport himself accordingly. Those who, for their own creative reasons, were searching for more modern forms of musical expression and, being apolitical in Goebbels's benign sense, were not attuned to the complicated political developments inside the Reich, sometimes had reason to feel unsure and even fearful regarding their professional activities. A case in point is that of Carl Orff, who, like his erstwhile student Werner Egk, initially influenced by Stravinsky, was searching for modern forms of musical expression, albeit tonal ones, far removed from the experimental Weimar and Vienna Schools. His *Carmina Burana* was at first sufficiently idiosyncratic to be suspect in Rosenberg's and even Goebbels's circles, so that Orff, for a while at least, had reason to fear the heavy hand of censorship on anything else he might write in the future. Although it may not have been necessary, the Frankfurt producers secured the formal approval of Raabe as RMK president even before the premiere of the work at the ADMV's last annual festival in June 1937. A year later Orff still had reason to be wary of Rosenberg's stooges, and he was apprehensive about Drewes's new censorship office, not knowing what sort of victims it was looking for. Although Orff's professional fortunes were then noticeably on the upswing, his publisher, Schott's Söhne, cautioned that Raabe and Drewes, not to mention Rosenberg's men, were suspiciously watching his every move regarding the performance of his next work, *Der Mond* (which was musically much less daring than *Carmina Burana*). "An official rejection would mean a very severe reversal for you. We have to choose the most secure path," he was warned. Although this proved to be an overstatement, Schott's Söhne believed that "those people have a hundred ways to finish you off, if they only want to." Thus, a continued association with the modern-oriented Frankfurt troupe of Hans Meissner was believed to be somewhat risky. Even as late as 1943 Orff, already nationally famous, thought it politic to visit the Promi in person in order to ensure an officially friendly reception of his latest work, the scenic cantata *Catulli Carmina,* and on his return from Berlin he gleefully reported an overall attitude of benevolence on the part of Promi bureaucrats. In July 1944 Orff had the personal satisfaction of being informed that Gauleiter Karl Hanke of Silesia, a former Promi state secretary, had had a talk with Goebbels about the composer's entire artistic output, and "hence there is no more danger."[45]

Recalling his (real or imagined) travails with the Nazi censors in the immediate aftermath of World War II, and recognizing that he had compromised himself more than necessary during the regime on very specific counts, Orff apparently considered the possibility of an instant whitewash with the new American military government: why not portray himself as a victim of Nazism and thus escape cumbersome and possibly detrimental denazification procedures? As he sensed an opportunity to participate in the rebuilding of democratic structures in the cultural sector under the Allied aegis, Orff claimed to have been persecuted by Nazi authorities because of the "un-German" character of his compositions and his sympathy with Jews. Moreover, early in 1946 he told a U.S. intelligence officer, who just happened to have been a student of his in Munich during 1938–39, that he had been a founding member of the "White Rose," a political resistance group whose members, under the spiritual leadership of Munich professor Kurt Huber, were arrested, tried for treason, and executed in 1943. As the former officer, New York chamber music conductor Newell Jenkins, later told me in an interview in March 1993, Orff claimed "that he had worked together with Huber, they had founded some kind of a youth group. The danger came when he and some kids or maybe Huber himself were discovered passing out leaflets. Huber was arrested and killed. Orff, as far as I remember, told me that he had gotten help through some friends and had fled into the mountains. He did not tell me where. And he stayed there until it was safe for him to come back." Based on this testimony, and without further ado, the Americans consigned Orff to the "gray-acceptable" category of suspected Nazis and allowed his just-finished opera, *Die Bernauerin*, to be premiered in Stuttgart in June 1947, starring his own daughter Godela in the title role.[46]

Orff's story was a clever fabrication, for although the composer and Huber had been friends and had collaborated in musical matters, Orff was never privy to the "White Rose" conspiracy. Huber's widow, Clara, has insisted that Orff "neither cofounded the 'White Rose' nor was ever a member," and Orff's own widow, Gertrud, attests that "Orff was not a participant in the plot, was not involved."[47] Because he himself knew that the truth would be damaging to his postwar career, Orff kept quiet about the details of his association with Jenkins and what he had told him, up to his death in 1982, having made an attempt to discredit the American intelligence officer after he had returned to the United States in 1947.[48]

But, to be fair, what was the extent of Orff's deviation from the straight Nazi Party line, and in what fashion did he affiliate himself with the regime? Orff, born in 1895, had been touched by Stravinsky as a young composer in the early 1920s, and he had composed songs based on texts by the Jewish poet Franz Werfel and the Marxist playwright Brecht. Politically, he tended toward indifference, but Brecht's revolutionary stance impressed him. Among his musical friends were several Jews; at the end of the republic he had dealings with Kestenberg, Jöde, and Scherchen. After the political change in 1933, like Hindemith, he was regarded with suspicion by the tone-setting Rosenberg clique, and Orff, too, tried to reach an understanding with the regional Kampfbund chapter. Having failed in this by 1934, and being politically an unknown quantity in circles other than Rosenberg's own, he composed *Carmina Burana* in some trepidation, knowing that the medieval Latin text alone might irk the Nazis. Without fail it did, as did the sexually explicit German translation, and so did the (to some) strange-sounding music.[49]

Notwithstanding the partial success of the work by 1937 and shortly thereafter, a strongly democratic-minded Orff would have had reason enough to resort to a state of inner emigration—in fact, he could have left the country altogether. He was offered an opportunity in the fall of 1938, at the time of the Sudeten crisis, by his student Jenkins, who had important connections in the United States. But Orff refused, arguing that he was too deeply rooted in Bavarian soil and knew no English.[50]

The truth is that, being extremely conscious of his need to conceal his partly Jewish ancestry from the authorities, Orff had already decided to accommodate himself to a regime that at heart he detested. He had been trying, if unsuccessfully, since 1934 to pawn off sections of his pedagogic music from the *Schulwerk*, which was to augment his international fame after 1945, for use by the Hitler Youth. In 1938 he composed ersatz *Ein Sommernachtstraum* music as part of an official Nazi scheme to replace Mendelssohn's celebrated original; it was performed in Frankfurt a year later. By early 1942 he had entered into a contractual arrangement with Vienna's culturally ambitious Gauleiter Baldur von Schirach, the son of the Wiesbaden intendant, that paid 1,000 marks a month. By the end of the war he had been granted one of the RMK's major prizes, was explicitly exempted from any kind of conscription, and was being courted for musical contributions by Goebbels's broadcast network and cinematic news services. Throughout the entire period Orff had been no hero, asserts his daughter in her memoirs, but according to a variety of evidence, he was no Nazi villain either. A sensitive and original artist in the Weimar Republic, Orff became something of a politico-cultural opportunist in the face of uncertainty and the threat of persecution, especially early in the regime. After overcoming initial suspicions, his music remained consistently modern yet tonal and somehow archetypally Germanic. As Gerald Abraham has written, perhaps somewhat hyperbolically: "The only kind of modernism acceptable in the Third Reich was the rhythmically hypnotic, totally diatonic neo-primitivism of Orff's scenic cantatas." Acceptable, that is, at least to the point where, at the height of the war, many leading Nazis, including Goebbels and Schirach, could reckon Orff among the few promising talents they needed for a genuine cultural revolution in their Reich, even though he seems never to have been their first choice.[51]

In June 1942 a disgruntled Hans Pfitzner mentioned composer Rudolf Wagner-Régeny, along with Orff and Egk, as one of the moderns who were currently being favored.[52] In several respects his comment was not too far off the mark. For one thing, Egk and Orff considered Wagner-Régeny a kindred spirit. Nevertheless, whether officially favored or not, Wagner-Régeny himself, some colleagues, and not a few critics have described his activities during the Third Reich as having been perilously close to social and political opposition.[53] His biography suggests that he may have been predestined for such a turn of events from his early career in the Weimar Republic. Rudolf Wagner was born into the ethnic German community of Siebenbürgen in Hungary in 1903; his hometown of Sächsisch-Regen (Szaszrégen) later provided his nom de plume. In 1920, after the town had fallen to the Romanians, he studied piano in Leipzig, then from 1921 to 1923 he attended the Berlin Hochschule für Musik. Through the 1920s he worked variously in the cabaret, jazz, and light-music fields of Weimar Germany, in the provinces and in Berlin, sometimes with the dance teacher Rudolf von Laban, and increasingly close to the circle surrounding Weill and Brecht. He naturally met Darius Milhaud, Hindemith, and Hanns Eisler; after 1929 his constant collaborator and close friend was Caspar Neher, the stage designer and librettist who worked equally intimately with Weill and Brecht. In 1923, the year he became a German citizen, Wagner-Régeny married Leli Duperrex, a sculptor, born in Bucharest to a French Huguenot father and a Viennese Jewish mother.[54]

In February 1935 the composer's friend Karl Böhm premiered his first significant opera, *Der Günstling*, in Dresden, with a libretto by Neher, based on Victor Hugo's drama *Mary Tudor*. It contained certain passages that could have been interpreted as oppositional to Hitler's dictatorial regime: allusions to the executioner's axe, a land laid waste, the overthrow of a tyrant. Wagner-Régeny's musical style here was classically simple, reminiscent of Handel, sparsely orchestrated and within the boundaries of conventional tonality. Böhm, not averse to experimentation, loved it so much that within a few months his opera company had presented the work no fewer than eleven times. The opera was accepted by other companies in and outside Germany, and at thirty-two, Wagner-Régeny suddenly found himself a celebrity.[55]

After guest conductor Herbert von Karajan had led Wagner-Régeny's second major work, *Die Bürger von Calais*, at Tietjen's bidding, at the Preussische Staatsoper on 28 January 1939 (it was repeated there five times), it was called "problematical" by some critics—probably not because of Neher's libretto, but possibly because of his gray-on-gray stage design, symbolizing the foreshadowings of war, and also on account of the music, which now uncannily reminded some of the Weimar street-song style of Weill.[56]

Wagner-Régeny met his Waterloo in early April 1941 in Vienna, where, under the patronage of Schirach, his next opera, *Johanna Balk*, was premiered, with the help of the progressive stage director Oskar Fritz Schuh and conductor Leopold Ludwig. There were several reasons for the scandal that ensued, the most important being the complicated relationship between Goebbels and Schirach, who sought an extraordinarily large measure of cultural autonomy for himself (even though, in principle, both men were in favor of staging modern operas of the kind that Egk, Orff, and Wagner-Régeny were creating).[57] Shortly before, Wagner-Régeny had had a tussle with Goebbels's own man, Generalintendant Wilhelm Rode of the Deutsche Oper in Berlin, who had earlier been favorably disposed toward both him and Neher. At any rate, Rode had rejected *Johanna Balk* before the Viennese cultural establishment accepted it. Moreover, Neher's script this time was politically risky because it spoke of a seventeenth-century Hungarian prince who raped and subjugated German Saxons in Wagner-Régeny's home province of Siebenbürgen. This could have been taken as a diplomatic affront by the Axis-allied fascist Hungarian regime of Nikolaus Horthy. Hence, overnight the Hungarian names of the principals and locales were changed to German ones; the Hungarian villain Prince Bathory became the safely German Prince Balthasar. But perhaps not as safely as Wagner-Régeny might have wished, for now as a German, the tyrant possessed an obvious likeness to Hitler. Goebbels was furious that his explicit order to Schirach to scrap the piece had been ignored and that the Gauleiter had in fact delivered a speech in which he defended his very own idea of cultural pluralism. And again, it was to Wagner-Régeny's disadvantage that his musical style— rhythmically pronounced, tonally angular—so closely resembled Weill's. On opening night anti-Schirach Nazi agents provocateurs who had been planted in the audience hollered and booed, thus demonstrating to the outside world and Goebbels's own satisfaction that *Johanna Balk* was a "shoddy effort." Although the minister had sufficient authority to proscribe the work for the rest of Germany (Freiburg, Darmstadt, and Wuppertal had to go without), the opera persisted in Vienna for two more seasons. Goebbels, who had been rather more indifferent toward Hindemith and neutral to positive toward Orff and Egk, now displayed a singular hostility to Wagner-Régeny, a good part of which was grounded in his personal feud with Schirach. The composer became almost an incidental victim, being cut off from the RMK prizes that the Graeners, Orffs, Knabs, and Distlers were collecting, and not being placed on the favored broadcast list. Most seriously for a composer of his sensitivity, Wagner-Régeny was declared nonexempt from military service.[58]

Thus, on 5 February 1943 the musician was conscripted for duty at the eastern front. He spent eight weeks in a Wehrmacht training camp, where he endured physical and psychological hell, being thrown together with boorish men who indulged in dirty jokes and knew nothing of his kind of culture. He developed insomnia, intermittent crying fits, and a phobia about loaded guns. The man who had once been well nourished and flamboyantly handsome became emaciated. Yet after eight weeks he was shipped out not to Charkov, as expected, but to a much softer posting in occupied Paris—on the initiative of a prominent regime opponent with exquisite connections to important Nazis. His condition not having improved significantly, Wagner-Régeny found himself back in Berlin at the end of 1943, with a desk job but still in the army. One insider wrote in November of that year: "I know that there are currents running against him in the Propaganda Ministry." By now his wife, the "half-Jewish" foreigner, was thought to be in jeopardy, and to make matters worse, she had breast cancer. As a composer he had become a nonentity; his works were ignored. By early 1945, stationed in Mecklenburg, plagued by chronic migraine, his dying wife beside him, he was learning Russian as an antidote to the Red Army offensive threatening to overtake his little village at any moment.[59]

Wagner-Régeny's former close friend Gottfried von Einem, whose mother the baroness had pried him loose from service at the eastern front in 1943, said to me in 1994: "Wagner-Régeny was a character in and of himself, who could not be bribed. . . . He wrote his music according to his conscience, as a man whom you could not buy, and is that not a lot?"[60] Indeed, it would have been had Wagner-Régeny's integrity been as sacrosanct as Einem described it. But there was an underside to this man's character as well, dark enough to make one doubt his often-stated anti-Nazi commitment. In 1934, for instance, he was approached by Rosenberg's NS-Kulturgemeinde to write music for *Ein Sommernachtstraum*, and the play with his music, netting him a tidy 2,000 marks, was publicly performed in 1935. Much later he excused this as a harmless sequel to Orff's effort in that direction—but Orff did not succumb to the temptation until four years later.[61] Wagner-Régeny's musical style, its simplicity set in conscious contrast to the late Romantics' music, as in the case of the Confessionalist church musicians, was just what suited the Nazis and was accepted by some as innovative. The "nontheatrical" individuality of his music as it resounded from his *Der Günstling* and *Die Bürger von Calais* was applauded for the same reason. But after trenchant analysis, Claudia Maurer Zenck today ascribes to Wagner-Régeny's neo-Weillian constructivism in *Johanna Balk* a disturbingly apocryphal quality, the end result of a recasting of certain elements of a Weimar musical style "for the collectivism of the Hitler dictatorship."[62] Moreover, Neher's libretto for *Die Bürger von Calais* was adapted to Nazi ideology to the extent that what was celebrated here was the willingness of selfless individuals to sacrifice their lives for the sake of the community, a heroic theme Hitler himself might have inspired in Neher.[63] And Wagner-Régeny, like Orff, was on the payroll of a nefarious Nazi leader, Vienna Gauleiter von Schirach, from the beginning of 1942, even though he received just over half the amount his more famous colleague Orff was able to command.[64]

According to his own contemporary utterances and postwar testimonies, conductor Wilhelm Furtwängler consciously attempted to oppose Nazi rule from the first time he decided to remain in Germany early in 1933, and then again when he might have emigrated in early 1935, again in late 1936, and at Christmas 1938. So was he really that "saintly musician (with human little foibles), proud but shy, with fine, crusty *altmitteleuropäische* manners," as the Briton Ronald Harwood has cast him in his play *Taking Sides?*[65] Furtwängler's self-defense for staying in the

Third Reich was that one could do so as an apolitical artist, especially if one tried to intercede on behalf of Jews.[66] Indeed, Furtwängler's intervention for the sake of the Jewish members of his Berlin Philharmonic Orchestra, notably the concertmaster Simon Goldberg, is well documented, and is now almost legendary. Because of him, several musicians were able to stay and work in Germany much longer than would otherwise have been possible.[67] Furtwängler supported Schoenberg, in temporary exile in Paris, by strongly urging the composition professor's former employer, Education Minister Rust, "not to turn him into a martyr."[68] Furtwängler also spoke for the non-Jewish Hindemith, personally imploring Goebbels and, in the summer of 1937, even the Führer, always with unhappy results.[69] One of Furtwängler's more credible biographers has recounted that the conductor acted on behalf of at least eighty persons, and probably many more, since conversations and telephone calls were not documented.[70]

So large a number, however, is in itself suspicious. Upon closer examination, one finds not just Jews and known opponents of the Nazi regime on that list but also anti-Semites, Nazis, and musicians sympathetic with the Nazi cause. Pfitzner is there, whom Furtwängler tried to help in a very controversial pension settlement when the personal safety of that composer was not at stake.[71] Furtwängler intervened on behalf of singing instructor Anna Bahr-Mildenburg, composer Georg Vollerthun, and conductor Franz von Hoesslin, each of whom was at the time pro-Nazi.[72] Especially questionable was his support of the Nazi Max Trapp after he had been caught in his affair with a married student; Furtwängler's laconic explanation was that "Trapp is being pursued by a woman" (in this particular instance it may have been the case of one notorious womanizer covering for another).[73]

Furtwängler used his influence not just to help people, however, but also to harm those who he thought were in his way. He did his best to avoid producing any of Strauss's operas in Berlin until he lost his permanent post at the Staatsoper in December 1934. Frequently in Goebbels's presence he intrigued against Strauss, his rival of long standing, until the very end, when, in a sudden bout of compassion, he sought to protect the eighty-year-old composer from the compound wrath of the Promi minister and Hitler.[74] Furtwängler's constant machinations against Karajan have already been mentioned, as has the injurious letter he penned against Clemens Krauss in 1936. And there is circumstantial evidence that Furtwängler tried to undermine Karl Böhm's new position in Vienna after 1942, if we can believe Böhm's assistant Oskar Fritz Schuh. After the war, Furtwängler, although approached, withheld assistance from Otto Klemperer, his erstwhile Berlin colleague and now a possible competitor, when he needed it badly for a European comeback.[75]

This much meddling, whether for a positive or a negative purpose, suggests that Furtwängler was not an altruist but a man obsessed with personal connections, who always had to be at the center of things. At the end of the republic Pfitzner called him a *Primadonnerich,* one who was wont "to pull everything in his direction and cast it off again, as soon as he has been recognized."[76] To be sure, during the Third Reich Furtwängler seems not to have relinquished any position of control once he had it—dozens of panels, committees, offices, and societies (including the honorary presidency of the Hans Pfitzner Society)—just to keep as many irons in the fire as possible. He always had to play a role, or to be seen playing one; this gave him a sense of omnipotence. This sense, which led to his pathological urge "to help," is expressed in a line he wrote to his mother in Heidelberg toward the end of the Reich in 1944, when much of Germany already lay in ruins: "Even though I may often be far away, I can, at most times, assist you immediately."[77]

As the British historian Richard J. Evans has suggested, in evaluating Furtwängler during the Third Reich, one cannot be too careful in assessing his mandarin upbringing as the son of a famous archaeology professor during the outgoing Wilhelmine era, and, accordingly, as an arch-conservative upper-bourgeois professional, forging ahead in the political environment of a republic he despised.[78] It was his constant respect for authority, inherited from the Wilhelmine days, that preconditioned Furtwängler to be elitist and antidemocratic, a man who not only welcomed the return of rule and order under Hitler (who he thought would undo the injustices of Versailles, among others), but even was partial to certain precepts of Nazi anti-Semitism. The "Jewish Question," of course, he saw as a cultural rather than a racial problem: he knew Jews with a propensity for greatness (at one time he said that only Jews knew how to play the violin), and others with a penchant for the trashy, cheap, and decayed. Early on in the Third Reich, he agreed with Goebbels that the destructive elements must be removed. In 1933, in defending Hindemith's teacher Sekles, Furtwängler remarked that this scholar was "one of the few Jews I have known for fifteen years who has been *positively constructive,* to the point where he was able to demonstrate a natural feeling of affinity with German music." Such an argument is suggestive of the dangerously selective, even discriminatory verdicts that led to the stereotypes Nazi musicologists identified with "Jewish" composers such as Mendelssohn.[79]

One key phrase in Furtwängler's recurring reflections is "German," an attribute he also was to invoke in his public defense of Hindemith. Somewhere, he believed, there was a secret, genuine Germany which the vulgar excrescences of Hitler's rule, the totalitarian exaggerations that weighed heavily on his soul, could not touch, so long as people like himself, who understood this real Germany, stood by it and did not emigrate. Ultimately, of course, this amounted to a futile attempt on the part of the conductor "to be even more German than German, in the belief that one could defend the true German against the false German redolent of tyranny." Schiller, Goethe, Beethoven, and Brahms were the champions and symbols of the true Germany, and if he, Furtwängler, with his all-encompassing humanistic *Bildung,* did not hold them in high esteem, then the ugly, plebeian, brownshirted Germans would get the upper hand (and more of the good Jews would perish). Furtwängler's cardinal mistake here was that he did not realize to what extent the Nazis—and not only Hitler, Goebbels, and Göring, whom he generally respected as the highest bearers of temporal authority—claimed, in fact monopolized, those very same German men of culture and used them for their own devious purposes. He also did not see that such a split between a good and a bad Germany was conceptually—that is, morally and historically—quite impossible, as other great men such as Thomas Mann had already realized. But mindful of the true Germany that had to be rescued, Furtwängler could indulge in his naively idealistic role as everybody's savior on a much larger scale, and so this mental construct well served his pathological persona. He was convinced that the upright Germans had to enter into perhaps distasteful alliances, and, at least early on, Furtwängler thought he could forge such alliances without betraying his private and artistic integrity. "Every German of standing today is facing the question whether he wishes to maintain and carry through with his position or not. Having opted for the affirmative, he somehow *has to* make a practical pact with the ruling party, or else, he *will* have to go," Furtwängler told his disbelieving émigré friend Ludwig Curtius in September 1934.[80]

As with several tenets touching on law and order (and showing once again the conductor's proximity to dictatorship which he himself was not willing to acknowledge), Furtwängler agreed with the new authoritarian government regarding the place of so-called degenerate music in German culture; in his lexicon this too was not part of the real Germany. In this category Furtwängler, who himself composed in a long-winded post-Romantic style, included vulgar dance music, jazz (which he termed "indigestible" and "a lie"), and atonal music, particularly Schoenberg's serial music. He also disliked Hindemith's earlier, more experimentally dissonant sound—for instance, his *Neues vom Tage*—a disgust for which he admitted sharing with Hitler. All these to him were manifestations of a modernity that he thought "deviant," quite in the same way that the Nazis detested Weimar culture. Why, then, did he offer his assistance to Schoenberg and to Hindemith? He admired and had conducted some of Schoenberg's earlier nonserialist works, and even the serial *Variationen für Orchester* of 1928. Schoenberg had been an important composition teacher in Berlin, and now, as a Jew, the composer had become an object of his fraternal care. Besides, Furtwängler, albeit authoritarian, was not censorial; unlike even Richard Strauss, he believed that audiences ought to be given a chance to recognize quality on its own merits (no doubt he thought that they would all come round to his point of view eventually), and, while some of this actually met with Hitler's and Goebbels's guarded conception of artistic freedom, he was fatally wrong in thinking that the Führer would allow for *total* liberty in cultural expression and reception. "When I stood up for Hindemith," mused Furtwängler in 1935, "I actually did not do so as a demonstration for his art—its ultimate worth still is very much up in the air and his mode of making music far removed from my own. Rather, as a matter of principle, I wanted the public, the nation at large, to be provided with an opportunity to pass judgment *by themselves.*"[81]

The maestro's pact with the National Socialists turned out to be beneficial to both sides. In the highest party echelons he was known and courted as the preeminent conductor of the Weimar period. Goebbels was in touch with him in May 1933, after having become the minister of propaganda and before he institutionalized his Reich Culture Chamber, which would make Furtwängler Goebbels's subordinate as chief conductor of the Berlin Philharmonic. Göring, who was Furtwängler's superior at the Preussische Staatsoper, made him a Preussischer Staatsrat, or state counselor, on 15 September. In addition to his orchestra-directing duties, Furtwängler immediately went to work for the new leaders in other ways: as a musical consultant and as vice-president of the Reich Music Chamber, in which capacity he several times represented the absent Strauss.[82]

What followed was a power struggle in which Furtwängler, thinking himself indispensable, tested the political waters during the controversy surrounding Hindemith: he published his provocative article in a Berlin daily on the morning of 25 November 1934 and conducted a public performance only a few hours later, which was received with ostentatious applause by Berlin's culture enthusiasts. This irked the regime leaders, who now decided to put the conductor in his place. The result was his removal from most of his official posts (except the state counselorship). Early in 1935 this chain of events could have provided the second chance for him to emigrate. Thomas Mann, who followed the spectacle from Switzerland, was impressed by his behavior.[83]

Instead, Furtwängler decided to extend his alliance with the rulers for the time being, for there continued to be something in it for both parties. Without the famous conductor, the Berlin Philharmonic was losing money and prestige, and that meant a huge publicity loss for a dictatorial regime trying to polish its image abroad. Furtwängler knew that he had a chance for a rapprochement because neither the Philharmonic nor the Staatsoper had cut him off their payrolls, at least until the spring of 1935.[84] And so on 28 February 1935 the conductor and Goebbels had a reunion, in which they ironed out their differences and arrived at a new modus vivendi. Trying to live up to his nominally apolitical image but knowing that in fact he was embroiled in a political dispute, Furtwängler compromised his initial position of strength by publicly, and mendaciously, claiming that he had written his famous article in Hindemith's defense solely from a musical point of view and that he regretted any political consequences. It had never been his intention, he said, to interfere with the direction of cultural policy, which, naturally, was the sole prerogative of the Führer and his minister. After Furtwängler's abrogation of all official claims to power, Goebbels received him back into the fold, claiming "a great moral victory" for himself. Furtwängler was to stay on as a regular guest conductor for the Philharmonic and, eventually, the Staatsoper as well. To symbolize the new agreement, the maestro, to ovations from a roaring Berlin audience, once again conducted the Berlin Philharmonic on 25 April.[85]

After the war, during his denazification trial, Furtwängler claimed not only that he had continued his service in the Third Reich as an "apolitical artist," but also that he had never again entered into any contractual relations with the Nazi state. Moreover, he said that he had resisted Nazi attempts to coopt his talents for propaganda purposes.[86] The available evidence today shows that on all of these counts the conductor had not spoken the truth. To begin with, given his enormous prestige, he did not need a permanent position to find continuous employment. Also, many of his future performances were to take place within highly propagandistic frameworks, rendering his art eminently political. Among the first of these, ironically, was his directing Wagner's *Die Meistersinger* at the same party rally that ushered in the anti-Jewish Nuremberg Race Laws of September 1935—an action on the part of Furtwängler that made a mockery of his broad pledge to save Jews. This all the more so since, as the composer's great-granddaughter Nike Wagner has reminded us, Hitler had made *Die Meistersinger* into the "representative festive opera of the Nuremberg party rally."[87] In the service of Hitler, Goebbels, and Göring, Furtwängler continued to conduct just as he had before. The delight of the Führer and his propaganda minister has been profusely documented—notwithstanding occasional minor squabbles with the conductor, perhaps involving the still open question of Hindemith or the situation of non-"Aryans."[88]

Furtwängler had another chance to emigrate when, on Toscanini's recommendation, he was offered the position of chief conductor of the New York Philharmonic in the spring of 1936. A number of factors intervened, however. First, the Nazi regime, and especially Göring, applied pressure on him to stay in the Reich; he was not to be allowed back in if he left. Second, the New York artistic community was divided over the issue of having a man like Furtwängler, who had already compromised himself, assume the preeminent musical position in the United States. After all, New York had a highly visible Jewish population, which heavily subsidized the arts. "I am quite sure that the Jewish subscription to the Philharmonic represents fifty per cent of the total number of seats sold," cautioned a member of the Philharmonic executive committee. Of course, non-Jewish patrons were also concerned. One agitated Protestant clergyman threatened: "Because of the appointment of the apostle and tool of Naziism, Furtwaengler, I must decline to attend concerts of your orchestra. Moreover, I intend using my influence with my great number of relatives, friends, and parishioners against their subscription renewals or attendance at any of your concerts." Furtwängler himself was indecisive, although in late February 1936 he had agreed to conduct a season of forty-two concerts for $35,000 in twelve weeks, to begin in November.

Ultimately, the entire proposition confronted him once more with the existential question of emigration, exile, and his Germanness, and the original dictates of his conscience could not allow this. In any case, by mid-March a virtual U.S. boycott, which he did not have the moral strength to counter, prompted him to remain in Germany.[89]

For this Furtwängler was handsomely rewarded by the regime. In spite of being anything but friendly with Winifred Wagner, with the backing of Hitler and Goebbels he was able to conduct at the Bayreuth Festival in 1936 and 1937. In February 1937 he directed a concert for the Nazi charity Winterhilfswerk. He gave advice in the question of recruiting musicians, and in February 1938 conducted a special Philharmonic concert for the Berlin Hitler Youth. The Philharmonic continued to do impressively well financially under Furtwängler as guest conductor. The maestro was considered by Hitler himself a candidate for the new Nazi National Prize designed to rival the international Nobel Prize, and although he was not among the recipients, he was able to improve his financial situation after repeated consultations with Goebbels. Proceeds from the orchestra and other earnings seem to have netted the conductor at least 206,000 marks in fiscal 1939 alone. No wonder he refused yet again to emigrate when Richard Wagner's granddaughter Friedelind begged him not to return to the Reich from a stay in Paris at Christmas 1938.[90]

As the pall of war slowly settled over Europe, Furtwängler became important to the Third Reich in his capacity as a cultural ambassador, a role he, on the whole, accepted willingly. Again ironically, the conductor was poised to demonstrate to non-German audiences the musical personae of Beethoven, Brahms, and Bruckner, whom the Nazis themselves thought to be the only legitimate representatives, but whom he, according to his postwar testimony, relegated to another Germany. "He once again has done us excellent service abroad," noted Goebbels in his diary in November of 1939.[91] Furtwängler and his second wife, Elisabeth, both boasted after the war that one thing the conductor never stooped to do was to advance Nazi propaganda by conducting in occupied countries. Not only was this a lie in that Furtwängler worked in occupied Denmark in February 1942, but also it is false in terms of a wider sense of "occupied" that would include Nazi satellite states, for Furtwängler conducted the Vienna Philharmonic in Prague, in the Nazi Protectorate of the vanquished Czechs, in November 1940 on a mission specifically designated as propaganda by Goebbels and then again in March 1944. He toured Oslo one week before Norway was attacked by German troops. He also sanctioned a trip by the Berlin Philharmonic to occupied Holland, Belgium, and France in 1940, though without taking part himself. Furtwängler concertized in Axis-allied Hungary as well as in Switzerland and Sweden, two neutral countries in which his mere presence blew the horn of the Nazis.[92]

Standard biographies of Furtwängler have attempted to exculpate the conductor.[93] Not only can this not credibly be done for the period before the war, but also recently discovered evidence shows clearly that the longer the war of aggression dragged on for Germany, the stronger became Furtwängler's inner commitment to the National Socialist regime. It also demonstrates that because of this, the maestro earned rave character reviews from Goebbels and the unflagging admiration of the Führer, not only as a musician but also as a loyal follower of government policy. In 1942, after Furtwängler's tour to Scandinavia, Goebbels noted that he was "overflowing with national enthusiasm." Two years later the minister remarked that "the tougher things become, the closer he moves to our regime." What is more, "Furtwängler shows himself from his best side. He is a genuine patriot and warm adherent and advocate of our politics and martial leadership. All one has to do these days is to tell him what one wants from him and he will immediately deliver." In contrast to Strauss, with Furtwängler there was no suspicion of treason or opposition.[94]

After April 1940 Furtwängler once again enjoyed a more stable relationship with an orchestra, as "permanent conductor" of the Vienna Philharmonic. Goebbels at the time was considering him as successor to Raabe as president of the Reich Music Chamber, a post Furtwängler himself apparently craved. But failing this, Furtwängler was just as happy to conduct the Berlin Philharmonic on the occasion of Hitler's birthday in April 1942, as so many lesser colleagues were doing in those days. The ever grateful Hitler at first wanted to give him a new house close to a scenic Bavarian lake, but then, as he feared for the maestro's safety, ordered a special bunker to be built for him, an expenditure Furtwängler had the tact to decline. In the last months of the war the conductor's recordings of Beethoven and Hitler's beloved Bruckner seem to have cheered the Führer and his propaganda minister during those dark hours which Goebbels became so fond of cursing in his diary. In December 1944, after a visit to Switzerland, Furtwängler had an audience with Goebbels in which he reported "hair-raising things about the political conviction of leading Swiss citizens." But then suddenly, early in 1945, he himself vanished from the country across the Swiss border, after his family had already moved there. The conventional interpretation of this incident is that Himmler suspected him of complicity in the July 1944 plot against the Führer and that the conductor was forewarned of impending arrest by a Berlin physician close to the Himmler household. At most, Furtwängler's name may have been placed on a conspirators' list without his knowledge, but not even that has been proved. As Peter Hoffmann, the authoritative historian of the July plot, has informed me, "Furtwängler does not appear in my work because I know of no evidence why he should." In any event, it is much more likely that Furtwängler found it expedient to desert the sinking ship after he had reaped as many of the material and psychological benefits from the regime as was humanly possible without serious harm to himself. This, then, was his final exit. Furtwängler was not the devil's music master, as has hyperbolically been claimed, but he was not a man of the Resistance either. He was an elitist, beholden to authority, and with a strongly conservative bent, a man who decided to ride out a dangerous political storm, assuaging his ego with occasional humanitarian commitments which for him, the powerful culture broker, entailed very few risks. In the end, spokesmen for the free world were impelled to point out to him that he had accommodated himself to a tyranny, whose long-lasting success he had helped ensure through precisely the sorts of cultural-political tasks Goebbels was convinced that music should perform.[95]

Balancing Acts: Strauss and Pfitzner

For lack of a firm grip on the man, Richard Strauss has lately been described, by one of the more astute music scholars, as a "consummate wearer of masks," a person of many enigmas.[96] One of the masks that Strauss chose to wear was that of an apolitical artist, in the manner of Wilhelm Furtwängler: "I have never meddled in politics," he said of himself at the start of the Nazi era.[97] That credo has been uncritically adopted by his defenders and detractors alike.[98] In reality, Strauss was even more consciously and more skillfully political than Furtwängler and most of his artistic contemporaries, and he had the requisite background and several good reasons for such an attitude. That his politics were largely to fail him even in the early stages of the Third Reich was part of the personal tragedy of this composer, whom his famous librettist Stefan Zweig, before his suicide in Brazil in February 1942, called "the last in a great line of German master musicians."[99]

What, then, determined Strauss's role as *homo politicus?* To begin with, Strauss was politically conditioned as a loyal subject and servant of temporal rulers in at least three different jurisdictions before the turn of the century. He was born in 1864 in Munich, the seat of the Bavarian Wittelsbach dynasty, which, like his father the horn player and professor, he served artistically in state-supported orchestras after he had assumed his first important post as conductor of the court orchestra for the duke of Saxe-Meiningen in 1885. From 1898 to 1910 he was conductor of the Royal Prussian Opera in the service of Kaiser Wilhelm II in Berlin. In his formative years, therefore, Strauss developed to an unusual degree not only his artistic personality but also a firm sense of political authority and social hierarchy.[100]

The awareness of his own place in that hierarchy caused him quite naturally to claim responsibility in the shaping of artistic policy at the beginning of the Weimar Republic. The fact that he, the grand bourgeois who was brought up in the diehard conservative monarchist tradition, detested the republic was beside the point; actually, it motivated him even more strongly to help restore and safeguard order in the land.[101] Permanently settling in Bavarian Garmisch in 1924 after a conducting stint in

Vienna, Strauss observed what he diagnosed as endemic faults of the republic in disgust and greeted the coming of Hitler in January 1933 filled with hope, not because he had a preference for totalitarianism, as has wrongly been alleged,[102] but because he believed that a dictatorial regime could help him implement the changes in the musical culture of his country for which he had been vainly striving for decades. By the same token, Strauss admired in Mussolini not the Fascist with a neocolonial, imperialist ideology but the political strongman who seemed to agree with his own interpretation of public music performance, particularly of his own works.[103]

As we saw in the first chapter, Strauss's intended reforms mainly involved a general improvement of the musical culture, especially the opera culture, through proper policing, education, and training, as well as royalty and copyright protection for composers. On behalf of the latter he had been active since 1898; in 1903 he had founded the Genossenschaft Deutscher Tonsetzer (GDT), or League of German Composers, an officially recognized lobby that safeguarded the copyright of musical content in their oeuvre for composers vis-à-vis their publishers.[104] By 1933 Strauss's objective was to extend the copyright and royalty period from the existing thirty to fifty or even seventy years after a composer's death. It was contact with Goebbels over legislative questions concerning these issues in the first few months after Hitler's takeover that, combined with Strauss's prestige as the leading German composer (he had long been president of the ADMV), led directly to Goebbels's offer of the Reich Music Chamber presidency on 10 November 1933. Thinking that the first fierce storms of revolution would blow over soon, and realizing the full executive potential such an office entailed not only for the copyright issue but also for his overall plans, Strauss accepted.[105]

Strauss, being fully conscious of his unique position at the helm of German composers specifically and all musicians generally, and frequently engaging in personal audiences with Goebbels, Göring, and Hitler, where he used the powers of the neocorporatist music chamber, proceeded to toil in the interests of the very specific goals he had set himself. In the matter of composers' rights he found an ally in Bavarian Justice Minister Hans Frank, who was an avid music lover, and who helped him overcome objections advanced by Goebbels. He also collaborated closely with Winifred Wagner, who wished to broaden monopoly rights over her late father-in-law's operas, in particular a repatriation of Parsifal to Bayreuth as the exclusive performance stage, which Hitler himself had promised her in 1923. (According to the old law, the copyright for Parsifal had expired in 1913, along with the Wagner family's sole right to stage the work.) The Wagner acolyte Strauss could not but agree, promising to do his best. Still in 1933, Goebbels had implemented a restructuring of the German system for collecting and distributing royalties, using a newly constituted body, the Stagma, which came under the direction of the RMK. By its formula "a disproportionately high percentage of royalties" was awarded to serious musicians, the nearest colleagues of Strauss. In addition, by early 1935 a new copyright law had extended the protection period for a composer's works from thirty to fifty years (a period long observed in countries other than Germany) to benefit the family after his death.[106]

Until 1935 the Olympian was obviously successful in looking after the professional and material interests of his lesser composer colleagues. And though he has often been accused of favoring them at the expense of other members of the RMK, such as orchestra musicians,[107] it must be remembered that Strauss's own lobbying expertise had been for decades limited to the composers' arena. Another related charge is that by advancing composers' interests he was primarily advancing his own, since no composer in Germany (save some in the light-music industry) was earning more money than he was. On the whole this complaint is valid. Nonetheless, Strauss's materialism has all too often been exaggerated, as even one of his harshest critics, George Marek, concedes. Nobody, for instance, has as yet seen fit to malign Furtwängler for the money he collected, especially in the Third Reich, when, if the records are reliable, his earnings exceeded Strauss's. While Strauss was still a young conductor, until about the time he began his work for the GDT, he earned just enough money to support his family in modest comfort—so he averred later. His early operas, especially *Der Rosenkavalier*, had made him rich by the time World War I broke out, and he was able to build a charming villa in Garmisch, at the foot of the Bavarian Alps. But because he had deposited the bulk of his sizable fortune in British banks, it was confiscated by Germany's enemies, never to be returned. With a wife and son to support, he had to start anew, although he had hoped to retire from conducting and work solely as a composer. This he was finally able to do in 1924, after resigning his job in Vienna, although when he did conduct, his fee was commensurate with his high stature. Hitler's dictatorship ensured the continued performance of many of his works, but it also inconvenienced him materially through the loss of potential royalties after repeat performances of his opera *Die schweigsame Frau* were forbidden in 1935. And of course, every time a major opera house was destroyed during air raids, the composer shuddered, for where would his operas be staged in the future? Strauss despaired at the thought that after a lost war, the German opera culture, of which he was a part and from which he had substantially and justly benefited, would lie in ruins forever.[108]

This opera culture was very much on his mind when he entered into deliberations with Nazi authorities even before his appointment to the RMK in November 1933, and far beyond. Strauss's wish list was a lengthy one. He had long objected to carelessly assembled potpourris of opera snippets and to the influx of what he considered inferior foreign operas, such as certain French or Italian works, which were either cheap to produce or required no royalties whatsoever. He proposed state subventions for a few major German opera companies and the disbanding or merging of the provincial remnants, for both economic and aesthetic reasons: brilliant opera stars should receive financial bonuses. These plans entailed a downgrading of Goebbels's own Deutsche Oper in Berlin, for the benefit of Göring's Preussische Staatsoper, to which measure the minister understandably objected. Music content in radio should also be enriched, he thought, with ever larger audiences listening to German operas of good quality. All manner of operetta, however, with the exception of the works of Johann Strauss, Jr., and perhaps the Berliner's Paul Lincke (who had collaborated with Strauss in GDT matters), should be suppressed. Strauss deemed operetta tasteless, exploitable in most public venues by salon orchestras such as at seaside and mountain resorts, and, of course, in unfair competition with the nobler species of opera, including his own massive oeuvre.[109]

To implement what Ştrauss viewed as necessary improvements in the broader music culture, in ordinary times he might have preferred persuasion, but with the failure of his plans in the Weimar Republic, the coercion that could be applied by a dictatorial regime appealed to his autocratic nature. Fundamentally, he thought that education was the key to any necessary changes, and that would have to begin with the nation's youth. For instance, he objected to the mindless belching-out of "patriotic, hiking, and battle songs" in the schools and Hitler Youth associations, again for aesthetic but also for health reasons, since he feared that the voices of adolescent males would be ruined. So that they might eventually understand the high art of opera and classical concert music, he wanted pupils to be taught basic harmony and theory, music appreciation, and the mastery of an instrument in the secondary schools. Properly trained music teachers would be in charge of such instruction, not amateur musicians whose main occupation was the teaching of mathematics or geography.[110]

From the start, and quite predictably since the reforms were to occur in cooperation with Goebbels's ministry, Strauss was fought by Rosenberg and his minions. Rosenberg, the Kampfbund, and thereafter the NS-Kulturgemeinde seized on the fact that Strauss's erstwhile librettist Hugo von Hofmannsthal had been by Nazi standards half Jewish, and Stefan Zweig, his current one since 1932, was fully Jewish. They were also well aware that the master's longtime publisher Otto Fürstner was a Jew. In August 1934 Rosenberg himself insinuated to Goebbels that Strauss was beholden to "a Jewish emigrant" and demanded the proscription of Strauss's and Zweig's opera Die schweigsame Frau, to be premiered in mid-1935. Goebbels countered by charging Rosenberg with willful obfuscation, claiming that Zweig was not an emigrant but an Austrian citizen, possessed of no particular hostility toward the Reich. This acrid exchange of notes ushered in the specter of anti-Semitism in Strauss's life and work, and it helped to precipitate the infamous letter affair which, in the summer of 1935, reversed the aged Strauss's political and personal fortunes for the remainder of the Nazi regime.[111]

Strauss's working relationship with Zweig was still embedded in, and frequently suffered from, a genteel, largely economically, religiously, and culturally motivated anti-Semitism on the part of Strauss, which, since the time of the Hohenzollern empire, was in vogue in German upper-class circles and from which even the urbane Thomas Mann was not entirely free.[112] In Strauss's case, although by his own admission he had benefited much from the patronage and friendship of Jews, the older companion of his youth, Alexander Ritter, as well as Cosima Wagner had instilled in him a cultural anti-Semitism that shows through in his correspondence.[113] Not unlike Wagner's, but to a far less virulent degree, Strauss's aversion to Jews was not personal but was rather most likely directed at a perceived cultural stereotype, as is illustrated by his distasteful encounter with Otto Klemperer around 1932. As Klemperer, the champion of modern music, which Strauss hated, tells it, Strauss made derogatory remarks when his wife, Pauline Strauss, suggested that Klemperer seek their help if the Nazis ever took power.[114] But it would be distorting this issue to say that Strauss, by conducting the Berlin Philharmonic in March 1933 in Bruno Walter's stead, committed an "act of anti-Semitism," as has been claimed: although the two musicians never cared much for each other, and Strauss disparaged Walter in correspondence with third parties, he took over the Berlin concert free of charge to help the cash-stricken orchestra in an emergency.[115]

Strauss's fecund partnership with Zweig, from the start of the Third Reich until they parted ways in the summer of 1935, was marred by the composer's overbearing attitude as the most famous musician of his time, as one for whom working with any librettist short of Hofmannsthal would amount to slumming, although he did accept Zweig as making the grade. Between the lines, Strauss tried to impress Zweig as the "Aryan" president of the Reich Music Chamber, an admittedly Nazi creation which would nonetheless, because of Strauss's level of personal tolerance and his intervention with an otherwise dangerous minister, elect to accommodate Zweig, if only he would agree to continue working for the maestro as librettist. In their correspondence, and increasingly until June 1935, this led Strauss to adopt a degree of condescension toward Zweig which the novelist, whose admiration for Strauss was bottomless, in the end found unbearingly humiliating. What must have insulted him especially was that he knew that in order not to antagonize the authorities unduly on account of the "Jewish" ingredient of *Die schweigsame Frau,* Strauss had offered to postpone the premiere of the opera indefinitely, but in the autumn of 1934 had been assured by Hitler and Goebbels that, despite Zweig, they would not stand in the way of the performance.[116]

The formal reason for Strauss's overthrow from his throne in July 1935 was that he, in a letter to Zweig on 17 June, had claimed merely to have acted in the role of the RMK president in order to prevent worse things from happening.[117] Given the cultural and political agenda Strauss had been advancing since 1933, the composer's assertion is simply not persuasive. The fact is that Strauss had assumed his office in November 1933 with high expectations, but he had become disenchanted along the way, not least because he never spent much time in Berlin and trusted unreliable men in his absence. One day it was Furtwängler, his deputy, who in his eyes did not measure up; another he was apprehensive about the planned radicalization of anti-Jewish measures. In October 1934 Strauss grumbled that Goebbels had repudiated "my extensive, well-considered proposals for reform." Throughout November and beyond he was seriously contemplating resigning, but he refrained from it because, first, he did not wish to be seen in solidarity with the disliked Furtwängler (who was fated to be dismissed from his posts at the end of the year), and second, some of his proposed 3tagma changes were about to be pushed through and on no account did he want to forestall that process. Nonetheless, he had already thought of a successor. Even as late as May 1935, shortly before his departure, he was complaining that RMK managing director Ihlert had made important judgments "without asking me in advance"—which on most accounts had of course been the practice all along.[118] It is therefore quite likely that Strauss would have resigned in 1935 in any event had not the Zweig affair of June–July obviated that decision.

Recently historians have maintained that after Strauss's official governmental functions had come to an end, the composer and the regime found a new and much less onerous mode of communication and mutual understanding.[119] If this is to suggest that from the summer of 1935 onward Strauss's Nazi career really took flight, such verdicts could not be more wrong. After an obsequious letter to Hitler penned on 13 July[120]— possibly a final, desperate attempt to regain the leader's good graces, to effect a reappointment for better or for worse, and to ensure continued performances of *Die schweigsame Frau*—Strauss's professional and personal life entered a roller-coaster phase that took him from the depths of disaster to exalted heights, and then back down to the abyss again. Even after copious analysis of those events, the historian can detect little logic.

Strauss was to suffer the carrot-and-stick treatment throughout the remainder of the regime because for the longest time the Reich's leaders could not forgive his intransigence regarding the "Jewish Question," his arcane yet personally vested reform proposals, and the unmistakable anti-Nazi insults contained in the Strauss–Zweig letter intercepted by the Gestapo and sent to Hitler by the same Saxon provincial regime that had caused the downfall of conductor Fritz Busch two years earlier. It was ironic that Hitler and Goebbels should reject an autocrat who refused fully to fit into their own autocracy—but perhaps Strauss was really an aesthetocrat.[121] The other side of the coin was that Strauss was still useful for official advertising in the outside world. And, despite everything, Hitler and Goebbels still loved his music.[122] This is not to say that Strauss composed in a style congenial to fascism, or composed fascist music, as some critics, including Thomas Mann, have insinuated; so long as the parameters of fascist aesthetics are undefined, such remains merely subjective conjecture.[123]

It was humiliating for Strauss never to receive an answer from Hitler to that craven letter of 13 July. For the balance of 1935 Strauss remained persona non grata, as defamatory remarks against him abounded, and performances of several of his operas were suppressed.[124] The pall did not lift until the summer of 1936, when Strauss's *Olympische Hymne* was performed at the games in Berlin, a minor work that had been commissioned not by the German government but by the Olympic Committee. Goebbels once more was impressed, and Strauss was allowed to conduct his own works at the Reich Music Festival in Düsseldorf in May 1938.[125] Thereafter things tightened again, with the occurrence of Kristallnacht in the fall. Months before, Reinhard Heydrich's SS security service had reminded the Promi of the Zweig affair, adding a new dimension to the old problem by maliciously mentioning Strauss's Jewish daughter-in-law, Alice, née von Grab. Born into a wealthy Prague industrialist family, she was married to the music patent lawyer Franz Strauss, the composer's only son and, yet another ironic twist, an ardent Nazi who loved to show off the accoutrements of his party status.[126] Perhaps to keep Strauss in check, the authorities planned to arrest Alice during the pogrom of 9–10 November, but she was away at the time. Instead, her young children, Richard and Christian, were physically molested and taken to the Garmisch square, where, in tears, they were forced to spit at Jews already rounded up there. Later they suffered at the hands of their "Aryan" schoolmates. Alice Strauss was kept under curfew in the Garmisch villa for a time, and her personal papers were confiscated indefinitely.[127]

Although Strauss's professional honor seemed vindicated on the occasion of his seventy-fifth birthday in June 1939, when he received another round of public accolades,[128] the harassment of members of his immediate family, whom he loved dearly, sounded warnings about his precarious situation in the Reich that were a foreshadowing of worse to come. There is no question that the Nazis could have left his Jewish relatives alone had they wanted to, especially in view of Franz Strauss's party rank. But the strategy was to use and abuse the composer at one and the same time, to make him pay for the sins of his past and nip further rebellion in the bud. It escalated when World War II broke out, for now Strauss was threatened with the loss of his household staff and his chauffeured car, which he needed to make his regular trips to Munich, Vienna, and his spa in Switzerland.[129] Since Strauss now lacked any direct leverage with the Berlin government, he began to use agents, such as the Japanese imperial government, for which he composed his *Festliche Musik* on condition that it intercede on his family's behalf in Berlin.[130]

It may reasonably be doubted whether such intercession actually took place, for by late 1941 Strauss had decided to entrust himself and his family to the care of Baldur von Schirach, the new, art-flaunting Gauleiter of Vienna, where the Strauss family owned a second home. Schirach tried as much as he could to shield the composer and his family; Strauss had known Schirach's father, the intendant, back in the town of Weimar.[131] Goebbels was immediately alarmed, all the more so since he had reason to fear oppositional politics out of Vienna by the self-assertive Schirach.[132] In addition to the continued problems with his Garmisch villa, which was either to be stripped of household help or occupied by civilian war evacuees (while Furtwängler was being offered a new lakeside villa), Strauss increasingly suffered fears for his non-"Aryan" family members. Paula Neumann, an octogenarian and grandmother of his daughter-in-law, at the end of 1941 was holding out in the Prague ghetto, where she had already been robbed of all vital possessions and was in danger of being sent to a concentration camp. Her daughter Marie von Grab, Alice's mother, was safe in Lucerne and eager to receive the old lady, but the German authorities would not let her go, despite the fact that she had already been granted a Swiss visa. During the summer of 1942, other children of Paula Neumann were dispatched from Prague to the camp at Theresienstadt. At that point Strauss himself wrote to the SS in Prague asking for compassion, but without results; he also drove his large car right up to the Theresienstadt camp gates, only to be turned back by dumbfounded SS guards. Schirach, despite hosting the Strauss family in Vienna and sponsoring the master's compositions at special performances, was powerless to help, as was Hans Frank, Strauss's old admirer and now the ruthless governor of occupied Poland. Frau Neumann was allowed to stay in Prague until the summer of 1943, but was then sent to Theresienstadt, where she perished. Other relatives of Alice Strauss were taken to the ghetto in Lodz and from there, presumably, to extermination camps. Altogether by 1945 twenty-six members of the Neumann family had been murdered.[133]

Richard Strauss survived the Third Reich an embittered man, insufficiently sheltered by Schirach, cynically tolerated by Hitler and Goebbels, and with his immediate family members harassed by numerous police searches and constantly threatened with arrest, the withdrawal of civil liberties, deportation, and punitive conscription by the armament industry. His eightieth birthday in June 1944 was celebrated nationally, out of ornamental necessity, but with minimal publicity, Goebbels just barely bringing himself to submit his compliments. In Vienna Karl Böhm could still conduct Ariadne auf Naxos, and in Salzburg a few weeks later Clemens Krauss directed the dress rehearsal of Strauss's new opera Die Liebe der Danae, planned for the Salzburg Festival; but then Goebbels canceled the festival and closed down all the theaters. For the remainder of the year Hitler strictly forbade Strauss any contact with members of his government or party and, as a personal slight, prohibited the ailing composer from traveling to the Swiss sanatorium he so badly needed. The beginning of 1945 found Richard and Pauline Strauss ill and trembling with fear, not knowing how the future Allied victors would regard them.[134]

In sum, it can be shown that Strauss's engagement with the Nazi regime, deplorable as it was, was far less committed and durable, and far less motivated by personal, egocentric concerns, than has hitherto been held. Besides Hindemith, whom Strauss respected despite his dislike of the Weimar modernists, he also tried to help other victims of the regime, although not with the public fanfare of a Furtwängler.[135] In addition, there is now a large body of evidence to prove that Strauss and his family were punished by the regime to a degree of viciousness never thought possible in the case of a supposed Third Reich collaborator. Hence, it is fair to conclude that, just as Furtwängler's portrait in the Third Reich has, for decades now, been far too flatteringly drawn, that of Strauss has been painted much less charitably, and redressing this imbalance is in order.

Both Strauss and Hans Pfitzner died in 1949, although Pfitzner was five years younger. If historical judgment over Strauss is divided, what is today's verdict on Pfitzner? Was he a "party ideologue,"[136] a "most ruthless cooperator with the Third Reich,"[137] a "convinced National Socialist"[138] and an artist who "essentially subscribed to the Nazi creed"?[139] Did he adopt a "posture that suggested solidarity with the regime"?[140] Was he a man who furthered his career "through good behavior,"[141] one who was "being raised up by the authorities as a rival pope" to the progressively declining Strauss?[142] Or did he maintain a "distanced" or even "critical stance vis-à-vis Nazi ideology,"[143] so that his works were "ignored and prohibited"?[144] These often contradictory opinions suggest that Pfitzner's life and personality may have been at least as much a riddle as Strauss's own.

Born of German parents in Moscow and trained at the Hoch'sche Konservatorium in Frankfurt, Pfitzner occupied several ill-paying and unsatisfying positions until he landed a job as director of musical institutions in Strasbourg—then in the German Empire—in 1907. His first major work came late, the opera *Der arme Heinrich,* harking back to Wagner and Weber, and generally displaying what Pfitzner became noted for during his lifetime, a "nostalgia for the midday of German Romanticism." The opera's premiere in Cologne was poorly performed but was saved by the heldentenor in the title role—Bruno Heydrich, the father of Reinhard, who would later confront the composer in his SS quarters over the matter of Pfitzner's Jewish friend Paul Cossmann. Without becoming active in party politics, Pfitzner displayed a highly internalized, consummate conservatism, upholding German values and the Second Empire's right to victory during World War I. The end of that conflict saw him leave the once more French city, at great material and emotional cost to himself and his family; he moved to the environs of Munich, where munificent friends had bought him a house.[145] Meanwhile, he had been able to build on the success of his second opera, *Palestrina,* premiered in 1917 by the then largely unknown Bruno Walter in Munich, which dealt with a morally and aesthetically weighty Reformation theme: at the center was a lonely Christian church-music composer, called by the pope to account for his work at the Council of Trent. This hero may well have been a stand-in for Pfitzner. The opera impressed Thomas Mann, spawning a friendship of several years' duration. It was a stiff and somewhat dry opus, if often hauntingly beautiful. Although again it was beholden to mainstream German Romanticism, the second act showed harmonic boldness that paralleled some creations of the modernists. Yet it was pathbreaking for neither the librettist nor the composer, Pfitzner, who remained a Romantic epigone for the balance of his career, especially during the republic. Indeed, he hated that republic for its manifestations of what he—along with other conservative critics—termed its cultural Bolshevism, referring not only to its political democracy and the Treaty of Versailles it had signed but also to the new modernism in art and culture, which he equated with internationalism and Jewry. A new opera of his entitled *Das Herz,* maudlin and with a shoddily written libretto by an undistinguished student, was neither a financial nor an artistic success after 1931, yet at the same time it demonstrated that there was still creative potential left in the sixty-eight year-old Pfitzner.[146]

It is important to understand Pfitzner as a leading conservative composer of the Weimar Republic who, along with the albeit much more universally recognized Strauss, was the last serious representative of the bygone nineteenth-century style. To do so, one must look more closely at this self-appointed "German composer," in addition to what he identified with modernism and Jewry. "Pfitzner the German" was an image that, owing to a small but regionally influential Pfitzner cult, was carried over into the Third Reich, the new order that for Pfitzner signaled a collection of mixed blessings. In 1940 the Nazi musicologist Josef Müller-Blattau, one of the composer's many Third Reich admirers, called Pfitzner "musically German." Like the man, Pfitzner's music tended to be sternly introspective, redolent of heroism and self-sacrifice, and suffused with religious and metaphysical symbolism. Unlike in Strauss's oeuvre, in most of Pfitzner's stage works there was no eroticism, no expansiveness, irony, or pranks, none of the rich colors, and of course no happy endings, only toil, severity, and resignation. In that sense Pfitzner's music by the early 1930s was closer to Wagner's *Parsifal.* His music has often been called "torn," a credible reference to the dualist Faustian state of being that his countrymen, and not just dyed-in-the wool post–World War I nationalists, held to be quintessentially German. In particular, the frequent intimations of death, the embrace thereof as a motif, and the ready references to pure Romanticism were linked to an axiomatically purist German quality, which Pfitzner himself extolled in his various caustic writings during the republic, particularly the programmatic major treatise "The New Aesthetics of Musical Impotence: A Symptom of Decay." His "Romantic cantata" *Von deutscher Seele* (1921) aimed to articulate a German confession; conversely, it was meant as an indictment of anything he deemed alien and offensive. Typically overstating his case, Pfitzner said during the

Third Reich that it had originated at a time "when the word 'German' could hardly be uttered in Germany with impunity."[147]

"Decay," of course, was the term the National Socialists, with whom Pfitzner did not overtly sympathize during the Weimar Republic, had especially reserved for everything Jewish. In regard to that particular connotation of "decay," however, there was never any serious disagreement between Pfitzner and the Nazis. In generalizing fashion, and unlike Strauss and Furtwängler, Pfitzner thought that the Jews as a whole were anathema to true German existence; in the cultural realm he started with the formula of "national" equaling "German" and "international" equaling "Jewish" (or, by extension, Bolshevist). To him Jews as individual persons were less important than Jewry as a collective; in the manner of some Nazis later on, he conceded that there were certain Jews who could behave like Germans and Germans who would act against the interests of Germany, and thus be more like Jews and Bolshevists. These categorizations initially had no lethally racist implications. Pfitzner failed to realize, however, how easily any collective, culturally motivated stereotype could be turned in that direction, nor did he see that his own ad hominem attacks on Jews, undertaken in the 1920s with great vehemence— as against the critics Paul Bekker and Alfred Einstein—came close to expressing the virulence that routinely characterized the Nazis' anti-Semitism then and later. Apologists for Pfitzner have maintained that two or three of the composer's closest friends were Jews, mainly Bruno Walter and the publicist Paul Cossmann. Walter, as we have seen, was a practicing Jew of a politically conservative bent who would eventually break with Pfitzner over the Nazi regime's policies. As a highly assimilated Jew, Cossmann, like his contemporaries the writer Otto Weininger and the politician Walther Rathenau, was an anti-Semite who shared the sentiments of political right-wingers before converting to Catholicism in 1905. This did not prevent his arrest by the Gestapo in 1933 and his death in Theresienstadt in 1942; the first of these Pfitzner was able to undo, but the second further embittered an already bitter man. In sum, it is clear that Pfitzner never advocated the killing, incarceration, or expulsion from Germany of Jews; but he did want their influence in Germany curtailed, and hence he served as an intellectual forebear of the much more virulent anti-Semites to come. This was another dreadful consequence of applauding Wagner's archetypal anti-Semitism by naively giving credence to his characterization of Jews, going so far as to say that sensible Jews at the time had agreed with Wagner.[148]

After Hitler's ascension to power in January 1933, some high-placed Nazis thought that they could use Pfitzner to the same extent to which he hoped to see his own star rise.[149] He appears to have been a candidate to succeed Max von Schillings as intendant of the Berlin municipal opera after Schillings's death in July 1933. Most likely Pfitzner was favored in his bid by Rosenberg and his Kampfbund, and for that reason alone Goebbels as Gauleiter of Berlin did not approve of him but instead

backed Kammersänger Wilhelm Rode, who, unlike Pfitzner, was supported by the Führer himself.[150] In any case, some sort of working alliance between Pfitzner and the Kampfbund was shaping up, without
the composer's understanding or caring about the intricacies of intraparty wranglings in the Third Reich. In the early years of the regime,
first the Kampfbund and then its successor organization the NS-
Kulturgemeinde organized special concerts of Pfitzner's works, at some of
which the maestro himself conducted, and which were sometimes cast
into the mold of festivals in honor of Pfitzner, mostly in his new hometown of Munich, but also in other venues such as Berlin, Kiel, and
Gera.[151] There were additional, non–politically motivated Pfitzner events
staged by municipal bureaucracies, radio, and public concert organizations; Pfitzner's oeuvre made a noticeable impact on advertising bill-
boards.[152] In fact, the composer's music suddenly seemed to be so
fashionable that in November 1934 a Viennese friend expressed his satisfaction that "everywhere in Germany your name is finally mentioned."[153]

Until the end of the regime, including a stretch when the composer's
productivity was lagging, Pfitzner's music continued to be performed
routinely in regular concert and opera programs, and he collected his fair
share of prizes and public distinctions, especially on his seventieth birthday in May 1939.[154] This in itself is not remarkable in the case of a man
whose music was safely traditionalist and whose national prestige had
been pristine since World War I. But what is worthy of mention is that
Pfitzner's music, in addition, continued to be favored by a number of
party and government organizations that were as self-contained as they
were self-important, not reporting in these matters to the RMK, Goebbels, Göring, or Hitler himself, and thus once again signifying the high
degree of decentralization in the cultural landscape of the Third Reich.

Not unexpectedly, invitations by the NS-Kulturgemeinde and, later, by
KdF organizations continued on course, especially since they came to
oversee the newly styled "Pfitzner Society."[155] Moreover, several Gauleiter and their administrations increasingly saw fit to invite Pfitzner to their
regional seats of power and demonstratively paid homage to him personally and to his "German" music, most of which he himself was asked to
conduct or accompany on the piano. This occurred, for example, in the
framework of official Nazi celebrations in Bremen (1938), Salzburg
(1940), Strasbourg (1940), and Poznan (1942).[156] Of special significance
were the Pfitzner concert series organized by the Cracow-based governor
of Poland, Hans Frank, who loved his compositions no less than Richard
Strauss's. But whereas Strauss successfully resisted putting in a personal
appearance in Cracow, despite repeated invitations by the governor,
Pfitzner cravenly betook himself there in 1942 and 1944 and presented a
special piece, *Krakauer Begrüssung*. Frank knew how to reciprocate:
whenever possible he offered his personal railway coach to fetch Pfitzner
and delighted the composer with rare delicacies for Christmas.[157]

But from the beginning of his professional life and beyond the Third

Reich, Pfitzner suffered from peculiar problems; he was always a troubled man. One of these problems had to do with money. By family background not as generously endowed as Strauss or even Furtwängler, Pfitzner found it difficult to make ends meet until his Strasbourg appointment in 1907. A decade later, expelled from that city, he was indigent again. After he received a post at Berlin's Akademie der Künste in 1919 (where in 1921 he became an absentee professor, somehow trying to instruct students out of his Bavarian home), things changed for the better, but since his works were performed relatively seldom in the republic and did not draw large crowds, he was mainly dependent on arduous guest conducting and piano recitals all over the land. For September 1929 Pfitzner accepted a position as full professor at the Bayerische Akademie der Tonkunst, where he was supposed to teach a master class in composition, and he was also guaranteed a fixed number of guest-conducting spots with the Munich opera (then under Franckenstein and Knappertsbusch), in addition to the freedom to conduct on a freelance basis elsewhere. Hence, at the beginning of the Third Reich in January 1933 (despite the recent commercial misfortune of *Das Herz*), Pfitzner was doing reasonably well, albeit in the shadow of Strauss and Furtwängler. But his moderate affluence reinforced his belief that under National Socialist rule his time had finally come and things could only improve.[158]

This positive feeling changed abruptly to one of angry disbelief when in mid-1934, on the occasion of his sixty-fifth birthday, Pfitzner was pensioned off at the Bavarian academy, and his Munich conducting privileges were reduced as well. This occurred at a time when it had just been made clear to the composer by Franckenstein that as far as the Bayerische Staatsoper was concerned, his stage works were not netting much money and therefore could not be performed as often as Pfitzner might have wished. Although the composer later claimed that he had been "purposely lied to and defrauded," his dismissal was legal strictly on the grounds of his having reached the usual retirement age of sixty-five. And although it was not uncommon for artists of his stature to be kept on longer, Pfitzner had not particularly distinguished himself at either the academy or the opera. At the academy he had merely taught a dramaturgical seminar and in the five years of his influence there had had only two students, whereas his colleagues, particularly Joseph Haas, had trained many more. As to his work at the opera, Franckenstein and Knappertsbusch complained that ever since Pfitzner had started there in 1929, his efforts had amounted to an "unwanted burden in financial as well as, especially, artistic respects." Pfitzner had never adapted there and was permanently regarded as an outsider by the *corps d'opéra;* and he had exhausted the entire opera staff and materials during rehearsals and performances, creating expenses not guaranteed by his initial contract.[159] To add insult to injury, the Berlin Deutsche Oper, which had been on the verge of hiring Pfitzner as intendant, informed him, toward the end of the year, that rather than present his Christmas stage work *Christelflein*

(1906–17), the directorate had decided on the always reliable *Hänsel und Gretel* by Humperdinck.[160]

The nasty business of Pfitzner's Munich dismissal left him in financial limbo for some years, for it was clear neither how large a pension was due to him nor how it was to be balanced against his freelance income and music royalties. The matter occasioned humiliating letters and even personal visits by the composer to government ministries and party offices in Munich and Berlin, until by 1937 Goebbels and Hitler seem to have decided to end the ugly squabbles by allotting Pfitzner an "honorary pension" on account of his unofficial status as "Pfitzner the German," but doubtless also because the authorities were simply getting tired of his grousing. In the end, Pfitzner was granted a pension large enough to allow him to maintain his new Munich house and a car with chauffeur, as well as to assist in the support of an incurably ill son and two other children partially dependent on him. With Pfitzner's compositions being patronized by various official agencies in the Reich, which he was often invited to conduct, he still had to continue his strenuous schedule as a concert musician throughout Germany, something Strauss had largely given up by 1924. Pfitzner must have known that without such authoritative backing his compositions would have brought in very meager earnings on a freely competitive basis in the marketplace. This is reflected, not least, by the comparative dearth of commercial recordings of his works from that period.[161]

Hence, it should be sufficiently clear that, contrary to the belief of even some modern musicologists, Pfitzner's relationship with the Third Reich was a fractured one, nor was he, who never deigned to join the party, a model N nal Socialist. After the neglect of his operas on German stages in the early 1930s, the pension affair, and the rebuff he experienced at the Berlin Deutsche Oper, this chronically frustrated and intemperate man adopted the personal credo that even though he had been prepared to serve the Third Reich at a suitably high level after many personal and artistic sacrifices in the Weimar Republic, he had instead been repudiated. Apart from the finances, much of the problem was that Pfitzner, although politically and aesthetically a reactionary, did not comprehend the politically conservative aims of the regime, yet neither could he understand what few signs of modernism it displayed. He resented being prevented from conducting in Salzburg in 1933, at a time when the regime's political relations with Austria were critical, and he remained deeply suspicious of all the manifestations of its day-to-day anti-Semitism, particularly since friends of his came to suffer from it. Yet he also rejected what to him seemed to be the new champions of art, such as Orff, Egk, and Wagner-Régeny. The mystical Christian content in some of his own compositions, notably *Palestrina* and *Christelflein,* was of a sort not congenial to either the official Nazi version of "Aryan," assertive German Christianity (though Pfitzner also had no ties with the regenerative Confessionalist church musicians à la Distler), or the Hitler Youth–style celebrations, which, rancorous elitist that he was, he openly despised. After much brooding, Pfitzner therefore concluded that the Third Reich was ungrateful to him (a conclusion not borne out by the evidence to 1945) because inexplicably the government had not constituted the desired antidote to the Weimar perversions but had instead brought about new ones. Tragically, Pfitzner was a marginal man, a latter-day Romantic, perhaps a protofascist who was asynchronously tied to an immutably ensconced fascist regime. He misjudged Hitler's Third Reich to the same extent that it appeared to misjudge him. "I denounce this Germany from the deepest bottom of my heart," Pfitzner exclaimed to his composition student and sometime paramour Lilo Martin in 1934. The sad irony was that he was ready to denounce his home country in virtually any productive phase of his life, since he always believed it owed him something it simply would not yield.[162]

Throughout various phases of his professional life Hans Pfitzner was haunted by three demons he could not shake off, try as he might. Their names were Hermann Göring, Adolf Hitler, and Richard Strauss. In the matter of his retirement, after he had attempted in vain to get Bavarian Minister-President Rudolf Siebert and Goebbels to reverse the decision of July 1934, Pfitzner wrote to Göring in December to inform him that he was thinking of taking the Bavarian government to court, and what a shame that would be for Germany. Would Göring be able to receive him in Berlin for an hour or so? Pfitzner would be in the capital in January.[163] Göring replied early in the new year to say that he had been prepared to support Pfitzner financially but recently had learned that the composer was much better off than he had been led to believe. Pfitzner responded that his actual financial status was not the issue, but rather that his honor had been violated, not least through a neglect of his operas on Prussian stages. He compared himself with Mozart, who (Pfitzner said) had once been kicked by a Salzburg bishop—yet the fault had not been Mozart's. An infuriated Göring then ordered Pfitzner to appear in his Berlin offices on 5 January 1935. At this meeting, of which we have only Pfitzner's notes, Göring seems to have threatened the composer with the concentration camp, but after much shouting, in the course of which Göring belittled all German artists, the premier conceded that he liked Pfitzner's *Das Herz* yet found much of *Palestrina* intolerable—one of several explanations why "Pfitzner operas never brought any money into the till."[164] The standoff ended with a formal apology by Pfitzner to the Prussian opera chief, in which he repeated that he had viewed the Nazis' assumption of power as the "longed-for awakening of the German nation" for which he had fought so ardently, only to be disappointed "not to have been called to an eminent post, in order to accomplish the cultural reconstruction."[165] For the time being Göring acquiesced, promising to pay more attention to Pfitzner's oeuvre at his own Staatsoper. But although he later sent the composer a courteous notice of his upcoming marriage to Emmy Sonnemann, in future Pfitzner had good cause to be wary of the crafty politician, who in his own injured pride could always seek revenge through tricky cultural politics, therein using his Mephistophelian servant Heinz Tietjen, whose machinations Pfitzner, like so many musicians in the Third Reich, would constantly have reason to dread.[166]

If, all things considered, Göring was more like a troll to Pfitzner than a demon, Pfitzner's mostly hidden relationship with Hitler always had something truly demonic about it, and it ultimately explains why the composer could never be certain of his place in the Third Reich.

Hitler was born in 1889, the year Pfitzner enjoyed his first public success while still a student at the Frankfurt conservatory, with the performance of his Scherzo for Orchestra composed two years earlier. None other than Paul Cossmann arranged a personal meeting between the Führer of the Nazi Party and Pfitzner, who was in a Munich hospital in February 1923, for that hypernationalistic publicist wanted the conservative composer and the reactionary revolutionary to become acquainted. Hitler arrived with an entourage, including his mentor, the seedy poet Dietrich Eckart. The two men—with Hitler in his shabby trenchcoat at the foot of the bed—conversed about "the future of Germany" and World War I, for which "the Jews alone were responsible." Otto Weininger was mentioned, whom, according to Pfitzner's memory, Hitler wished to acknowledge because as a Jew he had, through suicide, "removed himself from this world." Characteristically, Hitler did most of the talking. As the visitors were leaving, Hitler said to Eckart on the stairway that he did not want anything to do with this old rabbi— evidently mistaking the bearded Pfitzner for a Jew.[167]

Pfitzner did not learn of Hitler's devastating verdict until 1934, when he was disinvited to conduct during the September party rally in Nuremberg, because, as the musician lamented to Lilo Martin, Hitler thought him to be half Jewish. Apparently this impression stuck with the Führer till the end of the regime, for as late as June 1943 Goebbels noted in his diary that Hitler was not opposed to honoring the composer on his seventieth birthday, but only modestly, for "the Führer really is very much against Pfitzner, since, contrary to all evidence, he thinks him to be a half-Jew."[168]

After Hitler's aborted Beer Hall Putsch in November 1923, Pfitzner prepared to send a token of his sympathy to the Führer's Landsberg prison cell; it was a small biography of Ulrich von Hutten, the German Peasants' War hero and contemporary of Luther. Pfitzner dedicated it to "Adolf Hitler the great German." Dated 1 April 1924, this offering was never mailed, nor was Pfitzner's accompanying letter, in which he reminded the Nazi Führer that for brave nationalists such as himself, it was Germans who were the worst traitors.[169]

After January 1933, whenever Pfitzner tried to seek out Hitler in person, the Führer attempted to avoid him. After a Pfitzner concert in Weimar, Hitler invited all the participants to his hotel for the customary late-hour chat, save Pfitzner, who was purposely left out. Hitler ignored a

Pfitzner visit to Munich party headquarters, where the composer hoped to speak to him about the Gestapo's incarceration of his old friend Cossmann, the man who had introduced them in 1923. The main reason why Pfitzner complied with the Salzburg concert ban (which Strauss had chosen to ignore) was that he feared to antagonize Hitler. When in Berlin, Pfitzner would pointedly invite Hitler to his performances—invariably without success. Moreover, the musician was at great pains to establish his "Aryan" lineage once the suspicion about his Jewishness had been raised officially in 1934. In addition, Pfitzner poured forth public praise of the Führer: "Today there is no one beside him with the strength of body, spirit or soul, him whom we have known as our German Führer for the past ten years." And although Hitler could not refrain from influencing the controversial matter of Pfitzner's pension settlement, by 1939 Berlin insiders were saying openly that he neither liked Pfitzner personally nor cared for his music. No wonder that in the spring of that year Pfitzner thought he had valid grounds to assume that Hitler himself had forbidden a round of festivities in honor of his seventieth birthday, which had been planned in Munich.[170]

For better or worse, Pfitzner was able to accommodate himself to Göring, and he could force himself to live with the fact that Hitler, the political leader he idolized, failed to grasp his significance as an artist and a cultural prophet. But what cast a "permanent shadow over his life" and made him question his raison d'être was the towering aloofness of Richard Strauss.[171] Whereas Strauss was a much more politically minded man and a manipulator of ideas, systems and people for his long-term goals, including the service of his sacred egotism, Pfitzner was never in control of anything but his own compositions. Strauss, for a while at least, was shaping events in the Third Reich, until he became one of its most prominent victims. Pfitzner, however, always just barely survived.

The rivalry between Pfitzner and Strauss is said to date from 1900, when, after a joint concert in Berlin, Strauss was acclaimed by the audience, whereas a cooler reception greeted Pfitzner's *Die Rose vom Liebesgarten*, which was wedged in between *Tod und Verklärung* and *Ein Heldenleben*.[172] This need not have worried Pfitzner unduly; after all, Strauss was older and better established. But it could not be overlooked that from then on, Strauss consistently reaped more attention, although the two composers remained on a friendly footing for years. The physical and temperamental differences between the two men, however, could hardly be ignored: Strauss, tall and urbane, with wealth and solid upbringing behind him, married to a general's daughter, and the petit-bourgeois Pfitzner, small and frail, hunched over, and with the sad facial expression of a night owl.[173] In their aesthetics they were never far apart, though Pfitzner favored the traditional approach of Schumann and Brahms over what he demeaned as Wagnerian chromatics in Strauss's music. Nor did Pfitzner share Strauss's very high esteem of Mozart. But they were united in their opposition to foreign influences, particularly "cheap" Italian and French music, as well as that of the moderns, which Pfitzner subsumed under his rubric of cultural Bolshevism.[174]

Pfitzner must have viewed Strauss's early cultural-political ascent in the Third Reich with envy, and he felt constrained as a member of the RMK presidial council, since he did not wish to be made into a "vassal of the Arabella composer."[175] Pfitzner came to experience the real impact of Strauss's influence when, in the aftermath of the Hindemith debacle, over the New Year 1934–35 his opera Der arme Heinrich and other works that had been tentatively scheduled by Furtwängler were removed from the program of the Preussische Staatsoper by Tietjen and Clemens Krauss in favor of a solid program of Strauss.[176] For the remainder of the Third Reich this was the prevailing theme. In Pfitzner's eyes his own works were consistently neglected for the benefit of Richard Strauss.[177] And the statistics bear this out: from early 1933 to the end of 1943, at the Bayerische Staatsoper alone, 317 performances of Strauss operas were staged as opposed to only 61 of Pfitzner's works.[178]

Such differences in artistic fortune were, naturally, also reflected on the international scene and in both men's earnings. Although Pfitzner sometimes conducted in other capitals of Europe, he was performed only once in New York, when at Carnegie Hall Artur Bodansky presented his cantata Von deutscher Seele in October 1923. Another attempt to feature Pfitzner's music in America in 1929 failed. This was the price that "Pfitzner the German" had to pay—the rather more provincial German reception his music got over the years, including in the Third Reich.[179] Compare this with Strauss's endless worldwide success, whether in Rio de Janeiro, Buenos Aires, or New York, where the composer personally conducted. Strauss, of course, earned more too—approximately double—even though during the war both composers were placed in the highest national prize category, along with the much lesser composer Paul Graener.[180]

Strauss remained quite sanguine despite the slights he received at the hands of Pfitzner and his small but fanatical following, particularly Pfitzner's acolyte the Berlin music critic Walter Abendroth, who in his contemporary biography of Pfitzner likened Strauss to the devil incarnate.[181] Pfitzner was "a capable composer," as were Graener, von Reznicek, and Vollerthun, Strauss noted gratuitously in May 1935, but a few weeks later anger overcame him, and he ranted that "this man constantly behaves most maliciously against me," a remark obviously not without justification.[182]

In the end, terrible personal misfortune almost united them, even geographically, for Pfitzner spent some months toward the end of his life, impoverished, in a nursing home in Garmisch. His eyesight had deteriorated, most of his family and many friends had died, he himself had nearly been killed in air raids, and his Munich house had been destroyed by bombs in 1943. By 1945 his faith in Adolf Hitler, National Socialism, and the Third Reich had been shaken. Of Strauss's final years the chronicles are full. But experts tell us that the music the two men composed in their very last years bears a certain resemblance.[183]

Forms of Resistance

Karlrobert Kreiten was born on 26 June 1916 in Bonn, the son of a piano teacher and a singer. He grew up in Düsseldorf, where his father was professor of piano and composition at the municipal conservatory. An extremely gifted child, Karlrobert showed a talent for languages, the fine arts, and, above all, violin and piano. Having decided to become a pianist, he took lessons from his father's students, giving his first public concert at the age of ten. From then on his career was prodigious. In 1929, still in Gymnasium, he was awarded a scholarship to study at the Cologne Conservatory. Two years later, at fifteen, he mastered the difficult *Paganini-Variationen* by Brahms. Among more than 250 serious contestants, he won first prize at an international piano competition under the patronage of Clemens Krauss in Vienna in June 1933; he had been the youngest entrant. What secured him the prize was his rendition of Franz Liszt's technically challenging Dante Sonata. In October of that year Kreiten also won the coveted Mendelssohn Prize in Berlin. The following years saw him perfecting his art in Vienna and, in Berlin, as a star pupil of Claudio Arrau. By 1938 and on into the war years, he was concertizing all over Germany, with Liszt, Chopin, Beethoven, and Mozart among his specialties. By 1941 critics were comparing him to Wilhelm Backhaus, by 1943 to Germany's master pianist Walter Gieseking.[184]

Then one day in May 1943 music lovers were waiting for him to appear for a recital at the Auditorium Maximum of the University of Heidelberg. Karlrobert Kreiten never showed up. That morning, 3 May, he had been arrested in his hotel by the Gestapo. He was taken to the Gestapo prison in Berlin, where, during the next several weeks, he was prepared to be tried for high treason and defeatism by Hitler's infamous People's Court. During this period he was without protection from frequent air raids on the capital, and reportedly was afraid that he might be burned alive in a bomb attack. On 3 September the court sentenced him to death. The regional Nazi Party in Düsseldorf thwarted all attempts by his family to appeal for clemency at the highest levels. Kreiten was hanged at Plötzensee penitentiary on 7 September.[185]

What had he done? The pianist had committed one of the most serious political crimes German civilians could be held accountable for during the Second World War: he had listened to anti-Nazi news on the BBC and had spread this, along with his own scathing analysis of the status of Hitler's war and the current political system, to his landlady, a Nazi Party member and former friend of his mother, a woman he thought he could trust. She then had passed the information on to other Nazis, ensuring that Kreiten would be charged.[186]

In connection with the Kreiten case, two essential questions must be asked that might actually serve as benchmarks for judging other cases of disobedience by German musicians against Nazi authority. First, was Kreiten's action truly politically motivated? And second, did the aesthetics of his musical art influence his anti-regime attitude to the extent that his opposition would have been a function of his vocation, as in the case of a physician who opposes war because his priority is to save human lives?

On the first count, there is no doubt that Kreiten was politically sensitized by his upbringing, for his was a cosmopolitan, not a narrowly chauvinist background. His father, Theo Kreiten, originally hailed from Holland, and his maternal grandmother, whom he loved dearly, was a Frenchwoman born in Spain. From her Karlrobert learned fluent French as a child, and he spent many vacations in western Europe. In 1933, while a conservatory student in Cologne, he successfully resisted attempts by the Nazi student organization to recruit him (although Nazi sources have it that later he applied for membership in the party, evidently unsuccessfully). He may also have been conditioned by Hedwig Rosenthal-Kanner, a Jewish piano teacher from his Vienna days, who later emigrated to the United States and in 1937 begged him to join her and her husband in exile, promising him a career that most surely would have rivaled that of the slightly older Rudolf Serkin. He seems to have felt true outrage at Hitler's unconscionable direction of the war and at the obviously repressive politics inside Germany—outrage that could arise only in a politically aware person. And although he may have trusted his Berlin landlady, he must have known of the risks involved every time a resident of the Reich spread news from the BBC to others, especially since the number of death sentences to counter this crime was known to have risen since 1941.[187]

On the second count the answer is ambiguous. Although Kreiten allegedly said to the Nazi woman that "the Führer hasn't got a clue about how to wage a war, nor about music, he just sticks his nose into everything," this is not clear proof that a professional ethos motivated him to assume a political stance against the regime.[188] This observation is important, for it raises the subsequent question whether a professional ethos among musicians ever was sufficiently potent to cause such opposition in the Third Reich.

Hence, in the much-celebrated case of Kreiten, two hitherto widespread assumptions may be safely laid to rest, one being Furtwängler's predictable characterization of the young artist as a "totally unpolitical personage" (whom he once again felt compelled to rescue), and the other being Theo Kreiten's judgment that the Nazis would not consider clemency for his son because they purposely wished to select "a victim of high rank from among artistic circles."[189] Contrary to Furtwängler's (and probably Goebbels's own) conjecture, and as has, from a different angle, already been observed in the case of Strauss, artistic professionalism and political awareness were not mutually exclusive. And because of the relative importance the Nazi regime ascribed to artistic productivity even during the war, and since artists had not been seen as egregious political lawbreakers, there was no particular reason for the authorities to make an example of an errant musician such as Kreiten. On the face of the sometimes threadbare evidence so far, the relationship between politics and the cultural arts (whose premise is and was a degree of freedom of individual expression that even Goebbels did not deny), the fundamental formula was relatively simple: if one wanted to practice one's art, one had to be physically free, and this required that one insured oneself politically, or at least tried to stay clear of politics. "I wanted to play in the theater and not be in a concentration camp," stated the famous actor Bernhard Minetti unequivocally after the war.[190] If one felt this was impossible under the constraints of a totalitarian dictatorship, one had either to change jobs, as did Max Butting, a minor composer, or to emigrate, as did Thomas Mann. Neither of these two options was absolute or simple. Butting, though he chose to become a businessman, continued to compose occasionally, only to realize that he was a failure.[191] As for Mann, even the circumstances of his "emigration" are still not entirely clear. Erika Mann recalls how, in a long telephone conversation from Munich on 11 March 1933, she pleaded with her father, who was in Swiss Arosa, not to return to Germany, until he finally agreed.[192] What would have happened had he returned? What would have happened had Hitler allowed the performance of Hindemith's opera *Mathis der Maler* in 1935, or had Göring given Fritz Busch a post at the Preussische Staatsoper in 1933?

Among the majority of non-Jewish musicians who remained in the Third Reich, there were many demonstrations of discontent that did not, in and of themselves, signify a consistent political attitude that could have long-term personal consequences. Nor were they usually motivated by aesthetics. Bass-baritone Hans Hotter, who in 1933 in Prague had proved to have a sardonic sense of humor, once was sitting with conductor Hans Schmidt-Isserstedt in a pub when a stranger entered, greeting everyone with a rousing "Heil Hitler!," whereupon Hotter replied to him with a cool "Very well!"[193] Soprano Marta Fuchs, the Kundry in Bayreuth's *Parsifal*, admired by Goebbels and Hitler alike, approached the Führer after a performance of the *Ring* during the 1938 season and half-jokingly warned him not to start a war. Hitler allegedly assured her that he had had enough of wars from his last experience, when, during World War I, his eyes had suffered from gas attacks. A year later the two met again in Bayreuth and Hitler asked the prima donna if he had waged a war or not. In her broad Swabian accent Fuchs replied: "Herr Hitler, I just don't trust you!" The mere omission of the Führer title in addressing Hitler could have landed an ordinary person in a concentration camp. But Fuchs knew she could rely on her prestige—and, besides, she had been one of the very few artists in Dresden who did not endorse the firing of Fritz Busch, whom Hitler liked, in 1933.[194] Less well known figures who balked, especially during the war, could fare much worse, as did one Hamburg voice teacher, who had lost two sons in the war and repeatedly criticized Hitler. He received a light sentence of one year in jail only because he was credited with having a good National Socialist record and having brought up all of his children in the Nazi faith.[195] Such an offense would have been comparable to listening to the BBC in wartime, which several musicians, like so many other Germans, did. They did not get caught, however, because they wisely did not spread the news.[196] Tuning in to the BBC may have been a much worse crime than casually fraternizing with Jews or clandestinely playing Hindemith's music—the latter strictly for aesthetic reasons.[197]

But there were musicians who exposed themselves less irresponsibly and more systematically than Karlrobert Kreiten had done, fully aware of the possible consequences, whether as professional artists or politically mature citizens. Eberhard Rebling was a young Berlin pianist who felt himself drawn to left-wing refugee politicians in Prague. He himself almost joined the communist underground, but in 1937 he decided to get out and move to Holland, where he then met and married a Jewish dancer.[198] The Viennese composer and clarinetist Friedrich Wildgans joined an Austrian resistance group around the Catholic theologian Karl Roman Scholz; in 1940 the group was caught, and Wildgans was incarcerated by the Gestapo for more than two years. After his release he continued his resistance and miraculously survived.[199]

In Berlin, Helmut Roloff's was a similar case. Born in 1912 in Giessen, where his father was a history professor, Roloff had studied in Leipzig and Berlin. Unlike most musicians—in fact, unlike most members of the haute bourgeoisie—Roloff was conditioned against the Nazi state in an anti-Hitler home. And so, like Kreiten, as a student he stayed aloof from Nazi organizations. While still taking private lessons around 1940, he met the dentist Hans Helmuth Himpel and his "half-Jewish" girlfriend Marie Terwiel, who collaborated with the communist resistance organization Rote Kapelle. "We were not communists," Roloff explained later, "we were simply—well, how shall I put it?—liberal-minded citizens who just did not accept the Third Reich and therefore tried to do something." The group became involved in anti-Nazi activities through the distribution of handbills and several conspiratorial meetings. Evidently, while they were being observed by the Gestapo, Terwiel and Himpel asked Roloff to hide a suitcase for them, so the pianist put it in his Berlin flat, under his grand piano, without knowing what was in it. Roloff, no fool, understood the danger. On 19 September 1942 Terwiel and Himpel were arrested, and the Gestapo found the suitcase in Roloff's apartment. When a transmitter was discovered, he denied having had any knowledge of it. During interrogation at Gestapo headquarters, Roloff kept insisting that he had not known about either the radio or the activities of his Resistance friends; they had met only for the sake of listening to music. The friends, in turn, did not betray him either, even under torture. In January 1943 Roloff was released unharmed, since no hard evidence against him had been found. The dentist and his girlfriend, along with many other members of the Rote Kapelle, were sentenced to death and beheaded later that year. For the remainder of the regime Roloff was able to continue a modest series of concerts, favoring in particular the more modern composers, such as Orff, Egk, and Wagner-Régeny.[200]

Unlike Roloff, the pianist Margarethe Klinckerfuss did not have a brush with death; instead, she was treated like a pariah and taken out of circulation. But, like Roloff, she possessed a mature sense of responsibility. This Stuttgart musician was the daughter of a wealthy piano manufacturer; her mother, Johanna, had been a piano prodigy, a student of Liszt, and a close friend of Clara Schumann. Margarethe Klinckerfuss herself had been well acquainted with composers such as Hugo Wolf and Ferruccio Busoni. In addition, she was the aunt of Rüdiger Schleicher, an expert on international aviation law and, after 1933, a high official in Göring's Reich Air Ministry. Schleicher, a brother-in-law of Dietrich Bonhoeffer, like that courageous theologian became caught up in the July 1944 plot against Hitler and was murdered by the SS in April 1945.[201]

Deeply religious in the Lutheran-Pietistic faith that characterizes so many Swabians, Klinckerfuss, apart from being a professional pianist, was a member of the Protestant Johanniter Order. During World War I, in her thirties, she had been moved to help wounded soldiers behind the trenches and from then on had despised anything having to do with arms and war. This, in addition to her faith in the integrity of music and her unshakable religious beliefs, made her an early antagonist of Hitler and his Third Reich. In September 1937 Reich Youth Leader Baldur von Schirach (who, we recall, had appointed Wolfgang Stumme and later extended protection to Orff and Strauss) claimed in a public speech in Stuttgart's town hall that there were no more Protestants and Catholics, only adherents to the Nazi weltanschauung. All dissenters would automatically be regarded as traitors. Incensed, Klinckerfuss heckled him from the audience and was duly beaten up by Brownshirts afterwards. When she lodged a complaint with the Stuttgart public health authorities, a physician declared her mentally disturbed and Gestapo officers delivered her to an insane asylum. For a total of six years she was forcibly confined to several institutions, including Eglfing-Haar near Munich, where many of the infamous "euthanasia" murders of the early 1940s were perpetrated. An early release was prevented by the fact that, even after the original incident, she was still being denounced for having attacked, on various occasions, the Nazi struggle against the churches, the persecution of the Jews, and the "euthanasia" killings. In May 1943 she ended up in the sanatorium of Christophsbad near Stuttgart, where, under a sympathetic physician, she was allowed to try her hand at music therapy among the genuinely disturbed inmates. Luckily for Klinckerfuss, Christophsbad possessed the rare distinction of shielding most of its inmates from "euthanasia" murder.[202]

There can be no doubt that her resilience was religiously and politically, even aesthetically, motivated. In the case of the composer Gottfried von Einem and his teacher Boris Blacher, a friend of Helmut Roloff, the formula for opposition to the Nazi regime and its various elements is not nearly so certain.

On 28 September 1938 twenty-year-old Gottfried von Einem was having breakfast at the venerable Adlon Hotel in Berlin, when three Gestapo officers burst in and arrested him. He was taken to Gestapo headquarters at Prinz-Albrecht-Strasse and interrogated for several hours before being released. Einem had no idea why he had been singled out, but he glimpsed a piece of paper lying on a Gestapo officer's desk, which had been signed by Heydrich, the chief of the secret police. It read: "Taken into protective custody for suspicion of having betrayed his country, and high treason." The Gestapo came for Einem again, repeatedly, sometimes keeping him for several days. His entire, not inconsiderable, assets were confiscated, most of which he co-owned with his mother, Baroness Gerta Louise von Einem, who had been arrested along with him.[203]

If young Baron von Einem, after weeks of intermittent grilling at Gestapo headquarters, still did not know the formal reasons for the charges, he knew he was guilty by association, for he was extremely close to his mother. Einem had a colorful family history; in comparison with other members of his generation, his was an unconventional upbringing, and his mother was exotic. His father, Baron William von Einem, a general under the Habsburg monarchy, had been posted to the Austro-Hungarian embassy in Bern, where Gottfried was born in 1918. What the son found out only later from Gestapo officials was that his real father was not William but the Hungarian Count Laszlo von Hunyady, a former Habsburg colonel, also stationed in Bern. Gottfried's beautiful mother, who was descended from the Hessian nobility, had been in the habit of traveling to Africa with him to engage in lion-hunting safaris, always taking along an upright piano, for the count adored music no less than Gerta Louise and played the piano well. On one of these outings sometime in the 1920s, the count was torn apart by a severely wounded feline on the shores of the Nile near Khartoum. Happily, by that time Gottfried had been adopted by the forbearing Baron William.[204]

Because the baronial couple traveled internationally, socially and on business, and were quite wealthy, Gottfried grew up and went to school in the countryside of Holstein, in northern Germany. On the large estate of the Einems near Plön, young Gottfried, who saw his parents only occasionally, and who, with his Austrian heritage, did not relate easily to this stern north German milieu, became socially isolated and, with the passage of time, very much dependent on his own devices. He had always been a loner among his peers, but when the National Socialists took power in early 1933, his Gymnasium was turned into an elite Nazi school. As a foreigner he was not allowed to wear the new uniform of the cadres, nor was he admitted to the inner core of his nazified classmates. Indeed, among his north German schoolmates, who were mostly blond and blue-eyed, Gottfried, with his dark, curly hair and prominent nose, was thought to be a Jew. When he switched to a school in nearby Ratzeburg, things improved. Ratzeburg was the burial place of the Expressionist painter Ernst Barlach, and it featured sculptures of his that fell under the Nazi rubric of degenerate art. For Gottfried von Einem these became an inspiration. The young, hitherto introverted baron, not exceptionally good at school but obviously musically gifted, began to develop an eclectic life-style. It may have been influenced by the cosmopolitan acquaintances of his urbane parents who occasionally visited—aristocrats of all sorts, entrepreneurs, artists, and financiers, and sometimes also "Aunts" Paula and Olga, the sisters of Hermann Göring, childhood friends of Gerta Louise from shared summer vacations in neighboring country chalets in south Austrian Styria. In his new school Gottfried finally found a sympathetic teacher who encouraged his creative talents; at home he took piano lessons, and he started writing letters to people such as Gerhart Hauptmann, Hermann Hesse, and Richard Strauss. Sometimes he was rewarded with an answer. The character-forming highlights of this phase were a more intimate acquaintance with Wagner's operas and, in the company of his august relatives, regular visits to the Salzburg summer festival, where he resided in the swankiest quarters and came to meet not only more aristocrats but also Bruno Walter, Arturo Toscanini, and Lotte Lehmann. And there was more of Wagner's music.[205]

What was in the making here was an extremely sensitive man with a great gift for the arts, especially music, the composition of which came easily to him by 1936. He was conditioned no less by the cosmopolitanism of his immediate family (around this time his parents had residences in Vienna as well as in London, where they socialized with the Rothschilds and other highly placed Jews), strengthening ties with musicians of the caliber of Walter, Furtwängler, and Tietjen. He was beginning to nurture a deep suspicion of the dictatorial extremes of Nazi supporters, although the singular personality of Hitler fascinated him for a long time. In 1937 Einem visited Kent; a marked predilection for custom-tailored suits, as well as a good feel for the English language, was the result. Then in London he met with German emigrants, and that sharpened his eye for the intolerances practiced by the Nazi regime.[206]

By that time there was no doubt that Einem wanted to be a composer. In early January 1938 he and his mother moved to Berlin, where they conversed in English when discussing confidential subjects; they lived in an apartment at the Hotel Adlon while waiting for a luxurious private flat to be finished. Significant for his musical tastes even then, he had wanted to take lessons from Hindemith at the Hochschule für Musik, but the composer had already left the Hochschule permanently, and Furtwängler and Kammersänger Max Lorenz advised him to acquire some practical experience at the Preussische Staatsoper with Generalintendant Tietjen. The omnipotent music master took him in, and this made Einem an opera coach in Berlin and, soon enough, in Tietjen's second sphere of influence, Bayreuth.[207]

At the time Einem and his mother were arrested in September, she had been about to travel to Luxembourg to meet her Jewish friend Edward Albert Leonard, a businessman from England. (Later it became clear that the Nazis suspected her of treason and currency violations.) Einem already had his second Bayreuth season behind him, on which occasion he had had a personal encounter with Hitler, who had chatted with him about the arts, and also with Friedelind Wagner, the older daughter of Winifred and a critic of the regime. Something like a courtship ensued, very much encouraged by Winifred and by the baroness, who had been released from prison in late fall 1939. Gerta Louise traveled with her son and Friedelind to Venice and Lucerne, where the Bayreuth heiress met up with her fatherly mentor Toscanini. The baroness may not have known what to make of this, but Gottfried's antennas were receptive: Friedelind and Toscanini, both enemies of Hitler! Yet, despite a few more encounters and some correspondence, nothing came of the hoped-for liaison, and Friedelind soon fled Germany forever.[208]

Musically, the young man needed more coaching. Although the ambience of the Berlin Staatsoper under Tietjen and especially the music at Bayreuth had been exciting, and he had become well versed in the arts of opera directing and ballet accompaniment on the piano, the experiences had not moved him closer to his goal, which was composition. In 1938, as his dream of studying with Hindemith was evaporating, he learned more about the modernist composer Boris Blacher, whose just-premiered Symphony opus 12 intrigued him but whom, at that point in time, he did not dare approach for guidance. Through his manifold connections he finally managed an introduction to Blacher, who took him on as an advanced student from April 1941 to summer 1943. If anything, Blacher only perfected the composition techniques Einem had already mastered, but it was in the atmosphere around that somewhat eccentric musician that Einem really thrived. Clandestinely they studied much that now was on the index—Stravinsky, Hindemith, Milhaud, Schoenberg, and the condemned jazz—from records or the many foreign radio stations that played it on the air. Altogether and definitively Blacher squelched in Einem any vestiges of the admiration he had felt for Hitler.[209]

If there was a conspiratorial air about these exercises, it tended to be enforced by the circle of musical friends with whom both teacher and student soon affiliated. These were men who were equally imaginative, inclined toward modernism, and with roots in the culture of Weimar, although, admittedly, politically merely on the margins of resistance, if at all, as were Orff, Egk, Wagner-Régeny, Intendant Oskar Fritz Schuh of

Vienna, and the former Brecht and Weill intimate Caspar Neher, the progressive stage designer and librettist, who appeared to be all but untouched by the censoring demons of the Third Reich.[210]

Not so Boris Blacher and his student and friend Gottfried von Einem. After 1940 the baroness was residing once more in a well-equipped flat in Berlin's Brückenallee, which became a haven for dissidents in artistic, diplomatic, and high military circles. At her soirées cultural and culinary pleasures abounded. Here, the baroness once again, if always under the eyes of the Gestapo, played at her old game of power, amours, money, and connections. It was because of her that Wagner-Régeny's lot as a soldier was eventually eased. Her son was living in much more modest rented quarters, and from here he attempted to help Jews (so-called U-boats) hiding in the capital who needed papers, money, and food ration stamps, and active opponents to the regime, frequently old communist stage hands. One of the men whom he had assisted was eventually shot by the Gestapo in broad daylight. Through his mother he knew Leipzig's former lord mayor Karl Goerdeler, who had protested the removal of the Mendelssohn statue in front of the Gewandhaus in 1936 and in 1944 became embroiled in the plot against Hitler. He also met General Hans Oster of Admiral Canaris's Abwehr (rumor had it Canaris himself was a former beau of the baroness), and Fabian von Schlabrendorff, who tried to kill Hitler with a bomb in 1943 and who survived to marry into the Einem family.[211]

As a young composer in the last two years of the Reich, Gottfried von Einem found himself in an ambiguous situation. Three compositions of his were publicly presented before Goebbels put an end to all music performances in late summer 1944. The first was his *Capriccio*, played by the Berlin Philharmonic under Leo Borchard in 1943; it was well received. The second was his ballet *Turandot*, premiered under Karl Elmendorff in Dresden on 5 February 1944. This was a resounding success, but some orthodox critics such as Hans Schnoor felt that it had touched on atonality, albeit not without clear characteristics of "the profound Romanticism indicative of feeling." The reason for this was that, although he never abandoned conventional tonality, von Einem had managed, undoubtedly under the influence of Blacher, to strive for extended harmonic dissonances, which, however, always returned the listener to the governing tonality.[212]

The young composer got into hot water with his third piece, a concerto that had been commissioned by Herbert von Karajan, who meant to use it, after the tremendous success of *Turandot*, to give a boost to his own sagging career, particularly in his never-ending feud with Furtwängler. In this work, musically very similar to the two preceding ones, von Einem clearly showed the influence of his master Blacher, in that during the final Allegro he utilized not only syncopations, as had been his wont, but also thematic variations very much reminiscent of improvisation in jazz, which was of course taboo. In April 1944 Karajan conducted the Berlin

Philharmonic with his customary verve. Magda Goebbels, an acquaintance of the Einem family and not a stranger to the jazz subculture, was in the audience, but so was Werner Naumann, Goebbels's state secretary in the Promi. According to Einem, Naumann's report to the minister was not favorable. He was hauled before Heinz Drewes in the ministry and formally interrogated: "What were you thinking when you wrote this piece?" The composer answered cockily: "Music does not need words." Goebbels himself, however, in his perpetual quest for that "new" German music, and perhaps under the influence of his wife, seems to have held much more positive views. Not only did he order Karajan to make a studio recording of the work for closer examination (and on the basis of this allowed Einem to move from Berlin to Elmendorff's Dresden), but also he instructed the national radio network once again to broadcast more modern music such as works by Einem.[213]

In many respects the baron's life in the Third Reich was precarious, for despite some struggle, he had found his ideological and political bearings early on in his youth, and professed aesthetic principles that could have gotten him into trouble with the prevailing laws. Danger was lurking not least because of his close association with Blacher. Once in 1941 (he had just begun his studies under that composer) Einem was returning to Berlin from a Mozart festival in Vienna when who should be seated across from him in the train compartment but that archetypal Nazi music critic Herbert Gerigk of former Kampfbund fame. Soon they were talking. When Blacher's name was mentioned, Gerigk said: "Blacher is an ingenious composer. Too bad that he is a Jew." Gerigk insisted that in Zurich he had seen documents proving that Blacher's father had been an elder of the Jewish congregation in Riga.[214]

Blacher was surprised by this encounter and, after von Einem had returned to the capital, played down his allegedly Jewish pedigree. The fact was that Blacher had not been born in Germany and at the time was living in Berlin on the strength of a Nansen passport customarily issued to stateless persons by the League of Nations. Baroness von Einem managed, as only she could do, to secure for Blacher German citizenship papers in the middle of World War II.[215]

The passport story exemplifies how in the Third Reich Boris Blacher constantly led a borderline existence between acceptance and rejection. His personal background was almost as checkered as Einem's. His partly Jewish ancestry and an early proclivity toward avant-garde elements in music made integration into Third Reich society problematic at best, even at the barest functional level. Like Einem, he came to Germany long before the Nazis took over, attracted by the modernism of Weimar, centered in Berlin. His father had been a wealthy Baltic German businessman working for a tsarist Russian bank in northern China, where Boris was born in 1903. As in the young baron's case, his home was a cultivated one, and Boris was tutored in several languages by governesses. He seems to have suffered the same detachment from his father as Einem did, compensated once more by an unusual closeness to his mother, who accompanied him on his way to Berlin in 1922 via Paris.[216]

Blacher's arrival in Berlin marked the beginning of his musical career. As soon as he started formal studies at the Hochschule für Musik, his father stopped sending a monthly check. His mother returned to the Baltics in 1925. Left to his own devices, Blacher played piano and harmonium in movie theaters and started arranging for dance bands. This introduced him to jazz music, but he also developed a strong preference for Schoenberg and Stravinsky. He became friendly with Rudolf Wagner-Régeny, whose musical interests were similar. In light of this one of his first works was remarkable: *Jazz-Koloraturen* for soprano voice, alto saxophone, and bassoon, in two movements, "Slowfox" and "Charleston" (1929). But the slightly built Blacher had to watch himself: his heavy smoking and a penchant for hard liquor tended to play havoc with his health, and he had latent tuberculosis, a disease the Nazis, in their eugenic fanaticism, were later to use as a criterion for "negative selection."[217]

Not knowing very much about him, Rosenberg's NS-Kulturgemeinde performed Blacher's *Capriccio* for orchestra in Berlin in 1935. Immediately Fritz Stege poured out his criticism of the composer and his composition with a vengeance: "This piece, as it is characterized by noisy effects and rhythmic crudities, represents the spiritual legacy of a Stravinsky and Kurt Weill." Henceforth, Stege's sarcastic commentaries, especially regarding Blacher's typical jazz inflections, became a permanent thorn in the composer's side. In December 1937, through a stroke of luck, Carl Schuricht conducted Blacher's *Konzertante Musik für Orchester* with the Berlin Philharmonic. Because the musicians had trouble playing the complicated jazzlike syncopation correctly, Schuricht repeated the eleven-minute piece, and hence there were two successive curtain calls. This special circumstance was then reflected in the press; ironically, it instantly rebounded positively on the composer, who now saw his work performed many times in Germany as well as internationally, and suddenly found himself a celebrity.[218] One consequence of this was that Blacher was included as a participating composer in the program of the Düsseldorf Reich Music Festival in May 1938. But Blacher's Music for Violin in Three Movements predictably proved to be controversial, in that progressive reviewers such as Theo Kreiten lauded it, while strident Nazi critics found it "cold." Although later that year Karl Böhm managed to get him appointed as a professor of music at the Dresden Conservatory, Blacher was forced to give up the position after only a few months because he had used works by Hindemith and Milhaud, along with politically acceptable ones, in his classes.[219]

At the beginning of World War II Blacher was well known in Germany; his *Konzertante Musik*, for instance, was scheduled to be played in Leipzig, Breslau, Duisburg, and Darmstadt, among other cities, and he was beginning to attract students of the caliber of von Einem.[220] But by 1940 Blacher was again being subjected to a concentrated attack by Stege for his allusions to jazz. It was around this time that the Reich Music Chamber made an official entry in its registry about Blacher's maternal grandmother, one Louise Feliciana Boerling, who was the daughter of baptized Jews. Although Goebbels had earlier decided that so-called quarter-Jews should be treated as "Aryans," the combination of even a partially Jewish heritage, a dissonant musical language, and an unconventional life-style or history could, for many Nazi bigots, give rise to xenophobic suspicion, dangerous innuendo, and chicanery, as the incident involving Einem and Gerigk in the train compartment demonstrates. If to this one adds the factor of questionable social intercourse, one has all the ingredients of a time bomb ready to explode with each progressive step of radicalization in formal Nazi policy. Blacher befriended Einem, who with his family was increasingly suspect. In addition, his new girlfriend was the young pianist Gerty Herzog, who shared her piano teacher with the political dissident Helmut Roloff and had Jewish relatives herself. And his own works were being performed by the pianist Edith Picht-Axenfeld, who was herself not fully "Aryan."[221]

Until the end of the Third Reich, Boris Blacher's compositions continued to be performed, and he had a staunch following of admirers, some of whom were writing for Goebbels's highbrow broadsheet *Das Reich*.[222] But by the same token, vicious commentaries regarding his music could never be suppressed, and could assume an immeasurable degree of danger when combined with questions about family background and political comportment. Toward the end of the regime, Blacher was privy to the political activities of his friend Einem and his circle, and in fact harbored a Jewish "U-boat" himself for a while. Complimentary official rewards, such as endowed national prizes of the kind Strauss, Orff, Pepping, and Müller enjoyed for money and for recognition, were denied him, and he was always in great need of funds. The reason the prize committee gave was that he was a "quarter-Jew." But that did not prevent attempts to induct him into the Wehrmacht, even though he had had another bout with tuberculosis. That odious conscription order reached him in early April 1945, soon after he had become a German citizen. At that time Blacher deemed it safe to disregard it; luckily he emerged from the Third Reich unscathed.[223]

Karl Amadeus Hartmann did something no other musician of promise could afford to do by way of resistance to the Third Reich in that in 1933 he denied himself and his art to the public within Germany's borders. For an artist who depended for his success on the public exposure of his output, this amounted to professional suicide. "I realized," he later wrote, "that it was necessary to give testimony, not out of despair and fear of that regime, but as a counter-measure. I said to myself that freedom will eventually prevail, even if we ourselves are obliterated."[224] Short of fighting the Nazis weapon in hand, this may have been the most effective form of political opposition; it called for a similar degree of courage, and morally it was equally defensible.

Hartmann, born 1905 in Munich, together with his three brothers was socialized from childhood by parents who were firmly on the political left. When in the early 1920s his father died, his mother, though a good Roman Catholic, continued that educational work in the Social Democratic tradition. Hence, Hartmann was a dedicated antifascist long before Hitler came to power. His brother Richard, a card-carrying communist, early in 1933 suddenly left Munich for Switzerland after having taken part in a last-ditch effort to distribute anti-Hitler leaflets. Hours later the SA were at his mother's house, but Richard was already on his way to St. Gall, where Karl Amadeus knew the young Swiss conductor Ernst Klug.[225]

Hartmann's musical education up until 1933 had been squarely in the modernist tradition that also influenced Orff, Egk, Wagner-Régeny and Blacher, and in which Stravinsky was such a major force. Like Orff, he became estranged early from his traditionalist composition teachers at the Munich Akademie der Tonkunst, in his case Joseph Haas; as an instrumentalist he acquired technical proficiency on piano and especially trombone. In 1932 Hartmann directed a program of children's games to the music of Hindemith and Egk, in cooperation with rhythmic ballet students from Orff's music classes in the progressive Güntherschule. In the same year his *Sonate für Klavier* and *Burleske Musik* (for horns, piano, and percussion), both recent compositions, were performed in a concert also featuring chamber works by Bartók, Poulenc, and Hindemith, as well as Satie's *Jack in the Box* (1899). And, as it had for Křenek, Hindemith, Blacher, and Weill, jazz became an important catalyst in Hartmann's work. "In the Munich audience there were only a few circles that were receptive to new and contemporary art," he recalled. "I myself blended Futurism, Dada, jazz, and other currents in a carefree manner, in a number of compositions," one of these being the *Jazztoccata und Fuge für Klavier* of 1928. Hartmann had also written vocal works to texts by Karl Marx and the German communist poet Johannes R. Becher.[226]

Aesthetically and politically, therefore, Hartmann was already well defined when in 1933 he decided to take further training with the notorious antifascist Hermann Scherchen. As I noted in chapter 3, the beginning of his collaboration with Scherchen was a watershed in both his personal and his professional life. Elisabeth Reussmann, a former high school sweetheart who married Karl Amadeus in 1934, remembered the overpowering presence of Scherchen in her husband's artistic development. Hartmann posed the question that actor Bernhard Minetti and so many others had also asked themselves and then answered in a different way: how to practice one's art, oppose the political dictatorship, and not end up in Dachau. Hartmann elected not to suppress his political impulses but to renounce publicity instead. In 1994 his wife rationalized his behavior thus: "The Nazis left him alone because he kept quiet. It would not have made any sense to take to the streets in protest, for they would have knocked him down and sent him to Dachau." And so it was that

Hartmann, during his key developmental phase in the country of his birth, kept musically silent at the expense of his career. To be sure, he could not have done that without the abiding generosity of his father-in-law, who kept the young family afloat for years; but then it took much effort for a German man of Hartmann's generation to swallow his personal pride.[227]

Hartmann's silence was only on the outside, however, for he internalized his ideological opposition. In an ingenious and imaginative way he used his creative talents to build up a very private monument of protest against the Hitler regime—by expressing his sentiments in his compositions, including text and music, and striving to get them performed abroad. In 1934 he started to compose his stage work *Des Simplicius Simplicissimus Jugend,* based on a story by the seventeenth-century poet Hans Jakob Christoph von Grimmelshausen, whose hero, a farm lad, like that historic poet, survives the horrors of the Thirty Years' War (1618–48). Scherchen and Wolfgang Petzet helped Hartmann with the libretto, which was directed against political oppression and terror. Simplicius was cast as an antihero with an endless capacity for suffering—the very opposite of Hitler's ideal of steely, resilient German youth, which Stumme and Bresgen were embracing. As a sign of empathy with Hartmann's many Jewish friends, there were hints of Jewish melody in the second act, as the war dead are mourned.[228]

Hartmann's next confessional work was the symphonic poem *Miserae,* which, under the baton of Scherchen, was presented at the ISCM festival in Prague in the summer of 1935. This composition was dedicated to "friends, who had to die in the hundreds," and was dated "Dachau 1933/34." One could hardly be more explicit. It impressed the Italian composer Luigi Dallapiccola, once a follower of Mussolini until his marriage to a Jewish woman had made him think again, and who was also at the festival. Dallapiccola thought *Miserae* a "painful, solemn, and sometimes depressing composition." In April 1936 the Hungarian newspaper *Népszava* spoke of the work's "sad tone colors, depicting the fate of German political victims."[229] One month later Hartmann wrote to a friend in Budapest that he was now working on a cantata for contralto and orchestra, with a modified text, originally by Walt Whitman (by 1938 known as his *Symphonisches Fragment,* later incorporated into his First Symphony): "In it I am describing our life. The poems, which I have considerably altered, embrace the entire difficult, hopeless life, and yet no idea is being stifled by death. I think I have made some progress with this work in the direction of a kind of music that concerns all humankind."[230]

It is understandable if, after the beginning of the war, Hartmann's anxiety about the Nazi regime intensified. This was manifested by his *Concerto funèbre* for solo violin and strings, composed under the impact of the early war days and premiered in St. Gall by Ernst Klug, on which occasion Karl Amadeus traveled to Switzerland, where he was reunited with his brother Richard. It may have been in recognition of both Richard and Scherchen, who was then in nearby Winterthur, that Hartmann cited in this piece the Russian workers' song "Immortal Victims."[231] In the first nine months of 1940 Hartmann composed a *Sinfonia tragica,* which he dedicated to his Belgian friend, the antifascist musicologist and conductor Paul Collaer, and which could not be performed; after the war its first and second movements were integrated with what was to become Hartmann's Third Symphony.[232] No other politically inspired work came forth until 1944. Perhaps struck by a paralyzing desperation, the composer buried all his scores in an airtight zinc container two meters below ground in the Bavarian Alps.[233] In the winter of 1944–45, when he learned of the Gestapo arrest of the Marxist scientist and philosopher Robert Havemann, he wrote his symphony *Klagegesang* in honor of that scholar. After the war he told him that he had had trouble finding an ending for the original version "under the terrible blow of the events just transpired," but that now, in 1946, it was possible to finish the symphony "in brilliant D-flat major."[234] His last ideologically founded work once again was written with Dachau on his mind, after he had watched a queue of thousands of concentration camp inmates shuffle by his house on their death march at the end of April 1945, a few days before American troops liberated the camp. Thus originated his Second Piano Sonata, with its inscription: "Endless was the queue—endless was the misery—endless was the suffering." Here a connection had been forged with his earlier *Miserae.*[235]

Unable to present this "confessional music" in Nazi Germany, Hartmann was eager to have it performed abroad, to make a political statement and also, if possible, to earn some money.[236] But for a number of reasons such opportunities turned out to be fraught with problems. By and large, only international concerts, foreign radio productions, and festivals, chiefly those of the ISCM until the war, were available for the distribution of Hartmann's music, and of the last-mentioned, until the war there was only one a year. That, observed Elisabeth Hartmann, "was simply not enough" to make a composer well known internationally.[237] Hence, in Swiss music competitions Hartmann's chances were limited from the start because the Swiss culture brokers tended to favor their own musicians; indeed, the Bern composer Heinrich Sutermeister had beaten Hartmann in a Zurich competition in early 1937.[238] Conductor Paul Sacher wrote Hartmann in June 1938 from Basel, "I still know very little about your style of music; at first hearing it was rather strange to me." A few months later Sacher informed Hartmann that for purposes of live performance he was compelled to consider local rather than foreign talent. Radio Bern, too, found Hartmann's *Simplicius Simplicissimus* "strongly modern for our Swiss listeners" (one may be tempted to see in this judgment that peculiar brand of bigoted provincialism that has recently been identified as having ruled most of the conservative Swiss cultural establishment during this period).[239] It must also be admitted, however, that Hartmann was, after all, not Stravinsky, who was at the top of Sacher's foreign artists' list. Hartmann's works were not in great demand in other places either, for instance, Budapest, judging from a 1937 opinion of that city's most prominent music publisher. Nor were the British rushing to publish Hartmann's string quartet *Carillon* in February 1939, even though it had been successfully performed in London by the Kutscher Quartet some six months earlier.[240] It was, therefore, somewhat presumptuous of Hartmann to write to the New York League of Composers shortly before World War II, asking them to find American musicians willing to take *Carillon* on a tour of the United States, although the League was known to champion modern works.[241]

Much of Hartmann's isolation, apart from his reaction to the Nazis, had to do with Hermann Scherchen. As I remarked earlier, that avant-garde conductor treated Hartmann as his personal composer, not free to act on his own. Other than that, he ignored Hartmann or even worked against him. Some of this was Hartmann's fault because he unnecessarily complained to Scherchen how isolated he felt in Nazi Germany, thereby rendering himself completely dependent on his mentor.[242] Before an international competition in Zurich in January 1937, for example, he confided to Scherchen that his chances of winning a prize for his cantata *Anno '48/Friede,* just completed, were slim because one of the judges was Ernst Křenek, whose own cantata for choir began with the same stanzas from a poem by the Baroque poet Andreas Gryphius that Hartmann had used.[243] Not surprisingly, therefore, in the case of the Hungarian publishing house, Hartmann was told that during his recent visit Scherchen had casually mentioned the composer's name, without expressly endorsing him.[244] Scherchen, who was partly responsible for the conception of *Simplicius Simplicissimus,* tacitly assumed that he had a monopoly on the option for its premiere, but did nothing to bring it about, although Hartmann repeatedly reminded him and even withheld from other conductors the opportunity of staging the opera. "Only twice have you ever conducted anything of mine," Hartmann complained in December 1938.[245] During the war Scherchen once more used Hartmann to further his own reputation as a modernist by suggesting to Radio Beromünster in Zurich that a composition for strings by the Munich composer be performed there, but despite Hartmann's subsequent efforts nothing ever came of it.[246]

A third complicating factor was the complexity and length of Hartmann's works. Hartmann had long since gone beyond the late Romantic school in style, though several days of intensive study with Anton Webern in Vienna in November 1942 did not push him into a serial style. His works, strong on rhapsodic elements and rhythm and vibrantly expressive, were more reminiscent of Stravinsky, Kodály, and Bartók than of Schoenberg, Berg, or Webern.[247] Concerning the harmonics in what later became his *Carillon* string quartet, "there are a lot of those which you cannot play (actually getting them to sound)," wrote violinist Felix Galimir from Vienna in December 1934. Therefore, on a tour to Spain, the Galimir Quartet decided not to perform Hartmann at all, opting instead for a piece by Wladimir Vogel. This complaint was repeated more than a year later by the Hungarian String Quartet. In addition, cellist Vilmos Palotai complained that Hartmann's scores were so carelessly written as to be hardly legible.[248] In addition to Scherchen's dilatory behavior, another reason why *Simplicius Simplicissimus* could not be premiered during the Brussels World's Fair in 1935 was that Hartmann simply was not able to complete the elaborate score in time.[249] His cantata for contralto and orchestra (*Symphonisches Fragment*) was rejected as an entry at the International Music Festival of the ISCM in Paris in December 1936 because it was too long.[250] Dante Fiorello, a minor New York composer (and a plagiarist who for years took an interest in Hartmann's works, presumably in order to exploit them), characteristically informed him that the cantata, though a "masterpiece," did not attract any instrumental groups because "they object to the Work being so large and for voice."[251] A more serious matter for Hartmann was Sacher's charge of undue "technical difficulty" in his rejection of the composer's oeuvre.[252]

Considering all this, it is astonishing how much success Hartmann still was able to enjoy on the international music scene outside of Germany. In early 1936 he received first prize from the Gesellschaft für Zeitgenössische Kammermusik "Carillon" in Geneva for his string quartet, hence named *Carillon*—the same piece that was allegedly so difficult to play and which he had dedicated to Scherchen. The jury included the Italian composer Gian Francesco Malipiero and the Swiss conductor Ernest Ansermet.[253] Then, in May 1937 the Viennese Emil Hertzka Memorial Foundation gave *Anno '48/Friede* an honorable mention, behind works by two prominent Austrians who shared the money prize. This time the Viennese composers Franz Schmidt and Anton Webern were members of the jury.[254] At the annual ISCM festivals throughout Europe Hartmann was fairly regularly invited, with the ones in Prague (1935) and London (1938) according him special recognition and honors.[255] In 1938 he enjoyed a spate of individual successes with premieres and broadcast performances in Belgium, dampened only by the outbreak of the war.[256]

It is amazing that, through his trials and tribulations, Hartmann was able to make a living at all, let alone care decently for his family—his wife and son Richard, born in 1935. Because of his relatively frequent international trips, his status was suspended in a vacuum, for he neither bothered to join the RMK in any formal sense nor had any official standing in the ISCM, Germany having left that body in 1933 in order to set up its own, fascist-controlled organization under Strauss and Emil Nikolaus von Reznicek. RMK functionaries, who treated Hartmann as if he were a member while apparently being willing to wait forever for his proof of "Aryan" lineage, knew that before 1939 he had been wont to go abroad; in fact, they had asked him to report on the 1935 Prague meeting. Hartmann seems to have been aware that he needed formal permission to travel thereafter, and indeed the records suggest that he applied for and received such permission. In 1941 the RMK noted that the composer had been "championed by a very specific, mostly Jewish clique"—a possible reference to Galimir (who escaped to the United States in 1938) and to Jewish musicians in Switzerland and, until 1940, Belgium, but for unknown reasons the music chamber's inquiry went no further.[257]

Hartmann and his small family managed to subsist beyond V-E Day in May 1945 by virtue of the generosity of his father-in-law, a prosperous Munich merchant who supplied him with the material means of existence, for his taxable earnings were laughable: four pfennigs from the Stagma in 1935, nothing in 1939, and 7.14 marks in 1940. He and his wife were isolated; there was no contact with other established Munich composers such as Orff, Pfitzner, or Egk. But the couple did belong to a loose circle of like-minded souls, mostly academics and some artists, who gathered informally for music-making, exchange of ideas, frequently politically charged ones, and communal listening to the BBC. Among these people was a highly placed military physician who several times in the 1940s arranged for Hartmann to be exempted from conscription into the Wehrmacht. After 1942 the family lived, almost continuously, in a small house belonging to his in-laws near Lake Starnberg south of Munich, without giving up their urban flat in the Wilhelmstrasse, also paid for by the in-laws. Here, in Kempfenhausen, young Richard went to school with the daughter of Interior Minister Wilhelm Frick, who had a summer retreat nearby. One might think that this connection could have afforded the family a certain degree of protection; but it also meant danger, in that the parents had to be careful lest Richard betray something of their antiregime conversations, during which he was often present, or their samplings from the BBC, which also did not escape the child.[258]

After Germany's surrender on 8 May 1945, Bavaria was occupied by the Americans, with Munich as their military and administrative headquarters. Their most pressing problems, apart from strictly economic ones, involved denazifying German society and reconstituting democratic structures. In the latter process, culture was assigned a special role. Since uncontaminated German democrats were very scarce, especially those with expertise, it was not surprising to find Karl Amadeus Hartmann as a member of that diminutive circle of dedicated local patriots who, with their insider knowledge, were able to help. Apparently Hartmann was at first offered the post of Generalintendant of the Bayerische Staatsoper, but he found these responsibilities too demanding. He then settled for the position of dramaturge, which for the time being gave him a mandate to help direct the musical life of the city.[259]

This mandate he used toward reintroducing an international music repertoire, in particular the cultivation of modern music beyond the narrow range permitted by the National Socialists. The first task was to try to remove the enormous handicap that consumers of high culture had suffered under Nazi rule, for they were virtually ignorant of developments in

Western music since 1933. Hindemith, Schoenberg, and Stravinsky had become all but forgotten, and even French composers such as Debussy were now largely distant memories. Among Germans wishing to put the Nazi tyranny behind them, particularly younger ones, there was great eagerness to learn and be reeducated.[260] At first in small and primitive settings, but after October 1945 in the Prinzregententheater, still standing amid all the ruins, Hartmann began to produce modern-music performances that continued to flourish, even after his death in 1963, as regular concert series under the name Musica Viva. He specialized in compositions once considered avant-garde, but increasingly patronized younger masters—for example, Hans Werner Henze, a student of Wolfgang Fortner. During the early stages of this series Hartmann worked with Hans Rosbaud, a seasoned champion of modern music, who had easily cleared his name with the occupation forces and, until 1948, acted as Generalmusikdirektor of Munich's Philharmonic.[261] Hartmann again brought works by Stravinsky, Schoenberg, Křenek, Bartók, Shostakovich, and Hindemith to Munich, but an attempt to present the German premiere of Hindemith's opera *Mathis der Maler* failed, even though the composer, now at Yale, had shown polite interest in the scheme in March 1946.[262]

Hartmann immediately made sure that his own works, including some new ones enriched with older themes, were not neglected. But from the late 1940s into the 1960s he was of course becoming much better known in Germany, in particular since his old collaboration with Scherchen was resumed, if at a less emotionally charged level. True to his concern for the welfare of humanity in general, in the immediate postwar years Hartmann became extremely worried about the global atomic threat. But Germany remained his special concern, and here he continued to fear for social and political justice. In particular, sensing a resurgence of anti-Semitism in the country, he had reason to dread the renewed rise of National Socialism. As he put it in a letter to Křenek in 1948, he was afraid that the tender flower of democracy, which he had done his best to nurture, might be trampled under foot by old and new advocates of dictatorship.[263]

In the coming decades, and after Hartmann's untimely death, this was not to happen. Although musicians in the Third Reich had not acquitted themselves in exemplary fashion, they had not been sufficiently silenced, or corrupted, by the tyrants to be prevented from taking their place in the gradual cultural regeneration of their country.

Notes

INTRODUCTION

1. I am indebted to Kristen K. Stauffer of the University of Kentucky at Lexington and Stephan Lindeman of Rutgers University for helping me to identify the music.

2. See Ian Kershaw, *The Nazi Dictatorship: Problems and Perspectives of Interpretations*, 2nd ed. (London, 1989), esp. 61–81.

3. With particular reference to Hitler and Göring, see Ian Kershaw, *Hitler* (London, 1991); Hans Mommsen, "Reflections on the Position of Hitler and Göring in the Third Reich," in Thomas Childers and Jane Caplan, eds., *Reevaluating the Third Reich* (New York, 1993), 86–97.

4. With the following qualification: Erhard Bahr's view that an initial phase of functionalism in Nazi cultural politics (to about 1937) was followed by a phase of intentionalist control is not borne out by the evidence presented either in his study or elsewhere, although his ideal-typical depiction of the two phenomena agrees fairly well with models from reality. The problem with his view is that, contrary to what he aims to show, there was a constant merging and separating of the two patterns; neither ever existed in a self-contained state long enough to establish a trend, and so Bahr's distinction in the context of actual historical events is meaningless. See Erhard Bahr, "Nazi Cultural Politics: Intentionalisms vs. Functionalism," in Glenn R. Cuomo, ed., *National Socialist Cultural Policy* (New York, 1995), 5–37.

5. Pertinent discussions of these problems may be found in Ian Kershaw, ed., *Why Did German Democracy Fail?* (New York, 1990); and Harold James, "Innovation and Conservatism in Economic Recovery: The Alleged 'Nazi Recovery' of the 1930s," in Childers and Caplan, *Reevaluating*, 114–38.

6. Hans Mommsen, *Die verspielte Freiheit: Der Weg der Republik von Weimar in den Untergang, 1918 bis 1933* (Frankfurt am Main, 1990), 10 (quote).

7. Peter Gay, *Weimar Culture: The Outsider as Insider* (New York, 1970); George L. Mosse, *Nazi Culture: Intellectual, Cultural, and Social Life in the Third Reich* (New York, 1968).

8. Gerald D. Feldman, "Right-Wing Politics and the Film Industry: Emil Georg Stauss, Alfred Hugenberg, and the UFA, 1917–1933," in Christian Jansen et al., eds., *Von der Aufgabe der Freiheit: Politische Verantwortung und bürgerliche Gesellschaft im 19. und 20. Jahrhundert: Festschrift für Hans Mommsen zum 5. November 1995* (Berlin, 1995), 219–30 (quote 220). See also Siegfried Kracauer, *From Caligari to Hitler: A Psychological History of the German Film* (Princeton, N.J., 1974).

9. Pamela Potter, "The Nazi 'Seizure' of the Berlin Philharmonic, or the Decline of a Bourgeois Musical Institution," in Cuomo, *Policy,* 39–40. For a similar view, see Michael Walter, *Hitler in der Oper: Deutsches Musikleben, 1919–1945* (Stuttgart, 1995), viii, 118. With some reason, Potter chides me for having adhered too closely to Gay's interpretation in my pilot study of music in the Weimar Republic, "The Revenge of the Fathers: The Demise of Modern Music at the End of the Weimar Republic," *German Studies Review* 15 (1992), 295–315; see Potter, "Philharmonic," 40, 58, n. 1.

10. Potter, "Philharmonic," 40. In mentioning that "individual studies have already begun to chip away at these [monolithic] assumptions," Potter correctly includes jazz in the Third Reich along with other good examples. Indeed, two studies of my own make exactly this point, one as early as 1989. See my "Forbidden Fruit? Jazz in the Third Reich," *American Historical Review* 94 (1989), 11–43; and *Different Drummers: Jazz in the Culture of Nazi Germany* (New York, 1992).

CHAPTER 1

1. BDC Grimm.

2. BDC Kirchner, Walther, Klein, and Rohr.

3. Christoph Sachsse and Florian Tennstedt, *Der Wohlfahrtsstaat im Nationalsozialismus* (Stuttgart, 1992), 38–39; Richard J. Overy, *War and Economy in the Third Reich* (Oxford, 1994), 42–43, 216.

4. Michael H. Kater, "The Revenge of the Fathers: The Demise of Modern Music at the End of the Weimar Republic," *German Studies Review* 15 (1992), 303–4; Albert Richard Mohr, *Die Frankfurter Oper, 1924–1944: Ein Beitrag zur Theatergeschichte mit zeitgenössischen Berichten und Bildern* (Frankfurt am Main, 1971), 178, 239–40, 308; Peter Muck, *Einhundert Jahre Berliner Philharmonisches Orchester: Darstellung in Dokumenten,* 3 vols. (Tutzing, 1982), 2:102; Alan E. Steinweis, *Art, Ideology, and Economics in Nazi Germany: The Reich Chambers of Music, Theater, and the Visual Arts* (Chapel Hill, N.C., 1993), 76.

5. Voigt to Reich Interior Ministry, 29 July 1933, BA, R55/1139; Munich Music Library to Culture Office, 6 June 1936; "Betrifft: Konzertbund München," [1936], SMK, 395.

6. Steinweis, *Art,* 96; Sachsse and Tennstedt, *Wohlfahrtsstaat,* 38; Heinz Ihlert, *Die Reichsmusikkammer: Ziele, Leistungen und Organisation* (Berlin, 1935), 23.

7. Fritz Stein, "Berufsfreudiger Orchesternachwuchs," in Alfred Morgenroth, ed., *Von deutscher Tonkunst: Festschrift zu Peter Raabes 70. Geburtstag* (Leipzig, 1942), 213–14.

8. See letter dated January 1938 in Cornelia Zimmermann-Kalyoncu, *Deutsche Musiker in der Türkei im 20. Jahrhundert* (Frankfurt am Main, 1985), 218.

9. *TG* 3:394; BDC Otto Schad; Steinweis, *Art*, 81–82.

10. Meyerhofer to Schemm, 17 May 1933, SMK, 177; BDC Otto Schad and Hans Ortleb.

11. Berlin Philharmonic to Promi, 24 Mar. 1936 and 10 June 1937; Furtwängler to Promi, 23 Dec. 1937, BA, R55/197; Michael H. Kater, *Doctors Under Hitler* (Chapel Hill, N.C., 1989), 31–34.

12. Von Keudell to Rüdiger, 9 July 1934, BDC Furtwängler; Stegmann to Goebbels, 24 Feb. and 26 Sept. 1938, BA, R55/951; Göring certification, 21 May 1935, BH, MK/45196; remuneration statement for Furtwängler, 1939, ZNF.

13. Radio Frankfurt to Rosbaud, 10 Nov. 1934, LP, 423/1/9.

14. BDC Walter Lutze; Rohr to Rasch, 8 May 1937 (BDC Hanns Rohr); Mayer to Konzertverein München, 10 Apr. 1935, SMK, 208.

15. Michael H. Kater, "Carl Orff im Dritten Reich," *Vierteljahrshefte für Zeitgeschichte* 43 (1995), 30.

16. Meyer et al., "Arbeitsblatt, Finanzamt Garmisch-Partenkirchen," Aug.–Oct. 1946, AM, Strauss; "Meldebogen Pfitzner," 24 Apr. 1946, AM, Pfitzner.

17. Ihlert, *Reichsmusikkammer*, 15; see also at nn. 48, 111, 175.

18. Minutes, fourth meeting of RMK-Präsidialrat, 20 Jan. 1934, RG; Michael H. Kater, *Different Drummers: Jazz in the Culture of Nazi Germany* (New York, 1992), 41.

19. Ihlert, *Reichsmusikkammer*, 18; Steinweis, *Art*, 76; Clement to Siebert, 7 Feb. 1935, BH, MA/107460.

20. Steinweis, *Art*, 99. See also *TG* 2:709, 717; *TG* 3:314, 318; *DDP*, 3 Dec. 1937, 2; *AMR*, 15 Dec. 1940, BA, RD33/2–2. For representative cases of potential beneficiaries (including candidates eventually rejected), see BDC Paul de Nève, Spero Kochmann, Otto Klein, Karl Fiedler.

21. BDC Lore Schepers. For the background of Goebbels's wartime cultural requirements, see Kater, *Different Drummers*, 111–52. For examples of huge earnings, see BDC Hans Hotter, Eugen Jochum, Michael Raucheisen.

22. Sample of 1,152 *n* (musicians) was culled from RMK questionnaires in the RMK section of the BDC. Results of the analysis are statistically significant at the 95 level. On the questionnaires, see Kater, *Different Drummers*, 35. Fred K. Prieberg's estimate that two-thirds of all musicians were unemployed is unproved and wholly unlikely (*Musik und Macht* [Frankfurt am Main, 1991], 209).

23. According to figures in Steinweis, *Art*, 96; Ihlert to Strauss, 19 May 1934, RG.

24. Clemens Hellsberg, *Demokratie der Könige: Die Geschichte der Wiener Philharmoniker* (Zurich, 1992), 464.

25. Hans Uldall, "Weltanschauliche Grundlagen einer neuen Musik," *DM* 29 (1937), 674. Critical reflections on this issue are found in Albrecht Riethmüller, "Komposition im deutschen Reich um 1936," *Archiv für Musikwissenschaft* 38 (1981), 241–78.

26. Wolfgang Stumme, "Musikaufgaben in der Nationalsozialistischen Deutschen Arbeiterpartei," in Stumme, ed., *Musik im Volk: Gegenwartsfragen der deutschen Musik* (Berlin-Lichterfelde, 1944), 162–63.

27. Pfitzner to Göring, 9 Jan. 1938, OW, 211.

28. According to Hermann Zilcher, "Zur deutschen Musikerziehung," *ZM* 101 (1934), 925. See also Steinweis, *Art,* 37.

29. Strauss to Stange, 19 Apr. 1935, RG.

30. See Ian Kershaw, *The Nazi Dictatorship: Problems and Perspectives of Interpretation* (London, 1985); Hans Mommsen, *From Weimar to Auschwitz* (Princeton, N.J., 1992).

31. Kärnbach to Strauss, 9 Jan. 1934, RG; RRG circular, Berlin, 6 Mar. 1935, BA, R78/693; memorandum for Generalintendanz Bayerische Staatstheater, 29 July 1936, BH, MK/40985; Rosbaud declaration, 4 Jan. 1947, LP, 423/8/127; Max Butting, *Musikgeschichte, die ich miterlebte* (Berlin, 1955), 214.

32. BDC Stiebler.

33. BDC Holzinger.

34. BDC Lutze.

35. Baldur von Schirach, *Ich glaubte an Hitler* (Hamburg, 1967), 18–28; *Wer ist's?*, 10th ed., ed. Herrmann A. L. Degener (Berlin, 1935), 1388; *TGII* 4:579.

36. Berthold Goldschmidt, in Karoly Csipak, "Berthold Goldschmidt im Exil: Der Komponist im Gespräch über Musiker-Exil und Musikleben," in Habakuk Traber and Elmar Weingarten, eds., *Verdrängte Musik: Berliner Komponisten im Exil* (Berlin, 1987), 61; *DM* 26 (1934), 363 (quote).

37. Harald Focke and Monika Strocka, *Alltag der Gleichgeschalteten: Wie die Nazis Kirche, Kultur, Justiz und Presse braun färbten* (Reinbek, 1985), 54; *ZM* 109 (1942), 400–401.

38. *ZM* 109 (1942), 401–2.

39. BDC Hans Gansser; *DM* 16 (1934), 875; *Skizzen* (June–July 1935), 15; Nicolas Slonimsky, *Music Since 1900,* 4th ed. (New York, 1971), 667 (quote).

40. Examples for all three are found in *DDP,* 22 Jan. 1937, 1; *ZM* 109 (1942), 304; *MK* 2 (1944), 34.

41. Prieberg, *Macht,* 180; see the collection in BS, Ana/306, and the characteristic letter by Bormann to Kähler, 4 July 1933, in that collection.

42. *TG* 3:491 (quote); Rasch to Promi, 24 Apr. 1935, BA, R55/1177.

43. BDC Kaehler.

44. BDC de Nève (for quote, see his curriculum vitae [May 1938]).

45. Kulturamt München to Wartisch, 14 Jan. 1937, SMK, 213/2; BDC Müller-Rehrmann.

46. *TG* 2:718; Hindemith quoted in Geoffrey Skelton, *Paul Hindemith, the Man Behind the Music: A Biography* (London, 1975), 111.

47. *DKW,* no. 11 (1933), 10–12 (quote on 10).

48. Kater, "Revenge," 304–7; idem, *Different Drummers,* 24.

49. *DKW,* no. 3 (1932), 19; no. 19 (1933), 15.

50. *DKW,* no. 1 (1933), 13; no. 8 (1933), 20 (quote); BDC Hans Rössert.

51. *DKW,* no. 9 (1933), 19; no. 10 (1933), 20; no. 11 (1933), 20.

52. *DKW,* no. 25 (1933), 13; no. 29 (1933), 14.

53. Strecker to Hindemith, 5 Apr. 1933, PF, Schott Korr.

54. *AMZ* 60 (1933), 607. In his postwar memoirs Meyer-Giesow successfully (and typically) deemphasizes his Nazi affiliations (*Taste, Taktstock, Tinte: Ein Leben für die Musik* [Frankfurt am Main, 1968]).

55. Kater, "Orff," 8.

56. Ulrike Gruner, *Musikleben in der Provinz, 1933–45: Beispiel: Marburg: Eine Studie anhand der Musikberichterstattung in der Lokalpresse* (Marburg, 1990), 67.

57. Pfitzner to Spiegel, 13 May 1933; Spiegel to Pfitzner, 26 May 1933, OW, 64.

58. BDC Krämer.

59. Willi Hammer, "Die Grundlagen des künstlerischen Schaffens im neuen Staat," Hamburg, 23 May 1933, BDC Hammer.

60. Hans Heinz Stuckenschmidt, *Zum Hören geboren: Ein Leben mit der Musik unserer Zeit* (Munich, 1979), 134.

61. Donald W. Ellis, "Music in the Third Reich: National Socialist Aesthetic Theory as Governmental Policy" (Ph.D. diss., University of Kansas, 1970), 111–16. On Gerigk, see Kater, *Different Drummers*, 33.

62. *DM* 26 (1934), 933–36; *Angriff,* 24 Sept. 1934; Heim to Hess, 25 Sept. 1934, BDC Havemann.

63. Jeserich to lord mayors et al., 3 July 1937, SMK, 846; Ellis, "Music," 118.

64. Maschat to Oberste Theaterbehörde, 6 Feb. 1941, BH, MK/40975; *MK* 1 (1943), 107; "Spielplan der Staatstheater vom 31. Januar mit 6. Februar 1944," [Munich], BH, Staatstheater/14395; Anton Dermota, *Tausendundein Abend* (Vienna, 1978), 144.

65. Mertin Thrun, "Die Errichtung der Reichsmusikkammer," in Hanns-Werner Heister and Hans-Günther Klein, eds., *Musik und Musikpolitik im faschistischen Deutschland* (Frankfurt am Main, 1984), 75–76.

66. See Konrad H. Jarausch, *The Unfree Professions: German Lawyers, Teachers, and Engineers, 1900–1950* (New York, 1990); Kater, *Doctors,* 19–25.

67. Thrun, "Errichtung," 77.

68. *DKW,* no. 3 (1933), 12; Kater, *Different Drummers,* 24.

69. Thrun, "Errichtung," 77; Steinweis, *Art,* 34.

70. Ellis, "Music," 99–101; Kater, *Different Drummers,* 24, 34.

71. Willy Hoffmann and Wilhelm Ritter, *Das Recht der Musik: Eine erläuternde Darstellung der für das musikalische Urheberrecht geltenden Gesetze, Verordnungen und Anordnungen in alphabetischer Form* (Leipzig, 1936), 248–56; compulsory membership was announced in Ihlert to Rosbaud, 17 Dec. 1934, LP, 423/1/9.

72. Goebbels telegram to Strauss, 10 Nov. 1933, AM, Strauss; Ihlert to Bouhler, 11 Apr. 1934, BDC Ihlert; *DM* 26 (1934), 361–62; Muck, *Jahre* 2:106; Steinweis, *Art,* 48.

73. Gerhard Splitt, *Richard Strauss, 1933–1935: Ästhetik und Musikpolitik zu Beginn der nationalsozialistischen Herrschaft* (Pfaffenweiler, 1987). Eager to discredit Strauss, Splitt goes to the absurd length of characterizing his music as aesthetically fascistic. An excellent though not quite exhaustive critique of Splitt's tendentious work is in Pamela M. Potter, "Strauss and the National Socialists: The Debate and Its Relevance," in Bryan Gilliam, ed., *Richard Strauss: New Perspectives on the Composer and His Work* (Durham, N.C., 1992), 93–113.

74. See his letters from the period 1918–33 in Franz Grasberger, ed., *Der Strom der Töne trug mich fort: Die Welt um Richard Strauss in Briefen* (Tutzing, 1967), 233–344.

75. By and large this information was supported by Strauss's erstwhile RMK employee Julius Kopsch during Strauss's denazification trial. See Kopsch deposition, 1 Mar. 1947, AM, Strauss.

76. See Steinweis, *Art,* 51.

77. An example of Strauss's infrequent presence in Berlin on RMK business (addressing an RMK council meeting) is "Arbeitstagung der Reichsmusikkam-

mer," Berlin, 13–17 Feb. 1934, OW, 250. Characteristically, Strauss's main reason for being in Berlin seems to have been to conduct his opera *Arabella* in the Preussische Staatsoper on 17 February.

78. See Ihlert to Kopsch, 14 Mar. 1934; Stange to Strauss, 25 May 1935, RG; Ihlert to Bouhler, 11 Apr. 1934; enclosure with letter Hempel and Bullerian to Hess, 20 July 1934, BDC Havemann; Ihlert to Hinkel, 22 May 1935, BA, R56I/18; Hinkel to Heydrich, 7 Jan. 1937, BA, R56I/136.

79. BDC Kurt Markwart; Greulich to Hess, 17 July 1934, SMK, 197; Willms to Orff, 31 Dec. 1934, CM, Schott Korr.; Kater, *Different Drummers*, 34–37.

80. Minutes of eighth meeting of RMK-Präsidialrat, 26 Mar. 1934, RG.

81. Strauss to Zweig, 17 June 1935, BDC Strauss; *TG* 2:490, 492; *AMZ* 62 (1935), 485 (quotes).

82. Walter Deppisch, *Richard Strauss: Mit Selbstzeugnissen und Bilddokumenten* (Reinbek, 1989), 140–45; George R. Marek, *Richard Strauss: The Life of a Non-Hero* (London, 1967), 277–84.

83. Kopsch deposition (see n. 75).

84. Strauss to Rasch, 14 Dec. 1934, RG. See chapter 5, at nn. 6–17.

85. The best treatment of this topic is Claudia Maurer Zenck, "Zwischen Boykott und Anpassung an den Charakter der Zeit: Über die Schwierigkeiten eines deutschen Komponisten mit dem Dritten Reich," *Hindemith-Jahrbuch* 9 (1980), 65–129.

86. *DM* 27 (1935), 607–8; Raabe in Harry E. Weinschenk, *Künstler plaudern* (Berlin, 1941), 250; Franz Rühlmann, "Peter Raabe: Bild seines Wesens und Wirkens," *ZM* 109 (1942), 473–79; Robert C. Bachmann, *Karajan: Anmerkungen zu einer Karriere*, 2nd ed. (Düsseldorf, 1983), 117; Ernst Haeussermann, *Herbert von Karajan: Eine Biographie*, 2nd ed. (Vienna, 1983), 50.

87. BDC Raabe; *DM* 26 (1933), 148–49; Peter Raabe, *Die Musik im Dritten Reich: Kulturpolitische Reden und Aufsätze* (Regensburg, 1935); idem, *Kulturwille im deutschen Musikleben: Kulturpolitische Reden und Aufsätze* (Regensburg, 1936).

88. *TG* 2:627; *TG* 3:301. See also Peter Raabe, *Franz Liszt*, 2 vols. (Stuttgart, 1931), 1:169, 179, 181; 2:passim.

89. Joseph Wulf, ed., *Musik im Dritten Reich: Eine Dokumentation* (Reinbek, 1966), 205.

90. Steinweis, *Art*, 138–39; Kater, *Different Drummers*, 45.

91. *TG* 2:627, 752; Wulf, *Musik*, 205–8; Steinweis, *Art*, 53–54; Kater, "Orff," 9.

92. Petschull to Strecker, 11 Oct. 1936; Gertrud Hindemith to Strecker, 28 Oct. 1936; Hindemith to Strecker, 1 Nov. 1936, PF, Schott Korr.

93. *JdM* 1944, 106–7; BDC Drewes.

94. For an explanation of this leadership principle, see Reinhard Bollmus, *Das Amt Rosenberg und seine Gegner: Studien zum Machtkampf im nationalsozialistischen Herrschaftssystem* (Stuttgart, 1970), 236–50; Kershaw, *Dictatorship*, 61–81. Quote is from Overy, *War*, 255.

95. Ordinance of 12 July 1937 in *AMR*, 15 July 1937, BA, RD33/2–1; Steinweis, *Art*, 54.

96. *TG* 3:243 (quote), 270, 273, 294–95, 307, 310, 392, 408, 412, 423, 436, 451, 528; Schmidt-Leonhardt to Hinkel, 6 Nov. 1937; Raabe to Goebbels, 15 Jan. 1938; Raabe to [Hanke], 31 Jan. 1938, BDC Raabe.

97. *TG* 3:273; *JdM* 1943, 22.

98. "Sonderbericht" Müller-Andress, Berlin, 29 July 1937, BA, R56I/141; Raabe, Krebs, and Benecke, "Dienstanweisung für Kreis-und Städtische Musikbeauftragte," Berlin, 1 Aug. 1938, SMK, 393.

99. Kater, *Different Drummers.*

100. Kater, "Orff," 9–11, 20–21.

101. *TG* 3:273, 310.

102. Hinkel to Funk, 22 July 1935, BA, R56I/93; *Unterhaltungsmusik*, 4 July 1941, 618.

103. *TG* 2:752 (quote); and see chap. 5.

104. *ZM* 107 (1940), 516, 660; 108 (1941), 200, 490, 620, 680; 109 (1942), 183.

105. *TG* 3:419, 457–58; *TG* 4:114–15, 329, 378, 406, 408–9, 419.

106. *Podium der Unterhaltungsmusik*, 15 Apr. 1943, 100 (quote); *TGII* 10:412; Mayer to Raabe, 9 Sept. 1944, SMK, 477.

107. NSDAP membership card, BDC Havemann; Berthold Goldschmidt in Karoly Csipak, "Berthold Goldschmidt im Exil: Der Komponist im Gespräch über Musiker-Exil und Musikleben," in Traber and Weingarten, *Musik*, 49.

108. *Das Deutsche Führerlexikon, 1934–35* (Berlin, n.d.), 175.

109. Walter Trienes, *Musik in Gefahr: Selbstzeugnisse aus der Vergangenheit* (Regensburg, 1940), 53; *The Memoirs of Carl Flesch*, ed. Hans Keller (Harlow, 1973), 317; Stuckenschmidt, *Hören*, 115, 139; Luther Noss, *Paul Hindemith in the United States* (Urbana, Ill., 1989), 6.

110. Kraemer to NSDAP-Verbindungsstab, 21 Dec. 1933, BDC Havemann.

111. *DKW*, no. 2 (1932), 13; no. 4 (1932), 12; no. 1 (1933), 13; no. 3 (1933), 14–15.

112. Willy to Ludwig Strecker, 4 Aug. 1933, PF, Schott Korr. See also A. Backhaus memorandum, 28 Aug. 1934, BDC Havemann.

113. "Eine Anklage gegen den Kampfbund für Deutsche Kultur. Fachgruppe Musik," Berlin, 23 Feb. 1933, BA, R55/1138; BDC Havemann; Steinweis, *Art*, 39.

114. See n. 109.

115. Havemann to Hess, 21 Dec. 1933, BDC Havemann.

116. Havemann to NSDAP-Reichsleitung, 24 Feb. 1934, BDC Havemann.

117. Hindemith to Strecker, 15 Nov. 1934, PF, Schott Korr.; *Frankfurter Zeitung*, 16 Nov. 1934 (quote); Stenger to Schulte-Strathaus, 24 Nov. 1934, BDC Havemann. See chap. 5.

118. Havemann to Hitler et al., 18 June 1935, BDC Havemann; *TG* 2:490; Maurer Zenck, "Boycott," 93.

119. Gaugericht Kurmark to Oberstes Parteigericht, 3 Aug. 1937, BDC Havemann.

120. "Neue Abschlüsse . . . seit 1. Oktober 1939," BH, Staatstheater/-14506; *ZM* 107 (1940), 432; *ZM* 108 (1941), 413–14, 554, 615–16; *ZM* 109 (1942), 136.

121. Kochanowski to Hinkel, 22 Oct. 1941, BDC Havemann; *LI*, 235–36, 317–18, 480–81, 654–55, 698–99.

122. Graener in Weinschenk, *Künstler*, 93–98 (quote on 97).

123. *Musikblätter des Anbruch* 9 (1927), photo opposite p. 198; Eugen Schmitz, "Zum 70. Geburtstag Paul Graeners," *ZM* 109 (1942), 3; Kater, "Revenge," 296, 299.

124. See Schmitz, "Geburtstag," 1–4; *GLM* 3:350–51.

125. BDC Graener; *Führerlexikon,* 152; Strauss to Rasch, 21 July and 12 Oct. 1935, BS, Ana/330, I, Rasch, Hugo.

126. *Melos* 12 (1933), 307; *Artist,* 19 June 1933; Muck, *Jahre* 2:108, 110; Rudolf Hartmann, *Das geliebte Haus: Mein Leben mit der Oper* (Munich, 1975), 105–6.

127. *Melos* 13 (1934), 208.

128. *Frankfurter Zeitung,* 27 Feb. 1934; Willi Schuh, ed., *A Confidential Matter: The Letters of Richard Strauss and Stefan Zweig, 1931–1935* (Berkeley, 1977), 94–95; TG 2:556.

129. On Hitler, see Graener in *Skizzen* (Jan. 1936), 11; for quote see Graener in *DKW,* no. 12 (1933), 1. On performances, see *Skizzen* (Feb. 1936), 18; "Abonnement-Konzerte 1935/36," [Munich], SMK, 212; *DM* 29 (1936), 56; *DDP,* 5 Mar. 1937, 2.

130. Walch to Hinkel, 28 Feb. 1936; Walch to Graener, 14 May 1936; Hinkel to Hanke, 17 Feb. 1938; Hinkel to Goebbels, 23 Feb. 1938, BA, R56I/135; Richartz to Radio Frankfurt (also to Radio Hanover, Munich, etc.), 11 Mar. 1936, BDC Graener.

131. See anon. to Graener, 17 Jan. 1936, BDC Graener; Kater, *Different Drummers,* 29–110.

132. Graener to Hinkel, 18 Aug. 1936; Owens to Hinkel (with Hinkel's annotations), 30 Nov. 1936; Hinkel to Hanke, 23 June 1937; BA, R56I/135; *Unterhaltungsmusik,* 21 Jan. 1937, 70–71; *Unterhaltungsmusik,* 14 Apr. 1938, 454 (quote).

133. Hinkel to Goebbels, 8 Mar. 1938; Hinkel to Walch, 19 Mar. 1938; Hinkel to Christoffer, 27 Apr. 1938, BA, R56I/135; TG 4:3.

134. Hinkel to Goebbels, 19 Feb. 1938, BA, R56I/135. See also *Frankfurter Zeitung,* 23 Aug. 1938; "Städtische Bühnen Frankfurt am Main, 'Woche der Lebenden' vom 19. bis 26. März 1939," CM, Allg. Korr.; *Generalanzeiger,* Frankfurt am Main, 25 Aug. 1939; "Neue Abschlüsse . . . seit 1. Oktober 1939," BH, Staatstheater/14506; *ZM* 108 (1941), 123; *ZM* 109 (1942), 18, 113, 254; *JdM 1943,* 198–99; Muck, *Jahre* 3:302; Albrecht Dümling and Peter Girth, eds., *Entartete Musik: Zur Düsseldorfer Ausstellung von 1938: Eine kommentierte Rekonstruktion* (Düsseldorf, [1988]), 107.

135. *ZM* 107 (1940), 303, 422, 717.

136. *MK* 1 (1944), 228; *Reichsrundfunk,* no. 10 (Jan. 1944), 203–4. See also Aulich to Orff, 22 Mar. 1943, CM, Allg. Korr.; *Reichskulturkammer,* no. 3/4 (1944), 61.

137. BDC Graener; *Reichsrundfunk,* no. 21/22 (Jan. 1942), 409; *Leipziger Neueste Nachrichten,* 11 Jan. 1942; RMK minutes, [Berlin, May–July 1942], BDC Werner Egk.

138. Kopsch to Strauss, 24 Jan. 1941, RG; TG 4:521, 653; *ZM* 108 (1941), 484. See also at n. 103.

139. Graener corr. (1943–44), BA, R56I/135; Ritter to Egk, 25 May 1944, BDC Richard Strauss; *Reichskulturkammer,* no. 7 (1944), 114.

140. Friedrich Welter, *Musikgeschichte im Umriss: Vom Urbeginn bis zur Gegenwart* (Leipzig, n.d.), 320–21; *ZM* 107 (1940), 460; *MK* 1 (1943), 65.

141. Kater, "Revenge," 304–5; *ZM* 107 (1940), 460; Eleonore van Hoogstraten, ed., *Elly Ney: Briefwechsel mit Willem van Hoogstraten: Erster Band 1910–1926,* (Tutzing, 1970), 260; Muck, *Jahre* 2:82.

142. BDC Trapp; *DKW*, no. 3 (1932), 19; Welter, *Musikgeschichte*, 321 (quote).

143. *DKW*, no. 13 (1933), 9.

144. Muck, *Jahre* 2:146, 151; 3:289–90, 292; Rimnitz to Strauss, 24 June 1935, RG; "Programmvorschlag," Munich, 31 July 1936, SMK, 214; *TG* 4:230; *Unterhaltungsmusik*, 11 July 1940, 633.

145. See ZM 107 (1940), 90; ZM 109 (1942), 354; MK 1 (1943), 48. For the exception, see ZM 107 (1940), 698.

146. Welter, *Musikgeschichte*, 322; *DKW*, no. 3 (1932), 19; Hans Heinz Stuckenschmidt, "German Season Under the Crisis," *Modern Music* 10 (1932), 167 (quote).

147. Vollerthun in Carl Niessen, ed., *Die deutsche Oper der Gegenwart* (Regensburg, 1944), 270 (quote). See also Vollerthun in *DKW*, no. 13 (1933), 2–3; no. 28 (1933), 6–7; no. 12 (1933), 16.

148. *DKW*, no. 12 (1933), 16.

149. *Artist*, 19 May 1933; *TG* 2:432; Strauss to von Niessen, 16 Apr. 1933, RG.

150. *Deutsches Musiker-Lexikon*, ed. Erich H. Müller (Dresden, 1929), 1502; BDC Vollerthun; corr. regarding Vollerthun (1936), BA, R55/223. See also ZM 101 (1934), 1155; DM 27 (1935), 759; *Artist*, 24 Sept. 1936, 1215; Muck, *Jahre* 3:268.

151. ZM 107 (1940), 298–99 (quote); 109 (1942), 277–78; 110 (1943), 134; *Artist*, 24 Sept. 1936, 1215; MK 2 (1944), 109.

152. BDC Rode; *Führerlexikon*, 389; Goldschmidt in Csipak, "Evil," 61; Oliver Rathkolb, *Führertreu und gottbegnadet: Künstlereliten im Dritten Reich* (Vienna, 1991), 93.

153. BDC Rode; BDC Walter Lutze; *TG* 3:1.

154. BDC Reichwein; *VB*, 30 Sept. 1932; ZM 103 (1936), 281–83; Rathkolb, *Führertreu*, 47; *NG* 7:311.

155. Michael Tanner in *New York Review of Books*, 26 June 1994, 23.

156. Strauss to Rasch, 14 Dec. 1934, RG; Junk to Pfitzner, 8 Nov. 1934, OW, 958. See also BDC Reichwein; Reichwein to Boepple, 23 Mar. 1935, BH, MK/36795; corr. Reichwein (1936), SMK, 213/2; *Echo* (Vienna), 3 Aug. 1934.

157. Muck, *Jahre* 3:278, 286, 290; ZM 109 (1942), 69, 122, 176, 307, 427, 546.

158. Corr. BDC Stadelmann; Stadelmann to Hinkel, 3 Aug. 1933, ibid. (quote).

159. BDC Stadelmann; Ehlert to Esser, 4 Apr. 1934, BH, MWi/2817 (quote); corr. in SMK, 275 and 97/5; ZM 108 (1941), 747; ZM 110 (1943), 120.

160. *JdM 1943*, 130–31; Ney in Weinschenk, *Künstler*, 225–27; ZM 109 (1942), 391–92.

161. Ney to Ley, 15 July 1943, EB/26 (1st quote); Hoogstraten, *Ney*, 240 (2nd quote), 303–4; Matthes to Pfitzner, 23 Dec. 1932, OW, 299; *Westdeutscher Beobachter* (Bonn), 20 June 1938; Max Strub in Elly Ney, *Erinnerungen und Betrachtungen: Mein Leben aus der Musik*, 4th ed. (Aschaffenburg, 1957), 165. On Seiss, see *MGG* 12:477.

162. Ney in Weinschenk, *Künstler*, 229; Ney to van Hoogstraten, 23 Mar. 1939, EB/26.

163. See the various contributions in Eleonore van Hoogstraten, ed., *Worte*

des Dankes an Elly Ney (Tutzing, 1968), and Willem van Hoogstraten in Ney, *Erinnerungen,* 170.

164. See Ney to van Hoogstraten, [23 Mar. 1933], EB/6; Ney telegram to Hinkel, 20 Apr. 1937; Ney to Hinkel, 29 Nov. 1943; von Hansemann memorandum, May 1944, BDC Ney; *Nationalzeitung* (Essen), 16 Mar. 1938.

165. Ney in *DM* 27 (1935), 346–47; Ney to Raabe, 2 Aug. 1935, EB/26; *Skizzen* (Jan. 1937), 11, 18; *ZM* 108 (1941), 340; photograph of Ney in *JdM 1943,* opposite p. 129. On Nazi Beethoven mania and Ney, see Nanny Drechsler, *Die Funktion der Musik im deutschen Rundfunk, 1933–1945* (Pfaffenweiler, 1988), 58–68; Elly Ney, "Bekenntnis zu Ludwig van Beethoven," in Morgenroth, *Tonkunst,* 59–67.

166. Muck, *Jahre* 3:268; *Skizzen* (Nov. 1937), 19; (Aug.–Sept. 1939), 18; *ZM* 108 (1941), 280; *ZM* 109 (1942), 42, 234, 467; *ZM* 110 (1943), 21; *MK* 1 (1943), 145; *ZM* 2 (1944), 64, 112; Wolf-Eberhard von Lewinsky, *Ludwig Hoelscher* (Tutzing, 1967), 46.

167. Opinion of the American conductor Newell Jenkins, who was studying in Germany before World War II (recorded interview, Hillsdale, N.Y., 20 Mar. 1993, APA). See *Skizzen* (Dec. 1935), 18; *Skizzen* (Jan. 1939), 20; *ZM* 106 (1939), 1134; *ZM* 108 (1941), 482; Gert Kerschenbaumer, *Faszination Drittes Reich: Kunst und Alltag der Kulturmetropole Salzburg* (Salzburg, [1988]), 162, 172.

168. Ney to van Hoogstraten, 2 Jan. 1944, EB/7 (1st quote); Ney to van Hoogstraten, 12 Nov. 1939, EB/6 (2nd quote); Ney to van Hoogstraten, [Mar.] 1933, EB/6 (3rd quote). Also Ney to van Hoogstraten, 27 July 1936 and 13 May 1939, EB/6; Grete Busch, *Fritz Busch: Dirigent* (Frankfurt am Main, 1970), 57.

169. Ney to van Hoogstraten, 14 Feb. 1933 (1st and 3rd quotes); Ney to van Hoogstraten, 8 May 1938 (2nd quote), EB/6.

170. Ney to Franz [recte Framm], 30 Oct. 1935; Ney to Hinkel, 3 Dec. 1936, BDC Ney; *TG* 3:516.

171. Ney to van Hoogstraten, [23 Mar. 1933] and 16 May 1933, EB/6.

172. Ney to van Hoogstraten, [July 1936], EB/6. See also *DM* 27 (1935), 346; *ZM* 107 (1940), 444; *ZM* 109 (1942), 123; David B. Dennis, *Beethoven in German Politics, 1870–1989* (New Haven, 1996), 155–56.

173. BDC Ney; *ZM* 109 (1942), 392; Ney telegram to Hinkel, 20 Apr. 1937; Ney telegram to Hitler, 17 Dec. 1938, BDC Ney; Ney to van Hoogstraten, 18 July 1938 and 12 Nov. 1939 (quote), EB/6.

174. See Ney corr. in EB.

175. Von Waltershausen to Bavarian Culture Ministry, 5 Mar. 1928, BH, MK/36611 (quote); Max Neuhaus, "Das nationalsozialistische Reichs-Symphonie-Orchester," *ZM* 100 (1933), 916–19; *Unterhaltungsmusik,* 17 Dec. 1936, 1608–9; *VB,* 9 Aug. 1938; *ZM* 109 (1942), 28–29.

176. Huebner to Göring, 27 Jan. 1933, BDC Willy Huebner.

177. Erwin Bauer, "Westmarkreise des N.S. Reichssymphonie-Orchesters," *ZM* 100 (1933), 919–22; *ZM* 106 (1939), 1136; *ZM* 107 (1940), 111; RRG to Hadamovsky, 31 Aug. 1933, BA, R78/909; *AMZ* 63 (1936), 402; *Musik-Woche,* 9 Oct. 1937, 6.

178. *ZM* 107 (1940), 308; *ZM* 108 (1941), 472; *ZM* 109 (1942), 139, 186–87, 380; *ZM* 110 (1943), 42, 146; *Unterhaltungsmusik,* 13 Dec. 1941, 153; *Podium der Unterhaltungsmusik,* 8 Jan. 1942, 9; Mayer to Städtisches Kulturamt, 5 Sept. 1944, SMK, 477.

179. Wolfgang Wagner, *Lebens-Akte: Autobiographie* (Munich, 1994), 38.
180. See Erich Ebermayer, *Magisches Bayreuth: Legende und Wirklichkeit* (Stuttgart, n.d.), 61–225; Zdenko von Kraft, *Der Sohn: Siegfried Wagners Leben und Umwelt* (Graz, 1969); Kraft, *Das Festspielhaus in Bayreuth: Zur Geschichte seiner Idee, seines Werdegangs und seiner Vollendung*, 4th ed. (Bayreuth, 1969); Dietrich Mack, *Bayreuther Festspiele: Die Idee, der Bau, die Aufführungen* (Bayreuth, 1974).
181. Wagner, *Lebens-Akte*, 12.
182. See, e.g., Frederic Spotts, *Bayreuth: A History of the Wagner Festival* (New Haven, 1994), 76–77, 104–5, 112–13.
183. Jacob Katz, *The Darker Side of Genius: Richard Wagner's Anti-Semitism* (Hanover, N.H., 1986); Alan David Aberbach, *The Ideas of Richard Wagner: An Examination and Analysis of His Major Aesthetic, Political, Economic, Social, and Religious Thoughts* (Lanham, Md., 1988); Dieter Borchmeyer, "Richard Wagner und der Antisemitismus," in Ulrich Müller and Peter Wapnewski, eds., *Richard-Wagner-Handbuch* (Stuttgart, 1986), 137–61; Hartmut Zelinsky quoted in Klaus Umbach, "'Zu schönen Klängen eine brutale Ideologie': Spiegel-Gespräch mit Wagner-Forscher Hartmut Zelinsky über 'Parsifal' und dessen Auswirkungen auf Hitler und Holocaust," in Umbach, ed., *Richard Wagner: Ein deutsches Ärgernis* (Reinbek, 1982), 38–41, esp. 38. The most prominent conventional biographer of Wagner, Martin Gregor-Dellin, *Richard Wagner: Sein Leben, sein Werk, sein Jahrhundert*, 4th ed. (Munich, 1991), 310–14, 606–7, 766–69, typically analyzes Wagner's anti-Semitism at too superficial a level.
184. August Kubizek, *The Young Hitler I Knew* (Westport, Conn., 1976), 187–92 (quote on 191).
185. Adolf Hitler, *Mein Kampf*, 26th ed. (Munich, 1933), 15; Henry Picker, *Hitler's Tischgespräche im Führerhauptquartier, 1941–1942*, ed. Gerhard Ritter (Bonn, 1951), 364, 382; Ernst Hanfstaengl, *Zwischen Weissem und Braunem Haus: Memoiren eines politischen Aussenseiters* (Munich, 1970), 56; Hans Severus Ziegler, *Adolf Hitler aus dem Erleben dargestellt*, 3rd ed. (Göttingen, 1965), 70; Michael Karbaum, *Studien zur Geschichte der Bayreuther Festspiele (1876–1976)*, 2 vols. (Regensburg, 1976), 1:72.
186. Zelinsky in Umbach, *Klängen*, 39; Karl Grunsky, *Der Kampf um die deutsche Musik* (Stuttgart, 1933), 63.
187. Karbaum, *Studien* 1:72; 2:114; Picker, *Tischgespräche*, 97, 349; Spotts, *Bayreuth*, 140–43.
188. Ebermayer, *Bayreuth*, 186; Hans Mayer, *Richard Wagner in Bayreuth, 1876–1976* (Stuttgart, 1976), 104; Wagner, *Lebens-Akte*, 44–45; allegation regarding Wieland Wagner is in *International Herald Tribune* (Paris), 29 Aug. 1994.
189. Winifred Wagner (1947) cited in Spotts, *Bayreuth*, 203; Wagner, *Lebens-Akte*, 47; Friedelind Wagner, *Nacht über Bayreuth: Die Geschichte der Enkelin Richard Wagners* (Bern, [1946]), 160–61. See also Karbaum, *Studien* 2:115; Kraft, *Sohn*, 307–8; and Spotts's own heedless repetition of that legend, *Bayreuth*, 165.
190. Alfred Rosenberg, *Der Mythus des 20. Jahrhunderts: Eine Wertung der seelisch-geistigen Gestaltenkämpfe unserer Zeit* (1930), 41st/42nd ed. (Munich, 1934), 316, 388–89, 401–2, 427–34, 443–44 (quote 428).
191. Kater, *Different Drummers*, 24; *DKW*, no. 14 (1933), 16.

192. Gruner, *Musikleben*, 106, 126; *DKW*, no. 1 (1933), 9–10; Trienes, *Musik*, 10.

193. *TG* 2:648–49; *TG* 3:211, 214; *TGII* 12:47; *DKW*, no. 18 (1933), 8; Walter Rischer, *Die nationalsozialistische Kulturpolitik in Düsseldorf, 1933–1945* (Düsseldorf, 1972), 76; Karbaum, *Studien* 1:72; William E. Dodd, Jr., and Martha Dodd, eds., *Ambassador Dodd's Diary, 1933–1938* (New York, 1941), 164–65; Goebbels quoted in *DM* 28 (1936), 721.

194. *AMR*, 1 June 1938, BA, RD33/2-1. See also *TGII* 2:573.

195. *Münchener Neueste Nachrichten*, 16/17 Apr. 1933.

196. *ZM* 107 (1940), 239; Hohenschwanstein corr. (1933), SMK, 239; *VB*, 22 Dec. 1933; Hartmut Zelinsky, ed., *Richard Wagner—ein deutsches Trauma: Eine Dokumentation zur Wirkungsgeschichte Richard Wagners, 1876–1976*, 3rd ed. (Berlin, 1983), 195, 230; Karbaum, *Studien* 2:78, 80; Berndt Wilhelm Wessling, ed., *Bayreuth im Dritten Reich: Richard Wagners politische Erben: Eine Dokumentation* (Weinheim, 1983), 272–74.

197. Wagner, *Lebens-Akte*, 47. Winifred Wagner's assertion is in Ziegler, *Hitler*, 159.

198. Werner Jochmann, ed., *Adolf Hitler: Monologe im Führerhauptquartier, 1941–1944: Die Aufzeichnungen Heinrich Heims* (Hamburg, 1980), 235; Ebermayer, *Bayreuth*, 205–7; Ziegler, *Hitler*, 179–80; Carl Vinzent Krogmann, *Es ging um Deutschlands Zukunft, 1932–1939: Erlebtes täglich diktiert von dem früheren Regierenden Bürgermeister von Hamburg*, 2nd ed. (Leoni, 1977), 314–15; sketch of seating arrangement, "Abendtafel am Dienstag, dem 25. März 1935," PA Dr. Martin Haushofer, Herrsching. On Tietjen, see Rudolf Augstein in *Spiegel*, 25 July 1994, 156.

199. Ziegler, *Hitler*, 173; Wagner, *Nacht*, 178–336; Picker, *Tischgespräche*, 236, 369; *TGII* 7:512.

200. Abendroth to Pfitzner, 12 Mar. 1938, OW, 288.

201. Winifred Wagner to Strauss, 9 June 1933, RG. See also Susanna Grossmann-Vendrey, *Bayreuth in der deutschen Presse: Beiträge zur Rezeptionsgeschichte Richard Wagners und seiner Festspiele* (Regensburg, 1983), 256.

202. Ziegler, *Hitler*, 171; Wessling, *Bayreuth*, 176; Karbaum, *Studien* 2:79–80; Mayer, *Wagner*, 137, 140, 149.

203. *Manchester Guardian* quoted in Wessling, *Bayreuth*, 190; Meta Kropf, *Ein Beitrag zur Zeitgeschichte: Bayreuther Festspielsommer von damals*, 2nd ed. (Munich, 1978), 18.

204. Fred Hamel in *Reich*, 28 July 1940, 18; Wolfgang Golther in *ZM* 108 (1941), 584–86; *MK* 1 (1943), 107; Heinz Boberach, ed., *Meldungen aus dem Reich: Die geheimen Lageberichte des Sicherheitsdienstes der SS, 1938–1945*, 17 vols. (Herrsching, 1984), 8:2675–76; Zelinsky, *Wagner*, 243–44.

205. Paul Bülow, "Adolf Hitler und der Bayreuther Geistesbezirk," *ZM* 100 (1933), 677; *ZM* 108 (1941), 346; *Münchener Neueste Nachrichten*, 14 Aug. 1933; "Aufruf an alle Bühnen, an denen Opern gespielt werden!" [1938], SMK, 396; Wessling, *Bayreuth*, 260; Drechsler, *Funktion*, 68–78.

206. Verdi surpassed Wagner in 1942–43. See Hubert Kolland, "Wagner-Rezeption im deutschen Faschismus," in Christoph-Hellmut Mahling and Sigrid Weismann, eds., *Bericht über den Internationalen Musikwissenschaftlichen Kongress Bayreuth 1981* (Kassel, 1984), 501–2; also Franz-Heinz Köhler, *Die Struktur der Spielpläne deutschsprachiger Opernbühnen von 1896 bis 1966* (n.p.,

n.d.), 35–36; Petra Maria Valentin, "Die Bayerische Staatsoper im Dritten Reich" (M.A. thesis, University of Munich, 1985); table showing opera productions from 1 Jan. 1933 to 2 Oct. 1943.

207. *VB*, 22 Dec. 1933.

208. Karl Laux, "Bayreuth," *Melos* 12 (1933), 302–3.

CHAPTER 2

1. Sittmann et al. to Epp, 3 Dec. 1934, BH, Reichsstatthalter/669/8; Knappertsbusch memorandum for Bavarian Culture Ministry, Nov. 1935, BH, MK/41010 (quote).

2. Sittmann et al. to Epp (see n. 1).

3. *LI*, 380; Kurt Blaukopf, *Grosse Dirigenten* (Teufen, n.d.), 108–12; Helge Rosvaenge, *Mach es besser, mein Sohn*, 2nd ed. (Leipzig, 1963), 66.

4. Paul Ehlers, "Die Musik und Adolf Hitler," *ZM* 106 (1939), 359; Hans Rudolf Vaget, "Präludium in München: Bruno Walter und die Vertreibung Thomas Manns," *Frankfurter Allgemeine Zeitung*, 14 May 1994; Vaget, "Musik in München," *Thomas Mann Jahrbuch* 7 (1994), 55–58; Edith Stargardt-Wolff, *Wegbereiter grosser Musiker* (Berlin, 1954), 244.

5. Donald W. Ellis, "Music in the Third Reich: National Socialist Aesthetic Theory as Governmental Policy" (Ph.D. diss., University of Kansas, 1970), 36–41.

6. Thomas Mann, "Tischrede auf Pfitzner" (1919), in *Gesammelte Werke*, 13 vols., 2nd ed. (Frankfurt am Main, 1974), 10:417–22; idem, ["Für Bruno Walter"] (1936), ibid., 10:479–83; idem, "Aufruf zur Gründung des Hans Pfitzner-Vereins für Deutsche Tonkunst" (1918), ibid., 11:744–45; idem, ["Geist und Wesen der Deutschen Republik"] (1923), in Mann, *Reden und Aufsätze*, 2 vols. (Frankfurt am Main, 1965), 2:53–60; Gabriele Busch-Salmen and Günther Weiss, eds., *Hans Pfitzner: Münchener Dokumente/Bilder und Bildnisse* (Regensburg, 1990), e.g., 63–65; Mann to Pfitzner, 23 June 1925, OW, 80; Pfitzner to Fürstner, 8 Sept. 1932, MMP; Vaget, "Musik," 57–58; Hans Pfitzner, *Gesammelte Schriften*, 3 vols. (Augsburg, 1926–29), 2:244–49; Katia Mann, *Meine ungeschriebenen Memoiren*, ed. Elisabeth Plessen and Michael Mann (Frankfurt am Main, 1981), 49–53; Michael H. Kater, "The Revenge of the Fathers: The Demise of Modern Music at the End of the Weimar Republic," *German Studies Review* 15 (1992), 298.

7. See Pfitzner to Hartmann, 29 Apr. 1927; Knappertsbusch to Pfitzner, 9 June 1931, OW, 297; Pfitzner to Kanppertsbusch, 3 June 1931, OW, 300.

8. Thomas Mann, "Über die Kunst Richard Wagners" (1911), in *Reden* 2:693–95; idem, "Wie stehen wir heute zu Richard Wagner?" (1927), ibid., 2:757–59.

9. Alfred Rosenberg, *Der Mythus des 20. Jahrhunderts: Eine Wertung der seelisch-geistigen Gestaltenkämpfe unserer Zeit*, 41st/42nd ed. (Munich, 1934), 388, 421; Katia Mann, *Memoiren*, 96–98; Paul Egon Hübinger, *Thomas Mann, die Universität Bonn und die Zeitgeschichte: Drei Kapitel deutscher Vergangenheit aus dem Leben des Dichters, 1905–1955* (Munich, 1974), 124–25.

10. Editor's quotation in Thomas Mann, *Pro and Contra Wagner* (London, 1985), 91.

11. Ibid.

12. Thomas Mann, "The Sorrows and Grandeur of Richard Wagner," ibid., 91–148, esp. 98, 107–8, 135, 140–41, 148.

13. Thomas Mann, *Tagebücher, 1933–1934,* ed. Peter de Mendelssohn (Frankfurt am Main, 1977), 209, 307; idem, *Wagner,* 165; Hübinger, *Mann,* 129–30, n. 83.

14. Walter Panofsky, *Richard Strauss: Partitur eines Lebens* (Munich, 1965), 276.

15. "Protest der Richard-Wagner-Stadt München," 16 Apr. 1933, reprinted in Hartmut Zelinsky, ed., *Richard Wagner—ein deutsches Thema: Eine Dokumentation zur Wirkungsgeschichte Richard Wagners, 1876–1976* (Berlin, 1983), 195; Knappertsbusch to "Euer Hochwohlgeboren" [here Hans Pfitzner], 3 Apr. 1933, OW, 282. On Matthes, see Muck to Matthes, 10 Mar. 1929; Knappertsbusch to Matthes, July 1933, BDC Matthes. See also Vaget, "Musik," 47–50.

16. Pfitzner to Knappertsbusch, 13 Apr. 1933, OW, 282; Pfitzner to Abendroth, 22 Jan. 1934, OW, 289.

17. "Protest der Richard-Wagner-Stadt München" (see n. 15).

18. *LI,* 380; Erika and Klaus Mann, *Escape to Life: Deutsche Kultur im Exil,* 2nd ed. (Munich, 1991), 128; Karl Böhm, *Ich erinnere mich ganz genau: Autobiographie* (Zurich, 1968), 47; Panofsky, *Strauss,* 304; Frederic Spotts, *Bayreuth: A History of the Wagner Festival* (New Haven, 1994), 207; Hugo Burghauser, *Philharmonische Begegnungen: Erinnerungen eines Wiener Philharmonikers* (Zurich, 1979), 195; Hubert Hackenberg and Walter Herrmann, *Die Wiener Staatsoper im Exil, 1945–1955* (Vienna, 1985), 23; "Gutachten," 8 Jan. 1947, AM, Strauss; Knappertsbusch to [Leer], 28 Dec. 1947, AM, Pfitzner; Knappertsbusch to Bavarian State Ministry, 15 Apr. 1952, BH, MK/45179.

19. Mezger to Bavarian Theater Administration, 23 Sept. 1952, BH, MK/45179; Ellis, "Music," 197; Herta and Kurt Blaukopf, *Die Wiener Philharmoniker: Wesen, Werden, Wirken eines grossen Orchesters* (Vienna, 1986), 188.

20. Rath-Rex to Hinkel, 7 Sept. 1933, BDC Friedrich Schery; Neuschwanstein file (1933–36), SMK, 239, in particular Fiehler to Winifred Wagner, 8 Feb. 1933.

21. On continued friction between Pfitzner and Knappertsbusch, see Knappertsbusch to Pfitzner, 15 May 1934, BH, MK/44737; Knappertsbusch to Walleck, 11 Sept. 1934, BH, Staatstheater/NA Pfitzner; corr. Knappertsbusch/Pfitzner (May 1934), OW, 282.

22. Sittmann et al. to Epp, 3 Dec. 1934, BH, Reichsstatthalter/669/8; Mezger, "Zur Frage der Leitung der Staatsoper," 27 Feb. 1936, BH, MK/41010; *Melos* 13 (1934), 254; Ellis, "Music," 192–93.

23. Mezger to Generalintendanz, 31 Dec. 1933; Boepple to Bavarian State Chancellery, 13 July 1934, BH, MK/41010.

24. Schemm to Goebbels, 7 Feb. 1935, BH, MK/40991; Strecker to Hindemith, 16 May 1935, PF, Schott Korr.

25. Knappertsbusch memorandum, Nov. 1935, BH, MK/41010 (quote); Walleck to Köglmaier, 15 June 1937; Mezger to Bavarian Theater Administration (see n. 19).

26. Knappertbusch memorandum, Nov. 1935, BH, MK/41010.

27. Mezger to Bavarian Theater Administration (see n. 19). See also *Reichsgesetzblatt I* (1933), 175–77. For the apologists, see n. 18.

28. Mezger memorandum, 4 Mar. 1936, BH, MK/41010; Boepple to Goebbels, 13 Mar. 1936, BH, MK/40993; Walleck memorandum, 4 Dec. 1937, BH, MK/45196; Leute to Geiger, 22 Nov. 1935, BDC Knappertsbusch.

29. *Wiener Freie Presse*, 20 Nov. 1934; *Neues Wiener Journal*, 25 Nov. 1934; Ruhne to Promi, 3 Jan. 1935, BA, R55/1184; Knappertsbusch quoted in Signe Scanzoni and Götz Klaus Kende, *Der Prinzipal: Clemens Krauss: Fakten, Vergleiche, Rückschlüsse* (Tutzing, 1988), 173.

30. *TG* 2:551–52.

31. Traim to Referat 28, 22 Oct. 1952, BH, MK/45179 (1st quote); Ranczak in Hermann Proebst and Karl Ude, eds., *Denk ich an München: Ein Buch der Erinnerungen*, 2nd ed. (Munich, 1967), 233 (2nd quote); Henry Picker, *Hitlers Tischgespräche im Führerhauptquartier, 1941–42*, ed. Gerhard Ritter (Bonn, 1951), 396; Hans Severus Ziegler, *Adolf Hitler aus dem Erleben dargestellt*, 3rd ed. (Göttingen, 1965), 168–69.

32. *ZM* 107 (1940), 33, 89; *ZM* 108 (1941), 520–21; W. T. Anderman [Walter Thomas], *Bis der Vorhang fiel: Berichtet nach Aufzeichnungen aus den Jahren 1940 bis 1945* (Dortmund, 1947), 135; Otto Strasser, *Und dafür wird man noch bezahlt: Mein Leben mit den Wiener Philharmonikern* Vienna, 1974), 146–47, 153; Hackenberg and Herrmann, *Staatsoper*, 24, 29; Clemens Hellsberg, *Demokratie der Könige: Die Geschichte der Wiener Philharmoniker* (Zurich, 1992), 462, 475.

33. Burghauser, *Begegnungen*, 123.

34. Peter Muck, *Einhundert Jahre Berliner Philharmonisches Orchester: Darstellung in Dokumenten*, 3 vols. (Tutzing, 1982), 2:152; 3:289, 300, 308; *Generalanzeiger* (Frankfurt), 28 May 1939; Rudolf Sonner, "Kriegsauftrag von 'Kraft durch Freude,'" *DM* 33 (1940), 11; *ZM* 107 (1940), 118; *ZM* 108 (1941), 70, 126, 492, 690; *ZM* 109 (1942), 471.

35. Hellsberg, *Demokratie*, 477; *ZM* 108 (1941), 30; Werner Präg and Wolfgang Jacobmeyer, eds., *Das Diensttagebuch des deutschen Generalgouverneurs in Polen, 1939–1945* (Stuttgart, 1975), 407.

36. Baldur von Schirach's recollection of Braun in Spandau Prison, May 1948, quoted in Albert Speer, *Spandauer Tagebücher* (Frankfurt am Main, 1975), 156; Muck, *Jahre* 3:305, 309; Hinkel to Reichspropagandaamtsleiter Wien, 15 Mar. 1943, BDC Knappertsbusch; von Borries to Tackmann, 1 July 1943, BDC Werner Egk; *TGII* 8:132; *TGII* 12:155, 204; Hellsberg, *Demokratie*, 478.

37. Hustert to Gauleitung Wien, 5 Feb. 1945, OSW, Gauakt/139835.

38. Corr. Giesler/Knappertsbusch (1944), SMK, 383.

39. Traim to Referat 28, 22 Oct. 1952, BH, MK/45179.

40. See Alfred E. Frauenfeld, *Und trage keine Reu': Vom Wiener Gauleiter zum Generalkommissar der Krim: Erinnerungen und Aufzeichnungen* (Leoni, 1978), 54–55.

41. Burghauser, *Begegnungen*, 36–37; Blaukopf, *Dirigenten*, 113–17; Oskar von Pander, *Clemens Krauss in München* (Munich, 1955), 25; Anderman [Thomas], *Vorhang*, 118; Rudolf Hartmann, *Das geliebte Haus: Mein Leben mit der Oper* (Munich, 1975), 178; Berndt Wilhelm Wessling, *Hans Hotter* (Bremen, 1966), 62; Hans Heinz Stuckenschmidt, *Zum Hören geboren: Ein Leben mit der Musik unserer Zeit* (Munich, 1979), 103–4 (quote).

42. "Lebenslauf" [Krauss], n.d., BH, Staatstheater/14444; Krauss in Harry E. Weinschenk, *Künstler plaudern* (Berlin, 1941), 132–36; von Pander, *Krauss*, 9–11.

43. UE memorandum, 1 June 1931, WC, Weill/UE corr.; Blaukopf, *Dirigenten*, 113, 115; Heinrich von Kralik, *Die Wiener Philharmoniker: Monographie eines Orchesters* (Vienna, 1938), 91; John L. Stewart, *Ernst Krenek: The Man and His Music* (Berkeley, 1991), 175–76; Egon Seefehlner, "Die Direktoren und ihre Ensembles," in Andrea Seebohm, ed., *Die Wiener Oper: 350 Jahre Glanz und Tradition* (Vienna, 1986), 107–12. Gerhard Botz authoritatively qualifies the concept of Austro-Fascism in his *Krisenzonen einer Demokratie: Gewalt, Streik und Konfliktunterdrückung in Österreich seit 1918* (Frankfurt am Main, 1987), 211–36.

44. *Neue Freie Presse* (Vienna), 11 Dec. 1934; Rosenzweig to anon., 16 Apr. 1946, OSW, Unterrichtsministerium/12; von Kralik, *Philharmoniker*, 92–93; Stewart, *Krenek*, 175; von Pander, *Krauss*, 26; Erik Maschat, "Nachruf auf Klemens Krauss—'politisch,'" *Blätter der Bayerischen Staatsoper*, no. 9 (1987), 28–29.

45. Gottfried von Einem, recorded interview, Vienna, 30 Nov. 1994, APA; Friedrich Saathen, *Einem Chronik: Dokumentation und Deutung* (Vienna, 1982), 40.

46. Tietjen to Strauss, 21 Feb. 1935, RG.

47. See Hartmann, *Haus*, 104; Tietjen to Strauss, 8 Apr. 1935, RG.

48. Furtwängler to Strauss, 9 May 1936, BH, MK/45196.

49. *TG* 2:492; Fred K. Prieberg, *Kraftprobe: Wilhelm Furtwängler im Dritten Reich* (Wiesbaden, 1986), 195–289.

50. See text at n. 39.

51. This is implausibly suggested by Maschat, "Nachruf," 28.

52. Oliver Rathkolb, *Führertreu und gottbegnadet: Künstlereliten im Dritten Reich* (Vienna, 1991), 108. But see the qualifying remarks in Hartmann, *Haus*, 110, 117–20.

53. *TG* 2:530; Walleck memorandum, 24 Oct. 1935, BH, MK/45196. The collusion between Hitler and Goebbels is also apparent from *TG* 2:646.

54. Details in various documents in BH, MK/45196; BH, MK/41010. The Promi's pressure is apparent from Walleck to Wagner, 6 Feb. 1936, BH, MK/45196.

55. *VB*, 7 Jan. 1937.

56. See Walleck to Wagner, as early as 28 Apr. 1936, BH, MK/45196. Also [Walleck] to Wagner, 31 Aug. 1936, ibid.

57. "Dienstvertrag" for Bavaria and Krauss, Munich, 1 Sept. 1936, BH, MK/45196.

58. Ibid.

59. [Krauss] memorandum, n.d., BH, MK/45196; Ranczak in Proebst and Ude, *München*, 235; Joseph Gregor, *Clemens Krauss: Seine musikalische Sendung* (Bad Bocklet, 1953), 125; von Pander, *Krauss*, 30, 74.

60. Hotter in Josef Müller-Marein and Hannes Reinhardt, eds., *Das musikalische Selbstportrait von Komponisten, Dirigenten, Instrumentalisten, Sängerinnen und Sängern unserer Zeit* (Hamburg, 1965), 280.

61. Ranczak in Proebst and Ude, *München*, 234.

62. Krauss memorandum, 22 Apr. 1938, BH, MK/41010. On the contract renewal, see Krauss contract, 2 July 1938, BH, MK/45196.

63. *VB*, 30 Apr. 1938; Hartmann, *Haus*, 140; Scanzoni and Kende, *Prinzipal*, 217. On friction, see *TG* 3:178; Walleck "Vormerkung," 4 Dec. 1937, BH, MK/45196; Scanzoni and Kende, *Prinzipal*, 215–16.

64. Gertrud to Paul Hindemith, 15 Mar. [1939], PF, 3.144.22–37.

65. Walleck, "Vormerkung," 4 Dec. 1937, BH, MK/45196. See also Hartmann, *Haus*, 128.

66. Ney to van Hoogstraten, 23 Mar. 1939, EB, 0.26. See also Abendroth to Pfitzner, 9 Jan. 1937, OW, 211.

67. Krauss to Hitler, 25 Apr. 1938, BDC Krauss.

68. Adolf Hitler, *Mein Kampf*, 26th ed. (Munich, 1933), 55 (quote); *TGII* 8:538–40; Scanzoni and Kende, *Prinzipal*, 247. On Hitler's continued admiration, see Picker, *Tischgespräche*, 396; *TGII* 9:584; Hartmann, *Haus*, 151.

69. *TGII* 3:249; Anderman [Thomas], *Vorhang*, 132–33.

70. Von Pander, *Krauss*, 112; "Dienstvertrag" for Krauss, [Jan. 1941, retroactive 1 Apr. 1940], BH, MK/45196.

71. Details are in the designated files in BH, i.e., MK/41010 and 45196.

72. Mezger to Krauss, 20 Jan. 1942, BH, MK/45196; Ellis, "Music," 220.

73. Götz Klaus Kende and Willi Schuh, eds., *Richard Strauss Clemens Krauss: Briefwechsel* (Munich, 1963), 228–31; Krauss to Hitler, 24 Sept. 1944, BH, Staatstheater/14739.

74. Bormann office to Giesler, 1 Sept. 1943, BH, MK/45196; *TGII* 7:310.

75. *Richard Strauss: Briefwechsel mit Willi Schuh* (Zurich, 1969), 56; Giesler to Bormann, 3 Jan. 1943 [recte 1944], BH, MK/45196; Ellis, "Music," 225.

76. *TGII* 10:112, 132, 137, 192, 194; Müller to Press, 9 May 1944, BDC Krauss; Giesler telex to Bormann, received 1 Sept. 1944, BH, MK/45196; *Strauss: Briefwechsel Schuh*, 68; Kende and Schuh, *Briefwechsel*, 269; Scanzoni and Kende, *Prinzipal*, 230.

77. Krauss to Hitler, 24 Sept. 1944, BH, Staatstheater/14739.

78. Strauss to Thomas, 16 Oct. 1944, RG; Bormann telegram to Giesler, 4 Nov. 1944, BH, Staatstheater/14846.

79. Cited in Rathkolb, *Führertreu*, 110. Upon hearing Krauss conducting in Berlin in April 1935, the American ambassador William Dodd referred to him as "the Austrian Nazi conductor" (William E. Dodd, Jr., and Martha Dodd, eds., *Ambassador Dodd's Diary, 1933–1938* [New York, 1941], 232). See also Ernst Lothar, *Das Wunder des Überlebens: Erinnerungen und Ergebnisse* (Hamburg, 1960), 356. In his memoirs Frauenfeld acknowledges having known Krauss privately but mentions nothing political (*Reu'*, 54). On Ursuleac, see Stephan Stompor, "Oper in Berlin von 1933 bis 1945," *Beiträge zur Musikwissenschaft* 28 (1986), 30.

80. Elisabeth Wamlek-Junk, ed., *Hans Pfitzner und Wien: Sein Briefwechsel mit Victor Junk und andere Dokumente* (Tutzing, 1986), 101.

81. I owe this information to Gerhard Botz.

82. Gottfried von Einem, recorded interview, Vienna, 30 Nov. 1994, APA (quote); see also von Einem to Orff, 23 Aug. 1943, CM, Allg. Korr.; Maschat, "Nachruf," 29; Hotter to author, Munich, 12 Dec. 1994, APA. Hotter also writes that Krauss tried to shield two non-"Aryan" artists. This is corroborated in Scanzoni and Kende, *Prinzipal*, 169.

83. Nazi Party judgments of 15 Feb., 3 Mar., and 27 June 1941 in BDC Krauss; Rosenberg judgment quoted in Rathkolb, *Führertreu*, 112.

84. Hartmann, *Haus*, 129; Maschat, "Nachruf," 31; Michael H. Kater, *Different Drummers: Jazz in the Culture of Nazi Germany* (New York, 1992), 101; *TGII* 7:297, 509.

85. Krauss to Reinhard, 13 Oct. 1937, SMK, 97/7 (1st quote); von Pander, *Krauss*, 35 (2nd and 3rd quotes).

86. Egk proposal [for Goebbels, Oct. 1941], BDC Egk. Schultze was not really a "serious" composer. See the list in von Pander, *Krauss*, 12–20, which curiously omits Orff's *Der Mond* (Feb. 1939).

87. Orff to Strecker, 4 Feb. 1938 and 25 Jan. 1939, CM, Schott Korr.; Preussner to Orff, 13 Nov. 1942, CM, Allg. Korr.; *JdM 1944*, 129 (quote); Michael H. Kater, "Carl Orff im Dritten Reich," *Vierteljahrshefte für Zeitgeschichte* 43 (1995), 11, 20–21.

88. See n. 67.

89. Pfitzner to Schütz, 21 Aug. 1940, OW, 958; Hans Pfitzner, *Sämtliche Schriften*, ed. Bernhard Adamy (Tutzing, 1987), 323.

90. Reimer to [Hanke], 21 Oct. 1943, BA, R55/198; Wagner to Schaub, 13 Mar. 1942; Mezger "Aktenvormerkung," 22 July 1943; Giesler to Mezger, 28 Aug. 1943; Giesler to Bormann, 3 Jan. 1943 [recte 1944]; Mezger "Vormerkung," 21 Feb. 1944, BH, MK/45196; Krauss to Hitler, 24 Sept. 1944, BH, Staatstheater/14739; Bormann to Giesler, 1 Jan. 1945, BH, Staatstheater/18846; *TGII* 7:78.

91. There is plenty of evidence in the appropriate files in BH (see n. 71).

92. ZM 109 (1942), 420; Hellsberg, *Demokratie*, 478.

93. *JdM 1943*, 78–80; *TG* 4:210.

94. Hellsberg, *Demokratie*, 480; Präg and Jacobmeyer, *Diensttagebuch*, 618, 660, 776.

95. Krauss to Wagner, 9 Mar. 1942, BH, MK/45196; ZM 109 (1942), 237; von Westerman to Promi, 21 May 1942, BA R55/198; Kende and Schuh, *Briefwechsel*, 231.

96. ZM 107 (1940), 368; Kurt Preis, *München unterm Hakenkreuz: Die Hauptstadt der Bewegung: Zwischen Pracht und Trümmern* (Munich, 1980), 211–12.

97. *LI*, 364; Ernst Haeussermann, *Herbert von Karajan: Eine Biographie*, 2nd ed. (Vienna, 1983), 43–63; Hansjakob Kröber, *Herbert von Karajan: Der Magier mit dem Taktstock* (Munich, 1986), 42–67, 89 (quotes on 43–44). On the characteristics of his style, see Blaukopf, *Dirigenten*, 85; Hans Hotter in Wessling, *Hotter*, 71. On Karajan's early Berlin successes, see *DAZ*, 9 Apr. 1938; *DM* 31 (1939), 564.

98. ZM 107 (1940), 767.

99. Tietjen to Strauss, 9 Mar. and 26 Oct. 1940, RG (1st quote); Strauss to von Prittwitz, 13 Aug. 1940, BS, Ana/330/I/, Prittwitz, E. von (2nd quote).

100. Kater, "Orff," 21; *Reich*, 28 Dec. 1941; Orff to List, 11 Feb. 1941, and to Pitz, 10 Jan. 1942 (quote), CM, Allg. Korr.

101. Karajan's Salzburg party number was 1607525; when he joined again in Ulm on 1 May 1933, he received the number 3430914. See Mitgliedschaftsamt to Lehmann, 5 Jan. 1939; Karajan's (provisional) Salzburg and (regular) Ulm party membership cards, BDC von Karajan. For Karajan's denial and distortions, see Paul Robinson, *Karajan* (Toronto, 1975), 12; Roger Vaughan, *Herbert von Karajan: A Biographical Portrait* (New York, 1986), 107–8; Peter Csobády, ed., *Karajan oder die kontrollierte Ekstase: Eine kritische Hommage von Zeitzeugen* (Munich, 1990), 169–70; Rathkolb, *Führertreu*, 206, 211.

102. Karajan declaration, Vienna, 18 Mar. 1946; Pernter et al., "Begut-

achtungskommission für die politische Einstellung . . . Bundesministerium für Unterricht," Vienna, 25 Mar. 1946, OSW, Unterrichtsministerium/12.

103. Mitgliedschaftsamt to Lehmann, 7 July 1939, BDC von Karajan.

104. Luis Trenker, *Alles gut gegangen: Geschichten aus meinem Leben* (Munich, 1975), 439–41; Kröber, *Karajan*, 49; *Spiegel*, 24 July 1989, 144–49.

105. See Werner Oehlmann's praise of Karajan in these terms in *Reich*, 27 Oct. 1940.

106. *Globe and Mail* (Toronto), 3 Aug. 1989.

107. Robert C. Bachmann, *Karajan: Anmerkungen zu einer Karriere*, 2nd ed. (Düsseldorf, 1983), 137; Rathkolb, *Führertreu*, 212; Vaughan, *Karajan*, 127; BDC Rudolf Vedder.

108. Haeussermann, *Karajan*, 40; Kröber, *Karajan*, 58–59, 63; Bachmann, *Karajan*, 85, 88–89, 94–95; Rathkolb, *Führertreu*, 206.

109. Bachmann, *Karajan*, 111; Rathkolb, *Führertreu*, 208–9.

110. Rathkolb, *Führertreu*, 207; Gottfried von Einem, recorded interview, Vienna, 30 Nov. 1994, APA.

111. Berndt Wilhelm Wessling, *Furtwängler: Eine kritische Biographie* (Stuttgart, 1985), 327.

112. Karla Höcker, ed., *Wilhelm Furtwängler: Dokumente—Berichte und Bilder—Aufzeichnungen* (Berlin, 1968), 94; Daniel Gillis, *Furtwängler and America* (New York, 1970), 73–78; Wessling, *Furtwängler*, 330, 334.

113. Hartmann, *Haus*, 156.

114. *TG* 4:432, 441; Muck, *Jahre* 2:172; Bachmann, *Karajan*, 137, 149; Kröber, *Karajan*, 89.

115. Marie Vassiltchikov, *Berlin Diaries, 1940–1945* (New York, 1987), 36.

116. Egon Seefehlner, *Die Musik meines Lebens: Vom Rechtspraktikanten zum Opernchef in Berlin und Wien* (Vienna, 1983), 70 (quote); *TGII* 8:386–87; *TGII* 12:59–60.

117. Abendroth to Pfitzner, 5 Aug. 1942, OW, 288; Wessling, *Furtwängler*, 338; Rathkolb, *Führertreu*, 216.

118. For examples, see Bachmann, *Karajan*, 119, 122, 125–26, 132, 134; Kröber, *Karajan*, 64, 84; Rathkolb, *Führertreu*, 210, 214; Muck, *Jahre* 3:290.

119. This is borne out by many entries in Goebbels's diaries (*TG* and *TGII*).

120. Elmendorff to [Gerdy Troost], 13 Jan. 1942, BDC Karl Elmendorff; *TG* 4:383–84; *TGII* 5:207; Ziegler, *Hitler*, 178; Bachmann, *Karajan*, 133; Kröber, *Karajan*, 92–93, 95–96; Karajan as told to Csobádi, *Karajan*, 171; *LI*, 209; Werner Jochmann, ed., *Adolf Hitler: Monologe im Führerhauptquartier, 1941–1944: Die Aufzeichnungen Heinrich Heims* (Hamburg, 1980), 198, 235, 318, 438, 444, 454.

121. BDC von Karajan; Bachmann, *Karajan*, 144; Haeussermann, *Karajan*, 67; Kröber, *Karajan*, 96; Rathkolb, *Führertreu*, 217–19. On the dangers and rarity of resigning one's party membership, see Michael H. Kater, *The Nazi Party: A Social Profile of Members and Leaders, 1919–1945* (Cambridge, Mass., 1983), 159.

122. IfZ, Munzinger-Archiv/Int. Biograph. Archiv; Legge-Schwarzkopf to author, Zumikon, 9 May 1994, APA.

123. Cf. the versions in Schwarzkopf declaration, [1945–46], OSW, Unterrichtsministerium/12; Rathkolb, *Führertreu*, 97; Bachmann, *Karajan*, 366, n. 9a; Peter G. Davis in *Opera News*, 9 Dec. 1995, 33 (quote).

124. Legge-Schwarzkopf to author, Zumikon, 9 May 1994; Ritter to author, Vaduz, 27 May 1994; author to Legge-Schwarzkopf, Toronto, 6 Jan. 1992 and 18 May 1994; author to Ritter, Toronto, 15 June 1994, all APA.

125. Schwarzkopf quoted in David Patrick Stearns, "The Schwarzkopf," *Opera News*, 9 Dec. 1995, 28; and *International Herald Tribune*, 18 Mar. 1983; see also Rathkolb, *Führertreu*, 96–97.

126. Vollerthun to Rühlmann, 7 Sept. 1935, BDC Georg Vollerthun; Schwarzkopf's short curriculum vitae, n.d.; Schwarzkopf "Personal-Fragebogen," 6 May 1938, BDC Schwarzkopf.

127. Schwarzkopf "Personal-Fragebogen," 6 May 1938, BDC Schwarzkopf; Alan Jefferson, *Elisabeth Schwarzkopf* (London, 1996), 24. On the political significance of her office, that of "Fachschaftsführerin der ANSt," see Jacques R. Pauwels, *Women, Nazis, and Universities: Female University Students in the Third Reich, 1933–1945* (Westport, Conn., 1984), 55–70, 74–75.

128. Schwarzkopf declaration, 3 May 1938; Rode and Schwarzkopf "Dienstvertrag," 3 and 9 May 1938, BDC Schwarzkopf.

129. Schwarzkopf "Personalfragebogen" [1940], BDC Schwarzkopf. Rode's self-serving interest in Schwarzkopf is well documented in his letter to Keppler, 29 Oct. 1941, BDC Schwarzkopf.

130. Schwarzkopf file, BDC Schwarzkopf. Quote from Batteux "Meldung," 9 June 1939, ibid.

131. According to Rathkolb, *Führertreu*, 97.

132. Her NSDAP number was 7548960. She had applied to join on 26 Jan. 1940. Her registration card is in BDC Schwarzkopf. For her NSV membership, see Fischer memorandum, 6 Dec. 1940, ibid. Examples of her letters are Schwarzkopf to Generalintendant [Rode], 30 Oct. 1939 and 24 Feb. 1940, ibid.

133. *TGII* 7:65 (quote); *TGII* 8:568.

134. Rathkolb, *Führertreu*, 97; Rode to Schlösser, 11 July 1942; Schwarzkopf "Urlaubs-Gesuch," 17 Feb. and 15 Apr. 1941; Schwarzkopf to Hinkel, 22 Apr. 1942, BDC Schwarzkopf. Also see text below at n. 185.

135. For the season 1 Aug. 1942–31 July 1943 Schwarzkopf was to be offered 14,000 marks. See draft of "Dienstvertrag," [1942], and related documents (1940–41) in BDC Schwarzkopf; Rode to Schlösser, 11 July 1942; Rode to Schwarzkopf, 11 July 1942, ibid.

136. Corr. (1943–44) in BDC Schwarzkopf. Goebbels's decision is documented in Hinkel memorandum, 20 May 1944, ibid.

137. *LI*, 663; IfZ, Munzinger-Archiv/Int. Biograph. Archiv.

138. *Ostdeutscher Beobachter*, 7 Sept. 1942 (quote); ZM 109 (1942), 558; Winkler to Greiser, 17 Sept. 1942; Schwarzkopf to Pfitzner, 21 Sept. 1942, OW, 61.

139. "Amt Truppenbetreuung . . . Betr.: Einzeleinsatz der Sängerin Elisabeth Schwarzkopf," 25 Jan. 1943, BDC Schwarzkopf.

140. *TGII* 2:171; IfZ, Munzinger-Archiv/Int. Biogr. Archiv. Lothar passed on the information about the liaison to composer Gottfried von Einem in Salzburg (Gottfried von Einem, recorded interview, Vienna, 30 Nov. 1994, APA), but it has yet to be documented in archival records. Right after the war Jury avoided trial by committing suicide (IfZ, Munzinger-Archiv/Int. Biogr. Archiv). On Lothar's function, see his *Wunder*, 258–62.

141. Blaukopf, *Dirigenten*, 58–59; *LI*, 76; Anton Dermota, *Tausendundein Abend* (Vienna, 1978), 146.

142. Adolph to Strauss, 7 Feb. 1935, RG; Strauss to Drewes, 22 Aug. 1938, BS, Fasc. germ. (Drewes); *Strauss: Briefwechsel Schuh,* 57; Pfitzner to Nieland, 28 Dec. 1941, OW, 261.

143. Böhm, *Ich,* 73; *Skizzen* (Feb. 1938), 23; Kater, "Orff," 21.

144. *Skizzen* (Feb. 1938), 23; Rathkolb, *Führertreu,* 102–3; Kater, *Different Drummers,* 90–92. See also chapter 5, at n. 24.

145. Schuh to Egk, [1942?], BS, Ana/410; Böhm, *Ich,* 84; Hans Heinz Stuckenschmidt, *Boris Blacher* (Berlin, 1963), 14. On Schuh, see *GLM* 7:291; on Neher, see Ronald Taylor, *Kurt Weill: Composer in a Divided World* (London, 1991), passim. See also chapter 5, at n. 219.

146. See text at n. 136; Hinkel memorandum, 20 May 1944, BDC Schwarzkopf (quote); Rathkolb, *Führertreu,* 124; minutes of broadcast planning committee, 2 Aug. 1944, BA, R55/556; *TGII* 12:228.

147. Böhm, *Ich,* 86–88; Böhm in Müller-Marein and Reinhardt, *Selbstportrait,* 80.

148. Böhm, *Ich,* 68 (1st quote); Böhm's letter to Willy [Rode] of 25 Apr. 1934, quoted in Scanzoni and Kende, *Prinzipal,* 200 (2nd quote); Ahrens to Hinkel, 2 Sept. 1933, BDC Karl Muck; *Melos* 12 (1933), 351.

149. Rathkolb, *Führertreu,* 45, 99.

150. Böhm quoted in Albrecht Dümling and Peter Girth, eds., *Entartete Musik: Zur Düsseldorfer Ausstellung von 1938: Eine kommentierte Rekonstruktion* (Düsseldorf, [1988]), 58; and Rathkolb, *Führertreu,* 104.

151. *Skizzen* (Oct. 1937), 22.

152. Böhm, *Ich,* 83; *TG* 3:84, 260; *TGII* 2:344, 409, 415; *TGII* 7:401; Pietzsch to Orff, 23 Nov. 1941, CM, Allg. Korr.; Anderman [Thomas], *Vorhang,* 131; Kende and Schuh, *Briefwechsel,* 233.

153. *TGII* 3:129, 508; *TGII* 5:207; Hinkel to Reichspropagandaamtsleiter Wien, 15 Mar. 1943, BDC Hans Knappertsbusch.

154. Hellsberg, *Demokratie,* 478.

155. "Biographie von Hans Rosbaud," [1945], LP, 423/1/2; Gertrud Hindemith to Rosbaud, 20 June [1929], 423/1/8; Hartmann to Paul Hindemith, 4 Feb. 1946, BS, Ana/407; *LI,* 615.

156. See Joan Evans, *Hans Rosbaud: A Bio-Bibliography* (New York, 1992), 19–21, 48–50.

157. Ibid., 29–30; statement of appreciation by Stravinsky, Paris, Sept. 1936, LP, 423/1/3.

158. Evans, *Rosbaud,* 28–29; Kater, "Orff," 20; "5. Musikvereinskonzert," Münster, 10 Feb. 1939, LP, 423/8/134.

159. Rosbaud to Bartók, 18 July 1935, LP, 423/33/603.

160. Quoted in Evans, *Rosbaud,* 34.

161. Ibid., 31–34; Böhm interview, *Zeit,* 15 Dec. 1978.

162. Seiber to Orff, 12 Oct. 1932, CM, Allg. Korr.

163. See Rosbaud in Müller-Marein and Reinhardt, *Selbstportrait,* 198 (quote); "Biographie von Hans Rosbaud," [1945], LP, 423/1/2.

164. The first quote is from private notes taken by jazz fan Dietrich Schulz-Köhn, "Vortrag vom Intendanten Herrn Otto Fricke Frankfurt/M am 9.12.35," APA. The second is from *DM* 28 (1936), 292. See also Kater, *Different Drummers,* 49.

165. Observation by Swiss composer Heinrich Sutermeister, a Nazi sympathizer, in letter to Orff, [summer 1936], CM, Allg. Korr.

166. Details regarding the case (1936–37) are in BDC Felix Josef Hess; Koch, "In Sachen Hess/Reichssender Frankfurt a.M.," 3 July 1936, LP, 423/1/2.

167. Hessen to Schueller, 5 Apr. 1933, LP, 423/1/2. An example of blatant anti-Semitism is Prince Hessen to Rosbaud, 8 Mar. 1941, LP, 413/5/74.

168. Rosbaud declaration, [post-1945], LP, 423/33/755; Rosbaud in Müller-Marein and Reinhardt, Selbstportrait, 199.

169. Hildebrand/Rosbaud agreement, Münster, 16 Oct. 1937, LP, 423/1/2.

170. "15.-22. April Gau-Kulturwoche Westfalen-Nord 1939: Eröffnungsfeier," and other relevant documents in LP, 423/8/134; ZM 107 (1940), 274.

171. "Gaukulturwoche Westfalen-Nord 1940," LP, 423/8/134.

172. Gerhard L. Weinberg, A World at Arms: A Global History of World War II (Cambridge, 1994), 514.

173. TGII 9:75; "Die Reichsuniversitäten Strassburg und Posen," Deutscher Wochendienst, 174/43, no. 7488, 4 Sept. 1942, BA; Lothar Kettenacker, Nationalsozialistische Volkstumspolitik im Elsass (Stuttgart, 1973), 91.

174. ZM 109 (1942), 38.

175. Newspaper fragment, 28 Feb. 1941, LP, 423/8/134 (quote); Kettenacker, Volkstumspolitik, 91.

176. Rosbaud to Lange, 24 July 1943, LP, 423/1/10.

177. The phrase is Evans's (Rosbaud, 36).

178. Elisabeth Furtwängler, Über Wilhelm Furtwängler (Wiesbaden, 1979), 128; Annemay Schlusnus on behalf of her husband, baritone Heinrich Schlusnus, in Eckart von Naso, Heinrich Schlusnus: Mensch und Sänger (Hamburg, 1957), 180–81.

179. Rosbaud declaration, [post-1945], LP, 423/33/755; Rosbaud in Müller-Marein and Reinhardt, Selbstportrait, 199. See also Evans, Rosbaud, 37.

180. Evans, Rosbaud, 38–39; ZM 108 (1941), 690; MK 2 (1944), 78. Material on Frederick the Great in LP, 423/1/10. As a typical example, the king is glorified in an article exalting "tough education" in the SS journal SS-Leitheft 9, no. 1 (Jan. 1943), 12–14. See also TGII 4:135; TGII 7:292, 294–95; TGII 8:281, 365, 425, 536. On the Strasbourg orchestra, see Peter Heyworth, Otto Klemperer: His Life and Times, 2 vols. (Cambridge, 1983, 1996), 2:64.

181. See n. 179. See also "Biographie von Hans Rosbaud," [1945], LP, 423/1/2; Paul Rosbaud to Hans and Edel Rosbaud, 18 Nov. 1946, LP, 423/1/13; Ludwig to Maitre [Rosbaud], 17 Feb. 1946, LP, 423/3/46.

182. RMK comment on registration card for Valentin Grimm, 20 May 1941, BDC Grimm.

183. On conscription, see Kettenacker, Volkstumspolitik, 92.

184. BDC Schneiderhan; Rathkolb, Führertreu, 91; Friedelind Wagner, Nacht über Bayreuth: Die Geschichte der Enkelin Richard Wagners (Bern, [1946]), 184.

185. Sketch of seating arrangement, "Abendtafel am Dienstag, dem 25. März 1935," PA Martin Haushofer, Herrsching; TG 2:556; TG 4:298; TGII 5:157, 194; TGII 8:414; TGII 12:78, 120; AMR, 15 Mar. 1942, BA, RD33/2–2; minutes of broadcast planning committee, 24 Sept. 1942, BA, R55/696; BDC Raucheisen (1941–44); LI, 58, 590.

186. LI, 298; sketch of seating arrangement, see n. 185; Hinkel to Stang, 27 Aug. 1936; Grümmer to Hinkel, 23 Nov. 1936; Grümmer to Reichsminister [Goebbels], 15 Dec. 1941, BDC Grümmer.

187. Skizzen (Oct. 1937), 20 (quote); "Erster Abend im Gürzenich mit dem Reichssender Köln: 'Vom goldnen Überfluss,'" 18 Oct. 1939, LP, 423/8/134;

Gieseking to Hinkel, 3 Nov. 1933; Hinkel to Gieseking, 17 Nov. 1933 and 22 Mar. 1944; Lammers to Hinkel, 15 Nov. 1933, BDC Gieseking; *ZM* 107 (1940), 298; Hans-Peter Range, *Die Konzertpianisten der Gegenwart: Ein Musikliebhaber berichtet über Konzertmilieu und 173 Klaviervirtuosen,* 2nd ed. (Lahr, 1966), 116; Karl Grunsky, *Der Kampf um deutsche Musik* (Stuttgart, 1933), 34; Cornelia Zimmermann-Kalyoncu, *Deutsche Musiker in der Türkei im 20. Jahrhundert* (Frankfurt am Main, 1985), 56. On Backhaus, Fischer, and Kempff, see Konzertverein München e.V. to Siebert, 21 Mar. 1936, BH, MA/107486; *TGII* 8:443; *MK* 2 (1944), 33; BDC Edwin Fischer; Funk to Wiedemann, 9 Aug. 1935, BDC Johannes Strauss.

188. Hotter to author, Munich, 14 Dec. 1994, APA; author's telephone conversation with Hotter, Munich, 14 Dec. 1994; Rössner to [Fischer], 21 Sept. 1943, BDC Hotter; Hitler paraphrased by Goebbels in *TGII* 4:408. Nonnenbruch is documented in *Wer ist's?,* 10th ed., ed. Herrmann A. L. Degener (Berlin, 1935), 1151.

189. *MGG* 12:1638; *NG* 18:310; Fred K. Prieberg, *Lexikon der Neuen Musik* (Freiburg, 1958), 155–56; Karl H. Wörner, *Neue Musik in der Entscheidung* (Mainz, 1954), 287–88; William W. Austin, *Music in the 20th Century from Debussy Through Stravinsky* (New York, 1966), 492; Bruno Stürmer, "Die Neue Tonalität," *DM* 24 (1931), 118–20.

190. *ZM* 107 (1940), 727; *ZM* 108 (1941), 171, 241, 265, 344; *ZM* 109 (1942), 71, 311; *MK* 1 (1943), 117; *MK* 1 (1944), 230; *JdM 1944,* 24, 28–30; Nanny Drechsler, *Die Funktion der Musik im deutschen Rundfunk, 1933–1945* (Pfaffenweiler, 1988), 91; Ulrike Gruner, *Musikleben in der Provinz, 1933–45: Beispiel Marburg: Eine Studie anhand der Musikberichterstattung in der Lokalpresse* (Marburg, 1990), 75, 132.

191. See *MGG* 12:1638; Eberhard Preussner, "Das Singen in den gemischten Chören," in Wolfgang Stumme, ed., *Musik im Volk: Grundfragen der Musikerziehung* (Berlin, 1939), 170.

192. *Melos* 12 (1933), 307; *Melos* 13 (1934), 112; Bachmann, *Karajan,* 120.

193. Friedrich Welter, *Musikgeschichte im Umriss: Vom Urbeginn bis zur Gegenwart* (Leipzig, n.d.), 315; Gerhart Winter, "Über den heutigen Stand der deutschen Blasmusik," *ZM* 107 (1940), 13; *M* 109 (1942), 472; *JdM 1943,* 51.

194. Wilhelm Ehmann, *Musikalische Feiergestaltung: Ein Werkweiser guter Musik für die natürlichen und politischen Feste des Jahres* (Hamburg, 1938); Winter, "Stand," 13; *ZM* (108), 267–68; *Musik der Hitler-Jugend* (Wolfenbüttel, 1941), 32; *MK* 1 (1944), 228; *MK* 2 (1944), 117; *Reichskulturkammer,* no. 3/4, 1944, 61 (BA, RD33/1); Schaal to Pfitzner, 29 Dec. 1943, OW, 257; Gruner, *Musikleben,* 72.

195. *ZM* 108 (1941), 707; *ZM* 109 (1942), 39–40; *MK* 1 (1943), 116; *Musik,* 26; Ehmann, *Feiergestaltung,* 40, 45, 82–83.

196. Ludwig F. Schiedermair, *Musiker Schicksale: Aus dem Leben grosser Komponisten* (Berlin, 1990), 214.

197. Hans and Rosaleen Moldenhauer, *Anton von Webern: A Chronicle of His Life and Work* (New York, 1979), 391, 395, 473 (quote).

198. Louis Krasner, as told to Don C. Seibert, "Some Memories of Anton Webern, the Berg Concerto, and Vienna in the 1930s," *Fanfare* 11 (1987), 335.

199. Schoenberg quoted in Moldenhauer, *Webern,* 410. See also ibid., 411–12; Schoenberg to Webern, 4 Aug. 1933, AI, gen. corr.; Ernst Hilmar, "Arnold

Schönberg an Anton Webern: Eine Auswahl unbekannter Briefe," in Hilmar, ed., *Arnold Schönberg: Gedenkausstellung 1974* (Vienna, 1974), 57.

200. Moldenhauer, *Webern*, 408, 414, 474 (1st quote from Webern); Schoenberg and Webern quoted in Nuria Nono-Schoenberg, ed., *Arnold Schönberg, 1874–1951: Lebensgeschichte in Begegnungen* (Klagenfurt, 1992), 339; remaining quotes from Krasner, "Memories," 337. See also Peter Stadlen in *Österreichische Musikzeitschrift* 43 (1988), 195.

201. Hans Severus Ziegler, *Entartete Musik: Eine Abrechnung* (Düsseldorf, [1938]), 17; Moldenhauer, *Webern*, 491, 497–98, 503, 516–17, 531.

202. Webern quoted in Moldenhauer, *Webern*, 527; Walter Trienes, *Musik in Gefahr: Selbstzeugnisse aus der Verfallszeit* (Regensburg, 1940), 37 (3rd quote).

203. Moldenhauer, *Webern*, 522, 543–44.

204. Webern to Rasch, 9 Nov. 1940, BDC Webern.

205. Webern, "Fragebogen betr. Spende 'Künstlerdank,'" 27 Nov. 1940; RMK postscript, ibid., 21 Feb. 1941; Rasch's recorded decision of 24 Feb. 1941, ibid., BDC Webern.

CHAPTER 3

1. Paragraph 3, *Reichsgesetzblatt I* (1933), 175; Uwe Dietrich Adam, *Judenpolitik im Dritten Reich* (Düsseldorf, 1979), 51–71.

2. Michael H. Kater, *Doctors Under Hitler* (Chapel Hill, N.C., 1989), 186–200.

3. *Das Schwarzbuch—Tatsachen und Dokumente: Die Lage der Juden in Deutschland 1933* (1934; rpt., Frankfurt am Main, 1983), 406; Walter L. Laqueur, *Weimar: Die Kultur der Republik* (Frankfurt am Main, 1974), 198–206; Fred K. Prieberg, *Kraftprobe: Wilhelm Furtwängler im Dritten Reich* (Wiesbaden, 1986), 12.

4. Petra Maria Valentin, "Die Bayerische Staatsoper im Dritten Reich" (M.A. thesis, University of Munich, 1985), 106; Oliver Rathkolb, *Führertreu und gottbegnadet: Künstlereliten im Dritten Reich* (Vienna, 1991), 128; Clemens Hellsberg, *Demokratie der Könige: Die Geschichte der Wiener Philharmoniker* (Zurich, 1992), 464.

5. Goebbels as quoted in *AMR*, 1 June 1938, BA, RD33/2–1.

6. See Albrecht Riethmüller, *Die Walhalla und ihre Musiker* (Laaber, 1993).

7. Karl Adler to Rieger, 27 Feb. 1933, LBI, AR-7276/IV/2/15.

8. Richard Eichenauer, "Über die Grundsätze rassenkundlicher Musikbetrachtung," in Guido Waldmann, ed., *Musik und Rasse* (Berlin, 1939), 22–48 (quote on 23).

9. Friedrich Blume, *Das Rasseproblem in der Musik: Entwurf zu einer Methodologie musikwissenschaftlicher Rasseforschung* (Wolfenbüttel, 1939), esp. 3, 82–83.

10. Albrecht Riethmüller, "German Music from the Perspective of German Musicology after 1933," *Journal of Musicological Research* 11 (1991), 178–79.

11. Michael Alt, *Deutsche Art in der Musik* (Leipzig, 1936); Siegfried Günther, *Musikerziehung als nationale Aufgabe* (Heidelberg, 1933), 16, 51, 53, 55; Friedrich W. Herzog, "Was ist deutsche Musik? Erkenntnisse und Folgerungen," *DM* 26 (1934), 801–6; Karl Hasse, *Von deutschen Meistern: Zur Neugestaltung unseres Musiklebens im neuen Deutschland: Ausgewählte Aufsätze* (Regensburg,

1934), 115; Robert Pessenlehner, *Vom Wesen der Deutschen Musik* (Regensburg, 1937), 176; Richard Eichenauer, *Polyphonie—Die ewige Sprache deutscher Seele* (Wolfenbüttel, 1938), 70; Friedrich Welter, *Musikgeschichte im Umriss: Vom Urbeginn bis zur Gegenwart* (Leipzig, n.d.), 279.

12. Pessenlehner, *Wesen,* 163, 169–71, 176, 184–85; Karl Grunsky, *Der Kampf um deutsche Musik* (Stuttgart, 1933), 5; Fritz Metzler, "Rassische Grundkräfte im Volkslied," in Waldmann, *Musik,* 70–71; Karl Blessinger, *Mendelssohn, Meyerbeer, Mahler: Drei Kapitel Judentum in der Musik als Schlüssel zur Musikgeschichte des 19. Jahrhunderts* (Berlin, 1939), 38; Hans Severus Ziegler, *Entartete Musik: Eine Abrechnung* (Düsseldorf, [1938]), 28–29; for a critical view, see Albrecht Riethmüller, "Die Erneuerung der Kirchenmusik im Dritten Reich—Eine Legende?," *Kirchenmusiker* 40 (1989), 165–66. On the lur, see *GLM* 5:169–70; *NG* 11:338–39 (quote).

13. Richard Litterscheid, "Mendelssohn, Mahler und wir," *DM* 28 (1936), 413–17; Herzog, "Was," 802, 805–6; Pessenlehner, *Wesen,* 160–62, 178; Blessinger, *Mendelssohn,* 29; Günther, *Musikerziehung,* 55; Hasse, *Meistern,* 9.

14. Walter Abendroth, "Opernideale der Rassen und Völker," *DM* 28 (1936), 424; Pessenlehner, *Wesen,* 162, 166, 173; Eichenauer, "Grundsätze," 32; Hans Brückner, "Judentum und ernste Musik," *DDP,* 10 July 1936, 1.

15. Strecker to Nadia Boulanger, 15 Mar. 1937, PF, Schott Korr.; Litterscheid, "Mendelssohn," 414 (quote).

16. Brückner, "Judentum," 1–4; Pessenlehner, *Wesen,* 161–62, 175–76, 178–79; Herzog, "Was," 801–2; Blessinger, *Mendelssohn,* 9–10, 19, 29, 38; Litterscheid, "Mendelssohn," 415; Welter, *Musikgeschichte,* 276, 282; Abendroth, "Opernideale," 424; Eichenauer, "Grundsätze," 32.

17. Pessenlehner, *Wesen,* 167–77; Blessinger, *Mendelssohn,* 11, 77 (1st quote), 94; Welter, *Musikgeschichte,* 279–80, 282 (2nd quote); Eichenauer, "Grundsätze," 32; Litterscheid, "Mendelssohn," 413–17; Wolfgang Stumme, "Musikpolitik als Führungsaufgabe," in Stumme, ed., *Musik im Volk: Gegenwartsfragen der deutschen Musik* (Berlin-Lichterfelde, 1944), 13; Albrecht Dümling and Peter Girth, eds., *Entartete Musik: Zur Düsseldorfer Ausstellung von 1938: Eine kommentierte Rekonstruktion* (Düsseldorf, [1988]), 15.

18. Pamela M. Potter, "The Deutsche Musikgesellschaft, 1918–1938," *Journal of Musicological Research* 11 (1991), 168–71. Also see her "Musicology under Hitler: New Sources in Context," *Journal of the American Musicological Society* 49 (1996), 70–113.

19. Ziegler, *Musik; Führer durch die Ausstellung Entartete Kunst* [Munich, 1937]. See also Fred K. Prieberg, *Musik und Macht* (Frankfurt am Main, 1991), 175, 179.

20. *VB,* 27 May 1938.

21. Walter Rischer, *Die nationalsozialistische Kulturpolitik in Düsseldorf, 1933–1945* (Düsseldorf, 1972), 66–68; Kim H. Kowalke, "Accounting for Success: Misunderstanding *Die Dreigroschenoper,*" *Opera Quarterly* 22, no. 3 (1989), 22.

22. Ziegler, *Musik,* 6, 12.

23. Ibid., passim; Michael H. Kater, *Different Drummers: Jazz in the Culture of Nazi Germany* (New York, 1992).

24. Volkmann to Bavarian Culture Ministry, 31 Mar. 1933, BDC Fritz Volkmann; Müller to Hinkel, 24 Aug. 1933, BDC Hans Schwieger; Snaga to Hinkel, 8 Oct. 1933, BDC Franz Snaga; Hüneke to Preussischer The-

aterausschuss, 21 Feb. 1934, BDC Gerhard Hüneke; Max Butting, *Musikgeschichte, die ich miterlebte* (Berlin, 1955), 199.

25. Adam, *Judenpolitik*, esp. 82–90.

26. *DKW*, no. 8 (1933), 5–6; Paul Schwers in *AMZ* 60 (1933), 151 (1st quote); "Einführung des neuen Direktors der Hochschule für Musik," [Berlin, spring 1933], BDC Fritz Stein; Furtwängler to Rust, 4 June 1933, BDC Furtwängler (2nd quote).

27. Toscanini et al. quoted in Nicolas Slonimsky, *Music Since 1900*, 4th ed. (New York, 1971), 564; Ferdinand Beussel, "Im Zeichen der Wende," *DM 25* (1933), 671; George R. Marek, *Toscanini* (New York, 1975), 7–8; Harvey Sachs, *Toscanini* (Philadelphia, 1978), 222–23; Hartmut Zelinsky, ed., *Richard Wagner—ein deutsches Thema: Eine Dokumentation zur Wirkungsgeschichte Richard Wagners, 1876–1976*, 3rd ed. (Berlin, 1983), 211; Frederic Spotts, *Bayreuth: A History of the Wagner Festival* (New Haven, 1994), 170–71.

28. The original letter is in Berta Geissmar, *Musik im Schatten der Politik*, 4th ed., ed. Fred K. Prieberg (Zurich, 1985), 86–89 (my translation according to Slonimsky, *Music*, 571). See also Erika and Klaus Mann, *Escape to Life: Deutsche Kultur im Exil*, 2nd ed. (Munich, 1991), 239; memorandum "Kunst und Judentum," 10 Apr. 1934, BA, R55/1181; Zelinsky, *Wagner*, 236; *IBD*, 544–45.

29. Alan E. Steinweis, *Art, Ideology, and Economics in Nazi Germany: The Reich Chambers of Music, Theater, and the Visual Arts* (Chapel Hill, N.C., 1993), 107.

30. Friedelind Wagner, *Nacht über Bayreuth: Die Geschichte der Enkelin Richard Wagners* (Bern, [1946]), 129–30; Spotts, *Bayreuth*, 168.

31. Ihlert to Strauss, 12 Dec. 1933, RG; Hans-Joachim Weinbrenner, ed., *Handbuch des Deutschen Rundfunks 1938* (Heidelberg, 1938), 266–70 (1st quote on 268); Karl-Friedrich Schrieber, *Die Reichskulturkammer: Organisation und Ziele der deutschen Kultupolitik* (Berlin, 1934), 28–29; Steinweis, *Art*, 107; Kater, *Different Drummers*, 35, 38–39; Achterlitz certification for Barnet Licht, 26 Sept. 1934, in Fred K. Prieberg, "Musik unterm Davidsstern," in *Geschlossene Vorstellung: Der Jüdische Kulturbund in Deutschland, 1933–1941* (Berlin, 1992), 113. See the case of Jewish opera singer Adolf Schwersenz, who completed the questionnaire on 12 July 1934 but was not expelled from the RMK until 3 Dec. 1936, and of violinist Betty Francken, questionnaire dated 19 Oct. 1934, expulsion 12 Mar. 1936 (BDC Schwersenz and Francken).

32. Strauss's draft of RMK statute, Garmisch, 38 Dec. 1933; Strauss to Rasch, 5 Mar. 1935 (quote); Ihlert to Hinkel, 22 May 1935; Stueckgold to Strauss, 28 Jan. 1947, RG; Weinbrenner, *Handbuch*, 268; *AMR*, 25 Apr. 1934, in Dümling and Girth, *Musik*, 48; Rasch to Strauss, 18 Jan. 1935, NWH, 975/15; Steinweis, *Art*, 52.

33. *AMR*, 14 Aug. 1935 and 25 May 1937, BA, RD33/2–1; *TG* 3:223, 294; Andress special report, 29 July 1937, BA, R561/141; Adam, *Judenpolitik*, 114–44; Kater, *Different Drummers*, 46.

34. Richartz to Schönicke, 28 Nov. 1935, BA, R78/912.

35. Adam, *Judenpolitik*, 204–46; Gerhard Botz, *Wien vom "Anschluss" zum Krieg: Nationalsozialistische Machtübernahme und politisch-soziale Umgestaltung am Beispiel der Stadt Wien 1938/39* (Vienna, 1978); Rathkolb, *Führertreu*, 56–57.

36. Amt für Konzertwesen, circular no. 3, Berlin, 1 Aug. 1938, SMK, 393 (1st quote); *TG* 3:669 (2nd quote).

37. *AMR*, 15 Feb. and 1 July 1939, BA, RD33/2–2; Steinweis, *Art*, 116; *TGII* 8:207 (quote).

38. *TGII* 8:207.

39. Schuricht's file (1933) in BA, R55/1181. See Demann to Schuricht, 25 Sept. 1933, ibid.

40. Michael H. Kater, "Carl Orff im Dritten Reich," *Vierteljahrshefte für Zeitgeschichte* 43 (1995), 30–31.

41. BDC Kaminski; Bucherer judgment, Bad Tölz, 18 Sept. 1940, ibid. (quote).

42. "Zum Recht der jüdischen Mischlinge nach dem Stande vom Mai 1938," BA, R56I/114; Adam, *Judenpolitik*, 114–44.

43. *TG* 2:540. See Steinweis, *Art*, 117. As an illustration, see the case of violinist Willy Seemann, BDC Seemann.

44. Steinweis, *Art*, 111.

45. Rudolf Hartmann, *Das geliebte Haus: Mein Leben mit der Oper* (Munich, 1975), 111. On Blech, see text accompanying n. 78.

46. RRG to Reichsrundfunkkammer, 22 Feb. 1938, BA, R78/1162; *TG* 3:470; *TG* 4:113; Joseph Wulf, ed., *Musik im Dritten Reich: Eine Dokumentation* (Reinbek, 1966), 437–39, 454; Fred K. Prieberg, *Musik im NS-Staat* (Frankfurt am Main, 1982), 190.

47. *AMR*, 1 Feb. 1939, BA, RD33/2–2; Steinweis, *Art*, 117, Kohler memorandum, 29 Sept. 1939; Stegmann to Promi, 13 Oct. 1939, BA, R55/197.

48. Adam, *Judenpolitik*, 303–54; Jeremy Noakes and Geoffrey Pridham, eds., *Nazism, 1919–1945*, 3 vols. (Exeter 1983, 1984, 1988), 3:1125–35.

49. *TGII* 3:432.

50. BDC Ganns; see also Kater, *Different Drummers*, 112–18.

51. Adam, *Judenpolitik*, 329–30; *TGII* 8:126; *TGII* 9:318.

52. *Schwarze Korps*, 28 Aug. 1935, 5; *Schwarze Korps*, 5 Sept. 1935, 5; *Bayreuther Festspielführer 1937*, 245; BDC Alfred Cortot; RRG to Reichsrundfunkkammer, 21 Feb. 1938, BA, R78/1162; Kater, *Different Drummers*, 94–95.

53. Kater, *Different Drummers*, 43; *DM* 28 (1936), 278–79; *TG* 3:478, 481, 494; Staatliche Akademie der Tonkunst to Bayerisches Kultusministerium, 2 Dec. 1935; NS-Rassenpolitisches Amt to Bayerisches Kultusministerium, 22 Feb. 1936, BH, MK/14818.

54. Christa Maria Rock and Hans Brückner, eds., *Judentum und Musik: Mit dem ABC jüdischer und nichtarischer Musikbeflissener*, 2nd ed. (Munich, 1936); Kater, *Different Drummers*, 43–44.

55. Report for Reichssendeleiter, 20 Apr. 1934, BA, R78/909; memorandum for Schönicke, 8 Aug. 1935, BA R78/912; RRG to RKK, 10 Mar. 1938; [Naumann] to Schuck, 29 June 1939, BA, R78/1162.

56. Theo Stengel and Herbert Gerigk, *Lexikon der Juden in der Musik: Mit einem Titelverzeichnis jüdischer Werke* (Berlin, 1941), 233; Rock and Brückner, *Judentum*, 194; Herbert Gerigk, "Themen des Tages," *MK* 1 (1943), 43.

57. Stengel and Gerigk, *Lexikon*, 404; *DM* 34 (1942), 168; Moshe Lazar, "Arnold Schoenberg and His Doubles: A Psychodramatic Journey to His Roots," *Journal of the Arnold Schoenberg Institute* 17 (1994), 37.

58. Robert Craft, ed., *Stravinsky: Selected Correspondence*, 3 vols. (New York, 1982–85), 3:236–37, n. 29 (1st quote); interview in *Komponierende Frauen im Dritten Reich: Eine Veranstaltung im Rahmen der Reihe "1933—*

Zerstörung der Demokratie, Machtübergabe und Widerstand" (Berlin, 1983), 79 (2nd quote).

59. Strauss to von Niessen, 11 May 1935; Papesch memorandum, 24 May 1939 (quote); Strauss to Moralt, 8 July 1939, RG.

60. Raabe quoted in *DDP*, 27 Mar. 1936, 1.

61. Peter Muck, *Einhundert Jahre Berliner Philharmonisches Orchester: Darstellung in Dokumenten*, 3 vols. (Tutzing, 1982), 3:255; George W. F. Hallgarten, *Als die Schatten fielen: Erinnerungen vom Jahrhundertbeginn zur Jahrtausendwende* (Frankfurt am Main, 1969), 182; Claudia Maurer Zenck, "Erich Itor Kahn: Ein früh Unvollendeter," in Manfred Briegel and Wolfgang Frühwald, eds., *Die Erfahrung der Fremde: Kolloquium des Schwerpunktprogramms "Exilforschung" der Deutschen Forschungsgemeinschaft* (Weinheim, 1988), 240, n. 5; Salon Bergin-Bronsgeest to Exzellenz, 17 Oct. 1933, BA, R55/1141; *DM 25* (1933), 621; *Melos* 13 (1934), 28; Hartmann, *Haus*, 96 (quote); Hermann Stoffels, "Das Musiktheater in Krefeld von 1870–1945," in Ernst Klusen et al., *Das Musikleben der Stadt Krefeld: 1870–1945*, 2 vols. (Cologne, 1980), 2:216; Joan Evans, *Hans Rosbaud: A Bio-Bibliography* (New York, 1992), 21.

62. Stumme, "Musikpolitik," 11–12.

63. *MK* 1 (1944), 229; Gerigk to Drewes, 24 June 1944, facs. in Dümling and Girth, *Musik*, 61.

64. Hartmann, *Haus*, 156–57.

65. Hinkel to Richartz, 30 May 1936, BA, R78/908.

66. Volker Dahm, "Kulturelles und geistiges Leben," in Wolfgang Benz, ed., *Die Juden in Deutschland, 1933–1945* (Munich, 1988), 115; Eichenauer, *Polyphonie*, 67 (quote), 71; Erik Levi, *Music in the Third Reich* (New York, 1994), 77–81.

67. Prieberg, *NS-Staat*, 351–52; Ulrike Gruner, *Musikleben in der Provinz, 1933–45: Beispiel: Marburg:Eine Studie anhand der Musikberichterstattung in der Lokalpresse* (Marburg, 1990), 102–3, 127; Christopher Hogwood, *Handel* (London, 1984), 271–73.

68. *NG* 12:134–52; *Skizzen* (Mar. 1935), 6; Fritz Müller, "Der Fall Mendelssohn," *ZM* 106 (1939), 259–61; Blessinger, *Mendelssohn*, 23–24.

69. Dietrich Schulz-Köhn, *Die Schallplatte auf dem Weltmarkt* (Berlin, 1940).

70. See *Skizzen* (Apr. 1934), 13; (Oct. 1934), 14; (Nov. 1934), 15; (Feb. 1935), 15; (Mar. 1935), 15, 16; (Apr. 1935), 13–14, 16; (June–July 1935), 13; (Aug.–Sept. 1935), 14, 17; (Dec. 1935), 18; (Dec. 1936), 15; (Aug.–Sept 1937), 20; (Jan. 1938), 16; *DM 25* (1933), 467; *ZM* 102 (1935), 478 (quote); Kater, *Different Drummers*, 50–51.

71. I have discussed this phenomenon with respect to Jewish physicians in *Doctors*, 206–7.

72. Louis Lochner, *Fritz Kreisler* (New York, 1950), 280–83; *IBD*, 662–63; *LI*, 395–96.

73. *IBD*, 737; *LI*, 431; Spotts, *Bayreuth*, 155, 168, 171.

74. Hans-Peter Range, *Die Konzertpianisten der Gegenwart: Ein Musikliebhaber berichtet über Konzertmilieu und 173 Klaviervirtuosen*, 2nd ed. (Lahr, 1966), 207–8; Artur Schnabel, *My Life and Music: Reflections on Music* (Gerrards Cross, 1970), 108; *LI*, 651–52.

75. *LI*, 284–85; *The Memoirs of Carl Flesch*, ed. Hans Keller (Harlow, 1973), 317; Muck, *Jahre* 2:112; Prieberg, *Kraftprobe*, 177–78.

76. Michael H. Kater, "The Revenge of the Fathers: The Demise of Modern Music at the End of the Weimar Republic," *German Studies Review* 15 (1992), 307; *VB*, 24 Feb. 1933; David Drew, ed., *Über Kurt Weill* (Frankfurt am Main, 1975), 110–11; Albrecht Dümling, *Lasst euch nicht verführen: Brecht und die Musik* (Munich, 1985), 365–66; Weill to UE, 16 Jan. 1933, WC, Weill/UE corr.

77. Eggert to Parteigenosse, 17 Jan. 1933, BDC Paul Eggert; Blech in Josef Müller-Marein and Hannes Reinhardt, eds., *Das musikalische Selbstportrait von Komponisten, Dirigenten, Instrumentalisten, Sängerinnen und Sängern unserer Zeit* (Hamburg, 1965), 121–22; Hans Heinz Stuckenschmidt, *Zum Hören geboren: Ein Leben mit der Musik unserer Zeit* (Munich, 1979), 159; Hartmann, *Haus*, 100, 109; Rathkolb, *Führertreu*, 82; Tietjen to Strauss, 26 Oct. 1934, RG.

78. See Holthoff to Roennecke, 23 June 1933, BDC Georg Meyer.

79. Graener to Hinkel, 27 July 1939; Hinkel telegram to Fiehler, 28 July 1939, BDC Graener. Also Stengel and Gerigk, *Lexikon*, 172. On deportations from Munich, see Else R. Behrend-Rosenfeld, *Ich stand nicht allein: Erlebnisse einer Jüdin in Deutschland, 1933–1944*, 2nd ed. (Frankfurt am Main, 1963), 119–70.

80. Wagner, *Nacht*, 147, 292–94, 311; Frida Leider, *Das war mein Teil: Erinnerungen einer Opernsängerin* (Berlin, 1959), 182, 184, 189–90.

81. BDC Klingler; Edith Stargardt-Wolff, *Wegbereiter grosser Musiker* (Berlin, 1954), 281.

82. BDC Hoesslin; Hoesslin to Führer, 3 Aug. 1939, and Rössner to von Borries, 14 Aug. 1944, ibid. (quotes). See also *TG* 3:543; 4:98; *LI*, 330; Spotts, *Bayreuth*, 148, 153, 178, 193.

83. BDC Güden; Güden "Formblatt," n.d., BH, Staatstheater/14444; Krauss to Güden, 13 Nov. 1941, BH, Staatstheater/14480; Flügel to Staatssekretär, 12 Aug. 1943; Hinkel to Flügel, 20 Aug. 1943 (quote), BA, R55/125; Hinkel to Naumann, 31 Jan. 1944, BA, R55/1254; *Die Reichskulturkammer*, no. 1 (1944), 13 (BA, RD33/1); Hartmann, *Haus*, 164; Steinweis, *Art*, 118–20.

84. Erich Lüth, *Hamburger Theater, 1933–1945: Ein theatergeschichtlicher Versuch* (Hamburg, 1962), 65; *Zündende Lieder—Verbrannte Musik: Folgen des Nationalsozialismus für Hamburger Musiker und Musikerinnen: Katalog zur Ausstellung in Hamburg im November und Dezember 1988* (Hamburg, 1988), 136; Stefan Wulf in Heister et al., *Musik im Exil: Folgen des Nazismus für die internationale Musikkultur* (Frankfurt am Main, 1993), 149–51.

85. Sinzheimer to Orff, 28 May 1933, CM, Allg. Korr. (quote); Stengel and Gerigk, *Lexikon*, 260.

86. Schoenberg to Casals, 20 Feb. 1933; Schoenberg to Maria Freund, 15 May 1933, AI, gen. corr.; Ernst Hilmar, ed.,*Arnold Schönberg: Gedenkausstellung 1974* (Vienna, 1974), 326–27; Erwin Stein, ed., *Arnold Schoenberg: Letters* (New York, 1965), 116, 177; Hans Heinz Stuckenschmidt, *Arnold Schoenberg* (London, 1964), 92–110; Michael Mäckelmann, *Arnold Schönberg und das Judentum: Der Komponist und sein religiöses, nationales und politisches Selbstverständnis nach 1921* (Hamburg, 1984), 203–4.

87. *IBD*, 631; *TG* 2:374 (1st quote); Abendroth to Pfitzner, 16 Feb. 1933, OW, 289; John Sargent Rockwell, "Prussian Ministry of Culture and the Berlin State Opera, 1918–1931" (Ph.D. diss., Berkeley, 1972), 302–3; Heinrich Strobel, "Kunstleben 1933," *Melos* 12 (1933), 67–68; Peter Heyworth, *Otto Klemperer: His Life and Times*, 2 vols. (Cambridge, 1983, 1996), 1:391–417 (2nd and 3rd quotes, 413, 415); *Artist*, 2 Aug. 1934.

88. *IBD*, 1205–6; Bruno Walter, *Theme and Variations: An Autobiography* (New York, 1966), 295–300; Stargardt-Wolff, *Wegbereiter*, 275–79; Walter quoted in Beussel, "Zeichen," 669; *Münchener Neueste Nachrichten*, 19 Mar. 1933; *New York Times*, 21 Mar. 1933; Kopsch deposition, 1 Mar. 1947, AM, Strauss. On Hitler's hatred, see Henry Picker, *Hitlers Tischgespräche im Führerhauptquartier, 1941–42*, ed. Gerhard Ritter (Bonn, 1951), 395–96. If Strauss can be believed, the agent Wolff asked him the first time, musicians (Julius Kopsch and Hugo Rasch from the RMK) the second time, Walter having indicated his approval to Wolff. Strauss to Karpath, 6 Apr. 1933, printed in Beussel, "Zeichen," 670.

89. Internment in a concentration camp is not documented, but on the face of the evidence one cannot come to any other logical conclusion. See BDC Erwin Gottschalk, Herbert Klüger, and Willy Lange.

90. Karoly Csipak, "Berthold Goldschmidt im Exil: Der Komponist im Gespräch über Musiker-Exil und Musikleben," in Habakuk Traber and Elmar Weingarten, eds., *Verdrängte Musik: Berliner Komponisten im Exil* (Berlin, 1987), 64–66; Traber and Weingarten, *Musik*, 246; *Süddeutsche Zeitung*, Munich, 7 Oct. 1994.

91. *IBD*, 988; Rosenstock to Strauss, 12 Apr. 1933, RG.

92. *IBD*, 892–93; Adolph to Franz Strauss, 11 May 1933, RG; Stengel and Gerigk, *Lexikon*, 211.

93. Albert Richard Mohr, *Die Frankfurter Oper, 1924–1944: Ein Beitrag zur Theatergeschichte mit zeitgenössischen Berichten und Bildern* (Frankfurt am Main, 1971), 154–55 (quote on 154); *LI*, 698.

94. *LI*, 334–35; Rischer, *Kulturpolitik*, 58–60.

95. BDC Fritz Mach and Herbert Gillis-Neubert.

96. Nicolai to Hinkel, 27 Aug. 1935, BDC Nicolai.

97. Otto Sedlmayr file, BA, R55/226 (quote in Sedlmayr to Hitler, 3 Mar. 1938).

98. BDC Praetorius; Cornelia Zimmermann-Kalyoncu, *Deutsche Musiker in der Türkei im 20. Jahrhundert* (Frankfurt am Main, 1985), 64–65; Fritz Neumark, *Zuflucht am Bosporus: Deutsche Gelehrte, Politiker und Künstler in der Emigration, 1933–1953* (Frankfurt am Main, 1980), 122.

99. Herbert Freeden, *Jüdisches Theater in Nazideutschland* (Tübingen, 1964), 14–16, 19; *Zündende Lieder*, 31–32; Dahm, "Leben," 85–86, 90.

100. "Aufruf," [1935], LBI, AR-A726/2590; *Jüdische Rundschau*, 20 Aug. 1935; Freeden, *Theater*, 25, 59; Dahm, "Leben," 93, 105, 120; Kurt Düwell, "Der Jüdische Kulturbund Rhein-Ruhr, 1933–1938: Selbstbesinnung und Selbstbehauptung einer Geistesgemeinschaft," in Jutta Bohnke-Kollwitz el al., eds., *Köln und das rheinische Judentum: Festschrift Germania Judaica, 1959– 1984* (Cologne, 1984), 428; Steinweis, *Art*, 121.

101. *Israelitisches Familienblatt*, Berlin, 26 Oct. 1933; *Schild*, 12 June 1936; Singer in *Jüdische Rundschau*, 21 July 1936 (quote).

102. Freeden, *Theater*, 22–23, 94; Dahm, "Leben," 87, 89, 108; Joseph Walk, ed., *Das Sonderrecht für die Juden im NS-Staat: Eine Sammlung der gesetzlichen Massnahmen und Richtlinien—Inhalt und Bedeutung* (Heidelberg, 1981), 221; Rosy Geiger-Kullmann, "Lebenserinnerungen," ms., Feb. 1961, 59 (LBI, ME/180).

103. Goebbels paraphrased by Freeden, *Theater*, 61; Hinkel in *Israelitisches Familienblatt*, Berlin, 1 Aug. 1935; *Zündende Lieder*, 36.

104. See Gestapo, "Richtlinien für die Tätigkeit des Reichsverbandes der Jüdischen Kulturbünde in Deutschland," Berlin, 13 Aug. 1935, LBI, AR-A726/2590/63 + 64; Freeden, *Theater,* 52.

105. Hinkel in *Frankfurter Zeitung,* 13 May 1937;)C Wilhelm Guttmann, Erich Rosenow, and Hugo Stern; Dahm, "Leben," 109; Steinweis, *Art,* 121.

106. Singer to Berlin Gestapo, 7 Sept. 1934; Gestapo to Kulturbund, 11 Sept. 1934, LBI, AR-C1210/3100; Dahm, "Leben," 114; Steinweis, *Art,* 122.

107. *Hamburger Fremdenblatt,* 6 Feb. 1936; communication by Jüdischer Kulturbund Hamburg, 10 Mar. 1936, LBI, AR-A727/2591; program of Jüdischer Kulturbund Hamburg for Thursday, 6 Nov. 1936, LBI, AR-A728/2592; Steinweis, *Art,* 123.

108. *Hamburger Israelitisches Familienblatt,* 21 May 1936; Kulturbund Hamburg to "Sehr geehrtes Mitglied," Mar. 1937, LBI, AR-A728/2592; Freeden, *Theater,* 92–93, 104; Dahm, "Leben," 120.

109. Freeden, *Theater,* 160, 163–64; Dahm, "Leben," 245–46, 251, 257; *Zündende Lieder,* 40.

110. Dahm, "Leben," 121–22.

111. *Israelitisches Familienblatt* (Berlin), 2 Nov. 1933; *Jüdisches Gemeindeblatt für Berlin,* 13 Feb. 1938; Christine Fischer-Defoy, *Kunst, Macht, Politik: Die Nazifizierung der Kunst- und Musikhochschulen in Berlin* (Berlin, [1988]), 156.

112. "Abend Frankfurter Komponisten," 27 Jan. 1934, LBI, AR-7049/13; Rosy Geiger-Kullmann, "Lebenserinnerungen," ms., Feb. 1961 (LBI, ME/180).

113. Sinzheimer of Orff, 20 Jan. 1934, CM, Allg. Korr.; Dahm, "Leben," 94.

114. *Jüdisches Gemeindeblatt für Berlin,* 21 Apr. and 16 June 1935, 2 Feb. 1936; catalog, "'Lukraphon' Schallplatten," [1935/36], PA Eike Geisel, Berlin.

115. Traber and Weingarten, *Musik,* 291, 305, 308, 341, 344; "Jüdischer Kulturbund Hamburg: Abschieds-Abend," 25 Nov. 1936, LBI, AR-A727/2591; *Jüdisches Nachrichtenblatt,* 2 May 1941; *Jüdisches Gemeindeblatt für Berlin,* 12 Apr. 1936; Weiss to Misch, 3 Jan. 1965, LBI, AR-C738/2073. On Misch, see NG 12:362.

116. *Israelitisches Familienblatt* (Berlin), 8 Mar. and 19 Apr. 1934; *Jüdisches Gemeindeblatt für Berlin,* 17 Nov. 1935, 3 May 1936, 2 May 1937, 24 Oct. 1937, 16 Jan 1938; "Gastspiel Alexander Kipnis," Düsseldorf, 9 Feb. 1937, LBI, AR-A835/3047; "Alexander Kipnis," Hamburg, 10 Feb. 1937, LBI, AR-A728/2592; "Stuttgarter Jüdische Kunstgemeinschaft," 15 Oct. 1938, LBI, AR-7276/IV/2/15; *LI,* 373–74.

117. *Jüdisches Gemeindeblatt für Berlin,* 4 Apr. 1937; Stefan Wulf in Heister et al., *Musik,* 154.

118. *Schild,* 24 Apr. 1936; *Jüdisches Gemeindeblatt für Berlin,* 3 May 1936; Flesch to Herr Doktor, 5 July 1936, LBI, AR-7049/2 (quote). Strangely, Flesch was using the Nazi expression "Rassegenossen."

119. *Israelitisches Familienblatt* (Berlin), 11 Jan. and 13 Sept. 1934; *Schild,* 30 Oct. 1936; *Jüdisches Gemeindeblatt für Berlin,* 12 July 1936; Berlin Künstlerhilfe to Kowalski, 14 Apr. 1935, LBI, AR-7049/4; Jüdischer Kulturbund Hamburg to subscribers, [May 1936], LBI, AR-A727/2591.

120. *Israelitisches Familienblatt* (Berlin), 26 Oct. 1933; "Konzert" at Dr. Meyer's, 10 Feb. 1935, LBI, AR-7049/13; "Stimmen im Tempel," 30 Aug. 1938, LBI, AR-7040/13; Freeden, *Theater,* 74, 123, 126.

121. Hinkel quoted in *Frankfurter Zeitung*, 13 May 1937; Freeden, *Theater*, 162; Dahm, "Leben," 115; Steinweis, *Art*, 122.

122. *Schild*, 12 Apr. 1935; *Jüdisches Gemeindeblatt für Berlin*, 22 Sept. 1934, 19 May 1935, and 16 June 1937; "Konzert," 31 Jan. 1935, LBI, AR-A726/2529; "Klavierabend Bernhard Abramowitsch," 20 Nov. 1935, LBI, AR-A726/2590; Berlin Kulturbund program, Mar. 1934, LBI, AR-A834/3046; Maurer Zenck, "Itor Kahn," 241.

123. *Jüdisches Gemeindeblatt für Berlin*, 5 Jan. 1935 and 28 Apr. 1936; *Schild*, 28 June 1935; "Abend Frankfurter Komponisten," 27 Jan. 1934, LBI, AR-7049/13; program, "Jüdischer Kulturbund Hamburg," Dec. 1935, LBI, AR-A726/2590; "Konzert Tempelchor," Feb. 1938, LBI, AR-A729/2593; Prieberg, "Davidsstern," 124.

124. *Schild*, 26 Nov. 1933 and 12 Apr. 1935; *Israelitisches Gemeindeblatt* (Berlin), 23 Nov. 1933; Dahm, "Leben," 191.

125. Craft, *Stravinsky* 3:243, n. 42 (quote); also Dahm, "Leben," 114.

126. *Schild*, 27 Oct. 1933; *Israelitisches Familienblatt* (Berlin), 13 Sept. 1934; *Jüdisches Gemeindeblatt für Berlin*, 27 Mar. 1938; Freeden, *Theater*, 75.

127. "Jüdischer Kulturbund Hamburg," 12 Nov. 1935, LBI, AR-A726/2590; Freeden, *Theater*, 101; *Zündende Lieder*, 33, 37; Dahm, "Leben," 93.

128. Freeden, *Theater*, 102–3 (calculation according to figures, 114).

129. Dahm, "Leben," 242, 247, 255; Prieberg, "Davidsstern," 126.

130. Katz to Orff, 22 July 1933 (quote), 2 and 11 Aug. 1933; Doflein to Orff, 9 Sept. 1933; Kohrs to Orff, [1938], CM, Allg. Korr.; *IBD*, 600; Grunsky, *Kampf*, 47; Traber and Weingarten, *Musik*, 277; *NG* 9:828.

131. Polizeipräsidium Stuttgart to Adler, 14 Mar. 1933; Gestapo "Bescheinigung," 15 Nov. 1938, LBI, AR-7276/V/3/2; Adler, "Ergänzende Bemerkungen zum Fall Baach," 9 Nov. 1966, ibid., V/3/3. On capriciousness in spring 1933, see Michael H. Kater, "Everyday Anti-Semitism in Prewar Nazi Germany: The Popular Bases," *Yad Vashem Studies* 16 (1984), 138–46.

132. Stargardt and Wolff, *Wegbereiter*, 256; Mohr, *Oper*, 157–58; Otto Strasser, *Und dafür wird man noch bezahlt: Mein Leben mit den Wiener Philharmonikern* (Vienna, 1974), 170; Hellsberg, *Demokratie*, 464.

133. Traber and Weingarten, *Musik*, 222; Stengel and Gerigk, *Lexikon*, 40.

134. Gabriele E. Meyer, "Münchener Philharmoniker," n.d., 12 (SM, Av.-Bibl./23933).

135. Freeden, *Theater*, 167; Stargardt-Wolff, *Wegbereiter*, 170–71; 228; Slonimsky, *Musik*, 759; Mohr, *Oper*, 156; Strasser, *Und*, 155; Stengel and Gerigk, *Lexikon*, 90; Eckhard John in Heister et al., *Musik*, 263, 268.

136. *Den Opfern der Gewalt: 2. Baden-Württembergische Musikhochschultage, Stuttgart, 11.–18. Oktober 1989: Europäische Komponisten—gestorben in den Weltkriegen und Konzentrationslagern* (n.p., n.d.), 61; Prieberg, *Macht*, 265–67; *NG* 19:326–27; Peter Kien, libretto, "Der Kaiser von Atlantis oder Der Tod Dankt ab: Legende in vier Bildern," ms., LBI, AR-A1368/4403; *New Yorker*, 6 June 1977, 111–12; *Focus*, 26 Sept. 1994, 158, 160; compact disk London 440854-2 (1994).

137. Rainer Licht in Heister et al., *Musik*, 238; Stein weis, *Art*, 72, 110; Mohr, *Oper*, 157; Traber and Weingarten, *Musik*, 330; *Die Vertreibung des Geistigen aus Österreich: Zur Kulturpolitik des Nationalsozialismus*, 2nd ed. (Vienna, n.d.), 336; *LI*, 616. For an unsympathetic portrait of Rosé in Auschwitz, see Fania Fénelon, *Das Mädchenorchester in Auschwitz*, 4th ed. (Munich, 1984), 33–235.

138. Horst Möller, *Exodus der Kultur: Schriftsteller, Wissenschaftler und Künstler in der Emigration nach 1933* (Munich, 1984), 47.

139. Boris Schwarz, "The Music World in Migration," in Jarrell C. Jackman and Carla M. Borden, eds., *The Muses Flee Hitler: Cultural Transfer and Adaptation, 1930–1945* (Washington, D.C., 1983), 137; Kater, "Orff," 31–32.

140. Bernard Wasserstein, *Britain and the Jews of Europe, 1939–1945* (Oxford, 1979); Marion Berghahn, *German-Jewish Refugees in England: The Ambiguities of Assimilation* (London, 1984); *TGII* 3:423; *TGII* 8:286; *TGII* 11:31, 399, 554; *TGII* 12:145.

141. Stefan Wulf in Heister et al., *Musik*, 152–54; *LI*, 91, 731–32.

142. Graudan file, BA, R55/197; *Vertreibung*, 337, 343; *LI*, 616.

143. *Vertreibung*, 351; *IBD*, 1233–34; *Israelitisches Familienblatt* (Berlin), 13 Sept. 1934; Goldschmidt in Csipak, "Goldschmidt," 67–68; *Spiegel*, 5 Sept. 1994, 204; *Süddeutsche Zeitung* (Munich), 7 Oct. 1994.

144. Herbert A. Strauss, "Jewish Emigration from Germany: Nazi Policies and Jewish Responses (II)," *Leo Baeck Institute Yearbook* 26 (1981), 343–409; Kater, *Doctors*, 213–15.

145. Salomon to Orff, 4 June and 15 July 1933, and [1935], CM, Allg. Korr.; Peter Gradenwitz, "Der deutsch-jüdische Beitrag zur Entwicklung des Musiklebens in Israel," in Traber and Weingarten, *Musik*, 83–84.

146. Gradenwitz, "Beitrag," 93–94; idem in Heister et al., *Musik*, 120–31.

147. Traber and Weingarten, *Musik*, 271; Prieberg, *Lexikon*, 173; *IBD*, 544; Slonimsky, *Music*, 637; Marek, *Toscanini*, 184–86; Gradenwitz, "Beitrag," 85–86.

148. Reinhard Voigt in *Zündende Lieder*, 45–54; Traber and Weingarten, *Musik*, 356–57; Gradenwitz, "Beitrag," 91–92; Austin Clarkson, "Stefan Wolpe's Berlin Years," in Maria Rika Maniates and Edmond Strainchamps, eds., *Music and Civilization: Essays in Honor of Paul Henry Lang* (New York, 1984), 371–93; *Spiegel*, 30 Oct. 1995, 219.

149. Clarkson, "Years," 391–93.

150. *IBD*, 1131; Stiedry to Schoenberg, 8 Dec. 1937, AI, gen. corr.; Traber and Weingarten, *Musik*, 278, 325–26, 334; Eckhard John in Heister et. al., *Musik*, 272–63, 268–69.

151. Möller, *Exodus*, 47.

152. Saul S. Friedman, *No Haven for the Oppressed: United States Policy Toward Jewish Refugees, 1938–1945* (Detroit, 1973), 20–27 (Tincher cited on 21); Strauss, "Emigration," 358–62; David S. Wyman, *The Abandonment of the Jews: America and the Holocaust, 1941–1945* (New York, 1985).

153. Schoenberg circular [to his friends in Europe], Nov. 1934, LBI, AR-7049/10; German Embassy, Washington, D.C., to Auswärtiges Amt, Berlin, 11 July 1935; RMK memorandum, 11 July 1935, BA, R55/1177; Walter H. Rubsamen, "Schoenberg in America," *Musical Quarterly* 37 (1951), 475; Hilmar, *Schönberg*, 63; Charlotte Erwin, "Ernst Toch in America," in Traber and Weingarten, *Musik*, 112–16; Harvey Sachs, *Music in Fascist Italy* (London, 1987), 130; *NG* 4:714.

154. *IBD*, 662–63; Albrecht Betz, *Hanns Eisler: Musik einer Zeit, die sich eben bildet* (Munich, 1976), 142–59; Traber and Weingarten, *Musik*, 232–33; *Vertreibung*, 325.

155. *LI*, 651–52; Traber and Weingarten, *Musik*, 254, 297, 327; Juan Allende-Blin in Heister et al., *Musik*, 115–16; Maurer Zenck, "Itor Kahn," 246–

50; Itor Kahn to Rosbaud, 30 July 1947, LP, 123/1; Hahn to Margarete Adler, 3 Aug. 1973, LBI, AR-7276/V/3/17.

156. Schoenberg to Görgi [Georg Schönberg], 28 Oct. 1934; Schoenberg to Kolisch, 8 Dec. 1934, AI, gen. corr.; Schoenberg circular [to his friends in Europe], Nov. 1934, LBI, AR-7049/10; Rubsamen, "Schoenberg," 472; Stuckenschmidt, *Schoenberg*, 111–14.

157. Slonimsky, *Music*, 583; Stein, *Schoenberg Letters*, 202–3.

158. Schoenberg to Görgi [Georg Schönberg], 10 June 1934; Schoenberg to Bartlett Fraenkel, 26 Nov. 1935 (1st quote); Schoenberg to Hirschmann, 11 June 1938; Schoenberg to RCA Victor, 8 Feb. 1939 (2nd quote); Schoenberg to Rankl, 9 Feb. 1939 (3rd and 4th quote); Schoenberg to Buck, 10 Apr. 1941 (5th quote), AI, gen. corr.

159. I owe my insight into this comparison to Joan Evans of Toronto.

160. Schoenberg to Mahler-Werfel, 23 Jan. 1936; Schoenberg to Felt, 12 Sept. 1937; Schoenberg to Görgi [Georg Schönberg], 22 May 1939; Schoenberg to Richard [Hoffmann], 17 Oct. 1944; Schoenberg to Powell, 4 Jan. 1945; Schoenberg to Trudi, 3 Feb. 1945, AI, gen. corr.; Ploss to Gertrud Schoenberg, 23 July 1951; University of California to Schoenberg, 23 Apr. 1936, 6 May 1938, 28 Mar. 1939, 14 July 1939, AI, Gertrud Schoenberg Collection; Rubsamen, "Schoenberg," 471–72, 479–80; Dika Newlin, *Schoenberg Remembered: Diaries and Recollections (1938–76)* (New York, 1980), 250–52; Nuria Nono-Schoenberg, ed., *Arnold Schönberg, 1874–1951: Lebensgeschichte in Begegnungen* (Klagenfurt, 1992), 397.

161. Newlin, *Schoenberg*, 21, 33, 53, 94, 106, 322–33; Richard Taruskin, "The Dark Side of Modern Music," *New Republic*, 5 Sept. 1988, 33.

162. See, e.g., Newlin, *Schoenberg*, 14, 249; see also Schoenberg to Křenek, 1 Dec. 1939, AI, gen. corr.

163. See Rubsamen, "Schoenberg," 474; Peter Stephan Jungk, *Franz Werfel: Eine Lebensgeschichte*, 2nd ed. (Frankfurt am Main, 1987), 302, 309.

164. Katia Mann, *Meine ungeschriebenen Memoiren*, ed. Elisabeth Plessen and Michael Mann (Frankfurt am Main, 1981), 133 (1st quote); Thomas Mann, *Tagebücher, 1940–1943*, ed. Peter de Mendelssohn (Frankfurt am Main, 1982), 617 (other quote).

165. Schoenberg to Mann, 28 Dec. 1938 and 15 Jan. 1939; Mann to Schoenberg, 9 Jan. 1939 (quote), AI, gen. corr.

166. Schoenberg to Klatzkin, 13 June 1933, AI, Jew/8; Schoenberg memorandum, Arcachon, 12/13 Aug. 1933, AI, Jew/7.

167. Schoenberg to Jalowetz, 19 Aug. 1933, and to Shubow, 23 Dec. 1933, AI, gen. corr.; Denis Arnold, ed., *The New Oxford Companion to Music*, 2 vols. (Oxford, 1990), 2:1637.

168. Schoenberg to Wise, 12 May 1934, AI, gen. corr.

169. Arnold Schoenberg, "A Four-Point Program for Jewry" [1938], *Journal of the Arnold Schoenberg Institute* 3 (1979), 49–67; Mäckelmann, *Schönberg*, 276, 310; Rubsamen, "Schoenberg," 476, 478.

170. Schoenberg quoted in liner notes, compact disk *Deutsche Grammophon* 437 036-2 (1986); Schoenberg to Hermann [Greisle], 15 Oct. 1943, AI, gen. corr.; Slonimsky, *Music*, 792; Arnold, *Companion*, 2:1637. See also Stuckenschmidt, *Schoenberg*, 119–26.

171. Klemperer telegram to Schoenberg, 6 Feb. 1934 and 17 Oct. 1936; Schoenberg to Klemperer, 8 Nov. 1934 and 18 Mar. 1936; Schoenberg to Engel,

2 Apr. 1936; Schoenberg to Charlotte Dieterle, 30 July 1936; Schoenberg to Greissle, 3 Feb. 1937; Schoenberg to Herz, 2 May 1938; Schoenberg to Smallens, 25 May 1938; Schoenberg to Jalowetz, 7 June 1938; Klemperer to Schoenberg, 24 Nov. 1940; Schoenberg to Johanna Klemperer, 13 Sept. 1941, AI, gen. corr.; Slonimsky, *Music,* 606; Newlin, *Schoenberg,* 65; Nono-Schoenberg, *Schönberg,* 325.

172. Schoenberg to Stiedry, 2 Apr. 1940 (1st quote); Schoenberg to Greissle, 22 July 1944; Schoenberg to Klemperer, 25 Sept. and 28 Nov. 1940; Klemperer to Schoenberg, 29 Sept. 1940 (2nd quote); Schoenberg to Usher, 4 Jan. 1945; Schoenberg to Trudi, 3 Feb. 1945, AI, gen. corr.; Otto Klemperer, *Meine Erinnerungen an Gustav Mahler und andere autobiographische Skizzen* (Freiburg, 1960), 26, 47; Newlin, *Schoenberg,* 243.

173. Otto to Johanna Klemperer, 6 Nov. 1933 (1st quote), 25 Nov. 1933 (2nd quote), 15 Dec. 1933 and 13 Feb. 1934 (3rd quote), all PA Lotte Klemperer, Zollikon; Lotte Klemperer to author, Zollikon, 2 Feb. 1991, APA; Lotte Klemperer, interview, Zollikon, 5 Dec. 1990; Prieberg, *NS-Staat,* 45; Heyworth, *Klemperer* 2:48.

174. Strecker to Hindemith, 27 Apr. and 22 Oct. 1934, PF, Schott Korr.; Zirato to Walter, 11 June 1934, NYA, Walter Collection; Lotte Klemperer to Gertrud Schoenberg, 15 Apr. 1941, AI, gen. corr.; Slonimsky, *Music,* 636; Hans and Rosaleen Moldenhauer, *Anton von Webern: A Chronicle of His Life and Work* (New York, 1979), 470–71; Newlin, *Schoenberg,* 119–20, 276; Thomas Mann, *Tagebücher, 1937–1939,* ed. Peter de Mendelssohn (Frankfurt am Main, 1980), 204, 212; Mann, *Tagebücher, 1940–1943,* 328, 579, 625; Luther Noss, *Paul Hindemith in the United States* (Urbana, Ill., 1989), 51; *IBD,* 631; Klemperer, *Erinnerungen,* 46–47; Kurt Blaukopf, *Grosse Dirigenten* (Teufen, n.d.), 104 (1st quote); *NG* 10:106; Lotte Klemperer, interview, Zollikon, 5 Dec. 1990 (2nd quote); *LI,* 377; Heyworth, *Klemperer* 2:121.

175. Schoenberg circular [to his friends in Europe], Nov. 1934, LBI, AR-7049/10.

176. *IBD,* 1205; Walter, *Theme,* 340; Judson memorandum of conversation with Walter, 23 Feb. 1932; New York Philharmonic, "Contract Suggestions for Bruno Walter—Season 1933–1934," 24 Jan. 1933; New York Philharmonic telegram to Walter, 24 Mar. 1933; Walter to Judson, 12 Apr. 1933, NYA, Walter Collection.

177. Philharmonic-Symphony Society of New York, press release, 15 Dec. 1933; Zirato to Walter, 23 May 1934, NYA, Walter Collection; Lotte Walter Lindt, ed., *Bruno Walter: Briefe, 1894–1962* (Frankfurt am Main, 1969), 243. On Feuermann, see *IBD,* 295–96; *LI,* 228.

178. Program, "Florentiner Musikfestspiele," 27 Apr.–9 June 1937, LP, 413/4/54; Walter to Toscanini, 20 Feb. 1938, in Harvey Sachs, "Salzburg, Hitler und Toscanini: Unbekanntes Briefmaterial aus den dreissiger Jahren," *Neue Zeitschrift für Musik* 148 (July–Aug. 1987), 22; Walter Lindt, *Walter: Briefe,* 159–60; Walter, *Theme,* 303, 312–21, 328; Schoenberg to Wise, 12 May 1934, AI, gen. corr.; Sachs, *Music,* 93–94, 175.

179. Sachs, *Music;* Fiamma Nicolodi, *Musica e musicisti nel ventennio fascista* (Florence, 1984); Jürg Stenzl, *Von Giacomo Puccini zu Luigi Nono: Italienische Musik, 1922–1952: Faschismus—Resistenza—Republik* (Buren, 1990).

180. Rathkolb, *Führertreu,* 115–16.

181. *IBD,* 1205; Walter, *Theme,* 337–42; Newlin, *Schoenberg,* 292–93;

Mann, *Tagebücher, 1940–1943*, 344, 358, 391, 395, 648–49; Walter Lindt, *Walter: Briefe*, 264–66, 268–69; Slonimsky, *Music*, 751, 775; Walter to Judson, 11 Dec. 1942; Field to Walter, 15 Mar. 1944 (1st quote); Walter to Field, 15 Mar. 1944 (2nd quote), NYA, Walter Collection.

182. Weill to UE, 15 July 1931; Hertzka to Weill, 17 July 1931; Weill to Heinsheimer, 3 Apr. 1933, WC, Weill/UE corr.; Ronald Taylor, *Kurt Weill: Composer in a Divided World* (London, 1991), 217.

183. Kapp to Weill, 4 Jan. 1944, WC, 48/28; Weill to parents, 18 Jan. 1944, WC, Weill/Parents corr.; Weill to Cheryl [Crawford], 30 Jan. 1944, WC, 48/26; Taylor, *Weill*, 216–83.

184. Weill–Dietrich corr. (1942), WC, 47/3 and 48/29; Weill to parents, 14 Aug. 1943, WC, Weill/Parents corr.; Taylor, *Weill*, 277. Cf. the story about Dietrich's musical saw antics in Donald Spoto, *Blue Angel: The Life of Marlene Dietrich* (New York, 1992), 176–80.

185. Weill to Dreyfus, 31 Dec. 1943, WC, 47/3; Taylor, *Weill*, 261.

186. Weill to parents, 24 June 1942, WC, Weill/Parents corr. (1st quote); Weill to [Werfel], 3 Aug. 1936, WC, 47/15 (2nd quote); Weill to parents, 30 Apr. 1945, WC, Weill/Parents corr. (3rd quote); Weill to Lyons, 15 Sept. 1939, WC, 47/10; Taylor, *Weill*, 282.

187. See, in the year of Weill's death, Heinrich Strobel, "Erinnerung an Kurt Weill," *Melos* 17 (1950), 133–36; more recently Jürgen Schebera, *Kurt Weill: Leben und Werk* (Königstein, 1984), 203; and Taylor, *Weill*, e.g., 224.

188. Jerome Barry, "Kurt Weill: 'Von Berlin zum Broadway': Lecture-Recital," in Otto Kolleritsch, ed., *Die Wiener Schule und das Hakenkreuz: Das Schicksal der Moderne im gesellschaftspolitischen Kontext des 20. Jahrhunderts* (Vienna, 1990), 161, 163 (quote).

189. Stephen Hinton, review of Taylor in *Kurt Weill Newsletter* 10, no. 2. (Fall 1992), 17. In the same vein, see Drew, *Weill*, 46.

190. Weill to Kalmus, 28 July 1937, WC, Weill/UE corr.

191. Weill to Lyons, 12 Feb. 1941, WC, 47/10.

192. Brecht to Weill, [Mar.–Apr. 1942], WC, 48/22; Weill to Brecht, 20 Apr. 1942, WC, Brecht corr.; Weill to Maurice [Speiser], 22 Jan. 1944, WC, 47/14 (quote); Taylor, *Weill*, 270–72.

193. Taylor, *Weill*, 227–28; Lys Symonette and Kim H. Kowalke, eds., *Speak Low (When You Speak Love): The Letters of Kurt Weill and Lotte Lenya* (Berkeley, 1996), passim.

194. Weill to Frank, 17 June 1940, WC, 47/4; Weill to Bob, 12 Dec. 1941, WC, 47/17; Weill to Wechsler, 9 Feb. 1943, WC, 47/15; Taylor, *Weill*, 255–57, 274.

195. Taylor, *Weill*, 7–8, 22–23, 73.

196. Weill to Curjel, 19 Apr. 1934, WC, Curjel corr.; Weill to [Reinhardt], 6 Oct. 1934, WC, 47/13; Reinhardt to Weill, 27 Nov. 1935, WC, 49/58; Weill to [Werfel], 3 Aug. 1936, WC, 47/15; Taylor, *Weill*, 206, 225–27; Drew, *Weill*, 61–62.

197. Weill to parents, 5 Feb. and 17 Apr. 1943 (quote), WC, Weill/Parents corr.; Putterman to Weill, 13 May 1946, WC, 49/55.

198. Toch quoted in *Auszug des Geistes: Bericht über eine Sendereihe* (Bremen, 1962), 185.

199. *IBD*, 1167; *Auszug*, 176–85; Prieberg, *Lexikon*, 427–28; Erwin, "Toch," 109–16; Mann, *Tagebücher, 1940–1943*, 613; Newlin, *Schoenberg*,

122, 139–40 (1st quote); *Neue Zeitschrift für Musik* 128 (1967), 499–500 (Slonimsky quote on 499); Albrecht Dümling in Heister el at., *Musik*, 316–19; Traber and Weingarten, *Musik*, 342–43.

200. Konrad H. Jarausch, *The Unfree Professions: German Lawyers, Teachers, and Engineers, 1900–1950* (New York, 1990); Kater, *Doctors*.

201. Erika and Klaus Mann, *Escape*, 242–44.

202. *LI*, 420; Stargardt-Wolff, *Wegbereiter*, 280–81; Erna Berger, *Auf Flügeln des Gesanges: Erinnerungen einer Sängerin*, 2nd ed. (Zurich, 1989), 55; Wagner, *Nacht*, 205–6; Berndt Wilhelm Wessling, *Furtwängler: Eine kritische Biographie* (Stuttgart, 1985), 258; Mann, *Tagebücher, 1940–1943*, 126, 281; Spotts, *Bayreuth*, 171. Alan Jefferson places the altercation in April 1933 (*Lotte Lehmann, 1888–1976* [London, 1988], 146–49).

203. Carl Schuricht in Müller-Marein and Reinhardt, *Selbstportrait*, 427; *LI*, 662 (quote); *GLM* 7:301; *NG* 16:873.

204. Strasser, *Und*, 154; Claudia Maurer Zenck, *Ernst Krenek—Ein Komponist im Exil* (Vienna, 1980), 89.

205. Stuckenschmidt, *Hören*, 142–43; *IBD*, 1144; Prieberg, *NS-Staat*, 225–33.

206. Busch memorandum, 8 Mar. 1933, BDC Fritz Busch; Fritz Busch, *Pages from a Musician's Life* (Westport, Conn., 1971), 192–215; Grete Busch, *Fritz Busch: Dirigent* (Frankfurt am Main, 1970), 52–129.

207. Richard Engländer, "Fritz Busch," *Musikblätter des Anbruch* 7 (1925), 457 (quote); German Embassy at The Hague to Auswärtiges Amt, 18 Oct. 1933, incl. memorandum of 17 Oct. 1933, BA, R55/1181; Wagner, *Nacht*, 137.

208. Lüddecke et al., "Denkschrift," 18 Mar. 1933, BDC Fritz Busch; Busch, *Pages*, 192–206; Busch, *Busch*, 52–62; *Münchener Neueste Nachrichten*, 19 Jan. 1933; *DKW*, no. 7 (1933), 13; Stargardt-Wolff, *Wegbereiter*, 283.

209. Strauss to Fürstner, 10 and 28 Mar. 1933, BS, Ana/330/I/Fürstner; Adolph to Strauss, 14 Mar. and 12 Apr. 1933; Strauss to Adolph, 17 Mar. 1933, RG; Busch, *Pages*, 210.

210. Posse to Adolph, 15 Mar. 1933, BDC Fritz Busch; Bauer to Strauss, 20 Mar. 1933, RG (quotes). In her memoirs Berger falsely claims that she resisted signing (*Flügeln*, 47). See also Busch, *Pages*, 210; Prieberg, *Kraftprobe*, 62.

211. Bauer to Strauss, 20 Mar. 1933, RG.

212. Gustav Bosse, " 'Führerverantwortlichkeit' oder 'Revolution der Strasse'?," *ZM* 100 (1933), 484–85.

213. Busch, *Pages*, 196–98 (1st quote on 197); Busch, *Busch*, 62–63; Picker, *Tischgespräche*, 380 (2nd quote).

214. Furtwängler to Rust, 4 June 1933, BDC Furtwängler; *Melos* 12 (1933), 257; Busch, *Pages*, 206–15; Rathkolb, *Führertreu*, 101; Prieberg, *NS-Staat*, 42; Prieberg, *Kraftprobe*, 109–10; Spotts, *Bayreuth*, 170–71.

215. Busch, *Pages*, 211; Busch, *Busch*, 66. In a story of equally dubious veracity, Busch in 1938 presented himself to the American violinist Louis Krasner in Stockholm as both a friend of Hermann Göring and an anti-Nazi patriot who had hurriedly left Germany for Switzerland without even telling his wife. Louis Krasner as told to Don C. Seibert, "Some Memoirs of Anton Webern, the Berg Concerto, and Vienna in the 1930s," *Fanfare* 11 (1987), 342.

216. Hinkel to Demann [?], Oct. 1933, BDC Fritz Busch; Beussel, "Zeichen," 670; Prieberg, *Kraftprobe*, 110–13; Signe Scanzoni and Götz Klaus Kende, *Der Prinzipal: Fakten, Vergleiche, Rückschlüsse* (Tutzing, 1988), 198–99; Sam H.

Shirakawa, *The Devil's Music Master: The Controversial Life and Career of Wilhelm Furtwängler* (New York, 1992), 393.

217. Braun to Hinkel, 10 Apr. 1933; Busch to Hinkel, 26 Apr. 1933; Brandt to Hinkel, 22 Sept. 1933, BDC Fritz Busch.

218. *LI,* 104–5; *GLM* 1:394–95; memorandum about Busch, 12 Mar. 1934, BA, R55/1181; Thomas Mann, *Tagebücher, 1933–1934,* ed. Peter de Mendelssohn (Frankfurt am Main, 1977), 84, 261, 269, 271, 290, 375; Mann, *Tagebücher, 1940–1943,* 138; Otto Erhardt, "Fritz Busch," in Martin Müller and Wolfgang Mertz, eds., *Diener der Musik* (Tübingen, 1965), 141; Busch, *Busch,* 77–252; J. Hellmut Freund in Heister et al., *Musik,* 75.

219. J. Hellmut Freund in Heister et al., *Musik,* 75.

220. *LI,* 104–5, 376–77; Helge Rosvaenge, *Mach es besser, mein Sohn,* 2nd ed. (Leipzig, 1963), 41 (quote).

221. Pfitzner to Brockhaus, 24 Nov 1923, MMP; König to Minister [Goebbels], 27 Feb. 1933, BDC Theo König; Joel Sachs, "Some Aspects of Musical Politics in Pre-Nazi Germany," *Perspectives of New Music* 9 (Fall–Winter 1970), 93; Stuckenschmidt, *Hören,* 117–18; Willi Reich, "Erich Kleiber and Alban Berg," *Schweizerische Musikzeitung* 98 (1958), 375; Kater, "Revenge," 303–4. See also text at n. 53.

222. Tietjen to Strauss, 1 Apr. and 19 May 1933, RG; Strauss to Fürstner, 8 Apr. 1933, BS, Ana/330/I/Fürstner; John Russell, *Erich Kleiber: A Memoir* (London, 1957), 142–43; Douglas Jarman, *Alban Berg: Lulu* (Cambridge, 1991), 1–38; Karen Monson, *Alban Berg: A Biography* (London, 1980), 253–97, 311–14.

223. *NG* 2:535–36; Burgartz's critique in *DM* 27 (1935), 262–63; Reich, "Kleiber," 376; Stuckenschmidt, *Hören,* 141; Russell, *Kleiber,* 144–47; William E. Dodd, Jr., and Martha Dodd, eds., *Ambassador Dodd's Diary, 1933–1938,* (New York, 1941), 198, 217 (2nd quote).

224. Berlin telegram to *De Telegraaf,* 6 Dec. 1934, BA, R55/1182; Berliner Philharmonisches Orchester to von Keudell, 30 Jan. 1935, BA, R55/1148; RMK file card on Kleiber, n.d., BDC Kleiber; Russell, *Kleiber,* 147–58 (quote on 147).

225. Russell, *Kleiber,* 159–97; Erika and Klaus Mann, *Escape,* 72; Prieberg, *Macht,* 185; Sachs, *Music,* 177–89.

226. Ernst Krenek in *Österreichische Musikzeitschrift* 43 (1988), 183; Laqueur, *Weimar,* 63, 205; Traber and Weingarten, *Musik,* 289; Kater, "Revenge," 296, 304–5; Ziegler, *Musik,* 7, 13, 16–18, 20; Wulf, *Musik,* 38, 223, 386, 392, 415, 468; Françoise Giroud, *Alma Mahler or the Art of Being Loved* (Oxford, 1991), 134.

227. See Elisabeth Klamper, "Die böse Geistlosigkeit: Die Kulturpolitik des Ständestaates," in *Kunst und Diktatur, Bildhauerei und Malerei in Österreich* (Vienna, 1994), 124–33; Helmut Wohnout, "Im Zeichen des Ständeideals: Bedingungen staatlicher Kulturpolitik im autoritären Österreich, 1933–1938," ibid., 134–41; Maurer Zenck, *Krenek,* 88–93; John L. Stewart, *Ernst Krenek: The Man and His Music* (Berkeley, 1991), 154–85.

228. Maurer Zenck, *Krenek,* 93–101 (quote on 94).

229. Křenek in Müller-Marein and Reinhardt, *Selbstportrait,* 187; Křenek in *Österreichische Musikzeitschrift* 43 (1988), 183–84; Erika and Klaus Mann, *Escape,* 258–59; Stewart, *Krenek,* 185, 217; Maurer Zenck, *Krenek,* 102–5.

230. Křenek to Schoenberg, 5 Sept. 1939, AI, gen. corr.

231. Hans W. Heinsheimer, *Best Regards to Aida: The Defeats and Victories of a Music Man on Two Continents* (New York, 1968), 265 (quote); Křenek in *Österreichische Musikzeitschrift* 43 (1988), 184–85; Křenek in Müller-Marein and Reinhardt, *Selbstportrait*, 187–88; Maurer Zenck, *Krenek*, 110–18; Stewart, *Krenek*, 218–35.

232. *GLM* 5:9; Prieberg, *Lexikon*, 237; Stewart, *Krenek*, 240–71; Traber and Weingarten, *Musik*, 289.

233. Lothar Kempter, ed., *Das Musikkollegium Winterthur* (Winterthur, 1959), 286; Stewart, *Krenek*, 45.

234. Weill to Hans [Weill], 20 June 1919, WC, Hans and Rita Weill Collection; Weill to UE, 24 Aug. 1930, WC, Weill/UE corr.

235. Blaukopf, *Dirigenten*, 135–39; Rolf Liebermann in Müller-Marein and Reinhardt, *Selbstportrait*, 270; Kater, "Orff," 6; Hansjörg Pauli in Heister et al., *Musik*, 58; Pfitzner to Scherchen, 23 Nov. 1920, BS, Autograph Pfitzner.

236. Hermann Scherchen, *Alles hörbar machen: Briefe eines Dirigenten, 1920 bis 1939*, ed. Eberhardt Klemm (Berlin, 1976), 371–74; Harry Goldschmidt, *Um die Sache der Musik: Reden und Aufsätze*, 2nd ed. (Leipzig, 1976), 207; Alexander von Bormann, "Das nationalsozialistische Gemeinschaftslied," in Horst Denkler and Karl Prümm, eds., *Die deutsche Literatur im Dritten Reich: Themen—Traditionen—Wirkungen* (Stuttgart, 1976), 266.

237. *DKW*, no. 18 (1933), 14 (quote); Grunsky, *Kampf*, 29.

238. "Strasbourg—Conservatoire de Musique," 7–16 Aug. 1933, BS, Ana/410; Scherchen to Hartmann, 3 Jan. 1937; "Société Philharmonique de Paris," [1938], BS, Ana/407; Scherchen, *Alles*, 368, 374–75; Hermann Scherchen, *Aus meinem Leben: Russland in jenen Jahren: Erinnerungen*, ed. Eberhardt Klemm (Berlin, 1984), 57–58; Rolf Liebermann in Müller-Marein and Reinhardt, *Selbstportrait*, 269; Moldenhauer, *Webern*, 500–501; Habakuk Traber, "Exil und 'Innere Emigration': Über Wladimir Vogel und Karl Amadeus Hartmann," in Traber and Weingarten, *Musik*, 168.

239. With the exception of Athens, which Scherchen visited in the early 1940s. See Speckner to Orff, 17 Oct. 1940, CM, Allg. Korr.; Scherchen, *Alles*, 373; Moldenhauer, *Webern*, 551.

240. Scherchen, *Alles*, 264–67, 271; Hansjörg Pauli in Heister et al., *Musik*, 64–65; Elias Canetti, *The Play of the Eyes* (New York, 1986), 42–50.

241. Hindemith to Strecker, 8 Sept. 1931, PF, Schott. Korr.; Orff/David corr. (1932), CM, Allg. Korr.

242. Hartmann cited in Andrew D. McCredie, *Karl Amadeus Hartmann: Sein Leben und Werk* (Wilhelmshaven, 1980), 31; Elisabeth Hartmann, recorded interview, Munich, 13 Dec. 1994, APA.

243. Röntgen to Hartmann, 22 Sept. 1935; Scherchen to Hartmann, 4 Dec. 1935 and 3 Jan. 1937; Hartmann to Osterc, 15 Oct. 1936, BS, Ana/407; Elisabeth Hartmann, recorded interview, Munich, 13 Dec. 1994, APA.

244. Scherchen to Hartmann, 11 May 1937, 19 June 1937, 2 Feb. 1938, 19 May 1938, 14 Nov. 1938, 17 Jan. 1939, 17 July 1940; Hartmann to Scherchen, 2 Dec. 1938; Jemnitz to Hartmann, 8 Mar. 1944 (quote), BS, Ana/407.

245. Jemnitz to Hartmann, 24 Nov. 1938, 19 Sept. 1941, 19 Mar. 1942, BS, Ana/407; Sutermeister to Orff, 25 Dec. 1934, CM, Allg. Korr.

246. Hansjörg Pauli in Heister et al., *Musik*, 61, 65–68; Goldschmidt, *Sache*, 207.

CHAPTER 4

1. See August Reissmann, *Die Hausmusik* (Berlin, 1884); *NG* 8:313–14; *GLM* 4:48; James J. Sheehan, *German History, 1770–1866* (Oxford, 1989) 144–206, 324–88, 524–87, 793–852; Thomas Nipperdey, *Deutsche Geschichte, 1800–1866: Bürgerwelt und starker Staat,* 2nd ed. (Munich, 1984), 403–594; Hans-Ulrich Wehler, *Deutsche Gesellschaftsgeschichte* (Munich, 1995), 3:373–448, 1169–1249. Wagner quoted in Johann Peter Vogel, *Hans Pfitzner: Mit Selbstzeugnissen und Bilddokumenten* (Reinbek, 1986), 77.

2. Werner Kindt, ed., *Die deutsche Jugendbewegung, 1920 bis 1933: Die bündische Zeit* (Düsseldorf, 1974), 1624–71; Pamela M. Potter, "The Nazi 'Seizure' of the Berlin Philharmonic, or the Decline of a Bourgeois Musical Institution," in Glenn Cuomo, ed., *National Socialist Cultural Policy* (New York, 1995), 56.

3. Kindt, *Jugendbewegung*, 1627; Pamela M. Potter, "German Musicology and Early Music Performance, 1918–1933," in Bryan Gilliam, ed., *Music and Performance During the Weimar Republic* (Cambridge, 1994), 102.

4. *ZM* 108 (1941), 292; *ZM* 109 (1942), 123; *MK* 1 (1943–44), 187; *MK* 1 (1944), 234.

5. Henry A. Turner, Jr., *German Big Business and the Rise of Hitler* (New York, 1985); Thomas Childers, *The Nazi Voter: The Social Foundations of Fascism in Germany, 1919–1933* (Chapel Hill, N.C., 1983).

6. Rudolf Maria Breithaupt, "Zum Tag der Hausmusik," *DM* 26 (1933), 81; Peter Raabe, *Kulturwille im deutschen Musikleben: Kulturpolitische Reden und Aufsätze* (Regensburg, 1936), 47; Hermann Blume, "Musikerschaft und Hausmusik," *DDP,* 20 Nov.1936, 5–6; *ZM* 105 (1938), 1091; Raabe in *ZM* 109 (1942), 521; Johannes Hodek, *Musikalisch-pädagogische Bewegung zwischen Demokratie und Faschismus: Zur Konkretisierung der Faschismus-Kritik Th. W. Adornos* (Weinheim, 1977), 163–65; Albrecht Riethmüller, "Die Bestimmung der Orgel im Dritten Reich," in Hans Heinrich Eggebrecht, ed., *Orgel und Ideologie: Bericht über das fünfte Colloquium der Walcker-Stiftung für orgelwissenschaftliche Forschung 5.–7. Mai 1983 in Göttweig* (Murrhardt, 1984), 49–50; Michael H. Kater, "The Revenge of the Fathers: The Demise of Modern Music at the End of the Weimar Republic," *German Studies Review* 15 (1992), 303.

7. "Arbeitsgemeinschaft für Hausmusik bei der Landesmusikerschaft Bayern: Besprechung am 14.9.34," SMK, 321; *VB,* 11 Dec. 1934.

8. *VB,* 11 Dec. 1934; Hans Brückner, "Was hat der Unterhaltungsmusiker mit der Hausmusik zu tun?," *DDP,* 13 Nov. 1936, 1–3; Blume, "Musikerschaft," 5–7.

9. Raabe, *Kulturwille,* 17, 44–45; Raabe in *ZM* 108 (1941), 290; Fritz Reusch, *Musik und Musikerziehung im Dienste der Volksgemeinschaft* (Osterwieck, 1938), 17; Ulrike Gruner, *Musikleben in der Provinz, 1933–45: Beispiel: Marburg: Eine Studie anhand der Musikberichterstattung in der Lokalpresse* (Marburg, 1990), 155.

10. George L. Mosse, *The Crisis of German Ideology: Intellectual Origins of the Third Reich* (New York, 1964); Michael H. Kater, *Different Drummers: Jazz in the Culture of Nazi Germany* (New York, 1992); Peter Fritzsche, *A Nation of Flyers: German Aviation and the Popular Imagination* (Cambridge, Mass., 1992), 185–219.

11. *Mitteilungen des Kampfbundes für deutsche Kultur* 1 (1929)–5 (1933); *DKW* (1932–33).

12. *AMZ* 62 (1935), 38; Blume, "Musikerschaft," 5; Wilhelm Ehmann, *Musikalische Feiergestaltung: Ein Werkweiser guter Musik für die natürlichen und politischen Feste des Jahres* (Hamburg, 1938), 15; *AMR*, 15 Oct. 1941, BA, RD33/2-2; ZM 107 (1940), 225; ZM 109 (1942), 555–56; Gruner, *Musikleben*, 156. On parallels in medicine, see Michael H. Kater, "Die Medizin im nationalsozialistischen Deutschland und Erwin Liek," *Geschichte und Gesellschaft* 16 (1990), 440–63.

13. Karl Hasse, *Vom deutschen Musikleben: Zur Neugestaltung unseres Musiklebens im neuen Deutschland: Ausgewählte Aufsätze* (Regensburg, 1933), 114; Breithaupt, "Tag," 82; *AMZ* 64 (1937), 514; ZM 104 (1937), 1416; ZM 108 (1942), 728.

14. Raabe, *Kulturwille*, 48; Raabe quoted in *AMR*, 15 Nov. 1941, BA, RD33/2-2. See also the revealing memoirs by Margarete Hannsmann, *Der helle Tag bricht an: Ein Kind wird Nazi* (Munich, 1984), and Jost Hermand, *Als Pimpf in Polen: Erweiterte Kinderlandverschickung, 1940–1945* (Frankfurt am Main, 1993).

15. Michael H. Kater, "Die deutsche Elternschaft im nationalsozialistischen Erziehungssystem: Ein Beitrag zur Sozialgeschichte der Familie," *Vierteljahrschrift für Sozial-und Wirtschaftsgeschichte* 67 (1980), 484–512.

16. *VB*, 11 Dec. 1934; Hasse, *Musikleben*, 114; Raabe, *Kulturwille*, 16; "Vorwort" in Erich Lauer, *Das völkische Lied: Erstes Buch: Lieder des neuen Volkes aus dem ersten Jahrfünft des Dritten Reiches*, 3rd ed. (Munich, 1939); Eberhard Preussner, "Hausmusik," in Alfred Morgenroth, ed., *Von deutscher Tonkunst: Festschrift zu Peter Raabes 70. Geburtstag* (Leipzig, 1942), 37; Herbert Just, "Hausmusik als Führungsaufgabe," in Wolfgang Stumme, ed., *Musik im Volk: Gegenwartsfragen der deutschen Musik* (Berlin-Lichterfelde, 1944), 95.

17. Kurl Lamerdin in ZM 105 (1938), 1091–92.

18. The RMK section (since 1933) was "Arbeitsgemeinschaft für Hausmusik" (see ZM 107 [1940], 369). For Hitler Youth *Hausmusik*, see *MJV* 1 (1937–38), 154–55; Eugen Mayer-Rosa, "Musikerziehung der Hitler-Jugend und Hausmusik," *MJV* 3 (1940), 266–69; ZM 109 (1942), 176; *MK* 1 (1943–44), 196.

19. On this friction, see Michael H. Kater, "Hitler-Jugend und Schule im Dritten Reich," *Historische Zeitschrift* 228 (1979), 572–623; on *Hausmusik* in schools, see "Wie feiert München den Tag der Hausmusik?" [1933]; Gutknecht to Ehrenberg, 6 Oct. 1942, SMK, 321; *VB*, 29 Sept. 1934 and 30 Oct. 1936; *AMR*, 1 Nov. 1939, BA, RD33/2-2; Michael Alt, "Die Musikerziehung in der deutschen Schule," *Internationale Zeitschrift für Erziehung* (1939), 332; ZM 109 (1942), 556; Walter Rischer, *Die nationalsozialistische Kulturpolitik in Düsseldorf, 1933–1945* (Düsseldorf, 1972), 188.

20. Heinz Boberach, ed., *Meldungen aus dem Reich: Die geheimen Lageberichte des Sicherheitsdienstes der SS, 1938–1945*, 17 vols. (Herrsching, 1984), 2:114; Just, "Hausmusik," 93.

21. ZM 108 (1941), 58, 130; ZM 109 (1942), 555; *AMR*, 31 Dec. 1943, BA, RD33/2-2.

22. *AMR*, 15 July 1941, 15 Jan. 1943, and 31 Dec. 1943, BA, RD33/2-2; *JdM* 1943, 39–40; *MK* 1 (1943–44), 186; *Podium der Unterhaltungsmusik*, 14 July 1944, 365; Just, "Hausmusik," 94, 97.

23. "Programm: Hausmusikstunde am Sonntag, 22. November," [Munich, 1942], SMK, 321; ZM 108 (1941), 23; ZM 110 (1942), 44; *MK* 1 (1943–44), 187, 193.

24. Ulrich Günther, "Musikerziehung im Dritten Reich—Ursachen und Folgen," in Hans-Christian Schmidt, ed., *Geschichte der Musikpädagogik* (Kassel, 1986), 105–24; idem, "Musikerziehung im Dritten Reich: Ursachen, Folgen, Folgerungen," *Musik und Bildung* 15 (1983), 13–14; Siegfried Günther, *Musikerziehung als nationale Aufgabe* (Heidelberg, 1933); Raabe, *Kulturwille*, 22; Eckhard Nolte, *Lehrpläne und Richtlinien für den schulischen Musikunterricht in Deutschland vom Beginn des 19. Jahrhunderts bis in die Gegenwart: Eine Dokumentation* (Mainz, 1975), 161–62; Reusch, *Musik*, 9–10, 14–15, 19–20; Alt, "Musikerziehung," 325–37; Sybille Neumann in *Zündende Lieder—Verbrannte Musik: Folgen des Nationalsozialismus für Hamburger Musiker und Musikerinnen: Katalog zur Ausstellung in Hamburg im November und Dezember 1988* (Hamburg, 1988), 76; Kater, "Hitlerjugend," 572–623.

25. Wolfgang Stumme, "Musikpolitik als Führungsaufgabe," in idem, *Musik im Volk*, 11; Just, "Hausmusik," 99–100; HJ and SS leader Karl Cerff quoted in *MJV* 1 (1937–38), 76.

26. Wolfgang Stumme, *Was der Führer der Einheit vom Singen wissen muss: Eine erste musikalische Hilfe für Jugendführer und Laiensingwarte*, 2nd ed. (Wolfenbüttel, 1942), 5; *Reich*, 5 Oct. 1941 (quote).

27. Schirach in Dorothea Hemming, ed., *Dokumente zur Geschichte der Musikschule (1902–1976)* (Regensburg, 1977), 131.

28. Michael H. Kater, "Bürgerliche Jugendbewegung und Hitlerjugend in Deutschland von 1926 bis 1939," *Archiv für Sozialgeschichte* 17 (1977), 169–71.

29. Otto Zander in Hemming, *Dokumente*, 119.

30. Guido Waldmann, "Reichsmusiktage der Hitlerjugend, Stuttgart 1937," *MJV* 1 (1937–38), 95–98; idem, "Bekenntnis zur deutschen Musik: Reichsmusiktage Düsseldorf—Beethovenfest der HJ. in Wildbad," *MJV* 1 (1937–38), 329–40; idem, "Das dritte Reichsmusik-Schulungslager der RJF in Braunschweig," *Deutsche Musikkultur* 1 (1936–37), 303–5; Richard Eichenauer, *Polyphonie—Die ewige Sprache deutscher Seele* (Wolfenbüttel, 1938), 3; Wolfgang Stumme, "Musik in der Hitler-Jugend," in Stumme, *Musik im Volk*, 29; Ulrich Günther, *Die Schulmusikerziehung von der Kestenberg-Reform bis zum Ende des Dritten Reiches: Ein Beitrag zur Dokumentation und Zeitgeschichte der Schulmusikerziehung mit Anregungen zu ihrer Neugestaltung* (Neuwied, 1967), 64, 252.

31. ZM 104 (1937), 1416; *JdM* 1943, 59–60; *MK* 1 (1943), 116; Stumme, "Musik," 24; Stumme, "Der Musikerzieher in der Hitler-Jugend," in Stumme, *Musik im Volk*, 63 (quote); Günther, *Schulmusikerziehung*, 55; Hemming, *Dokumente*, 131, 156–63.

32. ZM 108 (1941), 60, 749; "Anweisung für den HJ-Dienst in Orchesterschulen," appended to Krieger to Ehrenberg, 4 June 1941, SMK, 396; Patutschnik memorandum, 5 Nov. 1943, SMK, 865.

33. Felix Oberborbeck, "Gegenwartsaufgaben der deutschen Musikhochschulen," in Stumme, *Musik im Volk*, 134.

34. For purposes of this book, and to keep the proliferation of German technical terms to a minimum, the original designation will be used consistently.

35. Stumme, "Musikerzieher," 62; ZM 107 (1940), 176.

36. Bieder to Stumme, 29 Sept. 1936, BDC Stumme.

37. ZM 108 (1941), 429; Michael H. Kater, "Carl Orff im Dritten Reich," *Vierteljahrshefte für Zeitgeschichte* 43 (1995), 16–17; Wilhelm Twittenhoff, *Orff-Schulwerk: Einführung in Grundlagen und Aufbau* (Main, 1935).

38. ZM 107 (1940), 175; Gert Kerschenbaumer, *Faszination Drittes Reich: Kunst und Alltag der Kulturmetropole Salzburg* (Salzburg, [1988]), 179–80.

39. Wolfgang Stumme, "Musik in der Hitler-Jugend," in Stumme, ed., *Musik im Volk: Grundfragen der Musikerziehung* (Berlin, 1939), 19–20.

40. Felix Oberborbeck, "Landschaftlicher Musikaufbau dargestellt am Beispiel der Steiermark," ZM 107 (1940), 680–90; idem, "Gegenwartsaufgaben," 142–43; Helmut Brenner, *Musik als Waffe? Theorie und Praxis der politischen Musikverwendung, dargestellt am Beispiel der Steiermark, 1938–1945* (Graz, 1992), 72–203.

41. Marx to Ehrenberg, 29 Apr. 1941, SMK, 47; Marx to Orff, 1 Apr. 1944, CM, Allg. Korr.; *AMZ* 62 (1935), 314; ZM 107 (1940), 362; ZM 108 (1941), 357; MK 2 (1944), 75; Ehmann, *Feiergestaltung*, 27, 85; Carl Hannemann, *Neues Singebuch für Männerchor* (Hamburg, 1940), 9–10; Georg Götsch, *Singende Mannschaft: Einfache Chorlieder für drei gleiche Stimmen* (Kassel, [1940]), 35, 52–53; *Musik der Hitler-Jugend* (Wolfenbüttel, 1941), 22, 31, 33–34; Kater, "Orff," 6, 8. Note the typically apologetic post-1945 biography of Marx (Gudrun Straub et al., *Karl Marx* [Tutzing, 1983], esp. 34–36).

42. BDC Ruth Gottschalk, Eva Keck, Willi Träder, Urte Wabbel, Hans-Achim Weicker, Traute Zastrow, Ingeborg Zetsche, and Liselotte Zezulka.

43. "2. Niederbergisches Musikfest am 23./24. Mai 1935 in Langenberg-Rhld.," OW, 119; Grost to Reinhard, 12 Nov. 1938, SMK, 396; Amt für Konzertwesen, circular no. 3, 1 Aug. 1938, SMK, 393; Stumme, "Musik" (1939), 26; Stumme, "Musik" (1944), 23; ZM 107 (1940), 438, 796; *Musik*, 15; Stumme, *Führer*, 7; Dietz Degen, "Jugend komponiert," MK 2 (1944), 122–25; MK 1 (1944), 198; Ernst Klusen, *Volkslied: Fund und Erfindung* (Cologne, 1969), 177–80; Gruner, *Musikleben*, 72.

44. Ludwig Kelbetz, "Hans Baumann als Komponist der Hitlerjugend," ZM 105 (1938), 1100–1102; Jay W. Baird, *To Die for Germany: Heroes in the Nazi Pantheon* (Bloomington, Ind., 1990), 155–71 (quote on 155).

45. Lauer, *Lied* (biography 233); "Süddeutsche Tonkünstlerwoche 7.–13. Juni 1941 München," SMK, 47; ZM 107 (1940), 616–17.

46. Grost to Reinhard, 12 Nov. 1938, SMK, 396; Ehrenberg to Schmitt, 30 Mar. 1941; Schmitt to Ehrenberg, 25 Apr. 1941, SM., 47; Franz Köppe, "Die jugenderzieherischen Aufgaben der Hitlerjugend im Rundfunk," 67–69; Stumme, "Musik" (1939), 25; Stumme, "Volksliedsingen der Jugend," in Johannes Hoepp, ed., *Deutsche Liederkunde: Jahrbuch für Volkslied und Volkstanz* (Potsdam, 1939), 1:16; Stumme, "Musik" (1944), 26–27; *LI*, 643.

47. Reinhold Hartmann, "Musik unterm Hakenkreuz: Musikalische Beeinflussung im faschistischen Deutschland," *Musiktherapeutische Umschau* 8 (1987), 31; *TGII* 12:126; Hermand, *Pimpf*, 81–83.

48. Büchtger to Reinhard, 1 July 1937, SMK, 319; Amt für Konzertwesen, circular no. 3, 1 Aug. 1938, SMK, 393; Ehmann, *Feiergestaltung*, 10, 12, 16, 27; Stumme, "Volksliedsingen," 13–14; *Musik*, 18, 26, 32, 36, 44, 49; ZM 107 (1940), 422; MK 1 (1943), 102–3, 134; JdM 1944, 33; Nanny Drechsler, *Die Funktion der Musik im deutschen Rundfunk, 1933–1945* (Pfaffenweiler, 1988), 105; Gerd Kratzat in *Zündende Lieder*, 97; *GLM* 1:378.

49. ZM 110 (1943), 16–17; MK 1 (1944), 227.

50. Rudolf Kluge and Heinrich Krüger, *Verfassung und Verwaltung im Dritten Reich (Reichsbürgerkunde)* (Berlin, 1937), 91 (1st quote); Hitler in *Der Kongress zu Nürnberg vom 5. bis 10. September 1934* (Munich, 1934), 167 (2nd quote);

Der Kongress, 167 (3rd quote). See also Helmut Majewski, "Blasmusik auf dem Reichsparteitag 1938," *MJV* 1 (1937–38), 547–48; Ehmann, *Feiergestaltung,* 27 35, 81; Majewski, "Neugestaltung deutscher Blasmusik," in Stumme, *Musik im Volk* (1939), 34; Reinhold Heyden, "Ursprung und Gestaltung des Offenen Volksliedsingens," in Stumme, *Musik im Volk* (1939), 186; *JdM 1944,* 33.

51. Hans-Jochen Gamm, *Führung und Verführung: Pädagogik des Nationalsozialismus* (Munich, 1964); Werner Klose, *Generation im Gleichschritt: Ein Dokumentarbericht* (Oldenburg, 1964).

52. Majewski, "Neugestaltung," 31–45 (quote 35); *Musik,* 36.

53. Ludwig Kelbetz, *Zur Neugestaltung der deutschen Hochschulen für Musik* (Wolfenbüttel, 1941), 12 (quote); Götsch, *Mannschaft,* esp. 34–35, 52–53; Oberborbeck, "Gegenwartsaufgaben," 144; Klusen, *Volkslied,* 182; Hermand, *Pimpf,* 61.

54. *MJV* 3 (1940), 26–31; *ZM* 107 (1940), 782–83; Hermann Wagner, "Ergebnisse einer Frankreichfahrt der Standortspielschar Nürnberg der HJ.," *ZM* 108 (1941), 113–15; *ZM* 108 (1941), 267–68; *Musik,* 19; Stumme, "Musik" (1944), 29; Oberborbeck, "Gegenwartsaufgaben," 152.

55. "Historisches Konzert der SS," 31 Jan. 1934, BA, R78/1142; Josef von Golitschek, "60 Jungen—zwei Orchester: Die Musikschule der Waffen-SS," *ZM* 109 (1942), 398–400; Stumme, *Führer,* 33; *MK* 1 (1943), 107.

56. *Musik,* 22–23; Boberach, *Meldungen* 14 (1943), 5591–92; Erika Funk-Hennigs, "Über die instrumentale Praxis der Jugendmusikbewegung—Voraussetzungen und Auswirkungen," in Karl-Heinz Reinfandt, ed., *Die Jugendmusikbewegung: Impulse und Wirkungen* (Wolfenbüttel, 1987), 231; Hartmann, "Musik," 30. On soldiers, girls, and promiscuity, see Boberach, *Meldungen* 10 (1942), 3896–97; *Meldungen* 16 (1944), 6484–88.

57. BDC Stumme, *ik,* 60; Hodek, *Bewegung,* 115–16.

58. Bresgen in Carl Niessen, ed., *Die deutsche Oper der Gegenwart* (Regensburg, 1944), 100 (1st quote); Cesar Bresgen, *Mittersill 1945—Ein Weg zu Anton Webern* (Vienna, 1983), 48 (2nd quote); Rudolf Lück, *Cesar Bresgen* (Vienna, 1974), 8, 11–12; Lauer, *Lied,* 229; Erich Schütze, "Cesar Bresgen," *Nationalsozialistische Monatshefte* 12 (1941), 605–9; *ZM* 105 (1938), 1106–7.

59. "XIII. Vortragsabend: Kompositionen von Studierenden der Akademie," Munich, 27 June 1934, SMK, 475.

60. "Olympia-Sommer 1936," 30 Aug. 1936, SMK, 323/3; ADMV, "Mitteilungen," May 1937, BDC Peter Raabe; *VB,* 18 Oct. 1937 (1st quote); Eichenauer, *Polyphonie,* 74 (2nd quote); "Reichs-Musiktage 1939: Düsseldorf 14.–21. Mai," BS, Ana/410; *ZM* 107 (1940), 536–37; *ZM* 109 (1942), 227; *MK* 2 (1944), 76–77; Lück, *Bresgen,* 60–77.

61. Strecker to Orff, 15 Sept. 1937, CM, Schott Korr. (quote); Bresgen to Rosbaud, 6 May 1942, LP, 423/1/12.

62. *MK* 1 (1943), 60.

63. Bresgen in Lück, *Bresgen,* 19–20.

64. "Festsommer 1938 München," SMK 97/6; Lauer, *Lied,* 48–49, 60–61; Bresgen to Ehrenberg, 19 Dec. 1940 and 21 Feb. 1941, SMK 47; *Musik,* 40, 47–48; *ZM* 108 (1941), 471; *ZM* 110 (1943), 95; *MK* 1 (1943), 135; *MK* 2 (1944), 75 (quote); *JdM 1944,* 31; Peter Muck, *Einhundert Jahre Berliner Philharmonisches Orchester: Darstellung in Dokumenten,* 3 vols. (Tutzing, 1982), 3:309; Richard Eichenauer, *Von den Formen der Musik* (Wolfenbüttel, 1943), 72; Kerschenbaumer, *Faszination,* 152, 262–63.

65. Bresgen, *Mittersill,* 19, 71.

66. Büchtger to Reinhart, 1 July 1937, SMK, 142; Bresgen to Orff, 29 Mar. 1939, CM Allg. Korr.; Schmitt to Ehrenberg, 25 Apr. and 20 May 1941; "Süddeutsche Tonkünstlerwoche 1941," SMK, 47; *ZM* 108 (1941), 357; *ZM* 109 (1942), 89; Bresgen to Rosbaud, 10 June 1942, LP, 423/1/12; Kerschenbaumer, *Faszination,* 153, 171, 260–63; Brenner, *Musik,* 249.

67. Minutes of *Musikbeiräte* meeting, [Munich], 27 Sept. 1938, SMK, 909; "Verwaltungsbericht des Kulturamtes für das Rechnungsjahr 1938," SMK, 828; RMK minutes [Berlin, May–July 1942], BDC Werner Egk; *ZM* 109 (1942), 281, 372, 561; Lück, *Bresgen,* 15, 22; Kerschenbaumer, *Faszination,* 262 (quote).

68. Felix Raabe, *Die Bündische Jugend: Ein Beitrag zur Geschichte der Weimarer Republik* (Stuttgart, 1961); Kater, "Jugendbewegung," 127–74.

69. Dorothea Kolland, *Die Jugendmusikbewegung: "Gemeinschaftsmusik"—Theorie und Praxis* (Stuttgart, 1979); GLM 4:255; Fritz Jöde, "Die singende Jugend und die Musik," in Elisabeth Korn et al., eds., *Die Jugendbewegung: Welt und Wirkung: Zur 50. Wiederkehr des freideutschen Jugendtages auf dem Hohen Meissner* (Düsseldorf, 1963), 59–64; Günther, "Musikerziehung" (1986), 138–44. On Kestenberg, see *IBD,* 617–18.

70. Fricke to Kallmeyer, 18 Jan. 1933, BDC Jöde (1st quote); Jöde to Adler, 10 Sept. 1927, LBI, AR-7276/IV/2/7; Jöde to Orff, 26 Jan. 1932; Orff to Preussner, 28 Dec. 1932; Katz to Orff, 28 Aug. [1932] (2nd quote), CM, Allg. Korr.; Kallmeyer to Stege, 14 Dec. 1932, BDC Jöde; Fritz Jöde, "Musik und Gesellschaft: Eine Einleitung," *Musik und Gesellschaft* 1 (Apr. 1930), 1–3; *DKW,* no. 1 (1933), 13; Karl Grunsky, *Der Kampf um deutsche Musik* (Stuttgart, 1933), 46; Ernst Krieck, *Musische Erziehung* (Leipzig, 1933); Georg Götsch, "Musische Erziehung, eine deutsche Aufgabe," *Völkische Musikerziehung* 2 (1936), 5–11; Reusch, *Musik,* esp. 12–13, 30; Kurt Sontheimer, *Antidemokratisches Denken in der Weimarer Republik: Die politischen Ideen des deutschen Nationalismus zwischen 1918 und 1933,* 4th ed. (Munich, 1962), esp. 35, 315; Herman Lebovics, *Social Conservatism and the Middle Classes in Germany, 1914–1933* (Princeton, N.J., 1969); Karl-Heinz Reinfandt, "Fritz Jödes Schaffen zwischen Idee und Wirklichkeit," in Reinfandt, *Jugendmusikbewegung,* 283; Hodek, *Bewegung,* 105–9; Günther, "Musikerziehung" (1986), 144–45.

71. Jöde in *ZM* 100 (1933), 581 (1st quote); Fritz Jöde, *Deutsche Jugendmusik: Eine Frage nach dem Wesen im Wandel der Zeit* (Berlin, [1934]), 46–48 (remaining quotes); Kallmeyer to Rust, 9 Feb. and 10 Mar. 1933; Kallmeyer, "An die Gegner Professor Jödes, wenn sie die Wahrheit hören wollen," Apr 1933; Kallmeyer, "An die Freunde der Arbeit Professor Fritz Jödes!," Apr. 1933; "Erklärung," May 1933; Jöde, "In eigener Sache (Bericht)," June 1934; *ZM* 100 (1933), 571, 582–91; Günther, "Musikerziehung" (1986), 147; Hodek, *Bewegung,* 110–11; Christine Fischer-Defoy, *Kunst, Macht, Politik: Die Nazifizierung der Kunst- und Musikhochschulen in Berlin* (Berlin, [1988]), 99, 321; Wolfgang Stumme, "Die Musikschule im 20. Jahrhundert: Bericht eines Zeitzeugen," in Reinfandt, *Jugendmusikbewegung,* 255; Günther, "Jugendmusikbewegung und reformpädagogische Bewegung," in Reinfandt, *Jugendmusikbewegung,* 176; Reinfandt, "Schaffen," 285.

72. Stumme, "Musikschule," 255; Reinfandt, "Schaffen," 285; Günther, *Schulmusikerziehung,* 48; Hodek, *Bewegung,* 112; Kerschenbaumer, *Faszination,* 178; Napiersky's testimony in Fred K. Prieberg, *Musik im NS-Staat* (Frankfurt am Main, 1982), 244.

73. *VB*, 28 Feb. 1933 (quote); Hasse and zur Nedden, "In Ihrem eigensten Interesse!" [1933]; Zimmermann to Krieck, [1933]; Hasse to Kallmeyer, 2 Apr. 1933, BDC Jöde; Kittel to Graener, 18 Mar. 1933, BDC Bruno Kittel; Zimmermann to Frick, 8 Mar. 1933, BDC Willy Zimmermann; Niechciol to Rust, 10 Mar. 1933, BDC Traugott Niechciol; Hasse to Hinkel, 17 June 1933, BDC Karl Hasse; Grunsky, *Kampf*, 48–49, 66; *ZM* 100 (1933), 572–81; Hodek, *Bewegung*, 103–4.

74. Jöde RMK registration card with information from the security service of the SS dated 26 July 1940; von Staa to [Bieder], 25 Feb. 1937; Kunisch to Jöde, 11 Feb. 1935; Kunisch "Beschluss," 19 Mar. 1935; Kunisch to Vorsitzenden, 19 Mar. 1935, BDC Jöde; Bahmann et al., "Abschrift zu Va 153/39," 8 Oct. 1936; Miederer to Bavarian Culture Ministry, 8 Feb. 1939, BH, MK/36711. See also Reinfandt, "Schaffen," 277; Heinrich M. Sambeth in Reinhold Stapelberg, ed., *Fritz Jöde: Leben und Werk: Eine Freundesgabe zum 70. Geburtstag* (Trossingen, 1957), 93.

75. Heinrich Lades in Stapelberg, *Jöde*, 10; Jörn Thiel, ibid., 133; Jöde to Staatliche Hochschule, 18 June 1937 (all but last quote); Baudissin to [Bieder], 6 Aug. 1937; Poller to Best, 1 Aug. 1938, BDC Jöde; Kunisch to Bavarian Culture Ministry, 19 Dec. 1938 (last quote) and 11 May 1939, BH, MK/36711; Eichenauer, *Polyphonie*, 69; Ehmann, *Feiergestaltung*, 8, 11, 82; Reinhold Heyden, "Ursprung und Gestaltung des Offenen Volksliedsingens," in Stumme, *Musik in Volk* (1939), 183, 185.

76. The apologetic contention, published after 1945 by his disciples, that Jöde left Salzburg because of political difficulties and also left the Nazi Party, is a fabrication. As in the case of Karajan (see chapter 2 at n. 121), a retreat from the Nazi Party would have been recorded in Jöde's personal papers, which have been preserved. See Reinfandt, "Schaffen," 287–88; Heinrich Lades in Stapelberg, *Jöde*, 10–11. See also Bresgen, ibid., 145; Bresgen, *Mittersill*, 132; BDC Jöde; Günther, "Jugendmusikbewegung," 176; Götsch, *Mannschaft*, 2; Carl Hannemann, "Der Gemeinschaftsabend," *MJV* 3 (1940), 214; Stumme, *Führer*, 43; *MK* 1 (1943), 104, 106; *MK* 1 (1943–44), 183.

77. Oberborbeck, "Gegenwartsaufgaben," 140 (quote). See also Fritz Stein, "Aus der Arbeit der Staatl. akademischen Hochschule für Musik in Berlin," *ZM* 107 (1940), 388–95; *ZM* 108 (1941), 450.

78. *IBD*, 1070; Michael Fend in Hanns-Werner Heister et al., eds., *Musik im Exil: Folgen des Nazismus für die internationale Musikkultur* (Frankfurt am Main, 1993), 171–73; Donald W. Ellis, "Music in the Third Reich: National Socialist Aesthetic Theory as Governmental Policy" (Ph.D. diss., University of Kansas, 1970), 73–76; Joseph Wulf, ed., *Musik im Dritten Reich: Eine Dokumentation* (Reinbek, 1966), 29.

79. Kreutzer to Hinkel, 15 June 1933, BDC Kreutzer; [Stein] to [Rust], 23 Oct. 1933, BDC Vollerthun; [Stein] to [Rust], 9 Mar. 1939, BDC Wilhelm Lamping; KfdK, "Wünsche der Fachgruppe Musik," [late 1932], BDC Fritz Stein; Ferdinand Beussel, "Im Zeichen der Wende," *DM* 25 (1933), 672; Habakuk Traber and Elmar Weingarten, eds., *Verdrängte Musik: Berliner Komponisten im Exil* (Berlin, 1987), 219, 295; Fischer-Defoy, *Kunst*, 72, 126.

80. BDC Vollerthun.

81. BDC Trapp; *ZM* 107 (1940), 460; *ZM* 109 (1942), 470; Michael Mäckelmann, *Arnold Schönberg und das Judentum: Der Komponist und sein reli-*

giöses, nationales und politisches Selbstverständnis nach 1921 (Hamburg, 1984), 205; *GLM* 8:161.

82. Gotthold Frotscher, "Der Begriff 'Volksmusik,'" in Stumme, *Musik im Volk* (1939), 234 (quote); idem, "Die Musikarbeit im Kriegsjahr 1942," in Hemming, *Dokumente*, 164–67; idem, "Die Aufgabe der Musikwissenschaft," in Stumme, *Musik in Volk* (1944), 356–68; *GLM* 3:183–84.

83. KfdK, "An die deutschen Universitäten und Hochschulen," [30 Apr. 1932]; Hasse to Hinkel, 14 July 1933, BDC Hasse; Adler to Hasse, 18 May 1933, LBI, AR-7276/IV/2/12; Hasse to Stege, 27 July 1942, OW, 40; Karl Hasse, *Von deutschen Meistern: Zur Neugestaltung unseres Musiklebens im neuen Deutschland: Ausgewählte Aufsätze* (Regensburg, 1934); Siegmund Helms, *Musikpädagogik zwischen den Weltkriegen: Edmund Joseph Müller* (Wolfenbüttel, 1988), 101; *GLM* 4:43.

84. Karl Blessinger, *Mendelssohn, Meyerbeer, Mahler: Drei Kapitel Judentum in der Musik als Schlüssel zur Musikgeschichte des 19. Jahrhunderts* (Berlin, 1939); idem, *Judentum und Musik: Ein Beitrag zur Kultur- und Rassenpolitik* (Berlin, 1944); Wulf, *Musik*, 283, 475–76.

85. *GLM* 8:186; BDC Trunk; Fiehler memorandum, 15 Oct. 1942, SMK, 734; *VB*, 9 July 1934; *Münchener Neueste Nachrichten*, 9 July 1934; *Das Deutsche Führerlexikon 1934/35* (Berlin, n.d.), 497–98; Nicolas Slonimsky, *Music Since 1900*, 4th ed. (New York, 1971), 575. On Wessel, see Baird, *To Die*, 73–107.

86. Josef Müller-Blattau, "Das Horst Wessel-Lied," *DM* 26 (1934), 322–28 (quote on 328); idem, *Germanisches Erbe in deutscher Tonkunst* (Berlin, 1938); *ZM* 109 (1942), 185; *GLM* 5:385; Prieberg, *NS-Staat*, 285.

87. *Musik im Zeitbewusstsein*, no. 4 (4 Nov. 1933), 1–2; Friedrich Blume, "Musik und Rasse," *DM* 30 (1938), 736–48; *Podium der Unterhaltungsmusik*, 15 June 1944, 344; Prieberg, *NS-Staat*, 110–11; Kurt Gudewill, "Zur Geschichte des Faches Musikwissenschaft an der Christian-Albrechts-Universität in Kiel," in Carl Dahlhaus and Walter Wiora, eds., *Musikerziehung in Schleswig-Holstein: Dokumente der Vergangenheit, Aspekte der Gegenwart* (Kassel, 1965), 19–20; Pamela M. Potter, "The Deutsche Musikgesellschaft, 1918–1938," *Journal of Musicological Research* 11 (1991), 160–62. See n. 18 in chap. 3.

88. Jeremy Noakes, "The Ivory Tower Under Siege: German Universities in the Third Reich," *Journal of European Studies* 23 (1993), 371–407.

89. *ZM* 108 (1941), 62.

90. Schünemann "Fragebogen," 13 Aug. 1933, BDC Schünemann; *Wer ist's?*, 10th ed., ed. Herrmann A. L. Degener (Berlin, 1935), 1450; *GLM* 7:301; *The Memoirs of Carl Flesch*, ed. Hans Keller (Harlow, 1973), 316; John L. Stewart, *Ernst Krenek: The Man and His Music* (Berkeley, 1991), 27–32, 35–37.

91. *Wer ist's?*, 1450; *GLM* 7:281, 301.

92. Schünemann "Fragebogen," 13 Aug. 1933, BDC Schünemann; *GLM* 7:301; *Wer ist's?*, 1450; Niechciol to Rust, 10 Mar. 1933, BDC Niechciol; Kittel to Graener, 18 Mar. 1933, BDC Kittel; Schwartz to Hinkel, 26 Mar. 1933, BDC Schwartz; Rasch to Schünemann, 29 Mar. 1933, BDC Rasch; Schünemann to Hinkel, 8 Apr. 1933, BDC Fritz Stein; Kralle to [Hinkel], 21 June 1933, BDC Schünemann (1st quote); Hindemith to Strecker, 15 Apr. 1933 (2nd quote); Willy to Ludwig Strecker, 4 Aug. 1933, PF, Schott. Korr., Trinius to Hinkel, 30 May 1933, BDC Hans Trinius; Havemann to Hess, 21 Dec. 1933, BDC Havemann; Wulf, *Musik*, 20; Prieberg, *NS-Staat*, 44.

93. Gertrud to Paul Hindemith, 14 Apr. [1937], PF, 3.144.12–21; *TG* 3:348; Bruno von Niessen, "Bestätigung," 13 Aug. 1946, AM, Strauss; *AMZ* 64 (1937), 730; *ZM* 107 (1940), 232; *ZM* 108 (1941), 446, 471; Victor Junk, "Die Mozartwoche des Deutschen Reiches in Wien," *ZM* 109 (1942), 11; *MK* 1 (1943), 28; Georg Schünemann, *Die Singakademie zu Berlin, 1791–1941* (Regensburg, 1941), 186–89; *JdM* 1944, 27; *Podium der Unterhaltungsmusik,* 15 Feb. 1944, 263; Rudolf Hartmann, *Das geliebte Haus: Mein Leben mit der Oper* (Munich, 1975), 157; Fred K. Prieberg, *Musik und Macht* (Frankfurt am Main, 1991), 261; Schünemann quoted in Prieberg, *NS-Staat,* 408; Pamela M. Potter, "Musicology under Hitler: New Sources in Context," *Journal of the American Musicological Society* 49 (1996), 85–86.

94. Walter Rumpel as quoted in "Vermerk," 12 Dec. 1946, BDC Stein.

95. *Deutsches Musiker-Lexikon,* ed. Erich H. Müller (Dresden, 1929), 1388–89; *Führerlexikon,* 471–72; Stein to Herren, 30 July 1933, BDC Stein; Gudewill, "Geschichte," 18.

96. Lehmann to RSK, 30 Sept. 1941, BDC Stein; BDC Walter Teschendorff; *Artist,* 14 Apr. 1933; *DKW,* no. 11 (1933), 20. Stein's final falling out with the Kampfbund (1934) is portended in his letter to Hinkel, 16 June 1933, BDC Stein.

97. Rumpel, "Vermerk," 12 Dec. 1946, BDC Stein; Claudia Maurer Zenck, "Zwischen Boykott und Anpassung an den Charakter der Zeit: Über die Schwierigkeiten eines deutschen Komponisten mit dem Dritten Reich," *Hindemith-Jahrbuch* 9 (1980), 87, n. 90.

98. Stein, "Ansprache," 2 May 1933, BDC Stein; Wulf, *Musik,* 100.

99. Stein to [Franz Strauss], 6 Apr. 1934, RG; Alfred Morgenroth, "Peter Raabe und sein Weg," in Morgenroth, *Tonkunst,* 21.

100. BDC Stein; Stein to Hinkel, 22 July 1935, PF, Musikhochschule Berlin; *Melos* 12 (1933), 351; *Melos* 13 (1934), 72; Fritz Stein, "Chorwesen und Volksmusik im neuen Deutschland," *ZM* 101 (1934), 281–88 (quote on 284).

101. BDC Stein (on Stuckenschmidt, see Stein to Hinkel, 25 Nov. 1933).

102. *Skizzen* (Aug.–Sept. 1937), 15; *Skizzen* (Oct. 1937), 17; *Skizzen* (Mar. 1938), 18; *DDP,* 26 June 1936, 1–2.

103. H. J. Therstappen, "Fritz Stein," *ZM* 106 (1939), 1141–46; Carl Adolf Martienssen, "Fritz Stein als Musikerzieher und als Lehrer," *ZM* 106 (1939), 1146–50, 1150–51; Fritz Stein, "Aus der Arbeit der Staatlichen Akademischen Hochschule für Musik in Berlin," *ZM* 107 (1940), 388–95; *ZM* 108 (1941), 33, 586–87; *AMR,* 15 Jan. 1940 and 15 Jan. 1943, BA, RD33/2-2.

104. Petschull to Strecker, 11 Oct. 1936, PF, Schott. Korr.; Stein to Gossrau, 22 Dec. 1936, and to Furtwängler, 22 Mar. 1937, PF, Musikhochschule Berlin; Maurer Zenck, "Boykott," 96, 105–6; Andres Briner, *Paul Hindemith* (Zurich, 1971), 113; Orff to Strecker, 18 Feb. 1938, CM, Schott. Korr.

105. Alfred Rosenberg, *Der Mythus des 20. Jahrhunderts: Eine Wertung der seelisch-geistigen Gestaltenkämpfe unserer Zeit,* 41st/42nd ed. (Munich, 1934), esp. 616–17; idem, *An die Dunkelmänner unserer Zeit: Eine Antwort auf die Angriffe gegen den Mythus des 20. Jahrhunderts* (Munich, n.d.).

106. For the religious-political background, see Victoria Barnett, *For the Soul of the People: Protestant Protest Against Hitler* (New York, 1992); John S. Conway, *The Nazi Persecution of the Churches* (Toronto, 1968).

107. For background see works cited in n. 106.

108. Britta Martini, "Der Weg der Kirchenmusik in der nationalsozialistischen

Zeit im Spiegel der Zeitschrift 'Musik und Kirche,'" *Kirchenmusiker* 40 (1989), 89.

109. On Söhngen, see *GLM* 7:377. Quotations from "Erklärung," Berlin, 17–18 May 1933, ZM 100 (1933), 599–600.

110. Hasse, *Musikleben*, 8; Hasse to Hinkel, 16 June 1933 (quote) and 17 June 1933, BDC Hasse; Karl Hasse, "Deutsche Christen, Kirchenmusik und Orgelbewegung," ZM 100 (1933), 712–17; Stein to Hinkel, 1 July and 6 Oct. 1933, BDC Stein; ZM 108 (1941), 275; Wulf, *Musik*, 71; Jörg Fischer, "Evangelische Kirchenmusik im Dritten Reich: 'Musikalische Erneuerung' und ästhetische Modalität des Faschismus," *Archiv für Musikwissenschaft* 46 (1989), 186–225.

111. Fred Hamel, "Zur Erneuerung der Kirchenmusik," *Melos* 12 (1933), 276–81 (1st quote on 276); remaining quotes, enclosures with Emilie von Freyhold to Goebbels, 6 Sept. 1933, BA, R55/1140. See also Martini, "Weg"; Albrecht Riethmüller, "Die Erneuerung der Kirchenmusik im Dritten Reich—Eine Legende?" *Kirchenmusiker* 40 (1989), 161–74; Fischer, "Kirchenmusik," 200–209.

112. Hamel, "Erneuerung," 281.

113. Quote according to Hans Prolingheuer, "1937—Das Jubeljahr des Oskar Söhngen: Zum 'Fest der deutschen Kirchenmusik' vor 50 Jahren," *Neue Stimme* 14 (1987), 28. See also *Fest der deutschen Kirchenmusik: Werke unserer Zeit* (Berlin-Steglitz, [1937]); Oskar Söhngen, *Die neue Kirchenmusik: Wandlungen und Entscheidungen* (Berlin-Steglitz, 1937), 23–24, 41 (n. 9); Martini, "Weg," 91–93; Söhngen, *Kämpfende Kirchenmusik: Die Bewährungsprobe der evangelischen Kirchenmusik im Dritten Reich* (Kassel, n.d.), 42–44; Fischer, "Kirchenmusik," 228; Prieberg, *NS-Staat*, 37.

114. Hans Prolingheuer, *Ausgetan aus dem Land der Lebendigen: Leidensgeschichten unter Kreuz und Hakenkreuz* (Neukirchen-Vluyn, 1983), 102–41; idem, *Wir sind in die Irre gegangen: Die Schuld der Kirche unterm Hakenkreuz nach dem Bekenntnis des "Darmstädter Wortes" von 1947* (Cologne, 1987) (Söhngen's quote reproduced in facs., ibid., 156); idem, "Die 'Entjudung' der deutschen evangelischen Kirchenmusik zwischen 1933 und 1945: Vortrag in der Ev. Akademie Arnoldshain am 28.1.1989," *Kirchenmusiker* 40 (1989), 121–37; AMZ 62 (1935), 542; *Schwarze Korps*, 5 Sept. 1935, 5; Wolfgang Gerlach, *Als die Zeugen schwiegen: Bekennende Kirche und die Juden* (Berlin, 1987), 194–200; Fischer, " Kirchenmusik," 209, 225–28, 232; Martini, "Weg," 94–95.

115. Oskar Söhngen, *Die Wiedergeburt der Kirchenmusik: Wandlungen und Entscheidungen* (Kassel, 1953), 43, 58.

116. RMK minutes [Berlin, May–July 1942], BDC Werner Egk; Oliver Rathkolb, *Führertreu und gottbegnadet: Künstlereliten im Dritten Reich* (Vienna, 1991), 176; ZM 109 (1942), 562 (quote); Slonimsky, *Music*, 760; Fred K. Prieberg, *Lexikon der Neuen Musik* (Freiburg, 1958), 99.

117. *Melos* 12 (1933), 421, 431; *Melos* 13 (1934), 207; AMZ 66 (1939), 114; ZM 107 (1940), 299; Karl Laux, *Musik und Musiker der Gegenwart* (Essen, 1949), 1:65–72; Karl H. Wörner, *Neue Musik in der Entscheidung* (Mainz, 1954), 294; Prieberg, *Lexikon*, 98–99; Fischer, "Kirchenmusik," 212, 215–18 (Distler quote on 231).

118. Laux, *Musik*, 65; *GLM* 2:325.

119. BDC Distler; BDC Heilwig Thieme; *Deutsche Musikkultur* 1 (1936–37), 238 (1st quote); Ehmann, *Feiergestaltung*, 40–41, 85; Fischer, "Kirchenmusik,"

204 (Distler's 2nd quote), 211, 219 (Distler's 3rd quote); Eric Levi, *Music in the Third Reich* (New York, 1994), 153.

120. Ernst Pepping, *Stilwende der Musik* (Mainz, 1934) (quotes on 79–81); Adam Adrio, "Ernst Pepping," *Melos* 13 (1934), 142–47; Laux, *Musik*, 193–201; Wörner, *Musik*, 294; Fischer, "Kirchenmusik," 230–31.

121. *NG* 11:795–96.

122. Victor Klemperer, *"LTI": Die unbewältigte Sprache: Aus dem Notizbuch eines Philologen* (Munich, 1969).

123. Quotes Gau-Dozentenbundsführer to Drissen, 19 Oct. 1938, BDC Pepping. See also Friedrich Blume, "Ernst Pepping" (1937), in Heinrich Poos, ed., *Festschrift Ernst Pepping zu seinem 70. Geburtstag am 12. September 1971* (Berlin, 1971), 51; Ehmann, *Feiergestaltung*, 39; *VB*, 1 Aug. 1939; *Reich*, 23 Mar. 1941; *ZM* 107 (1940), 171, 463; *ZM* 108 (1941), 603; Adam Adrio, "Ernst Pepping," *ZM* 109 (1942), 49–53; *ZM* 109 (1942), 112, 234, 403–4; *MK* 2 (1944), 77; Muck, *Jahre* 2:173.

124. David to Orff, [1943], CM, Allg. Korr.; Munich Philharmonic, "Städtische Philharmonische Konzerte 1942–43," SMK, 177; Friedrich Welter, *Musikgeschichte im Umriss: Vom Urbeginn bis zur Gegenwart* (Leipzig, n.d.), 317; *JdM* 1943, 134–44, 196–97; *JdM* 1944, 82; *ZM* 107 (1940), 273, 563–64, 574, 611, 744, 797; *ZM* 108 (1941), 55, 101, 447, 474, 796–97; *ZM* 109 (1942), 91, 114, 160, 184, 377, 493; *ZM* 110 (1943), 117–18; *MK* 1 (1943), 34; *MK* 2 (1944), 65, 68; Bernhard Kohl, "'Ein Kunstwerk aus der Hand der Götter': Johann Nepomuk David in Leipzig," in Johannes Forner, ed., *Festschrift 150 Jahre Musikhochschule 1843–1993: Hochschule für Musik und Theater "Felix Mendelssohn Bartholdy"* (Leipzig, 1993), 156–73.

125. *VB*, 12 Oct. 1937; RMK minutes, [Berlin, May–July 1942], BDC Werner Egk; Ehmann, *Feiergestaltung*, 83; *ZM* 108 (1941), 450; *ZM* 110 (1943), 45, 71, 118; *MK* 1 (1943), 115–16. Kohl's attempt to downplay David's role in the creation and performance of the Führer motet amounts to an apologia, still rampant in Germany ("Kunstwerk," 160–61). On this, see Prieberg, *NS-Staat*, 10.

126. Günter Hartung, "Analyse eines faschistischen Liedes," *Wissenschaftliche Zeitschrift der Martin-Luther-Universität Halle-Wittenberg* 23, no. 6 (1974), 53; Hartmann, "Musik," 29.

127. Söhngen, *Wiedergeburt*, 42.

128. *GLM* 7:406–7; Bieder to Spitta et al., 13 Feb. 1935, BDC Fritz Jöde; Guido Waldmann, "Musikschulungslager und Musiktage der Hitlerjugend: Erfurt 1935," *Deutsche Musikkultur* 1 (1936–37), 58 (quote); Spitta in Lauer, *Lied*, 238; Welter, *Musikgeschichte*, 308.

129. Quotations from "Der Führer hat Gerufen" in Prolingheuer, *Irre*, 107. Also see ADMV, *Mitteilungen*, no. 113 (May 1937), BDC Peter Raabe; Ehmann, *Feiergestaltung*, 26, 39, 41, 46, 82, 85; Spitta's fanatical Nazi letter from the front in *MJV* 3 (1940), 29–31; *Musik*, 12–17, 22, 27, 30, 32–33, 42, 45–46, 49; *ZM* 108 (1941), 722; *ZM* 109 (1942), 184, 188, 372, 423; *ZM* 110 (1943), 23, 123; *MK* 2 (1944), 34.

130. Franz Krautwurst in Krautwurst et al., *Armin Knab* (Tutzing, 1991), 37–40; Friedrich Zipp, ibid., 93–120; Bieder to Knab, 17 Jan. 1944 (2nd quote), BDC Knab; other corr., ibid.; Söhngen, *Kämpfende Kirchenmusik*, 48; Lauer, *Lied*, 232; *DAZ*, 19 Feb. 1941 (1st quote); *Melos* 12 (1933), 422, 431; Welter, *Musikgeschichte*, 314–15; *ZM* 108 (1941), 60, 477, 681; *ZM* 109 (1942), 90–

91; *JdM 1944*, 32; *MK* 2 (1944), 104; Oskar Lang, *Armin Knab: Ein Meister deutscher Liedkunst* (1937; rpt. Würzburg, 1981), 32–75.

131. Krautwurst in *Knab*, 36, 41 (quotes); Hans Schmidt-Mannheim, ibid., 55; Knab "Fragebogen," 28 June 1934, BDC Knab; Michael H. Kater, *The Nazi Party: A Social Profile of Members and Leaders, 1919–1945* (Cambridge, Mass., 1983), 67, 108, 112, 134; Konrad H. Jarausch, *The Unfree Professions: German Lawyers, Teachers, and Engineers, 1900–1950* (New York, 1990), 141.

132. Vollerthun to Rühlmann, 7 Sept. 1935 and 16 Apr. 1936, BDC Vollerthun; Knab to [Bieder], 12 Apr. 1938, BDC Knab; *DAZ*, 19 Feb. 1941; *ZM* 101 (1934), 1274–75; *ZM* 109 (1942), 424; *ZM* 110 (1943), 116; Ehmann, *Feiergestaltung*, 26, 38–42, 45–46, 82, 85–86; Lauer, *Lied*, 29–31, 122–23; Welter, *Musikgeschichte*, 308; Hannemann, *Singebuch*, 33–35, 126–28; Carl Hannemann, "Der Gemeinschaftsabend: Alte und neue Geselligkeit," *MJV* 3 (1940), 215; Götsch, *Mannschaft*, 67; *Musik*, 15, 22, 26–27, 29–30, 32–33; Fischer-Defoy, *Kunst*, 101–2, 221.

133. RMK minutes, [Berlin, May–July 1942], BDC Werner Egk; *VB*, 22 July 1940; *ZM* 108 (1941), 74; *MK* 1 (1943), 115.

134. Söhngen, *Kämpfende Kirchenmusik*, 42–43; idem, *Wiedergeburt*, 42; Ulrich Dibelius, *Moderne Misik: Voraussetzungen, Verlauf, Material* (Munich, 1966), 36 (1st quote); Heinrich Lindlar, ed., *Wolfgang Fortner: Eine Monographie: Werkanalysen, Aufsätze, Reden, Offene Briefe, 1950–1959* (Rodenkirchen, n.d.), 47 (2nd quote).

135. *NG* 13:104–5 (quote on 104); Robert Hill, "'Overcoming Romanticism': On the Modernization of Twentieth-Century Performance Practice," in Gilliam, *Music*, 37–58; Richard Taruskin, *Text and Act: Essays on Music and Performance* (New York, 1995), 256.

136. *GLM* 3:137–38; Dibelius, *Musik*, 35; Lindlar, *Fortner*, 14–17; Laux, *Musik*, 97–104; *Melos* 13 (1934), 71, 111, 157; *AMZ* 63 (1936), 174; Helmut Heiber, *Die Kapitulation der Hohen Schulen: Das Jahr 1933 und seine Themen*, 2 vols. (Munich, 1992, 1994), 2:501–3; Welter, *Musikgeschichte*, 309 (quote).

137. Ehmann, *Feiergestaltung*, 47; Gau-Dozentenbundführer to Drissen, 18 Dec. 1937 (quotes); Besseler to Stein, 12 Feb. 1938, BDC Fortner.

138. RMK minutes, [Berlin, May–July 1942], BDC Werner Egk; BDC Fortner; Fortner quoted in Fischer, "Kirchenmusik," 230; *Musik*, 17, 22, 30, 34; *ZM* 107 (1940), 574, 744, 798; *ZM* 108 (1941), 74, 560; *ZM* 109 (1942), 85, 114, 159; *MK* 1 (1943), 37; *MK* 1 (1943–44), 187; *MK* 2 (1944), 113.

139. Peter Williams, "The Idea of *Bewegung* in the German Organ Reform Movement of the 1920s," in Gilliam, *Music*, 135–53.

140. Josef Müller-Blattau in Müller-Blattau, ed., *Bericht über die zweite Freiburger Tagung für die deutsche Orgelkunst vom 27. bis 30. Juni 1938* (Kassel, 1939), 5–6; "Erklärung," Berlin, 17–18 May 1933, *ZM* 100 (1933), 599–600; Auler to Goebbels, 20 May 1933, BA, R55/1138; Karl Hasse, "Deutsche Christen, Kirchenmusik und Orgelbewegung," *ZM* 100 (1933), 712–17; Werner David, "Zukunftshoffnungen heutiger Orgelkunst," *ZM* 110 (1943), 9–12; Oskar Söhngen, *Wandel und Beharrung: Vorträge und Abhandlungen über Kirchenmusik und Liturgie* (Berlin, 1965), 60, 128; Söhngen, *Kämpfende Kirchenmusik*, 137; Riethmüller, "Bestimmung," 38.

141. David, "Zukunftshoffnungen," 11.

142. Manfred Mezger, "Inquisition: Der 'Nationalsozialist' Günther Ramin," *Musik und Kirche* 59 (1989), 291–92; Wolfgang Dallmann, "Kirchenmusi-

kalische Erneuerung in schwerer Zeit," *Musik und Kirche* 59 (1989), 109–10; *DM* 29 (1936), 34 (picture of Ramin opposite page 16); Riethmüller, "Bestimmung," 40–41.

143. Müller-Blattau paraphrased by Riethmüller, "Bestimmung," 35 (1st quote); 2nd quote is Riethmüller's phrase, ibid.

144. Prieberg, *NS-Staat*, 359; Michael H. Kater, *Das "Ahnenerbe" der SS, 1935–1945: Ein Beitrag zur Kulturpolitik des Dritten Reiches* (Stuttgart, 1974), 18, 80–81.

145. Stumme in *Die Orgel in der Gegenwart* (Wolfenbüttel, 1939), 2–4; idem, "Musik in der Hitler-Jugend," in Stumme, *Musik im Volk* (1939), 30; idem, "Musikaufgaben in der Nationalsozialistischen Deutschen Arbeiterpartei," in Stumme, *Musik im Volk* (1944), 172; idem, "Musik in der Hitler-Jugend," in Stumme, *Musik im Volk* (1944), 30–31; BDC Helmut Majewski, Kurt Tantau and Karl Friedrich Waack; Prolingheuer, "Entjudung," 134; Dallmann, "Erneuerung," 111.

146. Herbert Haag in *Die Orgel*, 14–16.

147. Ibid., 85.

148. Josef Müller-Blattau, "Orgel und Gegenwart," in Müller-Blattau, *Bericht*, 147.

149. *MJV* 3 (1940), 28–29; Jochum to Orff, 2 Apr. 1942, CM, Allg. Korr. (1st quote); Schulz to Strauss, 8 Jan. 1944, RG (2nd quote).

150. Fischer-Defoy, *Kunst*, 219; Söhngen, *Kämpfende Kirchenmusik*, 99; ZM 107 (1940), 556–57; *MK* 1 (1943–44), 197; *MK* 2 (1944), 33; *JdM 1944*, 29; Prolingheuer, "Jubeljahr," 28.

151. "Erklärung," Berlin, 17–18 May 1933, ZM 100 (1933), 599–600; ZM 107 (1940), 501.

152. Gotthold Frotscher, *Geschichte des Orgelspiels und der Orgelkomposition*, 2 vols. (Berlin-Schöneberg, 1935–36) 2:1260; idem in *Die Orgel*, 7; idem, "Amerikanismus in der Musik," *MJV* 6 (1943), 94–97; *Musiker-Lexikon*, 373–74; *GLM* 3:183–84; BDC Frotscher; *DM* 31 (1939), 502 (quote); *Musik*, 14–15, 59; ZM 110 (1943), 44; Prolingheuer, "Entjudung," 133; Riethmüller, "Bestimmung," 36.

153. Adolf Aber, "Günther Ramin," *DM* 20 (1928), 333–38; Charlotte Ramin, *Günther Ramin: Ein Lebensbericht* (Freiburg, 1958), 15–41, 60; *LI*, 587.

154. *VB*, 21 Oct. 1993; Ramin, *Ramin*, 67, 99, and passim; ZM 107 (1940), 463; ZM 108 (1941), 48, 316, 588; ZM 109 (1942), 255, 541; Muck, *Jahre* 3:308.

155. Ramin, *Ramin*, 79.

156. Ibid., 73–79; corr. BA, R55/1177 and R55/1184. Goebbels's initials are on several of those letters.

157. Ullo von Bülow to Vicco von Bülow, 8 Nov. 1934, BA, R55/1177; Ramin, *Ramin*, 79–80; Erich Stockhorst, *Fünftausend Köpfe: Wer war was im Dritten Reich* (Velbert, 1967), 50, 158; Fritzsche, *Nation*, 146, 179.

158. Söhngen, *Kämpfende Kirchenmusik*, 44.

159. Prieberg, *NS-Staat*, 139, 141. Tension is documented in Ramin, *Ramin*, 88–89, 98–99; and *LI*, 588. See also ZM 107 (1940), 148–49; ZM 110 (1943), 17.

160. ZM 107 (1940), 273, 463; ZM 108 (1941), 48 (quote), 450, 795; ZM 109 (1942), 208; ZM 110 (1943), 144; F. A. Hauptmann, "Johann Sebastian Bach und wir: Ansprache vor Junkern der Waffen-SS," ZM 110 (1943), 101–4.

CHAPTER 5

1. Gottfried von Einem, recorded interview, Vienna, 30 Nov. 1994, APA.

2. On the Nazis as modernizers, see Jens Alber, "Nationalsozialismus und Modernisierung," *Kölner Zeitschrift für Soziologie und Sozialpsychologie* 41 (1989), 346–65; Michael Prinz and Rainer Zitelmann, eds., *Nationalsozialismus und Modernisierung* (Darmstadt, 1991). One of the glaring defects of these works is their neglect of culture.

3. Quoted in *Münchener Neueste Nachrichten*, 1 July 1936.

4. I am adopting this concept from Reinhard Bollmus, *Das Amt Rosenberg und seine Gegner: Zum Machtkampf im nationalsozialistischen Herrschaftssystem* (Stuttgart, 1970), esp. 236–50.

5. On the graphic arts, see *Führer durch die Ausstellung Entartete Kunst* [Munich, 1937]; Joseph Wulf, ed., *Die bildenden Künste im Dritten Reich: Eine Dokumentation* (Gütersloh, 1963); Stephanie Barron et al., *"Degenerate Art": The Fate of the Avant-Garde in Nazi Germany* (Los Angeles, 1991). Generally and with emphasis on music, see *DM* 25 (1933), 917; Amt für Konzertwesen, circular no. 3, 1 Aug. 1938, SMK, 393; Goebbels quoted in Albrecht Dümling and Peter Girth, eds., *Entartete Musik: Zur Düsseldorfer Ausstellung von 1938: Eine kommentierte Rekonstruktion* (Düsseldorf, [1988]), 57; *TG* 2:627; *TGII* 7:115; *TGII* 8:245, 267, 320–21, 346, 548; Goebbels in *Münchener Neueste Nachrichten*, 1 July 1936; W. T. Anderman [Walter Thomas], *Bis der Vorhang fiel: Berichtet nach Aufzeichnungen aus den Jahren 1940 bis 1945* (Dortmund, 1947), 236–37.

6. Hindemith to Strecker, 15 Apr. 1933; Willy to Ludwig Strecker, 4 Aug. 1933; Hindemith to Strecker, 5 Feb. 1934; Strecker to Hindemith, 8 Feb. 1934, PF, Schott. Korr.; Hindemith to Toch, 23 Sept. 1933, ETA, 36 (1st quote); Havemann to Hess, 21 Dec. 1933, BDC Havemann; Fritz Stege in *Westen* (Berlin), 18 Nov. 1934; *Mitteldeutsche National-Zeitung* (Halle), 6 Nov. 1934; *Melos* 13 (1934), 112; *Skizzen* (Nov. 1934), 18; Claus Neumann, "Moderne Musik— Ein 'Ja' oder 'Nein'?," *ZM* 100 (1933), 546 (2nd quote); Hans Heinz Stuckenschmidt, *Zum Hören geboren: Ein Leben mit der Musik unserer Zeit* (Munich, 1979), 130; Alban Berg, *Briefe an seine Frau*, ed. Helene Berg (Munich, 1965), 627; Andres Briner et al., *Paul Hindemith: Leben und Werk in Bild und Text* (Mainz, 1988), 132, 143, 146; Geoffrey Skelton, *Paul Hindemith, the Man Behind the Music: A Biography* (London, 1975), 108, 115–17; Giselher Schubert, *Paul Hindemith: Mit Selbstzeugnissen und Bilddokumenten* (Reinbek, 1990), 79; Peter Muck, *Einhundert Jahre Berliner Philharmonisches Orchester: Darstellung in Dokumenten*, 3 vols. (Tutzing, 1982), 3:259; Claudia Maurer Zenck, "Zwischen Boykott und Anpassung an den Charakter der Zeit: Über die Schwierigkeiten eines deutschen Komponisten mit dem Dritten Reich," *Hindemith-Jahrbuch* 9 (1980), 72, 118.

7. James E. Paulding, "Mathis der Maler—The Politics of Music," *Hindemith-Jahrbuch* 5 (1976), 112; Maurer Zenck, "Boykott," 119 (1st quote); Hermann Danuser, *Die Musik des 20. Jahrhunderts* (Regensburg, 1984), 227–28, 241–42; Heinrich Strobel in *Melos* 13 (1934), 96 (2nd quote); Strobel, "Hindemiths neue Symphonie," *Melos* 13 (1934), 127–31.

8. Wilhelm Pinder, *Die deutsche Kunst der Dürerzeit: Text* (1943; rpt. Cologne, 1953), 253–75; *Führer*, 9; Barron et al., *"Degenerate Art,"* 315–24; Peter Selz, *German Expressionist Painting* (Berkeley, 1974); Michael H. Kater,

"Anti-Fascist Intellectuals in the Third Reich," *Canadian Journal of History* 16 (1981), 275–76.

9. Maurer Zenck adroitly takes umbrage at earlier postwar versions of Hindemith's "inner emigration." See her "Boykott," 69–70, 117, 120, 125, 127; and Heinrich Strobel, "Mathis der Maler," *Melos* 14 (1947), 65–68; Andres Briner, *Paul Hindemith* (Zurich, 1971), 108.

10. Karl Grunsky, *Der Kampf um deutsche Musik* (Stuttgart, 1933), 25, 30; DM 26 (1933), 150 (quote); Briner et al., *Hindemith*, 132; Skelton, *Hindemith*, 108, 113–14, 120; Schubert, *Hindemith*, 80. On Hitler, See Michael Walter, *Hitler in der Oper: Deutsches Musikleben, 1919–1945* (Stuttgart, 1995), 193.

11. Hindemith to Strecker, 15 and 18 Nov. 1934, PF, Schott Korr.; Westen (Berlin), 18 Nov. 1934; Skelton, *Hindemith*, 117; Briner et al., *Hindemith*, 143; Fred K. Prieberg, *Musik und Macht* (Frankfurt am Main, 1991), 137.

12. Furtwängler, "Der Fall Hindemith," in *DAZ* (Berlin), 25 Nov. 1934.

13. *VB*, 2 Dec. 1934; Hindemith to [Stein], 5 Dec. 1934, PF, Musikhochschule Berlin; DM 27 (1935), 246–47; Skelton, *Hindemith*, 122; Prieberg. *Macht*, 174; Maurer Zenck, "Boykott," 83; Oliver Rathkolb. *Führertreu und gottbegnadet: Künstlereliten im Dritten Reich* (Vienna, 1991), 87–88.

14. Briner, *Hindemith*, 101.

15. This is the tenor of Maurer Zenck, "Boykott."

16. Hans Severus Ziegler, *Entartete Musik: Eine Abrechnung* (Düsseldorf, [1938]), 31–32; Briner et al., *Hindemith*, 148–70; Schubert, *Hindemith*, 86–105.

17. Strecker to Hindemith, 20 Apr. 1936; "Vortrag Dr. Fritz von Borries anlässlich eines Hindemith-Konzerts im März 1941"; Rösch to Herren, 29 Jan. 1943; Kinzel to Hindemith, 19 Aug. 1943; Brandt to Schott's Söhne, 31 July 1944, PF, Schott Korr.; Kabasta to Reinhard, 19 Feb. 1940, SMK, 177; *Melos* 14 (1947), 187; Skelton, *Hindemith*, 133; Maurer Zenck, "Boykott," 108–10; Rudolf Stephan, "Zur Musik der Dreissigerjahre," in Christoph-Hellmut Mahling and Sigrid Wiesmann, eds., *Bericht über den Internationalen Musikwissenschaftlichen Kongress Bayreuth 1981* (Kassel, 1984), 144; Cesar Bresgen, *Mittersill 1945—Ein Weg zu Anton Webern* (Vienna, 1983), 76.

18. Igor Stravinsky, *An Autobiography* (New York, 1962), 171; Thomas Mann, *Tagebücher, 1940–1943*, ed. Peter de Mendelssohn (Frankfurt am Main, 1982), 497; Richard Taruskin, "The Dark Side of Modern Music," *New Republic*, 5 Sept. 1988, 32; Taruskin in *New York Review of Books*, 15 June 1989, 57; Michael H. Kater, *Different Drummers: Jazz in the Culture of Nazi Germany* (New York, 1992), 62; Harvey Sachs, *Music in Fascist Italy* (London, 1987), 167–69.

19. *DKW*, no. 15 (1993), 7–8; Strecker to Hindemith, 5 Apr. 1933, PF, Schott. Korr.; Stuckenschmidt in *BZ am Mittag* (Berlin), 15 Nov. 1934; Stege in *Westen* (Berlin), 18 Nov. 1934; Fred K. Prieberg, *Musik im NS-Staat* (Frankfurt am Main, 1982), 41; Joan Evans, "Die Rezeption der Musik Igor Strawinskys in Hitlerdeutschland," paper, international colloquium, "Zur Situation der Musik in Deutschland in den dreissiger und vierziger Jahren," at Carl-Orff-Zentrum, Munich, 23 Nov. 1994.

20. Evans, "Rezeption"; Bergese to Orff, 8 Apr. 1936, CM, Allg. Korr. (quotes); Abendroth to Pfitzner, 5 Apr. 1938, OW, F68, 288; *VB*, 5 July 1937; *DAZ* (Berlin), 25 May 1938; *Skizzen* (Nov. 1938), 17; "Statistik," [Berliner Philharmonie], 1938–39, BA, R55/197; *AMR*, 15 Feb. 1940, BA, RD33/2–2;

Ziegler, *Musik*, 22; Muck, *Jahre* 3:278, 284; Hermann Stoffels, "Das Musiktheater in Krefeld von 1870–1945," in Ernst Klusen et al., *Das Musikleben der Stadt Krefeld: 1870–1945*, 2 vols. (Cologne, 1980), 2:178; Gerigk's warning in *Nationalsozialistische Monatshefte* 10 (Jan. 1939), 86. Sam H. Shirakawa's incorrect statement that to perform Stravinsky in Nazi Germany in 1938 was "all but a capital crime" reflects the overall shoddiness of his book (*The Devil's Music Master: The Controversial Life and Career of Wilhelm Furtwängler* [New York, 1992], 451).

21. *DKW*, no. 13 (1933), 10; Justitiar to Dressler-Andress, 8 Mar. 1934, BDC Gustav Havemann; *AMR*, 5 Dec. 1934, SMK, 393; Stegmann to Promi, 1 Feb. 1935, BA, R55/1148; Strauss/Laubinger memorandum, 11 Feb. 1935, NWH, 975/16–4; RRG to Promi, 29 May 1935, BDC Wilhelm Buschkötter; [Ehrenberg?] memorandum, 28 Aug. 1935, SMK, 214; Fischer to Generalintendanz, 16 Sept. 1935, BH, MK/40991; *ZM* 102 (1935), 1258; Goebbels quoted in *Münchener Neueste Nachrichten*, 1 July 1936; Mayer memorandum, 29 Nov. 1937; Joseph Wulf, ed. *Musik im Dritten Reich: Eine Dokumentation* (Reinbek, 1966), 460–71; Guido Waldmann, "Bekenntnis zur deutschen Musik: Reichsmusiktage Düsseldorf—Beethovenfest der HJ. in Wildbad," *MJV* 1 (1937–38), 330–33; Muck, *Jahre* 2:105.

22. Egk in *Melos* 13 (1934), 233.

23. Rimnitz to Strauss, 24 June 1935, RG; Krieger to Hinkel, 13 Mar. 1936, BDC Theodor Seeger; Mayerhofer memorandum, 9 Sept. 1936, SMK, 468; Sander to Hinkel, 4 Jan. 1937, BDC Max Trapp; *VB*, 18 Oct. 1937; *AMZ* 65 (1938), 379; *Unterhaltungsmusik*, 21 Apr. 1938, 491; Walter Rischer, *Die nationalsozialistische Kulturpolitik in Düsseldorf, 1933–1945* (Düsseldorf, 1972), 63–64; Nanny Drechsler, *Die Funktion der Musik im deutschen Rundfunk, 1933–1945* (Paffenweiler, 1988), 87–91.

24. Strecker to the Hindemiths, 9 Apr. 1936, PF, Schott Korr.; Büchtger to Reinhard, [1937], SMK, 142; Rosbaud, "Der Rundfunk als Erziehungsmittel für das Publikum," [1937], LP, 423/4/54; *VB*, 2 June 1937; Albert Richard Mohr, *Die Frankfurter Oper, 1924–1944: Ein Beitrag zur Theatergeschichte mit zeitgenössischen Berichten und Bildern* (Frankfurt am Main, 1971), 165; Joan Evans, *Hans Rosbaud: A Bio-Bibliography* (New York, 1992), 27–33; Prieberg, *NS-Staat*, 286–87; Kater, *Different Drummers*, 90, 92; Kater, "Carl Orff im Dritten Reich," *Vierteljahrshefte für Zeitgeschichte* 43 (1995), 8–11.

25. See Ernst Pepping, *Stilwende der Musik* (Mainz, 1934), 84–88; Walter Trienes, *Musik in Gefahr: Selbstzeugnisse aus der Verfallszeit* (Regensburg, 1940), 25.

26. Hans-Günter Klein, "Atonalität in den Opern von Paul von Klenau und Winfried Zillig—zur Duldung einer im Nationalsozialismus verfemten Kompositionstechnik," in Mahling and Weismann, *Bericht*, 490–94; Albrecht Dümling, "Zwölftonmusik als antifaschistisches Potential: Eislers Ideen zu einer neuen Verwendung der Dodekaphonie," in Otto Kolleritsch, ed., *Die Wiener Schule und das Hakenkreuz: Das Schicksal der Moderne im gesellschaftspolitischen Kontext des 20. Jahrhunderts* (Vienna, 1990), 97–98; Claudia Maurer Zenck, "'Aufbruch des deutschen Geistes' oder Innere Emigration: Zu einigen Opern der 30er und 40er Jahre," paper, international colloquium, see n. 19; *NG* 20:682 (quote); *GLM* 4:45–46.

27. *TG* 2:729, 744; Hans Heinz Stuckenschmidt, "German Season under the Crisis," *Modern Music* 10 (1933), 165 (1st quote); *TG* 3:116 (2nd quote), 131;

Müller to Wiedemann, 23 Mar. 1938, BDC Gottfried Müller (3rd quote); *DM* 25 (1933), 917; Georg Schünemann, *Die Singakademie zu Berlin, 1791–1941* (Regensburg, 1941), 188; Friedrich Welter, *Musikgeschichte im Umriss: Vom Urbeginn bis zur Gegenwart* (Leipzig, n.d.), 317; Oskar Söhngen, *Kämpfende Kirchenmusik: Die Bewährungsprobe der evangelischen Kirchenmusik im Dritten Reich* (Kassel, n.d.), 42–43; Fred K. Prieberg, *Kraftprobe: Wilhelm Furtwängler im Dritten Reich* (Wiesbaden, 1986), 294; Rischer, *Kulturpolitik*, 63.

28. "Vereinigung für zeitgen. Musik," [1931], SMK, 143; *Melos* 12 (1933), 350; *Bayerischer Kurier*, 10 Apr. 1934 (1st quote); *Neueste Zeitung* (Frankfurt), 23 May 1935; *VB*, 25 Mar. 1936; *TG* 2:534 (2nd quote), 624; *AMZ* 63 (1936), 347; *Skizzen* (Nov. 1936), 9 (3rd quote); Welter, *Musikgeschichte*, 304; Stege in *Unterhaltungsmusik*, 10 Feb. 1938, 157. On Goebbels and "melody," see *AMR*, 1 June 1938, in Dümling and Girth, *Musik*, 123.

29. *TG* 3:567; *TG* 4:51; Petschull to Strecker, 17 Apr. 1939, PF, Schott Korr.; *Augsburger National-Zeitung*, 11 May 1939 (quote); "Reichs-Musiktage 1939 Düsseldorf 14.–21. Mai," BS, Ana/410; *Düsseldorfer Tageblatt*, 7 May 1939; *DAZ*, 20 May 1939; *VB*, 22 May 1939; Ehrenberg report, 27 May 1939, SMK, 396; *Frankfurter Zeitung*, 4 and 5 July 1940; ZM 107 (1940), 364; Julius Kapp, *Geschichte der Staatsoper Berlin* (Berlin, n.d.), 235; Mohr, *Oper*, 695; Werner Egk, *Musik—Wort—Bild: Texte und Anmerkungen—Betrachtungen und Gedanken* (Munich, 1960), 205–9; Egk, *Die Zeit wartet nicht* (Percha, 1973), 241–53, 311–14; Ernst Krause, *Werner Egk: Oper und Ballett* (Wilhelmshaven, 1971), 193–94.

30. ZM 107 (1940), 149, 171, 180–82, 231, 273, 276, 421, 431, 580, 662, 793; ZM 108 (1941), 55, 102, 460, 780; ZM 109 (1942), 41; ZM 110 (1943), 19; MK 1 (1943), 35; *JdM* 1944, 31; Gertrud to Paul Hindemith, 15 Mar. [1939], PF, 3.144.22–37 (1st quote); *TGII* 12:204 (2nd quote), 234.

31. *DM* 25 (1933), 917; Kater, "Orff," 8–10.

32. Kater, "Orff," 1–35.

33. *VB*, 22 May 1939; Dietrich Stoverock, "Paul Höffer," ZM 110 (1943), 56–59; *GLM* 4:102–3.

34. Munich Philharmonic, "Städtische Philharmonische Konzerte 1942–43," 2 June 1942, SMK, 177; Victor Junk, "Die 'Woche zeitgenössischer Musik in Wien,'" ZM 109 (1942), 243; "Mitteilungen der Fachschaft Komponisten in der Reichsmusikkammer" (Nov. 1940), 4 (OW, 40); Sachs, *Musik*, 132; *TGII* 4:211–12; *GLM* 4:111.

35. RMK minutes, [Berlin, May–July 1942], BDC Werner Egk; Scharping to [Goebbels], 25 Apr. 1944, BA, R55/559. Müller's name, curiously, is absent from this list.

36. *Unterhaltungsmusik*, 9 Mar. 1939, 322, and 23 Mar. 1939, 414–15; minutes of *Musikbeiräte* meeting, [Munich], 27 Sept. 1938, SMK, 909; "Denkschrift über die Programmgestaltung des Konzertvereins," 26 May 1939, SMK, 177; Büchtger to Reinhard, [July 1940]; Reinhard, "Süddeutsche Tonkünstlerwoche München 1941," 12 Nov. 1940, SMK, 142; *Saarbrücker Zeitung*, 4 June 1941; *VB*, 25 May 1939; *JdM* 1944, 54–55; Manfred Wagner, *Kultur und Politik: Politik und Kunst* (Vienna, 1991), 289–90.

37. Egk to [Goebbels], [1941], and related documents in BDC Egk; *TG* 4:653; *AMR*, 15 July 1941, BA, RD33/2–2; *Deutsche Zeitung Norwegen*, 19 July 1941; Werner Egk, "Musik als Ausdruck ihrer Zeit," in Alfred Morgenroth, ed., *Von*

deutscher Tonkunst: Festschrift zu Peter Raabes 70. Geburtstag (Leipzig, 1942), 25 (quote); Egk in *VB*, 14 Feb. 1943; Ehrenberg memorandum, 14 Nov. 1943; Fiehler to Kabasta, 18 Feb. 1944, SMK, 97/7; *JdM 1943*, 90–91, 169; *JdM 1944*, 82.

38. See my forthcoming book *Composers of the Nazi Era: Eight Portraits.*

39. Minutes of program meeting, 26 July 1944, BA, R55/556.

40. See e.g., Karl Dietrich Bracher, *The German Dictatorship: The Origins, Structure, and Effects of National Socialism* (New York, 1972).

41. "Richtlinien für die Musikarbeit der NS-Kulturgemeinde," *DM* 26 (1934), 933–36.

42. *JdM 1944*, 50–55 (quote on 52); Prieberg, *NS-Staat*, 276–78, 355–56; Alan E. Steinweis, *Art, Ideology, and Economics in Nazi Germany: The Reich Chambers of Music, Theater, and the Visual Arts* (Chapel Hill, N.C., 1993), 138–42.

43. Steinweis, *Art*, 138.

44. *TG* 2:483; *TG* 4:274, 294–95; *TG* 8:261–62; *TG* 9:288; *TG* 10:200; *TG* 11:583; *TG* 15:408, 638; Michael H. Kater, "Inside Nazis: The Goebbels Diaries, 1924–1941," *Canadian Journal of History*, 25 (1990), 233–43; Albert Speer, *Spandauer Tagebücher* (Frankfurt am Main, 1975), 401–2.

45. Strecker to Orff, 6 Mar. 1937, 9 June (1st quote), 13 July 1938 (2nd quote) and 18 Nov. 1943; Orff to Strecker, 24 Mar. 1938 and 26 May 1943; CM, Schott Korr.; Petschull to Orff, 6 Apr. 1938; Theater am Nollendorfplatz to Orff, 17 July 1944 (3rd quote), CM, Allg. Korr. (3rd quote); *TGII* 13:466; Kater, "Orff," 1–35.

46. Newell Jenkins, recorded interview, Hillsdale, N.Y., 20 Mar. 1933, APA. On Jenkins's career, see Nicolas Slonimsky, ed., *Baker's Biographical Dictionary of Musicians*, 8th ed. (New York, 1992), 849–50; *NG* 9:598. See also Kater, "Orff," 3–4, 23–26.

47. Clara Huber to author, Munich, 30 Sept. 1993; Gertrud Orff to author, Munich, 12 Nov. 1993, APA.

48. Kater, "Orff," 29.

49. Ibid., 4–11.

50. Ibid., 20–21; Newell Jenkins, recorded interview, Hillsdale, N.Y., 20 Mar 1993, APA.

51. Godela Orff, *Mein Vater und ich: Erinnerungen an Carl Orff* (Munich, 1992), 41; Gerald Abraham, *The Consice Oxford History of Music* (Oxford, 1986), 840; Kater, "Orff," 14–35.

52. Pfitzner to Abendroth, 3 June 1942, OW, 288.

53. Gottfried von Einem, recorded interview, Vienna, 30 Nov. 1994, APA; Rudolf Wagner-Régeny, *Begegnugen: Biographische Aufzeichnungen, Tagebücher, und sein Briefwechsel mit Caspar Neher* (Berlin, 1968), 82–83; Dieter Härtwig, *Rudolf Wagner-Régeny: Der Opernkomponist* (Berlin, 1965), 36; Dominik Hartmann, *Gottfried von Einem* (Vienna, 1967), 11; Carl Dahlhaus, "Politische Implikationen der Operndramaturgie: Zu einigen deutschen Opern der Dreissiger Jahre," in Mahling and Wiesmann, *Bericht*, 152.

54. *GLM* 8:325–26; Fred K. Prieberg, *Lexikon der Neuen Musik* (Freiburg, 1958), 442; Härtwig, *Wagner-Régeny*, 19–35; Rudolf Wagner-Régeny, *An den Ufern der Zeit: Schriften, Briefe, Tagebücher*, ed. Max Becker (Leipzig, 1989), 107.

55. Max Becker in Wagner-Régeny, *Ufern*, 20–21; Karl Böhm, *Ich erinnere*

mich ganz genau: Autobiographie (Zurich, 1968), 73; Adolph [?], memorandum, 26 Nov. 1935, BDC Karl Böhm.

56. Härtwig, *Wagner-Régeny*, 43; Wagner-Régeny, *Begegnungen*, 82; Kapp, *Geschichte*, 237; Welter, *Musikgeschichte*, 335.

57. Rathkolb, *Führerkult*, 68–78.

58. Wagner-Régeny, *Begegnungen*, 83; Becker in Wagner-Régeny, *Ufern*, 21–25; *TGII* 3:469 (quote); von der Null to Orff, 18 Sept. 1937; Ruppel to Orff, 9 July 1941; Jarosch to Orff, 9 Apr. 1941, CM, Allg. Korr.; Junk to Hans [Pfitzner], 18 Mar. 1942, SMM, 9; BDC Werner Egk; Scharping to [Goebbels], 25 Apr. 1944, BA, R55/559; ZM 108 (1941), 420; Baldur von Schirach, *Ich glaubte an Hitler* (Hamburg, 1967), 286–87; Anderman [Thomas], *Vorhang*, 119–20; Härtwig, *Wagner-Régeny*, 46; Dahlhaus, "Implikationen," 152–53; Andrea Seebohm, "Unbewältigte musikalische Vergangenheit: Ein Kapitel österreichischer Musikgeschichte, das bis heute ungeschrieben ist," in Liesbeth Waechter-Böhm, ed., *Wien 1945: Davor/danach* (Vienna, 1985), 144.

59. Photographs no. 15 and 16 in Wagner-Régeny, *Ufern*; Becker, ibid., 25–26; Gorvin to Orff, 8 Nov. 1943; Neher to Orff, 5 June 1944, CM, Allg. Korr.; Wagner-Régeny, *Begegnungen*, 110–221; Härtwig, *Wagner-Régeny*, 50.

60. Gottfried von Einem, recorded interview, Vienna, 30 Nov. 1994, APA.

61. Alfred Burgartz, *Rudolf Wagner-Régeny: Bildnis eines Schaffenden* (Berlin-Schöneberg, [1935]), 16; Herbert Gerigk, "Zehn Jahre nationalsozialistisches Musikleben," *DM* 35 (1943), 106; Wagner-Régeny, *Begegnungen*, 80; Härtwig, *Wagner-Régeny*, 41; Prieberg, *NS-Staat*, 151; Nicolas Slonimsky, *Music Since 1900*, 4th ed. (New York, 1971), 594; Dümling and Girth, *Entartete Musik*, ix.

62. Karl Laux, *Musik und Musiker der Gegenwart* (Essen, 1949), 1:230; Eugen Schmitz, "Oper im Aufbau," *ZM* 106 (1939), 382 (1st quote); Claudia Maurer Zenck, "'Aufbruch des deutschen Geistes'" (the author quotes Theodor W. Adorno's phrase).

63. Robert C. Bachmann, *Karajan: Anmerkungen zu einer Karriere*, 2nd ed. (Düsseldorf, 1983), 128–29.

64. "Verträge mit den Komponisten Carl Orff und Rudolf Wagner-Régeny zur Förderung ihres künstlerischen Schaffen," Vienna, 27 Mar. 1942, OSW. I owe my knowledge of this document to Hans Jörg Jans, Orff-Zentrum, Munich, whose assistance is gratefully acknowledged. See also Anderman [Thomas], *Vorhang*, 151, and the intentionally downplayed version in Wagner-Régeny, *Begegnungen*, 84.

65. Quoted in *Financial Times* (London), 5 July 1995.

66. No one has done more to validate this position in recent years than the German musicologist Fred K. Prieberg. See his *Kraftprobe*, esp. 100–101; and the forceful criticism of Prieberg's scholarship by Richard J. Evans, "Playing for the Devil: How Much Did Furtwängler Really Resist the Nazis?," *Times Literary Supplement* (London), 13 Nov. 1992, 3–4. See also Wilhelm Furtwängler, *Notebooks, 1924–1954*, ed. Michael Tanner (London, 1989), 160; Bachmann, *Karajan*, 139.

67. Prieberg, *Kraftprobe*; Berta Geissmar, *Musik im Schatten der Politik*, 4th ed., ed. Fred K. Prieberg (Zurich, 1985); Berndt Wilhelm Wessling, *Furtwängler: Eine kritische Biographie* (Stuttgart, 1985), 266–67.

68. Furtwängler to Rust, 4 June 1933, BA, R56/140; Furtwängler/Schoenberg corr. (1933) in AI, gen. corr.

69. *TG* 2:701; Furtwängler to Stein, 18 Aug. 1937, PF, Furtwängler Korr.

70. Prieberg, *Kraftprobe*, 443–44, n. 37.

71. Ibid., Geissmar to Pfitzner, 6 July 1934, OW, 123; Furtwängler to Pfitzner, 23 Feb. 1937, OW, 211.

72. Prieberg, *Kraftprobe*, 147, 443–44, n. 37.

73. Trapp to Hess, 10 Oct. 1935; [Furtwängler] to Görlitzer, 7 Feb. 1936 (quote), BDC Max Trapp.

74. Tietjen to Strauss, 29 Dec. 1934; Winifred Wagner to Strauss, 9 June 1935, RG; *TG* 2:646; *TGII* 12:238; Ernst Krause, *Richard Strauss: The Man and His Work* (Boston, 1969), 57.

75. See chap. 2 at nn. 48, 116; Schuh to Egk, [1943], BS, Ana/410; Peter Heyworth, *Otto Klemperer: His Life and Times*, 2 vols. (Cambridge, 1983, 1996), 2:241–42.

76. Pfitzner to Paul [Cossmann], 1 Sept. 1932 (1st quote; the typically Pfitznerian neologism *Primadonnerich* has not found its way into any dictionary); Pfitzner to Brockhaus, 24 Apr.1930 (2nd quote), MMP.

77. *Melos* 12 (1933), 236; Furtwängler to Matthes, 20 Apr. 1937, ZNF; Wilhelm to Adelheid Furtwängler, [Feb. 1944], in Frank Thiess, ed., *Wilhelm Furtwängler: Briefe*, 3rd ed. (Wiesbaden, 1965), 108 (quote); Prieberg, *Kraftprobe*, 81, 218–19.

78. Evans, "Playing," 3–4.

79. Furtwängler memorandum, [1933], BDC Wilhelm Furtwängler (quote). See also Furtwängler, *Notebooks*, e.g., 157; Wessling, *Furtwängler*, 260; Prieberg, *Kraftprobe*, 107, 220–21, 354.

80. Albrecht Riethmüller, "Musik, die 'deutscheste' Kunst," paper at colloquium "Verfemte Musik," Dresden, Jan. 1993 (1st quote); Furtwängler to Curtius, 10 Sept. 1934, in Thiess, *Furtwängler: Briefe*, 77 (2nd quote) and 80; advertisement, "Furtwängler and Beethoven," *Skizzen* (Jan. 1938), 15; Berg, *Briefe*, 628; Wessling, *Furtwängler*, 268; Furtwängler, *Notebooks*, 161; Prieberg, *Kraftprobe*, 199, 361; Rathkolb, *Führertreu*, 194–99.

81. Furtwängler quoted by Stege in *Artist*, 23 July 1936, 843; Furtwängler, *Notebooks*, 58, 122 (2nd quote); Furtwängler, "Denkschrift," Jan.–May 1935, ZNF (3rd quote); Schoenberg to Furtwängler, 16 Aug. 1928 and 4 June 1929, AI, gen. corr.; Thiess, *Furtwängler: Briefe*, 89; Prieberg, *Kraftprobe*, 53–55; Shirakawa, *Music Master*, 59–60. See Schoenberg's characteristic notation (n.d., AI, Text Manuscript Furtwängler): "Furtwängler's [postulated] 'biological inferiority' of twelve-tone music is nonsense from every possible perspective. Especially semantically." On Furtwängler as a frustrated composer, see *TG* 2:604; Abendroth to Pfitzner, 3 Nov. 1937 and [Spring 1940], OW, 288; *VB*, 20 Mar. and 28 Oct. 1937; Karla Höcker, ed., *Wilhelm Furtwängler: Dokumente—Berichte und Bilder—Aufzeichnungen* (Berlin, 1968), 85–87; Thiess, *Furtwängler: Briefe*, 76–77, 101, 104–6, 113; Elisabeth Furtwängler, *Über Wilhelm Furtwängler* (Wiesbaden, 1979), 16–17; Wessling, *Furtwängler*, 320–21.

82. *TG* 2:317, 425; BDC Kurt and Senta Hösel; minutes, eighth meeting of RMK-Präsidialrat, 27 Mar. 1934; Ihlert to Strauss, 13 Apr. 1934, RG; Wessling, *Furtwängler*, 274.

83. Prieberg, *Kraftprobe*, 186–94; Geissmar, *Musik*, 125–36; Thomas Mann, *Tagebücher, 1933–1934*, ed. Peter de Mendelssohn (Frankfurt am Main, 1977), 581.

84. Furtwängler to Funk, 3 Jan. 1935; Kohler to Furtwängler, 24 Jan. 1934,

BDC Furtwängler; Furtwängler to Göring, 23 Dec. 1937, in Theodor Richard Emessen, ed., *Aus Görings Schreibtisch: Ein Dokumentenfund* (Berlin, 1947), 40–41; Prieberg, *Kraftprobe*, 194, 201.

85. "Furtwängler bedauert," *DM*, 27 (1935), 437; *TG* 2:483 (quote); Skelton, *Hindemith*, 126; Maurer Zenck, "Boykott," 86; Wessling, *Furtwängler*, 293–94.

86. Furtwängler cited in Rathkolb, *Führertreu*, 196.

87. *TGII* 2:513; Nike Wagner, "'. . . Uns bliebe gleich die abendländ'sche Kunst': Entsorgungsanlage Neubayreuth," *Gehört gelesen: Die besten Sendungen des Bayerischen Rundfunks* 37 (Sept. 1990), 12 (quote).

88. For expressions of rapture by party leaders, see *TG* 2:513, 534, 567, 649, 737, 753, 760; *TG* 3:40–41, 211, 214, 216–17, 260, 307, 489.

89. True to Triller, 9 Mar. 1936 (1st quote); Abramson to Whitney, 7 Mar. 1936 (2nd quote); "Cables Interchanged Between Mr. Triller & Dr. Furt-waengler," 2 Mar. 1936, NYA, Furtwängler Collection; Thiess, *Furtwängler: Briefe*, 87; Wessling, *Furtwängler*, 308–9; Prieberg, *Kraftprobe*, 254–59.

90. *TG* 2:648–49; *TG* 3:40–41, 211, 214, 216–17, 252, 299, 358; *VB*, 5 Feb. 1938; Berlin Philharmonic to Goebbels, 26 Sept. 1938, BA, R55/951; "Bericht des kaufmännischen Leiters über das Haushaltsjahr 1938/39," BA, R55/197; remuneration statement for Furtwängler, 1939, ZNF; Friedelind Wagner, *Nacht über Bayreuth: Die Geschichte der Enkelin Richard Wagners* (Bern, [1946]), 321; Dorothea Hemming, ed., *Dokumente zur Geschichte der Musikschule (1902–1976)* (Regensburg, 1977), 120.

91. *TG* 3:650.

92. *TG* 4:7–8, 94, 352, 391; Höcker, *Furtwängler*, 95; Furtwängler, *Furt-wängler*, 128; Wessling, *Furtwängler*, 349, 355–57; Bachmann, *Karajan*, 140; Muck, *Jahre* 3:311; Prieberg, *Kraftprobe*, 370.

93. Geissmar, *Music*; Prieberg, *Kraftprobe*; Shirakawa, *Music Master*, 129–337. Michael Meyer, *The Politics of Music in the Third Reich* (New York, 1991), 331–72, adds no new nuances to Prieberg's version.

94. *TG* 4:55, 82, 114, 210; *TGII* 2:383; *TGII* 3:387 (1st quote); *TGII* 10:228–29; *TGII* 11:82 (2nd quote); 169, 407, 472, 541 (3rd quote); *TGII* 12:204; Henry Picker, *Hitlers Tischgespräche im Führerhauptquartier, 1941–42*, ed. Gerhard Ritter (Bonn, 1951), 396.

95. See Shirakawa, *Music Master*; *TG* 4:114–15, 378; *TGII* 4:135; *TGII* 8:448–49, 536; *TGII* 12:160; *TGII* 14:400 (1st quote); *TGII* 15:180; Furt-wängler file, BA, R3/1578; Bachmann, *Karajan*, 141; Wessling, *Furtwängler*, 363; *Spiegelbild einer Verschwörung* (Stuttgart, 1961), 446; Muck, *Jahre* 3:302; Clemens Hellsberg, *Demokratie der Könige: Die Geschichte der Wiener Philhar-moniker* (Zurich, 1992), 472; Peter Hoffmann, McGill University, Montreal, to author, 7 Sept. 1995, APA (2nd quote).

96. Leon Botstein, "The Enigmas of Richard Straus: A Revisionist View," in Bryan Gilliam, ed., *Richard Strauss and His World* (Princeton, N.J., 1992), 3–32 (quote on 6).

97. Strauss to Fürstner, 10 Mar. 1933, BS, Ana/330/I/Fürstner.

98. Roesen to Öffentlicher Kläger, 17 Jan. 1948, AM, Strauss; George R. Marek, *Richard Strauss: The Life of a Non-Hero* (London, 1967), 270; Stephan Kohler, "'Ich als "Verfemter des Geistes". . . .': Richard Strauss und das Dritte Reich," *Neue Zeitschrift für Musik* 144, no. 1 (1983), 4; Walter Deppisch, *Ri-chard Strauss: Mit Selbstzeugnissen und Bilddokumenten* (Reinbek, 1989), 139; Pamela M. Potter, "Strauss and the National Socialists: The Debate and Its Rele-

vance," in Bryan Gilliam, ed., *Richard Strauss: New Perspectives on the Composer and His Work* (Durham, N.C., 1992), 97.

99. Stefan Zweig, *Die Welt von Gestern: Erinnerungen eines Europäers* (Berlin, 1965), 335. See Zweig's vita in *IBD*, 1288–89.

100. Deppisch, *Strauss*, 7–127.

101. See Strauss's statement reproduced by Gerhard Splitt, *Richard Strauss, 1933–1935: Ästhetik und Musikpolitik zu Beginn der nationalsozialistischen Herrschaft* (Pfaffenweiler, 1987), 86; and Franz Grasberger, ed., *Der Strom der Töne trug mich fort: Die Welt um Richard Strauss in Briefen* (Tutzing, 1967), 232, 236–40, 250, 262, 296–97, 301–3; Günter Brosche, ed., *Richard Strauss—Frank Schalk: Ein Briefwechsel* (Tutzing, 1983), 53; Walter, *Hitler*, 144.

102. Splitt, *Strauss*, 97.

103. Strauss cited ibid., 80; Strauss to Fürstner, 28 Dec. 1932 and 30 Nov. 1936, BS, Ana/330/I/Fürstner.

104. Strauss's address in *ZM* 101 (1934), 288–90; Kopsch deposition, 1 Mar. 1947, AM, Strauss; Deppisch, *Strauss*, 77–78; Barbara A. Peterson, *"Die Händler und die Kunst:* Richard Strauss as Composers' Advocate," in Gilliam, *Perspectives*, 118–19.

105. Strauss to Kippenberg, 29 Mar. 1933; Strauss to Goebbels, 6 and 27 Aug. 1933, RG; Strauss to Rasch, BS, Ana/330/I/Rasch; Strauss to Ritter, 12 Sept. 1933, NWH, 975/16–1; *TG* 2:450; Ruediger telegram to Strauss, 10 Nov. 1933, AM, Strauss. Strauss's written acceptance has so far not been found in the records.

106. Funk, "Verordnung zur Durchführung," 15 Feb. 1934; Strauss to Kopsch, 15 Mar. 1934; Winifred Wagner to Strauss, 28 Dec. 1934, RG; Grasberger, *Strom*, 353; Michael Karbaum, *Studien zur Geschichte der Bayreuther Festspiele (1876–1976)*, 2 vols. (Regensburg, 1976), 2:97; Krause, *Strauss*, 49; Frederic Spotts, *Bayreuth: A History of the Wagner Festival* (New Haven, 1994), 101, 120, 133–34, 140, 170; Steinweis, *Art*, 51 (quote).

107. See, e.g., Prieberg, *Macht*, 222.

108. Strauss to Ritter, 25 Dec. 1940, RG; Roesen to Öffentlicher Kläger, 17 Jan. 1948, AM, Strauss; Grasberger, *Strom*, 398; Walter Thomas, *Richard Strauss und seine Zeitgenossen* (Munich, 1964), 365; Marek, *Strauss*, 325; Rudolf Hartmann, *Das geliebte Haus: Mein Leben mit der Oper* (Munich, 1975), 213; Deppisch, *Strauss*, 118, 130.

109. Strauss to Göring, 9 Jan. 1934; Strauss to Goebbels, 4 July and 1 Nov. 1934; Goebbels to Strauss, 25 Aug. 1934; Strauss to Laubinger, 12 Dec. 1934, RG; *Melos* 13 (1934), 255; Grasberger, *Strom*, 352; Willi Schuh, ed., *A Confidential Matter: The Letters of Richard Strauss and Stefan Zweig, 1931–1935* (Berkeley, 1977), 102.

110. Strauss to Stein, 28 Feb. 1934 (quote); Strauss to Goebbels, 5 June 1934, RG.

111. *DKW*, no. 28 (1933), 7–8; Strauss to Richter, 14 Dec. 1934, NHW, 975/16–3; Rosenberg to Goebbels, 20 Aug. 1934 (quote); Goebbels to Rosenberg, 25 Aug. 1934, IfZ, MA 596/737–44; *Richard Strauss Jahrbuch* (1959/60), 125; Donald W. Ellis, "Music in the Third Reich: National Socialist Aesthetic Theory as Governmental Policy" (Ph.D. diss., University of Kansas, 1970), 201.

112. On Mann, see Mann, *Tagebücher, 1940–1943*, 526; Ronald Hayman, *Thomas Mann: A Biography* (New York, 1995), 193, 213–14, 232, 238–39,

413; Johannes Saltzwedel in *Spiegel,* 17 Apr. 1995, 211; Gordon A. Craig, "The Man Nobody Knew," *New York Review of Books,* 29 Feb. 1996, 36.

113. Here, see Brosche, *Strauss,* 28–29, 84, 93, 172, 203, 222, 224, 318–19, 360; Krause, *Strauss,* 29.

114. Otto Klemperer, *Meine Erinnerungen an Gustav Mahler und andere autobiographische Skizzen* (Freiburg, 1960), 39–40.

115. Splitt, *Strauss,* 58 (quote); see also Walter Panofsky, *Richard Strauss: Partitur eines Lebens* (Munich, 1965), 273; Thomas, *Strauss,* 201; Potter, "Strauss," 103. In his letter to Zweig, 17 June 1935 (BDC Strauss), Strauss called Walter a "slimy rascal." Consult chap. 3 at n. 88

116. Strauss to Rasch, [1933]; Goebbels to Strauss, 1 Sept. 1934; Strauss to Goebbels, 20 Sept. 1934; Strauss to Richter, 14 Dec. 1934, RG; Goebbels to Rosenberg, 25 Aug. 1934, IfZ, MA 596/737–39; Strauss to Zweig, 17 June 1935, BDC Strauss; Schuh, *Matter,* xiii, 45, 59, 69, 101; Zweig, *Welt,* 335–41.

117. Strauss to Zweig, 17 June 1935, BDC Strauss; *TG* 2:490. See also chap. 1 at n. 81.

118. Grasberger, *Strom,* 349–50; Strauss to [Kopsch], 4 Oct. 1934 (1st quote); Strauss to Tietjen, 13 Nov. 1934; Strauss to Funk, 10 Dec. 1934; Strauss to Ihlert, 27 May 1935 (2nd quote), RG.

119. Splitt, *Strauss,* 225; copied almost verbatim by Peter Reichel, *Der schöne Schein des Dritten Reiches: Faszination und Gewalt des Faschismus,* 2nd ed. (Munich, 1992), 348.

120. Printed in full in Marek, *Strauss,* 282–83.

121. Panofsky, *Strauss,* 292; *TG* 2:493.

122. Ernst Hanfstaengl, *Zwischen Weissem und Braunem Haus: Memoiren eines politischen Aussenseiters* (Munich, 1970), 56; *TG* 2:450, 630; *TG* 3:454; *TG* 4:60, 523; *TGII* 2:436; *TGII* 8:132; *TGII* 12:527.

123. Mann, *Tagebücher, 1940–1943,* 218; Splitt, *Strauss,* 13. On "fascist music," see the remarks by Jens Malte Fischer in *Süddeutsche Zeitung* (Munich), 14 Mar. 1995.

124. Zeitschel memorandum, 24 Sept. 1935; Fabricius to Körner, 18 Oct. 1935, BDC Strauss; Walleck to Strauss, 5 Dec. 1935, AM, Strauss.

125. *TG* 2:630; Strauss to Fürstner, 16 Apr. 1938, BS, Ana/330/I/Fürstner; *TG* 3:419; Dümling and Girth, *Musik,* 109.

126. Six to Pruchtnow, 22 July 1938, RG; Kaltenbrunner to Himmler, 6 Sept. 1944, BDC Strauss.

127. [Alice Strauss], "Tatsachenbericht über die Vorgänge im November 1938," n.d.; Tietjen to Strauss, 6 Jan. 1939, RG; personal communication from Richard and Dr. Christian Strauss, Garmisch, 5 June 1993.

128. *Unterhaltungsmusik,* 15 June 1939, 821.

129. Götz Klaus Kende, *Richard Strauss und Clemens Krauss: Eine Künstlerfreundschaft und ihre Zusammenarbeit an "Capriccio"* (Munich, 1960), 41.

130. *Richard Strauss: Briefwechsel mit Willi Schuh* (Zurich, 1969), 29; Panofsky, *Strauss,* 297; *TG* 4:198.

131. Henriette von Schirach, *The Price of Glory* (London, 1960), 162.

132. *TGII* 3:474.

133. Paula Neumann to Swiss consulate general, 24 Oct. 1941; Jüdische Kultusgemeinde, "Einbekenntnis zur Kultussteuer," 2 Jan. 1942; Paula Neumann to Zentralstelle für jüd. Auswanderung, 2 Feb. [?] 1942; Strauss to Günther,

11 Aug. 1942; Marie von Grab certification, 21 Jan. 1947; Strauss to Thomas, 19 and 24 May and 1 July 1942, and 13 and 29 Sept. and 6 Nov. 1943; Schiede to Strauss, 30 Oct. 1943, RG; Frank to Strauss, 19 Nov. 1942, AM, Strauss; Maschat to Holthoff, 9 July 1942, BH, Staatstheater/NA Ursuleac; Anderman [Thomas], *Vorhang*, 233–35; Franz Trenner, "Alice Strauss: 3. Juni 1904–23. Dezember 1991," *Richard Strauss-Blätter*, no. 27 (June 1992), 6; personal communication from Richard and Dr. Christian Strauss, Garmisch, 5 June 1993.

134. *TGII* 11:82, 102, 169, 407, 473; *TGII* 12:527; Bormann, "Bekanntgabe 16/44," 24 Jan. 1944; Brandt to Kraus, 25 Apr. 1944; Hinkel to Schrade et al., 28 June 1944; Kaltenbrunner to Himmler, 6 Sept. 1944, BDC Strauss; Strauss to [Drewes], 3 Feb. 1944; Strauss to Funk, 25 Apr. 1944; Goebbels to Strauss, 11 June 1944; Strauss to Böhm, 11 Jan. 1945; Alice Strauss declaration, 22 and 26 Feb. 1946, RG; Klaus to Strauss, 6 Sept. 1944; Reiser declaration, 9 July 1947, AM, Strauss; *Strauss: Briefwechsel Schuh*, 77; Panofsky, *Strauss*, 327–28; Deppisch, *Strauss*, 150–53.

135. I deal in detail with this and other aspects of Strauss's Third Reich career in my forthcoming book *Composers of the Nazi Era: Eight Portraits.*

136. Allan Kozinn in the *New York Times*, 25 Aug. 1992.

137. Wessling, *Furtwängler*, 255.

138. Marek, *Strauss*, 284.

139. Robert Wistrich, *Who's Who in Nazi Germany* (New York, 1982), 233.

140. John Williamson, *The Music of Hans Pfitzner* (Oxford, 1992), 301.

141. See Reichel, *Schein*, 348.

142. Norman Del Mar, *Richard Strauss: A Critical Commentary on His Life and Works*, 3 vols. (Philadelphia, 1972), 3:397.

143. Leer defense plea, 12 Jan. 1948, AM, Pfitzner (1st quote); Gabriele Busch-Salmen and Günther Weiss, eds., *Hans Pfitzner: Münchner Dokumente/ Bilder und Bildnisse* (Regensburg, 1990), 86 (2nd quote).

144. Leer defense plea, 12 Jan. 1948, AM, Pfitzner.

145. Paul Griffiths in Denis Arnold, ed., *The New Oxford Companion to Music*, 2 vols. (Oxford, 1990), 2:1418 (quote); Williamson, *Music*, 18; Johann Peter Vogel, *Hans Pfitzner: Mit Selbstzeugnissen und Bilddokumenten* (Reinbek, 1986), 8–88.

146. Pfitzner to Klein, 30 Apr. 1932, OW, 299; Berndt Wilhelm Wessling, *"Verachtet mir die Meister nicht!" Ein Buch der Erinnerung an Rudolf Bockelmann* (Celle, 1963), 52–54; Bernhard Adamy, *Hans Pfitzner: Literatur, Philosophie und Zeitgeschehen in seinem Weltbild und Werk* (Tutzing, 1980), 296; Winfried Zillig, *Von Wagner bis Strauss: Wegbereiter der Neuen Musik* (Munich, 1966), 155. For an uncritical view, see Josef Müller-Blattau, *Hans Pfitzner* (Potsdam, 1940), 78–98.

147. Erich Valentin, "Hans Pfitzner, der Deutsche," *ZM* 101 (1934), 481–83; Walter Abendroth, "Hans Pfitzner, der Deutsche," *DM* 26 (1934), 561–65 (both 1st quote); Müller-Blattau, *Pfitzner*, 79–83, (2nd quote on 65); *DKW*, no. 36 (1933), 7–8; *Skizzen* (May 1938), 14; Vogel, *Pfitzner*, 52–53, 71, 77–80; Pfitzner to lord mayor, 6 Oct. 1935, OW, 120 (3rd quote).

148. Pfitzner to "geehrter Herr," May 1930, OW, 300; Pfitzner to Abendroth, 8 Mar. 1933, OW, 289; Hans Pfitzner, *Gesammelte Schriften*, 3 vols. (Augsburg, 1926–29) 2:107–11, 244–48; Müller-Blattau, *Pfitzner*, 78, 80, 98; Vogel, *Pfitzner*, 77–81; Adamy, *Pfitzner*, 304–11; Williamson, *Music*, 15, 20–21, 330. On Rathenau, Weininger, and Jewish "self-hatred," see Peter Loewenberg, "An-

tisemitismus und jüdischer Selbsthass: Eine sich wechselseitig verstärkende sozialpsychologische Doppelbeziehung," *Geschichte und Gesellschaft* 5 (1979, 455–75.

149. See Erich Valentin, *Hans Pfitzner: Werk und Gestalt eines Deutschen* (Regensburg, 1939), 651.

150. Anon. to Fiehler, [?] Aug. 1933; Pfitzner to Fiehler, 3 Aug. 1933, OW, 218; corr. about this case in MMP; *Berliner Tageblatt,* 28 July 1933; Elisabeth Wamlek-Junk, ed., *Hans Pfitzner und Wien: Sein Briefwechsel mit Victor Junk und andere Dokumente* (Tutzing, 1986), 102–3. See also chap. 1 at n. 152.

151. KfdK, "1. Orchester-Konzert," 2 Oct. [1933], OW, 64; Schrott to Pfitzner, 16 Oct. 1934, OW, 298; Herzog to Pfitzner, 3 Oct. 1934; "Pfitzner-woche der NS-Kulturgemeinde München," 3–8 May 1935; OW, 283; NSKG, "Tagung der Kleist-Gesellschaft," 1–3 Nov. 1935, OW, 120; NSKG-Gauobmann to Kultusministerium, 8 Feb. 1936, BH, MK/40975; *VB,* 10 May 1935 and 6 May 1936.

152. Franckenstein to Pfitzner, 11 Aug. 1933, BH, Staatstheater/NA Pfitzner; [Tonhalle München], "4. Jubiläums-Konzert," 27 Feb. 1934, SMK, 473; Stein to Musikverlag Fürstner, 7 July 1934, MMP; Schmitz to Pfitzner, 5 Oct. 1934, OW, 122; Boepple to Goebbels, 13 Nov. 1934, BH, MK/40993; *DKW,* no. 22 (1933), 15; *AMZ* 62 (1935), 769; *DM* 27 (1935), 957; Muck, *Jahre* 3:265; Wamlek-Junk, *Pfitzner,* 109; Mohr, *Oper,* 158.

153. Junk to Pfitzner, 1 Nov. 1934, OW, 958.

154. Meissner to Pfitzner, 15 June 1938, OW, 74; Ohlendorf to Pfitzner, 20 Jan. 1943, OW, 65; Munich program for "Hans Pfitzner-Ehrung," 8 Mar 1939, BH, MA/107486; *VB,* 28 Aug. 1937; *Unterhaltungsmusik,* 25 May 1939, 743; *ZM* 106 (1939), 1196; *ZM* 107 (1940), 572; *ZM* 110 (1943), 20; *MK* 1 (1943), 111; *MK* 1 (1943–44), 187; *MK* 2 (1944), 68, 77, 107, 112; *Reichs-kulturkammer,* no. 1 (1944), 11; Mohr, *Oper,* 334.

155. Schrott to Braun, 5 May 1937, SMK, 506; Abendroth to Pfitzner, 23 Dec. 1937, OW, 288; Böck to Pfitzner, 27 Nov. 1939, OW, 259; Gebhardt to Pfitzner, 10 Dec. 1941, OW, 126; Geissler to Pfitzner, 30 Apr. 1943, OW, 65; *ZM* 109 (1942), 137; Muck, *Jahre* 2:142.

156. *Unterhaltungsmusik,* 8 Dec. 1938, 1601; corr. regarding Salzburg (1940), OW, 259; *ZM* 107 (1940), 363; Reichspropagandaamt Baden to Pfitzner, 3 Oct. 1940, OW, 245; *Frankfurter Zeitung,* 17 Nov. 1940; *Ostdeutscher Beobachter,* 7 Sept. 1942; Scheffler to Pfitzner, 1 Oct. 1942, OW, 61; [Greiser] to [Graf von Krosigk], 3 Dec. 1942, BDC Hans Pfitzner.

157. Corr. Pfitzner/Frank/Eisenlohr/Stampe (1941–45), OW, 68, 220, and 417; Werner Präg and Wolfgang Jacobmeyer, eds., *Das Diensttagebuch des deutschen Generalgouverneurs in Polen, 1939–1945* (Stuttgart, 1975), 572, 840, 885, 887; Williamson, *Music,* 320.

158. Pfitzner to Fürstner, 20 Nov. 1931, MMP; Franckenstein, "Anweisung," 14 June 1933, BH, Staatstheater/NA Pfitzner; Müller-Blattau, *Pfitzner,* 87; Vogel, *Pfitzner,* 88–99; Busch-Salmen and Weiss, *Pfitzner,* 36.

159. Franckenstein to Pfitzner, 7 Feb. 1934, BH, Staatstheater/NA Pfitzner; Franckenstein to Pfitzner, 5 Mar. 1934, OW, 297; Pfitzner to Junk, 7 Nov. 1934, in Wamlek-Junk, *Pfitzner,* 117 (1st quote); Knappertsbusch to Kultus-ministerium, 12 June 1934, BH, Staatstheater/NA Pfitzner (2nd quote); Boepple to Goebbels, 21 July 1934, BH, MK/44737.

160. Eckardt to Musikverlag Fürstner, 1 Oct. 1934, MMP.

161. Walleck to Diemer, 8 Nov. 1934; Schrott to Wagner, 21 Aug. 1936, BH, Staatstheater/NA Pfitzner; Pfitzner to Fiehler, [Oct 1935], OW, 120; Pfitzner to Reichssender Wien, 17 Feb. 1940, OW, 259; ZM 102 (1935), 785–86; Busch-Salmen and Weiss, *Pfitzner*, 41–56; Vogel, *Pfitzner*, 91, 113.

162. See Pfitzner to Abendroth, 27 May 1933, OW, 289; Pfitzner to Paproth, 2 Apr. 1934, OW, 218; Pfitzner to Krebs, 3 Nov. 1934, OW, 297; Pfitzner, "Deutsche Opernkunst in Berlin ausge-Rode-t," appended to Pfitzner to Rosenberg, 23 Nov. 1938, OW, 179; Pfitzner to Witt, 20 Mar. 1942, OW, 958; Pfitzner to Abendroth, 20 June 1936 and 31 Mar. 1943, OW, 288; Pfitzner to [Junk], 5 Dec. 1933, SMM, 9/99; Pfitzner to [Martin], 19 June 1934, SMM, 20 (quote); Pfitzner to Hinkel, 6 Sept. 1933 and 6 Feb. 1934, BDC Pfitzner; Pfitzner to Walter, 1 Sept. 1936, AM, Pfitzner; *Berliner Illustrierte Nacht-Ausgabe,* 14 July 1933; Adamy, *Pfitzner*, 319–20; Williamson, *Music*, 329.

163. Pfitzner to Geissmar, 5 July 1934, OW, 123; Pfitzner to [Göring], 17 Dec. 1934, OW, 211; Pfitzner to Siebert, 13 June 1934, BH, MK/44737.

164. Göring to Pfitzner, 8 Jan. 1935; Pfitzner to Göring, 30 Jan. 1935; Göring telegram to Pfitzner, 2 Feb. 1935; Pfitzner protocol, 9 Feb. 1935 (quote), OW, 211.

165. Pfitzner to Göring, 8 Feb. 1935, OW, 211.

166. Göring to Pfitzner, 12 Feb. 1935; Göring's marriage announcement for 12 Apr. 1935; Pfitzner to Göring, 26 Apr. 1935; Furtwängler to Pfitzner, 10 June 1937; Pfitzner to Göring, 9 Jan. 1938, OW, 211.

167. Pfitzner to Abendroth, 11 Apr. 1934, OW, 289/326; Pfitzner's handwritten sketches, [post-1945], OW, 331 (quotes); Herzog to Grohe, 16 July 1947, AM, Pfitzner; Abendroth, *Pfitzner*, 252; Zillig, *Wagner*, 153; Vogel, *Pfitzner*, 145.

168. Pfitzner to [Martin], 23 Aug 1934, SMM, 20; *TGII* 8:448 (quote).

169. The original is in BS, 8 L. impr. cn. mss. 229; see Conrad Ferdinand Meyer, *Huttens Letzte Tage: Eine Dichtung* (Leipzig, 1922); Pfitzner to Hitler, [1 Apr. 1924] (this letter was not mailed), BS, Autograph Pfitzner.

170. Pfitzner to Lulu [Cossmann], 9 July 1933, OW, 160; Pfitzner to Abendroth, 1 Feb. 1934, OW, 289; also 9 Oct. 1937; Abendroth to Pfitzner, 16 June 1939, OW, 288; Pfitzner to Riebe, 20 June 1939, OW, 300; Pfitzner to Fürstner, 26 July 1933, MMP; Pfitzner to [Junk], 5 Dec. 1933, SMM, 9/99; Wetzelsberger declaration, 11 Dec. 1947, AM, Pfitzner; Pfitzner quoted in *Tag* (Berlin), 15 Aug. 1934; Adamy, *Pfitzner*, 330; Williamson, *Music*, 327.

171. The phrase is Walter Abendroth's; see letter to Pfitzner of 9 Jan. 1936, OW, 288.

172. Thomas, *Strauss*, 204; Vogel, *Pfitzner*, 47.

173. See Pfitzner to Brockhaus, 12 Feb. 1919; Pfitzner to Oertel, 12 Sept. 1927, MMP; Hans Pfitzner, *Briefe*, 2 vols., ed. Bernhard Adamy (Tutzing, 1991), 1:77, 93, 135, 141, 176–78, 186–87, 192–96, 229–30, 236–38; Vogel, *Pfitzner*, 48–49; Williamson, *Music*, 10–11; Thomas, *Strauss*, 207–15.

174. See Pfitzner, *Schriften* 2; and Adamy, *Pfitzner*, 280–81; Thomas, *Strauss*, 207, 217–18.

175. Pfitzner to Abendroth, 27 Feb. 1934 (quote), OW, 289; Pfitzner to Franckenstein, 13 Mar. 1934, OW, 297.

176. Tietjen to Strauss, 29 Dec. 1934, RG; Pfitzner to Schlösser, OW, 123; Pfitzner to Schrott, 9 Apr. 1935, OW, 283; Pfitzner to [Martin], 10 Apr. 1935, SMM, 20.

177. Pfitzner to Hampe, 14 Oct. 1941; Pfitzner to Schlösser, 15 Nov. 1941; Pfitzner to Morgenroth, 21 Nov. 1941, OW, 261; Pfitzner to Abendroth, 3 June 1942, OW. 288; Pfitzner to anon., 13 June 1944, OW, 300/82; Pfitzner to Deschler, 19 June and 19 July 1943, BS, Cod. germ. 8251; Pfitzner to Kraus, 10 Sept. 1939, SMM, 24.

178. Figures calculated from table in Petra Maria Valentin, "Die Bayerische Staatsoper im Dritten Reich" (M.A. thesis, University of Munich, 1985).

179. Friedberg to Fürstner, 13 Sept. 1929, MMP; Abendroth, *Pfitzner*, 253; Thomas, *Strauss*, 216; Adamy, *Pfitzner*, 331; Vogel, *Pfitzner*, 93.

180. See chap. 1 at n. 16; Ritter, "Verwendung des Staatszuschusses zur Verteilung an Komponisten ernster Musik 1941–42," BDC Richard Strauss.

181. Walter Abendroth, *Hans Pfitzner* (Munich, 1935), passim; Thomas, *Strauss*, 206–7.

182. Strauss to von Niessen, 11 May 1935 (1st quote); Strauss to Hadamovsky, 1 July 1935 (2nd quote), RG.

183. Pfitzner's handwritten sketches, [post-1945], OW, 331; Vogel, *Pfitzner*, 112–22.

184. Vita in Theo Kreiten, "Wen die Götter lieben . . . Erinnerungen an Karlrobert Kreiten," in Friedrich Lambart, ed., *Tod eines Pianisten: Karlrobert Kreiten und der Fall Werner Höfer* (Berlin, 1988), 28–75; ZM 107 (1940), 147, 209; ZM 108 (1941), 244; ZM 109 (1942), 38, 468; ZM 110 (1943), 115; DAF, "Fünfter Abend im Gürzenich mit dem Reichssender Köln," 21 Feb. 1940, LP, 423/8/134; Reinhard memorandum, 6 Mar. 1941, SMK, 396; Muck, *Jahre* 3:290, 298.

185. Kreiten, "Wen," 74–96; Lambart, *Tod*, 103–16.

186. Kreiten, "Wen," 80–81; Lambart, *Tod*, 103–8; Kater, *Different Drummers*, 139.

187. Kreiten, "Wen," 28, 35, 38, 42, 48–52; Lambart, *Tod*, 103–5, 111.

188. Quotation from the official indictment of 1 Sept. 1943; facsimile in Lambart, *Tod*, 106.

189. Furtwängler quoted in Kreiten, "Wen," 99; ibid., 94 (2nd quote). Prieberg, *NS-Staat*, 342, has uncritically adopted Theo Kreiten's "making an example" version.

190. Bernhard Minetti, *Erinnerungen eines Schauspielers*, ed. Günther Rühle (Stuttgart, 1985), 140.

191. Max Butting, *Musikgeschichte, die ich miterlebte* (Berlin, 1955), 218–23.

192. Erika and Klaus Mann, *Escape to Life: Deutsche Kultur im Exil*, 2nd ed. (Munich, 1991), 106. Cf. Katia Mann, *Meine ungeschriebenen Memoiren*, ed. Elisabeth Plessen and Michael Mann (Frankfurt am Main, 1981), 100–104; Thomas Mann, *Tagebücher, 1933–1934*, 3–110.

193. Reported by Paul Hans Schmidt-Isserstedt in Berndt Wilhelm Wessling, *Hans Hotter* (Bremen, 1966), 51.

194. The Bayreuth episodes were closely witnessed by Fuchs's and Friedelind Wagner's friend the young composer Gottfried von Einem (Gottfried von Einem, recorded interview, Vienna, 30 Nov. 1994, APA). See also *TG* 2:646; *TG* 3:211, 216; Posse to Adolph, 15 Mar. 1933, BDC Fritz Busch; Wessling, *Furtwängler*, 312; *LI*, 252.

195. BDC Albrecht Thausing.

196. Annemay Schlusnus in Eckart von Naso, *Heinrich Schlusnus: Mensch*

und Sänger (Hamburg, 1957), 205; Frida Leider, *Das war mein Teil: Erinnerungen einer Opernsängerin* (Berlin, 1959), 197; Steinweis, *Art,* 172.

197. BDC Elsa Teschner; Heinrich Strobel, "Mathis der Maler," *Melos* 14 (1947), 66, 187.

198. Lin Jaldati and Eberhard Rebling, *Sag nie, du gehst den letzten Weg: Erinnerungen* (Berlin, 1986), esp. 97, 114–15.

199. *Die Vertreibung des Geistigen aus Österreich: Zur Kulturpolitik des Nationalsozialismus,* 2nd ed. (Vienna, n.d.), 352; Rathkolb, *Führertreu,* 162.

200. Roloff told me his story in Berlin in 1960. See also Roloff's testimony in Christine Fischer-Defoy, *Kunst, Macht, Politik: Die Nazifizierung der Kunst- und Musikhochschulen in Berlin* (Berlin, [1988]), 190–96 (quote on 192); ZM 108 (1941), 539, 609; MK 1 (1943), 65; MK 2 (1944), 105, 113, 118; Gail to Orff, [1943], CM, Allg. Korr.; Hans-Peter Range, *Die Konzertpianisten der Gegenwart: Ein Musikliebhaber berichtet über Konzertmilieu und 173 Klaviervirtuosen,* 2nd ed. (Lahr, 1966), 199; GLM 7:112; Leopold Trepper, *Die Wahrheit: Autobiographie* (Munich, 1978), 151, 350, 375, 377.

201. Margarete [*sic*] Klinckerfuss, *Aufklänge aus versunkener Zeit* (Urach, 1948), 117–18, 133–37; Schleicher to Klinckerfuss, 16 Oct. 1942; Morgenroth to [Raabe], 17 Oct. 1942, BDC Klinckerfuss; Wessling, *Furtwängler,* 150; Klinckerfuss eulogy in *Esslinger Zeitung,* 5 Feb. 1959; Annedore Leber, ed., *Das Gewissen steht auf: 64 Lebensbilder aus dem deutschen Widerstand, 1933–1945* (1960), 134–36.

202. Klinckerfuss eulogy in *Esslinger Zeitung,* 5 Feb. 1959; Klinckerfuss to Geiser, 3 June 1956, KSM; Klinckerfuss, *Aufklänge,* 118–19; Michael Burleigh, *Death and Deliverance: "Euthanasia" in Germany, 1900–1945* (Cambridge, 1995), 139.

203. Gottfried von Einem, recorded interview, Vienna, 30 Nov. 1994, APA (quote); Friedrich Saathen, *Einem Chronik: Dokumentation und Deutung* (Vienna, 1982), 85–86, 90, 92.

204. Saathen, *Einem Chronik,* 22–40.

205. Ibid., 40–61.

206. Ibid., 61–71.

207. Ibid., 75–79; Gottfried von Einem in Josef Müller-Marein and Hannes Reinhardt, eds., *Das musikalische Selbstportrait von Komponisten, Dirigenten, Instrumentalisten, Sängerinnen und Sängern unserer Zeit* (Hamburg, 1965), 84; Gottfried von Einem, recorded interview, Vienna, 30 Nov. 1994, APA.

208. Saathen, *Einem Chronik,* 67, 75, 79–80, 82–84, 86, 89, 91, 95, 97; Wagner, *Nacht,* 313–14.

209. Saathen, *Einem Chronik,* 92, 100–102; Hartmann, *Einem,* 6, 10; Einem in Müller-Marein and Reinhardt, *Selbstportrait,* 85; Gottfried von Einem, recorded interview, Vienna, 30 Nov. 1994, APA.

210. Gottfried von Einem, recorded interview, Vienna, 30 Nov. 1994, APA; pocketbook diaries Werner Egk for 1942–44, BS, Ana/410; Einem to Orff, 17 Sept. and 7 Oct. 1942; Orff to Einem, 3 Oct. 1942; Blacher to Orff, [Apr. 1942], CM, Allg. Korr.; Wagner-Régeny, *Begegnungen,* 105, 196; Hartmann, *Einem,* 17, 19; Saathen, *Einem Chronik,* 76, 90, 103, 105.

211. Saathen, *Einem Chronik,* 87, 98–99, 112–14; Hartmann, *Einem,* 18; Leber, *Gewissen,* 146–48, 155–57.

212. Hans Schnoor in MK 1 (1944), 225 (quote); Laux, *Musik,* 91–94; Saathen, *Einem Chronik,* 109–10.

213. Quotations according to Gottfried von Einem, recorded interview, Vienna, 30 Nov. 1994, APA; minutes of broadcast planning committee, 26 July 1944, BA, R55/556; *TGII* 13:466; Einem in Müller-Marein and Reinhardt, *Selbstportrait*, 86; Prieberg, *Lexikon*, 109; Saathen, *Einem Chronik*, 110–11.

214. Gottfried von Einem, recorded interview, Vienna, 30 Nov. 1994, APA; Kater, *Different Drummers*, 35, 101, 224, n. 43.

215. Gottfried von Einem, recorded interview, Vienna, 30 Nov. 1994, APA.

216. Friedrich Saathen, *Von Kündern, Käuzen und Ketzern: Biographische Studien zur Musik des 20. Jahrhunderts* (Vienna, 1986), 288–92.

217. Ibid., 293–95; Blacher in Müller-Marein and Reinhardt, *Selbstportrait*, 409–11; Ulrich Dibelius, *Moderne Musik, 1945–1965: Voraussetzungen, Verlauf, Material* (Munich, 1966), 53; Hans Heinz Stuckenschmidt, *Boris Blacher* (Berlin, 1963), 11, 15–16; Michael H. Kater, "Die 'Gesundheitsführung' des Deutschen Volkes," *Medizinhistorisches Journal* 18 (1983), 363–66.

218. Stege quoted in Prieberg, *NS-Staat*, 127; Blacher in Müller-Marein and Reinhardt, *Selbstportrait*, 411–12; *Skizzen* (May 1939), 10.

219. Dümling and Girth, *Entartete Musik*, 106; Kreiten quoted by Werner Schwerter, ibid., 114; Stuckenschmidt, *Blacher*, 13–14; Heinz Maassen quoted in Prieberg, *NS-Staat*, 275–76; Guido Waldmann, "Bekenntnis zur deutschen Musik: Reichsmusiktage Düsseldorf—Beethovenfest der HJ. in Wildbad," *MJV* 1 (1937–38), 332 (both Maassen and Waldmann use the adjective "cold").

220. "Neue Abschlüsse bevorstehender Aufführungen unserer Orchesterwerke—seit 1. Oktober 1939," BH, Staatstheater/14506; *ZM* 107 (1940), 29, 178, 308, 492; Stoffels, "Musiktheater," 180.

221. Stege in *ZM* 107 (1940), 535, 766; BDC Blacher; Stuckenschmidt, *Blacher*, 19; *LI*, 557; Saathen, *Kündern*, 299; Newell Jenkins, recorded interview, Hillsdale, N.Y., 20 Mar. 1993, APA; Prieberg, *NS-Staat*, 286.

222. See Werner Oehlmann in *Reich*, 3 Nov. 1940; Peter Funk, ibid., 27 July 1941; H. Oehlerking (Wuppertal) in *ZM* 108 (1941), 199, 683; Oswald Schrenk in *JdM 1943*, 186.

223. RMK minutes, [Berlin, May–July 1942], BDC Egk; Reinhold Zimmermann in *ZM* 107 (1940), 792; Saathen, *Kündern*, 300–304.

224. Karl Amadeus Hartmann, *Kleine Schriften*, ed. Ernst Thomas (Mainz, 1965), 12.

225. Elisabeth Hartmann, recorded interview, Munich, 13 Dec. 1994, APA.

226. Hartmann, *Schriften*, 12 (quote); *Melos* 11 (1932), 29; Andrew D. McCredie, "Die Jahre der schöpferischen Reifung (1927–1935) und die postum veröffentlichten Kompositionen der Kriegszeit (1939–1945)," in *Karl Amadeus Hartmann und die Musica Viva: Essays. Bisher unveröffentlichte Briefe. Katalog* (Munich, 1980), 46–57, 362; Habakuk Traber, "Exil und 'Innere Emigration': Über Wladimir Vogel und Karl Amadeus Hartmann," in Traber and Elmar Weingarten, eds., *Verdrängte Musik: Berliner Komponisten im Exil* (Berlin, 1987), 167.

227. Elisabeth Hartmann, recorded interview, Munich, 13 Dec. 1994, APA.

228. Ibid.; Andrew D. McCredie, *Karl Amadeus Hartmann: Sein Leben und Werk* (Wilhelmshaven, 1980), 35–37; Andreas Jaschinsky, *Karl Amadeus Hartmann—Symphonische Tradition und ihre Auflösung* (Munich, 1982), 12.

229. McCredie, *Hartmann*, 37, 40–41 (1st and 2nd quotes); Luigi Dallapiccola, "Meine Erinnerungen an Karl Amadeus Hartmann," *Melos* 37 (1970), 333

(3rd quote); typescript excerpt from *Népszava,* signed Alexander Jemnitz, in BS, Ana/407 (4th quote). See also Sachs, *Music,* 142, 146.

230. Hartmann to Jemnitz, 7 May 1936, BS, Ana/407 (quote); McCredie, *Hartmann,* 45.

231. McCredie, *Hartmann, 54–55; Karl Amadeus Hartmann,* 240; Jaschinski, *Hartmann,* 12.

232. McCredie, *Hartmann,* 56; *Karl Amadeus Hartmann,* 358.

233. McCredie, *Hartmann,* 61. Desperation and fear leap off the page in Hartmann's letter to Schlee, 22 Dec. 1942, BS, Ana/407.

234. McCredie, *Hartmann,* 63; Hartmann to Havemann, 4 Feb. 1946, BS, Ana/407 (quotes).

235. McCredie, *Hartmann,* 63; *Karl Amadeus Hartmann,* 242. On the liberation of Dachau, see Nerin E. Gun, *The Day of the Americans* (New York, 1966).

236. McCredie, "Die Jahre," 59 (quote). The economic aspect is mentioned in Hartmann to Scherchen, 9 Feb. 1937 and 2 Dec. 1938, BS, Ana/407.

237. Elisabeth Hartmann, recorded interview, Munich, 13 Dec. 1994, APA. The ISCM was banned in Nazi-controlled countries starting in 1938, and in Italy in 1939 (*NG* 9:275).

238. Hartmann to Scherchen, 9 Feb. 1937, BS, Ana/407.

239. Sacher to Hartmann, 30 June 1938 (1st quote), 31 May and 5 June 1939; Studio Radio Bern to Hartmann, 14 Apr. 1939, BS, Ana/407 (2nd quote). On Swiss culture, see Theo Mäusli, *Jazz und geistige Landesverteidigung* (Zurich, 1995), 21–35.

240. Rôzsavölgyi & Co. to Hartmann, 20 Nov. 1937; Gibson to Hartmann, 1 Feb. 1939, BS, Ana/407.

241. Hartmann to League of Composers, Inc., 25 July 1939, BS, Ana/407.

242. See Hartmann to Jemnitz, 20 June 1936, BS, Ana/407.

243. Hartmann to Scherchen, 5 Jan. 1937, BS, Ana/407.

244. Rôzsavölgyi & Co. to Hartmann, 20 Nov. 1937, BS, Ana/407.

245. Hartmann to Scherchen, 22 May 1937, 17 Jan. 1938, and 2 Dec. 1938 (quote), BS, Ana/407.

246. Scherchen to Karl [Hartmann], 30 Nov. 1940; Haug to Hartmann, 27 July 1942; Hartmann to Haug, 1 Oct. 1942, BS, Ana/407.

247. Karl H. Wörner, *Neue Musik in der Entscheidung* (Mainz, 1954), 125–26; *Karl Amadeus Hartmann,* 82–86.

248. Galimir to Hartmann, 30 Dec. 1934; Palotai to Hartmann, 13 Mar. 1936, BS, Ana/407.

249. McCredie, *Hartmann,* 38.

250. Hartmann to Scherchen, 27 Dec. 1936, BS, Ana/407; Dragotin Cvetko, "Aus H. Scherchens und K. A. Hartmanns Korrespondenz an S. Osterc," in Heinrich Hüschen, ed., *Musicae Scientiae Collectanea: Festschrift Karl Gustav Fellerer am 7. Juli 1972* (Colonge, 1973), 73–75; *Karl Amadeus Hartmann,* 272.

251. Fiorillo to Hartmann, 27 Apr. 1937 (1st quote); and 27 May 1938 (2nd quote), BS, Ana/407. On Fiorillo, see *The New Grove Dictionary of American Music,* 4 vols., ed. H. Wiley Hitchcock and Stanley Sadie (London, 1986), 2:129.

252. Sacher to Hartmann, 5 June 1939, BS, Ana/407.

253. McCredie, *Hartmann,* 45–46; *Karl Amadeus Hartmann,* 238.

254. Memorandum "Emil Hertzka-Gedächtnis-Stiftung Wien," [1937]; Scheu to Hartmann, 21 May 1937, BS, Ana/407; McCredie, *Hartmann,* 47; *Karl Amadeus Hartmann,* 298–99.

255. McCredie, *Hartmann*, 50; idem, "Die Jahre," 58; *Karl Amadeus Hartmann*, 235–38; Dallapiccola, "Erinnerungen," 333; Windham to Hartmann, 1 Jan. 1938; Kutscher to Hartmann, 2 Aug. 1938, BS, Ana/407.

256. Skulsky to Hartmann, 3 Nov. 1938; Hartmann to Onnou, 24 May 1939; Belgisch Nationaal Instituut voor Radio-Omroep to Hartmann, 14 Mar. 1940; Collaer to Hartmann, 9 Jan. 1941; Hartmann to Collaer, 6 Oct. 1941, BS, Ana/407; McCredie, *Hartmann*, 51–52, 56.

257. Registration card, 11 July 1941, BDC Hartmann (quote); RMK to Hartmann, 21 Sept., 9 Oct., 4 Dec. 1935, and 22 Jan. 1936; Hartmann to Scherchen, 1 Jan. 1936; Devisenstelle, Oberfinanzpräsident München, to Hartmann, 17 June 1939; Hartmann to Haug, 15 Aug. 1942, BS, Ana/407; Dallapiccola, "Erinnerungen," 334; Prieberg, *NS-Staat*, 208–9; *LI*, 258–59.

258. Stagma to Hartmann, 6 Apr. 1940 and 2 Jan. 1941; Hartmann to USFRT Paris, 20 Apr. 1946, BS, Ana/407; Elisabeth Hartmann, recorded interview, Munich, 13 Dec. 1994, APA; *Karl Amadeus Hartmann*, 234; McCredie, *Hartmann*, 40; Andreas Jaschinski, "Anmerkungen zu Karl Amadeus Hartmann: Musik als Widerstand," *Fono Forum* (Nov. 1981), 29; Jaschinski, *Hartmann*, 11; Traber, "Exil," 169.

259. Hans-Erich Volkmann, ed., *Ende des Dritten Reiches—Ende des Zweiten Weltkriegs: Eine perspektivische Rückschau* (Munich, 1995); Hajo Holborn, *American Military Government: Its Organization and Policies* (Washington, D.C., 1947), 53–73; Lutz Niethammer, *Entnazifizierung in Bayern: Säuberung und Rehabilitierung unter amerikanischer Besatzung* (Frankfurt am Main, 1972); Jost Hermand, *Kultur im Wiederaufbau: Die Bundesrepublik Deutschland, 1945–1965* (Munich, 1986), 89–218, 277–88, 447–61; Elisabeth Hartmann, recorded interview, Munich, 13 Dec. 1994, APA; Traber, "Exil," 179.

260. Hartmann to Sacher, 23 Dec. 1945; Hartmann to Scherchen, 28 Jan. 1947, BS, Ana/407; Elisabeth Hartmann, recorded interview, Munich, 13 Dec. 1994, APA; Ulrich Dibelius, "Karl Amadeus Hartmann ist tot," *Melos* 31 (1964), 14.

261. Hartmann to Schlee, 15 Jan. 1946; Hartmann to Riisager, 30 Dec. 1946, BS, Ana/407; Elisabeth Hartmann, recorded interview, Munich, 13 Dec. 1994, APA; Edmund Nick, "München im Winterschlaf," *Melos* 14 (1947), 180–82; Karl Heinz Ruppel, "Komponist, Vorkämpfer und Organisator: Karl Amadeus Hartmann," *Melos* 22 (1955), 251–52; Dibelius, *Musik*, 70; *Karl Amadeus Hartmann*, 306; *LI*, 615.

262. Elisabeth Hartmann, recorded interview, Munich, 13 Dec 1994, APA; Hartmann to Hindemith, 4 Feb 1946; Hindemith to Hartmann, 5 Mar. 1946, BS, Ana/407; *Melos* 14 (1947), 90, 125, 266, 308, 352; *Karl Amadeus Hartmann*, 316, 318, 322. The German premiere of *Mathis* took place at the Frankfurt Opera in 1947.

263. Hartmann to Scherchen, 28 Jan. 1947 and 15 Apr. 1948; Hartmann to Křenek, 20 May 1948, BS, Ana/407; Elisabeth Hartmann, recorded interview, Munich, 13 Dec. 1994, APA; *Melos* 14 (1947), 90, 261, 341, 425; *Melos* 15 (1948), 184; Karl Heinz Ruppel, "Komponist, Vorkämpfer und Organisator: Karl Amadeus Hartmann," *Melos* 22 (1955), 249–51; Jaschinski, "Anmerkungen," 29.

Index

Printed in the United States
1034400002B

Made in the USA